Logic and Contemporary Rhetoric

The Use of Reason in Everyday Life

THIRTEENTH EDITION

Frank Boardman
Visiting Assistant Professor, Dickinson College

Nancy Cavender
Professor Emeritus College of Marin

Howard Kahane
Late of University of Maryland Baltimore County

 CENGAGE

Australia • Brazil • Canada • Mexico • Singapore • United Kingdom • United States

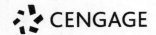

Logic and Contemporary Rhetoric: The Use of Reason in Everyday Life, Thirteenth Edition
Boardman, Cavender, Kahane

Product Director: Paul Banks

Content Developer: Sarah Edmonds

Content Development Manager: Megan Garvey

Product Assistant: Staci Eckenroth

Senior Marketing Manager: Jillian Borden

Senior Content Project Manager: Andrea Wagner

Senior Art Director: Marissa Falco

Interior Design: c miller design

IP Analyst: Alexandra Ricciardi

IP Project Manager: Carly Belcher

Manufacturing Planner: Julio Esperas

Cover Design: c miller design

Production Service/Compositor: Lumina Datamatics Inc.

Cover Image: xijian/iStock/Getty Images Plus/Getty images

For product information and technology assistance, contact us at **Cengage Customer & Sales Support, 1-800-354-9706 or support.cengage.com.**

For permission to use material from this text or product, submit all requests online at **www.cengage.com/permissions.**

Library of Congress Control Number: 2016952387

ISBN-13: 978-1-305-95602-5
ISBN-10: 1-305-95602-8

Cengage
200 Pier 4 Boulevard
Boston, MA 02210
USA

Cengage is a leading provider of customized learning solutions with employees residing in nearly 40 different countries and sales in more than 125 countries around the world. Find your local representative at: **www.cengage.com.**

To learn more about Cengage platforms and services, register or access your online learning solution, or purchase materials for your course, visit **www.cengage.com.**

Printed in Mexico
Print Number: 04   Print Year: 2020

To Ellie, Lisa, and John

Contents

Preface

I do not pretend to know what many ignorant men are sure of.
—CLARENCE DARROW

To know that we know what we know, and that we do not know what we do not know. That is true knowledge. —HENRY DAVID THOREAU

We have met the enemy and he is us. —WALT KELLY'S "POGO"

Education is not simply the work of abstract verbalized knowledge.
—ALDOUS HUXLEY

Many people would sooner die than think. In fact, they do. —BERTRAND RUSSELL

You can fool too many of the people too much of the time.—JAMES THURBER

Our loftiest ambition for the thirteenth edition of *Logic and Contemporary Rhetoric* is that it should encourage responsible and meaningful engagement in public discourse. *Responsible* engagement requires reason above all else, and so much of the text is devoted to introducing proper methods of identifying, analyzing, evaluating, and making arguments. *Meaningful* engagement requires an understanding of the actual state of rhetoric today, and so the text also focuses on some of the primary contexts of persuasion and argument in our daily lives.

The need is great and the moment is critical. We are faced with seemingly constant changes to the technology and norms of mass communication, just as social and political life is becoming more divided, more vitriolic, and less constrained by reason. We offer *Logic and Contemporary Rhetoric* as both a guide and an antidote to this condition.

The text contains examples and exercise items drawn from a broad range of sources—newspapers, websites, social media, film, television, advertisements, literature, political speeches, newspaper columns, and so on. Students get to sharpen their ability to think critically by reasoning about important topics and issues: Internet ethics, political trends, media biases, economic downturns, steroid abuse, and government doublespeak, to name just a few.

It quotes from or refers to writings and comments of Aristotle, Bertrand Russell, Barack Obama, Jerry Seinfeld, Ralph Ellison, Winston Churchill, Ann Coulter, Jane Austen,

Rush Limbaugh, Jonathan Swift, Fyodor Dostoevsky, Pliny the Elder, Donald Trump, William Shakespeare, Kwame Anthony Appiah, and a host of others. The text is sprinkled with relevant cartoons from the *New Yorker*, the Sunday papers, and the Internet. The trademarks of *Logic and Contemporary Rhetoric* always have been, and still are, ease of comprehension and up-to-date, interesting material. Textbooks need not be dull!

All this is done to sharpen students' abilities to think critically so that they can avoid being manipulated by the media, the advertisers, the political system, and a host of con artists—and ultimately to help them function independently and responsibly in our increasingly complex, challenging society.

The Instructor's Companion Site features an Instructor's Manual that provides useful suggestions for lectures and classroom activities, based directly on the content in this book. It also includes PowerPoint Lecture Slides offering a breakdown of the key points in each chapter. Interested instructors can find and access this content by adding the thirteenth edition of this book to their bookshelf on Cengage.com.

This edition is also accompanied by a digital solution for students and instructors: **MindTap for Philosophy: Logic and Contemporary Rhetoric,** a personalized, online digital learning platform providing students with an immersive learning experience that builds critical thinking skills. Through a carefully designed chapter-based learning path, MindTap allows students to easily identify the chapter's learning objectives; draw connections and improve writing skills by completing essay assignments; read short, manageable sections from the eBook; and test their content knowledge with critical thinking Aplia™ questions.

- **Chapter eBook:** Each chapter within MindTap contains the narrative of the chapter, offering an easy-to-navigate online reading experience.
- **Chapter Quiz:** Each chapter within MindTap ends with a summative Chapter Test covering the chapter's learning objectives and ensuring students are reading and understanding the material presented.
- **Chapter Aplia Assignment:** Each chapter includes an Aplia assignment that provides automatically graded critical thinking assignments with detailed, immediate feedback and explanations on every question. Students can also choose to see another set of related questions if they did not earn all available points in their first attempt and want more practice.
- **KnowNOW! Philosophy Blog:** The KnowNOW! Philosophy Blog connects course concepts with real-world events. Updated twice a week, the blog provides a succinct philosophical analysis of major news stories, along with multimedia and discussion-starter questions.

MindTap also includes a variety of other tools that support philosophy teaching and learning:

- The Philosophy Toolbox collects tutorials on using MindTap and researching and writing academic papers, including citation information and tools, that instructors can use to support students in the writing process.
- Questia allows professors and students to search a database of thousands of peer-reviewed journals, newspapers, magazines, and full-length books—all assets can be added to any relevant chapter in MindTap.
- ReadSpeaker reads the text out loud to students in a voice they can customize.
- Digital flashcards are premade for each chapter, and students can make their own by adding images, descriptions, and more.

MindTap gives students ample opportunities for improving comprehension and for self-evaluation to prepare for exams, while also providing faculty and students alike a clear way to measure and assess student progress. Faculty can use MindTap as a turnkey solution or customize by adding YouTube videos, RSS feeds, or their own documents directly within the eBook or within each chapter's Learning Path. MindTap goes well beyond an eBook and a homework solution. It is truly a personal learning experience that allows instructors to synchronize the reading with engaging assignments. To learn more, ask your Cengage Learning sales representative for more information, or go to www.cengage.com/mindtap.

New to the Thirteenth Edition

The principal changes in this edition are these:

1. Two entirely new chapters: one on changes to public discourse brought about by the emergence of cyberculture and new media (Chapter 12), and another on the argumentative and rhetorical function of fictional narratives (Chapter 13). The primary goal of both of these chapters (along with those on advertising and the news) is to capture and have students confront the contexts of argument and other modes of persuasion with which they are most familiar.

2. Ten new sections in existing chapters:
   - Arguments vs. Explanations (Chapter 1)
   - What Does "Winning an Argument" Mean? (Chapter 1)
   - Conditional Statements (Chapter 2)
   - Guilt by Association (Chapter 4)
   - Appeal to Tradition or Popularity (Chapter 4)
   - Appeal to Pity or Fear (Chapter 4)
   - Vagueness and Ambiguity (Chapter 7)
   - Some Subtle Issues (concerning language, Chapter 7)
   - Are Advertisements Arguments? Examples of Rhetoric? (Chapter 10)
   - Criteria for Theory Selection (Appendix)

3. Numerous new subsections, case studies, and expanded discussions throughout the text, including:
   - The "reproducibility crisis" in social psychology (Chapter 1)
   - High-profile cases of concocted and fabricated news stories (Chapter 3)
   - Domains where appeals to authority are never permissible (Chapter 3)
   - The significance of new evidence to appeals to ignorance (Chapter 4)
   - Criteria for determining an adequate sample size (Chapter 5)
   - The practical dangers of scapegoating, denial, and partisan mindsets (Chapter 6)
   - Cultural insensitivity versus politically correct overreaction regarding sports teams' names and mascots (Chapter 7)
   - Analyzing arguments with claims that serve as both premises and conclusions (Chapter 8)
   - Diagramming argument structure (Chapter 8)
   - The role of generalizations and rules in moral argumentation (Chapter 8)

- Overcoming the difficulty of starting essays (Chapter 9)
- Choosing claims that are neither too weak nor too strong (Chapter 9)
- The challenges and art of rewriting well (Chapter 9)
- Ads that create and exacerbate consumers' fears (Chapter 10)
- Ads that rely upon and promote stereotypes (Chapter 10)
- Push polls as advertisements (Chapter 10)
- The decline of both local and international news coverage (Chapter 11)
- The emergence of nonprofit newsrooms (Chapter 11)

4. Hundreds of new examples and exercises making the text more up to date and relevant to students, including updates to critical studies and stories featured in previous editions
5. Revisions to some parts of the text that maintain the overall mission, tone, and style of past editions
6. New cartoons chosen for both their wit and their relevance

Organization of the Text

The thought that sparked the original organization of material in *Logic and Contemporary Rhetoric* way back in 1969–1970 was that student reasoning about everyday topics could be improved by acquainting them with a few basic principles of good reasoning and, in particular, by enlightening them concerning common ways in which people are taken in by fallacious arguments and reasoning in everyday life. But a close examination of the ways in which reasoning, in fact, goes wrong in everyday life shows that it does so in a majority of cases, first, because of a lack of sufficient (or sufficiently accurate) background information; second, because of the psychological impediments (wishful thinking, rationalization, prejudice, superstition, provincialism, and so on) that stand in the way of cogent reasoning; and third, because of a poor understanding of the nature and quality of the various information sources.

Taking account of this insight has resulted in a book that divides into eight parts, as follows:

1. *Good and Bad Reasoning:* Chapter 1 introduces students to some basic ideas about good and bad reasoning, the importance of having good background beliefs, in particular of having well-pruned worldviews, as well as some very rudimentary remarks about deduction and induction and the three overarching fallacy categories employed in Chapters 3, 4, and 5.
2. *Deduction and Induction:* Chapter 2 contains more detailed material on deductive and inductive validity and invalidity.
3. *Fallacious Reasoning:* Chapters 3, 4, and 5 discuss fallacious reasoning, concentrating on how to avoid fallacies by becoming familiar with the types most frequently encountered in everyday life. The point is to help students increase their ability to spot fallacious reasoning by discussing the most common types of fallacious argument and by providing students with everyday life examples on which to practice.
4. *Impediments to Cogent Reasoning:* Chapter 6 discusses wishful thinking, rationalization, provincialism, denial, and so on, and how to overcome them. It explains the attraction and mistaken nature of belief in the paranormal and other pseudosciences. In some ways, this is the most important chapter in the

book, because these skewers of rational thought so severely infect the thinking of all of us. (Some instructors may argue that the topic is more appropriately taught in psychology classes, not in classes primarily concerned with critical reasoning. But the reality here is that many students do not take the relevant psychology classes and that those who do often are provided with a purely theoretical account divorced from the students' own reasoning in everyday life, not with a "how-to" discussion designed to help them overcome these obstacles to rational thought.)

5. *Language:* Chapter 7 discusses the ways in which language itself can be used to manipulate meaning, for instance, via doubletalk and long-winded locutions. (This chapter also contains a section, not common in critical-thinking texts, on the linguistic revolution that has tremendously reduced the use of sexist, racist, and other pejorative locutions in everyday discourse; and it also has a few things to say about the use of politically correct [PC] locutions.)

6. *Evaluating and Writing Cogent Essays:* Chapter 8 deals with the evaluation of extended argumentative passages—essays, editorials, political speeches, and so on. Chapter 9 addresses the writing of these kinds of argumentative passages. (Instructors are urged not to pass over Chapter 9 and urged to have students write *at least* two argumentative papers during the semester. Writing is very likely the best way in which we all can learn to sharpen our ability to reason well. Writing is indeed nature's way of letting us know how sloppy our thinking often is. But it also is the best way to learn how to sharpen our ability to think straight.)

7. *Important Sources of Information, Argument, and Rhetoric:* Chapter 10 discusses advertising (singling out political ads for special scrutiny); Chapter 11, the news media; Chapter 12, the Internet and new media; and Chapter 13, fiction.

8. *More on Cogent Reasoning:* The appendix provides additional material on deduction and induction; cause and effect; scientific method; theory selection; and so on.

Note also that a section at the back of the book provides answers to selected exercise items. It should be remembered, however, that most of the exercise items in this text are drawn from everyday life, where shades of gray outnumber blacks and whites. The answers provided thus constitute author responses rather than definitive pronouncements. Similar remarks apply to the answers to the exercise items provided in MindTap.

The Unique Nature of *Logic and Contemporary Rhetoric*

This book is unique among critical reasoning texts in bringing together all of these apparently diverse elements, in particular in stressing the importance of overcoming natural impediments to cogent reasoning; in bringing to bear good background information when dealing with everyday problems; and in so extensively discussing the most important information sources. In this complicated modern world, all of us are laypersons most of the time with respect to most topics; the ability to deal effectively with the "expert" information available to us via the media, textbooks, the Internet, and periodicals—to separate wheat from chaff—thus is crucial to our ability to reason well about everyday problems, whether of a personal or of a social-political nature.

Although the text contains much discussion of theory, this is *not* a treatise on the theory of cogent and fallacious reasoning. Rather, it is designed to help students learn *how* to reason well and *how* to avoid fallacious reasoning. That is why so many examples and exercise items have been included—arranged so as to increase student sophistication as they progress through the book—and why exercises and examples have been drawn primarily from everyday life. Learning how to reason well and how to evaluate the rhetoric of others is a skill that, like most others, requires practice, in this case practice on the genuine article—actual examples drawn from everyday life.

This text provides students with a good deal more than the usual supply of exercise items, but perhaps the most important are those requiring them to do things on their own: find examples from the mass media, write letters to elected officials, do research on specified topics.

A true critical reasoning course, or textbook, is unthinkable in a closed or authoritarian society and antithetical to the indoctrination practiced in that kind of culture. The authors of this text take very seriously the admonition that eternal vigilance is the price of liberty. Citizens who think for themselves, rather than uncritically ingesting what their leaders and others with power tell them, are the absolutely necessary ingredient of a society that is to remain free.

Acknowledgments

Many thanks to the reviewers for this thirteenth edition: David Hurst, College of the Sequoias; Agber Dimah, Chicago State University; Carrie Wasinger, Yuba College; Keira M. Hambrick, Marietta College; Robert V. Covert, Ph.D., Coastline Community College; Shant Shahoian, Glendale Community College; Meryl Siegal, Laney College; Odysseus Makridis, Fairleigh Dickinson University; Charles E. Weidler, Rowan University; and Jacqueline Ahl, State University of New York at New Paltz.

Thanks also to everyone who has aided in the preparation of this and previous editions, including Professors Thomas Allen, California Polytechnic University, San Luis Obispo; Don Anderson, Pierce College; Anatole Anton, San Francisco State University; Gary L. Baran, Los Angeles City College; Lawrence Beloof, West Hills Community College; William Bonis, California State University, Long Beach; Gene Booth, University of New Mexico; Donald Burrell, California State University, Los Angeles; Henry C. Byerly, University of Arizona; Carlotta Campbell, College of Alameda; Joseph Campbell, Washington State University; Alice Cleveland, College of Marin; Monte Cook, University of Oklahoma; Rosemary Cook, Saybrook Institute; Robert Covert, Coastline Community College; Wally Cox, Regent University; Leland Creer, Central Connecticut State University; Robert Cogan, Edinboro University; David Detmer, Purdue University, Calumet Campus; R. V. Dusek, University of New Hampshire; Frank Fair, Sam Houston State University; Dana R. Flint, Lincoln University; James Freeman, Hunter College; Marilyn M. Fry, Coastline Community College; Jonathan Gainor, Harrisburg Area Community College; Sidney Gendin, Eastern Michigan University; Norman L. Geisler, Liberty University; James A. Gould, University of South Florida; J. Anthony

Greybasch, Central State University; Paul J. Haanstad, University of Utah; Max O. Hallman, Merced College; Alan Hausman, Hunter College; James Heffernan, University of the Pacific; John Hernandez, Palo Alto College; Mark Herron, National University; Lori Hoffman, Moravian College; J. Thomas Howald, Franklin College; Sughra Hussain, Harrisburg Area Community College; John L. King, University of North Carolina; Charles Landesman, Hunter College and CUNY Graduate Center; Donald Lazere, California Polytechnic State University; Herschel Mack, Humboldt State University; Patrick Maher, University of Pittsburgh; Reed Markham, California Polytechnic University, Pomona; Judith McBride, somewhere in Arizona; Kate McCorkle, Butte College; Thomas McKay, Syracuse University; Donna Monahan, College of Marin; David Morgan, University of Northern Iowa; Clayton Morgareidge, Lewis and Clark College; Gonzalo T. Palacios, University of the District of Columbia; Ray Perkins, Jr., Plymouth State University; Linda Plackowski, Delta College; Nelson Pole, Cleveland State University; Merrill Proudfoot, Park College; Malcolm Reid, Gordon College; Vincent Riccardi, Orange Coast College; Paul O. Ricci, Cypress College; Paul A. Roth, University of Missouri; Arent H. Schuyler, Jr., University of California, Santa Barbara; Robert Schwartz, University of Wisconsin–Milwaukee; Roger Seanom, University of British Columbia; S. Samuel Shermis, Purdue University; Pamela Spoto, California State University, Chico; Douglas Stalker, University of Delaware; Ben Starr, Modesto Junior College; Joan Straumanis, Kenyon College; John Stroupe, Western Michigan University; Gregory P. Swartzentruber, Villanova University; Roye Templeton, University of Maryland, Baltimore County; John Titchener, University of Maryland, Baltimore County; and Perry Weddle, California State University, Sacramento.

Our very special thanks to the students of Whitman College, the University of Kansas, Bernard Baruch and Hunter Colleges of CUNY, the University of Maryland Baltimore County, and the College of Marin.

Finally, this being my first time working on this text, I'd like to take the liberty of switching to the first-person-*singular* and thank some people who made my own participation possible: Samantha Boardman, my wife and research guru; Alan Hausman, my friend and mentor; and Sarah Edmonds, Debra Matteson, and Andrea Wagner at Cengage, and Valarmathy Munuswamy at Lumina Datamatics. Most of all, though, I need to thank Nancy Cavender. This text is brimming with her (and Howard Kahane's) talent, passion, and hard work. Her help on this edition has also been invaluable. I can only hope that I have done some justice to her great generosity and trust.

FRANK BOARDMAN
Carlisle, Pennsylvania, and Brooklyn, New York

What is the use of philosophy, if all it does is enable you to talk . . . about some abstruse questions of logic, etc., and if it does not improve your thinking about the important questions of everyday life?

—Ludwig Wittgenstein

"Great speech! But let's cut your carefully reasoned conclusion and insert an uplifting sports metaphor."

Good and Bad Reasoning

1

It's much easier to do and die than it is to reason why. —H. A. Studdert Kennedy

Read not to contradict and confute, nor to believe and take for granted . . . but to weigh and consider. —Francis Bacon

You can lead a man up to the university, but you can't make him think. —Finley Peter Dunne

You can lead me to college . . . but you can't make me think. —Sweatshirt update seen at Duke University

Ignorance of reality provides no protection from it. —Harold Gordon

Reason is logic, or reason is motive, or reason is a way of life. —John Le Carré

MindTap® **Visit MindTap for more readings and resources.**

There is much truth to the old saying that life is just one problem after another. That's why problem solving is one of life's major preoccupations. **Reasoning** is the essential ingredient in problem solving. When confronted with a problem, those of us who are rational reason from what we already know, or have good reason to believe, or can find out, to new beliefs useful in solving that problem. The trick, of course, is to reason well. This book is about good reasoning—about how to reason well in everyday life—whether dealing with personal problems or those of a social or political nature.

All of us like to think of ourselves as rational human beings, yet most of what we know is passed on to us by other people. We know, for instance, that the earth is round because we've been told it is, even though our intuition is that it is flat because we walk on flat surfaces every day. In fact, for centuries, nearly everyone believed it was flat until scientific evidence proved without question that it isn't. Much of what we think we know is based on beliefs, sometimes unsupported by accurate information, instilled in us from childhood on. And too often, beliefs collapse into gut reactions to all manner of issues—from gun control to same-sex marriage to legalizing drugs. A gut reaction is not the same as a rational thought, however, nor is a belief, unless it has been examined for accuracy against conflicting ideas and evidence. Critical thinking, after all, requires information as well as the ability to reason well.

Fortunately, no one is an island. We all have available to us a great deal of knowledge others have gained through experience and good reasoning—accurate information and well-intended advice available to anyone who reaches out for it. Unfortunately, not all information is created equal. Charlatans and fools can speak as loudly as saints or geniuses. Self-interest often clouds the thinking of even the brightest individuals. The trick when evaluating the mountain of verbiage we all are exposed to is to separate the nourishing wheat from the expendable chaff. One way to become good at doing this is to think a bit about what makes reasoning good (cogent), as opposed to bad (fallacious).

1. Reasoning and Arguments

Here is a simple example of reasoning about the nature/nurture issue:

> Identical twins often have different IQ test scores. Yet these twins inherit exactly the same genes. So environment must play some part in determining a person's IQ.

Logicians call this kind of reasoning an **argument**. In this case, the argument consists of three statements:

1. Identical twins often have different IQ test scores.
2. Identical twins inherit the same genes.
So, **3.** environment must play some part in determining IQ.

The first two statements in this argument give reasons for accepting the third. In logic talk, they are said to be **premises** of the argument. And the third statement, which asserts the claim for which the premises offer support, is called the argument's **conclusion**.

In everyday life, few of us bother to label premises or conclusions. We usually don't even bother to distinguish one argument from another. But we do sometimes give clues called **logical indicators**. Words such as *because, since,* and *for* usually indicate that what follows is a premise of an argument. *Therefore, thus, consequently,* and *so* generally signal conclusions. Similarly, expressions such as "It has been observed that . . . ," "In support of this . . . ," and "The relevant data are . . ." are used to introduce premises, while expressions such as "The point of all of this is . . . ," "The implication is . . . ," and "It follows that . . ." are used to signal conclusions. Here is a simple example:

> *Since* it's always wrong to kill a human being [premise], it *follows* that capital punishment is wrong [conclusion], *because* capital punishment takes the life of [kills] a human being [premise].

Put into textbook form, the argument looks like this:

1. It's always wrong to kill a human being.
2. Capital punishment takes the life of (kills) a human being.
∴**3.** Capital punishment is wrong.[1]

In this form, we display only the premises and conclusion of the argument. We leave out logical indicators since the logical structure of the argument is shown by the way we arrange the sentences. Of course, an argument may have any number of premises and may be surrounded by or embedded in other arguments or extraneous material.

In addition to using logical indicators such as *since, because,* and *therefore,* we sometimes employ sentence order—the last sentence in a series stating an argument's conclusion—and occasionally even express a conclusion in the form of a question. Consider this section of President Obama's 2016 State of the Union address:

> Our unique strengths as a nation—our optimism and work ethic, our spirit of discovery, our diversity, our commitment to rule of law—these things give us everything we need to ensure prosperity and security for generations to come.
>
> In fact, it's that spirit that made the progress of these past 7 years possible. It's how we recovered from the worst economic crisis in generations. It's how we reformed our health care system, and reinvented our energy sector; how we delivered more care and benefits to our troops and veterans; and how we secured the freedom in every state to marry the person we love.
>
> But such progress is not inevitable. It's the result of choices we make to-gether. And we face such choices right now. Will we respond to the changes of our time with fear, turning inward as a nation, turning against each other as a people? Or will we face the future with confidence in who we are, in what we stand for, in the incredible things that we can do together?

The rhetorical questions at the end invite us to respond that we should face the future with confidence instead of fear. In the preceding paragraphs, Obama gave reasons for this con-clusion (and, of course, touted his administration's accomplishments while he was at it).

We should also note that, in daily life, premises and even the conclusions of arguments sometimes are implied rather than stated outright. Life is short, and we don't always bother to spell out matters that are obvious or not at issue or can be taken for granted. In the IQ example given earlier, for instance, the premise that IQ differences must be due either to genetic or to environmental factors was omitted as generally understood. When assessing arguments, we should by all means add unstated premises of this kind when they are relevant.

Sometimes people leave conclusions unstated as a kind of rhetorical device. We often feel more committed to beliefs we come to on our own, and leaving conclusions unstated can give us the impression that we've done just that. In a debate in Wisconsin during the 2016 presidential primary campaign season, Hillary Clinton had this to say about her opponent Bernie Sanders's plan for funding higher education:

> You know, I think, again, both of us share the goal of trying to make college affordable for all young Americans. And I have set forth a compact that would do just that for debt-free tuition.

---

[1]The symbol ∴ often is used as shorthand for the word *therefore* and thus indicates that a conclusion follows.

We differ, however, on a couple of key points. One of them being that if you don't have some agreement within the system from states and from families and from students, it's hard to get to where we need to go.

And Senator Sanders's plan really rests on making sure that governors like Scott Walker contribute $23 billion on the first day to make college free. I am a little skeptical about your governor actually caring enough about higher education to make any kind of commitment like that.

The unstated conclusion here is that Sanders's plan is impractical and unlikely to succeed. It was probably neither by accident nor mistake that Clinton left this out.

2. Exposition and Argument

Of course, only those groups of statements that provide reasons for believing something form arguments. Thus, anecdotes are not usually arguments, nor are most other forms of **exposition**. But even in these cases, arguments often are implied. Here is a sales clerk talking about the difference between the cameras on two phones, a Samsung and a Motorola. "Well, the Motorola has 21 megapixels and the Samsung has only 16. They both have terrific image quality, but the Samsung has optical stabilization. The Motorola right now is $150 less, but it has fewer features." Although the clerk's remarks contain no explicit argument because no conclusion is stated, a conclusion is definitely implied. You should choose the Samsung if you want more camera features; otherwise you should choose the Motorola.

The point is that talk generally is not aimless. A good deal of everyday talk, even gossip, is intended to influence the beliefs and actions of others and thus constitutes a kind of argument. In the phone example, the clerk provided information intended to convince the customer to draw either the conclusion, "I'll buy the Samsung because the additional features are worth the extra $150 to me," or the conclusion, "I'll buy the Motorola because high-powered options aren't worth $150 more to me." In other words, the point of the clerk's chatter was to sell a phone. Similarly, advertisements often just provide product information rather than advance explicit arguments, yet clearly every such ad has an implied conclusion—that you should buy the advertised product.

Nevertheless, it is important to understand the difference between rhetoric that is primarily expository and discourse that is basically argumentative. An argument makes the claim, explicit or implicit, that one of its statements follows from some of its other statements. It at least implies that acceptance of its conclusion is justified if one accepts its premises. A passage that is purely expository gives us no reason to accept any "facts" it may contain (other than the implied authority of the writer or speaker, as, for example, when a friend tells us that she had a good time at the beach).

3. Arguments vs. Explanations

One form of exposition that is especially likely to be confused for argument is the explanation. Explanations are often structured much like arguments and even use some of the same words to introduce them ("because," "since," etc.). But explanations are not arguments. Arguments are used to persuade an audience that some claim is true. Explanations are used to provide an audience with greater understanding about a given claim. When we explain something, we take its truth for granted. That is to say, arguments give us *reasons to believe* something, while explanations give us *the reasons why* something is (or has come to be) the case. To put it another way, explanations answer the question "Why is that claim true?" while arguments answer the question "Why should I believe that claim is true?"

For instance, have a look at this passage from Matthew T. Hall of the *San Diego Tribune* on the fact that the first presidential primary election is always held in New Hampshire:

> I've seen firsthand why New Hampshire should be first in line. Sure, the state isn't as diverse as it could be and its winners don't always get their party's nomination, but the state's complexion is going to change with the country's and its voters have shown the door to unfit candidates. Retail politics has real value there, and unsurprisingly for a state whose motto is "Live Free or Die," it has a huge share of independent voters. Put simply, I think they value their first-in-the-nation primary status in ways people in states getting the distinction every so often would not.

And then this from Mentalfloss.com: "New Hampshire's primaries have informally been the earliest since 1920, but over the years, the state has passed laws to ensure that its primaries will remain the first in the nation."

The first quote above is part of an attempt to persuade us that New Hampshire should hold the first primary. The second is an attempt to say why New Hampshire is first. The first one is an argument, the second an explanation.

Like just about any other form of exposition, explanations can be used to make implicit arguments. Still, the distinction between arguments and explanations is important to maintain as they call for different kinds of evaluation. (Did we just argue for or explain the claim that maintaining a distinction between arguments and explanations is important?)

4. What Does "Winning an Argument" Mean?

When we talk about an *argument* in this context, we clearly do not mean anything like a fight, and our sense of "argument" does not even imply any disagreement. So it is not clear that it is proper to ask what it means to "win" arguments as we understand them. That said, we are interested in the ways that arguments are actually used (hence the "and Contemporary Rhetoric" part of the title) and so we should take a moment to think about what it means for an argument to be successful.

From a strictly logical perspective, the only criterion for a successful argument is the quality of the argument itself, and we will turn in the next few sections to some ways of evaluating arguments in this respect. But an argument can be logically sound and still not very persuasive. That is to say, just because an argument *should* be convincing does not mean that it will be.

At the same time, we should not count as successful an argument that is persuasive but illogical. A truly "winning" argument is one that is *in fact* persuasive because it is rational to accept its conclusion on the basis of its premises. As we'll see throughout this text, the combination of logical integrity and rhetorical effect may be all too rare an accomplishment.

5. Cogent Reasoning

Our chief concern to this point has been the *identification* of arguments. We can now turn our focus to their *evaluation*. Reasoning can be either **cogent** (good) or **fallacious** (bad). We reason cogently when we satisfy the following conditions:

1. The premises of our reasoning are believable (**warranted**, justified), given what we already know or believe.
2. We consider all likely relevant information.[2]
3. Our reasoning is **valid**, or **correct**, which means that the premises we employ provide good grounds for accepting the conclusion we draw.[3]

When any of these three conditions of cogent reasoning are not satisfied, reasoning is said to be *fallacious*.

BELIEVABLE PREMISES

The first condition of good argument evaluation requires that we bring to bear whatever we already know or believe—our relevant **background beliefs** and information—to determine whether we should or shouldn't accept the premises of the argument in question. Take, for instance, the first premise of the capital punishment argument discussed earlier—the premise making the claim that taking the life of a human being always is wrong. Most of us are not pacifists—we don't believe that it always is wrong to take a human life. Bringing that background belief to bear thus should make us see the first premise of the capital punishment argument as questionable. So we should not accept the conclusion of that argument unless further reasons are presented in its support. (On the other hand, those of us who *are* pacifists obviously should reason differently.)

By way of contrast, consider the stated premise of the following argument:

> Novak Djokovic must be a terrific tennis player. He won the Wimbledon championship in 2015. (The implied premise is that anyone who wins the tournament at Wimbledon must be a terrific tennis player.)

---

[2]Satisfying this extremely stringent requirement is usually beyond the ability of most of us most of the time. The point is that good reasoners try to come as close as possible to satisfying it, taking into account the importance of drawing the right conclusion and the cost (in time, effort, or money) of obtaining or recalling relevant information. (One of the marks of genius is the ability to recognize that information is relevant when the rest of us fail to notice.)

[3]Provided we know nothing else relevant to the conclusion. Note that reasoning from an unjustified premise may still be cogent if it also employs justified premises that sufficiently support its conclusion. Note also that the term *valid* sometimes is used more broadly than we have used it here.

Tennis fans know that the Wimbledon Grand Slam championship is one of the most demanding tennis competitions in the world, and acceptance of the stated premise (that Djokovic won the tournament) is warranted by plenty of background information.

It's interesting to notice that, in effect, evaluating a premise of an argument by bringing background beliefs to bear entails constructing another argument whose conclusion is either that the premise in question is believable or that it isn't. For example, when evaluating the capital punishment argument discussed before, someone who is not a pacifist might construct the following argument: "I believe that it isn't wrong to kill in self-defense, or in wartime, or to kill those guilty of murder. So I should reject the premise that taking a human life always is wrong."

But what, you might be asking, about your own premise, that "it isn't wrong to kill in self-defense or in wartime, or to kill those guilty of murder"? Shouldn't that be subject to evaluation as well? This is a difficult question. We certainly should subject our own beliefs to scrutiny. But at the same time, if we evaluated every premise using another argument, including those premises used in the evaluating arguments, this process would never end! We will consider the use of background beliefs in greater detail later in this chapter. For now, let's just say that this process of evaluation should end in premises that are as self-evident as possible.

This brings to mind the fact that in daily life we often are exposed to assertions, or claims, that are not supported by reasons or arguments. Clearly, it is not rational to accept these assertions without evaluating them for believability, and, obviously, their correct evaluation requires us to do exactly what we do when evaluating the believability of the premises of an argument—namely, bring to bear what we already know or believe. Evaluating unsupported assertions thus involves just part of what is done when we evaluate arguments.

NO RELEVANT INFORMATION PASSED OVER

The second criterion of cogent reasoning requires that we not pass over relevant information. In particular, it tells us to resist the temptation to neglect evidence contrary to what we want to believe.

Here, for instance, is a part of a column written in December 2015 by David Brooks in the *New York Times* in which he predicted a precipitous decline in Donald Trump's support heading into the primary voting season:

> When campaigns enter that final month, voters tend to gravitate toward the person who seems most orderly. As the primary season advances, voters' tolerance for risk declines. They focus on the potential downsides of each contender and wonder, could this person make things even worse?
>
> When this mental shift happens, I suspect Trump will slide. All the traits that seem charming will suddenly seem risky. The voters' hopes for transformation will give way to a fear of chaos. When the polls shift from registered voters to likely voters, cautious party loyalists will make up a greater share of those counted.

The voting booth focuses the mind. The experience is no longer about self-expression and feeling good in the moment. It's about the finger on the nuclear trigger for the next 4 years. In an era of high anxiety, I doubt Republican voters will take a flyer on their party's future—or their country's future.

We can summarize Brooks' argument this way:

1. People are less likely to actually vote for risky candidates than they are to endorse them early in polls.
2. Voters who are more risk-averse are more likely to vote.
3. Trump is a risky candidate. (Implied)
∴4. Trump will not do as well in actual elections as he has in early polling and will do less well in polls that focus on likely voters.

Trump then won 14 of the first 20 primary contests. Brooks was hardly alone in underestimating Trump's campaign, but his argument seemed particularly strong. He looked to historical elections and likely voting behavior and came to a reasonable conjecture based on those things.

However, two factors worked against Brooks. First and foremost, he did not consider relevant information about the electorate, especially the high level of frustration Republican voters felt about their party's leadership and "cautious party loyalists." Second, Brooks may have been swayed by a bit of wishful thinking. As a moderate Republican and a (at least by *New York Times* standards) conservative, Brooks was very concerned about what a Trump nomination would mean for his party and country.

VALID REASONING

The third criterion of cogent reasoning requires that the premises of an argument genuinely support its conclusion; or, as logicians like to say, it requires that an argument be valid, or correct. It is vitally important to understand that the validity of an argument has nothing whatever to do with the truth of its premises or conclusion. Validity concerns the nature of the *connection* between the premises and conclusion of an argument, not the truth or believability of its premises. Determining that an argument is valid tells us that *if* we are justified in believing in its premises, *then* we also are justified in believing in the truth of its conclusion. It doesn't tell us *whether* its premises are true. An argument thus can be perfectly valid and have completely false premises, and even have a false conclusion. Here is an example:

1. The New York Mets have won more World Series games than any other major league team. (False premise, alas!)
∴2. They have won more World Series games than the New York Yankees. (False conclusion, and even more heartbreaking for Mets fans.)

The argument is valid because if the Mets *had* won more World Series games than any other major league team, then, obviously (well, it's obvious to baseball fans), they would have won more World Series games than the Yankees. The argument is valid, even though its premise and conclusion both are false. It's valid because anyone who is justified in believing its premise is justified in believing its conclusion.

6. Two Basic Kinds of Valid Arguments

Premises may correctly support conclusions in two fundamentally different ways. The first way yields *deductively valid* arguments; the second, *inductively valid* (or inductively strong) arguments.[4]

DEDUCTIVE VALIDITY

The fundamental property of a **deductively valid** argument is this: If all of its premises are true, then its conclusion must be true also, because the claim asserted by its conclusion already has been stated in its premises, although usually only implicitly.

Here is an example of a very simple deductively valid argument:

1. If this wire is made of copper, then it will conduct electricity. (Premise.)
2. This wire is made of copper. (Premise.)
∴.3. This wire will conduct electricity. (Conclusion.)

Taken alone, neither premise makes the claim that the wire will conduct electricity; but taken together, they do. We cannot imagine what it would be like for both premises of this argument to be true, yet its conclusion turns out to be false. Indeed, it would be contradictory to assert both of its premises and then to deny its conclusion.

It is important to see that it is the **form** of this argument—namely:

1. If some sentence, then a second sentence.
2. The first sentence.
∴.3. The second sentence—

that makes it deductively valid, not the truth values of its statements. Letting the capital letter *A* stand for the first sentence and *B* for the second sentence, the *form* of the argument can be stated this way:

1. If *A*, then *B*.
2. *A*.
∴.3. *B*.

Clearly, every argument having this form is deductively valid, another example being this argument:

1. If Sonia reads *Vogue* magazine, then she's up on the latest fashions.
2. Sonia reads *Vogue* magazine.
∴.3. She's up on the latest fashions.

---

[4]Some authorities believe that there is at least one other kind of legitimate argument—namely, the kind in which various alternatives are evaluated. The authors of this text incline to the view that evaluative arguments fall into one or the other of the two basic kinds about to be mentioned. Note also that some authorities restrict the use of the term *valid* so that it refers only to deductively good arguments, even though in everyday life, inductively strong arguments generally are said to be valid. In addition, note that the reasoning process called "mathematical induction" happens to be a kind of deductive reasoning. (Terminology sometimes is misleading.)

Logicians, by the way, call the form of this argument, and every argument having this form, *modus ponens*. (We will consider *modus ponens* again in the next chapter, along with other valid argument forms.)

It's very important to understand that the deductive validity of an argument guarantees that its conclusion is true *only if* its premises are true. Determining that an argument is deductively valid thus tells us just that *if* its premises are true, *then* its conclusion must be true also; it doesn't tell us *whether* its premises are true and thus doesn't tell us *whether* its conclusion is true.

Here, for instance, is a deductively valid argument having the form *modus ponens* that contains one true and one very likely false premise, and thus does not guarantee the truth of its conclusion:

1. If more people read Agatha Christie's mystery novels than read Shakespeare's plays, then her novels must be better than his plays. (False premise?)
2. Her novels have been read by more people than have Shakespeare's plays. (True premise.)
∴3. Her novels must be better than his plays. (False conclusion?)

Of course, a deductively valid argument that contains a false premise may have a true conclusion. But that would be a matter of luck, not of good reasoning.

Deductively valid arguments, then, can have false premises and a false conclusion, false premises and a true conclusion, or true premises and a true conclusion. The only combination that a deductively valid argument cannot have is all true premises and a false conclusion.

The fact that a deductively valid argument cannot move from true premises to a false conclusion constitutes its chief characteristic and great virtue. When you present someone with a deductively valid argument that has premises they know to be true, they must—on pain of irrationality—accept your conclusion! But deductive arguments are limited. They cannot yield conclusions that are not at least implicit in the premises from which they are derived. **Induction** is needed to perform this task.

INDUCTIVE VALIDITY

Inductively valid (inductively strong) arguments, unlike deductively valid ones, have conclusions that go beyond what is contained in their premises. The idea behind valid induction is that of *learning from experience.* We often observe patterns, resemblances, and other kinds of regularities in our experiences, some quite simple (sugar sweetening coffee), some very complicated (objects moving according to Newton's laws—well, Newton noticed this, anyway). Valid inductions simply project regularities of this kind observed in our experiences so far onto other possible experiences.[5]

Here is a simple example of an inductively valid argument, of the kind sometimes called *induction by enumeration,* expressed by a rather smart child in Jacksonville, Florida, explaining why he is doubtful about the existence of Santa Claus:

The tooth fairy turned out not to be real. The Easter Bunny turned out not to be real. So I'm beginning to wonder about Santa.

Admittedly this is a small sample, but perhaps not for a 4-year-old with a limited range of experience.

---

[5]This includes those experiences we can't have but might have if we had lived millions of years ago, or if, say, we could go into the interior of the sun without being incinerated.

We use inductive reasoning so frequently in everyday life that its nature generally goes unnoticed. Being informed about induction is a bit like being told that we've been speaking prose all our lives. We start drawing perfectly good inferences of this kind (and some klinkers) at a very early age. By age 5 or 6, the use of induction has taught us a great many of the basic truths that guide everyday behavior—for instance, that some foods taste good and some don't, the sun rises every morning and sets every evening, very hot things burn the skin, some people are trustworthy and some aren't (something most of us seem to need to relearn over and over), and so on.

The great virtue of inductive reasoning is that it provides us with a way of reasoning to genuinely new beliefs, not just to psychologically new ones that are implicit in what we already know, as in the case of valid deductions. However, this benefit is purchased at the cost of an increase in the possibility of error. As remarked before, the truth of the premises of a deductively valid argument guarantees the truth of its conclusion; but the premises of a perfectly good induction may all be true and yet its conclusion false. Even the best "inductive leap" may lead us astray, because the patterns noticed in our experiences up to a given point may not turn out to be the exact patterns of the whole universe. This happens all too often in daily life—for example, when a restaurant that has served excellent food many times in the past fails us on a special occasion. But it sometimes happens even in the lofty realm of physics. Scientists, for instance, believed for a long time—based on strong inductive reasoning—that particles could not be colder than absolute zero, but then researchers discovered that atoms could be cooled to negative absolute temperatures in a vacuum.

Nevertheless, rational people use induction in formulating their ideas about how things are going to turn out, whether in ordinary, everyday circumstances or in the rather special ones scientists bring about in the laboratory. Induction, thinking of Winston Churchill's famous remark about democracy, is the worst way to expand one's knowledge except for all of the other ways (guessing, wishful thinking, astrology, etc.).

7. Some Wrong Ideas About Cogent Reasoning

Having just presented three standards of cogent reasoning and having explained the nature of valid deduction and induction, perhaps we need to mention several recently voiced ideas about logic and good reasoning. According to these modestly trendy ways of looking at the topic, what counts as good reasoning is "culturally relative," or "gender-relative," or even "individually relative." We hear talk of "feminine logic," supposedly different from the "male logic" of logic classes (which has been developed, advanced, and taught by female logicians, but let that pass), and of "black intelligence," different from the "Eurocentric" variety foisted on us by white males, as though what makes reasoning good differs from group to group, from race to race, or from one sex to the other. We all too often hear students say things such as "That may well be true for you, but it isn't true for me," and listen to academics talk disparagingly of "Aristotelian linear reasoning," as opposed to a more "intuitive" type of reasoning, and so on.

> A wise person hears one word and understands two.
>
> —JEWISH PROVERB

Reading Between the Lines

The expression "reading between the lines" has several meanings. One captures the idea of grasping an intended thought that is not expressed, another of getting more information from a statement or argument than it explicitly—or even implicitly—contains, still another of noticing what rhetoric either deliberately or accidentally hides. Reading between the lines often is the essential ingredient in assessing a good deal of the everyday talk we all encounter, in particular political rhetoric and (interestingly) advertisements.

Take the Bufferin ad that states, "No regular aspirin product reduces fever better." Reading between the lines of this ad, we should conclude that Bufferin does *not* reduce fever better than some competing products, because if it did, the ad would make that stronger claim ("Bufferin reduces fever better than any other aspirin product") rather than the weaker one that none reduces fever better. The point is that our own background beliefs should lead us to expect an advertisement to make the strongest claim possible and thus lead us to at least tentatively conclude that a less strong claim is made because stronger claims would be false.

Reading between the lines is the linguistic equivalent of "sizing up" other people—for example, of gleaning information about their beliefs or likely actions from their overt behavior or way of saying something. A good poker player, for instance, looks for signs of bluffing—some players often unwittingly signal a bluff by increasing chatter or by nervous behavior; others do so by feigning lack of concern. Similarly, intelligent voters try to size up political candidates by looking for nonverbal clues and by reading between the lines of campaign rhetoric. (More will be said about campaign rhetoric in Chapters 7 and 10.)

But there is no truth to these ideas about what constitutes good reasoning. It is the height of folly to conclude, say, that an argument having the form *modus ponens* is not valid. Think, for example, what it means to assert seriously that all human beings have a right to life, and then in the next breath to claim, equally seriously, that a particular human being, Smith, has no right to life. What sense is there in first saying that if Jones has been to China, then he's been to Asia, and then asserting that he has indeed been to China but not to Asia? Yet accepting reasonings that violate the standards of deductive logic means precisely accepting some sorts of contradictory assertions or other, because the point of the principles of valid deduction (including the valid principles of mathematics) is to assure that we do not contradict ourselves when we reason from one thing to another. (That's why, to take just one of a thousand examples, double-entry bookkeeping works.)

Similarly, what reason could there be for violating the standards of good inductive reasoning—for denying what experience teaches us? That a large majority of the scientists who laid the groundwork in physics, chemistry, and biology were white males is totally irrelevant to the truth of their basic ideas and theories. *The way the world works does not differ depending on the race or sex of those trying to discover the way the world works!* That is why, to take an everyday example, it is foolish to toss away money on homeopathic medicines: Medical science has shown, over and over again, by means of inductive reasoning, to say nothing of very highly confirmed general biological principles, that homeopathy does not work. The point cannot be stressed too heavily. There simply is no truth whatsoever to the idea that standards of good reasoning differ from group to group, male to female, or person to person.

There is, however, a good deal of truth to three much different ideas. One is that self-interest, prejudice, and/or narrow-mindedness do in fact often lead people to reason invalidly. Bigotry has a bad name for good reason. Another is that self-interest often motivates us to neglect the values or interests of others, even when we share those values, so that some groups or individuals find their interests frequently neglected. For instance, rich people who believe fairness requires that everyone ought to have an equal chance when starting out in life often forget about equality of opportunity when they argue for the elimination of all inheritance taxes; in families in which both parents work, husbands notoriously tend to paper over their failure to share household and child-rearing duties; in the business world, high executives, while asserting their belief in equal rights for all, frequently overlook the ways in which women, Latinos, and blacks are often passed over for corporate advancement. In all of these cases, the problem is not with the principles of good reasoning. It is with the fallacious nature of the ways in which these principles sometimes are employed.

Those who champion other sorts of "logics" than the standard variety thus may well be mistaken in their target. They attack the principles of good reasoning rather than the failure of their opponents to employ these perfectly good (indeed the *only* good) standards of reasoning correctly, or to reason from acceptable moral or other kinds of values.

A good deal more will be said in later chapters on these matters, in particular about moral and other value claims. For now, the point is just that we must distinguish the principles of good reasoning, which are the same for all, from the ways in which these principles are employed (sometimes fallaciously), and from the differing values that enter into the premises of different reasonings.

8. Background Beliefs

Earlier, we characterized cogent reasoning in terms of three conditions: the validity of connections between premises and conclusions, the believability of premises, and the discovery and use of relevant information. Clearly, satisfaction of the last two of these three conditions requires the employment of background beliefs. That is why bringing one's background beliefs to bear is among the most important tasks in evaluating an argument for cogency.

Consider, for example, the argument frequently heard in the early 1980s that AIDS was essentially a gay plague inflicted on homosexuals as punishment for their perverse sexual conduct (a claim still occasionally heard). Setting aside illegitimate assumptions about diseases being punishments and the "perversion" of homosexuality, the key premise of this argument was that AIDS can be transmitted sexually only via homosexual conduct. This was supported by the evidence that in the United States, a large majority of those reported early on to have the disease were indeed homosexuals. But people with good background information did not accept this argument. For one thing, they knew that in other places around the world—for instance, in Haiti and parts of Africa—large numbers of heterosexuals also had contracted AIDS via sexual contact. And for another, those familiar with some of the basic scientific ideas concerning disease had theoretical (which means higher-level inductive) reasons for believing that AIDS could be transmitted via heterosexual behavior, as are syphilis, hepatitis B, herpes, and so on.

Today, most Americans know that AIDS is transmitted by both heterosexuals and homosexuals, but many people wrongly think that the disease is curable because they have heard about drugs used to treat HIV. In fact, these drugs suppress the viral infection but do not cure it, and no vaccine has been successfully developed to date. Unfortunately, many young people believe they can be cured if they become infected and thus fail to take adequate precautions.

The point is that, contrary to the old saying, ignorance is *not* bliss. It just renders us incapable of intelligently evaluating claims, premises, arguments, and other sorts of rhetoric we all are subject to every day. When evaluating arguments and issues, we can't bring relevant beliefs to bear if we don't have them, and we cannot make good judgments if what we believe is off the mark.

9. Kinds of Background Beliefs

Background beliefs can be divided up in many different ways, an important one being a separation into beliefs about *matters of fact* and beliefs about values. It is a factual question, for example, whether capital punishment is practiced in every society (it isn't); it is a question of values whether capital punishment is morally justified (is it?). In dealing with most social or political issues, we need to separate claims that are about matters of fact from those concerning values, because these two different sorts of claims are defended, or justified, in different ways. The statement, for example, that a given state has a death penalty is proved true, or false, by an examination of relevant government records; the judgment that capital punishment is, or isn't, morally justified as the punishment for heinous crimes is determined by bringing to bear an accepted moral code, or subjective intuitions.[6]

---

[6]Philosophers and others disagree seriously concerning the question whether there are such things as objective moral principles that all clear-minded, rational individuals are bound to see as correct, or whether moral right and wrong is a matter of subjective opinion—of feelings that can, and perhaps do, differ from person to person.

> Knowledge not renewed quickly becomes ignorance.
>
> —PETER DRUCKER

> Those who cannot remember the past are condemned to repeat it.
>
> —GEORGE SANTAYANA

Background beliefs also can be divided into those that are *true* and (unfortunately) those that are *false*. Someone who believes, for example, that capital punishment exists as a practice in every society has a false belief; those who believe that every society punishes murderers in one way or another has a belief that is true. An important reason for regularly testing our background beliefs in terms of our experiences and of what we learn from others is precisely to weed out background beliefs that are false. Education consists of a lot more than simply learning a mountain of facts; it also has to do with weeding out beliefs that turn out to be false (or unjustified).

Beliefs also differ as to how firmly they are or should be held. We feel completely sure, completely confident, of some beliefs (for example, that the sun will rise tomorrow); less sure, but still quite confident, of others (for example, that the United States will still be in existence in the year 2050); and a good deal less sure, but still mildly confident, of others (for example, that we won't get killed someday in an auto accident). The trick is to believe firmly what should be believed, given the evidence, and believe less firmly, or not at all, what is less well supported by evidence.

All of this relates directly to decisions we have to make in everyday life. Wise individuals take into account the probability of one thing or another happening and thus of the confidence they should place in their beliefs about what to do. That's a large part of the truth behind familiar sayings such as "A bird in the hand is worth two in the bush."

10. Worldviews or Philosophies

As we grow up from childhood into adults, we tend to absorb the beliefs and standards of those in the world around us—our families, friends, and culture. It is no accident that so many of us have the same religious affiliation, or lack of same, as do our parents, that we accept the principles and standards of our own society, and so on.

These beliefs constitute an important part of our **worldviews** or **philosophies**.[7] They tend to be the most deeply ingrained and most resistant to amendment of all of our background beliefs. They become so much a part of us that we often appeal to them without consciously realizing we have done so. They are so thoroughly woven into the fabric of our belief systems that we often find it hard to isolate and examine individual strands. And when we do examine them, our natural tendency is to reaffirm them without

---

[7]This includes religious beliefs in the case of those who have religious convictions.

thought and to disparage conflicting claims and evidence, quickly dismissing evidence that might count against them.

Most of these beliefs are general—for example, that killing always is morally wrong, that there is some good in virtually all human beings, or that we all die sooner or later. But not all are. Belief in a monotheistic deity, for instance, or rejection of such a belief, is a particular belief.

But in spite of the example just cited, general beliefs usually are more important than beliefs that are particular, or less general, because they tell us about a wider range of cases and thus tend to be more useful in everyday life. Believing that it rarely rains in July in Los Angeles, for instance, clearly is more useful than believing merely that it won't rain there, say, on July 16, 2024. That is why most of the important beliefs in one's worldview are general and also why most important scientific pronouncements are general—indeed, often extremely general. (Newton's laws, for example, don't just tell us about apples falling from trees or even just about items of all kinds falling toward Earth. They also tell us about the motion of Earth around the sun, about the motion of all planets around the sun, about how tides rise and fall, and, in fact, about the motions of all objects whatsoever.) It also is why it is so important, and useful, to expand our worldviews to contain at least a few modestly well-founded beliefs about important scientific theories—for example, about the theory of the evolution of all life on Earth.

Our Words and Worldviews

The worldviews of political parties are implied in the words and phrases they use repeatedly in their discourse. University of California linguist George Lakoff came up with a list of words used over and over in the speeches and writings of conservatives and liberals. It's worth examining them to figure out the dominant worldviews reflected in the language.*

Conservatives: character, virtue, discipline, tough it out, get tough, tough love, strong, self-reliance, individual responsibility, backbone, standards, authority, heritage, competition, earn, hard work, enterprise, property rights, reward, freedom, intrusion, interference, meddling, punishment, human nature, traditional, common sense, dependency, self-indulgent, elite, quotas, breakdown, corrupt, decay, rot, degenerate, deviant, lifestyle.

Liberals: social forces, social responsibility, free expression, human rights, equal rights, concern, care, help, health, safety, nutrition, basic human dignity, oppression, diversity, deprivation, alienation, big corporations, corporate welfare, ecology, ecosystem, biodiversity, pollution.

What worldviews are indicated by the repetition of these words? Reflect a moment on the assumptions you used to come to these conclusions. Specifically, which of the words above do you think were typically used with a negative connotation?

_____

*Taken from Lakoff, G. *Moral Politics: How Liberals and Conservatives Think*. Chicago: University of Chicago Press, 2002.

Compare the worldview reflected in this gem, excerpted from a 1950s women's magazine, to your worldview.

From "Runaway Husbands" by Barbara Heggie

Somehow, in her battle for equal rights, the American woman has convinced herself that one of these rights is the love of her husband. She should be reminded that love is not an obligation, but a reward for favors received—for affection, for solicitude, above all for making her husband feel he is the center of her own particular universe. What I had seen in the bleak faces of the deserted wives I had talked to was the knowledge they had failed in the biggest job a woman can accept.

—*GOOD HOUSEKEEPING*, OCTOBER, 1950

11. Insufficiently Grounded Beliefs

Most of us have strongly held beliefs about a great many controversial issues, and so we tend to respond automatically to arguments about these matters. We feel confident that we know whether marijuana should be legalized, whether we should privatize Social Security, whether this candidate or that is more likely to serve all of the people equally if elected to office, and so on. We hold these beliefs, often very strongly, even though a good deal of the time we have insufficient justifying background knowledge and have engaged in too little thought to be able to support our beliefs intelligently or defend them against informed objections. What, for example, do we usually know about candidates running for seats in the U.S. House of Representatives? (Every election year, a significant number of voters do not know the names of both major-party candidates for congressional seats in their districts; fewer still can name both candidates for state legislatures in their districts. Could you?) Too often, we base our vote on our party affiliation and not on the merit of individual candidates. Worse still, voters sometimes decide on the basis of name recognition alone. Clearly, then, weeding out insufficiently grounded background information is vital if we are to improve our reasoning about important, to say nothing of relatively trivial, matters. (It also might be a good idea to find out something about candidates for various offices before stepping into a booth and casting our ballots.)

Having well-supported background beliefs is particularly important with respect to those basic background beliefs that make up our worldviews. Worldviews are like lenses that cause us to see the world in a particular way or filters through which we process all new ideas and information. Reasoning based on a grossly inaccurate or shallow worldview tends to yield grossly inaccurate, inappropriate, or self-defeating conclusions (except when we're just plain lucky), no matter how smart we otherwise may be. Sometimes, the harm is relatively minor (gamblers who waste a few bucks playing "lucky" lottery numbers; astrology column readers who arrange vacation times to fit their sign), but at other times, the harm can be more serious (people with an overly rosy view of human nature who get taken by con artists; misanthropes who miss out on the benefits and joys of trusting relationships).

Obviously, then, we need to examine our background beliefs, especially those that make up our worldviews, for consistency and believability, and we need to amend them so as to square with newly acquired information. The point is that having a good supply of background beliefs is not just a matter of filling up one's "tank" with gallons of facts. It is at least equally important to improve one's existing stock of beliefs by weeding out those that experience proves to be false, to sharpen vague beliefs, and to replace crude beliefs with those that are more sophisticated—beliefs that penetrate more deeply into the complexities of life and the world.

People who hold different worldviews often clash on a personal level, but when cultures or nations have conflicting worldviews, they can create tension and spark antagonism internationally. One recent example involved a controversy over whether an Afghan should be sentenced to death because he converted from Islam to Christianity. Under Sharia law, a Muslim who rejects Islam may be tried and executed. So when it became known that the man had converted to Christianity, he was put on trial by the Afghan government, whose constitution allows prosecution under Sharia law. When Muslim clerics demanded that he be sentenced to death, prominent leaders in the Western world urged the government to honor human rights principles and free him. The conflicting worldviews caused an uproar on both sides. When the Afghan government looked for ways to drop the case in order to comply with international pressure, the clerics warned that if the man were freed, the people of Afghanistan would kill him. (The government resolved this dilemma by declaring him mentally unfit and citing "investigative gaps" in the case.) When clashes like this multiply and escalate, they can lead to serious international conflict and even large-scale violence.

The Cost of Entrenched Worldviews

It is worth noting here that widespread failure to revise worldviews often results in serious political and social unrest and injustice. E. M. Forster captures this poignantly in his novel *A Passage to India,* in which he depicts intense conflicts in colonial India between English masters and their conquered Indian subjects. Believing themselves socially and racially superior, the English relegate the Indians to subordinate positions, never allowing them equality under the British raj. The insensitivity of the British to the plight of their subjects is met with resentment, distrust, anger, and threats of violent retaliation by the Indians. (To make matters worse, the Indians are divided from one another by differing religious and cultural beliefs.) Very few of the British or Indians Forster depicts ever revise their biases and prejudices in the light of new information—for instance, in the light of obvious evidence about the competence of individual Indians or the glaring prejudice of English officials. The novel makes a compelling case for a widespread reexamination of worldviews and other background beliefs if human beings are to arrive at a peaceful, nonexploitative coexistence on planet Earth.

Socrates is said to have claimed that the unexamined life is not worth living.[8] While clearly an exaggeration, there surely is a great deal of truth in this idea. By the same token, there is a large dose of truth in the idea that an unexamined worldview is not likely to be worth holding, in particular because it will contain little more than an accumulation of the ideas and prejudices of others. Examining worldviews allows us to take control of our lives by actively sorting out our fundamental beliefs, testing them against ideas and information that point to conclusions contrary to what we already believe, and making whatever revisions are indicated in the light of what we have learned. *Doing this helps us to become our own person rather than just a passive follower of others!*

Unfortunately, it is no easy matter for us to examine our worldviews objectively. Psychological studies show that people hold on to their beliefs for dear life, ignoring evidence that undermines them and dredging up weak evidence to support them. This obstacle to rational thought is compounded by our natural tendency to take short-cuts in reasoning that reduce our mental effort, allowing us to slide past unwelcome evidence and leap to hasty conclusions that support our existing beliefs. All this makes rational self-analysis difficult, to say the least—but not impossible. To reason cogently, we need to fight this human tendency (discussed further in Chapter 6).

12. Two Vital Kinds of Background Beliefs

Background beliefs obviously differ greatly in their importance—that is to say, their propensity to affect (or even determine) our everyday judgments. Two kinds that are extremely important in this way concern the *nature of human nature* and the *reliability of information sources.*

THE NATURE OF HUMAN NATURE

Beliefs about what we ourselves and other people are like constitute a vital part of everyone's worldview. They are crucial in applying what we know to the problems encountered in everyday life, whether of a personal or a social nature. When can we trust our friends? Is an instructor to be believed who says that students are graded solely on the quality of their exams and not on agreement with the instructor's personal opinions? Will people be sufficiently motivated to work diligently under a socialistic system? Are large numbers of elected officials motivated by selfish interests that frequently override their sense of duty to those who have elected them?

Fortunately, we don't have to start constructing theories about human nature from scratch, since other people, including some of the great writers (Shakespeare, Aristotle, Darwin, Freud) have been at the task for some time now. (Of course, tapping these sources has its risks. Freud, for instance, had some way-off-target ideas on the subject to go along with some extremely penetrating ones.)

---

[8]Note, however, that psychology has just recently come out of its infancy. Note also that there is more chicanery in medical research (because of the profit motive?) than in most other areas of science.

THE RELIABILITY OF INFORMATION SOURCES

Thoughts about the accuracy, sufficiency, and truthfulness of information sources constitute another vital kind of background belief. As with computers, so also with the human mind: "Garbage in, garbage out." We therefore need constantly to reassess the reliability of important information sources—television, newspapers, magazines, friends, the Internet, teachers, textbooks, and so on. Under what conditions are these sources likely to provide truthful or, at least, sensible information or opinions? When are alleged experts likely even to possess the truth, much less be motivated to tell it to us straight? When are they likely to be prejudiced in ways that may cloud their judgment? We can't assume automatically that a source is reliable without some *reason* for believing this. As lamented a while back, many people seem to think that if they read it in print or hear it on the TV evening news, then it must be true. Sophisticated reasoners, however, realize that these information sources do not always furnish "the truth, the whole truth, and nothing but the truth"; they don't necessarily provide us with "All the news that's fit to print" (the *New York Times* motto), instead sometimes shaving matters either out of ignorance or from self-serving motives. Intelligent viewers of the scene thus try to determine when these sources are likely to be reliable and when not. That is why Chapter 10 deals with advertising as an information source, Chapter 11 with the reliability of the news media, and Chapter 12 with new media.

13. Science to the Rescue

The mention of Darwin and Freud a while back brings to mind the central place that science plays in modern life and in the construction of accurate stocks of background beliefs—in particular, in the formulation of sensible worldviews. Although no information source is absolutely reliable and no theory exempt from at least a small measure of doubt, the most reliable, the most accurate information comes from the well-established sciences of physics, chemistry, biology, and, to a lesser extent, psychology, the social sciences, and the applied sciences such as engineering. The scientific enterprise is an organized, ongoing, worldwide activity that builds and corrects from generation to generation. The method of science is just the rigorous, systematic, dogged application of cogent inductive reasoning, mixed with all sorts of deductive—including mathematical— reasoning from what has so far been observed over many centuries to theories about how the universe and the many things in it have functioned and are likely to function. Theories falsified by experience are tossed out, no matter whose pet ideas happen to get stepped on. Absolutely no one, starting from scratch, could hope to obtain, in one lifetime, anything remotely resembling the sophisticated and accurate conclusions of any of the sciences, even if that person were a Galileo, Newton, Darwin, and Einstein all rolled into one. *It is foolish indeed to dismiss what science has to say on any topic without very careful thought and without having extremely important reasons for doing so!*[9]

---

[9]It is worth noting that this comes to us from the "Apology," Plato's (probably somewhat fictionalized) account of Socrates's trial, where he was accused largely of "examining" himself and others and where he was ultimately sentenced to death.

Indeed, one justification for requiring all high school students to take at least one course in a physical or biological science is to allow them to gain an understanding of the great rigor with which scientific principles are tested and proved. But another, easier way to come to understand the power of science as compared to other ways of finding out about the world is to think carefully about the thousands of everyday items available to us today that did not exist 300 years ago, products that owe their existence to the tremendous advances in scientific theory that have been made since the days of Galileo and Newton. Without science, there would be no automobiles, no airplanes (not to mention spacecraft), no telephones, no electric lightbulbs, no air conditioning, no other electric devices of any kind (certainly no computers!), no batteries, no aspirin or other common painkillers, no anesthetics (alcohol used to be the painkiller used during amputations), no antibiotics (or even knowledge of the existence of microbes and thus the extreme importance of cleanliness), no ways to purify drinking water, no indoor plumbing, no eyeglasses, no insulin for diabetics, . . . the list goes on and on. Instead, there were plenty of mosquitoes and flies (and fly paper) everywhere on summer days, and people made do with commodes, outhouses, and well-drawn drinking and washing water. In those days, doctors could cure only a handful of ailments, horse dung and its foul smell were everywhere in every city and town, lighting after dark was furnished by candles or oil lamps, and so on. Before the existence of the scientific, modern, industrial world, the average life span almost everywhere was less than 50 years, much less in most societies.

Of course, to avoid having beliefs contradicted by scientific theory or to apply scientific principles successfully in dealing with everyday problems, one does have to have at least a casual acquaintance with what science has to say on various topics. The problem is that large numbers of people have no idea what science is up to and have only the tiniest stock of scientific facts about the nature of the world. This lack of knowledge about science can have unfortunate consequences. For instance, a growing number of parents have refused to vaccinate their children against measles on the mistaken belief that vaccines are ineffective preventatives and may even be harmful. They believe that a healthy diet and good living is enough and that their refusal to use vaccinations won't affect anyone but their own children. None of these assumptions is accurate, however. A study published in the *Journal of the American Medical Association* of measles cases over the last 15 years found that recent increases in measles cases correlate with the increase in vaccine refusals. For immunizations to be effective, a high percentage of children need to be vaccinated to protect the population at large. Ignoring the science has resulted in outbreaks of measles, which the Center for Disease Control was able to declare eradicated from the United States before the anti-vaccination movement took root.

Unfortunately, it isn't just the average person (or average college graduate?) who is more or less illiterate when it comes to science. Even those who need to know about specific scientific results in order to do their jobs adequately are frequently remiss in this way. During a quite severe drought in California, one government official defended his inaction by stating that "One problem [in deciding whether to enact water rationing measures] is that we have only 110 years of [precipitation] records. Our statistics [on California droughts] aren't very good." Yet, just prior to that time, a U.S. Geological Survey study of giant sequoia tree rings had yielded a record going back more than 2,000 years.

Students sometimes defend their ignorance of science by arguing that they only need to know the science, if any, that is relevant to the job they will perform after graduation from college. But this is a serious mistake. For one thing, it isn't possible to know now what basic scientific ideas will be relevant to a job held several years down the pike. (It isn't really possible, except in unusual cases, to know what sort of job it will *be*, much less what kinds of knowledge will be relevant to it.) In this increasingly technological age, more and more jobs require at least a general idea of what science has to say about various topics.

More to the point, a rudimentary understanding of science also is of immeasurable value when dealing with all sorts of everyday problems that aren't related to earning a living. Consumers spend millions of dollars every year on over-the-counter nostrums that don't work, or may even be harmful, because they don't know simple scientific facts— for instance, that no remedies they can buy will cure the flulike infections common in

A Crisis in Psychology?

It may be that not all fields that we call "science" are quite as reliable as the developed natural sciences (physics, biology, botany, etc.). This is not a disparagement of so-called "soft science" (roughly the social sciences: psychology, economics, political science, etc.). Work in these fields is often rigorous, fascinating, and useful. And we have much to learn from it.

But at the same time, it may not be quite as simple to rely on results in these fields. Take for instance a recent controversy in social psychology. One key criterion for a scientific result is reproducibility. A successful experiment ought to be able to be conducted again and again by anyone and always yield the same result. If not, then those results are at least subject to doubt if not thrown out entirely. However, in August 2015, a study by the "Reproducibility Project" found that the results of fewer than 40 percent of the 100 experiments published in major psychology journals were reproducible. Social psychology fared particularly badly, coming in at 25 percent.

To be fair, many experimental psychologists have argued that the controversy over these findings and the significant media coverage that followed them was overblown. As Lisa Feldman Barrett, a psychology professor at Northeastern claimed in the *New York Times*, "the failure to replicate is not a cause for alarm; in fact, it is a normal part of how science works . . . It is what leads us along the path— the wonderfully twisty path—of scientific discovery."

One problem with public scientific knowledge in general is that results of scientists' work are often publicized prematurely and misrepresented in the mass media. The lesson here is not that we shouldn't trust psychology or any other social science, but that maybe we should wait a bit until discoveries in these fields (and maybe to some extent in the hard sciences, too) are a little further along Professor Barrett's "wonderfully twisty path" before we fully take them on board. But once results *are* successfully replicated and agreement on a certain hypothesis approaches scientific consensus, we have all the reason in the world to accept it.

winter. Every day, people throw their money away on get-rich-quick schemes that defy the most basic principles of economics. Large sums are wasted on fortune tellers, mediums, and other charlatans whom science has proved over and over again cannot deliver the promised goods. (This point is discussed a bit more in Chapter 6.)

Students often are put off science by the sheer complexity of the subject matter. Biology, for example, has to be an extremely complicated science, given that the bodies of complex living organisms like humans contain trillions of cells, each one of which contains millions of atoms and subatomic particles. (Did you know this?) So the bad news is that every science quickly goes over the heads of almost all laypeople. But the good news is that with only modest perseverance, people who are reasonably intelligent can learn enough about science to greatly improve their everyday reasoning and thus their chances of success in everyday life. (Clearly, similar remarks apply to mathematics, particularly to arithmetic and simple algebra—note the confusion that occasionally results in supermarkets when the power goes out and clerks need to actually add and subtract to figure out what is owed.)

Summary of Chapter 1

Reasoning is the essential ingredient in solving life's problems. This chapter discusses some of the fundamentals of good reasoning and presents an overview of the material to be covered later on the topic of reasoning well in everyday life.

1. *Reasoning* can be cast into *arguments,* which consist of one or more *premises* (reasons) offered in support of a *conclusion.* In real life (as opposed to in textbooks), arguments usually are not labeled and divided from surrounding rhetoric, nor are their premises and conclusions neatly specified. But clues generally are given. *Logical indicators* such as *because, since,* and *for* usually signal premises; *hence, therefore,* and *so,* conclusions.

2. Not all groups of sentences form arguments. They may be anecdotes or other types of *exposition* or *explanation.* Explanations are especially prone to be confused for arguments. In most cases, explanations are meant to show how some claim came to be true, while arguments are meant to persuade us that some claim is true.

3. For our purposes, "winning an argument" means more than just persuading an audience. It means persuading an audience *based on a rational inference from premises to conclusion.*

4. Reasoning is either *cogent* (good) or *fallacious* (bad). Cogent reasoning must satisfy three criteria: It must (1) start with justified (warranted, believable) premises, (2) include all likely relevant information, and (3) be *valid* (correct).

5. There are two basic kinds of valid reasoning: *deductive* and *inductive.* The fundamental property of a *deductively valid* argument is this: If its premises are true, then its conclusion must be true also. This is so because the conclusion of a deductively valid argument already is contained in its premises, although usually implicitly, not explicitly. (Note that a deductively valid argument may have false

premises. What makes it valid is that *if* its premises are true, then its conclusion must be also.) Unlike deductively valid arguments, those that are *inductively valid* (inductively correct, strong) have conclusions that go beyond the claims made by their premises, projecting patterns stated in the premises onto additional cases.

6. There is no truth to claims about there being such things as "feminine logic," different from "male logic." Logic is not "gender-relative." Similarly, there is no truth to the idea that something exists called "black logic," different from the "Eurocentric" variety espoused by white male teachers. Good reasoning does not differ from sex to sex or from race to race; it is not in any way tied to ethnicity. Furthermore, with respect to facts, at any rate, the idea embodied in the idea that "It may well be true for you, but it isn't true for me" is without merit, as is the academic talk of there being something called "Aristotelian linear reasoning," different from a more "intuitive" type of reasoning. (But more needs to be said, and will be, about beliefs concerning values. The point made in this chapter is that, however we may arrive at value beliefs, reasoning from those beliefs must employ the same principles of logic as does reasoning about purely factual matters.)

7. Background beliefs can be divided in many ways, one being into beliefs about *matters of fact* (snow is white) and beliefs about *values* (Jane Austen's novels are better than those of Stephen King). (Note that when speaking of beliefs here, we have in mind a broad sense covering everything accepted as true, or very likely true, and all value judgments and convictions.)

8. Beliefs also, of course, can be divided into those that happen to be true and those that are false. They also can be differentiated in terms of how firmly they are or should be held, and with respect to whether they concern particular events (Jones went to the show last Wednesday) or those that are general (copper conducts electricity).

9. Our most important beliefs, taken together, make up our *worldviews* or *philosophies.* They are particularly important because they enter into decisions of all kinds—about what to do or what to believe—that we need to make in everyday life. **Examples:** We all die sooner or later; it's always wrong to betray a friend; the best way to find out about how things work is to use induction and deduction. Note that, although most beliefs in our worldviews are general— even extremely general—a few are not. **Example:** We don't know whether there is or isn't a God (part of the worldviews of agnostics).

10. Unfortunately, we all tend at least sometimes to hold a belief without sufficient reason for doing so—for example, when complicated social or political issues are discussed. This is true even with respect to some of the beliefs that make up our worldviews. But worldviews, just as any beliefs, need to be carefully examined: Does evidence support them? Do we really value this more than that? Having an

accurate supply of background beliefs is not just a matter of regularly acquiring more beliefs but also of pruning those we already have.

11.   We tend to absorb the beliefs of those around us as we mature from children into adults. Our worldviews, in particular, tend to grow out of family values, religious training, peer group attitudes, cultural heritages, and so on. We often hold these vital beliefs uncritically—indeed, often without realizing that we hold them. Good critical reasoners, on the contrary, try to become aware of and to critically evaluate their background beliefs, especially those making up their worldviews.

12.   Beliefs about human nature are of vital importance when reasoning in daily life, because the success or failure of everyday interactions depends on them. Whether we can trust this sort of person or that is an example. That is one reason why reading the writings of great literary and scientific figures is so useful (in addition to being entertaining).

13.   Beliefs about the accuracy and truthfulness of information sources also are of great importance, because, as the saying goes, "Garbage in, garbage out." We can't reason well from poor or false information. That is why later chapters in this book deal with several important information sources.

14.   Because science plays such an important part in everyone's life these days, it behooves us to become as well acquainted as we can, and as time permits, with the scientific view of the world and with the ways in which scientists come to their conclusions. No one on his or her own could possibly discover even a tiny fraction of what scientists have learned over hundreds of years about the way the world works. (Those who don't see the importance of science in their own lives should reflect on how much we depend, every day, on the fruits of scientific investigations. ***Examples:*** Electrical devices, painkillers and other modern medicines, toilet paper.) Unfortunately, most people do not have even a reasonably good grasp of what science is up to.

EXERCISE SET 1-1

Identify the premises and conclusions in the following arguments. (A few are from student exams—modestly edited.)[10] Remember, sometimes a premise or conclusion may be implied.

Example

Argument
   The barometer is falling sharply, so the weather is going to change.

Argument Structure
   Premise: The barometer is falling sharply.
   Implied premise: Whenever the barometer falls sharply, the weather changes.
   Conclusion: The weather is going to change.

---

[10]Starred (*) items are answered in a section at the back of the book.

1. Since everyone deserves health care, and 30 million Americans still don't have medical insurance, the United States should institute national insurance.

2. I have my doubts about genetically modified plants. To begin with, we don't have enough information about them to know if they are bad for us in the long run. Then there is the problem of cross contamination if they spread to other areas. The whole thing seems pretty questionable.

3. The legacy of the New England Patriots will forever be tarnished, no matter how many Super Bowls they win. They have a long history of cheating, whether we're talking about filming other teams' practices, lying about injuries, or deflating game balls. And that's just the stuff we know about! The truly legendary teams win like the Patriots, but unlike the Patriots, they do it the right way.

*4. William Shakespeare: "Forbear to judge, for we are sinners all."

*5. Why not legalize drugs? One thing for sure, we would get rid of the crime syndicates that run the show now. Instead of giving money to the drug lords, the government would rake in billions in taxes. Maybe even enough to pay down the debt.

6. Aristotle: "The Earth has a spherical shape. For the night sky looks different in the northern and the southern parts of the Earth, and that would be the case if the Earth were spherical in shape."

7. Human activities have become the major source of global warming. Over the past 200 years, they have been responsible for the rising carbon dioxide levels from burning fossil fuels and for increased concentrations of other greenhouse gases like methane and nitrous oxide.

*8. Several years ago, National Football League quarterback Michael Vick was convicted of sponsoring illegal dogfights and performing acts of cruelty to animals. But he served his time in federal prison and has worked with the Humane Society to help stamp out dogfighting among young people. So his criminal record shouldn't prevent him from getting into the Pro Football Hall of Fame. He was a great quarterback for the Atlanta Falcons before his prison time, and he made a great comeback with the Philadelphia Eagles. He deserves the honor.

9. College costs big bucks. When you put out that kind of money, you should be able to decide where your money goes. Students shouldn't have to take introductory courses if they don't want to. Besides, you don't need those basic courses for lots of careers.

10. Giving illegal aliens driver's licenses would undermine our immigration laws. After all, they are here illegally to begin with. Besides, there is the security issue. If anyone can get a license, so can terrorists, and that means they can fly anywhere in the country with just a license for an ID. Who knows how many planes they might blow up?

EXERCISE SET 1-2

Here are several passages. (Some are from student papers—again, modestly edited.) Indicate which contain arguments and which do not, label the premises and conclusions of those passages that do (as you did in the previous exercise), and explain why you think the other passages do not contain arguments.

Example

Passage from Agatha Christie's novel *Murder on the Orient Express: M. Hercule Poirot, having nothing better to do, amused himself by studying her without appearing to do so. She was, he judged, the kind of young woman who could take care of herself with perfect ease wherever she went. . . . He rather liked the severe regularity of her features and the delicate pallor of her skin. He liked the burnished black head with its neat waves of hair, and her eyes—cool, impersonal and gray.*

Evaluation: *This is not an argument. The author says Poirot judged (reasoned) that the woman could take care of herself, but does not describe his reasoning. And the rest of the passage simply says that Poirot liked certain features of the young woman.*

*1.   If we keep burning so much coal and oil, the greenhouse effect will continue to get worse. But it will be a disaster if that happens. So we've got to reduce dependency on these fossil fuels.

2.   We are never going to find a cure for diabetes, cancer, Alzheimer's, and a lot of other diseases unless we use the most promising research available. Stem cell research is the way to go.

3.   Stem cell research sounds like a good idea, but it costs a lot of money, and we don't really know if it will cure people. We don't know what the long-term effects will be either. What if it keeps people alive for 200 years—in a world that is already overpopulated? Besides, it's just wrong to take stem cells from embryos.

*4.   My summer vacation was spent working in Las Vegas. I worked as a waitress at the Tropicana and made tons of money. But I guess I got addicted to the slots and didn't save too much. That's why I'll try to find work outside a casino next summer.

5.   Legalizing prostitution is bound to increase sexually transmitted diseases. And look what it would do to women. It can't help but lead to their degradation. Besides, most people don't like the idea, anyway.

6.   The National Center for Education Statistics estimated that 20.2 million students would attend U.S. colleges and universities in 2015. The average cost of tuition, room, and board for in-state students at four-year public colleges and universities was $19,548, and at private schools, $43,921, according to the College Board's Annual Survey of Colleges.

7.   Some people in the field of medicine are keen on embedding computer chips inside the body, but I've got a problem with that. True, the chips could provide

helpful medical information if I'm unconscious or something, which I guess is the main reason for doing it, but I don't want to make that kind of information available to the government or anyone else, for that matter, who might want to invade my privacy.

8. Too much money is thrown at college football and basketball. It's almost like they are professional sports. In fact, lots of athletes go to college to train for pro teams, not to get an education. All the publicity and hero worship draws attention away from the reason for going to school to begin with. It's no wonder many students pick colleges because of their teams, not their academic standing.

9. West Virginia is a state today because Union-allied counties of what was then Confederate Virginia voted to separate shortly after Virginia's secession from the Union in 1861.

*10. Descartes: "Good sense is of all things in the world the most equally distributed, for everybody thinks himself so abundantly provided with it, that even those most difficult to please in all other matters do not commonly desire more of it than they already possess."

11. Since baseball players who take steroids have an unfair advantage over those who don't, it follows that they should not be inducted into the Hall of Fame, because giving them that honor would corrupt the basic fairness and integrity of the game.

12. Why shouldn't public schools take donations from private business? The government doesn't expend enough money to repair the buildings, let alone pay teachers a decent salary. Besides, big business would demand more for its money—like higher standards and better discipline.

13. Alexis de Tocqueville, *Democracy in America:* Men will never establish any equality with which they will be contented. . . . "When inequality of conditions is the common law of society, the most marked inequalities do not strike the eye: when everything is nearly on the same level, the slightest are marked enough to hurt it.

    Hence the desire for equality always becomes more insatiable in proportion as equality is more complete."

EXERCISE SET 1-3

Which of the following passages (modestly edited to make them more straightforward than arguments often are in daily life) do you think are deductively valid? Inductively valid? Defend your answers, showing the structure of those you believe to be valid.

1. A friend of mine told me that the herb echinacea would cure my cold or at least reduce the symptoms if I took it four times a day. So I did what he said, but I didn't get better any faster. A few months later I caught another cold and took echinacea again—this time at the first sign I was sick. But no luck. Next time I'll just take some aspirin. Echinacea doesn't work.

2. If I buy these potato chips, I know I'm going to eat the whole bagful at one sitting. But if I do that, I'll upset my stomach. Well, then, if I buy this tempting item, my guts are going to get upset again. Satan, get thee behind me!

3. My father has always voted for Republican candidates, and my mother has also. Hah! Now that I'm old enough to vote, I'm going to vote Democratic. That'll show them.

4. According to statistics compiled by the U.S. Bureau of Labor Statistics in 2015, full-time workers without high school degrees earned a median of $25,636 per year; high school graduates, $35,256 per year; community college graduates with associates degrees, $41,496 per year; college graduates with bachelor degrees, $59,124; college graduates with professional degrees, $89,960. Is college worth it? Yes, though these numbers are down significantly from 2008.

EXERCISE SET 1-4

1. Use Google or another search engine to search for Martin Luther King's "I Have a Dream" speech. Figure out which parts of the speech state or imply King's philosophy and explain his worldview.

2. Find at least one item on the Internet or in the mass media (a newspaper or magazine article or a television program) that seems to be based on a worldview contrary to the one you yourself hold. Explain your choice.

3. Find at least one item on the Internet or in the mass media that reflects a typically American point of view you happen to share, and explain what makes it typically American. (This is not as easy to do as it sounds. Recalling the content of the box on E. M. Forster's novel may help prod your memory.)

4. Describe a situation in which you changed your mind on some more or less fundamental belief, and explain what convinced you to do so. (This is a very difficult question for many people to answer, another bit of evidence for the fact that much of what goes on in the accumulation and emendation of important background beliefs happens only on the edge of consciousness.)

EXERCISE SET 1-5

1. When Barack Obama and Hillary Clinton ran for the Democratic presidential nomination in 2008, many people thought that the time had come to elect an African American or a woman as president. Never before in our history had two candidates from these politically underrepresented groups both come so close to leading the nation. Both presidential elections since 2008 have included a number of African Americans and women as major-party candidates. What changes in worldviews were reflected in voters' newfound willingness to elect a woman or an African American to the highest position in the country?

2.   According to the Pew Research Center, attitudes toward same-sex marriage in the United States shifted massively over the past 15 years, with 57 percent of those polled in 2001 opposing allowing gay and lesbian couples to wed, versus 55 percent of those polled in 2015 who supported legal same-sex marriages. How do you think these shifts were influenced by larger changes in worldview over those years? Also, attitudes toward gay rights in general seem to have shifted much faster in this country than did attitudes toward the rights of African Americans or women. Why do you think that is?

EXERCISE SET 1-6

How do the ideas expressed in the following excerpt from an essay by British philosopher Bertrand Russell compare with those in your own worldview and other background beliefs?

> *The aesthetic indictment of industrialism is perhaps the least serious. A much more serious feature is the way in which it forces men, women, and children to live a life against instinct, unnatural, unspontaneous, artificial. Where industry is thoroughly developed, men are deprived of the sight of green fields and the smell of earth after rain; they are cooped together in irksome proximity, surrounded by noise and dirt, compelled to spend many hours a day performing some utterly uninteresting and monotonous mechanical task. Women are, for the most part, obliged to work in factories, and to leave to others the care of their children. The children themselves, if they are preserved from work in the factories, are kept at work in school, with an intensity that is especially damaging to the best brains. The result of this life against instinct is that industrial populations tend to be listless and trivial, in constant search of excitement, delighted by a murder, and still more delighted by a war.*

Russell's essay, by the way, appeared in the June 1921 issue of the *Atlantic Monthly*. (The more things change, the more they remain the same?)

EXERCISE SET 1-7

Here is an excerpt from a speech delivered to the Utah chapter of NOW (National Organization of Women) in May 1997 by Elizabeth Joseph, in which she argues that polygamy is beneficial to women in the modern world:

> *I've often said that if polygamy didn't exist the modern American career woman would have invented it. Because, despite its reputation, polygamy is the one lifestyle that offers an independent woman a real chance to "have it all." . . .*
>
> *As a journalist, I work many unpredictable hours in a fast-paced environment. The news determines my schedule. . . . Because of my plural marriage arrangement, I don't have to worry [about coming home late]. I know that when I have to work late my daughter will be surrounded by loving adults with whom she is comfortable and who know her schedule without my telling them. My eight-year-old has never seen the inside of a day-care center, and my*

husband has never eaten a TV dinner. And I know that when I get home from work, if I'm dog-tired and stressed-out, I can be alone and guilt free. It's a rare day when all eight of my husband's wives are tired and stressed at the same time.

It's helpful to think of polygamy in terms of a free-market approach to marriage. Why shouldn't you or your daughters have the opportunity to marry the best man available, regardless of his marital status? . . .

Polygamy is an empowering lifestyle for women. It provides me the environment and opportunity to maximize my female potential without all the tradeoffs and compromises that attend monogamy. The women in my family are friends. You don't share two decades of experience, and a man, without those friendships becoming very special. . . . [P]olygamy [is] the ultimate feminist lifestyle.

Compare Joseph's view to your own on marital arrangements. Do you find her ideas persuasive? Does your worldview jibe with hers? Why or why not? Most of us think of monogamy as "natural," yet polygamy has been common in different parts of the world at different times in history. (Although Utah outlawed the practice in the nineteenth century as a condition of statehood, the anti-bigamy law is rarely enforced in that state. Estimates put the number of polygamists in Utah in the tens of thousands, even though it's impossible to verify the statistics, given the illegal nature of the activity.) Portions of Joseph's speech were reprinted in the February 1998 issue of *Harper's*.

EXERCISE SET 1-8

Here are some questions from a science knowledge quiz periodically given by the Pew Research Center as part of a study on the impact of science on society. Give it a try.

1.   Which kind of waves are used to make and receive cellphone calls?

    A. Radio waves   B. Visible light waves

    C. Sound waves   D. Gravity waves

2.   Which of these is the main way that ocean tides are created?

    A. The rotation of the Earth on its axis

    B. The gravitational pull of the moon

    C. The gravitational pull of the sun

3.   What does a light year measure?

    A. Brightness   B. Time

    C. Distance   D. Weight

4.   Denver, Colorado, is at a higher altitude than Los Angeles, California. Which of these statements is correct?

    A. Water boils at a lower temperature in Denver than Los Angeles.

    B. Water boils at a higher temperature in Denver than Los Angeles.

    C. Water boils at the same temperature in both Denver and Los Angeles.

5. Which of these elements is needed to make nuclear energy and nuclear weapons?

A. Sodium chloride   B. Uranium

C. Nitrogen   D. Carbon dioxide

Check your response against the percentage of adult Americans who answered the questions correctly.

1. A 72%   2. B 76%   3. C 72%   4. A 34%   5. B 82%

A canine induction by enumeration.

More on Deduction and Induction 2

MindTap® Visit MindTap for more readings and resources.

1. Deductive Validity

In Chapter 1, we distinguished between deductively valid and inductively valid arguments. Here now is a discussion of some of the basic principles of deductive reasoning, which, by the way, the vast majority of people find quite intuitive.

As pointed out in Chapter 1, different arguments may have the same *form,* or *structure.* Here are two arguments that have the same form—namely, *modus ponens:*

(1)   **1.** If it's spring, then the birds are chirping.
      2. It is spring.
   ∴**3.** The birds are chirping.
(2)   **1.** If a world government doesn't evolve soon, then wars will continue to occur.
      2. A world government isn't going to evolve soon.
   ∴**3.** Wars will continue to occur.

In Chapter 1, we noted that the form of *modus ponens* can be indicated this way:

1. If A then B.
2. A.
∴**3.** B.

Now, here is another commonly occurring deductively valid form, called *modus tollens*:

    Form: **1.** If *A* then *B*.
                     2. Not *B*.
                ∴**3.** Not *A*.

    Example: **1.** If it's spring, then the birds are chirping.
                     2. The birds aren't chirping.
                ∴**3.** It isn't spring.

Here is still another commonly occurring deductively valid argument form, usually called **hypothetical syllogism**:

    Form: **1.** If *A* then *B*.
                     2. If *B* then *C*.
                ∴**3.** If *A* then *C*.

    Example: **1.** If we successfully develop nuclear fusion power, then power will become cheap and plentiful.
                     2. If power becomes cheap and plentiful, then the economy will flourish.
                ∴**3.** If we successfully develop nuclear fusion power, then the economy will flourish.

And here is the deductively valid form called **disjunctive syllogism**:[1]

    Form: **1.** *A* or *B*.
                     2. Not *A*.
                ∴**3.** *B*.

    Example: **1.** Either Clinton won in 2016 or Trump did.
                     2. Trump didn't win.
                ∴**3.** Clinton did.

Note that, while the first premise is true, the second, unfortunately for Clinton, is false, as is the conclusion. Nevertheless, the validity of this argument guarantees that *if* both its premises had been true, *then* so would its conclusion have been true.

Finally, here are several argument forms of a different kind (all but the first two are called *syllogisms*):[2]

    Form: **1.** No *F*s are *G*s.
               ∴**2.** It's false that some *F*s are *G*s.

    Example: **1.** No police officers accept bribes.
              ∴**2.** It's false that some police officers accept bribes. (Uh-huh.)

---

[1]Strictly speaking, in spite of their names, *disjunctive syllogism* and *hypothetical syllogism* are not syllogisms.

[2]For additional material on deduction and induction see the Appendix, and see also: Hausman, Alan, Howard Kahane, and Paul Tidman. *Logic and Philosophy*. 12th ed. Boston: Wadsworth, Cengage Learning, 2013.

Form: **1.** All *F*s are *G*s.
∴**2.** If this is an *F*, then this is a *G*.
Example: **1.** All french fries are tasty.
∴**2.** If this is a french fry, then it is tasty. (No dispute on this one.)

Form: **1.** All *F*s are *G*s.
2. All *G*s are *H*s.
∴**3.** All *F*s are *H*s.
Example: **1.** All TV evangelists have high moral standards.
2. All who have high moral standards live up to those standards.
∴**3.** All TV evangelists live up to high moral standards. (Umm. . . .)

Form: **1.** All *F*s are *G*s.
2. This is an *F.*
∴**3.** This is a *G.* (Note that this is *not* the form called
modus ponens!)
Example: **1.** All elected officials always tell the truth.
2. Barack Obama is an elected official.
∴**3.** Barack Obama always tells the truth.

Form: **1.** All *F*s are *G*s.
2. No *G*s are *H*s.
∴**3.** No *F*s are *H*s.
Example: **1.** All males are chauvinist pigs.
2. No chauvinist pigs are likeable.
∴**3.** No males are likeable.

Form: **1.** No *F*s are *G*s.
2. Some *H*s are *F*s.
∴**3.** Some *H*s are not *G*s.
Example: **1.** No foreigners can be trusted.
2. Some newborn babies are foreigners.
∴**3.** Some newborn babies cannot be trusted. (Obviously.)

In daily life, arguments tend to get strung together into larger arguments leading up to a point, a grand conclusion or **thesis**. Here is an example (with logical structure exhibited to the left) in which the conclusion of the first argument is used as a premise in the second, and the conclusion of the second is used as a premise in the third and final argument:

1. If *A* then *B*.   **1.** If a world government doesn't evolve soon, then wars will continue to occur.

2. If *B* then *C*.   **2.** If they continue to occur, then nuclear weapons will proliferate

∴**3.** If *A* then *C*.   So, **3.** if a world government doesn't evolve soon, then nuclear weapons will proliferate.

4. If *C* then *D*.   **4.** If they proliferate, then a nuclear war will be inevitable, sooner or later.

∴**5.** If *A* then *D*.   Which proves that **5.** if a world government doesn't evolve soon, we'll end up fighting a nuclear war sooner or later.

6. Not *D*.   But **6.** it's ridiculous to think we'll actually have a nuclear war (that is, it's false that we'll have such a war).

∴**7.** Not *A*.   So **7.** a world government is going to evolve soon (that is, it's false that a world government won't evolve soon).

2. Deductive Invalidity

Any argument that doesn't have a deductively valid form is said to be **deductively invalid.**[3] The number of deductively invalid argument forms is legion, but a few occur so frequently that they've been given names. Here are two examples (to give the flavor):

Fallacy of **denying the antecedent**:
    Form: **1.** If *A* then *B*.
                2. Not *A*.
           ∴**3.** Not *B*
    Example: **1.** If abortion is murder, then it's wrong.
                2. But abortion isn't murder.
           ∴**3.** Abortion isn't wrong.

The conclusion doesn't follow: Even supposing abortion isn't murder, it may be wrong for other reasons.

Fallacy of **affirming the consequent**:
    Form: **1.** If *A* then *B*.
                2. *B*.
           ∴**3.** *A*.

    Example: **1.** If Trump is president, then a conservative is now president.
                2. A conservative is now president.
           ∴**3.** Trump is president.
The conclusion doesn't follow: some other conservative may now be president.

3. Conditional Statements

A number of the argument forms we just discussed—the valid *modus ponens, modus tollens, hypothetical syllogism,* and the invalid *denying the antecedent* and *affirming the consequent*—involve statements of the form "If *A* then *B*." We call these **conditional statements,** and they deserve a little specific attention here.

---

[3]A deductively invalid argument still may be a good argument if it is inductively correct. Arguments that have the forms about to be discussed are bad because they are neither deductively valid nor inductively correct.

The first thing to notice about conditional statements is that they are not themselves arguments. Sometimes people will implicate an argument using just a conditional statement. So, for example, Democratic presidential candidate Bernie Sanders said in a speech at Georgetown University that "if we are serious about transforming our country, if we are serious about rebuilding the middle class, if we are serious about reinvigorating our democracy, we need to develop a political movement which, once again, is prepared to take on and defeat a ruling class whose greed is destroying our nation." Clearly, we are meant to infer from this that we are in fact serious about these things, and so we do in fact need to develop a political movement as he describes.

But on its own, the conditional statement is not an argument. Indeed, it cannot be an argument because arguments must consist of premises and conclusions, and the conditional statement is only one claim. This claim has two parts, the *antecedent* (the part after the "if") and the *consequent* (the part after the "then"). Not all conditional statements will be stated exactly in the "If A then B" format, but they will all be reproducible in the form because they all have an antecedent and a consequent.

Here is University of North Carolina psychologist Lawrence Calhoun quoted in the *New Yorker* on his research on "post-traumatic growth": "We say that, if you do experience traumatic events, it is quite possible you will experience one or more elements of growth."[4] Notice that Calhoun is not claiming that his audience has experienced traumatic events or that they will experience growth, only that there is this connection between traumatic experiences and the possibility of growth. This is to say, a conditional statement does not claim that either its antecedent or consequent are true, only that there is some connection between them.

The second important point about conditional statements concerns the nature of that connection. To understand this, we need to take a step back and introduce two new concepts that are—in their own right—important in crafting and evaluating arguments. These are necessary and sufficient conditions. A given condition (i.e., a given fact, or state of things) is necessary for another just in case the first one must be present for the second to be present. So, being at least 35 years of age is necessary for being president of the United States, being a brother is necessary for being an uncle, and, in most restaurants, ordering food is necessary for eating dinner. One condition is sufficient for another if and only if the presence of the first one is enough to establish (or bring about) the second. So, having the flu is sufficient for being sick, being a sister is sufficient for being a daughter, and graduating from college is sufficient for earning a degree. Notice that none of the necessary conditions above are sufficient and none of the sufficient conditions above are necessary (for instance, much more than being at least 35 years old is required to make someone the president, and one can be sick without having the flu). Some conditions, though, are both necessary and sufficient for another. Being heated to 100 degrees Celsius (at sea level) is necessary and sufficient for water boiling, being in

---

[4]Kushner, David. "Can Trauma Help You Grow?" *New Yorker,* 15 March 2016.

an agreement to get married at some future time is necessary and sufficient for being engaged, and having a paying job is necessary and sufficient for being employed.

One really helpful way of thinking about conditional statements is in terms of necessary and sufficient conditions. Specifically, a conditional statement claims that the antecedent condition is sufficient for the consequent condition and that the consequent condition is necessary for the antecedent condition. Consider the statement "If Hillary Clinton lost the election, then the Democrats lost the White House ." This statement is true, not because Clinton lost or because the Democrats lost the White House, but because Clinton's loss is sufficient for the Democrats losing the White House and the Democrats losing the White House is necessary for Clinton losing the race (that is, Clinton can't have lost without it also being true that the Democrats lost the White House). Now consider: "If the economy improved, then there were major changes to the tax code." This is false because economic improvement is not sufficient for major tax changes, and major tax changes are not necessary for economic improvement.

Confusing necessary and sufficient conditions is awfully common, and explains the vast majority of cases of affirming the consequent and denying the antecedent. When evaluating someone's argument, it is useful to really consider what they're claiming when they make a conditional connection between two things. This is especially important (and sometimes difficult) when the statement in question is not in "If A then B" form. Consider this headline from MovieNewsGuide.com: "Daniel Craig Will Play James Bond Only if Wife Rachel Weisz Allows It." Well, here "Wife Rachel Weisz Allows It" follows an "if," but it is not the antecedent. "If" and "only if" don't mean quite the same thing. Think of it this way: Is the claim here that Weisz allowing it is enough to bring about Craig's playing Bond, or that it has to be the case that she allows it in order for him to play Bond? Obviously it's the latter. Craig wouldn't play Bond for free regardless of what his wife says. So the claim is that her approval is necessary for his taking the role and that his taking the role is sufficient for her having approved. So we could restate the same claim: "If Daniel Craig Plays James Bond, Then Wife Rachel Weisz Allows It." Notice that we'd provide the same analysis were the original headline "Only if Wife Rachel Weisz Allows It Will Daniel Craig Play James Bond." So you will not always be able to go by the order of appearance of phrases or even the mere placement of key words. It will always be important to consider what is really at stake and what someone is really trying to claim.

4. Syllogisms

A lot more needs to be said about invalid reasoning and will be in later chapters, in particular Chapters 3, 4, and 5, where various other kinds of fallacious reasoning are discussed. But let's now discuss a few more matters concerning the deductively valid reasonings called **syllogisms**.

We said before that arguments having the form called *hypothetical syllogism,*

   1. If *A* then *B*.
   2. If *B* then *C*.
∴**3.** If *A* then *C*.

are not true syllogisms (at least not in the sense intended by Aristotle, the inventor of syllogistic logic[5]), while those having the form

1. All *A*s are *B*s.
2. All *B*s are *C*s.
∴3. All *A*s are *C*s.

are the genuine article. What makes one the real thing and the other not? The difference between these two kinds of arguments that makes the difference should become clear in the following little exposition as to the nature of syllogisms in traditional syllogistic logic.[6]

In traditional syllogistic logic, a **categorical proposition** is a subject predicate proposition that asserts or denies a relationship between a **subject class** and a **predicate class**. There are exactly four kinds of categorical propositions (with one variation): **universal affirmative** (*A* propositions), having the form "All *S* are *P*" (*Example:* "All sinners are betrayers."); **universal negative** (*E* propositions), having the form "No *S* are *P*" (*Example:* "No chess players are imbeciles."); **particular affirmative** (*I* propositions), having the form "Some *S* are *P*" (*Example:* "Some men are chauvinists."); and **particular negative** (*O* propositions), having the form "Some *S* are not *P*" (*Example:* "Some logicians are not nitpickers.").[7] The one common variation is that statements such as "Socrates is a man," having as their subject a particular item rather than a class of items are often honorifically considered to be *A* propositions.

A *syllogism* is an argument containing three categorical propositions, two of them premises, one a conclusion. Here is one of the original examples (dechauvinized):

Syllogism	*Traditional Symbolization*
All humans are mortal.	MAP
All Greeks are human.	SAM
∴All Greeks are mortal.	∴SAP

The term *P*, the predicate of the conclusion, is said to be the syllogism's **major term**; the term *S*, the subject of the conclusion, its **minor term**; and the term *M*, which occurs once in each premise but not in the conclusion, its **middle term**. Every syllogism has exactly three terms (none used equivocally), each one repeated twice but not in the same proposition. So in the syllogism given above, *mortals* is the major term, *Greeks* is the minor term, and *humans* is the middle term. There are hundreds of different syllogistic

---

[5]It is often said today that *any* argument consisting of two premises and a conclusion is a syllogism. Obviously, something has changed since days of old, and that is why, for example, argument forms such as *hypothetical syllogisms* now sometimes are thought of as the genuine article. The point is that Aristotle and Aristotelians, until recently, would not have considered these other forms to be syllogisms.

[6]For now, let's just note that we replace the *A*s, *B*s, and *C*s in the form of *hypothetical syllogism* by whole sentences, as in "If Art goes to the show, then Betsy will stay home" but the *A*s and *B*s in "All *A* are *B*" are replaced by subjects of sentences, or predicates, as in "All women are fickle."

[7]A quick historical note: The "A," "E," "I," and "O" designations are not accidental. They come from the first two vowels in "affirmo," the Latin word for "I affirm" and "nego," Latin for "I deny."

forms (figure out how many), but, of course, only some are valid. The preceding one is valid, whereas the syllogism "All Greeks are human; all humans are mortal; therefore, all mortals are Greek" is not.

The valid syllogism about Greeks being mortal is said to be in the **mood** AAA (for obvious reasons). (In this case, the syllogism is said to be in the *first figure,* and its *form* is said to be AAA-I, but let's pass over this complication.) There are, of course, other moods (and figures). Here, for instance, is a syllogism in the mood AII (it happens to be in the third figure):[8]

Syllogism	*Traditional Symbolization*
All things made out of grass are green.	MAG
Some things made out of grass are cigarettes.	MIC
∴Some cigarettes are green.	CIG

5. Indirect Proofs

Another common everyday kind of reasoning is called an **indirect proof** or a **reductio ad absurdum** (reduce to an absurdity) **proof**. We reason in this way when we assume the opposite of what we wish to prove and then deductively derive a conclusion claimed to be false, indeed, often contradictory or otherwise absurd. The point is that if we validly reason to an obviously false conclusion, then our original assumption must be false and hence its negation—the thing we wish to prove—must be true. Here is an example:

> Assume for the moment that—as some people allege—the U.S. government actually faked the moon landings in the late 60s and early 70s. If that's true, then hundreds and hundreds of people were involved in a massive and (almost) entirely successful conspiracy to defraud the public. Of course there were the astronauts themselves, nearly everyone at NASA, and numerous film crews, not to mention the White House and probably many members of Congress. To pull off such an operation, the government would have to be amazingly good at perpetrating frauds and maintaining massive conspiracies. And it is not. Remember that this same government (at its very highest levels, mind you) was unable to successfully *break into an office* without the whole operation coming apart and the president resigning in disgrace. Just a decade later, another administration couldn't get away with a couple of relatively simple illicit arms deals. The U.S. government may well be morally bankrupt enough to perpetrate such a massive conspiracy, but there is just no way it is actually capable of pulling it off.

An indirect proof can be defeated in either of two ways. One is by showing that there is a mistake in reasoning. (In our example, there is no mistake in reasoning. The argument is deductively valid, which just means that if its premises are true, then its

---

[8]In the Middle Ages, students determined the validity of syllogistic forms by reciting a chant containing a name for each of the valid cases in each figure. For example, the name "bArbArA" occurs in the chant for the first figure, indicating that the form AAA-1 is valid.

conclusion must be true). The other way is to show that at least one of its premises (other than the assumed premise) is false. (In our example, the likely premise would be . . . ?)

6. Tautologies, Contradictions, and Contingent Statements

A **tautology** is a statement that is *logically,* or *necessarily,* true, or is so devoid of content as to be practically empty (and thus true because completely empty statements, making no claim, cannot be false).[9] *Example:* "The Mets will win the World Series, or they won't." A **contradiction** is a statement that is necessarily false (because it contradicts itself). *Example:* "The Mets will win and not win the World Series." All other statements are said to be **contingent**. *Example:* "The Mets will win the World Series."

We can determine the truth value of a contradiction or of a tautology by logical— deductive—means alone, without the need for any empirical investigation or inductive reasoning. Notice that we do not need to wait until the next baseball season plays out to know that the tautology above is true and the contradiction above is false. But determining the truth or falsity of a contingent statement requires observation by ourselves or others and, usually, the employment of inductive reasoning. *Example:* Tasting and disliking cooked vegetables several times has led many people to conclude inductively that in general, they will dislike cooked vegetables. (Note that there is no contradiction between always disliking cooked vegetables in the past and liking them sometime in the future. Nor does this past dislike guarantee that they always will be disliked in the future.)

7. Inductive Validity (Correctness) and Invalidity (Incorrectness)

As indicated before, we can think of induction as a kind of *patterning*. Perhaps the simplest form of induction is the one called **induction by enumeration**, mentioned in Chapter 1. In this kind of inductive reasoning, we reason from the fact that all *A*s observed so far are *B*s to the conclusion that, probably, all *A*s whatsoever are *B*s. We call the observed *A*s the **sample** (the instances observed so far) and all *A*s the **population** (the instances about which we're drawing a conclusion). For example, a study of 100 members of Congress no doubt would show that they all accept campaign contributions from lobbyists intent on influencing legislation, and finding this out would count as good evidence for the inductive conclusion that all 535 members of Congress accept funds of this kind.

Obviously, some inductions of this kind are better than others and make their conclusions more probable. Although there are several modestly different theories about how

---

[9]Note that logicians often use the term *tautology* in a more restricted manner, so as to cover only the logical truths provable by means of what is called *sentential logic.*

to determine the probability of the conclusions of enumerative inductions, almost all agree on a few points.

Greater sample size tends to yield greater probability. The more instances in a sample, the greater the probability of a conclusion reasonably drawn from that sample. A sample of 100 members of Congress who accept campaign contributions from lobbyists provides a higher degree of probability that all do than a smaller sample, say, of 50 members. The point is that more of the same sort of evidence doesn't change the conclusion of an induction; rather, it changes the degree of probability of that conclusion and thus changes the strength of belief a rational person should have in it.

More representative samples yield higher probabilities than those that are less representative. The quality of a sample is even more important than its size. (Indeed, the higher its quality, the smaller a sample needs to be to yield a given degree of probability.) When sampling apples in a barrel, for instance, it won't do just to sample a few from the top (the classic case); after all, rotten apples are more likely to be at the bottom than at the top of a barrel. Samples that neglect possible rotten apples at the bottom of metaphorical barrels are said to be *biased* or *unrepresentative*. Obviously, the less biased, more representative a sample, the higher the degree of probability of an inference based on that sample. We will consider representativeness again in Chapter 5.

One definite counterexample shoots down an enumerative induction. The most important reason why inductive reasoning is superior to many other kinds (for example, of the superstitious or the pseudoscientific variety to be discussed later) is that it does not allow us to pass over evidence that indicates a pet theory is false. For example, if one woman who takes a particular birth control pill as directed gets pregnant, then no valid enumerative induction about the pill's effectiveness can be drawn. (Note that it still may be possible to draw other kinds of valid inductive inferences, including the statistical kind to be discussed shortly.)

However, it often is hard to be sure that what looks like a counterexample really is one. A woman on birth control pills who becomes pregnant, for instance, may have accidentally neglected to take the pills properly, and we may not be aware of that fact. The moral is that it is risky to reject an enumerative induction on the basis of one counterexample, or even two, unless we are very sure that at least one is a genuine counterexample. But when we are sure, then an enumerative induction in question must be rejected.

REASONING BY ANALOGY

Several other kinds of inductive reasoning are very similar to enumerative induction, including **analogical reasoning**. In one version of this kind of inductive reasoning, we reason from the similarity of two things in several relevant respects to their similarity in another. Thus, if we know that two people have similar tastes in books, art, food, music, and TV programs and find out that one likes to watch *Downton Abbey* on public television (PBS), then we're justified in concluding by analogy that the other probably does also.

The trouble is that every two things resemble each other in one way or another.[10] Only *relevant* resemblances count in drawing correct analogies. But what makes a resemblance relevant? The answer lies in background beliefs about how, in general, things hang together. For example, if the stock market rises and falls in concert with ups and downs in the Olympic elk population over several years, only fools are likely to conclude that the two will fluctuate together in the future, because so much background information contradicts this idea. On the other hand, if stocks were to rise and fall over several years in concert with ups and downs in retail sales, we could reason by analogy that the next change in one will produce a similar change in the other. (Of course, given all of the other factors relevant to stock market prices, an induction of the kind just described would have to be assigned a very modest degree of probability.)

In another version of analogical induction, we reason from the fact that all examined items of a certain kind have a particular property to the conclusion that a particular as yet unexamined item of that kind will be found to have that property. Finding out that, say, 100 members of Congress accept money from lobbyists, we can conclude by this kind of analogy that a certain other member probably also does so.

As this last example shows, analogical inductions are much safer, and thus have a higher degree of probability, than their enumerative counterparts, because they have much weaker conclusions. Concluding, for example, that a particular member of Congress accepts money from lobbyists is a much weaker, hence safer, prediction than that all members of Congress do so.

STATISTICAL INDUCTION

When drawing a sample from a population, we often find that not all of the examined As are Bs, so that we cannot draw a valid enumerative induction. But having found that a certain percentage of the As have the property in question, we can conclude by a **statistical induction** that the same percentage of the total population of As have that property. Having found, say, that 480 of the first 1,000 observed tosses of a given coin land face up, we can conclude that 48 percent of all of the tosses with that coin will land face up (thus learning, incidentally, that the coin probably is slightly biased in favor of tails, as many coins are).

Of course, what was said about the quality and, hence, the degree of probability of enumerative inductions also applies to the statistical variety. The larger the sample employed and the more representative it is, the higher the degree of probability of a statistical induction based on that sample.

---

[10]Choose the two most wildly different things you can. They both share the characteristic of being an object of your present thought! But what if you weren't thinking about them? Then they would share the characteristic of being absent from your thoughts at the moment. It turns out that everything resembles everything else in an indefinitely large number of ways.

HIGHER-LEVEL INDUCTIONS

More general, **higher-level inductions** can be used to evaluate those that are less general. For example, we use higher-level induction when we conclude that an automobile engine eventually will wear out or need to be repaired, even though it has run perfectly for 100,000 miles. We overrule a low-level conclusion telling us that, because the car has run perfectly so far, it will do so forever, by appeal to a higher-level, more general induction such as this one: All mechanical devices with moving parts checked up on so far have eventually worn out or needed to be repaired, so very probably this particular mechanical device (the engine in question) also eventually will wear out or need to be repaired.

More general inferences, based on larger samples about more kinds of items, usually have higher degrees of probability than do those that are less general. That is why an enumerative induction about a particular automobile is overruled by a more general one about many mechanical devices. (There are, in fact, even higher-level reasons for tossing out this low-level induction by enumeration—for example, scientific inductions concerning basic principles of physics and chemistry having to do with the effects of friction.)

REASONING TO CAUSAL CONNECTIONS

When we reason inductively, we often are looking for explanations, or **causes**. For instance, early investigators of the connection between cigarette smoking and lung cancer, emphysema, and heart disease wanted to determine by means of statistical inductions whether smoking *causes* these death-dealing diseases. They found that smokers contract these diseases much more frequently than nonsmokers, and heavy smokers more than light. That is, they discovered a statistical link between smoking cigarettes and contracting these diseases. Finding no higher-level evidence to the contrary, they concluded that cigarette smoking does indeed cause these life-threatening illnesses. (That some people smoke like chimneys and never come down with these illnesses doesn't prove the contrary, but it does suggest that part of the cause of these diseases must be some other, very likely genetic, factor.[11])

The inductive patterns discussed in this chapter are relatively neat and simple. Enumerative induction is an example. But in daily life, and in particular in scientific theorizing, inductive reasoning often is much more complicated and may involve mathematical reasoning (a kind of deductive reasoning) as well. We believe cigarette smoking causes lung cancer, for example, not just because a certain percentage of those who smoke get that deadly disease, but also because the percentage of those who do not smoke and get lung cancer is much lower than for those who do smoke. It is the comparison of the two groups that proves the point. (In fact, the reasoning linking smoking and lung cancer is even more complicated than we have indicated here. For instance, we haven't mentioned how theorists ruled out certain other causal possibilities by carefully selecting the individuals in their samples to rule out the effects of other likely carcinogens.)

---

[11]See the section in the Appendix concerning necessary and sufficient conditions.

CONCATENATED INDUCTIONS

The cigarette–cancer example just discussed brings to mind the fact that in the vast majority of scientific cases, the reasoning employed is of the kind that can be called **concatenated reasoning**—a joining together of inductions and deductions in the discovery of a *pattern* that fits what has been observed or previously reasoned to. In scientific reasoning, inductively confirmed theories of several disciplines typically are brought to bear to reach a conclusion. This is done, for example, in determining the types and significance of the food our ancestors ate before the time of recorded history. Carbon-14 dating is used to determine the approximate date at which, say, animal feces, now fossilized, were deposited at the site of an archeological dig; chemical analysis to reveal what kind of food it was (grain, meat, etc.) and that it was eaten by human beings and not other animals—all of this coupled with anthropological theories about how this sort of food fit into the everyday diet of people in those days. Knowledge of this kind may then be used as part of the evidence in theories about the migrations of ancient peoples and the dispersal of and changes in various kinds of grains, fruits, and domesticated animals.

8. A Misconception About Deduction and Induction

There is a widespread but erroneous idea about the difference between deductive and inductive validity. This is the idea that in deductively valid reasoning, we go from the general to the particular, while in inductively valid reasoning, we move from the particular to the general. But little can be said in support of this idea. For instance, the deductively valid argument

  1. All Republican politicians are to the right of Barack Obama.
∴**2.** All who are not to the right of Barack Obama are not Republican politicians.

moves from the general to the equally general, while the inductively valid argument

  1. George Bush (the younger) made promises during the 2000 campaign that he didn't keep.
  2. George Bush made promises during the 2004 campaign that he didn't keep.
  3. Barack Obama made promises during the 2008 campaign that he didn't keep.
∴**4.** Donald Trump very likely won't keep all the promises he made during the 2016 campaign.

moves from the particular to the equally particular. And the inductively valid argument

  1. So far, all presidential candidates of the Republican Party have been male.
∴**2.** The next Republican Party presidential candidate will be male.

moves from the general to the particular, not the other way around.

  So there isn't much truth to the old idea that deductive reasoning moves from the general to the particular, while inductive reasoning moves from the particular to the general. More accurately, when we reason deductively, we reason to conclusions already contained (implicitly or explicitly) in our premises; when we reason inductively, we move to conclusions by extending patterns or resemblances from one set of events to another set.

Some of those who argue otherwise claim that the idea of deduction moving from the general to the particular is intended to be true only for syllogistic reasoning. Thus, the valid syllogism, "All humans are mortal; Socrates is human; therefore, Socrates is mortal," does indeed move from the general to the particular. The trouble, of course, is that this is not true for the vast majority of other valid syllogisms, including the one mentioned a while back, whose conclusion is that all Greeks are mortal.

9. Reasoning Cogently Versus Being Right in Fact

Reasoning correctly and getting a true conclusion are unfortunately not the same thing. We can reason correctly and get a false conclusion, and we can reason fallaciously and get a true conclusion.[12] *Examples:* Scientists in times past reasoned correctly from what was known then to the conclusion that superconductivity occurs only at temperatures very close to absolute zero, but we now know that this conclusion is false. Astrology buffs reason incorrectly that they will have a good day from the fact that a newspaper column says they will or that the stars are in a certain position in the sky, and then luckily they do have a good day (for completely different reasons having nothing whatever to do with astrology or where the stars happen to be).

On the whole, it's a lot better to reason incorrectly to true—right—conclusions than it is to reason well to false ones.[13] *But the most likely way to be right, in the long run, is to reason correctly!* When people who follow astrology columns thereby do better than they otherwise would have, they're just extremely lucky, not smart. (They're also an extremely rare species of speculator.) In daily life, however, people often equate being smart with being successful, as though success proves reasoning has been cogent. It doesn't, nor does failure prove reasoning fallacious. That's life. Smart people, as they say, "play the odds"—they try to reason well and take their chances in this not-quite-best of all possible worlds, and *in the long run in most cases, they do a lot better than those whose reasoning is excessively fallacious.*

---

[12]In philosophical jargon, we can be *epistemologically right* although *ontologically wrong,* and we can be *epistemologically wrong* but *ontologically right.*

[13]Philosophical slogan: "I'd rather be epistemologically wrong and ontologically right than vice versa, but the best way to be ontologically right is to be epistemologically right." (Philosophical jargon can be just as opaque as that of every other discipline.)

Summary of Chapter 2

1. Different arguments may have the same form, or structure. *Modus ponens, modus tollens, hypothetical syllogism,* and so on, are deductively valid argument forms. Note that in everyday life, arguments frequently get strung together, leading to a grand conclusion, a *thesis.*

2. But lots of other forms are deductively invalid. *Affirming the consequent* and *denying the antecedent* are examples of deductively invalid argument forms.

3. *Conditional statements* assert that one condition, described in the antecedent, is sufficient for another, described in the consequent; and that the consequent condition is necessary for the antecedent condition. While not always presented in the form "If A, then B," conditional statements can always be expressed in this form, where A is the antecedent and B the consequent.

4. A *categorical proposition* asserts or denies a relationship between a *subject class* and a *predicate class.* There are four kinds of categorical propositions: *universal affirmative* (*A* propositions), having the form "All *S* are *P*"; *universal negative* (*E* propositions), having the form "No *S* are *P*"; *particular affirmative* (*I* propositions), having the form "Some *S* are *P*"; and *particular negative* (*O* propositions), having the form "Some *S* are not *P*." Statements such as "Socrates is a man," having as their subject a particular item rather than a class of items, are often honorifically considered to be *A* propositions.

    A *syllogism* is an argument containing three categorical propositions, two of them premises, one a conclusion. ***Example:*** "No foreigners are trustable. Some newborn babies are foreigners. Therefore, some newborn babies cannot be trusted." The predicate of the conclusion of a syllogism is said to be its *major term;* the subject of the conclusion, its *minor term;* and the term that occurs once in each premise but not in the conclusion, its *middle term.* Every syllogism has exactly three terms (none used equivocally), each one repeated twice but not in the same proposition. There are hundreds of different syllogistic forms (figure out how many), but, of course, only some are valid. ***Example:*** The syllogism "All Greeks are humans; all humans are mortals; therefore, all mortals are Greek" is not valid.

    The *mood* of a syllogism is determined by the kinds of propositions it contains. Thus the syllogism just mentioned is in the mood AAA.

5. In an *indirect* or *reductio ad absurdum proof,* we assume the opposite of what we wish to prove and then deductively derive a conclusion claimed to be false, contradictory, or otherwise absurd. The point is that if we reason validly to a false, or absurd, conclusion, then our original assumption must be false and hence its negation—the thing we wish to prove—must be true.

6. A *tautology* is a statement that is *logically,* or *necessarily,* true or is so devoid of content as to be practically empty. ***Example:*** "Beyoncé is world-famous, or she isn't." A *contradiction* is a statement that is necessarily false (because

it contradicts itself). ***Example:*** "Beyoncé is world-famous and she isn't." All other statements are said to be contingent. ***Example:*** "Beyoncé is talented and world-famous."

The truth values of contradictions and tautologies can be determined by logical—deductive—means alone, but the truth or falsity of contingent statements cannot. They are justified by observation or by reasoning, part of which must be inductive, from what we and/or other people have observed.

7. There are several kinds of valid, or correct, inductions. One is *induction by enumeration,* in which we infer from the fact that all *A*s observed so far are *B*s, to the conclusion that all *A*s whatsoever are *B*s.

In general, the larger or the more representative a sample, the greater the probability of an induction based on it. Note that one definite counterexample invalidates an induction. (But we have to be sure that it really is a counterexample.)

Analogical reasoning is very much like induction by enumeration, the chief difference being that analogies yield conclusions about just one case (which is why they have higher degrees of probability than corresponding enumerative inductions), whereas enumerative inductions typically concern a great many.

Statistical inductions also are similar to the enumerative variety, but they move from the fact that a certain percentage of a sample has a given property to the conclusion that the same percentage in the population has that property.

We can use more general, *higher-level* inductions to correct, or overrule, lower-level ones. If experience shows that all mechanical devices eventually wear out or need to be repaired, then it isn't reasonable to conclude that a particular auto engine will not, even though it has run perfectly for 100,000 miles.

Inductive reasoning often is used to discover *causes,* as in the case of the statistical induction linking cigarette smoking and various life-threatening diseases.

Reasoning called *concatenated* often brings new evidence together with several already inductively established conclusions, combined with deductive reasoning, to obtain a further conclusion. This is especially true in the sciences. ***Example:*** Anthropologists or evolutionary theorists reason from principles of physics and chemistry in reaching conclusions from newly discovered evidence.

8. It often is said that deductively valid reasoning moves from general premises to particular conclusions, while inductively valid reasoning moves from particular premises to general conclusions. But this is not correct. ***Examples:*** The deductively valid argument "If you jump off the Brooklyn Bridge, then you'll be killed. So if you aren't killed, you haven't jumped off the Brooklyn Bridge," moves from the particular to the particular. (By the way, the form of this inference— "If *A* then *B*; therefore, if not-*B* then not-*A*"—is sometimes called *contraposition.*) The inductively valid reasoning "People who gain power tend to be corrupted by it. Speaker of the House Paul Ryan has gained tremendous power. So it is likely that he will be corrupted by it," moves from the general to the particular.

9. Life being what it is, reasoning correctly sometimes results in drawing false conclusions, even from a true premise. ***Example:*** The person who, having loaned a friend money many times before and having always been repaid, loans the friend money again and gets stiffed. Furthermore, again life being what it is, reasoning fallaciously sometimes results in drawing true conclusions, even sometimes from false premises. ***Example:*** risking one's life savings at a dice table in Las Vegas employing the "double the bet" method (discussed in the Appendix) and winning a small fortune.

But, still again, life being what it is, in a large majority of cases, those who reason cogently do better, often a great deal better, than those who reason fallaciously.

EXERCISE SET 2-1

1. Invent deductively valid arguments having the forms *modus ponens, modus tollens,* disjunctive syllogism, and hypothetical syllogism.

2. Use the conclusion of one of the arguments you have just constructed as a premise in another argument that is deductively valid.

EXERCISE SET 2-2

1. Invent an argument having the form of the fallacy *denying the antecedent,* and then show that it is deductively invalid by explaining how its premises might be true when its conclusion is false.

2. Do the same with an argument having the form *affirming the consequent.*

EXERCISE SET 2-3

Analyze each of the following conditional statements by identifying which condition is claimed to be sufficient for the other, and which is claimed to be necessary for the other. Then identify the antecedent and consequent.

Example

Statement

If you follow this pattern, you'll do well on these exercises.

Analysis

Your following this pattern is claimed to be sufficient for your doing well on these exercises, and your doing well on these exercises is claimed to be necessary for your following this pattern.
Antecedent: Your following this pattern.
Consequent: Your doing well on these exercises.

1. If there are more than 100 people on the platform, you're not likely to get a seat on the train.

2. Only if the bill has a chance of passing the whole House will they let it out of committee.

3. You can endorse the senator's argument provided you ignore all of the glaring fallacies.

4. In the event of a natural disaster, the state's lack of preparation will become clear.

EXERCISE SET 2-4

1. Invent a deductively valid syllogism that has the same form as the valid syllogism about Greeks being mortal mentioned in this chapter.

2. Invent another deductively valid syllogism in some other mood (but not the mood All).

3. Now invent a deductively invalid syllogism, and explain why you think that it is not valid.

*4. Explain why *disjunctive syllogisms* are not true syllogisms in the sense intended by Aristotle. (Try to do this before looking at the answer in the back of the book.)[14]

EXERCISE SET 2-5

Which of the following are tautologies, which are contradictions, and which are contingent statements? Defend your answers. (Be careful; at least one of these is sneaky.)

1. Either Donald Trump ran for president of the United States in 2016, or a lot of newspapers were mistaken.

2. Either Donald Trump was on the ballot in Georgia in 2016, or he wasn't.

*3. Trump didn't campaign both for the presidency and for the vice presidency.

4. Snow is always white, except, of course, when it isn't.

5. The news media always report the news accurately.

6. No politicians ever keep any of their campaign promises.

7. Those who laugh last, laugh best.

---

[14]Starred (*) items are answered in a section at the back of the book.

8. I learned in school that 2 + 2 always equals 4, but I don't believe it.

9. Either you're in favor of an equal rights amendment to the Constitution, or you're against it.

10. Trespassers will be shot and then they'll never trespass again.

11. If you don't play the state lottery, you can't win it.

12. If I didn't get all of the first ten questions here right, then I did get them all right.

EXERCISE SET 2-6

1. What is the difference between an induction by enumeration and analogical reasoning? Provide an example (not mentioned in the text) of each.

2. Explain in your own words what the difference is between an induction by enumeration and a statistical induction. Provide an example (not mentioned in the text) of a valid statistical induction.

3. What is meant by saying that an inference is a higher-level induction? Provide an example (not mentioned in the text).

"Having concluded, Your Highness, an exhaustive study of this nation's political, social and economic history, and after examining, Sire, the unfortunate events leading to the present deplorable state of the realm, the consensus of the council is that Your Majesty's only course, for the public good, must be to take the next step."

Question-begging advice, following oracular rule number 1: Make pronouncements as empty as possible to minimize the chance of being wrong.

Fallacies: Questionable Premises

3

MindTap® Visit MindTap for more readings and resources.

We said in Chapter 1 that we reason fallaciously when we fail to satisfy all three of the requirements of cogent reasoning. Using premises that we should doubt makes us guilty of the fallacy *questionable premise;* neglecting relevant evidence, guilty of the fallacy *suppressed evidence;* and drawing conclusions not sufficiently supported by evidence, guilty of the fallacy *invalid inference.*

Of course, we must remember that the arguments encountered in daily life tend to be vague, or ambiguous, and premises, and even conclusions, sometimes are omitted as understood. As a result, everyday arguments often can be construed in different ways. Consider the following claim, proudly proclaimed on the Hanes company website (in 2016):

> Hanes is America's #1 socks brand!

To their credit, Hanes does provide a reference to an independent consumer data study. So we probably have good reason to believe that Hanes is in fact the best-selling brand of socks. But what does that mean for us? Taken literally, this isn't an argument, but it clearly implies that the reader should buy Hanes socks. (Why else put the claim prominently on their website?) So the import of this claim may be put this way:

1. More people in America buy Hanes socks than any other brand. (Premise)
∴**2.** You, too, should buy Hanes socks.

Construed in this way, the ad does contain an argument, but the argument is defective because it contains an invalid inference. That a brand of socks is the most popular does not imply that you should buy it. The most popular socks, after all, may not be the best or the best value. However, you could just as well restate the argument this way:

1. More people in America buy Hanes socks than any other brand. (Premise)
2. The most popular brand is the best brand. (Implied premise)
3. You should buy the best brand (Implied premise)
∴4. You, too, should buy Hanes socks.

Now the argument is valid but contains at least one—and probably two—questionable premises. Just because something is popular does not make it good, much less the best. And it is not in general true that you should always buy the best brand—for instance, if you cannot afford the best brand, or if we're talking about a product for which quality doesn't matter *all* that much (maybe like socks!).

Like the Hanes example, most fallacious arguments can be stated in more ways than one. So there often isn't a single "right" label to apply to fallacious reasoning. This doesn't mean that there aren't plenty of wrong labels to apply, and it surely doesn't mean that merely applying a plausible label is sufficient. The point is to understand *why* an argument is fallacious and why a particular label can be shown to be right. In the Hanes case, for instance, it's important to see that being the most popular socks is not by itself sufficient reason for most people to conclude that they should go out and buy them. Labeling just helps us to see that an argument is fallacious (*if it is!*) and helps us to understand why it is fallacious.

Although all fallacious reasoning falls into one or more of the three broad categories just mentioned, over the years, a number of other, narrower fallacy species have been identified that crosscut the three basic types.[1] These labels have come into common use because experience has shown them to be helpful in spotting fallacious reasoning.

Let's now discuss some of the more important of these common fallacy categories and also add some comments concerning the broad fallacy category *questionable premise*.

1. Appeal to Authority

One of the most serious errors in reasoning is to accept the word of someone, in particular an alleged authority, when we should be suspicious. We all have to appeal to experts for information or advice—only fools don't do so with some regularity. In this technological age, we all are nonexperts in most fields. This makes us prone to take as cogent arguments that rely on inadequate authorities. Using the word of an authority, alleged or genuine, when we shouldn't make us guilty of the fallacy called **appeal to authority**.

But which appeals are proper and which fallacious? Clearly, it isn't a good idea to believe that an authority is reliable without having good reason for doing so. Some alleged authorities don't have the expertise they claim; others can't be relied on to tell it to

---

[1]That is, some instances of a narrower fallacy species may fall into one of the three broad genuses and some into another. Several hundred fallacy categories have been discussed in the literature, but no single source discusses all of them. Only those that occur frequently are discussed in this text, which means that our list is not exhaustive by any means. But the division into the three broad master categories *questionable premise, suppressed evidence,* and *invalid inference* is exhaustive.

us straight rather than feed us something more self-serving. Anyway, in some cases we need to do some of our own thinking and research.

So when seeking expert advice, four basic questions need to be addressed if we want to avoid committing the fallacy of appeal to authority:

1. Is the source likely to have the information or good judgment we need?
2. If so, can we trust the authority to tell it to us straight?
3. Do we have the time, desire, and ability to reason the matter out for ourselves (or to understand the expert's reasoning, so that we don't have to rely merely on the authority's word)?
4. Is the claim in question one that can *possibly* be justified by appealing to authority?

We usually know right away whether we have the needed time and inclination, but the other questions often are rather difficult to answer. However, a few rules of thumb should prove helpful.

SOME AUTHORITIES ARE MORE TRUSTWORTHY THAN OTHERS

Individuals who are regarded as authorities or experts are not created equal. Some are smart, others stupid; some are well trained in their field, some not; some are more or less honest (a completely honest person being a rarity in any case), others pretty much untrustworthy.

Characters who are less than completely ethical are found in every profession, but some fields attract this type more than others. The fields of law, financial advising, and politics, for instance, notoriously attract the unscrupulous, but even the clergy is not without its charlatans, and doctors who prescribe unneeded surgery are not unknown in the history of medicine.

The news media have its questionable characters as well. Take Rupert Murdoch, for instance, the owner of News Corporation in the United States and News International in Great Britain—and arguably the most powerful media mogul in history. When members of the British Parliament questioned him about the extensive, illegal phone tapping and computer hacking carried out by his tabloid reporters at *News of the World*, a flagship News International publication, he claimed he knew nothing about it, blaming it on staff members who betrayed him. "I think they have behaved disgracefully," he said, "And I think, frankly, that I'm the best person to see it through." Really? This from the man who ran a media empire in which thousands of phone and computer hackings occurred; officials in the police, armed services, and government were bribed for stories, and so were former employees—to keep their mouths shut. Why would anyone give him the authority to clean up the mess?

Unfortunately, untrustworthy information sources can be found at news institutions typically more respected than *News of the World*. In 2003, the *New York Times* reported that one of its own journalists, Jayson Blair, "misled readers and *Times* colleagues with dispatches that purported to be from Maryland, Texas and other states, when often he was far away, in New York. He fabricated comments. He concocted scenes. He lifted material from other newspapers and wire services. He selected details from photographs to create the impression he had been somewhere or seen someone, when he had not."[2] And in 2015, NBC suspended Brian Williams, the anchor and managing editor of its venerated *NBC Nightly News* program, for repeatedly making false claims about his own experience of the Iraq War a decade earlier. The lesson here may be that some news sources can be trusted not at all and no news source can be trusted entirely.

Even among more scrupulous people, the personal interests of experts are bound now and then to conflict with their duties to clients. Professionals are human, after all, just like the rest of us. Politicians elected to the U.S. Congress are bound to savor the perks, fame, power, and excitement that goes along with their jobs (who wouldn't?), making it rather difficult for them to refuse the fat-cat "campaign contributions" (bribes?) needed to gain reelection, and thus making it more difficult still for them to tell voters the straight truth on important issues. Remember, though, that politics is the art of compromise and, in particular, that candidates do need to get elected to do good work, so they often need at least to shade the truth for that purpose. (See the section in Chapter 10 on political rhetoric for more on this point.)

So when considering expert reasoning or pronouncements, we always need to make a judgment about believability. Does the authority have an axe to grind, a personal interest that might be furthered? Lawyers who speak out against no-fault auto insurance, as they usually do, have to be looked at with a jaundiced eye precisely because the point of no-fault insurance is to reduce legal costs. When members of Congress vote against gun laws, in spite of strong public sentiment favoring gun control in the wake of horrors like the shootings at Sandy Hook Elementary School in 2012, we aren't being overly skeptical if we wonder whether their judgment has been warped by campaign contributions from interested parties or by narrow constituent interests.

Perhaps we've learned by now to take anything a politician says with a grain (or pound) of salt. But we do—and largely must—rely heavily on medical advice with the expectation that medical experts are trustworthy sources. So you may have been excited in 2015 when Steven N. Blair posted a video online claiming that exercise rather than diet is the key to combating obesity, and that "Most of the focus in the popular media and in the scientific press is 'Oh, they're eating too much, eating too much, eating too much'—blaming fast food, blaming sugary drinks and so on. And there's really virtually no compelling evidence that that, in fact, is the cause." So you can run a few miles and then have potato chips and soda for dinner! Hooray! Hooray? No, wait. This is a pretty surprising claim. Maybe you should look into this Steven Blair a little bit. Well, Dr. Blair is a professor at the University of South Carolina and a well-trained expert in exercise science. Except the video wasn't posted to the University of South Carolina website, but as part of a new group called the Global Energy Balance Network (GEBN). Who are they exactly? Well, they're a nonprofit organization committed to fighting obesity. That sounds okay. Their membership includes numerous credentialed experts who have contributed to scientific journals. Their website reveals no obvious conflict of interest. That all checks out. But then the *New York Times* reveals that GEBN received $1.5 million and logistical support from Coca-Cola. Still, maybe everything is okay, because GEBN insisted that the funds in no way influenced the organization or its policies. Is it their

---

[2]"Times Reporter Who Resigned Leaves Long Trial of Deception." *New York Times,* 11 May 2003.

fault if Coca-Cola happens to benefit from their findings and message and therefore wants to support them? As long as they are truly independent, there is no real conflict of interest. Chips and soda! Hooray! Hooray? No, wait. The Associated Press then gets ahold of some emails between GEBN and Coca-Cola executives. It turns out Coca-Cola was instrumental in choosing GEBN's leadership and even edited its mission statement. One email from GEBN's president said, "I want to help your company avoid the image of being a problem in people's lives and back to being a company that brings important and fun things to them." Okay, maybe some vegetables instead.

On the other hand, we should be inclined, *other things being equal,* to accept the word of dentists who urge their patients to brush and floss regularly and of doctors who exhort us to quit smoking cigarettes, precisely because dentists make money when patients get cavities, and doctors profit when people get cancer, have heart attacks, or come down with emphysema. Advice to brush regularly or to quit smoking thus is more likely to be motivated by a professional intent to serve the interests of clients rather than by a desire to further selfish interests.

AUTHORITIES IN ONE FIELD AREN'T NECESSARILY EXPERTS IN ANOTHER

Famous athletes and movie stars who endorse all sorts of products in television commercials are good examples of professionals speaking outside their fields of expertise. There's no reason to suppose that someone who knows how to act, or to hit home runs, knows any more about washing machines, or shaving cream, than anyone else.

What exactly should we conclude from the facts that Jennifer Aniston was paid to endorse Smart Water and 50 Cent was paid to endorse Vitaminwater? How should these facts influence our choice of insanely expensive and nutritionally questionable alternatives to water? (Wait, why did we need an alternative to water again?) Should we choose Pepsi because they pay Beyoncé to drink their products, or Coke because they similarly pay Taylor Swift? There is very little reason to suppose a product is better than others because a celebrity chooses or promotes it. And there is *absolutely* no reason to suppose a product is better because a celebrity is paid to do so. Yet most of us, irrationally, are suckers when it comes to celebrity commercials. But at least in billboards and television commercials, it is clear that what we're seeing is in fact a paid endorsement. The situation gets a little more complicated when celebrities proclaim their love for a product on social media or a product shows up in a scripted TV show, beloved by the fictional characters therein. We'll consider both of these issues later in the text.

LEARN HOW BEST TO APPEAL TO AUTHORITIES

It generally is easy to know which sorts of experts to appeal to. Sick people need to consult doctors; someone sued for divorce, a lawyer. It's a lot more difficult to find experts in a particular profession who know their stuff and can be relied on. But even after finding them, we need to become adept at picking their brains. Experts often throw up roadblocks to understanding, especially by overwhelming us with professional lingo. They frequently find it tedious to explain complicated matters to laypeople, and anyway, they may not want to spend the time and effort necessary to do so.

It also is true that laypeople often are unable to follow the complicated reasonings of trained professionals, medical specialists being a case in point. But it usually is possible to get at least a rough idea of what authorities are up to if we are persistent and if we insist that they translate their professional lingo into ordinary discourse. It's hard not to be intimidated by professional jargon or by an authoritarian aura, but it is well worth the effort to resist that sort of intimidation.

UNDERSTAND WHAT AUTHORITIES CAN BE EXPECTED TO KNOW

All experts definitely are not created equal. It isn't just that some alleged authorities, as we mentioned before, don't know what they claim to know, or that some aren't completely on the up-and-up. It's also that a good deal more is known about some topics than about others, and that some kinds of information are much more expensive to obtain than others. True experts in some fields thus are more reliable than those in others.

We all are forced by the nature of modern life to seek advice and expert performance from doctors, lawyers, auto mechanics, and other kinds of trained (and often licensed) professionals. But we can't expect the same sorts of definitive answers to our questions or solutions to our problems when consulting these authorities as we can, say, when consulting physicists or chemists. Medicine, for example, while based on biological theory, still is an art. Doctors cannot always be sure of their diagnoses or of how to treat an ailment; the best of them are bound to be mistaken in their judgments now and then. Lawyers cannot be sure how jurors or judges will respond to evidence. Clergymen do not have direct lines to a higher authority.

Furthermore, some questions simply cannot be settled by appeal to authority; for instance, the kinds of questions you might encounter in a philosophy class. Critically, there are no authorities to whom we can appeal to settle difficult ethical questions. Some of us may be more moral (i.e., may act morally more often) than others, but deciding what one ought to do in a particular situation always requires contemplation and argument.

BECOME YOUR OWN EXPERT ON IMPORTANT CONTROVERSIAL TOPICS

When authorities disagree on a topic of importance, the rest of us need to become our own experts, turning to authorities for evidence, reasons, and arguments, but not conclusions. This is especially true with respect to social and political matters, because experts themselves disagree so much on these issues and because we have to watch out for the intrusion of self-interest into their stated judgments and opinions. Politicians, for example, may be beholden to special interests (as we noted before) or simply be going along with a misguided tide of public opinion. Conservative commentators generally see things differently than do those who are liberal.[3]

But politics is not by any means the only topic where the reasons and reasonings of experts should count for much more than their conclusions. Judges and juries, for example, too often uncritically accept the opinions of psychologists concerning the sanity of

---

[3]Although labels such as "conservative," "libertarian," "liberal," "right wing," and "left wing" tend to be vague and ambiguous, they still have some content: Those labeled by these terms do tend to differ in their viewpoints, and critical reasoners need to take these differences into account.

those charged with crimes, rather than delving into the reasons behind those opinions. After all, different opinions often can be obtained just by consulting other psychologists.[4] This holds true even in fields like medicine, where we tend to trust the opinions of experts. For instance, a woman who is advised to have a hysterectomy might be wise to seek a second opinion from another physician. (Women with relevant background information know that many unnecessary hysterectomies are performed for conditions that can be treated by less invasive means.)

One way to gauge the judgment of alleged experts is to check their past records. Professional sports people have a saying that when in doubt, you should go with a winner. Similarly, when expert advice is needed, it makes sense to go with a winner—someone whose track record is good. Those who have been right in the past are more likely than others to be right in the future, other things being equal. Remember, however, that other things are not always equal. Auto mechanics may get out of touch with the latest technology, lawyers who have made their pile may become lazy, and textbook writers (with at least three obvious exceptions!) may eventually go over the hill.

Note, by the way, that most fallacious appeals to authority fall under the broader category *questionable premise,* because underlying the appeal to the word of an authority is the implicit premise that it is wise to do so. In other words, the fallacy appeal to authority is committed by using expert advice or information when it isn't wise to do so, perhaps because the authority isn't likely to have the information we desire or may have a serious conflict of interest.

Before going on to a discussion of other fallacies, perhaps notice should be taken of the flip side of the fallacy of appeal to authority—namely, failure to take the word of authorities when we should. After all, salespeople frequently do give us the relevant facts straight; TV news programs do provide us with a good deal of useful information, even if they don't provide us with "the whole truth, nothing but the truth"; politicians sometimes do put aside self-interest and speak out against powerful interests. Being careful when evaluating information sources does not mean becoming completely cynical.

2. Inconsistency

We commit the fallacy of **inconsistency** when we present arguments that contain self-contradictory statements or statements that contradict each other.[5] Obviously, if two statements are contradictory, then one of them must be false.

Consider, for example, the ways in which inconsistencies intrude into campaign rhetoric. (Campaign rhetoric: The pronouncements of most politicians most of the time.) Candidates for public office do not explicitly say *A* and then immediately assert not-*A.* Instead, the contradictory nature of their pronouncements is concealed in one way or another. For instance, in the same speech, a candidate may assure voters that various government services or payments will significantly be increased (to curry the favor of voters who will profit from them), promise large tax reductions (to gain the support of

---

[4]This observation conforms to B. Duggan's Law of Expert Testimony: "For every Ph.D. there is an equal and opposite Ph.D."

[5]Recall the discussion in Chapter 2 about tautologies, contradictions, and contingent statements.

those burdened by high taxes), and favor a huge reduction in the national debt (to appeal to voter beliefs about the virtues of governmental thrift).[6]

That is how the vast majority of candidates for high office, including President Bush in 2000 and 2004, President Obama in 2008 and 2012, and both major presidential candidates in 2016, have played the game. But government services and benefits cost money, and a majority of government expenses are fixed (most notably interest payments on previously contracted debts), so that a package of increased services and benefits, coupled with significant tax and public debt reductions, can be regarded as inconsistent in the absence of a plausible explanation as to how this trick is going to be performed. (In recent times, extremely high military expenditures and huge financial bailouts have made this trick even more difficult than it otherwise would be.) Adding up the figures is one way of determining whether candidates are being consistent, and hence believable, when they promise us the moon.

Politicians hardly have a monopoly on inconsistency. In 2015, the National Football League, in response to a lawsuit brought by former players, denied a clear link between playing football and the degenerative brain disease chronic traumatic encephalopathy (CTE). The NFL argued that research has not "reliably determined" the cause of CTE, and dismissed the link between repeated concussions (like those suffered by professional football players) and CTE as "speculation" that "remains unproven."

But then a few months later, the NFL's executive for Health and Safety Policy told Congress that the answer to the question of a link between football and CTE is "certainly yes." And the NFL initially stood by the statements made to Congress before again backtracking and issuing a statement emphasizing that the scientific community does not recognize a cause of CTE.

All of that said, when evaluating the various kinds of rhetoric encountered in everyday life, it is important that we don't misjudge deliberately equivocal, ironic, or humorous rhetoric. It won't do, for example, to brand the literally contradictory bumper sticker that says "Good enough isn't good enough" as contradictory, since it isn't intended to be taken literally. It is saying that we should do better than merely minimally well.

Note that there are ways to be guilty of the fallacy of inconsistency in addition to the obvious one of being inconsistent within a single argument or statement. The earlier example about politicians who, in the same speech, promise lots of government services, lower taxes, and a reduction in the national debt is a case in point.

Another way to be inconsistent is to *argue one way at a given time and another way at some other time, or when talking to one person and then to another.* Of course, there is nothing wrong with changing one's mind—of believing *A* at one time and not-*A* at another. That, after all, is the point of learning from experience. It is when we continue to hang on both to *A* and to not-*A*, trotting out one for use when reasoning about one thing and the other when reasoning about something else, that we are guilty of being inconsistent.

---

[6]Their argument thus can be put this way: If elected, I won't destroy the government services and payments you want, I will significantly reduce taxes, and I will reduce the national debt. Therefore, you should vote for me.

In politics, being inconsistent over time or from audience to audience is called "blowing with the wind." What is popular with constituents in one place or at one time may not be in another. Circumstances thus push politicians into being inconsistent in order to keep up with the latest trends in public opinion or to placate particular audiences. Candidates for office try as much as they can to tell people what they want to hear, and different people want to hear different things. In a March 2016 debate among Republican presidential candidates on CNN, moderator Jake Tapper asked Donald Trump a question about violent incidents at his rallies: "Do you believe that you've done anything to create a tone where this kind of violence would be encouraged?"

"I hope not," Trump responded, "I truly hope not . . . I certainly do not condone that at all, Jake." Tapper then quoted some things Trump had said at his own rallies to his own supporters rather than to CNN's general audience, including "I'd like to punch [a protester] in the face," and "in the good ol' days, they'd have ripped him out of that seat so fast," and "knock the crap out of him, would you? Seriously, OK, just knock the hell. I promise you I will pay for the legal fees." Confronted with this inconsistency, Trump tried to shift the focus to "some protesters who are bad dudes" and some cheap-applause-seeking praise for local police.

To some extent, we all engage in this sort of inconsistency—politicians are just better at it than most of the rest of us. Occasionally, we do so deliberately, with conscious intent. But often we are trying to fool not just or even the other guy, but rather, ourselves. Virtually all of us, for instance, are against cheating others, yet at one time or another we can't resist the temptation to do so to our advantage while providing reasons (excuses) to justify what we have done; for example, the excuse that most other people do it, so it's not wrong for us to do so. (This point is discussed at greater length in Chapter 6, where impediments to cogent reasoning are the subject.)

It also must be noted that large organizations have an interesting way to be inconsistent that tends to be rather hard to notice: They have one representative speak out of one side of the mouth while another speaks from the other side. Let's call this sort of chicanery *organizational inconsistency,* thinking of a large organization as a kind of artificial person. In 2015, for instance, the state of Michigan informed its employees in Flint about the city's contaminated water supply and even brought in bottled water for them. It would be another six months before the state made a similar admission to the public.

We have just gone to some lengths to describe inconsistency as a serious mistake. Yet others have railed against being consistent; witness Ralph Waldo Emerson's famous remark, "A foolish consistency is the hobgoblin of little minds, adored by little statesmen, philosophers and divines."

But there need be no inconsistency in accepting both sides of this coin, provided we notice that consistency is an ambiguous concept. One sense requires us to be consistent in what we believe at any given time. This is roughly the sense meant in this chapter. The other requires us to be consistent now and forever, to stick to our guns no matter what contrary evidence we encounter. This, one must suppose, is the kind of consistency Emerson intended to disparage.

(In regarding this as a fallacy, we are, of course, stretching that concept a bit, but for a good purpose—namely, to call attention to this threat to consistent reasoning.)

Another kind of organizational inconsistency occurs when it seems expedient to ignore company policy—which brings us back to Rupert Murdoch. Although Murdoch's company policy was that the news should be gathered by legal means, many reporters found it expedient to tap phones and hack computers in order to land juicy stories. This practice continued for years before incriminating facts emerged. Indeed, Murdoch claimed his lawyers assured him "there was no illegality" except for one incident involving a single rogue reporter. However, whether Murdoch was ignorant of these nefarious activities or complicit in them, either way, there was inconsistency between company policy and actual practice.

Another way to be inconsistent is by *saying one thing while doing another.* Calling this a fallacy again stretches that concept to serve everyday purposes. Strictly speaking, saying one thing and doing another does not make one guilty of a fallacy, because it does not involve an inconsistency between one claim, idea, or argument and another. We include this discussion here to call attention to those who engage in this sort of behavior.

Al Gore was charged with this type of inconsistency when the media revealed that his private consumption of energy was at odds with his praiseworthy public campaign to reduce global warming. The day after he received an Oscar for the best documentary feature, *An Inconvenient Truth*, in which he urged Americans to curb their energy consumption, the Tennessee Center for Policy Research had this to say about Gore's personal energy use: "Gore's mansion . . . consumes more electricity every month than the average household uses in an entire year, according to the Nashville Electric Service . . . more than 20 times the national average. . . . In total Gore paid nearly $30,000 in combined electricity and natural gas bills for his Nashville estate in 2006." Considering how admirable his efforts have been to curb global warming, he might be forgiven a little personal inconsistency. Nonetheless, it would have looked better if he had walked the walk as well as talked the talk.

Inconsistency often is connected in people's minds with hypocrisy—with pretending to believe what one in fact does not, or to be what one is not. The vast majority of candidates for office in the United States during the past 40 years or so have run on platforms opposing legalization of drugs even though some of them smoked dope or sniffed cocaine. Bill Clinton did own up to smoking marijuana, but notoriously claimed that he did not inhale (ho, ho, ho). Should we say that those who were inconsistent in this way were guilty of the sin of *hypocrisy*? At least Barack Obama admitted past drug use in his teens, but attitudes have changed over the years, and Americans seem more willing to accept youthful lapses than they did before.

Readers may note, when they have completed reading the three fallacy chapters in this text, that a good deal more time is spent on the first two fallacies in this chapter than on any of the others. The reason is that these two are very likely the most important. The importance of the fallacy of appeal to authority is obvious: We all are nonexperts about most of the things that matter in everyday life and therefore regularly have to appeal to authorities for information and advice. The importance of the fallacy of inconsistency also should be obvious: It lies in the crucial importance of consistency to cogent reasoning. *At least one of a set of inconsistent statements must be false!*

That is why trying to be consistent is very likely the best way to improve the quality of one's stock of background beliefs (a point to be discussed again later). Having reasoned to a particular conclusion, consistency requires that we ask ourselves whether we would be willing to carry through that line of reasoning when it applies to other cases. If not, then we must give up that line of reasoning or admit to the intellectual crime of being *inconsistent*.

3. Straw Man

While the broad fallacy category *suppressed evidence* seldom is mentioned in traditional logic texts, several species of this genus are given great play. One of these is the **straw man** fallacy, which is committed when we (A) misrepresent an opponent's position, or a competitor's product, or go after a weaker opponent or competitor while ignoring a stronger one, (B) present an argument or claim against the misrepresentation or weaker version, and (C) make it seem like we've successfully attacked or refuted the original or stronger version.[7]

Straw man has always been the stock-in-trade of advertisers and political smear campaigns. A group called Common Sense Issues made a million automated phone calls to voters in the 2008 South Carolina primaries claiming that John McCain "has voted to use unborn babies in medical research." This was a gross distortion of his position to support research on stem cells gathered from embryos.

Politicians often use straw man arguments to undermine their opponents' positions. In 2016, Hillary Clinton's campaign ran an ad suggesting that she would make a better Democratic nominee than Bernie Sanders because, in part, she would "defend Planned Parenthood, not attack it," and "stand up to the gun lobby, not protect it." The ad was referring, we have to assume, to Sanders's comments about the leadership of Planned Parenthood being part of the "political establishment" and the fact that his position on gun control is somewhat weaker than Clinton's. Sanders took issue with both of these arguments, though, pointing out that he routinely called for increased funding for Planned Parenthood and received a "D-Minus" rating from the NRA.

But of course, these doors usually swing both ways. A press release from the Sanders campaign said, "Sanders was one of only three senators to vote in 2007 against barring the transfer of Guantanamo detainees to America," and that "Then-Sen. Hillary Clinton voted for the amendment that kept the prison open." The implied argument here is that Sanders is the better candidate in part because he has the right position on the controversial prison at Guantanamo and that Clinton's position is wrong. But the legislation in question said that Guantanamo prisoners "should not be released into American society," not that the prison should stay open. Clinton, in fact, cosponsored legislation that called for Guantanamo's closure.

---

[7]Note, however, that some cases of this fallacy do not fall into the category of *suppressed evidence*. Should we, by the way, replace the name "straw man" by, say, "straw person," or perhaps "false characterization"?

4. False Dilemma and the Either-Or Fallacy

In traditional logic, a **dilemma** is an argument that presents two alternatives, both claimed to be bad for someone, or some position. (Dilemmas are discussed further in the appendix.)

The general form of a dilemma can be put this way:

Either *P* or *Q*.
If *P* then *R*.
If *Q* then *S*.
Therefore, either *R* or *S*.

Sometimes the undesired outcomes *R* and *S* are identical, sometimes quite different. Here is an example in which they are not quite the same: "Either our fellow citizens are good or they're bad. If they're good, laws to deter crime aren't needed. But if they're bad, laws to deter crime won't succeed. So laws to deter crime either are not needed or won't succeed."

A **false dilemma** is a dilemma that can be shown to be uncogent because at least one of its premises is false (note that arguments of this form are always valid). One way to do this is to demonstrate that the premise having the form "Either *P* or *Q*" is false by showing that there is at least one other viable possibility. This is called "going between the horns" of the dilemma. In the case of the dilemma just mentioned, a viable alternative is that our fellow citizens may be both good (in some ways) and bad (in others).

Another way to defeat a dilemma is to challenge one or both of its other two premises. This is called "grasping the horns" of the dilemma. We might challenge the crime law dilemma, for example, by arguing that even if some citizens are bad, they still can be deterred by laws specifying harsh penalties.

False dilemmas usually are a species of the genus *questionable premise* because any set of statements that sets up a false dilemma needs to be questioned. (Note, by the way, that we can have false trilemmas, false quadrilemmas, and so on.)

The **either-or fallacy** (sometimes called the *black-or-white fallacy*) is very similar to that of *false dilemma*. We're guilty of this fallacy when we mistakenly reason from two alternatives, one claimed to be bad (that is, to be avoided) so that we ought to choose the other alternative. The general form of the fallacy is this:

Either *P* or *Q*.
Not *P*.
Therefore, *Q*.

where there is at least a third viable alternative, or it is questionable that *P* is bad. For example, "You have to vote either for the Republican or for the Democratic candidate. But you shouldn't vote for the Republican. So you should vote for the Democrat." A third alternative in this case would be to vote, say, for the Green Party candidate (this is like going between the horns of a dilemma), and some people would challenge the claim that you shouldn't vote for the Republican candidate (this would be like grasping a dilemma by its horns).

One notable example of the either-or fallacy was the second President Bush's battle cry after September 11, "You are either with us or against us in the fight against terror."

There were, of course, plenty of options in between. This simplification of a complex situation was a rhetorical device rather than an appeal to reason. A more recent example comes to us courtesy of the *New York Times* opinion pages. In a piece titled "Can Family Leave Policies Be Too Generous? It Seems So," Claire Cain Miller argues that, while U.S. family leave is too limited, women's professional lives can be hurt by having access to too much paid family leave. How so? According to Miller:

> Long leaves and part-time work protections might encourage women to scale back at work or stretch their leaves longer than they otherwise would have, according to the Cornell economists, Francine D. Blau and Lawrence M. Kahn, whose study was published last year in the *American Economic Review*. Employers, meanwhile, might "engage in statistical discrimination against women as a group, anticipating that women will take advantage of such opportunities," they wrote. Long absences are expensive for companies, particularly for jobs that build on training and promotions, and employers are understandably hesitant to hire people who might leave for a year at a time.

The implication here is that we can either mandate the availability of "too much" family leave and cause employers to discriminate against women, or we could mandate a smaller amount that would help families (Miller rightfully points out that there should also be more demand for and use of family leave among fathers). But surely there is a third option. We could allow for longer times (even paid time) for family leave while cracking down on the kind of discrimination—already illegal—that Miller describes. It may be "understandable" that employers would be hesitant. But isn't that exactly why we have antidiscrimination laws, to change behaviors when "hesitancies" are antithetical to fairness, justice, and other larger social interests?[8]

5. Begging the Question

When arguing, either with ourselves or with others, we can't provide reasons for every assertion and then reasons for the reasons, and so on. Some of what we assert must go unjustified, at least for the moment. But when we assume as a premise some form of the very point that is at issue—the very conclusion we intend to prove—we are guilty of the fallacy of **begging the question**.[9] In this sense, *to beg* means "to avoid." When the premise simply states another version of the conclusion, the question of proof is avoided, or *begged*. (The fallacy of begging the question usually falls into the broad category *questionable premise* because a statement that is questionable as a conclusion is equally questionable as a premise.)

---

[8]This very problem with this article was mentioned in *Extra!* (July/August 2015), "'Not Too Generous,' Please: NYT on Family Friendly Work Policies."

[9]In a sense, all deductively valid arguments beg the question, because what is said by their conclusions already is said in their premises. In the typical case, part of an argument's conclusion is said in one premise, part in another. That is the point of valid deduction; anyone who accepts the premises of a deductively valid argument and yet rejects its conclusion is being irrational. The difference in the case of the fallacy of begging the question is that the premises state the claim of the conclusion in a way that those who reject the conclusion also will reject the premises for being just as questionable as the conclusion.

In real life, of course, this fallacy rarely, if ever, has the form

> *A.*
> Therefore, *A.*

Few would be taken in by anything so obvious. Instead, a premise may state a conclusion in different but equivalent words, so that the conclusion is not so obviously begged. This is the way in which the question is begged in one of the classic textbook cases (from the nineteenth century—human gullibility tends to remain constant): "To allow every man unbounded freedom of speech must always be . . . advantageous to the state; for it is highly conducive to the interests of the community that each individual should enjoy a liberty, perfectly unlimited, of expressing his sentiments."[10]

Although the traditional fallacy of begging the question deals primarily with questions that are at issue, say, as in a debate, over time it has come to have a broader range so as to cover other sorts of questions. Thus, to take a textbook example, we can be said to fall for this fallacy when, having asked why chloroform renders people unconscious, we accept the answer that it does so because it is a soporific (a *soporific* being defined as something that induces sleep).

Doctors and other sorts of professionals are frequent perpetrators of this version of begging the question, but they aren't by any means the only ones who set us up for it. Indeed, many times questions are begged quite innocently. Here is an example taken from an article on exclusive men's clubs in San Francisco. In explaining why these clubs have such long waiting lists, Paul B. "Red" Fay, Jr. (on the roster of three of the clubs) said, "The reason there's such a big demand is because everyone wants to get in them."[11] In other words, there is a big demand because there is a big demand. Fay inadvertently (we hope) gave another version of the conclusion in the premise and thus avoided the question of proof.

Another way to beg the question is to offer premises that we have no reason to accept unless we already accept the argument's conclusion. Take the example of the "Freedom from Dogma Argument" for atheism as explained at argumentsforatheism.com: "Atheism is a convenient and accessible route to personal and societal freedom. The dogma of religion, on the other hand, is rigid and restrictive, and deliberately designed to act as a check on personal and group freedoms." To say that religious dogma is deliberately designed as a check on freedom is to *assume* that it is designed by human beings and reflects (rather untoward) human goals rather than the will of a deity. Of course a theist will not agree to this, but say that at least some religious dogma is designed to put us in line with the will of God. And the atheist will surely counter that there is no such being. The conflict once again turns back to the existence of God. But that is what the argument was meant to disprove. The atheist can't argue for the nonexistence of God using premises that assume the nonexistence of God. Nor, we should point out, can the theist argue for the existence of God by pointing to some holy text and say that its authority

---

[10]Cited by Richard Whately in his excellent book *Elements of Logic* (London, 1826). Whately's fallacy classification is more like the one used in this text than are those of any other text in use today.

[11]Quoted in: Lara, Adair. "The Chosen Few." *San Francisco Chronicle,* 18 July 2004.

demonstrateŝ God's existence. That authority is itself predicated on the existence of God, and so arguing from that authority assumes God's existence.

EVADING THE ISSUE

One effective way to beg the question at issue is simply to avoid it entirely. Doing this makes one guilty of the fallacy **evading the issue**. This approach succeeds when those taken in fail to notice that the issue has been evaded. Perhaps the best way to hoodwink an opponent or dodge a barbed question is to make it appear that the issue or question is indeed being addressed. Politicians frequently evade an issue concerning a complicated problem (the homeless, the national debt, whatever) by speaking instead about the pressing need to solve it. Savvy citizens are not taken in by this sort of chicanery.

Politicians are masters at evading the issue. When they are asked hard questions in interviews, they skirt the subject with responses like "That's a complex issue…" and then shift into the message they want to give. Or they claim the question is relevant, then dismiss it to clear the way for topics they do think are more relevant. Or they say things like "That's a good question, but before going into that I want to discuss…" and then go on to spin their own point of view. Evading the issue is so important to politicians that many of them hire media trainers to help them perfect the art.[12] We'll have more to say about evasion in Chapter 7, when we consider its function as a manipulative rhetorical device.

© Dilbert Cartoons

Two instances of begging the question.

6. Questionable Premise—Questionable Statement

As we noted earlier, most examples of the fallacies discussed so far fall into the broader category of *questionable premise.* But not all species of questionable premise have received specific names in the literature. So when a premise that is not believable is spotted in an argument and none of these more specific labels apply, we have to fall back on the general term **questionable premise**.

---

[12]For more on this see a fascinating article on media training: Lieberman, Trudy. "Answer the Question." *Columbia Review of Journalism,* January–February 2004.

Knowing for a fact that a statement is false obviously is a very good reason for questioning it—indeed, for dismissing it. Thus, when a colleague was alleged to be incompetent on grounds that she was an alcoholic, one of the authors of this text rejected the charge on the basis of personal knowledge that the allegation was false. Sometimes a premise that may be believable to one person can strike another as questionable or even false. Take, for instance, the comment of James Reda, Wall Street compensation consultant, about the Obama Administration's plan to limit to $500,000 the salaries of executives of companies that received large amounts of federal bailout money: "$500,000 is not a lot of money, particularly if there is no bonus." Well, maybe to the super rich it isn't a lot of money, but to the rest of us it is a fortune, and thus his premise is highly questionable.

Remember, though, that hearing something from a trustworthy expert often counts as a reason for believing it to be true. For example, the fact that the overwhelming majority of scientists believe the burning of fossil fuels, such as oil and coal, is polluting the air and causing a rise in worldwide temperatures ought to constitute good reason for believing that there very likely is a greenhouse effect resulting from the use of these fuels.

Finally, it is worth remembering here that in everyday life, statements generally do not come labeled as premises or conclusions and also that not all persuasive discourse is put into argumentative form. So there is a good deal of merit in expanding the fallacy of *questionable premise* so that it becomes, say, *questionable statement.*

7. Suppressed (Overlooked) Evidence

The general fallacy category **suppressed evidence**, introduced earlier along with questionable premise and invalid inference, has not received much attention in the fallacy literature, perhaps because theorists tend to see the suppression of evidence as an error in reasoning but not as a fallacy (as they define that concept). Whether thought of as a fallacy or not, however, it is important that we learn how to bring relevant evidence to bear on an argument and learn how to avoid being taken in by others when they suppress evidence.

Of course, people who suppress evidence often do so inadvertently, one reason that a more all-encompassing label for the fallacy might be *overlooked evidence,* or perhaps *slighted evidence.* It's easy, when strongly committed to a particular side of an issue, to pass over arguments and reasons on the other side. In recent years, advocates on both sides of issues such as capital punishment, abortion, the legalization of marijuana, the depiction of violence on TV, and the legalization of prostitution frequently have been guilty of slighting evidence damning to their side of the issue. Those opposed to "three strikes and you're out" legislation, for instance, tend to neglect the ways in which this kind of law might protect society from repeat offenders; those in favor don't like to talk about the high costs associated with keeping people in jail long past the age at which the vast majority of criminals have ceased to commit violent crimes, or about the fact that a great many of those sentenced under these laws have not committed violent or even serious crimes.

We all, of course, sometimes are motivated by more crass considerations than mere overzealousness. Self-interest is a powerful motivator of deliberately shady reasoning.

Take, for instance, the way drug companies manipulated data on drug trials that tested the effectiveness of antidepressants like Prozac and Paxil. The published trials showed that these drugs provided significant relief for 60 percent of people on the drugs, compared to only 40 percent for those on placebos. This evidence was convincing enough to persuade doctors and patients that the drugs were effective. But in January 2008, the *Journal of the American Medical Association* ran a report of a new analysis reviewing data from both the published and unpublished trials of the antidepressants. This analysis revealed that 94 percent of the positive trials were published, but only 14 percent of the unconvincing ones were. In effect, the drug companies were suppressing the negative data to win over the government and get FDA approval. Once the unpublished trials were taken into account, the antidepressants had only a slim edge over the placebos. No wonder physicians were puzzled that the drugs didn't seem to work as well on their patients as they did in the published trials.

The point of becoming familiar with the fallacy of suppressed evidence is to sharpen one's ability to spot cases in which relevant evidence is being passed over, whether by others or by ourselves. We need, in particular, to learn how to carry through reasoning so as to see whether all likely relevant information has been considered.

In December 2012, journalist Maria Bartiromo argued on *Meet the Press* that "Dividend taxes are not a rich tax, nor are capital gains." Her evidence was that "You're talking about pension funds, 401(k) plans, investments in companies that pay dividends." True enough, many people who aren't rich do rely on income from pensions and other retirement accounts. But the argument appears weaker when we learn that 401(k) withdrawals are not in fact taxed as dividends, and weaker still in light of the fact that the bottom 80 percent of earners gain just 0.7 percent of their incomes from dividends and capital gains.[13]

Shall I tell you what it is to know? It is to say you know when you know, and to say that you do not know when you do not know; that is knowledge.

—ATTRIBUTED TO CONFUCIUS
(WHICH MEANS THAT WE DO NOT KNOW FOR SURE THAT HE SAID IT)

We don't want to be too hasty, or too picky, in leveling a charge of begging the question. Although what Confucius is quoted as saying is literally question begging, it is very likely that what he meant to say (if he actually said it) is that a large part of wisdom is to know what you do and what you don't have good reason to believe and, by implication, not to believe what you do not have good reason to believe. Excellent advice, indeed.

---

[13]This problem was first noticed and publicized in the February 2013 issue of *Extra!* "When a Tax on the Rich Is Really a Tax on the Rich."

For lots of us, becoming adept at bringing to bear suppressed or overlooked relevant information is perhaps the most difficult knack required by good reasoning. Sometimes the difficulty is compounded by our limited understanding of the issue at hand. Take, for example, the Environmental Protection Agency's decision in 2002 to omit, for the first time in years, the chapter on global warming from its annual federal budget. In 2002, the *New York Times* reported that industrial lobbyists were "praising the decision, contending that carbon dioxide, which is believed to cause global warming, is not a pollutant." In one sense the lobbyists were right—carbon dioxide is not a pollutant; it's a natural gas—but scientists would argue that it has the side effect of trapping heat and thus causing temperatures to rise. Understanding the fallacious reasoning in the lobbyists' argument requires most of us to do a bit of research.

Many people have trouble distinguishing between having no evidence or proof for a claim and having evidence or proof that the claim is false. But having no evidence, say, that vitamin C helps us fight the common cold is quite different from having evidence that it does not do so. Similarly, a lack of clinical proof that marijuana has certain medicinal benefits is much different from having clinical proof that it does not. We will consider similar issues when we take up the "appeal to ignorance" fallacy in the next chapter.

8. Tokenism

Tokenism—mistaking a token gesture for the real thing, or offering a token gesture in lieu of something more concrete—is another common fallacy.

On May 13, 2015, Duke Energy issued a press release touting a new environmental initiative, which began this way:

> Solar energy use among South Carolina customers will increase significantly as a result of an agreement filed with the Public Service Commission of South Carolina on Tuesday.
>
> The agreement enhances Duke Energy's Distributed Energy Resource programs, which were filed with the S.C. Public Service Commission in February. The proposed programs are designed to grow solar capacity in Duke Energy's South Carolina service area from about 2 megawatts to about 110 megawatts.

Taken in by Tokens

In the Italian film *Il Postino* (*The Postman*), the big politician promises, again, that pipes will be built so that the people can have indoor running water, and he actually has construction begin before the election. People again vote him into office, and—surprise—construction immediately stops. Voters have again been suckered by a token gesture and only wake up to that fact when it is too late to make a difference.

Wow, that's really great. An energy company that is committed to helping the environment! However, the very next day . . . actually, we'll let the Environmental Protection Agency tell it (from their website):

> On May 14, 2015, three subsidiaries of Duke Energy Corporation were sentenced in federal court for multiple criminal violations of the Clean Water Act. Duke Energy Business Services LLC, Duke Energy Carolinas LLC, and Duke Energy Progress, Inc. were sentenced five years' probation for each charged count; fined $68 million; and will pay $34 million for environmental projects in North Carolina and Virginia. In the plea agreement, the defendants admitted that they had unlawfully failed to maintain equipment at the Dan River and Cape Fear facilities and unlawfully discharged coal ash and/or coal ash wastewater from impoundments at the Dan River, Asheville, Lee, and Riverbend facilities. The fine that Duke has agreed to pay would be one of the largest ever levied under the landmark Clean Water Act.

It is awfully difficult to view the Distributed Energy Resource program as anything but a token gesture in a cynical attempt at PR damage control. To be fair, Duke Energy has a number of similar environmental initiatives—though none of them are enough to keep the company off lists of America's worst companies for the environment.

Another example: A convincing case could be made that early attempts to include a "public option" (involving a government-run health insurance program) in President Obama's health care bill were simply token gestures to appease the progressive wing of the party. Obama never fought for it, and even supporters of the plan seemed to realize that it was little more than a bargaining chip in health care negotiations.

Actually, his token gesture was a variation on a related ploy—namely, behaving or speaking one way when the heat is on and another when it isn't sufficiently hot to force change. For as long as possible, George W. Bush satisfied those of his Texas constituents and his financial supporters who favored being "tough on criminals," changing when a wider constituency was being wooed during his presidential campaign, much as Texan and former President Lyndon Johnson did in political campaigns way back in the 1960s.

Summary of Chapter 3

All fallacious reasoning falls into one or more of the three broad categories of *questionable premise, suppressed evidence,* and *invalid inference.* But other fallacy categories, crosscutting these broad ones, have come into common use.

1.   *Appeal to authority:* Using the word of alleged authorities when there is not sufficient reason to believe that they have the information we seek or that they can be trusted to provide it to us (for example, when they have a vested interest), or doing so when we ought to figure the matter out for ourselves. ***Example:*** Taking the word of energy industry executives that nuclear power plants are safe.

When appeals must be made to authorities, we should remember that some are more trustworthy than others, and in particular, we should be wary of experts who have an axe to grind. We also should pay attention to the track records of alleged authorities.

2.   *Inconsistency:* Making an argument that has self-contradictory statements or statements that contradict each other. These contradictory assertions may be made (1) by one person at one time and place, (2) by one person at different times or places (without explaining the contradiction as a change of mind based on reasons), or (3) by different representatives of one institution. While not, strictly speaking, a fallacy, we need to note when there is a contradiction between what someone says and what that person does. ***Example:*** Al Gore's verbal support of energy conservation compared to his own excessive energy consumption to run his household.

3.   *Straw man:* Misrepresenting an opponent's position or a competitor's product to make it easier to attack him or to tout one's own product as superior, or attacking a weaker opponent while ignoring a stronger one, making it seem as though the stronger is the one that is being attacked. ***Example:*** Ads accusing Bernie Sanders of attacking Planned Parenthood and ads accusing Hillary Clinton of trying to keep the prison at Guantanamo open.

4.   *False dilemma:* A dilemma that can be shown to be uncogent either by "going between the horns" of the dilemma or by "grasping its horns." ***Example:*** Refuting the dilemma about the futility of laws to deter crime by pointing out that there is a third alternative—namely, that many citizens are both good and bad.

     The *either-or* (*black-or-white*) variation occurs when an argument is based on the assumption that there are just two viable alternatives, one of which is bad (so the other has to be chosen), although there is at least one other viable alternative. ***Example:*** Refuting the argument that you should vote for either a Republican or a Democrat to a third possibility, say, voting for a Green Party candidate.

5.   *Begging the question:* Assuming without proof the question, or a significant part of the question, that is at issue, or answering a question by rephrasing it as a statement. ***Example:*** In explaining why exclusive men's clubs have such long wait lists, "Red" Fay said, "The reason there is such a demand is because everyone wants to get in them." One way to beg the question is to avoid it entirely and thus evade the issue. ***Example:*** An elected official who skirts hard questions by shifting into a message he or she wants to give.

6.   *Questionable premise—questionable statement:* Using a less than believable premise or other statement. ***Example:*** James Reda's statement that "$500,000 is not a lot of money." (Note that the five fallacies just described are variations of this broader fallacy but that not all species of questionable premise have special names.)

7.   *Suppressed (overlooked) evidence:* Failing to bring relevant evidence to bear on an argument. ***Example:*** Advocates on both sides of the debates about the merits of "three strikes and you're out" laws who slight sensible arguments and objections of their opponents.

MindTap®   **Visit MindTap for more readings and resources.**

8. *Tokenism:* Offering or accepting a token gesture in lieu of the real thing. ***Example:*** Being satisfied with campaign rhetoric when there is little likelihood of serious intent to carry through.

EXERCISE SET 3-1

Determine which fallacies (if any) occur in the following passages and state reasons for your answers. For some of these, you may have to do some light research to gain relevant background knowledge. Note: Some items may contain more than one fallacy.

Example

Passage: Heard in a debate concerning capital punishment: "Capital punishment is morally wrong. After all, murder is just as wrong when committed by a government as it is when done by an individual person."

Evaluation: The speaker *begged the question at issue.* To say that capital punishment is murder is to say that it is a morally wrong killing (note that only wrongful killings are considered to be murder). But the issue was whether capital punishment—governmental killing—is morally wrong, so to assume without argument that it is (i.e., by calling it "murder") begs the question.

*1. Overheard in a laundry: "What makes me think abortion is murder? When my pediatrician refused to perform an abortion for me, she said she wouldn't be a party to murder. Babies and childbirth are her business, you know."[14]

*2. John Boehner, then House minority leader, had this to say about a minor provision to expand Medicaid family-planning services in President Obama's stimulus plan. "How can you spend hundreds of millions of dollars on contraceptives? How does that stimulate the economy?"

3. White House Press Secretary Josh Earnest in response to a question about overly partisan rhetoric: "But I guess the difference here, Margaret, is that at least [President Obama is] trying to bridge that partisan divide. And we see some other candidates who are trying—who have basically leased a backhoe and are seeking to deepen it and exploit it for their own personal political gain. It's not good for the country. It certainly is not good for the way our country is viewed around the world. And leaders have a responsibility to rise above that and condemn it when they see other people doing it. And again, I think this will mean some continued pointed questions for leaders in the Republican Party, because it's more than one presidential candidate on their side of the aisle who is engaged in these kinds of tactics."

4. Joe Morgan, announcing a Giants-Marlins baseball game and commenting on the Marlins pitcher: "He's been a little erratic, which explains why he hasn't been consistent."

---

[14]Starred (*) items are answered in a section at the back of the book.

5. From a description advertising L. Ron Hubbard's *Dianetics* at Scientology.org: "Containing discoveries heralded as greater than the wheel or fire, *Dianetics* has remained a bestseller for more than 50 years. And with over 20 million copies in print, generating a movement that spans over 100 nations, it's indisputably the most widely read and influential book ever written about the human mind."

6. Excerpt from the second President George W. Bush's 2004 State of the Union address:

    Black or white (the either or)

    either or & Straw man

    A strong America must also value the institution of marriage.... Congress has already taken a stand on this issue by passing the Defense of Marriage Act signed in 1996 by President Clinton. That statute protects marriage under federal law as the union of a man and a woman, and declares that one state may not redefine marriage for other states. Activist judges, however, have begun redefining marriage by court order, without regard for the will of the people and their elected representatives. On an issue of such great consequence, the people's voice must be heard. If judges insist on forcing their arbitrary will upon the people, the only alternative left to the people would be the constitutional process. Our nation must defend the sanctity of marriage.

7. Eric Jubler, in an article in which he argued that America should "open up" its wilderness areas: "The purist [conservationist] is, generally speaking, against everything . . . the purist believes that those who do not agree with him desire to 'rape the land.'"

    Straw man

*8. Donald Trump on Twitter responding to terrorist attacks in Brussels: "Europe and the U.S. must immediately stop taking in people from Syria. This will be the destruction of civilization as we know it! So sad!"

    Questionable premise

9. Calvin Coolidge is alleged to have been the first to say this: "We must keep people working—with jobs—because when many people are out of work, unemployment results."

10. In an interview with Sarah, Duchess of York, Larry King asked whether she was friends with Prince Charles. She replied, "Well, Larry, the important thing is that I have great respect for the royal family."

11. Argument in a student essay: "Prostitution should not be legalized because it encourages the breakdown of the family. Nevada, where prostitution is legal in ten counties, has the highest divorce rate in the nation, almost twice as high as the national average."

12. Notice from the Hyatt Regency Hotel in New Orleans: "We are pleased to confirm your reservation. It will be held on a space-available basis."

    Inconsistency

13. It is reported that when Socrates was condemned to death, his wife cried out, "Those wretched judges have condemned him to death unjustly!" To which Socrates is said to have replied, "Would you really prefer that I were justly condemned?"

    False dilemma / Questionable premise

*14. The American Heart Association and the American College of Cardiology select doctors who are experts in their fields to make independent evaluations of cardiovascular science and issue guidelines to doctors in clinical practice. But a

[handwritten: Supressed evidence]

[handwritten: Appeal to Authority, Questionable premise]

study published in 2011 by the *Archives of Internal Medicine* revealed that more than half the doctors (56 percent of 498) had conflicts of interest. Among those who led the panels, 81 percent had financial interests in companies affected by the guidelines. When the Institute of Medicine (the health branch of the National Academy of Science) recommended that the doctors responsible for setting guidelines cut their ties with conflict-of-interest companies, the president of the American Heart Association said that this could limit the number of doctors available for the work, adding that what makes it difficult is that some well-regarded experts in their field have conducted medical research sponsored by companies.

15. *[handwritten: Appeal to authority]* According to the trustworthy authors of *Logic and Contemporary Rhetoric*, you can believe everything in the book you're currently reading.

16. *[handwritten: Suppressed evidence]* Question to artist's model: "Why did he paint you so often?" Answer: "Because I'm his model."

*17. From a Dr. Joyce Brothers newspaper column: "Question: You should be more fearful of rape at home because rapes occur more frequently in private homes than in back alleys. Answer: TRUE. Studies indicate that more rapes are committed in the victim's home than in any other place. Almost half took place in either the victim's home or the assailant's; one-fourth occurred in open spaces; one-fifth in automobiles; one-twelfth in other indoor locations."

18. *[handwritten: STRAW MAN]* From *Slander,* by Ann Coulter, on the attitudes of liberals: "The liberal catechism includes hatred of Christians, guns, the profit motive, and political speech, and an infatuation with abortion, the environment, and race discrimination (or in the favored parlance of liberals, 'affirmative action')."

19. From a *New Republic* review of the James Michener book *Iberia:* "Michener leads off his chapter on bullfights with an argument between a quintessential American and Spaniard about brutal sports—which the Spaniard wins by pointing out that more young men get killed and maimed every year playing American football than in the bullring."

*20. Headline from CNN.com (and on-air): "Adult film actress in yanked Cruz ad endorses Trump" And from the Lead: "Erotic film actress Amy Lindsay returns to announce her endorsement after appearing in an ad for Ted Cruz that his campaign pulled off the air."

21. *[handwritten: either or]* A 2001 *Washington Monthly* article on celebrity chefs (July–August 2001) quoted Evan Kleinman, chef of Angeli Café in Los Angeles, as saying:

> Basically when it comes to food and food supply, I find it frightening that something so fundamental to life has been left to people whose only concern is profit.... I mean as far as I can see, because of that, there are only two kinds of people putting food in their mouths—the ones who have lost the notion that food is something made by human hands and then there are the others ... for whom there's still some link with food as a culture of nurturance. *[handwritten: implies only 2 options]*

22. Paraphrase of part of a letter to the editor (*Washington Post National Weekly Edition*, March 13–19, 1989):

> It's true that the Ayatollah Khomeini has gone too far with his death sentence for author Salman Rushdie [because of his "outrageous" book The Satanic Verses], but Rushdie also has gone too far by offending all Moslems. I am a strong believer in the ~~f~~ ~~...~~ech. However, books like Rushdie's ~~...~~aken the ties of people to each other. ~~...~~ ould be abolished.

[handwritten note:] 22 Inconsistancy: it supports free speech but not for particular book

[handwritten note:] 24 Inconsistancy claims he will not argue → continues to argue

~~...~~jority of Americans making over ~~...~~statement: "Poor people today have ~~...~~benefits without doing anything in

~~...~~ut to argue [as some sociobiologists ~~...~~re must be some heritable disposition ~~...~~ommon."

~~...~~the arrest of a Pakistani American sus-~~...~~Square: Michael Bloomberg, mayor ~~...~~ldn't lead to scapegoating by religion ~~...~~s was "Well, maybe somebody should ~~...~~ been threatening New York City and

~~...~~ proposed equal rights amendment to the state constitution of Iowa, Pat Robertson argued that the proposal was part of a "feminist agenda . . . a socialist, anti-family political movement that encourages women to leave their husbands, kill their children, practice witchcraft, destroy capitalism, and become lesbians."

27. An oil and gas industry–backed organization, energyfromshale.org, makes a case for increasing the production of "clean-burning, domestic, reliable supplies" of natural gas by developing more shale sites in this county. The process, known as fracking, involves injecting high-pressure fluid into deep rock formations to release natural gas. The issue is a contentious one, because fracking may cause groundwater contamination and air pollution, among other things, and disposal of waste may be mishandled. With assurances that the oil and gas industry will make sure that fracking is done responsibly, energyfromshale.org notes that "there are only two sides in the debate: those who want our oil and natural resources developed in a safe and responsible way, and those who don't want our oil and natural gas resources developed at all."

28. The day after the Mitchell Report was released detailing the widespread use of anabolic steroids in baseball, a fan made this comment on sfgate.com, the *San Francisco Chronicle*'s website (December 18, 2007): "This will send a shock wave through baseball and steroid usage will stop."

29. Bill O'Reilly in January 2016 felt the need to defend his journalistic integrity after receiving some criticism for being too soft on Donald Trump in an interview, and especially for saying to Trump, "Look, you know I'm looking out for you, right?" O'Reilly called the criticism "absolutely ridiculous" and aired the full clip to provide context:

> BILL O'REILLY: You know I am looking out for you, right? You know that? I am looking out for you. I look out for every honest politician. I do not care what party they are in.

30. O'Reilly had a diagnosis for the charge that he was supporting Trump: "This is the problem with American journalism today. There are no standards anymore—each individual outlet does pretty much what it wants to do with little accountability. That makes it harder for you the honest voter to decide who really is looking out for you."

31. Ad for an International Correspondence School journalism course: "Every successful writer started that first story or article with no previous experience. William Shakespeare, Alexander Dumas, Harold Robbins, Danielle Steel, Barbara Cartland—any famous writer you can name started just like you."

*32. In an interview with Vice President Joe Biden (*Meet the Press*, December 19, 2010), David Gregory asked him whether he agreed with Mitch McConnell that Julian Assange's WikiLeaks was high-tech terrorism or with others who said it is more like the Pentagon Papers (involving the unauthorized publication of top secret information about the government misleading the public over the US expansion of the Vietnam War). Biden replied, "I would argue that it's closer to being a high-tech terrorist than the Pentagon Papers."

33. Walter Burns, in an article in which he argues for capital punishment:

> When abolitionists speak of the barbarity of capital punishment ... they ought to be reminded that men whose moral sensitivity they would not question have supported [it]. Lincoln, for example, albeit with a befitting reluctance, authorized the execution of 267 persons during his presidency ... and it was Shakespeare's sensitivity to the moral issues that required him to have Macbeth killed.

34. Phyllis Schlafly, an outspoken opponent of the women's liberation movement, in her book *The Power of Positive Women*:

> The second dogma of the women's liberationists is that, of all the injustices perpetrated upon women through the centuries, the most oppressive is the cruel fact that women have babies and men do not. Within the confines of women's liberationist ideology, the abolition of this overriding inequality becomes the primary goal.

MindTap®   **Visit MindTap for more readings and resources.**

Drawing by H. Martin; © 1974 The New Yorker Magazine, Inc.

"If the coach and horses and the footmen and the beautiful clothes all turned back into the pumpkin and the mice and the rags, then how come the glass slipper didn't turn back, too?"

Two important factors in critical or creative thinking are the ability to bring relevant background information to bear on a problem and to carry through the relevant implications of an argument or position to determine whether they hang together. The cartoon illustrates the second of these factors: The child carries through the reasoning in the Cinderella story and finds it wanting. The first factor might be illustrated by a child who realizes there are millions of chimneys for Santa Claus to get down in one night and wonders how he could possibly manage to do so in time.

Fallacies: Invalid Inferences

4

MindTap® **Visit MindTap for more readings and resources.**

Most instances of the fallacies discussed in the previous chapter fall into the broad fallacy categories *questionable premise* or *suppressed evidence*. Most of the fallacies to be discussed in this and the next chapter belong to the genus *invalid inference*.

1. Ad Hominem Argument

There is a famous and perhaps apocryphal story lawyers like to tell that nicely captures the flavor of this fallacy. In Great Britain, the practice of law is divided between solicitors, who prepare cases for trial, and barristers, who argue the cases in court. The story concerns a particular barrister who, depending on the solicitor to prepare his case, arrived in court with no prior knowledge of the case he was to plead, where he found an exceedingly thin brief, which when opened contained just one note: "No case; abuse the plaintiff's attorney." If the barrister did as instructed, he was guilty of arguing **ad hominem**—of attacking his opponent rather than his opponent's evidence and arguments. (An *ad hominem* argument, literally, is an argument "to the person.")

Public ad hominem attacks reached a kind of zenith in the 2016 presidential campaign and especially in the person of Donald Trump. Trump often met the need for reasoned argument with abusive personal attacks and name-calling. In Trump's imagination and discourse, "losers," "dummies," "morons," "idiots," and "zeros" included a number of journalists, editors, activists, protestors, novelists, academics, congresspeople, presidents, cabinet members, fellow candidates, former members of his own staff, judges, athletes, musicians, filmmakers, business executives, foreign leaders, actors, radio hosts, comics, bloggers, websites, newspapers, individual Twitter users, and a brand of whiskey.

Even if Trump was extraordinarily bold about it, he is not alone in reducing himself to ad hominem attacks. Too many people in 2016 stooped down to his level. Senator Elizabeth Warren called Trump a "loser." Senator and presidential candidate Ted Cruz called him a "coward." And former presidential candidate Michael Dukakis called him "nuts."

It is important not to confuse ad hominem arguments with those in which the fallacy is *straw man*. The difference is that straw man attacks misrepresent an opponent's position, whereas those that are ad hominem abuse an opponent directly.

ATTACKS ON CHARACTER OR CREDENTIALS SOMETIMES ARE RELEVANT

Although attacks on a person usually are irrelevant to that individual's arguments or claims, sometimes they are very relevant indeed. Lawyers who attack the testimony of courtroom witnesses by questioning their expertise or character are not necessarily guilty of arguing ad hominem. They may be trying to gauge the integrity of the witness to determine whether his or her testimony is credible.

The judgment of expert witnesses may be particularly difficult to assess because they often express opinions or arguments against which the typical layperson is unable to argue directly. When doctors, lawyers, or other experts testify, often the best we can do is try to evaluate their honesty or judgment. Evidence that a psychologist testifying in court has been convicted of perjury, or spends a great deal of time testifying in court, would be a good reason to prefer the conflicting testimony of experts on the other side of the case.

Of course, negative evidence concerning an expert rarely proves that the authority's pronouncements are false. At best, character attacks just provide grounds for disregarding their testimony, not for deciding that it is false. If a doctor who advises operating on a patient turns out to be held in low esteem in the profession, it is rash to conclude that *therefore,* no operation is necessary.

What has just been said about attacking the credentials of experts applies to organizations and their pronouncements as well. For example, that a research organization receives most of its funds from the pharmaceutical industry and also regularly issues reports favorable to drug company interests constitutes a very good reason to be suspicious of its output.

The important thing to notice is that in none of these cases do we find instances of the ad hominem fallacy. Why not? Because the person is (explicitly or implicitly) part of the argument under attack. When a lawyer calls an expert (or alleged expert) to the stand, the implied argument is that the testimony is justified by his or her expertise. That is to say, that expertise is offered as a kind of premise in support of whatever they're called on to say. So, to try to impugn the witness's expertise is in effect an attempt to refute that implied argument, and so not an ad hominem fallacy. Similarly, in everyday life, we cannot cry "foul" if someone attacks us rather than our argument after we *insert* ourselves into the argument by claiming our own authority.

2. Guilt by Association

The fallacy **guilt by association** is related in some ways to the ad hominem fallacy, and you'll often see them discussed together. There are some important differences, however. When we commit the guilt by association fallacy, rather than attacking an arguer instead of an argument, we impugn an argument or policy by virtue of its being held by certain disreputable people or groups.

In American discourse, the gold standards for guilt by association arguments involve fascists or communists. It is enough to make a policy seem wrong and maybe even awful to point out that it was adopted in Hitler's Germany or Stalin's Soviet Russia. In fact, "Godwin's Law," first advanced in the early days of a mass public Internet by netizen and writer Mike Godwin, states that "As an online discussion grows longer, the probability of a comparison involving Nazis or Hitler approaches one."

Guilt by association arguments are common because they are persuasive. They make it seem like we must be defending Nazism, Stalinism, or some other atrocious ideology if we endorse some policy one of these groups also adopted. But even these epitomes of evil could not make an evil of everything they did.

For instance, in response to Congressman (and then vice presidential nominee) Paul Ryan's speech at the 2012 Republican National Convention, John Burton, the chairman of the Democratic Party in California, publicly compared him and other Republicans to Joseph Goebbels, the Nazi head of propaganda: "They lie and they don't care if people think they lie . . . Joseph Goebbels—it's the big lie, you keep repeating it." The complaint here is about the rhetoric Ryan used. But by attaching that complaint to the Nazis, Burton irrationally attaches to Ryan the air of monstrosity.

3. Two Wrongs Make A Right

Those who try to justify a wrong by pointing to a similar wrong perpetrated by others often are guilty of the fallacy sometimes called **two wrongs make a right** (traditional name: *tu quoque*—Latin, "you're another"). For example, in the 2000 presidential election, over 1,900 Palm Beach County, Florida, citizens voted for two candidates for the same office, thus invalidating their ballots. Democratic Party representatives claimed that the vast majority of these double votes resulted from confusion brought on by an illegally designed ballot, thwarting voter intent. A Republican Party spokesperson dismissed their complaint by pointing out that in the 1996 presidential election, over 15,000 ballots in Palm Beach County were invalidated for that reason, without creating a huge uproar. But surely, the fact that the 1996 election had a problem does not justify having the same problem in the year 2000.

Justifying a vengeful retaliation in sports may fall into this category as well. In recent years, the baseball commissioner has clamped down on aggressive acts of retaliation between players by fining and suspending them for violence on the field. But in the rough-and-tumble "good old days," retaliation was the way they settled scores. If a pitcher hit the batter, one of the players on the other team would take him down by sliding into first base, cleats high, when the pitcher was covering the base. The umpires would turn a blind eye, and the players would get revenge and the satisfaction of having taken care of the problem themselves.[1] Nonetheless, slamming into a player like a linebacker because a pitcher on the other team knocked down a batter is using one wrong to justify another.

---

[1]For more discussion of retaliatory behavior in baseball see: Chass, Murray. "End of an Age That Was Ruled by Retaliation." *New York Times,* 18 March 2008.

FIGHTING FIRE WITH FIRE

Like most other fallacies, the two wrongs fallacy seems plausible because of its resemblance to a more legitimate way of reasoning—in this case to the plausible idea that we sometimes are justified in "fighting fire with fire." Killing in self-defense illustrates this nicely. We feel justified in fighting one evil (the unjustified attack on our own life) by doing what otherwise would constitute another evil (taking the life of the attacker). So the two wrongs fallacy is not automatically committed every time one wrong is counteracted by another. The crucial question is whether the second wrong is genuinely needed to fight, or counteract, the first.[2]

The Handbook of Political Fallacies, *by British political philosopher and reformer Jeremy Bentham (1748–1832), is one of the classic works on political rhetoric and fallacies. Here are excerpts from his account of the first of four "causes of the utterance of [political] fallacies" (another excerpt appears in Chapter 6).*

First Cause . . .: Self-Conscious Sinister Interest

[I]t is apparent that the mind of every public man is subject at all times to the operation of two distinct interests: a public and a private one. . . .

In the greater number of instances, these two interests . . . are not only distinct, but opposite, and that to such a degree that if either is exclusively pursued, the other must be sacrificed to it. Take for example pecuniary interest: it is to the personal interest of every public man who has at his disposal public money extracted from the whole community by taxes, that as large a share as possible . . . should remain available for his own use. At the same time it is to the interest of the public . . . that as small a share as possible . . . should remain in his hands for his personal or any other private use. . . . Hence it is that any class of men who have an interest in the rise or continuance of any system of abuse no matter how flagrant will, with few or no exceptions, support such a system of abuse with any means they deem necessary, even at the cost of probity and sincerity. . . .

But it is one of the characteristics of abuse, that it can only be defended by fallacy. It is, therefore, to the interest of all the confederates of abuse to give the most extensive currency to fallacies. . . . It is of the utmost importance to such persons to keep the human mind in such a state of imbecility that shall render it incapable of distinguishing truth from error.

Students inclined to complain that too many of the fallacy examples in this text come from politicians should seriously reflect on Bentham's remarks, especially because government today deals with so many matters that determine the quality of all of our lives.

---

[2]This passes over questions concerning retributive justice. If retributivists are right, we sometimes are justified in punishing those guilty of unfairly harming others even though in doing so we fail to fight the original harm (or fail to rehabilitate the criminal or deter others from similar offenses).

TWO WRONGS AND HYPOCRISY

The two wrongs fallacy also sometimes seems plausible—not fallacious—for another reason: Those who argue this way may intend to imply that their opponents are being hypocritical, and often this charge is accurate and may even have some merit. The town drunk isn't the one to tell us we've had one too many and are making fools of ourselves, even if we are. (That's the import of the reply, "You're a fine one to talk.") Similarly, the philanderer who finds out about his wife's infidelity is hardly the one to complain that she has deceived him. But when we become outraged at the chutzpah of our accusers, we shouldn't lose sight of the fact that their hypocrisy doesn't justify our own failures. Also notice that hypocrisy doesn't make what we say wrong so much as it makes our saying it somewhat improper.

4. Appeal to Tradition or Popularity

Two more all-too-common fallacies involve the justification of claims or practices on the grounds that they are or have been accepted by others. In the first of these, the **appeal to popularity** (argumentum ad populam), an arguer moves from the fact that a given claim is widely believed to its truth, or from the fact that a lot of people engage in a practice to its acceptability or value. But being widely believed is not a reliable indicator of truth. If it were, then we would have to say that the truth of a claim changes along with public opinion about it.

So consider the following from Bernie Sanders, which was his evidence for the claim that he would provide better leadership as president than Hillary Clinton: "I am very happy in this campaign that we have had rallies with tens of thousands of people, mostly young people. What the polls are showing is that we are absolutely defeating the secretary among younger people. We're giving young people and working people hope that real change can take place in America. That's what the political revolution is about." What does Sanders's popularity among young people demonstrate about the quality of his leadership? Is it true that popular leaders are always better leaders? And if this were true, shouldn't we just vote for the candidate who has greater popular support? Why, then, have debates like the one in which Sanders said this? Why not just take some initial polls and let us decide from those?

We commit the second, the fallacy **appeal to tradition**, when we argue that some practice is acceptable because it has been done for some time. We can make some remarks about appeals to tradition similar to the ones we made about appeals to popularity. Were it true that a practice is made acceptable by its long standing, we would have no way to justify attempts to change common practices. There would be no way to do better, since whatever we happen to do (so long it is what we have done) would be right. But just as many people at once are capable of being wrong, so too can people be wrong over a long period of time. Notice, for instance, that appeals to tradition were common justifications for slavery, segregation, and all sorts of other atrocities. Such arguments were not fallacious because they justified evils, but because the fact that something has been done is no reason to think it should be.

Less dramatic examples are not difficult to find. In 2016, Hall of Fame pitcher Goose Gossage felt the need to weigh in on players today doing things like celebrating hitting home runs by flipping their bats in the air and showing some emotion going around the bases: "I went in the clubhouse and shook hands . . . We went in the clubhouse and went by each guy's locker and congratulated one another. That's how we did it. We didn't celebrate in front of everybody. But now, that's not the way. Now, it's all about 'dig me, dig me, man, I just hit a bomb.' " Gossage is not merely remarking on changing attitudes and mores. There is allegedly something *wrong* with the way the game is played today because it is not the way it was done in Gossage's day. But why think the old way was better? That a practice is long-standing is no evidence whatsoever that it is better.

Despite everything we've just said, there may be some reasons to doubt the general fallaciousness of appeals to popularity and tradition. We may pause over rejecting appeals to popularity because of the so-called "wisdom of crowds." In a 2004 book of that name, James Surowiecki made the case that the views of large crowds often track the truth better than individuals or (sometimes) even alleged experts. However, crowds turn out to be "wise" only in very specific circumstances, and not generally in moral decisions or when dealing with complex problems.[3] Also, crowds tend to be more correct only in aggregate, usually in the form of an average of opinions. Most appeals to popularity are to general agreements rather than averages of various views. Either way, we should not rely on popularity as a gauge of truth in important matters.

Regarding appeals to tradition, we may be uncomfortable denying the value of traditions. Traditions do serve important functions, especially binding families and cultures together by preserving a shared history. But recognizing the functions and even the value of tradition in general does not justify all traditions. That is to say, it is good for people to have some tradition or other. But doing the wrong thing does not get better because it has been done for a long time. We should then constantly question the value of our traditions, keeping the good ones and replacing the bad with better ones. As such, appeals to tradition make for poor arguments—and recognizing this does not deny the value that traditions genuinely hold.

5. Irrelevant Reason (Non Sequitur)

Traditional logic textbooks often discuss a fallacy called *non sequitur* (literally, "it does not follow"), usually described as being committed when a conclusion does not follow logically from given premises. In this sense, any fallacy in the broad category *invalid inference* can be thought of as a non sequitur. But other writers describe this fallacy more narrowly.

Let's replace the ambiguous term *non sequitur* with the expression **irrelevant reason**, used to refer to reasons or premises that are irrelevant to a conclusion when the error doesn't fit a narrower fallacy category such as ad hominem argument or two wrongs make a right.

At a 2011 Congressional hearing on climate change, a lawyer claimed that the EPA cannot declare that greenhouse gas emissions are a health threat. His reason? Public health has improved over the same period of time that greenhouse gas emissions have

---

[3]See Jaron Lanier's *You Are Not a Gadget* for similar (and other interesting) criticisms of the "wisdom of crowds" idea.

been rising.[4] Public health is better now because medical and scientific advances have decreased infant mortality, increased life expectancy, and improved our health in general, but these factors are irrelevant to the long-term effects of greenhouse gas emissions that require decades of study and have yet to be determined.

Sometimes irrelevant arguments defy logic. Shortly after the attack on the World Trade Center, Michael Kelly had this to say in "Pacifist Claptrap":

> Organized terrorist groups have attacked America. These groups wish the Americans to not fight. The American pacifists wish the Americans to not fight. If the Americans do not, the terrorists will attack America again. And now we know such attacks can kill many thousands of Americans. The American pacifists, therefore, are on the side of future mass murders of Americans. They are objectively pro-terrorist.[5]

Ah, those crafty pacifists. Little did we realize their murderous intent.

One perennial fallacy of this sort involves the claim that a president is ignoring or mishandling a situation on the basis of evidence he or she does anything else at all but fulfill presidential obligations every second of every day. So President Bush was alleged to be ignoring the war on terror and the failing U.S. economy because there was video of him playing golf. Every year President Obama filled out brackets for the NCAA basketball tournaments, and every year someone offered this as evidence that he wasn't appropriately dealing with some crisis or other. In one especially ridiculous example, Steve Hayes of the *Weekly Standard* argued on Fox News that President Obama was ignoring the political and military crisis in Ukraine in 2014 this way: "This is a disgrace. The way that the President of the United States and his administration is handling this is so unserious on so many different levels. You heard from the NATO Secretary General that this is a crisis, it's a crisis like we haven't seen in decades. What's President Obama doing? He's filling out his NCAA bracket. He's hosting a film ceremony for Cesar Chavez. This is not a serious response to what is, I think, a real crisis." In Hayes's imagination, Russia invades the Ukraine and the president says to himself, "Eh, that's not important. What's important is whether or not I think Syracuse can get past Kansas." This would indeed be a troubling and insufficiently serious response to the crisis. But it's fair to assume that filling out a bracket and attending a ceremony were *other* activities, and not part of the president's response.

Note, by the way, that a reason is not automatically irrelevant just because it is false. For example, the old superstition that walking under a ladder brings bad luck is false, but it isn't irrelevant to the question of whether a person should or shouldn't engage in this practice; were it true, it would be a very good reason indeed for not walking under ladders.

Note also that a reason may be irrelevant when looking at a matter from one point of view but not from another. Take, for example, the remark by a psychological clinician, quoted in *Science News* magazine, that abandoning the old and standard ways of classifying mental disorder in favor of new ones "will result in denial of insurance coverage

---

[4]Krugman, Paul. "The Truth, Still Inconvenient." *New York Times,* 4 April 2011.
[5]Kelly, Michael. *Washington Post* 26 September 2001, quoted in *Extra!* November–December 2001.

A humorous (we hope) equivocation.

for treatment of serious psychological disturbances." Looked at from the point of view of psychiatric *theory,* this remark is irrelevant, but from the point of view of psychiatric *practice,* it is very relevant indeed.

6. Equivocation

A term or expression is used *equivocally* in an argument when used to mean one thing in one place and another thing in another.[6] Making an argument that is invalid but appears valid because of an equivocal use of language makes us guilty of the fallacy that you will not be surprised to learn is generally called **equivocation**.

When a TV evangelist said that we all should stop sinning and "be like Jesus," someone in the audience expressed doubt that he was up to that, pointing out that, after all, "Jesus is the son of God." In reply, the evangelist told the doubter that he could indeed stop sinning because, "You're the son of God, too." But the evangelist was guilty of equivocation, because the doubter meant that Jesus is the son of God in the special way that (according to Christian doctrine) only Jesus is held to be, while the evangelist had to mean that the doubter was the son of God in the metaphorical sense in which (again, according to Christian theology) we all are children of God.

Equivocation is a common fallacy because it often is quite hard to notice that a shift in meaning has taken place. As might be expected, given human nature, less than completely ethical manipulators frequently take advantage of the ease with which people can be fooled in this way. The sugar industry, for instance, once advertised its product with the claim that "Sugar is an essential component of the body . . . a key material in all sorts of metabolic processes," neglecting the fact that it is *glucose* (blood sugar), not ordinary table sugar (sucrose), that is the vital nourishment. It's true, of course, that table sugar does turn into blood sugar in the body, but it provides that necessary ingredient

---

[6]As used in everyday life, the term *equivocation* often connotes the use of equivocation to deceive. As used here, it does not necessarily carry this connotation. We do, of course, have to remember that equivocation is frequently employed in daily life to make invalid arguments appear to be valid.

without also providing the other sorts of vital nutrients found in fruits, grains, and other more complete food sources that contain plenty of sucrose.

Advertisements of this kind for food and other health products are successful because a large majority of consumers know very little about how the body functions—what sorts of food are required for good health and what sorts are unhealthy. They tend to get their information about these vital matters from television commercials, other advertisements, TV talk shows, and websites of inconsistent reliability. So they are ready-made suckers for every fad that comes down the pike. For example, many food products have been advertised as especially healthy because they are low in cholesterol, or even cholesterol free, while containing the usual (high) levels of fats, which the body then uses to make cholesterol. The ambiguity taken advantage of here is, again, the difference between what is in a food and what is in the bloodstream. Low blood cholesterol levels are good; low food cholesterol levels combined with high fat content definitely are not good. (Note that some foods advertised to be cholesterol free or even fat free contain partially hydrogenated oils, which are much less heart healthy than the fats listed on packages by law.)

Sometimes legal action is taken against companies for misleading advertising. When Phillip Morris was sued for deceiving smokers into thinking "light" cigarettes were less harmful than regular ones, a company spokesman said that the word *light* referred to taste, not content, but surely he was equivocating. Most smokers would tend to think that "light" meant that the cigarettes had less tar and nicotine—if only to rationalize their bad habit.

7. Appeal to Ignorance

When good reasons are lacking, the rational conclusion to draw is that we just don't know. But when we greatly desire to believe something, it's tempting to take the absence of evidence, and thus absence of refutation, as justification for believing that it is

---

It is he that sitteth upon the circle of the earth.

—*ISAIAH 40:22*

Ambiguity

Almost any statement can be interpreted in various ways if we have a mind to do so. The Bible is a happy hunting ground for those intent on taking advantage of the ambiguity of natural languages, because so many people take what it says to be the word of the Ultimate Authority. This passage from Isaiah was once used to prove that the Earth is flat, but when the discoveries of Copernicus, Kepler, and Newton made the idea of a flat Earth untenable, the Isaiah quote was reinterpreted to prove that those who wrote the Bible knew the Earth is a sphere. We will return to a more in-depth discussion of ambiguity in Chapter 7.

true. Doing this makes us guilty of the fallacy **appeal to ignorance** (traditionally known as *argumentum ad ignorantiam*). Some people have argued, for example, that we should believe there is no intelligent life on other planets anywhere in our galaxy, since no one has been able to prove that there is; indeed, until recently, when the existence of other planets was confirmed, it was sometimes argued that there were no planets anywhere other than our own.

The fallacy in this sort of reasoning can be seen by turning it on its head. If appeals to ignorance could prove that no life exists on other planets, then it equally well could prove just the opposite. After all, no one has proved that life does *not* exist on any of these planets. In the absence of good evidence for a claim, the right thing to do is to be *agnostic* on the issue, to neither believe nor disbelieve. Ignorance proves nothing, except, of course, that we are ignorant. During the Iraq War, the Bush administration could have said that the opposition was guilty of appeal to ignorance when it claimed that because no weapons of mass destruction were found, there must not be any hidden weapons. As of this writing, they still haven't been found, but you never know—they may turn up.

There are, however, cases in which the failure of a search does count against a claim. That happens when whatever is searched for would very likely have been found if it existed. Given all the sky watching that has gone on in the past 10,000 years, the claim that there exists a planet-sized object between Earth and Mars is disproved by the failure of anyone to observe it. Similarly, the failure to find evidence of a virus in a blood test justifies a doctor's conclusion that the patient isn't infected with that virus. These are cases not of reasoning from ignorance, but rather of reasoning from the *knowledge* that we would have found the item looked for if it had been there to find.

Note, however, the importance of *appropriately* searching. That telescopes have searched the sky for several hundred years, and naked eyes for thousands, without spotting a god up there proves absolutely nothing about the existence of a god in the sky, since deities are not conceived of as the kind of entities that can be seen in this way.

Fallacies Can Be Dangerous

In 1950, when Senator Joseph R. McCarthy (Republican, Wisconsin), was asked about the fortieth name on a list of eighty-one names of people he claimed were communists working for the United States Department of State, he responded that "I do not have much information on this except the general statement of the agency that there is nothing in the files to disprove his communist connections."

Many of McCarthy's followers took this absence of evidence as proof that the person in question was indeed a communist, a good example of the fallacy of appeal to ignorance. This example also illustrates the importance of not being taken in by this fallacy. McCarthy never backed up his charges with a single bit of relevant evidence, yet for several years he enjoyed great popularity and power, and his witch hunt ruined many innocent lives before, finally, McCarthy and "McCarthyism" were brought down in congressional hearings that revealed the true character of this miserable person.

Sometimes new information about a search rather than its results can change the situation entirely. Take, for instance, the mystery concerning the final resting place of Queen Nefertiti. We still (as of this writing) do not know where Nefertiti is buried. But in 2015, archaeologist Nicholas Reeves published a paper providing evidence that the tomb of King Tutankhamun contains two previously unknown chambers. Now, before this discovery, it would have been perfectly reasonable to conclude that Nefertiti is not buried in King Tut's tomb, as the search appeared to have been exhaustive. The revelation that there is more to the tomb to be searched and discovered, however, means that that conclusion is no longer warranted.

8. Appeal to Pity or Fear

The fallacies appeal to fear (argumentum ad baculum, literally "argument to the cudgel" or "appeal to the stick") and appeal to pity (argumentum ad misericordiam) both involve inappropriate appeals to an audience's emotions.

In the appeal to fear fallacy, an arguer suggests that you should accept a claim for fear of the consequences of not accepting. To be sure, what we fear may provide more than ample reason to feign acceptance of a given claim (consider the proverbial and too often not-so-proverbial gun to the head). But such fear is never reason alone to actually accept a claim. This is not to say that our views and actions should not be informed by fear. Fear can be a great protector and educator. But too often our beliefs are determined entirely by fear, and it is all too easy to manipulate people using it. Appeals to fear are an unfortunate mainstay of electoral politics. In 2015, the *New York Times* did a detailed study of Donald Trump's rhetorical style and offered this apt description:

> "Something bad is happening," Donald J. Trump warned New Hampshire voters Tuesday night, casting suspicions on Muslims and mosques. "Something really dangerous is going on."
>
> On Thursday evening, his message was equally ominous, as he suggested a link between the shootings in San Bernardino, Calif., and President Obama's failure to say "radical Islamic terrorism."
>
> "There is something going on with him that we don't know about," Mr. Trump said of the president, drawing applause from the crowd in Washington.
>
> The dark power of words has become the defining feature of Mr. Trump's bid for the White House to a degree rarely seen in modern politics, as he forgoes the usual campaign trappings—policy, endorsements, commercials, donations—and instead relies on potent language to connect with, and often stoke, the fears and grievances of Americans.

It is often quite appropriate to appeal to an audience's feeling for others, and reasonable for the audience to be moved by such appeals. The capacity for such feelings and the willingness to act on them are a couple of our better qualities. But these qualities can also be manipulated and misused. We come upon the fallacy appeal to pity when we're asked to have feeling for others when it is not called for or when such feeling is irrelevant to the question or situation at hand. Every parent and every teacher has been approached with appeals to pity: "You can't make me do the dishes, I'm just too sad," or "You need to give me some make-up or extra credit work because I had a really rough semester and couldn't turn in work on time," or "My girl-friend broke up with me, so you need to let me off the hook about . . ." Any of these sound familiar?

9. Composition and Division

The fallacy of **composition**, also sometimes called the *salesman's fallacy,* is committed when someone concludes that a particular item must have a certain property because all of its parts have that property. Auto dealers, for example, frequently try to get prospective customers to fall for this fallacy by touting low monthly payments while neglecting total costs, hoping their marks will assume that if the monthly payments are low, then the total cost must be low also. Washers and dryers used to be sold by telling customers that it takes "only 50 cents a day" to buy one. Of course, 50 cents a day adds up to $365 in two years (a lot of money until rather recently), something buyers seldom thought to figure out even though the arithmetic involved was on the grade-school level.

The fallacy of **division** is committed when we conclude that all (or some) of the parts of an item have a particular property because the item as a whole has it. The fallacy of division thus is the mirror image of the fallacy of composition. While infrequently fallen for in everyday life, cases do happen. An example is concluding that all the rooms in a large, fancy hotel must be large, as guests often do when making reservations at places such as the posh Plaza Hotel in New York (where in fact lots of rooms are rather tiny).

10. Slippery Slope

In a typical **slippery slope argument**, an action is objected to on the grounds that once it is taken, another action, and then perhaps still another, is bound to be taken, down a "slippery slope," until some undesirable consequence results. According to a slightly different version, whatever would justify taking the first step would also justify all the others, but since the last step isn't justified, the first isn't, either.

Arguing that a slope is slippery without providing good reason for thinking that it is, or when the slope clearly is not, makes us guilty of the **slippery slope fallacy**. For example, a Canadian-style "single-payer" health care system has often been objected to on grounds that it is a kind of socialized medicine and that its adoption would lead to socialized insurance of all kinds, socialized railroads, airlines, and so on, without sufficient reason being presented for believing this would be the case. (Are there any?) It also sometimes is argued that whatever would justify a single-payer system of health care also would justify all sorts of other socialistic measures, again without justifying this conclusion.

Too often slippery slopes are used to incite fear or to demonize minority groups or movements. In 2010, when Muslims in Murfreesboro, Tennessee, attempted to build an Islamic center, people opposed to the plan rallied against it. In response, TV evangelist

The Domino Theory

Earlier editions of this text at this point had a section on a variation of the fallacy slippery slope called the *domino theory*. Back in the nasty old Cold War days, dominoes were alleged to be in danger of falling all over the globe. Perhaps the chief reason advanced by the Johnson and Nixon administrations for our involvement in the war in Vietnam was that if Vietnam fell to the communists, the rest of Southeast Asia would also, and then countries in Central America (Nicaragua, El Salvador, and so on) and even parts of South America (in particular, Chile). Although we were defeated in Vietnam, it is primarily communist dominoes that have fallen—perhaps the reason that the domino theory has gone out of fashion.

Pat Robertson had this to say on his show *The 700 Club* (Christian Broadcasting Network, August 19, 2010):

> You mark my word, if they start bringing thousands and thousands of Muslims into that relatively rural area, the next thing you know they're going to take over the city council. Then they're going to be having a public ordinance that calls for public prayers five times a day. Then they're going to be having ordinances... [for] foot washing in all the public restrooms . . . etcetera, etcetera. And before long, they're going to demand, demand, demand . . . and little by little, the citizens of Murfreesboro . . . are going to be cowed.

A malicious slippery slope if there ever was one—aimed at a group of people who represented only 1 percent of the town's population.

Note, however, that some slopes may well be slippery. The slippery slope fallacy is committed only when we present without further justification or argument the claim that that once the first step is taken, the others are going to follow, or that whatever claims (however inaccurate) would justify the first step would in fact justify the rest. Consider this explanation of an economic slide that could have occurred after the housing market crashed in 2007.[7]

> As homeowners see the value of their homes decline, they become more likely to delay purchases of the big items—like automobiles, electronics and home appliances—that are ballasts of the American economy. When those purchases decline, large manufacturing firms, suddenly short on funds, could begin laying off employees. Those workers, uncertain about the future, might in turn stop buying Starbucks lattes and movie tickets, and in a worst-case scenario, that could spur coffee shops and theaters to begin layoffs of their own.

This may seem like a slippery slope fallacy at first glance, but a similar chain reaction did occur during the Great Depression in 1929, resulting in persistent, widespread unemployment. It was, indeed, a slippery slope, and one that threatened to repeat itself when the credit markets froze up and the stock market plunged in 2008.

---

[7]Duhigg, Charles. "Depression, You Say? Check Those Safety Nets." *New York Times,* 23 March 2008.

Summary of Chapter 4

1.   *Ad hominem argument:* An irrelevant attack on an opponent rather than on the opponent's evidence or arguments. ***Example:*** Donald Trump calling opponents "losers," etc., rather than addressing their criticisms or arguments. Note, however, that not all character attacks are fallacious, as they may not be when challenging the integrity of a supposedly expert witness.

2.   *Guilt by association:* Judging a policy or claim wrong because it was adhered to or endorsed by some disreputable group. ***Example:*** The tendency in American public discourse to align opponents with either Nazis or Stalinists.

3.   *Two wrongs make a right:* Justifying a wrong by pointing to a similar wrong perpetrated by others. ***Example:*** Baseball players justifying aggressive retaliation against a pitcher on the other team because he hit a batter and knocked him down. Note, however, that when fighting fire with fire, what would otherwise be a wrong often isn't, as when someone kills in self-defense.

   Although there is an air of hypocrisy to a charge coming from an equally guilty party, this doesn't make an accurate charge any less on target.

4.   *Appeal to Popularity:* Justifying a claim, policy or action using evidence of its popularity—especially the number of people who hold or do it. ***Example:*** Bernie Sanders arguing that he would make the better leader because more young people endorse him than his opponent.

5.   *Appeal to Tradition:* Arguing that something should be done because it always has been done (or it has been done for a long time). ***Example:*** Goose Gossage arguing that baseball players shouldn't celebrate on the field because it wasn't done in his day.

6.   *Irrelevant reason:* Trying to prove something with evidence that is or comes close to being irrelevant. (Some other term, such as *ad hominem argument,* may also apply.) ***Example:*** The argument that greenhouse gas emissions are not a health threat because public health has improved over the same period that greenhouse gas emissions have increased.

7.   *Equivocation:* Using a term or expression in an argument in one sense in one place and another sense in another, with the result that the argument appears much better than it really is. ***Example:*** The TV evangelist's use of the expression "son of God" to refer to Jesus Christ and to a parishioner, in order to persuade the parishioner that he could "be like Jesus" and stop sinning. Note, however, that intentional ambiguity, even equivocation, is not always fallacious. It isn't, for example, when used for metaphoric effect.

8.   *Appeal to ignorance:* Arguing that the failure to find evidence refuting a claim justifies believing that it is true. ***Example:*** Arguing that there is no intelligent life on other planets since no one has been able to prove there is. Note,

however, that the failure of *appropriate* searches sometimes does support rejection of a claim.

9. *Appeal to fear:* Inappropriately using people's fear to persuade them of a given claim or to force a given action. ***Example:*** Donald Trump stoking voters' fears in order to rally their support.

10. *Appeal to pity:* Inappropriately using people's pity to persuade them of a given claim or to force a given action. ***Example:*** Demanding special (and perhaps unfair) treatment because of some relatively common hardship.

11. *Composition:* Assuming that an item has a certain property because all or most of its parts have that property. ***Example:*** Assuming a commodity is inexpensive because of low installment payments.

12. *Division:* Assuming that all or most parts of an item have a property because the whole item has it. ***Example:*** Assuming the rooms in a large hotel are large.

13. *Slippery slope:* Making a claim that a particular action must be avoided because, if taken, it would lead to another action, and another—down a slippery slope to undesirable consequences, without presenting sufficient (or any) reason to justify that claim. ***Example:*** Arguing that adoption of a single-payer health plan will lead to adoption of all sorts of other socialistic measures.

EXERCISE SET 4-1

Determine which fallacies (if any) occur in the following short passages and justify your answers (as you did when working on Exercise Set 3-1). (Some of these passages may contain fallacies discussed in the previous chapter.)[8]

1. During the mass protests in Egypt in 2011, Jim Lehrer, *News Hour* anchor, asked Vice President Joe Biden whether Egypt's President Hosni Mubarak should be seen as a dictator. Biden replied: "Look, Mubarak has been an ally of ours in a number of things and he's been very responsible . . . relative to geopolitical interests in the region . . . I would not refer to him as a dictator." (PBS *News Hour*, January 27, 2011, quoted in *Extra!* March 2011.)

2. Senator Marco Rubio on his 2016 Republican primary opponent Donald Trump, as described by NBC News: "In response to the property mogul calling him 'little Rubio,' Rubio conceded that Trump was taller than him. However, the Florida senator suggested Trump had small hands for his height. 'And you know what they say about guys with small hands,' Rubio said with a smile, prompting stunned laughter from the crowd. After a brief pause, he added: 'You can't trust 'em!' The crowd responded with applause."

3. Ted Gup (professor of journalism) writing for the *Washington Post* in response to arguments that Harvard Law School should retire its seal, which references a

---

[8]Starred (*) items are answered in a section at the back of the book.

slave-holding family that gave to the school 200 years ago: "I fear that if the university is bent on expunging all major remnants of what is today seen as morally repugnant, nothing will be left of Harvard as we know it. House names, professorships, busts and portraits will have to be removed, for if Harvard has been home to many great minds, it has also been home to many closed ones—like other American institutions. If this is followed to its logical conclusion, Harvard will undergo nothing short of total self-renunciation."

*4. Football player Roger Craig, on George Seifert's promotion to head coach of the National Football League's San Francisco 49ers: "I think George will do an excellent job, because he's been searching for a head coaching job for some time, and what better place to start his head coaching job." (In fact, Seifert did have an excellent record with the 49ers before being canned.)

5. From a 1972 article in the *Hartford Courant*, still relevant today, on the possibility of women priests in the Catholic Church: "Citing the historic exclusion of women from the priesthood,… the study [of a committee of Roman Catholic bishops] said, '… the constant tradition and practice, interpreted as divine law, is of such a nature as to constitute a clear teaching of the Ordinary Magisterium [teaching authority of the church].'"

*6. Bumper sticker seen in California when a handgun bill came before voters of that state:

Gun Registration Equals Mass Extermination
First Register Guns, Then Register the Jews

7. From a PBS *News Hour* interview with President Obama's secretary of labor, Thomas Perez, on extending unemployment benefits in 2014:

> *Gwen Ifill: … some Republicans who object to this particular proposal, this Dean Heller–Jack Reed proposal, are saying that they don't object to the idea of expanding benefits or renewing benefits. They object to the idea that we're not paying for it. Is that not a reasonable argument?*
>
> *Secretary of Labor Thomas Perez: Well, certainly, when President Bush signed five extensions, there were no strings attached, when President Bush signed it. I believe 14 out of the last 17 extensions of unemployment benefits have been signed with no strings attached.*
>
> *So historically, there has been an understanding that we call it emergency unemployment compensation for a reason, because people are in a state of emergency. And we're talking about a bill here that is of a three-month duration. And during that period of time, I'm hopeful that Congress can work together on a bipartisan fashion, once again, to come up with a longer-term fix.*

8. Venture capitalist Tom Perkins in *The Wall Street Journal*:

> *Writing from the epicenter of progressive thought, San Francisco, I would call attention to the parallels of fascist Nazi Germany to its war on its "one percent," namely its Jews, to the progressive war on the American one percent, namely the "rich."*

From the Occupy movement to the demonization of the rich embedded in virtually every word of our local newspaper, the San Francisco Chronicle, *I perceive a rising tide of hatred of the successful one percent. There is outraged public reaction to the Google buses carrying technology workers from the city to the peninsula high-tech companies which employ them. We have outrage over the rising real-estate prices which these "techno geeks" can pay. We have, for example, libelous and cruel attacks in the* Chronicle *on our number-one celebrity, the author Danielle Steel, alleging that she is a "snob" despite the millions she has spent on our city's homeless and mentally ill over the past decades.*

This is a very dangerous drift in our American thinking. Kristallnacht was unthinkable in 1930; is its descendant "progressive" radicalism unthinkable now?

9. Jan Berger in the *Baltimore Evening Sun:* "Weeks of patient investigation have revealed that the gas leaked at Bhopal [India—with thousands of casualties] because something went wrong."

*10. Rush Limbaugh, on his February 29, 2012, show, caused a furor when he lashed out at a college coed who testified before Congress in favor of religiously affiliated schools providing insurance coverage for contraception. Limbaugh's response was, "What does that say about the college coed . . . who goes before a congressional committee and essentially says that she must be paid to have sex? What does it make her? It makes her a slut, right? It makes her a prostitute. She wants to be paid for having sex. She's having so much sex she can't afford the contraception."

Slippery slope

11. A claim made by opponents of an initiative to legalize marijuana for medicinal purposes: "It would be foolish to permit the sale of marijuana to seriously ill people on the recommendation of their physicians. That just opens the floodgates to the complete legalization of that dangerous drug."

12. A letter to the editor of *Connoisseur* magazine defended a previous article favoring bullfighting from "the protesting letters you are sure to receive," by reminding readers that bulls selected for the arena live twice as long as those destined for McDonald's and die in a far more noble fashion.

13. Jerry Bergman, writing for the Institute for Creation Research: "The racism of evolution theory has been documented well and widely publicized. It is known less widely that many evolutionists, including Charles Darwin, also taught that women are biologically inferior to men. Darwin's ideas, including his view of women, have had a major impact on society. In a telling indication of his attitude about women (just before he married his cousin, Emma Wedgewood), Darwin listed the advantages of marrying, which included: '. . . constant companion, (friend in old age) who will feel interested in one, object to be beloved and played with—better than a dog anyhow—Home, and someone to take care of house . . .'"

equivocation

*14. Indian mystic Vivekananda: "There is no past or future even in thought, because to think it you have to make it present."

15. From a conversation with a friend (not verbatim): "Sure, I've told you before that I believe everyone's opinion counts on moral matters like abortion. But not *everyone's* opinion counts—I wouldn't want Hitler's to count. Well, [name deleted] isn't a Hitler, but she sleeps around like sex was going out of style next week or something. She's just a slut, and she's broken up at least one marriage I know about. Why should her opinion count on anything? Why should we listen to her opinion on the abortion business?"

16. From ACLU.org, a comment on a Justice Department suit against Apple that would have required the company to unlock an iPhone belonging to one of the perpetrators of a mass killing in San Bernardino, California: "Apple is engaged in a high-profile battle against a court order demanding it write, sign, and deploy custom computer code to defeat the security on an iPhone. As civil liberties groups committed to the freedom of thought that underpins a democratic society, this fight is our fight. It is the fight of every person who believes in a future where technology does not come at the cost of privacy or individual security and where there are reasonable safeguards on government power. This is a fight that implicates all technology users. There are already bad actors trying to defeat the security on iPhones, and an FBI-ordered backdoor will only assist their efforts. Once this has been created, malicious hackers will surely increase their attacks on the FBI and Apple, hoping to ferret out clues to this entrance route—and they may well succeed. The precedent created by this case is disturbing: It creates a new pathway for the government to conscript private companies into building surveillance tools. If Apple can be compelled to create a master key to unlock this iPhone, then little will prevent the government from ordering any company to turn its products into tools of surveillance, compromising the safety, privacy, and security of everyone. "

17. Jules Crittenden, an embedded journalist for the *Boston Herald* in the Iraq War, defended himself from criticism for bringing home some illegal "souvenirs" from Iraq (*Boston Herald*, April 23, 2003): "I understand and share the world's concern about the disappearance of legitimate Iraqi national treasures that are in fact treasures of human civilization," Crittenden wrote in an open letter to journalists in this country. "However, those are matters separate from the time-honored tradition among soldiers of bringing home reminders of some of the most intense experiences of their lives. There was no exception to that historical practice in this war … [until reporters and soldiers were subject to search by federal agents on returning to the United States]. "

appeal to ignorance

18. Argument heard all too frequently in introductory philosophy classes: "We're perfectly entitled to believe there is a God. After all, every effort by atheists to prove otherwise has failed. "

equivocation

19. Lewis Carroll, in *Through the Looking Glass:* "'You couldn't have it if you did want it,' the Queen said. 'The rule is jam tomorrow and jam yesterday—but never jam *today*.' 'It must sometimes come to jam *today*,' Alice objected. 'No it can't,' said the Queen. 'It's jam every *other* day: today isn't any *other* day, you know.'"

20. From NRA.org: "Here's the truth about the Hollywood celebrities, political elites and billionaires who attack the Second Amendment. The thought of average people owning firearms makes them uncomfortable. They don't like how the men and women who build their office buildings, vacation homes and luxury cars . . . who mop their floors, clean their clothes and serve their dinner . . . have access to the same level of protection as their armed security guards. They want you to surrender your freedom for a false promise of government-provided security they will never rely upon themselves."

21. Robert Ringer in *The Tortoise Report,* touting gold as an investment: "Two thousand years after the human flesh had disappeared, the gold that adorned it [an ancient Egyptian corpse] remained virtually unchanged. That's a real hard act for paper money to follow."

22. Margaret Morissey, an anti-garbage activist, was interviewed on *As It Happens,* a Canadian news program (February 2002) about her arrest for blocking trucks from dumping garbage on a hill overlooking St. Brides, Newfoundland. The arrest occurred despite the fact that it was illegal to use the hill as a dumpsite. When she asked the mayor why the dumping was still allowed, he said, "We've been doing it for 30 years."

23. Overheard on the bus to Atlantic City: "I just play the quarter slots when I go to Atlantic City. That way, I don't lose too much money."

*24. Sigmund Freud: "Our own death is . . . unimaginable, and whenever we make the attempt to imagine it we can perceive that we really survive as spectators."

25. A Robert Ringer writing for a site called WND.com: "While reading Walter Laqueur's biography of Josef Stalin, I was struck by a couple of similarities between Stalin and Obama. Even though Stalin's life and personality were for very different from Obama's [sic], there are a couple of important similarities between the two men. The most obvious one, which almost certainly laid the foundation for the hatred that was embedded in the souls of both leaders, was their extremely dysfunctional and unhappy childhoods. A second similarity is their remarkable success in portraying themselves to be men of great character and morality, the exact opposite of who they really were/are. Stalin, much like Obama today, succeeded in carrying out a nonstop propaganda campaign in which he was portrayed to the public as the kindly 'Uncle Joe,' notwithstanding his ruthless murdering of tens of millions of his own countrymen."

26. When John Bolton was nominated for the position of ambassador to the United Nations in 2005, repeated testimony was given in Senate hearings about his bad temper and his abrasive manner with subordinates. (One person went so far as to call him a "serial abuser.") But he was defended by Danielle Pletka, a vice president at the American Enterprise Institute, who said, "This is a disgrace, the idea that temperament is suddenly important. There are legions who have gone before John, as well as members of Congress, who have behaved appallingly."

27. St. Augustine, in *De Libero Arbitrio:* "See how absurd and foolish it is to say: I should prefer nonexistence to miserable existence. He who says, I prefer this to that, chooses something. Nonexistence is not something; it is nothing. There can be no real choice when what you choose is nothing."

28. Donald Trump, to a *Rolling Stone* reporter on his 2016 Republican primary opponent Carly Fiorina: "Look at that face! Would anyone vote for that? Can you imagine that, the face of our next president?! I mean, she's a woman, and I'm not s'posedta say bad things, but really, folks, come on. Are we serious?"

29. Item from the *Philadelphia Inquirer* (August 28, 2003) about an atheist, Sherrie Wilkins, suing a school board in Camden, New Jersey, over school uniforms: "Citing the equal protection clause of the U.S. Constitution, Wilkins' lawsuit argues that atheists should have the same rights as religious parents [since the school district allows parents to opt out of the requirement on religious grounds].… [Furthermore] as an atheist, Wilkins said in court documents, she objects to the uniforms because they 'hinder her children's creativity … and freedom of expression.' Uniforms also symbolize militarism, which she opposes, she said."

30. In the run-up to the Senate confirmation of appointments to the Supreme Court, Senate Republicans threatened to strip Democrats (the minority party) of their right to use the filibuster as a way to prevent the confirmation of judges. The Democrats argued that the filibuster had been around for 200 years and scrapping it would be "changing rules in the middle of the game." Further, it would undermine the constitutional principle of "checks and balances" that protected Americans from one-party rule. (Discussed in: Bai, Matt. "The Framing Wars." *New York Times Magazine*, 17 July 2005.)

31. A lobbyist, whose job is to get people to call or write to members of Congress, responding to the charge that this sort of activity makes the "political playing field" uneven (because big money can afford these endeavors much better than small): "Everyone knows that the playing field isn't level in this country in the business arena, or in others for that matter. Nobody complains about that. Why fuss about the funding for what I do?"

32. From the Institute for Creation Research: "In the entire fossil record, there is not a single unequivocal transition[al] form proving a causal relationship between any two species. From the billions of fossils we have discovered, there should be thousands of clear examples if they existed.

    "The lack of transitions between species in the fossil record is what would be expected if life was created."

*33. Phil Gramm, former senator from Texas, defending his argument that food stamps should be cut: "We're the only nation in the world where all our poor people are fat."

It's dangerous to conclude that A *is the cause of* B *just because* B *follows* A.

Fallacies: Misusing Induction

> *Figures don't lie, but liars figure.* —OLD SAYING
>
> *There are lies, damn lies, and statistics.* —BENJAMIN DISRAELI
>
> *It's very difficult to make predictions, especially about the future.* —CASEY STENGEL

MindTap® Visit MindTap for more readings and resources.

Let's now continue our discussion of fallacious reasoning with several fallacies that generally fall into the broad category of *invalid inference*, and typically involve an error of inductive reasoning.

1. Hasty Conclusion

The fallacy of **hasty conclusion** is committed when we draw a conclusion from relevant but insufficient evidence. This fallacy is committed in many different ways and circumstances, ranging from judging political candidates primarily on the basis of 30-second TV commercials to concluding that a neighbor is having an affair on the basis of one or two suspicious clues.

Of course, if we mere human beings were as lucky as Hercule Poirot or Miss Marple, or the other famous fictional detectives, our overly hasty conclusions would frequently turn out to be correct. Here, for example, is the archetype of the great fictional detective Sherlock Holmes making one of his amazing "deductions" when first introduced to Dr. Watson in Sir Arthur Conan Doyle's *A Study in Scarlet:*

> Here is a gentleman of the medical type, but with the air of a military man. Clearly an army doctor, then. He has just come from the tropics, for his face is dark, and that is not the natural tint of his skin, for his wrists are fair. He has undergone hardship and sickness, as his haggard face says clearly. His left arm has been injured. He holds it in a still and unnatural manner. Where in the tropics could an English army doctor have seen much hardship and gotten his arm wounded? Clearly in Afghanistan.

What Holmes observed about Watson was consistent with all sorts of other possibilities that in real life might have been actualities. Doctors don't look that much different from other professionals. Some men with a military air (whatever that might be) never have been in the military. Among Englishmen in those days, when Britain ruled the waves, naval military men were just as common as army types. Tanned faces can result from exposure to nontropical sunlight. A still and unnatural arm carriage may be the legacy of a childhood accident, a haggard expression due to anguish at the loss of a close relative. And even supposing the person in question were a military man who had been wounded in battle in Afghanistan, he still might just have come from a funeral in Italy, South Africa, Brighton, or Timbuktu. The conclusion drawn by Holmes may have been a good guess, but stated with the typical Holmes air of infallibility, it surely was hasty.

Fallacies are endemic to political rhetoric, and hasty conclusions are no exception. Over the last couple of decades, politicians have been eager to reform school performance under President Bush's No Child Left Behind and President Obama's Race to the Top, using the simplistic method of linking teacher evaluations to student performance on standardized tests. The theory is that good teachers will produce students who score well on these tests. But this fails to take into account many of the complex factors involved in student performance, such as problems with tests that may not reflect the actual curriculum or problems with students who have poor language or math skills to begin with and need more time and instruction than is available. It is therefore hasty to conclude that because a class scores below average, the teacher is ineffective.

2. Small Sample

Recall our previous discussion of inductive validity and invalidity, and especially arguments involving samples and populations. Statistics frequently are used to project from a sample to the population from which it was drawn. This is the basic technique that underlies several kinds of inductive reasoning and is the method employed by most polls, including those conducted by Gallup, Harris, and the Nielsen television ratings. But when we accept a conclusion based on a sample that is too small to be a reliable measure of the population from which it was drawn, we are guilty of the fallacy of the **small sample**, a variety of the fallacy *hasty conclusion.* No sample of 100 to 500 voters, for instance, can possibly reflect accurately the entire voting population of the United States.

Scientists, of all people, aren't supposed to commit statistical fallacies (or any fallacies, for that matter), but they're human. In an interesting, one might say comical, example, researchers drew a conclusion about the mating vocal responses of primate species based on a sample of three human couples (each observed engaged in sex exactly once), a pair of gibbons, and one troop of chacma baboons.

What constitutes a sufficiently large sample depends both on the population in question and on the conclusions we want to be able to draw about it. Clearly, a larger population will (all things being equal) require larger samples, but the constitution of the population is important, too. By and large, the more heterogeneous a population, the larger a sample of it needs to be. That is to say, the less alike the members of a population are, the more members of that population we need to sample. The (usually reasonable) assumption here is that we'll find greater consistency among more uniform populations. Consider pens coming off of an assembly line at a particular factory. These pens are made to be as exactly like one another as possible. Let's say you test five red pens and five blue pens and find that the red pens have red ink and the blue pens have black ink. It is perfectly reasonable to conclude that this pattern will continue for all or at least a great majority of the remaining pens. But let's say instead that you're testing pens from *various* manufacturers. It would be hasty to conclude from the same data from the same sort of sample (red ink in five red pens and black ink in five blue pens) that all red pens have red ink and all blue pens have black ink. This is not so much because the population is greater in the second case,[1] but because the population is more heterogeneous.

It also matters how exact we want our conclusions to be. Consider this headline from Salon.com in 2014: "9 out of 10 doctors are seriously concerned about what the meat industry's up to." The first line from the article reads, "over 95 percent of physicians are concerned about antibiotic resistance, a Consumer Reports poll found." That poll was conducted on 500 physicians. Now, according to the Henry J Kaiser Family Foundation, there are just over 900,000 physicians working in the United States. That means the poll in question sampled about 0.056 percent of the population. Since 95 percent of the sample (roughly 475 doctors) were concerned about antibiotic resistance from meat, the Salon headline could have been "19 out of 20 doctors are seriously concerned about what the meat industry's up to." Now, their choice of headline was probably driven by style as much as anything else, but it is also true that the "9 out of 10" claim is much safer than the "19 out of 20" claim, even though the latter is more accurate and startling. Why? Because the sample is so small, we should expect greater variation in a larger sample. If we sampled 10,000 doctors (just over 1.1 percent of the population) we might get a slightly different result. Assuming both samples are sufficiently representative (see section 3 below), it is unlikely that the results will be *extremely* different. Even so, while the data supports the "19 in 20" conclusion, the sample size might not support such an exact claim. "9 in 10" is safer. Safer still would be an even weaker claim about "a majority of doctors." But this would not be as attention-grabbing or as indicative of the attitudes of doctors as a whole. All of this may be to say that deciding on an adequate sample is tricky business!

Sometimes, however, a sample is clearly too small. One particularly egregious (and surprisingly common) sort of small sample fallacy involves the use of a sample with only one member. This is sometimes called "arguing from anecdote" or "anecdotal reasoning." We most commonly make this mistake when we take our own lives to be indicative of larger patterns or trends. We do it in part because we have a natural tendency to overvalue our own experiences. So while we don't want to belittle anyone, it is always worth remembering that no one person's experience is indicative of anyone else's. One author of this text had a very interesting conversation come up in class one day. A student said she thought that the prevalence of sexism in society

---

[1]To see why this is, imagine that there is only one manufacturer of pens. It wouldn't matter how large the population is!

was often exaggerated and offered as evidence the fact that she did not feel she had experienced sexism very much in her life. Another student responded that she experienced sexism almost daily, intimating that the first student must be wrong. Both of these students could be correct about their own lives. And while their attitudes and stories are germane and interesting, they are not necessarily indicative of anything larger. By the way, what does this one story say about how common anecdotal reasoning is? (Answer: Nothing!)

3. Unrepresentative Sample

In addition to being large enough, a good sample should be *representative* of the population from which it is drawn. Indeed, the more representative a sample is, the smaller it needs to be to be significant. When we reason from a sample that isn't sufficiently representative, we commit the fallacy of the **unrepresentative sample** (sometimes called the fallacy of **biased statistics**, although that name also applies to cases where known statistics that are unfavorable to a theory are deliberately suppressed).

> Sample size does not overcome sample bias.
>
> —SAYING POPULAR AMONG STATISTICIANS

The example mentioned earlier about primate mating responses illustrates the fallacy of the unrepresentative sample as well as that of the small sample. For one thing, only three of the dozens of primate species were checked—chimps, gorillas, lemurs, tarsiers, and so forth, may be quite different. (In fact, orangutans turn out to be much different from all other primates in their sex practices.) For another, there is plenty of reason to believe that no sample of three human couples could possibly be representative of all *Homo sapiens,* given the tremendous variety of sex practices engaged in by members of our species.

As usual, relevant background information is crucial when we try to determine whether a sample is likely to be representative of the population from which it was drawn (or is likely to be sufficiently large, for that matter). Good reasoning *always* requires good background information.

For instance, let's say you wanted to find out how many students in your school work full-time jobs. If you conducted a survey of students on campus at 11:00 am on a Monday, you'd have an unrepresentative sample. But in order to see that, you'd have to recognize that students who work full time are more likely to take evening and weekend classes and are less likely to be on campus at 11:00 am on a Monday. Notice though, that a survey of students' fashion or dietary habits could likely be conducted at 11:00 am on a Monday. This is just to reemphasize that the representativeness of a sample will always depend on the conclusions drawn from it.

4. Questionable Cause

We commit the fallacy of **questionable cause** when we label something as the cause of something else on the basis of insufficient or unrepresentative evidence, or when doing so contradicts well-established, high-level theories.[2] (Note that the fallacy of questionable cause often overlaps that of hasty conclusion or of small sample.)

As just mentioned, it isn't easy to determine whether a sample is sufficiently large or representative. This is true in particular because judgments on these matters often depend on seeing the relevance of background information and *bringing it to bear.* Similarly, people all too often make judgments about causal connections on the basis of observed correlations, often quite small, that contradict very general, very well-confirmed, and quite easily understood higher-level theories about what sorts of causes can result in what kinds of effects. People often do so because they lack the relevant and *accurate* background information; sometimes they are motivated by wishful thinking to ignore contrary evidence or theories (a topic to be discussed at some length in the next chapter).

Many people have little or no understanding of the general way in which things work in this world. As they experience life, they don't try to figure out how things work in general or attempt to gain some of the knowledge that has been gleaned over time by others. Instead, they attend almost exclusively to immediate events and problems. They may see science as some kind of magical box from which gadgets like television sets, computers, and jet planes are extracted by bearded drudges with German accents, or by youthful nerds. Having relatively little background information to bring to bear on experience, they are unable to assess either the adequacy of evidence or the possibility that a general idea might be true. Think, for instance, of those who believe in ESP (extrasensory perception) despite the failure of every scientific test to confirm it.

Consider the apparent rise in autism cases that certain groups have blamed on child immunizations, particularly the measles, mumps, and rubella vaccination (MMR).[3] They reason that since the rise in autism cases has coincided with an increase in recommended childhood vaccinations, certain vaccines must be the cause of autism in some children. The MMR immunization, given to toddlers between 15 and 17 months, comes at about the same time that parents begin to observe signs of

---

[2]This doesn't mean that these higher-level theories are exempt from refutation. Evidence that persistently runs contrary even to the highest-level, most general scientific theories eventually, and sometimes rather swiftly, overturns them—as, for example, old ideas about the motions of continents, and related matters, were overturned by evidence favoring the currently held theory concerning plate tectonics.

[3]For more on this see: Jacoby, Susan. *The Age of American Unreason.* New York: Pantheon Press, 2008. 219–220; and more specifically: Madsen, Kreesten, et al. "A Population-Based Study of Measles, Mumps, and Rubella Vaccination and Autism." *New England Journal of Medicine* 347 (7 November 2002).

autism. But this low-level reasoning fails to take into account the fact that autism typically begins to emerge at the end of the second year, whether the child is immunized or not, as rigorous scientific studies have shown. Yet the coincidental appearance of symptoms of autism at the time the vaccine is given, plus the media coverage of the plight of autistic children, have persuaded many people that vaccinations are the cause.

They continue to do so even after the original study, done in Great Britain, was roundly discredited and retracted by *The Lancet*, the British medical journal that first published it. A 2010 analysis found "clear evidence of falsification of data," and the *British Medical Journal* called it an "elaborate fraud." The main author of the study, Dr. Andrew Wakefield, and his colleagues were charged with altering facts to suit their hypothesis, and Dr. Wakefield was stripped of the right to practice medicine in Great Britain. Yet many parents cling to their belief that childhood vaccines cause autism.

And lest we forget that fallacies can be dangerous, there's this from the *New York Times* in 2013: "Last year, Britain had some 2,000 reported cases of measles, and it has already had more than 1,200 this year. The highest rates are among adolescents who were never vaccinated, some because they lacked easy access to vaccines, others because their parents feared autism."

The fallacy at the heart of many people's reasoning about autism and immunization is a special (and especially common) form of questionable cause called *post hoc ergo propter hoc* (literally "after this, therefore because of this"). All too often we attribute a given phenomenon to something that happens just before it. It is easy to see how superstitious thinking can emerge from the post hoc ergo propter hoc fallacy. At least one of the authors of this text is not immune from it. For a long time early in this decade, it seemed that every time I turned on the radio to listen to a Mets game, they would immediately do something terrible: commit an error, give up a run, hit into a double play, etc. Now of course, this was because my beloved Mets were a pretty bad team and not because I turned on the radio. But the superstitious thinking was something I had to fight against, so strong can the seduction to post hoc ergo propter hoc thinking be. We will discuss superstition more in the next chapter.

Politics and economics are breeding grounds for questionable cause fallacies. Critics were inclined to blame the second President Bush for the downturn in the economy during his last year in office. But the fact that the country slid into a recession during his last year doesn't prove that his policies caused the economy to slow down. True, his administration sank billions of dollars into the Iraq and Afghanistan wars, but wars tend to stimulate the economy in the short run. (The long run is another matter, as future generations will discover when the tax burden to pay for these wars falls on them.) The reasons are more complex, and economists are still sorting them out, but one cause was certainly the crash of the bloated housing market. When the housing bubble burst in 2007, inflated real estate values sank like a stone, home foreclosures skyrocketed, the stock market skittered around, and the nation's largest financial institutions teetered on the brink of bankruptcy as they looked for bailouts from the government. But President Bush did not cause the chain reaction. Although his administration certainly contributed to it by reducing government oversight of the financial industry, the groundwork was laid by previous administrations that deregulated financial markets over a period of thirty years, allowing an unregulated shadow banking system of hedge funds and investment banks to evolve, bypassing the safety regulations imposed on traditional banks, and thus paving the way for the credit crisis in 2008.

For a brief period when Barack Obama took office, President Bush continued to take the heat for the weak economy, but as the recession deepened and unemployment rose, the blame shifted to Obama. Republicans hammered him for driving up the deficit; Democrats fought back with the charge that the deficit was a toxic legacy from Bush. In fact, both presidents increased federal spending extensively, but other factors they had little control over had greater influence—not the least of which was the massive hit to the federal budget from the loss of tax revenues as the recession bottomed out. Nonetheless, when it's time for elections, the sitting president in a bad economy usually is held responsible no matter what other forces are at work. The economic well-being of the United States depends on many complex factors, here and around the world, that a president does not and cannot control. This doesn't mean that, by promoting unsound economic policies, a president cannot be a part of the cause of an economic downturn. The point is that it is simplistic to give him or her the lion's share of the blame without

The
General Surgeon
has determined that breathing
is dangerous to your health.
This conclusion
was drawn from a survey
of 100 Canadian rats
that have died
within the past 5 years.
All were
habitual breathers.

Reprinted by permission of American Greetings Corporation, Cleveland, Ohio.

Greeting card humor illustrating some fallacy or other, no doubt.

further argument. And just as we should be less quick to blame a president when the economy suffers, we should also be highly suspect when a presidential candidate claims that he or she can fix or make dramatic improvements to the economy (as they all seem to do).

The fallacy questionable cause is also sometimes committed because items are incorrectly classified—poorly sorted into different kinds. Any items, no matter how different from one another, have some things in common, so that there always is some reason for grouping them together in our thoughts. When we classify items to discover cause/effect relationships, we need to make sure we have bunched together just the right sorts of cases. In some areas of the United States, for instance, a larger percentage of nonwhite children do poorly in school compared to students who are white, a fact that has led some people to conclude that being nonwhite is the *cause* of their doing less well in school (that there is a genetic difference involved here), an interesting and very serious example of the fallacy questionable cause.[4]

As might be expected, the statistical variety of questionable cause, in which a mere statistical correlation is taken to provide proof of a causal connection, is quite common. We sometimes call this "confusing correlation and cause." It's true that every statistical correlation has some significance and, in the absence of reasons to the contrary, increases the likelihood (probability), however slightly, that there also is a causal connection between the things correlated. But when there are reasons to the contrary, or when the statistical sample in question is too small or unrepresentative, we make a mistake in jumping to the conclusion that we've found a causal connection.

Sometimes alleged causal connections based on statistical surveys are too silly to take seriously, because they are so obviously contrary to well-supported background beliefs. An example is the theory that smoking marijuana causes college students to get better grades, based on one dubious statistical study in which marijuana smokers averaged slightly higher grades than nonsmokers. This theory actually gained modest acceptance in some, ah, "high"-minded circles during the 1970s. (And what are the background beliefs that should make you doubt smoking dope causes an increase in grades?)

One final example: consider this excerpt from the beginning of a story at the *Huffington Post* under the headline "Soda May Cause Violence in Teens, Study Says":

> Refreshing? Yes. Healthy? Not so much. Soda is filled with caffeine, causes cavities—and even diet soft drinks have been linked to weight gain.
>
> But, a new study conducted by David Hemenway, a professor at the Harvard School of Public Health and Sara J Solnick, Department of Economics, University of Vermont found another reason to keep your kids away from the stuff. The research concludes that teenagers who consume large amounts of soda are more likely to be violent—a scary finding when you consider that 1 in 4 teens drink soda every day.
>
> The participants were 1,878 kids between 14 and 18-years-old, from 22 schools in inner city Boston. Each was asked how many soda cans he or she had

---

[4]Such discrepancies are much better explained by some combination of the legacy of social and economic inequality between whites and nonwhites and cultural bias in testing and instruction in schools.

consumed in the previous week—and also asked whether they drank alcohol or smoked, carried a weapon or acted violently, Fox News Latino reports.

Hemenway said that teens who drank more soft drinks were between nine and fifteen percent more likely to have violent tendencies.[5]

To the reporter's credit, she does later mention that this is not proof of causation. But is the headline—which certainly suggests the possibility of causation—appropriate? Is it more likely that drinking a lot of soda causes violent behavior, or that these two things both result from some other underlying causes—perhaps a lack of parental supervision or impulse control problems, to name a couple?

5. Questionable Analogy

We reason by *analogy* when we conclude from the observed similarity of two or more items in some respects to their similarity in another.[6] Sports fans, for example, may have reasoned by analogy when they concluded that the 2016 Olympic Games would be fun to watch, given that they were fun to watch in previous years. Caffeine lovers do so when they reason from the fact that coffee has kept them awake several nights in a row to the conclusion that drinking it again tonight will keep them awake.[7] The general form of such reasoning is that the items mentioned are alike in certain respects, so they will be alike in some other way.

But we aren't always justified in reasoning by analogy. When we do so anyway, we are guilty of the fallacy of **questionable analogy**, sometimes referred to as **faulty comparison**.

Analogical reasoning can be fallacious for several different reasons. The thing about which we're drawing a conclusion may not be like the thing to which it is being compared (its "analogue"), the basis of comparison between this thing and its analogue may not be relevant to the conclusion drawn about it, or there may be some critical dissimilarity between the thing and its analogue that speaks against the conclusion we're trying to draw about it.

Some analogies seem to be apt on the surface but collapse under closer scrutiny. For instance, in an op-ed article for the *New York Times* (January 1, 2007), the historian Arthur Schlesinger, Jr., used this analogy to illustrate the folly of ignoring the lessons of the past: "As persons deprived of memory become disoriented and lost, not knowing where they have been and where they are going, so a nation denied a conception of the past will be disabled in dealing with its present and its future." Although both examples deal with a loss of past experience, the first involves forgetting all experience, as Alzheimer's patients do, but the second involves ignoring past experience—quite a different phenomenon.

---

[5]Samakow, Jessica. "Soda May Cause Violence in Teens, Study Says." *Huffington Post,* 25 December 2011.

[6]Analogical reasoning thus is very similar to induction by enumeration. Indeed, the latter can be thought of as a kind of analogical reasoning.

[7]Recall, though, the earlier discussion of the fallacy questionable cause. It isn't easy to be positive that it's the coffee keeping us awake.

Not uncommonly, questionable analogies surface in a court of law. In 2003, many American tourists were annoyed to discover that credit card companies were charging a currency conversion fee for items purchased abroad. One irate customer filed suit against Visa and MasterCard for intentionally hiding the fee from cardholders. The attorney for MasterCard argued, "That's not hiding, that's not concealing—that's how business is done in this country." The defense went on to explain that "while consumers naturally understand that commercial suppliers of goods and services impose a mark-up over their costs, the proposed decision would condemn as 'embedding' the standard practice that a seller tells its customer its price to them, not which part of the price reflects its cost and which part its mark-up." However, to compare hidden credit card fees to the undisclosed markup of commercial goods is certainly questionable. The consumer knows the cost of an item in a retail store because it is clearly marked on the price tag, but when using a credit card abroad, the consumer has no idea of the total amount because of the hidden conversion fee.

In 2009, Congress passed the Credit Card Accountability Responsibility and Disclosure Act, requiring companies to disclose hidden fees on foreign transactions, among other things. But those crafty bankers figured out how to transform and bury that fee by redefining the term *foreign*. Now it includes any transaction that touches a foreign bank, even if the entire exchange takes place in U.S. dollars—like booking foreign flights on domestic planes through online travel sites. And now *that's* how business is done.

Some analogies are easily seen to be fallacious, others as clearly apt. But the evaluations of still others often require a good deal of thought. Consider this analogy in a letter to the editor arguing against stricter handgun control laws: When a drunk driver runs over a child, we go after the driver, not the car. When someone kills a child with a gun, we go after the gun. But shouldn't we go after the person who murders with a gun, not the gun itself? In this case, there clearly is a relevant resemblance between the two cases—killing with a car or with a gun—so there is something to the analogy. But there also are important differences, as there often are, and the question is whether they are both relevant and sufficient to make the analogy questionable. For example, private autos are an extremely important kind of transportation in our society; banning their use would dramatically change all sorts of things in everyday life. Handguns serve few legitimate purposes in private hands; AK-47s and the like, none at all. Restricting their use would make relatively little difference in most of our lives. Furthermore, most auto deaths result from accidents or negligence, rarely from deliberate intent to murder. Guns frequently are used deliberately to murder other people. Note that the letter writer omits the fact that, when people use guns for nefarious purposes, we go after the gun user as well as the gun itself, and also the fact that we outlaw autos believed to be unsafe to drive. The point of all of this is that we don't want to label analogies questionable, or apt, too quickly; in some cases, we need to consider all sorts of factors. Good critical reasoners need to become adept at bringing background information to bear when evaluating analogies, just as most other sorts of reasoning.

This example also illustrates the difficulty in bringing one's relevant background beliefs to bear when evaluating an argument. All of the relevant differences just mentioned are common knowledge, yet we often fail to bring information of this kind to bear when evaluating an argument. (Did you in this case?)

Before turning to a discussion of other fallacies, perhaps it should be noted that we need to distinguish between *explanatory* analogies used to explain and *argumentative* analogies used to prove a point. This distinction follows the general distinction between explanations and arguments discussed in Chapter 1. When we argue or reason analogically, we present evidence for a conclusion; when we use an analogy to explain, we merely liken the thing explained to something already familiar. In Plato's famous analogy of the cave, for example, the people in the cave who merely see the shadows of things are likened to those who restrict themselves to the ever-changing world of everyday experience, while the people who come out into the sunlight and see the objects themselves are likened to the philosophers who reason to the unchanging reality that lies behind everyday experiences. The analogy explains Plato's ideas about a world beyond that of mere everyday experiences, but it doesn't prove that there is such a world or in any way argue that there is. (Plato himself very likely intended his cave myth to be explanatory, not argumentative, but it is often construed otherwise.)

The point here is that we shouldn't accuse those whose analogies are intended to explain of being guilty of the fallacy questionable analogy. (They may, of course, serve very poorly to explain, but that is another matter.) Anyway, as just remarked, explanatory analogies sometimes are mistakenly taken to prove what they merely explain, and in this case, we are indeed justified in accusing those who do this of the fallacy questionable analogy.

Finally, we need to notice that, in everyday life, it often is difficult to determine whether an analogy is intended to explain or to prove; no doubt some are intended to serve both purposes. In any case, as with explanations in general, it is hard to separate the mere explanatory nature of an analogy from its power to persuade.

6. Questionable Statistics

Statistics always seem so precise and *authoritative*. It sounds so much more believable, for instance, to claim that the average child watches 1,680 minutes of TV per week rather than just that kids typically watch an awful lot of TV. But how could anyone know such an exact fact? There would have to be a lot of guesswork and extrapolation from relatively small samples to arrive even at an informed rough estimate as to these sorts of matters. This doesn't mean that we ought simply to dismiss these statistics; it just means that we have to understand their limitations.

Statistics on the state of the economy are a case in point. Take the ones published by the federal government on business conditions in the United States. One of the major problems with these statistics is that their *margins of error* (not always provided) are often greater than the "significant" differences they report. These problems become even starker when we consider that the government's later revisions of its own figures often reflect a change larger than the alleged margin of error.

In addition, problems arise from the need to use a base year in determining long-run trends. Those who want to show that a given year has had a high rate of growth can choose a low base year; those intent on proving a low rate of growth, a high base year. Meanwhile, a precisely true rate of growth may remain elusive.

In the case of figures concerning the gross national product, we have several other reasons for being suspicious. One is that a good deal of commerce in the United States today is illegal. Think only of racketeering, gambling, drug traffic, prostitution, and the hiring of illegal aliens to do migrant farm labor or household cleaning and other low-paying, tedious, and often backbreaking jobs. Reliable statistics concerning illegal activities are by their nature hard to come by. Calculating, say, the commerce in illegal drugs has to be done indirectly, by reference to the sale of legal drug equipment, drug busts, and so on. Another reason for suspicion is that a good deal of otherwise legal commerce is done "off the books," so that no taxes need to be paid or so that restrictive laws can be avoided. How are we to assess the value of goods when one kind is bartered for another?

Statistics on corrupt activities are just as hard to come by, particularly in countries where corruption is endemic and bribery is the norm rather than the exception. Brazil, for instance, has been the focus of international concern as well as domestic protest over government corruption. Such attention has increased since 2013, as Brazil prepared for the 2014 World Cup and the 2016 Olympics. One study from the Federation of Industries of Sao Paulo State suggested that the annual cost of corruption in Brazil at the time was as much as $53 billion. But that must have been an *awfully* rough estimate. How is it possible to come up with these statistics when bribery, by its very nature, usually occurs under the table?

Sometimes statistics are based on soft information and are thus questionable. For years, doctors have urged us to reduce our intake of fatty foods, but a 2006 study funded by the Women's Health Initiative (WHI) seemed to contradict this advice. The study—following 48,835 women aged 50–79 for an average of 8.1 years—revealed no significant statistical difference in the rates of colorectal cancer, heart disease, or stroke between the group on the low-fat diet and the comparison group on the normal diet. But the study was problematic because the data were drawn from the participants' memories of what they ate—sometimes up to a year earlier! (Do you remember what you ate last week, let alone a year ago?) Evidence that their memories were unreliable becomes clearer when we consider this finding: Women who weighed 170 pounds on average claimed they consumed 1,700 calories a day at the beginning of the study and 1,500 calories at the end. Yet these women lost only 1 pound over many years in the WHI study.[8] How could that be? Either their memories were faulty or they were shaving off calories. More likely, they consumed 500–700 more calories a day than they reported. Given the apparent unreliability of these reports, it is questionable that low-fat diets fail to protect women from certain illnesses. No matter, this dubious science made headlines and probably allowed many women to rationalize eating the fatty foods they craved.

The government's figures on unemployment also need to be viewed with a good deal of suspicion. These figures are calculated partly on the basis of information gathered via polls of "representative" individuals. How these people respond depends on the precise wording of the questions they are asked (a point soon to be discussed further), and this in part depends on what the government considers to be full-time, compared to

---

[8]For more on this see: Ness, Carol. "Down to a Science." *San Francisco Chronicle,* 16 March 2006.

part-time, employment, and who is said to be seeking employment, compared to those who have given up the search. (It also depends on how truly representative the government's samples happen to be.) Early in 2012, for instance, the Obama administration was upbeat about the drop in unemployment from a dismal 8.9 percent in October 2011, to a slightly less dismal 8.3 percent in January 2012. But that report was based on people out of work for less than a year, and didn't reflect the rate of those out of work for over a year. The total percentage of the unemployed, plus workers who wanted full-time jobs but had to settle for part time, is 15.1 percent, nearly double the amount cited. Of course, it is to the advantage of every administration to quote the official rate of the Bureau of Labor Statistics (BLS), which is the lowest, but all you have to do is check out the unemployment figures released monthly by the BLS to get a more accurate picture of the various categories and percentages of people out of work in this country.

All of this certainly does not mean that government statistics on commerce and employment should be tossed into the nearest wastebasket. But it does mean that precise official figures should be taken for what they are: the best *approximations* we have of economic activity—valuable primarily in showing very-long-term trends, but often calculated so as to serve short-term political interests.

By way of contrast, consider a correctly cautious claim typical of those frequently made by scientists (*Science News,* January 19, 1991): Scientists using sophisticated techniques to determine the age of ancient cliff drawings in west Texas estimated that the drawings were painted "3,865 years ago, *give or take a century*" (italics added).

Finally, it's important to have some idea as to which sorts of statistics can be known, even in theory. Some statistics simply are unknowable. Here is a letter one of the authors of this text received several years ago that contains examples of unknowable statistics it would be hard to top:

> Dear Friend: In the past 5,000 years men have fought in 14,523 wars. One out of four persons living during this time have been war casualties. A nuclear war would add 1,245,000,000 men, women, and children to this tragic list.

It's ludicrous to present such precise figures as facts. No one knows (or could know) the exact number of wars fought so far, to say nothing of the number of war casualties. (Does anyone even know the true casualty rates just for all of the wars that have occurred in the past ten years?) As for the numbers in a nuclear conflict, the casualty rate would depend on who fought such a war, and, in any event, it is a matter on which even experts can engage in only the wildest sorts of speculations.

7. Questionable Uses of Good Statistics

As we've just seen, statistics that are obviously questionable are a problem. But perfectly good statistics also can cause trouble—for two reasons. The first is the inability of so many people to understand the significance of this statistic or that, made worse by the natural tendency in all of us to pay attention to statistics that support conclusions we already have drawn. The second is the ability of charlatans to bamboozle the rest of us via cleverly employed statistics. (That's the import of the old saying that figures don't lie, but liars figure.)

Consider, for instance, the evidence often used by climate-change deniers that temperatures actually *decreased* between 1998 and 2012 despite no corresponding decrease in CO_2 emissions. This claim is statistically accurate, as the average global temperature was 58.3 degrees in 1998 and 58.2 degrees in 2012. Hooray! Hooray? No, wait. Accurate as it is, this statistic is extremely misleading. For one thing, 1998 was an abnormally hot year because of El Nino. The fact that global temperatures were only 0.01 degree cooler in 2012 without a significant El Nino weather event is actually extremely alarming. Second, climate scientists are generally not as concerned with 14-year numbers as they are with longer trends. And the average global temperature has risen 1.4 degrees since 1880.[9] But really, that doesn't sound so scary, does it? Only the most sensitive among us could even notice such a change. So maybe global warming isn't so bad after all. Hooray! Hooray? No, wait. We're confusing normal local fluctuation with global change. According to one source, "A one-degree *global* change is significant because it takes a vast amount of heat to warm all the oceans, atmosphere, and land by that much. In the past, a one- to two-degree drop was all it took to plunge the Earth into the Little Ice Age. A five-degree drop was enough to bury a large part of North America under a towering mass of ice 20,000 years ago." But that source was probably some alarmist fringe environmentalist, right? These people aren't exactly rocket scientists. We'll be fine, right? Wrong. That quote came from NASA.[10]

Then there are the politicians who made much of the fact that in 2011, 47 percent of Americans did not pay federal income tax. While this statistic is accurate according to the Tax Policy Center, it is misleading because some politicians misinterpret it to mean that almost half the people in this country pay no taxes at all. In fact, the great majority do pay other taxes. Nearly 90 percent of nontaxpaying households earn low incomes that exempt them from federal taxes, but not from payroll and excise taxes, state and local income taxes, or sales and property taxes.[11] So when politicians complain that half the population is getting a free ride, they are wrong. It is simply a ploy to con the public into thinking that nontaxpayers are scamming the system.

The misuse of statistics is just as common in economics as it is in politics. For instance, a libertarian defending the current economy on a radio talk show claimed that less than 10 percent of Americans used to own stocks, but now up to 45 to 50 percent do. Thus, an ordinary wage earner who saves can take part in the increase in wealth the stock market provides. Although his figures are about right, he neglects two important points. First, the 45 to 50 percent includes retirement funds invested by companies, not individuals—the ordinary earner simply draws a pension from the invested fund. Second, a tiny portion of stockholders own most of the stock and get rich, and the gap between the rich and the rest of us has been getting a good deal larger.

In another example, the Death Penalty Information Center indicated that from 1990 to 2006, the murder rate was higher in states with the death penalty than in those without it.

[9]Temple, James. "How Climate-Change Deniers Misuse Global Warming Data" *San Francisco Chronicle,* 21 July 2013.

[10]http://earthobservatory.nasa.gov/Features/WorldOfChange/decadaltemp.php

[11]Williams, Roberton. "Why Do People Pay No Federal Income Tax?" Tax Policy Center of the Urban Institute and Brookings Institution. Web. 27 July 2011.

Those opposed to the death penalty on grounds that it does not deter homicides take this to be evidence supporting that conclusion. But sophisticated critical reasoners wondered whether doing so made them guilty of the fallacy questionable cause (especially confusing correlation and cause). For it very well may be that states with death penalties had a higher rate of murder to start with and that perhaps they opted for this harsh penalty to try to reduce the amount of serious crime. To prove their point, those opposed to the death penalty on these grounds would have to present statistics showing that serious crime remained the same, or increased, after a death penalty was imposed in particular states. Otherwise, the comparison is of apples and oranges. (Remember that the number of serious crimes tends to increase in hard economic times and decreases in good.)

8. Polls: An Important Special Case

A well-conceived and well-executed poll can be a fruitful way to find out all sorts of things, from the voter strength of a political candidate to Fido's preferences in dog food. Unfortunately, not all polls are created equal.

One problem is that the way in which a question is asked seriously influences the answers one can expect. It is extremely difficult, if not impossible, to word a question in a way that is completely neutral. At the height of the Watergate scandal, for instance, a Gallup poll asked the question:

> Do you think President Nixon should be impeached and compelled to leave the presidency, or not?

Thirty percent said yes. But a Pat Caddell private poll asked the question this way:

> Do you think the President should be tried, and removed from office if found guilty?

Fifty-seven percent answered yes to that one. So 30 percent answered yes to the question worded one way, 57 percent when the same question was put another way.

Information left out of questions can skew poll results enormously. Here, for example, are two different questions on late-term abortion that had radically different responses.[12] An ABC poll asked "Do you think the late-term abortion procedure known as dilation and extraction, or partial birth abortion, should be legal or illegal?" Sixty-two percent said "illegal." But a follow-up question was asked, adding additional information. "What if it would prevent a serious threat to the woman's health?" Only 33 percent responded "illegal" to this question.

The importance of framing the issue has not escaped those intent on skewing poll results one way or the other. Here, for example, are a couple of loaded questions in the "2000 Official NRA Gun Owners Survey":

> Do you think gun owner names should be subject to surprise inspection by the Bureau of Alcohol, Tobacco, and Firearms?
>
> Do you think gun owners like you should be required to pay expensive liability insurance for every gun you own?

---

[12]Quoted in "Framing the Abortion Issue." *Extra!* July–August 2007.

Trouble with Statistics

Statistics seem to baffle almost everyone. Several years ago, when 200 educators were asked what percentage of children read at grade level or below, 78 percent failed to provide the correct answer—50 percent. Even teachers have a hard time keeping straight on the difference between comparative and absolute scales.

Another comparative rating that causes confusion is the IQ rating: Half of those who take the test must be rated at 100 or below, given that 100 merely marks the halfway point in results.

© Tom Meyer

What gun owners in their right minds would answer "yes" to these questions?

Sometimes problems with polling emerge not so much from their design as from their interpretation and reporting. Consider this case, as relayed by Paul Krugman in the *New York Times* as part of his argument that a lack of skills among workers does not explain high unemployment:

So how does the myth of a skills shortage not only persist, but remain part of what "everyone knows"? Well, there was a nice illustration of the process last fall, when some news media reported that 92 percent of top executives said that there was, indeed, a skills gap. The basis for this claim? A telephone survey in which executives were asked, "Which of the following do you feel best describes the 'gap' in the U.S. workforce skills gap?" followed by a list of alternatives. Given the loaded question, it's actually amazing that 8 percent of the respondents were willing to declare that there was no gap.[13]

The biggest problem with polls, though, is the difficulty of tapping a truly representative sample. The 1936 *Literary Digest* poll, based on names lifted from telephone directories and auto registration lists, is perhaps the most famous example of an extremely biased poll. It predicted that Alf Landon would defeat Franklin Roosevelt, while the actual result was a tremendous landslide for Roosevelt. The magazine (which went out of business shortly afterward—post hoc ergo propter hoc?) failed to take into account the fact that few people in the bottom half of the American population had telephones or autos in those days, so that their sample was completely unrepresentative of American voters.

Of course, the art of polling has come a long way since 1936, or even 1948, when polls predicted an easy victory for Thomas E. Dewey over Harry Truman. The *Chicago Tribune*—whose motto, incidentally, was and still is "The World's Greatest Newspaper"—was so sure Dewey would win that it grossly misinterpreted early returns and printed one of the most infamous headlines in newspaper history—"Dewey Defeats Truman"—which an exultant Truman held up to the crowd at his victory celebration.

But it still is difficult to get a representative sample of the voting population by polling only 1,500 or so potential voters—the standard practice today. In theory, a very carefully selected sample of roughly this size should be almost as reliable as one of 15,000 (a poll of this size would be much too expensive and is never conducted). But in practice, for all sorts of reasons, things frequently don't work as planned. This doesn't mean that we should not pay attention to polls. They often are the best or even the only way we have of testing the water. It just means we have to pay heed to them in an intelligent manner. A presidential election poll taken in September is of much less value, other things being equal, than one conducted in October; polls paid for by one side or the other are worth less than those conducted by truly independent organizations. But most important, we have to remember that even the best polls have a batting average well below 100 percent.

The reputation of the polling industry took a particularly hard beating following the 2016 election. Pundits and pollsters were shocked at how thoroughly the Clinton lead had been misjudged. Just one day prior to the election, Bloomberg predicted the race breaking in Clinton's favor 44% to Trump's 41%, with third-party candidates Gary Johnson and Jill Stein picking up 4% and 2% of votes, respectively. In a two-way race, Bloomberg gave Clinton an even larger margin of 46% to Trump's 43%. Similarly, Reuters/Ipsos called a two-way match-up for Clinton at 44% to Trump's 39% and even FOX News showed Clinton with a comfortable 48% to Trump's 44%. The L.A. Times/USC poll offered the only dissent, consistently predicting a Trump victory prior to Election Day with a generous 4–5% margin. Post-mortem articles noted that nearly all major polls leading up to the election gave Clinton the lead in her so-called "firewall" states: Michigan, Wisconsin, Virginia, Colorado, Pennsylvania and New Hampshire. Of those, she ultimately took only Virginia, New Hampshire and Colorado, and those by relatively slender margins. Likewise, polls predicted Clinton would capitalize on demographic shifts in local electorates in Florida and North Carolina, states which she would go on to lose.

---

[13]Krugman, Paul. "Jobs and Skills and Zombies." *New York Times,* 30 March 2014.

Note, by the way, that there is no such thing as a "poll fallacy," even though, as just illustrated, polls do give rise to fallacies such as questionable statistics and hasty conclusions.

9. False Charge of Fallacy

It often is all too easy to charge others with fallacious reasoning. This is particularly true when people change their minds and embrace positions they previously denied. The temptation is to charge them with the fallacy of inconsistency. But making a given statement at one time and one that contradicts it at a later time does not necessarily indicate inconsistency; we may have good grounds for changing our minds.

Take the person who says, "I used to believe that women are not as creative as men, because most of the intellectually productive people I knew about were men; but I've changed my mind, because I believe now (as I didn't then) that environment (culture, surroundings), not native ability, has been responsible for the preponderance of intellectual men." Surely, that person cannot be accused of the fallacy of inconsistency, since he (or she!) has explained the change of mind.

Let's say that those who falsely accuse others of fallacy are themselves guilty of making a **false charge of fallacy**. Of course, falsely accusing someone of inconsistency is not the only way in which someone might be guilty of false charge of fallacy. Recall, for example, the earlier discussion of the distinction between analogical reasoning and explanatory analogies; clearly, we are guilty of making a false charge of fallacy if we accuse someone of perpetrating a questionable analogy when his or her intent is not to prove something but merely, via an analogy, to explain it.

We are also guilty of falsely charging someone with a fallacy when we take literally an ironic jab at the opposition. In the following letter to the editor, for example, the writer clearly intends to be ironic:

> Billions of dollars and two decades later, the War on Drugs has successfully eliminated illegal drugs from the face of America. The country is finally free of pot, coke, and heroin. With this as a model, the War on Junk Guns is bound to be successful.

Claiming that the writer is guilty of questionable premise or suppressed evidence because the War on Drugs hasn't eradicated illegal drugs clearly constitutes a false charge of fallacy. The letter writer just employs sarcasm to remind us ironically that the War on Drugs has been a failure.

QUIBBLING

When deciding whether someone has or has not committed a fallacy, we don't want to **quibble**. We don't want to take advantage, for instance, of the fact that life is short, and, in everyday life, we don't usually bother to spell out every detail. Some things can, and should, be taken for granted.

Consider the American Medical Association (AMA) ad that stated:

> 100,000 doctors have quit smoking.
> Maybe they know something you don't.

File Under: Everyone Makes Mistakes

Exercise item from the second edition of a certain textbook on logic and contemporary rhetoric:

> *Newspaper story:* Thor Heyerdahl has done it again, crossing the Atlantic in a papyrus raft designed according to ancient Egyptian tomb carvings. Landing in the Western Hemisphere on the island of Barbados, he was greeted by the Barbados prime minister, Errol Barrow, who declared, "This has established Barbados was the first landing place for man in the Western World."

This was a very un-PC remark by Barrow, but that is not the point here. The point is that the correct answer to this exercise item was supposed to be hasty conclusion, but a student from Barbados pointed out that the prime minister was known for his sense of humor. Another false charge of fallacy, this time by the (here nameless) author of the critical reasoning textbook in question.

Students have called this ad fallacious because, among other reasons, it suppresses evidence as to what kind of doctors have quit. ("Maybe it was horse doctors." "They don't say if they were doctors of medicine.") But this sort of response amounts to nothing better than quibbling. It resembles the remark of a student who objected to Shakespeare's wonderful line, "He jests at scars, that never felt a wound" (*Romeo and Juliet*), on grounds that *he* (the student) had felt a wound—a mere scratch—and still jested at scars. (Other students have objected to the line on the grounds that Shakespeare incorrectly used *that* instead of *who,* but they [the students!] were guilty of another, grammatical sort of quibbling—to say nothing of hubris, in having the temerity to "correct" the grammar of someone who may well be the greatest writer to ever work in the English language.)

This (finally!) concludes our discussion of fallacies, unfortunately restricted to just a few of the more common varieties that have been discussed in one place or another in the literature. While it is useful to become adept at aptly applying specific names to cases of fallacious reasoning, the point of acquiring this skill, after all, is to learn how to improve one's own reasoning and to be better able to spot the fallacious reasoning of others. Remember, though, that what counts is not the ability to apply a label to poor reasoning. Labels certainly are useful in getting adept at spotting bad arguments, but seeing that they are bad and understanding why they are bad is the name of the game.

In any case, we will soon see that spotting fallacies is only part of the larger enterprise of evaluating more complicated passages containing related arguments that are intended to form a coherent whole. *Extended arguments* of this kind—argumentative essays—are discussed in Chapters 8 and 9.

Summary of Chapter 5

1. *Hasty conclusion:* Accepting an argument on the basis of relevant but insufficient information or evidence. ***Example:*** Sherlock Holmes's conclusion that Dr. Watson was an army man just back from Afghanistan.

2. *Small sample:* Drawing conclusions about a population on the basis of a sample that is too small to be a reliable measure of that population. ***Example:*** Conclusions drawn about primate mating habits based on a sample of three human couplings, a gibbon mating, and those of one troop of baboons.

3. *Unrepresentative sample:* Reasoning from a sample that is not representative (typical) of the population from which it was drawn. ***Example:*** The sample of primates just mentioned.

4. *Questionable cause:* Labeling *A* as the cause of *B* on evidence that is insufficient, negative, unrepresentative, or in serious conflict with well-established high-level theories. ***Example:*** Blaming President Bush or President Obama for the down-turn in the economy when other, more complex factors are at work.

5. *Questionable analogy:* Drawing an analogical conclusion when the cases compared are not alike, or when their similarity is not relevant to the conclusion drawn or when there is some crucial dissimilarity between them that speaks against the conclusion. ***Example:*** Comparing hidden fees to retail markups.

6. *Questionable statistics:* Employing statistics that are questionable without fur-ther support. ***Example:*** Accepting government statistics on short-term business trends as completely accurate rather than just educated approximations. *Extreme example:* Employing unknowable statistics about how many wars have been fought in the past 5,000 years and how many casualties there have been.

    Note, by the way, that the quality of statistics sometimes differs a great deal from time to time and place to place.

7. *Questionable uses of statistics:* Perfectly good statistics are also sometimes problematic—for two reasons. The first is the inability of so many people to understand the significance of this statistic or that, made worse by the natural tendency in all of us to see statistics as favoring conclusions we already have drawn. The second is the ability of charlatans to bamboozle the rest of us via cleverly employed statistics. ***Example:*** Accepting evidence that the murder rate in states that have adopted a death penalty for serious crimes is higher than in states that have not done so as proof that the death penalty does not deter crime, without further evidence that this statistical evidence has a causal founda-tion; it could well be, for example, that states adopting death penalties had even higher murder rates than other states and have adopted a death penalty in an attempt to do something about that unfortunate fact.

8. *Polls:* Although polls are an important source of information, they need to be dealt with cautiously. Polls can be misleading (1) because of the way in which

questions are worded—often deliberately to obtain the desired statistics; (2) because they ask the wrong questions; (3) because respondents don't want to appear ignorant, immoral, odd, or prejudiced; or (4) because they are based on a sample that is too small or unrepresentative. ***Example:*** The NRA survey asking loaded questions skewed to get negative responses to government control of gun owners.

9. *False charge of fallacy:* Erroneously accusing others of fallacious reasoning. ***Example:*** Accusing someone of inconsistency who has changed his mind about the lack of creativity of women in the light of contrary evidence.

    Note that ironic rhetoric that, if taken literally, would be fallacious, may well not be. Note also that we don't want to be overly critical of the reasoning of others to the point that we are guilty of *quibbling.*

EXERCISE SET 5-1

1. In the wake of terrorist attacks across Europe, the French National Assembly passed a law banning the Islamic burqa and niqab—full body veils that mask the identity of the wearer. This legislation provoked a wave of protests. In defense of the law, Jean-Francois Cope, the majority leader in the French Assembly, argued that covering the face poses a serious threat to public safety, particularly now that security cameras are commonly used to identify criminals.[14] As evidence, he cited a recent case in which criminals dressed in burqas committed armed robbery in a Paris suburb. He said that the French are "passionately attached" to individual liberty, but that sometimes they must compromise for the greater public good. To make his point, he argued that a U.S. law prohibiting people "from strolling down Fifth Avenue in the nude does not constitute an attack on the fundamental rights of nudists. Likewise, wearing headgear that fully covers the face does not constitute a fundamental liberty." Rather, it undermines the common good of the community.

    Identify the fallacies in this passage and explain them.

2. The National Science Foundation reported that two different polls conducted by telephone two weeks apart came up with much different results on the question of whether Americans support embryonic stem cell research—even through the pollsters used similar methodologies.[15] The Coalition for the Advancement of Medical Research (CAMR) found that nearly 75 percent of Americans supported this type of research, but a poll conducted two weeks later by the United States Conference of Catholic Bishops (USCCB) reported that "48 percent of Americans oppose federal funding of stem cell research that requires destroying human embryos." Only 39 percent approved. Why were the results so different? The answer is in the way the questions were framed.

---

[14]Cope, Jean-Francois. "Tearing Away the Veil." *New York Times,* 5 May 2010.

[15]For further discussion see "Public Attitudes about S & T [Science and Technology] in General," http://nsf.gov/statistics/, (2006).

CAMR question: *I'm going to read you a brief description of embryonic stem cell research, and then get your reaction. Embryonic stem cells are special cells that can develop into every type of cell in the human body. The stem cells are extracted from embryonic cells produced in fertility clinics and then frozen days after fertilization. If a couple decides that the fertilized eggs are no longer needed, they can choose to donate the embryos for research or the clinic will throw the embryos away. Scientists have had success in initial research with embryonic stem cells and believe that they can be developed into cures for diseases such as cancer, Parkinson's, heart disease, juvenile diabetes, and spinal cord injuries. Having heard this description, do you strongly favor, somewhat favor, somewhat oppose, or strongly oppose medical research that uses stem cells from human embryos?*

USCCB question: *Stem cells are the basic cells from which all of a person's tissues and organs develop. Congress is considering the question of federal funding for experiments using stem cells from human embryos. The live embryos would be destroyed in their first week of development to obtain these cells. Do you support or oppose using your federal tax dollars for such experiments?*

Evaluate the way the issue is framed in each question and explain how the questions likely influenced the survey results.

3. Here is a paraphrase of a letter to the editor of the *Nutrition Action Health Letter:*

   I am a diabetic who has found the artificial sweetener NutraSweet to be "a total nightmare." I thought it would be a good substitute for sugar [diabetics have to severely limit their intake of sugar]. But when I started using it, I began to have serious headaches that my doctor could not account for. So under my doctor's supervision, I stopped using NutraSweet and my headaches stopped. Going back onto NutraSweet was followed by a renewal of my headaches. I did this back and forth three times and the scenario was the same each time: "no NutraSweet, no headache; NutraSweet, headache."

   The unstated implication here is that taking the NutraSweet was the cause of the headaches. Is this a reasonable conclusion to draw on the basis of the evidence provided?

4. Comment on this quote (attributed to Rush Limbaugh) from an ad urging people to join the National Organization for Women: "What if a man claimed the right to rape using the same principle found in the theory that it is his body and he has the right to choose?"

5. Earlier in this chapter, we questioned the use of Death Penalty Information Center statistics concerning the death penalty to show that that extreme form of punishment does not deter crime more than lesser penalties. What about a *Harper's Index* item indicating that the chances of a white teenager arrested on a drug charge being tried in adult court, rather than a juvenile court, are about 1 in 70, while for blacks the chances are 1 in 18? Is the implied conclusion that black teenage offenders are discriminated against compared to whites justified on the basis of this evidence?

*6.   Comment on the following statistic listed in the November 2000 *Harper's Index:*
      Points by which the average SAT score of a home-schooled student exceeds that
      of other United States students—81.[16]

EXERCISE SET 5-2

Determine which fallacies (if any) occur in the following short passages and justify your
answers (as you did when working on Exercise Sets 3-1 and 4-1). (Note again that some
of these passages may also contain fallacies discussed in previous chapters, and some
may not contain fallacious reasoning.)

*1.   In 2014, when asked if he believes homosexuality is a disorder, then-Texas
      governor Rick Perry said the following: "Whether or not you feel compelled to
      follow a particular lifestyle or not, you have the ability to decide not to do that.
      I may have the genetic coding that I'm inclined to be an alcoholic, but I have the
      desire not to do that, and I look at the homosexual issue the same way."

2.   The *New York Times* (January 20, 2005) reported that Germaine Greer, a
      well-known Australian feminist and literary scholar, quit the cast of *Celebrity Big
      Brother,* a British reality show, after only five days. On this program, celebrities
      are confined in a house where they interact with one another while viewers vote
      on who should go or stay. Greer complained that contestants were encouraged
      to bully, living conditions were poor, food was stale, and towels were filthy. Even
      worse, she claimed that they were subjected to "lockdowns" in their bedrooms,
      where they were prohibited from eating, using the bathroom, or sleeping. When
      other contestants refused to join her revolt against *Big Brothers* thought police,
      she quit in disgust and denounced the show as a "fascist prison camp."

3.   From a Bob Schwabach "On Computers" newspaper column: "There aren't
      just a couple of brands [of IBM-compatible computers] for those [very low]
      prices; there are dozens. Do they work? Someone I know has been running one
      continuously for five months, and it's never missed a beat."

4.   During the wars in Afghanistan and Iraq, the U.S. government placed a value on
      human lives that suffered wrongful deaths caused by the U.S. military and made
      "condolence payments" to family members. They did the same for Americans
      killed in al Qaeda attacks on September 11, 2001. Here are some statistics on the
      worth of human life taken from "A Scale for the Price of Life," by Tom Engelhardt
      (*San Francisco Chronicle,* 20 May 2007).

        A civilian killed in Haditha, Iraq, by U.S. Marines: $2,500.
        A civilian killed near Jalalabad, Afghanistan, by U.S. Marines: $2,000.
        A civilian killed by al Qaeda terrorists on September 11: $1.8 million.

---

[16]Starred (*) items are answered in a section at the back of the book.

5. Smoking pot definitely leads to heroin use. A report by the U.S. Commissioner of Narcotics on a study of 2,213 hard-core narcotics addicts in the Lexington (Kentucky) Federal Hospital shows that 70.4 percent smoked marijuana before taking heroin.

6. Senator Ted Cruz in 2013 on some of his fellow Republicans' argument that they needed to fund "Obamacare" despite their misgivings about it: "Look, we saw in Britain, Neville Chamberlain, who told the British people, 'Accept the Nazis. Yes, they'll dominate the continent of Europe, but that's not our problem. Let's appease them. Why? Because it can't be done. We can't possibly stand against them.' And in America there were voices that listened to that. I expect the same pundits who say it can't be done, had it been in the 1940s, we would have listened to them."

7. From a student essay: "It is wrong to criticize advertisers for manipulating people through psychological ploys because that's what makes ads effective."

8. Overheard in a local bar: "You women are wrong to be for censoring pornography, even if it's true, and I'm pretty sure it isn't, that porno stuff makes a few men more likely to rape. Would you want to ban miniskirts, bikini outfits, low-cut dresses, and such—require women to wear Muslim-style outfits—if it's true that scanty clothes make some men more likely to rape?"

9. Donna Brazile, Democratic strategist, had this to say about women in politics (quoted in the *San Francisco Chronicle,* 4 August 2010): "If we had more women in politics this country would be farther ahead—because women are not afraid to ask for directions when they're lost."

10. The president of a college who shall go unnamed here justifying the reduction of salaries for adjunct (part-time) teachers who are paid only 75 percent of the rate paid to full-time staff per course: "I don't see the problem here. No other college in the state pays more than we do."

11. Comment in *Time* article (14 May 2001) by Tom Green, a self-proclaimed fundamentalist Mormon, who was indicted in Utah on four counts of bigamy: "Mormons say polygamy is immoral and wrong, but the church was founded by polygamists. That is hypocrisy."

*12. Bill O'Reilly on "The Age of Anger" (December 14, 2015):

   A new Gallup poll says 16% of Americans now believe terrorism is the most important problem facing the country today. Thirteen percent say dissatisfaction with government. The economy stands at nine percent.
   So you can see that anger and fear are presently driving American politics. Hint: Have a look back at what was in the news in November and December 2015.

13. In a speech at the Naval Postgraduate School in Monterey, California, Albert Gonzales, the president's White House counsel, justified the second President Bush invading Iraq without a congressional declaration of war. When one officer

asked how Bush could legally do this, Gonzales said that we had conducted 100 military actions in the past without a congressional declaration of war; further-more, past presidents often declared war without a congressional declaration.

14. Hendrik Hertzberg, *New Yorker* columnist, had this to say about Fox News in his "Talk of the Town" article, "The Debate Debate," February 13 and 20, 2012:

> *TV journalism's most pathological mutation, Fox News, propagandizes for the Republican right as faithfully, slickly, and humorlessly as Russian state TV does for Vladimir Putin.*

14. Apple, addressing FBI requests to build software to unlock the iPhone of one the San Bernardino killers (recall the ACLU statement quoted earlier on this same controversy): "We have great respect for the professionals at the FBI, and we believe their intentions are good. Up to this point, we have done everything that is both within our power and within the law to help them. But now the U.S. government has asked us for something we simply do not have, and something we consider too dangerous to create. They have asked us to build a backdoor to the iPhone."

James B. Comey, Jr., director of the FBI, responds: "There's already a door on that iPhone. Essentially, we're saying to Apple 'take the vicious guard dog away and let us pick the lock.'"

15. From a student essay: "The U.S. Department of Health states that only 3–5 percent of sexually transmitted diseases in this country are related to prostitution."

16. Paraphrase of part of a letter in a December 1990 "Ann Landers" advice column:

> *My parents didn't give me much guidance about social behavior, morals, or sex. But I read your column—you were one person I learned from. You said not to go for looks and popularity, but to pay attention to "the quiet one in the corner." So about nine years ago, I married an average-looking guy who is a "great father and a good provider," and have been very happy. Thanks very much for your excellent advice.*

17. President Obama, at a town hall meeting in Cannon Falls, Minnesota (August 15, 2011), had this to say about the House Republicans' refusal to compromise on closing the deficit by eliminating some tax loopholes for the wealthy as well as cutting trillions from the budget:

> *It's not that complicated, but it does require everybody being willing to make compromises . . . in my house if I said, you know, Michelle, honey, we got to cut back, so we're going to have you stop shopping completely, you can't buy shoes, you can't buy dresses, but I'm keeping my golf clubs. You know, that wouldn't go over so well.*

*20. A letter to the editor of the *New York Times* (August 6, 2010) argued that since same-sex marriage is "contrary to divine and natural law," it should be forbidden "by human law as well."

21. From Gail Collins, "A Gun on Every Corner," *New York Times* (February 2015):

> *Earlier this month—right between Groundhog Day and Valentine's Day—*
> *Senator John Cornyn of Texas introduced a bill that would allow people from*
> *states with lax gun laws to carry their concealed weapons all around the country.*
> *   The goal, Cornyn said in a press release, is to treat local gun permits "like*
> *drivers' licenses."*
> *   "This operates more or less like a driver's license," he told a reporter for* The
> Hill. *"So, for example, if you have a driver's license in Texas, you can drive in New*
> *York, in Utah, and other places subject to the laws in those states."*
> *   This is perfectly reasonable, except for the part about gun permits being*
> *anything whatsoever like drivers' licenses. If a citizen from Mississippi shows*
> *his driver's license to someone in Connecticut, the Connecticut person has a*
> *good reason to presume that the licensee can, um, drive . . . On the other hand,*
> *a permit to carry a concealed weapon from Mississippi is concrete proof of the*
> *owner's ability to fill out an application.*

22. Comment by Dr. James M. Orient, executive director of the Association of American Physicians and Surgeons, on President Clinton's February 2000 proposed $3,000 fine on tobacco manufacturers for each underage smoker:

> *What's next? Fining auto makers for each speeding driver, nailing Hershey*
> *for every diabetic who eats a candy bar, or gouging McDonald's for all obese*
> *people who order a Big Mac?*

EXERCISE SET 5-3

Here are a few more short passages to be evaluated.

*1. A response to the criticism of the danger of the *Cassini* space mission because it contained 72.3 pounds of plutonium: "Would you decide not to drive a car because you might have an accident and harm others?"

2. From a 2016 *Washington Post* article with the headline "Releasing low-level offenders did not unleash a crime wave in California" (The *Post*'s website stated under this headline that "California's experiment shows that these prison reforms are not dangerous"): "Some fear that reducing sentences for nonviolent crimes and letting low-level offenders back on the streets—key components of prison reform—could produce a new and devastating crime wave. Such dire predictions were common in 2011 when California embarked on a massive experiment in prison downsizing. But five years later, California's experience offers powerful evidence that no such crime wave is likely to occur."

3. When New York mayor Michael Bloomberg announced that New York public schools would use student test scores to evaluate teachers and to help decide which ones would get tenure, the teachers' union fought back, claiming that he put too much emphasis on standardized testing. Bloomberg defended his decision, claiming that banning the use of test scores would be like "saying to

hospitals, 'You can evaluate heart surgeons on any criteria you want—just not patient survival rates!' "

4. Taken from a student's paper (paraphrased):

    The prohibition amendment, which made drinking alcohol illegal early in this century, reduced consumption by 50 percent. When the amendment was repealed, the consumption of alcohol almost tripled. This shows that Americans take the law seriously; when something is illegal, they tend to stay away from it.
        Instructor's comment on the student's paper: "This must be why we have no drug problems today."

5. Missouri representative Todd Akin defended his position on abortion in a television interview when he was asked if he would support abortions on women who were raped. "It seems to me first of all, from what I understand from doctors, that's really rare," he said. "If it's legitimate rape, the female body has ways to try to shut the whole thing down" (KTVI, St. Louis TV station, August 18, 2012).

6. Newspaper Association of America's spokesperson Paul Luthringer (quoted in *Extra!* (September–October 1995), responding to a survey that found only 19 percent of sources quoted or referred to on newspaper front pages were women: "The fact that women are quoted less than men has nothing to do with the state of journalism, but has more to do with who—male or female—is the first to return a reporter's call."

*7. From a *Science News* article:

    [Scientists] produced their map of the vegetation existing 18,000 years ago by sifting through published reports on ancient pollen and other plant remains in sediments from around the world. They then estimated how much carbon dioxide was locked within the plants, soil and peat in specific regions. Continental vegetation and soils contained far less carbon dioxide during the Ice Age than they do today, researchers report.... Carbon storage on the continents totaled 968.1 billion tons 18,000 years ago, compared with 2,319.4 billion tons now, an increase of 140 percent.

8. The *New York Times* (17 June 1988) reported that, when several women's groups protested the Pakistani law that accords the legal testimony of women half the weight of the testimony of men, Qazi Hussain Ahmed, leader of the Islamic party, said, "These laws do not affect women adversely. Our system wants to protect women from unnecessary worry and save them the trouble of appearing in court."

9. Craig Stoll, a San Francisco restaurant owner, defended his decision to prohibit diners from bringing their own wine into his pizzeria. "I don't know why people feel so entitled to bring their own [bottle]. What if you collected fine tablecloths from all over the world and you don't ever cook at home so you want to bring one in to eat off of? It's ridiculous" ("The Taming of the Screw," *San Francisco Chronicle*, 6 April 2006).

*10. Item in *Science 80* (November–December 1979):

> *The chief trouble with the word "superstition" is that it always applies to the beliefs of someone else, not your own. The entire history of science shows that, in varying degrees, much that even the greatest scientists believed to be fact is today either false or else somewhat less than factual, perhaps even superstitious. It follows that what the best scientists today believe to be fact will suffer the same fate.*

11. On a segment of *Your World* (Fox News, January 4, 2008), host Neil Cavuto asked author Marc Rudov why he said that Hillary Clinton's nagging voice was the reason men overwhelmingly picked Barack Obama rather than Clinton in Iowa (at the Democratic caucuses). Rudov replied, "When Barack Obama speaks, men hear, 'Take off for the future.' And when Hillary Clinton speaks, men hear, 'Take out the garbage.'"

12. Rick Santorum had this to say in an interview on the Christian website Caffeinated Thoughts (October 2012): "Many in the Christian faith have said, 'Well, that's O.K. Contraception's O.K.' It's not O.K. because it's a license to do things in the sexual realm that is counter to how things are supposed to be."

13. A letter to the *San Francisco Examiner* from a physician argued that if juries award sums like $10.5 million to plaintiffs who have contracted toxic shock syndrome—even though that disease wasn't known to medical science when the damage took place—perhaps we can now expect lawsuits against pharmaceutical companies and physicians by the relatives of people who died of pneumonia before 1943, on the grounds that as-yet-undiscovered penicillin hadn't been prescribed.

*14. When it was pointed out to Stephen Schneider, a climatologist at Stanford's Institute for International Studies, that he was recommending action now even though he was only 90 percent sure that global warming was occurring because of atmospheric emissions, he replied, "Why do we need 99 percent certainty when nothing else is that certain? If there were only a 5 percent chance the chef slipped some poison in your dessert, would you eat it?"

15. Peter Singer in his book *Animal Liberation:* "The racist violates the principle of equality by giving greater weight to the interests of members of his own race when there is a clash between their interests and the interests of those of another race. The sexist violates the principle of equality by favoring the interests of his own sex. Similarly, the speciesist allows the interests of his own species to override the greater interests of members of another species. The pattern is identical in each case."

16. Former New York City mayor Michael Bloomberg, on the *PBS News Hour* in 2013 defending the NYPD's controversial "stop and frisk" policy after a federal judge ordered significant changes to it:

> *Today, we have the lowest percentage of teenagers carrying guns of any major city across the country, and the possibility of being stopped by—acts as a vital*

deterrent, which is critically important by—a critically important byproduct of stop, question, frisk.

The fact that fewer guns are on the street now shows that our efforts have been successful, and there is just no question that stop, question, frisk has saved countless lives. And we know that most of the lives saved, based on the statistics, have been black and Hispanic young men.

17. Hitler's version of Darwin's theory of evolution by natural selection (from *Mein Kampf*): "No more than Nature desires the mating of weaker and stronger individuals, even less does she desire the blending of a higher with a lower race, since if she did her whole work of higher breeding over perhaps hundreds of thousands of years, might be ruined with one blow."

18. When Sharif el-Gamal, a real estate developer, proposed building an Islamic Center near Ground Zero, the site of the 9/11 attack, Newt Gingrich opposed it (on *Fox and Friends*, August 16, 2010): "We would never accept the Japanese putting up a site next to Pearl Harbor. There is no reason for us to accept a mosque next to the World Trade Center." (Quoted in: Hulse, Carl. "G.O.P. Seizes On Islamic Center Near Ground Zero as Election Issue." *New York Times*, 17 August 2010.)

19. Part of a political column by George Weigel (November 29, 1992), in which he argued against the *Roe v. Wade* Supreme Court decision:

The hard sociological fact is that abortion on demand (the regime established by Roe*) has been the greatest deal for irresponsible or predatory men in American history. Why? Because whatever else is said,* Roe *frees men from responsibility for the sexual conduct they consensually enter.* Roe *is alleged to have empowered women; in fact,* Roe *legally disempowered women from holding men accountable for their sexual behavior where that behavior had unplanned results.*

*20. From an article in the January–February 1994 issue of *Quill* magazine about the claim by Dr. John Pierce (University of California, San Diego) that the Joe Camel cigarette ads were responsible for "a sharp increase in teen smoking":

His study shows that first-time smokers among Californians from the ages of 16 to 18 had steadily declined from 12.5 percent in 1975 to 6.2 percent in 1988, but then began sharply increasing again. Joe Camel, a cool-looking, cartoon-ish character, was introduced as the Camel symbol in 1988. Teenage smoking immediately began increasing by 0.7 percent a year, through 1990. In 1992, Pierce conducted another study that showed Joe Camel was as familiar a character as Mickey Mouse to children as young as six.

The *Quill* article also indicated that because of his research, Dr. Pierce stated that he believes we should ban all tobacco advertising. When asked whether this wasn't censorship contrary to the Constitution's First Amendment, he replied, "There is no free speech [issue] here. The issue is to protect our children from being influenced into an addiction that will cause cancer."

*21. Since the 55-mile-per-hour speed limit was introduced by President Carter, traffic fatalities in the United States have dropped almost in half. So now that the Republican Congress (in 1995) has repealed the 55-mph limit, we can expect traffic fatalities to go back to where they were—almost double what they are now. (*Note:* We now have the advantage of hindsight, since we can find out whether the repeal did or did not go back to where they were or significantly increased. But do this exercise item without resort to later information of this kind. By the way, did traffic fatalities significantly increase?)

22. The late Justice Antonin Scalia: "If we cannot have moral feelings against homosexuality, can we have it against murder? Can we have it against other things?"

*23. Taken from an item in *Extra!* (December 2003):

> *Fox News anchor Brit Hume argued (August 26, 2003) that U.S. soldiers were better off than Californians. "Two hundred seventy-seven U.S. soldiers have now died in Iraq, which means that statistically speaking U.S. soldiers have less of a chance of dying from all causes in Iraq than citizens have of being murdered in California, which is roughly the same geographical size. The most recent statistics indicate California has more than 2,300 homicides each year, which means about 6.6 murders each day. Meanwhile, U.S. troops have been in Iraq for 160 days, which means they're incurring about 1.7 deaths including illness and accidents each day.*

24. Fivethirtyeight.com explaining Bernie Sanders's shocking win over Hillary Clinton in the 2016 Michigan Democratic primary despite polls that showed Clinton with a commanding lead: "Mitchell Research and Communications, which showed a 37 percentage point Clinton lead in a poll conducted Sunday, found that people younger than 50 would make up less than a quarter of all voters; they made up more than half instead. Mitchell was one of the only pollsters in the state to poll using only calls to landlines, and most Americans younger than 45 live in households without landlines."

EXERCISE SET 5-4

*A letter to the editor of *Free Inquiry* (Winter 1999–2000) argues against hanging copies of the Ten Commandments in public schools on the grounds that it may promote church attendance, which may well be harmful. As evidence, the writer cites statistics from two different issues of *Scientific American*. The first (July 1999) notes the percentage of adults in the United States and in European countries who attended church

at least once a month in the 1990s. The second (August 1999) lists the criminal population per hundred thousand behind bars during that period. Evaluate these statistics
and explain why you think they do or don't support the claim that churchgoing may be
harmful.

40 Percent or More Attending Church

Country	Percentage Attending Church	Number in Jail per 100,000
Ireland	88	55
Poland	74	170
U.S.	55	668
Italy	47	85
Canada	40	115
Mean	61	219

Under 20 Percent Attending Church

France	17	95
Norway	13	55
Sweden	11	65
Finland	11	60
Iceland	9	40
Mean	12	63

EXERCISE SET 5-5

Find several fallacy examples of your own, perhaps gleaned from newspapers, websites, magazines, television programs, textbooks (including this one; no one is perfect!),
or what have you, provide a name in each case if you can, and carefully explain why the
passage is fallacious.

MindTap® **Visit MindTap for more readings and resources.**

Psychological Impediments to Cogent Reasoning: Shooting Ourselves in the Foot

> Memory says, "I did that." Pride replies, "I could not have done that." Eventually, memory yields. —NIETZSCHE
>
> Every dogma has its day. —ABRAHAM ROTSTEIN
>
> Think with your head, not your guts. —OLD SAYING
>
> Populus vult decipi. (The people want to be deceived.) —ANCIENT ROMAN SAYING
>
> Nothing is so firmly believed as what we least know. —MONTAIGNE
>
> How strange it is to see with how much passion People see things only in their own fashion. —MOLIÈRE
>
> I wouldn't have seen it if I hadn't believed it. —INSIGHTFUL TAKEOFF ON AN OLD SAYING

MindTap®   Visit MindTap for more readings and resources.

Good reasoning is a matter of character as well as brainpower. If human beings were completely rational animals, learning how to reason well would be a relatively easy task. We would simply learn which patterns of reasoning are good and which bad, and then make all of our reasoning conform to good patterns while avoiding the bad. Even if we started out with poor background beliefs, repeated use of valid deductive and inductive inferences, based on all of what we have experienced so far, would soon set things straight.

Unfortunately, human beings are not completely rational, although rationality is an important part of our makeup. This chapter is concerned with that other part of human nature—the nonrational, emotional component that prevents us from being perfect reasoners. While no one can completely eliminate these non-rational impediments to cogent reasoning, any more than a leopard can change its spots, understanding how they work can help us to reduce the harm they do to our attempts at genuinely rational thought.

1. Loyalty, Provincialism, and The Herd Instinct

Throughout history, individual chances for success at most things—getting enough food, attracting and holding a mate, successfully raising children—have depended on two fundamental factors. The first is the success of the groups we belong to in their competitions with other groups. Members of primary in-groups (nations, tribes, cultures) defeated by competing out-groups generally suffer serious harm to their chances of having a good life or any life at all. That is why we all feel a tug of **loyalty** to our own in-group; a society that has too many disloyal people has little chance against other, more cohesive groups. (Note, however, that the strength of this tug differs greatly from person to person.)

But being a member of a successful in-group is of little value if others in the group do not allow us reasonable chances for success in whatever it is we want to do. That is an important reason why we all are so anxious to get along with the other members of the groups to which we are loyal. The person who is completely out of step with everyone else is not likely to be successful, even if the group as a whole thrives and multiplies.[1] Enter the **herd instinct** that tends to keep our beliefs, and thus our actions, within the bounds of what society as a whole will accept. Finding ourselves in a culture in which everyone covers certain parts of the body, we feel uncomfortable leaving those parts naked. Those belonging to Muslim or Orthodox Jewish groups find eating any part of the pig abhorrent. In Western societies, virtually everyone avoids eating the meat of horses and dogs. In China, while it is not regularly consumed by the majority of the country, dog meat is the featured cuisine at an annual festival in the town of Yulin and enjoyed as a delicacy in other areas.

Of course, there is no harm in feeling embarrassed if caught in public with the wrong attire or in finding shellfish repugnant. But the herd instinct sometimes leads people to do horrendous things, as they do when mobs carry out vigilante "justice" or when whole nations acquiesce to unfair practices. Refraining from eating the flesh of the cow, as Hindus do, is one thing; branding some of one's compatriots as "untouchables" is another.

---

[1]For more on this way of looking at the human repertoire, see: Kahane, Howard. *Contract Ethics: Evolutionary Biology and the Moral Sentiments.* Lanham, Md.: Rowman & Littlefield, 1995; and Wilson, James Q. *The Moral Sense.* New York: Free Press, 1993.

The point is that it is part of human nature to find it easy and natural to believe what everyone else in our society believes, and to find it foolish to believe what others find foolish. This is no doubt one reason for what sociologists call **culture lag**, the tendency of practices and beliefs to persist long after whatever conditions made them useful or sensible have disappeared.

We all desire to have at least a minimal status in the groups to which we belong, for the reasons just mentioned. But the higher our status, the better our chances. That's why most of us have such a strong desire to make a better than minimally good appearance when in public. We want to look intelligent, informed, and decisive—to shine compared to others. And that is why, for instance, millions of Americans who had never heard of Osama bin Laden before the devastating terrorist attack on the World Trade Center, who had no idea what the Taliban was until it gave refuge to bin Laden, and who knew next to nothing about Islam and the Muslim religion, let alone the meaning of *jihad,* formed almost instant opinions on the invasion of Afghanistan and later Iraq. After the two-pronged war began, newspapers across the country were filled with letters to editors expressing demands for this action or that. The need to be in the swim, to talk "intelligently" about topics of the day, leads us to form and broadcast these quick opinions based on superficial evidence. And once we have pronounced them, the need to avoid appearing to have been wrong in public leads us to hang onto those beliefs, often in the face of conflicting evidence. Results from a Fairleigh Dickinson University poll conducted in 2014 (!) found that: "overall, 42 percent of Americans believe that U.S. forces found active weapons of [a] mass destruction program in Iraq." We can only guess that such a pervasive error results from a combination of the widespread belief prior to and during the war that the United States *would* find such weapons and the fact that we tend to be extraordinarily—and sometimes absurdly—reluctant to admit mistakes. All too often, we would rather continue to *be* wrong than own up to having *been* wrong. The underlying psychological mechanism at work here is the desire to gain, and retain, the status in the eyes of others in our group that is vital to success in everyday life.[2]

> Man is a social animal; only in the herd is he happy. It is all one to him whether it is the profoundest nonsense or the greatest villainy—he feels completely at ease with it—so long as it is the view of the herd, and he is able to join the herd.
>
> —SØREN KIERKEGAARD

It also should be noted that hardly any of the large societies common in today's world are completely cohesive. Nations such as the United States, Canada, India, China, and Russia are composed of all sorts of diverse subgroups, the United States being one of the two most diverse cultures in history. (The other was the Soviet Union before its

---

[2]Erving Goffman's fascinating book *The Presentation of Self in Everyday Life* (New York: Doubleday, 1959; Penguin, 1969) still is an excellent source of information on these matters.

disintegration.) Most people are completely loyal to their own nation but also have a special interest in the fates of subgroups. They therefore tend to see things not just from the point of view of the mainstream culture, but also from that of smaller groups within the primary culture. We see the results of this in current political rhetoric designed to appeal to "special interest" groups such as religious fundamentalists, African Americans, Latinos, Jews, and so on. (Note, by the way, that we all have a very special interest in the welfare of members of our own families.)

Provincialism stems in large part from this natural tendency to identify with the ideas, interests, and kinds of behavior favored by those in groups with which we identify. Think of the polls in the 2008 presidential primaries that showed men favoring Barack Obama and women favoring Hillary Clinton until well into the primaries. And in 2016 Donald Trump won largely by virtue of his advantage among white male voters. More locally, consider the beliefs and attitudes you share with your own family and friends. These are undoubtedly issues on which you disagree, but more likely than not you agree on much more than you disagree. Now some of this comes from having shared interests and from selecting friends with whom you already agree. But provincialism surely plays a role as well.

Of particular importance, though, is the fact that we tend to see things from the point of view and interests of our primary culture—our primary in-group—especially when there is conflict with other groups. The result is a kind of belief provincialism operating at various levels—leading Americans, for example, to pay relatively little attention to what happens to the peoples of the rest of the world and to misconstrue what is happening there. That is why, although the United States was founded on the principles of democracy and fair play, a great many Americans have failed to notice that since World War II, the U.S. government has helped to overturn several democratically elected governments around the world (for instance, in Chile) and attempted to murder Cuba's Fidel Castro. It is difficult to swallow unpleasant truths when loyalty and the herd instinct reinforce what others in our group vehemently assert, and when provincialism narrows our range of interests and tends to make us see everything in terms of the interests of our own primary group.

2. Prejudice, Stereotypes, Scapegoats, and Partisan Mind-Sets

Loyalty and provincialism often lead to **prejudice**, including prejudice against all or almost all members of other groups, and to thinking in terms of unverified **stereotypes** that support prejudicial beliefs. But being prejudiced against others is quite different from simply having a bad opinion of them. We are prejudiced only when our nasty beliefs about others are not justified by sufficient evidence. So prejudice can be defined as thinking ill of others without sufficient warrant.

African Americans in particular have been the victims of prejudice in this country, flagrantly before the civil rights movement, but after that in more devious ways. Racial slurs were masked in code phrases like "welfare mothers" or "crime in the streets" or "states' rights." Over time, these covert references were driven underground by politically correct attitudes that put the lid on anyone who "played the race card," but political correctness also tended to dampen healthy discussions about race. It wasn't until Barack Obama ran in the 2008 presidential primaries that robust discussions of prejudice and race returned to the public forum—and, sadly, so did racial slurs. Obama himself was dubbed the "food stamp president" by Newt Gingrich in the 2012 Republican primaries. This kind of sour rhetoric has hardly gone away since. Congressman Mo Brooks offered this in August 2014: "Well, this is a part of the war on whites that's being launched by the Democratic Party. And the way in which they're launching this war is by claiming that whites hate everybody else. It's part of the strategy that Barack Obama implemented in 2008, continued in 2012, where he divides us all on race, on sex, greed, envy, class warfare, all those kinds of things." Set aside for the moment the prima facie absurdity of Congressman Brooks's claims here. Why do you think he made them? What might he gain from saying things like this?

Prejudicial attitudes often lead to stereotypical thinking that involves attributing certain oversimplified characteristics, often negative, to a specific group of people. Of course, no group of any size is composed of people who resemble one another as do peas in a pod, so it is foolish to be prejudiced against every member of such a group. It's just silly to think that the French all are great lovers, that all Jews and Scots are unusually frugal, or that all women are more emotional than men. It *is* true, though, that people in a given large social group generally are different in many ways from those in other groups. The French as a group are modestly different from Germans, as are Iranians from Pakistanis, something anyone can notice simply by going from one of these countries to the other. The trouble with stereotypical thinking is rather that, even when accurate with respect to groups as a whole (and they often are not), it fails to take account of the differences among individual members.

> Ignorance—that is to say, fear of the unknown—is the source of the most invidious prejudice.
>
> —JUSTICE JOHN PAUL STEVENS

During the 2008 presidential primaries, Hillary Clinton was a lightning rod for stereotypical and sexist comments about women. Her positions on the issues were often drowned out by media hype on her appearance and her emotional control (or lack thereof). At various times, she was criticized for having thick ankles, wearing pants suits, styling her hair like a helmet, and—showing cleavage. If tears came to her eyes (which happened once), she was a weak sister; if she remained controlled, she was an ice princess. Contrast that brief, tearful show of emotion to John Boehner's frequent bouts of weeping in public over everything from funding Iraq troops to celebrating the Republican Party's victory in 2008. When that election won him the position of Speaker of the House, much was made of his crying, but never once was this seen as a sign of weakness. This curious reversal of the stereotype that tough men don't cry reflects a welcome change in attitude that allows men to express emotion, but no such latitude is given to women in public office. Imagine the reaction if Nancy Pelosi had burst into public tears just once when she was Speaker of the House.

Women in high position regularly face sexist scrutiny. When Elena Kagan was up for confirmation to the Supreme Court, the media commented on her dress and mannerisms in ways never directed at male justices. Like most professional women, Kagan had to appear highly qualified but not too masculine; well dressed, but not too feminine. A fashion columnist in the *Washington Post* had this to say about her appearance:[3] her "dowdy" style was "unabashedly conservative," with a "generous sprinkling of frumpiness"—all of which "made her so much older." As far as body language goes, she sat "hunched over," with "her legs ajar," and in fact never seemed to cross her legs at all. The column noted that although Kagan knew the cameras were on her, she didn't seem to care. She was just "intent on being comfortable"—which is damning with faint praise. No male Supreme Court nominee was ever subjected to this kind of sexist scrutiny. An ironic footnote: an article in the same edition was titled "Does the *Post* Treat Women Badly."

Now surely, attitudes have changed since the 2008 election, right? Well, no. One hardly knows where to begin in the craziness of the 2016 election cycle. One presidential candidate sends a tweet comparing his wife to the wife of a rival on their attractiveness. Another candidate retweets a claim that a reporter is a "bimbo." And another candidate had something negative to say about the appearances of all of his female opponents, and said of one that "all she's got is the woman card." (Okay, okay, that was all the same candidate.)

One of the most widely stereotyped groups, particularly in this country, is teenagers. Consider this quote: "Our youth now love luxury. They have bad manners, contempt for authority; they show disrespect for their elders, and love to chatter in places of exercise. They no longer rise when elders enter the room. They contradict their parents, chatter before company, gobble food, and tyrannize their teacher." And who is responsible for that rant against teens? None other than Socrates, that wise old philosopher, though whether he actually said it is debatable. Nonetheless, it reminds us that teenagers have had a bad rep throughout the ages and are stereotyped today much as they were in the fifth century BCE. Yet most people, even parents of teens, know that the great majority of young people are reasonably well-behaved, polite, and respectful of their elders.

The flip side of prejudice and intolerance directed against members of other groups is overtolerance of—even blindness to—the defects and foibles of our own group and its members. Loyalty tends to make us see our own leaders as a good deal more intelligent, informed, and honest than in fact they are (or than it would be reasonable to expect the leaders of any society to be) and to regard the general run of our compatriots as better on average than the people in other societies. People are particularly prone to loyalty to the government in times of war, as was evident during the early months

---

[3]See: Givhan, Robin. "Elena Kagan's Artful Plumage: D.C. Frump," *Washington Post,* 23 May 2010.

of the war in Iraq, when the media were so uniformly patriotic that it was considered taboo for journalists to break ranks and criticize the government—this, despite the fact that unprecedented protests were occurring throughout the world. (More discussion on this is in Chapter 11.) Clear thinkers need to overcome this reverse prejudice in favor of people in their own in-groups, especially of in-group leaders (an important reason for the inclusion in this text of so many examples illustrating the clay feet of quite a few elected officials).

Prejudice against members of other groups, particularly of minorities within a larger culture, often is reinforced by the need to find scapegoats—others we can blame for the ills of the world—when in fact we ourselves may bear a large measure of responsibility. That a group being trashed cannot possibly have produced the troubles it is charged with rarely makes a difference.

The classic scapegoat in the Christian world has always been the Jews. In days of old, when Christian theology was interpreted to say that lending money at interest constituted the sin of usury, Jews therefore became important moneylenders. Blaming them for calamities then sometimes had the practical motive of serving as an excuse for the repudiation of outstanding loans. But at most times, the primary point of anti-Semitism has been simply to place the blame for ills elsewhere.

Everyone nowadays is familiar with the way in which the Nazis used the Jews as scapegoats, and with their attempt to exterminate all European Jews. So it might be supposed that picking on the Jews would have little appeal these days. Yet anti-Semitism is still very common in many places. In Russia, to take one example, Jews are commonly held responsible for the ills produced by 70 years of Soviet communism. (The thin thread of truth behind this ridiculous idea—note that Stalin was not Jewish—is that a very few of the high officials in the Communist Party and in the Soviet government were Jews.) In other Eastern European countries, Jews were similarly often held responsible for the problems generated by Soviet domination. This was true even in Poland, where only about 10,000 out of more than 3 million Jews survived the German attempt at genocide and still resided in Poland.

One might suppose that the murder of millions of Jews in Europe during World War II, and the still existing anti-Semitism just described, would make Jews, of all people, the least likely to relegate others to second-class citizenship. And yet in Israel, the first primarily Jewish state in about 2,000 years, Israeli Arabs do not have the same status as Israeli Jews, and Arab lands in the West Bank have been taken from them and given to Jewish "settlers." Not that the Arabs have been paragons of virtue—think only of the stated objective of several Arab and other Islamic countries to destroy Israel.

And then there are the genocidal conflicts going on in Africa, the mass destruction and murder in the former Yugoslavia, hostilities between Hindus and Muslims in India, the savage revenge killings between Shiites and Sunnis in Muslim countries, and so on. In every case, those on both sides in these ethnic battles feel justified in their vindictive hatred and prejudice against the "enemy."

Prejudice and scapegoating, of course, also occur in the United States. As usual, small or less powerful groups tend to be the ones picked on, including people of African or Asian descent, Latinos, Native Americans (American Indians), and, naturally, Jews. Since the attack on the World Trade Center, an irrational prejudice against Middle

Easterners has sprung up in this country. Yet almost all Middle Easterners in the United States are peaceful, productive members of society who are just as horrified at the terrorist attacks as everyone else. Only a handful are involved in terrorist activities, as are a handful of whites. Why, we must ask ourselves, has the social status (and indeed for many the civil liberties) of people who look like Mohamed Atta (a ringleader of the 9/11 attacks) changed since 2001 when there was no such change for people who look like Timothy McVeigh after the Oklahoma City bombing in 1995?

Increasingly, we have been scapegoating immigrants, particularly Latinos. They are blamed for taking jobs from Americans, draining our education and medical resources, and posing the threat of terrorism. Anti-immigration sentiment is highest in areas where unemployment is at its worst, and people look for someone else to blame when faced with job losses and higher costs of living. Some politicians have been so riled up over the issue that they have introduced legislation to end the Fourteenth Amendment's guarantee of citizenship to children of unauthorized immigrants. Senator Lindsey Graham had this to say about it. "People come here to have babies. They come here to drop a child, it's called 'drop and leave' " (*Fox News*, July 28, 2010). The fear is that these "anchor babies" go back to their country only temporarily. Once grown, they will legally return to the United States for their education and bring the rest of their family with them. Yet PolitiFact (August 6, 2010) finds nothing in immigration research that supports the notion of "drop and leave." Rather, all the data suggest that people come here to work.[4] The loaded language used to describe these immigrants is designed to inflame and mislead the public.

Scapegoating immigrants has a long history in this country, as it has in most countries, for that matter. When a wave of Irish immigrated to the United States during the potato famine in the 1840s, they were stereotyped as dirty, ignorant, alcoholic, and violent, and were blamed for society's ills. The same thing happened to the Poles when a million and half swamped Ellis Island in the early twentieth century. That's when Polish jokes started making them out to be stupid, lazy, and inferior. It is a sad tendency of human nature that people tend to move blame and responsibility away from themselves and project it onto others by vilifying and blaming them for things they didn't do.

Some instances of scapegoating would be hilarious for their absurdity were they not so awful in their sentiment. Days after the 9/11 terrorist attacks, Jerry Falwell appeared on Pat Robertson's *700 Club* television show. Keep in mind that these were both religious figures with huge and devout followings. Falwell said of the attacks that "the pagans and the abortionists and the feminists and the gays and the lesbians who are actively trying to make that an alternative lifestyle, the ACLU, People for the American Way—all of them who have tried to secularize America . . . I point the finger in their face and say 'you helped this happen.' "

"Well, I totally concur," Robertson said in reply.

We're not sure a more ridiculous example could be found, but rabbi Yehuda Levin did his best to provide a few when he blamed a massively destructive earthquake in Haiti on high rates of HIV and AIDS in that country and blamed a very minor earthquake in

---

[4]See: Hollar, Julie. "Time to 'Drop and Leave' Loaded Language." *Extra!* March 2011.

Virginia on gay people. It seems that people living with AIDS in Haiti are just better at creating earthquakes than homosexuals in Virginia.

At this point, having discussed both the irrationality and unfortunate effectiveness of scapegoating for political gain, we have to talk once again about Donald Trump's run for president in 2016. Muslims, Mexicans, African Americans, the media, the Republican establishment, political correctness, Hillary Clinton, President Obama, and whatever and whoever else his campaign thought was easy to attack became the things that were causing all the ills of the world and difficulties in voters' lives. The really disturbing thing about this sort of ploy is just how well it works. Faced with fears about vastly complicated issues like the economy, public safety, and national security, people find a kind of comfort in the simplicity of scapegoating and the easiness of anger. And, as we've suggested, the chief psychological benefit to scapegoating may be that blaming someone else—even irrationally—means that we don't have to wonder or worry about our own behavior and complicity in bringing about our current condition.

We should point out that no one is immune from this tendency. There would be a terrible irony in patting ourselves on the back for not scapegoating while blaming the Jerry Falwells and Donald Trumps of the world for perpetuating its scourge.

Thinking in terms of unverified stereotypes and scapegoats often results from a **partisan mind-set** that leads people to perceive evidence and to judge arguments via an "us against them" or a "my right view against your wrong view" attitude. We all are tempted to arrange facts to fit our side of an issue and tend to be blind to the import of evidence supporting any other side. Good reasoners fight this tendency in all of us to favor ideas already held and see our side automatically as right and the other guy's as wrong. Those with a partisan mind-set give in to this all-too-human tendency, generally without being aware that they have done so. This is true, for example, of some individuals who are vigorously engaged in the social or political arenas. That is why it can be so maddening to discuss touchy issues with some very committed people—they tend to be deaf to counter-evidence and counterarguments. (Another reason, of course, is that we ourselves may be "hearing impaired" when it comes to the reasons and arguments of others.)

The partisan mind-set is on full display when politicians suddenly change their minds about a particular tactic or policy depending on who happens to be in office. In 1992, then-Senator Joe Biden argued that Republican president George H. W. Bush should not nominate a Supreme Court justice in the final year of his term. This position became uncomfortable in 2016 when *Vice President* Biden had to defend his own Democratic administration attempting to fill an empty seat in an election year. Similarly, allegedly principled arguments against the filibuster—a delaying tactic used by parties in the minority to prevent a particular vote from being held—come from the majority party, whichever that happens to be at the time. Now it could be that the parties simply change their minds, but then we have to ask why they did so. What changed for them other than the party in office?

A really good critical reasoner has a mind-set that is completely different from those who see everything from a partisan point of view. This does not mean that good reasoners lack a sense of loyalty! It means simply that they have an open mind rather than a mind that sees everything from the point of view that "our side always is right and the other side always wrong"—a mind open to the truth, wherever it may lie.

Mass Shooting   Terrorism

Forensics experts are hard at work
trying to determine the difference.

POLITICS.—

Tom Toles by Tom Toles

3. Superstitious Beliefs

Superstitions may not have quite the detrimental effects of prejudice and stereotyping, but they are no more helpful or rational. It is true, though, that superstitions often are based on some small scrap of evidence or other. Bad things obviously do occasionally happen after a mirror is broken. Coincidences do happen. And even newspaper astrology columns are moderately accurate once every blue moon. But so too is a broken clock right twice a day, and we wouldn't ever rely on such a clock or keep it hanging on the wall.

The difference between superstitious and sensible beliefs is that sensible beliefs are based on sufficient evidence that justifies those beliefs, not on carefully chosen scraps of support. Superstitious beliefs are generally based on biased evidence or on small or unrepresentative samples (discussed in Chapter 5)—evidence from which all negative cases have been removed. Bad things do happen on Friday the 13th, but so do lots of good things. And bad things happen on other days also, so that there is nothing remarkable about the fact that they happen on Friday the 13th. Superstitious people ignore facts of this sort and pay attention just to the evidence supporting their superstitious convictions.

The odd thing about superstitious beliefs is that their complete irrationality doesn't seem to stop even the most brilliant people from having them. Chess grand masters, for example, display amazing intelligence and insight when playing that great intellectual game, not to mention incredible memories. In the 2010 world chess championship match, for instance, grandmaster Veselin Topalov was so spooked out about playing a tiebreaker on May 13 with world champion "Vishy" Anand that he wound up losing the match the day before instead of going into overtime. Apparently he had lost a championship match on the 13th to Vladmir Kamik in 2006, and to avoid a tiebreaker on the 13th in 2010, he wound up playing an erratic final game on the 12th, losing what would have been the tie game. "I just didn't want to play on the 13th," he said, thus neatly combining a superstition with a rationalization. But the number 13 is not bad luck for every one. It was a lucky number for former world chess champ Garry Kasparov, who was born on April 13 (well, he was an Aries, so that explains his great ability) and he was the 13th world chess champion. Where is the logic in this logic-driven game?

4. Wishful Thinking and Self-Deception

As we have just seen, loyalty, prejudice, stereotypical thinking, the herd instinct, and superstition tend to give us beliefs that do not square with reality. Beliefs acquired in these nonrational ways often result from **wishful thinking**—believing what we would like to be true, often despite overwhelming evidence to the contrary—or from **self-deception**—consciously believing what at a deeper level we know to be dubious. It is a very human trait indeed to believe that which we would like to be true and to deny those things we find unpalatable (or, as in the case of our own eventual death, extremely hard to accept).

An extreme example in literature is Jay Gatsby's idealization of Daisy Buchanan in *The Great Gatsby* by F. Scott Fitzgerald. Gatsby persists in deceiving himself about her character despite mounting evidence that she not only is self-centered, irresponsible, and fickle, but also has let him take the blame for a crime she has committed. His self-deception is so great it could be called a **delusion**—one that leads tragically to his own death. Gatsby's adoration of Daisy is an exaggerated example of what many people feel in the early stages of love. We commonly indulge in wishful thinking about our lovers and deceive ourselves about their imperfections despite evidence to the contrary (hopefully imperfections of much less magnitude than Daisy's).

When the stakes are high, we have a natural tendency to deceive ourselves rather than face reality. This tendency is just as prevalent in world leaders as it is in the average person. A classic case is British prime minister Neville Chamberlain's decision to sign an agreement with Hitler in 1938 to achieve, in his words, "peace in our time." Chamberlain was so conscious of the horror another world war would bring, and so desperately anxious to spare his nation and the civilized world from such a disaster, that his judgment was destroyed, and he failed to see Hitler's intent in spite of all sorts of evidence that many others, including Winston Churchill, perceived for what it was.[5]

---

[5]In fairness to Chamberlain, note that a very few historians claim, on rather sparse evidence, that Chamberlain knew chances for peace were not great and wanted to gain time for Britain to rearm.

In more recent times, a few weeks after the Iraq War began in 2003, President Bush announced the end of major conflict in Iraq under the now infamous banner "Mission Accomplished." Well, eight years later when the war finally wound down, it wasn't hard to peg that one as wishful thinking. A lesser-known pronouncement made at the same time by Donald Rumsfeld, then secretary of defense, was that major conflict was at an end in Afghanistan as well. (Ho Ho Ho.)

Sometimes the stakes are so high that a world leader goes off the deep end, as was the case with the delusional Muammar Qaddafi, deposed Libyan dictator. In the midst of the Libyan insurgency of 2011, when rebels were pulling down posters of Qaddafi and putting up their own flag, reporters tried to get him to concede that the people had gone to the streets to protest.[6]

His reply? "They are not against us. No one is against us . . . They love me. All my people are with me, they love me all. They will die to protect me, my people." When a reporter asked him why, then, the rebels who captured Benghazi said they were against him, he said, "It's al-Qaeda. It's not my people," and then went on to blame the uprising on the hallucinogenic drugs that Osama bin Laden had given his people! And so Qaddafi, once a master of doublespeak, rambled into la-la-land, defending his delusions to the end. Fortunately, our self-deceptions tend to result in less global evils, although they still may have catastrophic consequences for ourselves or friends. Think of the large number of people who drink and then drive. Or consider the significant percentage of adults in every industrial country who still smoke cigarettes or chew tobacco in the face of over-whelming evidence linking tobacco to all sorts of fatal illnesses, including heart disease, various kinds of cancer, and emphysema. Millions of people everywhere continue to puff or chew away, undeterred even by warning labels on tobacco products like this one:

> SURGEON GENERAL'S WARNING: Smoking Causes Lung Cancer, Heart Disease, Emphysema, and May Complicate Pregnancy.

In Chapter 4, we presented the first of four "causes of the utterance of fallacies" that Jeremy Bentham described in his famous book The Handbook of Political Fallacies. *Here is an excerpt from the second of the four, which happens to be relevant to the topics discussed in this chapter:*

Second Cause: Interest-Begotten Prejudice

If every act of the will and hence every act of the hand is produced by interest, that is, by a motive of one sort or another, the same must be true, directly or indirectly,

---

[6]From an interview given by Qaddafi to BBC Middle East editor Jeremy Bowen and ABC's Christiane Amanpour, 1 March 2011.

of every act of the intellectual faculty, although the influence of interest upon the latter is neither as direct or as perceptible as that upon the will.

But how, it may be asked, is it possible that the motive by which a man is actuated can be secret to himself? Nothing, actually, is easier; nothing is more frequent. Indeed, the rare case is not that of a man's not knowing, but that of his knowing. . . .

By interest, a man is continually prompted to make himself as correctly and completely acquainted as possible with the springs of action which determine the conduct of those upon whom he is more or less dependent for the comfort of his life. But by interest he is at the same time diverted from any close examination into the springs by which his own conduct is determined. From such knowledge he would be more likely to find mortification than satisfaction.

When he looks at other men, he finds mentioned as a matter of praise the prevalence of . . . social motives. . . . It is by the supposed prevalence of these amiable motives that he finds reputation raised, and that respect and goodwill enhanced to which every man is obliged to look for so large a proportion of the comforts of his life. . . .

But the more closely he looks into the mechanism of his own mind, the less able he is to refer any of the mass of effects produced there to any of these amiable and delightful causes. He finds nothing, therefore, to attract him towards this self-study; he finds much to repel him from it. . . .

Perhaps he is a man in whom a large proportion of the self-regarding motives may be mixed with a slight tincture of the social motives operating upon the private scale. In that case, what will he do? In investigating the source of a given action, he will in the first instance set down the whole of it to the account of the amiable and conciliatory motives, in a word, the social ones. This, in any study of his own mental physiology, will always be his first step; and it will commonly be his last also. Why should he look any further? Why take in hand the painful probe? Why undeceive himself, and substitute the whole truth, which would mortify him, for a half-truth which flatters him?

5. Rationalization and Procrastination

Perhaps the most common form of self-deception is **rationalization**. We engage in this kind of psychological ploy when we ignore or deny unpleasant evidence so as to feel justified in doing what we want to do or in believing what we find comfortable to believe. Rationalization is nicely illustrated by the old joke about the psychiatrist and a delusional patient who believes he is dead. To prove to the patient that he is alive, the psychiatrist first gets him to agree that dead men don't bleed and then makes a cut in the man's arm, which, of course, bleeds. Smiling, the psychiatrist tilts his chair back and waits. "Well," says the dismayed patient, "I guess I was wrong. Dead men do bleed." He thus manages to sustain his delusion by rationalizing away undeniable proof to the contrary.

Another example, from the play *Cabaret:* a credulous German is reading the latest Nazi propaganda. Scowling, he says, "The Jews own all the banks. And they're behind an international communist conspiracy too." Whereupon his clearer-thinking companion observes, "But bankers are capitalists and communists are opposed to capitalism. How can Jews be both?" The first man pauses, then nods knowingly and rationalizes: "They're very crafty."

Rationalization is often used to justify an act that violates one's personal code. In a revealing study of prison staff who worked on execution teams, a group of Stanford psychologists found that team members were more likely to disengage themselves morally from executing criminals than prison guards not on the team.[7] The "executioners" were more inclined to dehumanize inmates on death row, to claim that they were a threat to society ("they can escape and kill again"), and to cite the financial burden on society of life imprisonments. Such rationalizations (buttressed by suppression and denial) let them slide out of taking moral responsibility.

And then there are media rationalizations, like the ones Nancy Grace and a CNN spokeswoman came up with after they aired a grueling interview with a mother who committed suicide not long after appearing on Grace's talk show. In it, Grace badgered the woman about the disappearance of her 2-year-old son, demanding that she disclose her whereabouts at the time her son went missing. The woman, a suspect in the case, stumbled over her words, groping for answers, as Grace pressed her for a confession. At the bottom of the screen, a text box appeared noting "Since show taping, body [of the mother was] found at grandparent's home." When a viewer called to ask if Grace thought she had pushed the woman over the edge, she replied that her show wasn't to blame for what happened. "The truth is not always nice or polite or easy to go down. Sometimes it's harsh and it hurts." Well, that's one way of rationalizing the effect of a brutal attack. A CNN spokeswoman justified the broadcast, saying that they decided to air the interview just hours after the suicide with the idea that it would continue to draw attention to the case in the hope of helping to find the missing 2-year-old. Right. So CNN was actually helping the police investigation—not rationalizing a sleazy attempt to sensationalize a tragic event.[8]

Rationalization often leads to procrastination—to putting off for tomorrow what common sense tells us needs to be done today. Young smokers often tell themselves that they'll quit a few years down the pike before any serious harm is done; students are famous for delaying work on term papers until the day before they're due. (Recall the old song about how "*Mañana* is good enough for me" and the Spanish saying *Mañana será otro día,* "Tomorrow will be another day.") It is an all-too-human tendency to favor immediate gratification at the risk of possible long-term harm. In general, the more likely or more serious the long-term harm, the less likely that an intelligent person will

---

[7]See more on this study in: Carey, Benedict. "When Death Is on the Docket, the Moral Compass Waivers." *New York Times,* 7 February 2006.

[8]From: Nevius, C. W. "CNN Talk Show Reaches a New Depth of Sleaze." *San Francisco Chronicle,* 15 September 2006. An unfortunate update: the boy remained missing as of 2014.

choose immediate gratification. The trouble is that most of us tend to weigh long-term harms or losses too lightly when compared with short-term gains.

Sometimes these types of self-deception affect an entire nation. When Thomas Jefferson wrote the line "all men are created equal" in the Declaration of Independence, apparently he didn't mean all men: he meant all property-owning men, and that certainly didn't include African Americans (let alone women). Nonetheless, he did not think slaves should be considered property and believed that slavery was morally at odds with the principles of the American Revolution. Yet he rationalized owning slaves himself (200, more or less, at any given time), selling them off when he needed the money, and freeing only a handful at his death. Jefferson was a complicated man who seemed able to hold two opposing ideas in his mind yet remain enough in denial of the moral contradictions not to worry too much. And so he procrastinated raising the issue of freeing the slaves, partly out of ambivalence and partly out of the very real opposition from the South, where slavery was endemic and fiercely defended. Eventually he said it was up to the next generation to free the slaves.[9]

The unwillingness of human beings to face unpleasant reality often is revealed strikingly in important works of fiction. In his novel *Heart of Darkness,* for example, Joseph Conrad describes the way in which Europeans who invaded Africa in the nineteenth century rationalized their exploitation and degradation of native populations. He thus chronicled a case of self-deception and rationalization engaged in by a whole group of people over an extended period of time. In his novel, set in the Belgian Congo at the turn of the century, European invaders claim that their aim is to enlighten and civilize the African natives—to "wean those ignorant millions from their horrid ways." But it becomes evident as the story develops that the colonial traders have only one mission— to plunder the land for ivory.

Although a work of fiction, *Heart of Darkness* was based on the true conditions that existed in the Belgian Congo at the turn of the century. In 1876, when the Belgians began their colonization of the Congo, their monarch, King Leopold, who literally took personal ownership of the Congo, described his intent as "to open to civilization the only part of our globe where Christianity has not yet penetrated and to pierce the darkness which envelops the entire population." But in fact, the king was a tyrant; the colonials, profiteers; and the Congolese, virtual slaves. When news of the atrocities committed against African natives reached Europe, a vague uneasiness rippled across the continent, but Europeans managed to deal with these reports by rationalization. If the natives rebelled, the sentries had to defend themselves, didn't they? Weren't some natives bound to die in the civilizing process in any case? Et cetera.

In *Heart of Darkness,* Conrad punctured European rationalizations about what they were doing in Africa in a graphic way by concentrating on a few characters whose development revealed the underlying truth that the European claim to be bringing civilization to the Africans was a smokescreen whose consequence (and unconscious intent?) was not to deceive the natives, but rather to deceive the Europeans themselves.

---

[9]For more on Jefferson's attitudes on slavery, see *American Sphinx,* an excellent, engaging biography of this complex man, by Joseph Ellis (New York: Alfred A. Knopf, 1997).

Here is a short excerpt from Jane Austen's celebrated novel Sense and Sensibility *that nicely reveals a kind of rationalization all too common in real life. The excerpt (from Chapter 2) starts with John Dashwood explaining to his wife Fanny why he intends to give his stepmother and half-sisters £3,000 (about $300,000 in present U.S. currency) from his very comfortable inheritance:*

Rationalization at Its Best (That Is, Worst)

"It was my father's last request to me, . . . that I should assist his widow and daughters."

"He did not know what he was talking of, I dare say; ten to one but he was light-headed at the time. Had he been in his right senses, he could not have thought of such a thing as begging you to give away half your fortune from your child. . . ." [In fact, it was very much less.]

"He did not stipulate any particular sum, my dear Fanny; he only requested me, in general terms, to assist them, and make their situation more comfortable than it was in his power to do. . . ."

"Well, then, *let* something be done for them; but *that* something need not be three thousand pounds. . . . [W]hen the money is once parted with, it never can return. Your sisters will marry, and it will be gone forever. If, indeed, it could ever be restored to our poor little boy—"

"Perhaps then, it would be better for all parties if the sum were diminished by one half—five hundred pounds [each] would be a prodigious increase in their fortunes!"

"Oh! beyond anything great! What brother on earth would do half so much for his sisters, even if *really* his sisters! And as it is—only half blood! . . ."

". . . As it is, without any addition of mine, they will each have above three thousand pounds on their mother's death—a very comfortable fortune for any young woman."

"To be sure it is: and, indeed, strikes me that they can want no addition at all. . . ."

"That is very true, and, therefore, I do not know whether, upon the whole, it would not be more advisable to do something for their mother while she lives rather than for them. . . . A hundred a year would make them all perfectly comfortable." . . .

"[I]t is better than parting with fifteen hundred pounds at once. But then if Mrs. Dashwood should live fifteen years, we shall be completely taken in. . . . [P]eople always live forever when there is an annuity to be paid them. . . ."

"I believe you are right, my love; it will be better that there should be no annuity in the case. . . . A present of fifty pounds now and then will prevent their ever being distressed for money, and will, I think, be amply discharging my promise to my father."

"To be sure it will. . . . Altogether they will have five hundred a-year amongst them, and what on earth can four women want for more than that?—They will live so cheap! Their housekeeping will be nothing at all. They will have no carriage, no horses, and hardly any servants; they will keep no company and can have no expenses of any kind! Only conceive how comfortable they will be! . . . They will be much more able to give *you* something!"

And so, the wealthy Dashwoods not only manage to rationalize their way out of helping John's stepmother and half-sisters but convince themselves that their much poorer relatives are better able to give something to them!

Reprinted by permission of Paul Miller.

Anyone who dismisses the *Heart of Darkness* portrayal of mass self-deception as just fiction—a story—or thinks that this sort of thing only happened a long time ago might reflect on the present-day confiscation of native lands in Brazil, Indonesia, and elsewhere, where the destruction of indigenous ways of life and peoples is justified in the name of "the integration of native populations into modern life" or "maximal use of resources."[10]

---

[10]It is worth noting that *Heart of Darkness* has itself come under fire for being racist in its depictions of Africa and Africans. See, for instance Chinua Achebe, "An Image of Africa: Racism in Conrad's 'Heart of Darkness.' " *Massachusetts Review,* vol. 18, no. 4 (Winter 1977).

6. Other Defense Mechanisms

When we rationalize or procrastinate, we usually are consciously aware of our actions. But there are a number of psychological strategies (defense mechanisms) that we generally are not consciously aware of using to avoid negative emotional feelings. Because they involve distortion of reality, these defense mechanisms can seriously undermine our ability to think critically.

In suppression, we avoid thoughts that are stressful by either not thinking about them or, more commonly, by thinking nonstressful thoughts. In this way, we manage to avoid the anxiety associated with the stress-provoking situation. Although suppression may reduce stress in the short run, it often has negative consequences later on. For instance, a student failing a statistics course may block his anxiety by thinking about happier events—his new girlfriend, an upcoming dance, a sports event—or anything else that will suppress his deep-seated fear of failure. Yet in the long run, he'd be better off facing the problem, getting help, and working to improve his grade.

Denial involves some suppression, but instead of replacing the stressful thoughts with more benign ones, we change our interpretation of the situation to perceive it as less threatening. When a love relationship goes bad, we may remain in denial until our partner walks out on us—even though the signs of discontent are apparent to other people. Instead of paying attention to these signs, we may reinterpret our partner's negative behavior by making excuses for it, or blaming ourselves, or ignoring it. Our need to protect ourselves against separation and loss may prevent us from facing the problems in our relationships and, perhaps, finding solutions.

Denial seems to be a common weakness of Internet users, who feel a false sense of privacy when they make provocative comments on sites like Facebook, YouTube, and Twitter. A good example is the UCLA student who posted a three-minute tirade on YouTube about ill-mannered Asian students who use cell phones in the university library. Speaking alone to a computer in the privacy of her room, she was surely in denial that her rant would have any consequences, let alone cause the firestorm of condemnation it sparked, including vitriolic charges of racial intolerance, and even death threats. Her instant notoriety was so poisonous that she dropped out of school because of—as she put it—"the harassment of my family . . . the death threats and being ostracized from an entire community." Maybe an inexperienced college student can be forgiven a lapse in judgment, but how do you explain two congressmen falling into the same trap? First there was Republican Chris Lee, who sent flirtatious emails plus a shirtless photo to a woman he met on Craig's List. Then we had Democrat Anthony Weiner, who tweeted lewd photos of himself—using the alias "Carlos Danger" (can't make this stuff up)—to a number of women. Both men resigned from Congress in the wake of their scandals. The apparent anonymity of the Internet seems to seduce even the most worldly people into denying that there may be consequences.

Albert Camus created an extreme case of denial and suppression in his existentialist novel *The Stranger*. The protagonist, Meursault, kills an Arab on an Algerian beach for no apparent reason and remains in denial about his own motivation, blaming it on the scorching heat of the sun instead. Thus, he reinterprets the situation to diminish his own responsibility and the psychological threat it entails. Later, in jail, he suppresses the anxiety one would expect him to feel about the upcoming trial and thinks instead about his bedroom at home. He spends literally hours recalling every crack in the wall, every chip in the paint, every item in the room—and successfully manages to avoid stress-provoking thoughts. Suppression and denial prevent him from devising his own best defense—that he shot the man in self-defense—a claim for which there is some evidence in the novel but which, of course, would undermine the existential theme.

People who remain in denial about life-threatening physical ailments run the risk of losing their lives or forfeiting the lives of others. A particularly troubling example is the AIDS "denialists," who claim that HIV is harmless, a belief that contradicts the scientifically proven fact that HIV causes AIDS.[11] These people advocate against taking antiretroviral drugs because they think such drugs cause AIDS rather than curb it. If only a few people were affected, this might be less of an issue, but when the head of a country advocates this claptrap, thousands suffer. In the last decade, the president of South Africa, Thabo Mbeki, so firmly persisted in denying the cause and treatment of AIDS that his administration curbed access to antiviral drugs. As a result, only about a quarter of those needing treatment received it, despite generous assistance from foreign donors. To make matters worse, the South African health minister, who believed antiviral drugs were poison, promoted nutritional alternatives like lemons, garlic, and olives to treat HIV, thus using pseudoscience to provide worthless "cures," which ultimately resulted in the deaths of many South Africans. Why people persist in this form of denial despite widely publicized evidence to the contrary is both puzzling and troubling.

In a piece for the Washington Post *in 2010 titled "What will future generations condemn us for?" philosopher Kwame Anthony Appiah makes the connection between the perpetuation of condemnable practices and widespread denial (as well as the kind of appeals to authority we discussed in Chapter 3).*

Widespread Denial and Social Evils

Once, pretty much everywhere, beating your wife and children was regarded as a father's duty, homosexuality was a hanging offense, and waterboarding was approved—in fact, invented—by the Catholic Church. Through the middle of the 19th century, the United States and other nations in the Americas condoned plantation slavery. Many of our grandparents were born in states where women were forbidden to vote. And well into the 20th century, lynch mobs in this country stripped, tortured, hanged and burned human beings at picnics.

Looking back at such horrors, it is easy to ask: What were people thinking?

Yet, the chances are that our own descendants will ask the same question, with the same incomprehension, about some of our practices today.

---

[11]For more on this, see: Moore, John, and Nattrass, Nicoli. "AIDS and South Africa: Deadly Quackery." *International Herald Tribune,* 4 June 2006.

Is there a way to guess which ones? After all, not every disputed institution or practice is destined to be discredited. And it can be hard to distinguish in real time between movements, such as abolition, that will come to represent moral common sense, and those, such as Prohibition, that will come to seem quaint or misguided. Recall the book burners of Boston's old Watch and Ward Society or the organizations for the suppression of vice, with their crusades against claret, contraceptives, and sexually candid novels.

Still, a look at the past suggests three signs that a particular practice is destined for future condemnation.

First, people have already heard the arguments against the practice. The case against slavery didn't emerge in a blinding moment of moral clarity, for instance; it had been around for centuries.

Second, defenders of the custom tend not to offer moral counterarguments but instead invoke tradition, human nature or necessity. (As in, "We've always had slaves, and how could we grow cotton without them?")

And third, supporters engage in what one might call strategic ignorance, avoiding truths that might force them to face the evils in which they're complicit. Those who ate the sugar or wore the cotton that the slaves grew simply didn't think about what made those goods possible. That's why abolitionists sought to direct attention toward the conditions of the Middle Passage, through detailed illustrations of slave ships and horrifying stories of the suffering below decks.

7. The Benefits of Self-Deception, Wishful Thinking, and Denial

Our account of human beings as self-deceivers, as well as rational agents, has been objected to on several grounds, perhaps the most important being that such a harmful device could not have evolved and, if it did, would long since have been weeded out by natural selection.[12] There are at least two important responses to this objection. First, whatever any theory may say, it seems clear that human beings do in fact deceive themselves and do engage in wishful thinking that sometimes results in harmful behavior. Those who accept a theory of evolution and natural selection have to make their theory conform to this fact—they cannot deny the fact because of their theory. (One of the great virtues of science is that scientists are not permitted to engage in this kind of monkey business.)

---

[12]That the rational, intelligent side of our nature should have evolved seems quite natural, given its immense value in solving life's problems, and this idea was held even in the nineteenth century, for instance, by Charles Darwin and Charles Peirce, among many others.

The second response is that self-deception and wishful thinking do in fact provide important survival benefits as well as harms; it thus makes sense to conclude that they evolved because of these beneficial effects. Although these benefits are not yet clearly understood, we now are beginning to grasp how this side of human nature works.

One important function of self-deception is to reduce anxiety or stress, giving us greater ability to make decisions and to act when delay might bring on disaster. One of the authors of this text, for example, was in a serious auto accident a few years ago during which he felt no fear whatsoever. He thus was able to control his car during the crucial moments in a way that would have been impossible had he been paralyzed by conscious fear. (After the accident was over, of course, he pretty much fell apart.) Psychologists would say that his fear was repressed during the crucial moments.

Anxiety reduction also is crucial with respect to long-term dangers and potential failures. Scientists are beginning to understand the biological effects of long-term anxiety on the body, and they are not good, to say the least. Stress is related to reduced effectiveness of the immune system and perhaps also to problems with other important body systems.[13] The relationship between anxiety or stress and belief systems is still not very well understood by psychologists, but this much seems to be true: Doubt, particularly doubt about important matters, produces anxiety in most people. Settling doubt and coming to some belief or other thus reduces anxiety and makes us feel better. So it isn't only the need to act, to do something, that sometimes leads us to premature or unwarranted beliefs. Even when there is nothing to be done right now, doubt may produce ongoing anxiety (sometimes referred to as *generalized anxiety*), and wishful thinking that eliminates this doubt may reduce the anxiety.

Self-deception also plays a positive role in life for those who tend to relive in memory the good experiences life has afforded them while tending to forget the bad ones. Why, years later, dwell on the bad? Why drag ourselves down in this way? (It's important, of course, to remember the mistakes one has made in order to make sure not to repeat them. The point is that nothing useful is accomplished by dwelling on them needlessly, as so many depressed people do.)

A widespread example of beneficial self-deception called the *placebo effect* occurs when people take dummy pills that they think are a form of medication but, in fact, are not. Because they expect the pills to make them well, they often do feel better even though the substance contains no medication whatsoever. Medical researchers have long understood the effect of placebos and regularly use them as a control in experiments to test the effectiveness of drugs. But a study published in the *Journal of the American Medical Association* (March 2008) showed that the cost of the pill as well as the pill itself raised patients' expectations. Investigators gave dummy pain pills to half of the 82 participants, who read that they cost $2.50 a dose. The other half read that the pills had been discounted to 10 cents each. Participants were asked to rate the pain caused

---

[13]For an excellent and very readable account of the relationship of self-deception to anxiety reduction and of how the unconscious mind selects what comes into consciousness, see: Goleman, Daniel. *Vital Lies, Simple Truths.* New York: Simon & Schuster, 1985. For a short account of one theory concerning the relationship between stress and the immune and endocrine systems, see the May 1987 *Scientific American,* pp. 68B–68D.

by electric shocks to their wrists before and after taking the pills. Although all the pills had a strong placebo effect on both groups, 85 percent of those taking the expensive ones said that they experienced significant pain relief compared to 61 percent taking the cheaper ones—yet the pills taken by both groups were identical. Studies like this illustrate the extent to which the mind will trick the body into responding, and in this sense, the self-deception is beneficial. People who take untested alternative medicines often experience similar placebo effects even though the drugs may be worthless. The danger is that they may be trying to cure serious ailments with bogus pills, and no amount of self-deception will do that.

In some countries, miracle potions are commonly accepted medications, though they may have little more than a placebo effect. A retired Tanzanian preacher concocted one such herbal remedy, hyping it as a cure for everything from AIDS to cancer to diabetes—all this and more for just 30 cents a cup.[14] It sold like hotcakes. Thousands of sick people poured into his village, waiting in lines so long that some of them died in the process. Rich and poor came—even Tanzanian politicians, who flew into the bush by helicopter for a swig of the magic medicine. "It's all about faith," one woman said. "If you believe that this works, it works." And it probably does, if all you need is a placebo, but the benefits stop short of curing AIDS or cancer, or diabetes—way short.

Perhaps the classic case in which self-deception helps people feel better occurs when, in spite of medical evidence, the terminally ill deny the proximity of death, thus reducing the numbing effect of terrible fear. We all need defenses against the knowledge of the certainty of death, those close to it much more than the rest of us. Similarly, it may be useful to be able to deny the seriousness of ailments that are not life-threatening, as it was for Franklin D. Roosevelt, whose denial for some time of the permanence and debilitating nature of his paralysis may well have been an important reason that he was able to persevere and become president of the United States.

In some cases, however, there may be a serious difference of opinion concerning the benefits of the denial that death lurks nearby. It is notorious, for example, that most young men who find themselves in the lethal killing zones typical of modern wars are able to function even though terrified in a way that most of the rest of us can hardly imagine. They can fight (those who can—many cannot) in large part because they tend to see the flying bullets and exploding shells hitting the other guy, not themselves. Soldiers tell stories of the extreme surprise some individuals show when they realize that they have been hit and are dying. The people who send young men into battle rely on this ability of the young to deny consciously what in some sense they know all too well—that they may be the next one to get it. The obviously good function of this kind of self-deception is that it enables soldiers to fight for their country when outside forces threaten its existence. The not entirely good consequence is that tyrants and other megalomaniacal leaders find it easier to get the young to risk their lives in immoral or foolish endeavors.

---

[14]Taken from a delightful article: Gettleman, Jeffrey. "Crowds Come Over Roads and by Helicopters for Tanzania's Cure-All Potion." *New York Times,* 29 March 2011.

8. The Pull of Pseudoscience and the Paranormal

That scientists, particularly those in the "hard sciences," generally know what they're talking about is vouchsafed by the everyday miracles that science makes possible, from computers to automobiles, TV sets, electric lightbulbs, nylon, toilet paper, eyeglasses, insulin, and clean water, hot or cold, flowing out of kitchen faucets. But **pseudoscientific theories** continue to be accepted by a significant number of people in spite of the fact that they produce no positive results whatsoever. Why is that?

A 2007 Harris interactive poll showed that a large number of Americans believe in ghosts (41%), UFOs (35%), witches (31%), and astrology (29%). We should assume that "UFO" is taken to mean alien spaceships and not merely flying objects that are not (yet) identified. A 2013 update on this poll showed about the same support for astrology and a very slight *uptick* in belief in ghosts. Why are they (you? we?) all so gullible? The answer lies in the strength of the various psychological mechanisms that we have been discussing in this chapter. Although science produces results, it doesn't always provide easy or satisfying answers to our problems. Instead, it often confirms what we would like very much to deny, including, unfortunately, the fact that we are not entirely rational animals; that the virtuous are not always rewarded, nor the guilty punished; that hard work is the fate of most of us; and that in the end we all die. (It also says nothing one way or the other about the possibility of life after death.)

Pseudoscience, on the other hand, while it often titillates with predictions of disasters others will experience, generally has rosy things to tell us about our own futures. It sometimes allays fears that it itself has generated—for instance, by transforming the fear that extraterrestrials lurk about by making them into benign cuddly creatures. It tends to be comforting, uplifting, optimistic. It often provides relatively easy solutions to our problems. Astrologers tell us that we, too, can be successful in business, provided, of course, that we schedule economic transactions on the "right" days. Fortune-tellers predict success in romance and marriage. Mediums claim to put us into contact with departed loved ones (implying the happy thought, by the way, that we too will survive death).

Nevertheless, it is bound to seem odd that pseudosciences are so widely believed, given that they are regularly proved worthless. Astrology, for example, has been disproved countless times over the centuries. Pliny the Elder (Roman scholar and naturalist, 23–79 CE), for instance, stated a simple yet devastating objection to astrology way back then when he said, "If a man's destiny is caused by the star under which he is born, then all men born under that star should have the same fortune. But masters and slaves and kings and beggars all are born under the same star." Can wishful thinking alone generate the considerable acceptance so many pseudosciences enjoy in the face of constant refutation? Whatever the answer to that question, it is clear that a pseudoscience like astrology retains much of its appeal in spite of crushing objections in part because charlatans have devised ways to make it seem plausible to the very suggestible (that includes most of us, in weak moments).

One weapon in the con artist's arsenal is what some psychologists call the "Barnum effect," after nineteenth-century circus magnate P. T. Barnum. Barnum is deservedly famous for remarking that "there's a sucker born every minute," but he also maintained that the secret of his immense success was in providing a little something for everyone. Con artists disguised as astrologers follow this advice very carefully. They word their horoscopes vaguely, so that virtually everybody who wants to can see themselves in the descriptions under their sign. Here is part of a "typical Barnum profile":

> You have a great need for other people to like you and admire you. You have a tendency to be critical of yourself. You have a great deal of unused capacity, which you have not used to your advantage. While you have some personality weaknesses, you are generally able to compensate for them. . . . You pride yourself on being an independent thinker and do not accept others' statements without satisfactory proof.

In fact, this description fits relatively few people, but it does fit how most of us think of ourselves—or want to think of ourselves.

Extrasensory perception (telepathy, clairvoyance, precognition, and so forth) is another form of pseudoscience widely believed by the public. But, in fact, over a century of research fails to confirm the existence of ESP in any of its alleged forms. After reviewing a large body of research in this area for the National Research Council, a scientific committee concluded that "despite a 130-year record of scientific research on such matters our committee could find no scientific justification for the existence of phenomena such as extrasensory perception, mental telepathy, or 'mind over matter' exercises. . . . Evaluation of the large body of the best available evidence simply does not support the contention that these phenomena exist."[15]

In the face of such findings, why do people continue to believe in ESP? We mentioned a few reasons a few pages back, but Thomas Gilovich, a cognitive psychologist at Cornell University, concludes (from surveys asking people to explain the origin of their beliefs) that personal experience also plays an important role. When by chance or coincidence people experience a run of good or bad luck, they often attribute it to some special power. Gamblers who have streaks of luck at blackjack or roulette have trouble accepting the fact that the theory of probability predicts that streaks of luck are likely to occur every once in a while. They often become convinced that some special power is at work—that unseen forces are on their side—rather than accept the fact that coincidences are bound to happen now and then.

Premonitions fall into the same category. A premonition is really a coincidence that occurs between someone's thoughts and actual events in the real world. A young man dreams about his ex-girlfriend, and lo and behold, she calls him the next day. If he thinks his dream is a premonition, he has forgotten for the moment the many times he has dreamed about her when she didn't call. After all, people frequently dream about ex-lovers, but rarely do they telephone the next day. When they do, it's coincidental. This element of chance applies as well to extraordinary premonitions that foretell an important event that really does occur. A woman has a dream that a passenger jet will crash in the Florida Everglades—and it does! Of what significance is this? The question to ask is whether such events occur more often than we would expect them to by

---

[15]*American Psychological Association Monitor,* January 1988—more recent evaluations come to the same conclusion.

The Task of Propaganda

Con artists are pikers in the great sweep of things. They titillate, comfort, and do a small amount of harm, and that's about it. But the great mesmerizers, the Benito Mussolinis and Ruhollah Khomeinis, who sell whole nations a bill of goods, are another matter. Here are a few pronouncements about mass propaganda by Adolf Hitler, an intuitive master at the game (culled from his writings by the Secular Humanist Bulletin, *March 1988):*

All propaganda must be popular and its intellectual level must be adjusted to the most limited intelligence among those it is addressed to.

All effective propaganda must be limited to a very few points and must harp on these slogans until the last member of the public understands what you want him to understand by your slogan.... [T]he masses are slow-moving, and they require a certain time before they are ready even to notice a thing, and only after the simplest ideas are repeated thousands of times will the masses finally remember them.

Propaganda's effect... must be aimed at the emotions and only to a very limited degree at the so-called intellect. [Italics added.]

The very first axiom of all propagandist activity: to wit, the basically subjective and one-sided attitude it must take toward every question it deals with. The function of propaganda is ... not to weigh and ponder the rights of different people, but exclusively to emphasize the one right that it has set out to argue for. Its task is not to make an objective study of the truth, ... its task is to serve our own right, always and unflinchingly.

Does this sound like the formula to which most political rhetoric in the United States today is tailored?

chance. People have an unfortunate tendency to believe premonitions that come true and to forget those that don't. This, by the way, nicely illustrates the difference between pseudoscience and science. Pseudoscience pays attention to successes and ignores failures; science never ignores failures. It puts its hypotheses to severe tests, requiring independent repetition of observations and experiments rather than relying simply on coincidence and anecdote.

9. Lack of A Good Sense of Proportion

The kinds of irrationality catalogued in this chapter so far—provincialism, self-deception, and so on—seem to have evolved primarily because they are advantageous in certain kinds of circumstances. Self-deception, as mentioned before, may reduce stress, and provincialism tends to increase group cohesiveness. But explanations as to why so many of us lack a good *sense of proportion* are much harder to come by.[16] In any case, there can be no doubt that on occasion we all lack a good sense of proportion when we make decisions and come to conclusions in everyday life. The trick is to learn how to minimize this natural impediment to cogent reasoning.

Prudence is one of the chief components of a good sense of proportion. In the sense intended here, prudence consists in being provident—of tempering what we do today to maximize our overall, long-run interests. Of course, being prudent does not mean becoming a drudge, or a workaholic. It doesn't mean always putting off until tomorrow pleasures that could have been had today. But it does mean carefully weighing today's pleasures against long-term interests.

Note, though, that imprudence frequently is not a factor when people lack a sense of proportion. The impediments to cogent reasoning already discussed certainly play an important role here. A sense of loyalty, for example, sometimes clouds the perspective of even the most level-headed among us, leading us to exaggerate the wonders of our own society while neglecting its defects. And wishful thinking certainly plays an important role. People play state lotteries not just because they have little understanding of what it means to say the odds are a million or a hundred thousand to one against winning the big prize, but also because of wishful thinking. ("This is my lucky day," or "I was born on 1/23/45, so 12345 is my lucky number.")

But there are plenty of cases, some of a much more serious nature, in which wishful thinking or self-deception plays little or no role. After the attack on the World Trade Center, for instance, Americans stopped flying just about everywhere. While this reaction was understandable, given the terrifying nature of the event, the odds against being killed in this way were millions to one. (Again, driving to work every day is much more life-threatening.) Many Americans refuse to fly commercial airplanes from one city to another even though driving is many times more dangerous. In fact, flying commercial airlines is just about the safest way to travel ever invented, yet lots

---

[16]Part of the explanation lies, no doubt, in the benefits of the psychological mechanisms already discussed. But perhaps another part lies in two important facts about human evolution. The first is that behavior guided by intelligence is a later arrival on the scene than responses motivated purely by desires and emotions (something that is confirmed by what is known about the development of the brains of vertebrate animals—in particular, mammals). Strong emotions that appropriately guided behavior at much earlier times now sometimes skew rational thought and motivate responses that are less than optimal. The second relevant fact is that until quite recently, very little was known about what philosophers used to call the "secret powers" that move things, and a great deal that was "known" has turned out to be false. (Think only of medicine until about 150 years ago, when doctors used bloodletting to treat almost every ailment.) If we go back, say, just 10,000 or 20,000 years in human history—an eyeblink on the evolutionary time scale—we are back to a time when exceedingly few accurate general beliefs about cause-and-effect relationships can have been known. So it is only recently in the great sweep of things that it has slowly become increasingly beneficial to moderate the urges of immediate desire and strong emotions in terms of what intelligence can learn from experience. Perhaps, then, the lack of a better sense of proportion is partly explained as being due to a kind of "evolutionary lag."

of people, including not one but two of the authors of this chapter on pseudoreasoning, have serious bouts with fear every time they fly.

In fact, failure to see things in proper perspective is one of the most serious errors in reasoning of which most of us are guilty. As might be expected, politicians frequently (one might say continually) take advantage of this tendency in our nature. They know that people can be diverted from important issues and problems by being given "bread and circuses," and that, for instance, the best time to announce unpopular measures is when the minds of masses of people are riveted on the private lives of celebrities like the British royal family or America's various Kardashians. Sometimes these measures slide under the radar when other, more riveting news hits the media. For instance, in 2007, when the subprime mortgage debacle surfaced and the stock market skittered around, President Bush vetoed a bill to expand health care coverage to include more children under the State Children's Health Insurance Program (SCHIP). The cost of this program—$60 billion over a five-year period—was a drop in the bucket compared to the staggering cost of the Iraq War at the time—$607 billion in direct funding, plus uncalculated billions in hidden costs. This, in itself, shows a skewed sense of proportion, but apparently members of Congress didn't get things in perspective, either, because they failed to muster enough votes to override the president's veto, and the American people, sidetracked by other issues, paid the matter little attention.

There are other ways for people in positions of power to release unflattering or unpopular news while trying to keep those releases relatively under our radar. One common strategy—common enough to have its own name—is the "Friday News Dump." Government agencies have a habit of releasing on Friday afternoons the news they'd rather not be covered too thoroughly. The White House and NSA are particularly adept at this. Why Friday afternoons? Because people tend to be occupied with other things Friday evenings and not home to watch the news on TV or to continually refresh a news website. And just as importantly, newspapers are read less on Saturdays than on any other day of the week.

Hard Hits, Hard Choices

It often is difficult to know whether someone is irrationally self-deceived, or perhaps imprudent, rather than being completely rational. Take the case of professional boxers and football players. Do they deceive themselves about the likelihood of permanent and serious damage to their bodies? Are they being extremely imprudent? Or do they so value their professional life (and its financial rewards) that to them it is worth the pain and suffering likely at a later date? Some retired professional football players, for instance, say that they were foolish to take the pounding week after week that has left them walking wounded; others say it was worth it. Are the latter still deceiving themselves?

Summary of Chapter 6

Human beings are not completely rational animals. There also is a nonrational component to our makeup that often interferes with our ability to argue or reason cogently.

1. Our reasoning sometimes is skewed because of *loyalty,* which inclines us to see our own society and its beliefs in a more favorable light than the evidence may warrant; because of *provincialism,* which tends to narrow our interests and knowledge of what goes on in the world; and because of the *herd instinct,* which makes it easy and natural for us to believe what most others in our society believe. ***Example:*** Failing to notice the undemocratic and nasty things our own government does on the international scene.

2. Loyalty and provincialism are related to *prejudice*—in particular, to prejudice against members of other groups, and to thinking in terms of unverified stereotypes. ***Example:*** The stereotype that was common in the United States until about the late 1950s, which pictured African Americans as foot-shuffling, obsequious children. But believing bad things about others constitutes prejudice only when not justified by sufficient evidence.

   Prejudice against others often is conjoined with an overtolerance of the defects and foibles of one's own group and its members, and it may be reinforced by the need to find *scapegoats*—others who can be blamed for our own troubles and mistakes. ***Example:*** Blaming the Jews for the transgressions of others.

   Thinking in terms of stereotypes and scapegoats often stems from a *partisan mind-set*—viewing everything in terms of "us against them" or "my right opinions against your wrong ones." Good reasoners, by way of contrast, have minds open to the truth, wherever it may lead.

3. *Superstitions* often are supported by a small amount of evidence. What makes them superstitions is that we believe them on the basis of insufficient and, frequently, biased samples from which all negative evidence has been eliminated. ***Example:*** Overlooking the fact that good things sometimes happen on Friday the 13th and bad things on other days.

4. Beliefs acquired in the irrational ways just described generally result from *wishful thinking*—believing what we want to believe, despite stronger evidence to the contrary—or from its variant, called *self-deception*—consciously believing what, at some deeper level, we know to be dubious. ***Example:*** British prime minister Neville Chamberlain wishfully believing that the Munich agreement with Hitler had assured "peace in our time."

5. Three other important ways to cut the wishful thinking pie are *rationalization, suppression,* and *denial.* ***Example:*** Smoking cigarettes after being exposed to all sorts of evidence that they're bad for one's health. Rationalization often supports

procrastination—putting off until tomorrow what ought to be done today. *Example:* Starting to write a term paper the day before it's due.

6. While we can't yet be sure why nonrational mechanisms have evolved, scientists are beginning to understand some of their beneficial effects. Loyalty and provincialism increase group cohesiveness when there is competition or strife with other groups. The herd instinct helps individuals to work well with others in their group. And self-deception frequently aids in the reduction of anxiety and stress, both of which can be harmful to health. Prolonged doubt about serious matters tends to produce stress and anxiety; coming to firm beliefs about these matters tends to combat depression and thus be good for one's physical well-being. ***Example:*** Denying the seriousness of a terminal illness, thereby reducing grief at the end of one's life.

7. *Pseudoscientific beliefs* are adopted, and endure, in spite of their failure to help us deal successfully with everyday problems, because of wishful thinking, self-deception, and similar psychological mechanisms. *Pseudoscience* is comforting and upbeat concerning our own welfare and the satisfaction of our deepest desires. ***Example:*** Seances that practitioners claim can put us into contact with deceased friends and relatives.

   But pseudosciences also gain widespread acceptance because charlatans have learned how to manipulate us in our unguarded or weak moments. ***Example:*** Alleged astrologers papering over the phoniness of their forecasts by larding them with "Barnum" profiles that tend to fit everybody. Note that the con artists who play on our weaknesses in this way are two-bit operators compared to such great political mesmerizers as Adolf Hitler, who expertly manipulate masses of their compatriots by clever and sophisticated appeals to the irrational side of the human psyche.

8. On occasion, most of us lack a good *sense of proportion,* a defect in reasoning that critical reasoners try to minimize. ***Example:*** Being persuaded by political rhetoric to pay more attention to relatively unimportant matters than to those that are more serious. Being *prudent,* in the sense of provident—acting so as to maximize long-run interests—is an important component of a good sense of proportion that we often lack. *Example:* Weighing today's small pleasure more highly than the long-run benefits of doing well on a final exam, thus not preparing until the last minute. But people often fail to see things in proper perspective for other reasons; for example, because of group loyalty or wishful thinking or because of other emotional interferences with cogent reasoning. *Example:* Being more afraid of small risks than of much bigger ones.

EXERCISE SET 6-1

1. How about this *Luann* cartoon?

LUANN GEC Inc./Dist. by United Feature Syndicate, Inc.

2. When France defied the United States and came out against the Iraq War in 2003, the same sort of stereotypes surfaced among some Americans as did at the end of World War II when the GIs liberated Paris: The French don't bathe, they're cowardly collaborators, French women are loose, and the like. Explain the psychological impediments involved and compare the political climates that gave rise to these attitudes.

3. Explain how this conversation between a student and a teacher (not quite verbatim) relates to topics discussed in this chapter:

   Student: I've come to your office to see about getting a B in this course.
   Teacher: But you're doing C work, the semester ends next week, and you missed two assignments. What makes you think you can get a B?
   Student: Well, I need to get a B to get into Berkeley [University of California at Berkeley] next fall.
   Teacher: But why didn't you come in sooner and talk to me about this and perhaps get help to do better work?
   Student: Yes. But I really need to get that B, or I can't get into Berkeley.

4. Do you believe that loyalty really does skew people's beliefs away from what the evidence will support? If so, support your belief with at least one example not mentioned in the text. If not, show that the examples given in the text are somehow mistaken.

5. Do human beings really have a herd instinct, or is that just true of cows and such? Defend your answer.

6. How does the text use the expression "belief provincialism"? Give some examples, other than those mentioned in the text, and explain why and how they fit the definition.

7. According to the text, what is wrong with categorizing, say, the French as great lovers, Germans as obedient automatons, and so on? After all, doesn't experience show that the members of a given group tend to be different from

the members of other groups, as Greeks are different from Pakistanis, and Mexicans from Nigerians?

8. Give at least two examples of other people engaging in self-deception or wishful thinking, and explain why you think their actions fit the relevant descriptions provided in the text. Do you ever engage in this sort of funny business? Explain and defend your answer. (Hint: You do.)

9. What are some of the good consequences of wishful thinking and self-deception that are mentioned in the text? Explain. Can you think of others?

10. Critically evaluate the following argument. (Does it contain a correct use of induction?) "Several of my friends have been very lucky in life so far, and I've read of quite a few other lucky souls. So when I say that my lucky friends will continue to have good luck, I'm basing my conclusion on experience, not wishful thinking."

11. If you had been interviewed for one of the Harris polls discussed in this chapter, would you have been among those expressing belief in at least one of the claims asked about? If so, explain. If not, do you hold any beliefs that are no more well-founded than these? (Note the temptation to engage in a tiny sort of "lie of silent assertion" by simply passing over this question!)

12. Carefully explain the so-called Barnum effect. How did the typical Barnum profile reprinted in this chapter fit you?

13. [Question is omitted because 13 is an unlucky number.]

14. We all suffer to some extent from the impediments to rational thinking described in this chapter, the authors of this text not being exceptions. Doesn't this textbook, for example, reflect the provincialism of its authors in some ways? If so, how? If not, why might some readers think otherwise? What about any other ways in which you think the text could be construed so as to indicate rational failures—of the kind discussed in this chapter—on the part of its authors? (Be brief, but do consider material from previous chapters and keep these questions in mind as you read the later chapters. You should, in fact, always keep such questions in mind!)

An important art of politicians is to find new names for institutions which under old names have become odious to the public.

—Talleyrand

Language

7

MindTap® Visit MindTap for more readings and resources.

anguage is the primary tool used in formulating arguments. We all are familiar (or should be!) with the power of language when it is employed by fine writers of fiction—Shakespeare, Fielding, Austen, Joyce (to name just a few who wrote in the English language)—the list is very long. The principal point of literature classes is precisely to make this apparent. But good writing can be equally effective when used in the construction of argumentative essays and other argumentative passages. (We will consider in Chapter 13 the possibility that literature can present its own sort of argument.) The trouble is that language can be used effectively in the service of fallacious as well as cogent arguments, deceiving the unwary or unknowing into accepting arguments they should reject.

1. Cognitive and Emotive Meanings

If the purpose of a sentence is to inform or to state a fact, some of its words must refer to things, events, or properties of one kind or another. These words must thus have what is commonly called **cognitive meaning**. (The sentences they compose also are said to have cognitive meaning.)

But most words also have **emotive meaning**, which means that they have positive or negative overtones. The emotive charges of some words are obvious. Think of the terms *wop, kike, nigger,* and *fag,* or the so-called four-letter words that rarely appear in textbooks, even in this permissive age.

The words just mentioned have negative emotive charges. But lots of words have positive overtones. Examples are *freedom, love, democracy, springtime,* and *peace.* And plenty of others have either neutral or mixed emotive force. *Pencil, run,* and *river* tend to be neutral words. *Socialism, politician,* and *whiskey* get mixed reviews.

In fact, almost any word that is emotively positive for some people or in some contexts may be just the opposite for others. One person's meat often is indeed another's poison. Perhaps the paradigm case is the word *God,* which has one kind of overtone for true believers, another for agnostics, and still another for strident atheists. To the average person, the word *student* has positive connotations, but not to a landlord or landlady.

Terms that on first glance may appear to be emotively neutral often turn out to have at least modest emotive overtones. The terms *bureaucrat, government official,* and *public servant,* for instance, all refer to the same group of people and thus have approximately the same cognitive import, but their emotive meanings are quite different. Of the three, only *government official* comes close to being neutral in tone.

2. Emotive Meanings and Persuasive Uses of Language

The fact that expressions have emotive as well as cognitive meanings has not escaped the notice of con artists, advertisers, politicians, and others whose stock in trade is the manipulation of attitudes, desires, and beliefs. Over the years, they have learned how to use the emotive side of language to further their own ends.

One common way in which the emotive force of language can be used to con, as Talleyrand observed some time ago, is to mask the odious nature of an institution or practice by giving it a nice name rather than a more accurate, nasty one. Why call the Chinese dictatorship by an accurate name when it can be called the *People's Republic of China?* When Saddam Hussein took control of Iraq, why should he have fiddled with the increasingly inaccurate name *Republic of Iraq?* The ruling clique in Myanmar (formerly Burma) surely had ample reason to call its thugs who engaged in mass murder and other kinds of nasty business anything other than the *State Peace and Development Council.* In a slightly different vein, why call diluted beer *watered-down beer* when you can call it *lite?* And doesn't *Department of Defense* have a much sweeter ring to it than the original and more accurate name *War Department?*

The names of political organizations are often heavily sanitized—not so much to hide their agenda as to suggest their agenda in the most generally agreeable terms. There is rhetorical (and so political) benefit in changing your name from the "National Abortion Rights Action League" to "NARAL Pro-Choice America." Lots of people are against abortion, but who could be against choice? Why should a minority political group call itself *The Moral Minority,* when it can puff itself up into *The Moral Majority*? (Note, by the way, the implication that the individuals in this group are more moral than other people.)

> I am firm, you are obstinate, he is pigheaded.
>
> —BERTRAND RUSSELL'S EXAMPLE OF WORDS HAVING SIMILAR COGNITIVE
> MEANINGS BUT MUCH DIFFERENT EMOTIVE SENSES

The language of diplomacy is particularly prone to tricky manipulation, especially when it refers to provocative international issues. A good case in point was cited by William Safire in his column on language.[1] In 2006, when things were heating up between Israel and the new Hamas government in Palestine, the prime minister, Ehud Olmert, wanted to move 90,000 Israelis from West Bank villages into secure areas behind the fence under construction, but instead of using the word *retreat,* he wanted a synonym that would neither suggest weakness for withdrawing nor imply that the new border was permanent. The Hebrew word chosen was *hitkansut,* or coming together (in a safe place), which seemed an appropriate choice for the Israelis, but the problem came with translating the term for the international community. After several false starts, Olmert and his aides decided on *realignment,* which suggests shifting of the lines to describe their withdrawal plan. Safire notes, "By adjusting the line of separation without seeking to establish a formal border, Israel's purpose is to minimize friction while retaining its historic claim on the land in dispute." Thus, the carefully chosen translation was an attempt to gain international support for establishing a firm line of separation from Palestine for the present, while leaving open the possibility of reclaiming the disputed land in the future. This type of language manipulation goes on all the time in diplomatic circles, where word choice is often critical in policy explanations.

In recent years, manipulative uses of language have been given a spate of emotively negative names, each with a slightly different connotation, including *double-speak* (deliberately ambiguous or evasive language), *bureaucratese* (governmental doublespeak), *newspeak* (media doublespeak), *academese* (the academic variety), *legalese* (lawyer talk), *gobbledygook, bafflegab,* and *jargon.*

Take *militaryese.* The military at all times and places has devised expressions intended as much as possible to hide the fact that war is, to put it mildly, unvarnished hell. For example, the term *waterboarding* sounds more like a harmless water sport than what it really is, a brutal method of torture. Here are some more examples:

Comfort women	Women of conquered countries forced to work as prostitutes "servicing" soldiers (term used by the Japanese during World War II).
Preemptive action	Our side attacking first.
Battle fatigue	Insanity suffered as a result of the unbearable horrors and strains of battle.
Incursion	Invasion.
Collateral damage	People who are inadvertently killed or property that is inadvertently destroyed in warfare.
Ethnic cleansing	Driving out unwanted citizens of a country, burning their houses, and killing some along the way (as in Kosovo, 1999).

---

[1]Safire, William. "When Diplolingo Does the Job." *International Herald Tribune,* 11 June 2006.

Enhanced interrogation technique	Torture.
Simulated drowning	Actual drowning that is interrupted.
Smart Bombs	Bombs.
Friendly fire	Shelling friendly villages or troops by mistake.
Servicing a target or visiting a site	Bombing a place flat (used during the Gulf War).
Information extraction	Torturing people into giving confessions.
Pacification center	Concentration camp (itself originally doublespeak).
Termination	Killing (also used by the CIA, where *termination with prejudice* means *assassination*).
Nuclear deterrent	Nuclear weapon.
Selective ordinance	Napalm (used to kill by incineration).
The Final Solution	Plan of the Nazis to murder all European Jews.

During World War II—one of the most awful of all wars—the expression *dehousing industrial workers* was used by the British and Americans to mean killing civilians, including women and children via *saturation* air raids. The indescribably horrible massive air raids on Germany and Japan that created incredible firestorms were said to result in *self-energized dislocation,* not widespread death by either incineration or asphyxiation. The term *war* itself has been euphemized into *conflict* or *operation.* Bush the elder waged "Operation Desert Shield"; Bush the younger, "Operation Iraqi Freedom." In the latter conflict, the term *war* was used to describe the War on Terrorism or the War for Peace (!), but not the Iraq War, until we were several years into the conflict. During that war, both sides manipulated terminology to suit their own bias. In the United States, the networks used the term *coalition forces* for what the Arab media called *occupation forces.* And when CNN reported that 16 "insurgents" were killed in an Iraqi uprising (May 7, 2004), the Arab media described them as "resistance fighters." George Orwell got it right when he said, "If thought corrupts language, language can also corrupt thought." Few people would realize that the harmless terms cited above were devised to sugarcoat the truth, or create a bias, or mask sinister, even hideous practices—unless it were pointed out to them.

Much less dramatic examples of doublespeak are prevalent in other ways. The law has its own version—legalese, a hybrid of French, English, and Latin that baffles the average person. In plain English, a *writ* is a claim form, and a *plaintiff* is someone who makes a complaint against another party. Meetings with the judge *in camera* are just private meetings behind closed doors. Why all this turgid terminology? The principal reason is to ensure certainty, to protect clients by using phrases defined by statutes or case law. Using different expressions may raise doubts as to precisely what is meant.

But why can't plain English accomplish the same thing? Another justification is that it's cheaper and less trouble to use archaic language than to rewrite everything. Maybe, but then again, lawyers might have to charge lower fees if legal documents were clear.

Of course, sometimes, doublespeak is just fuzzy thinking cloaked in garbled metaphors. Take, for example, this episode, bizarre even by the standards of the 2016 presidential election. Ted Cruz accused Donald Trump of planting a story in the *National Enquirer* alleging that Cruz had a number of extramarital affairs. His accusations focused largely on Trump advisor and long-time (some would say notorious) political operative Roger Stone: "I would note that Mr. Stone is a man who has 50 years of dirty tricks behind him. He's a man for whom a term was coined for copulating with a rodent. Well, let me be clear: Donald Trump may be a rat, but I have no desire to copulate with him." In addition to awkwardly stumbling around a profane expression, Senator Cruz seems to be intimating that he does not wish to have sex with Trump *even though* his opponent is a rat. It is highly unlikely, however, that he chose this moment to come clean about a sexual predilection for rodents.

In recent years, it's possible that doublespeak in the business world has managed to surpass even that of militaryese in its deviousness. Well, maybe not. But consider these examples of euphemisms used when someone is fired:

> *bumped, decruited, dehired, deselected, destaffed, discontinued, disemployed, dislocated, downsized, excessed, involuntarily separated, nonretained, nonrenewed, severed, surplussed, transitioned, vocationally relocated.*[2]

Firing large numbers of workers is *corporate rightsizing,* by the way, and the place where you get *downsized* is sometimes called the *outplacement office.*

The term *reform* is tricky in the business world. For instance, whereas tort reform suggests that limiting damage awards in a court of law is good for us, what it really means is that limiting the victim's right to sue is good for the profit margins of the corporations and people who may be at fault. A *Doonesbury* cartoon (November 20, 1999) nails the deceptive nature of business language by satirizing the owners of start-up companies that earn no money but make millions from IPOs (initial public offerings of stock). One character says, "We'll probably walk away with a fortune. It's only the small investors who get burned. It's called socializing the risk while privatizing the profit."

These examples illustrate the use of euphemistic language—locutions from which as much negative emotive content as possible has been removed—and the replacement of accurate names with more high-flown locutions. The point generally is to conceal or to mislead, which could be one reason that this kind of talk has become so popular with government officials, lawyers, military officers, doctors, and (alas) a large number of academics. (Is this one reason why so many other [!] textbooks are so dull?)

Interestingly, class differences have always been mirrored euphemistically. Average people *rent* apartments; the rich *lease* them. The nonrich talk of *social climbers;* social climbers like to think of themselves as *upwardly mobile* or (more recently) *changing*

---

[2]New York Times Service (8 March 1996); mentioned in the July 1996 issue of the *Quarterly Review of Doublespeak.*

DOUBLESPEAK FOR EVERYONE

Everyone knows that politics is fertile ground for doublespeak. All political parties use it when it suits their purposes. Here are a few examples noted in John Leo's article "Double Trouble Speak" (*U.S. News & World Report*, 4 July 2005).

REPUBLICAN	DEMOCRAT
climate change	global warming
trial lawyer	personal injury lawyer
faith-based	Religious
school choice	school vouchers
tax relief	tax cuts
illegal	Undocumented
fetus	uterine contents
military difficulties	Quagmire

TOLES the Buffalo News/Universal Press Syndicate

A play on words that distorts paying off the national debt to mean paying down the debt that this political character owes to his campaign contributors.

course, and not as *pushy* but rather as *emphatic.* The wealthy don't earn a *salary,* they receive *compensation* or have an *income.*

In the field of education, euphemisms abound. (And why should we be different?) One college gives placement tests in *Student Success Workshops,* presumably to soften the blow to the many students who place in remedial (uh, developmental) classes. Teachers no longer *teach* but *facilitate* in *comfort zones* where *collaborative learning* occurs.

Then there is academic doublespeak, especially deadly when it comes in whole sentences or runs on for whole paragraphs. Here, for example, is a tiny snippet from Zellig Harris's well-known text *Structural Linguistics* that makes a simple idea seem more profound:

> Another consideration is the availability of simultaneity, in addition to successivity as a relation among linguistic elements.

This seems to mean (there is a certain amount of vagueness here) that we can do two things at once, like gesture while we talk. (Didn't know that, did you?)

The deliberate use of euphemistic language has been going on at least since the beginning of recorded history, but it seems to have increased dramatically in recent years, perhaps because of the professionalization of most trades. Titled professionals want to sound objective and authoritative, not opinionated or biased. Also, controversial topics can be toned down when dressed in euphemistic language. For instance, to lessen its negative connotation, the term *abortion* comes in many guises nowadays: *effecting fetal demise, planned cessation of gestation, interrupted pregnancy, termination,* and *selective reduction.*

It's true that euphemisms can and often do serve useful, nonmanipulative functions. Circumlocutions used to replace offensive four-letter words are good examples. Using expressions like *put to sleep, passed gas,* and *for the mature figure* often is just a matter of politeness. Why shock or offend when we don't have to? Nevertheless, all too often euphemisms are used to further Machiavellian purposes. Indeed, the nastier something is, the greater the need to clothe it in neutral garb.

Doublespeak has become so common that we hardly notice it. Euphemisms slide past us without registering and soften our grasp of reality. When politicians "misspeak" rather than lie, we are less likely to hold them accountable. When the military "deploys troops" rather than invades a country, we are less alarmed. When mayors refer to neighborhoods with "substandard housing" rather than slums or ghettos, we are less likely to think of people living in poverty.[3] Doublespeak hoodwinks us into thinking wrong is right, dangerous situations are benign, poverty is nonexistent, and we are lulled into a deceptive calm. A misleading phrase here and there may not seem like much, but the cumulative effect is to erode our understanding of what is actually going on in the world. When doublespeak is a buffer between us and reality, we are more likely to be manipulated into mindless acceptance of half-truths, distortions, and lies.

Of course, sometimes attempts to whitewash bad news are so obvious that the American public simply rolls its collective eyes. When a recession loomed in 2008, President Bush avoided the "R word" and talked, instead, about "economic challenges"

---

[3]Examples are taken from *Doublespeak Defined* by William Lutz, a perceptive compilation and commentary of misleading language.

and "uncertainties," as in ". . . we have a dynamic economy, but there are some uncertainties." It didn't take an economist to recognize the code language for recession. Given the sinking economy and the drain on their pocketbooks, most people fully understood what was going on, and no amount of hedging could convince them otherwise. Unfortunately, many people have trouble seeing through doublespeak until they are personally affected, and sometimes that is too late.

Orwell on the Orwellian

The popularity of the writings of George Orwell is an important reason that doublespeak has received more than a usual amount of attention in recent years. In this excerpt from his 1948 classic "Politics and the English Language," he explains one reason why politicians favor this less-than-straightforward kind of rhetoric:

In our time, political speech and writing are largely the defence of the indefensible. . . . Thus political language has to consist largely of euphemism, question begging, and sheer cloudy vagueness. Defenceless villages are bombarded from the air, the inhabitants driven out into the countryside, the cattle machine-gunned, the huts set on fire with incendiary bullets: This is called *pacification*. Millions of peasants are robbed of their farms and sent trudging along the roads with no more than they can carry: This is called *transfer of population* or *rectification of frontiers*. . . .

The inflated style is itself a kind of euphemism. A mass of Latin words falls upon the facts like soft snow, blurring the outlines and covering up all the details. *The great enemy of clear language is insincerity. When there is a gap between one's real and one's declared aims, one turns as it were instinctively to long words and exhausted idioms, like a cuttlefish squirting out ink.* [These italics added.]

Language in every field, whether it be politics, law, medicine, or any other, is sometimes inflated or obscure and often larded with *jargon*. There are several senses of this term, one being nonsensical, incoherent, or meaningless talk; another, the specialized language used by professionals when talking (or writing) to each other. The trouble is that jargon intended in the professional sense can and often does turn out to be jargon in the meaningless or incoherent sense, making vacuous or otherwise simple and easily understood remarks appear to be profound.

We need to remember, though, that technical terms used by professional people generally do have an important function—namely, to ensure precision when it counts. Lawyers want contracts to be airtight. Doctors need to be sure they understand each other when they talk about patient illnesses. It may be adequate for a layperson to talk, say, about rapid or irregular heartbeats, but cardiologists need a more precise way of distinguishing the various kinds—distinguishing, for example, *supra ventricular tachycardia* from *atrial fibrillation* or from the immediately life-threatening *ventricular fibrillation*. Use of these technical expressions quickly conveys rather precise and absolutely vital information from one doctor to another. Technical jargon used by people in the same field is an essential form of communication, but when it deteriorates into incoherent or meaningless verbiage, it is puzzling at best and incomprehensible at worst.

And when professional lingo is not translated into ordinary language for the average person, it can be troubling, indeed. For example, doctors who tell patients they have a *malignant melanoma* without clarifying the term, may leave them ignorant of the fact that they have a form of skin cancer which quickly leads to death if untreated.

Language Change

As the world changes, language inevitably changes with it. New words come into common use for things and procedures that didn't exist just a few years ago; old words take on new meanings. The computer age illustrates this nicely. We now talk glibly of an inanimate variety of mouse, of clipless clipboards, nonedible menus, RAM, ROM, megabytes, and gigabytes. Terabytes are becoming part of everyday use, and we imagine petabytes can't be far behind. We cut and paste without scissors or glue, and not only delete but also unerase. We surf the (dry) Net and zero in on spiderless websites, navigating with a cursor.

Initially, these new locutions were used and understood primarily by computer nerds and functioned, as professionalese generally does, to exclude the uninitiated. But they quickly worked their way into the vocabularies of everyone who uses computers, even though much of what we do with them is word processing or game playing, not mathematical computation. So it goes.

Another common feature of jargon, by the way, is *padding*—adding significant-sounding sentences here and there that in fact say little or nothing. Here is an example typical of a common variety in psychological writings: "Although the effects of mental attitudes on bodily disease should not be exaggerated, neither should they be minimized." True. And here is an example of another type: "As soon as there are behaviors you can't generate, then there are responses you can't elicit." Yes. And another: "In order to achieve products, outputs, and outcomes through processes, inputs are required." Absolutely.

3. Ambiguity and Vagueness

We have already had one brief look at ambiguity when we discussed the fallacy of equivocation (in Chapter 4). Some ambiguity in speech and writing is unavoidable. But ambiguity can also be used to **obfuscate** (that is, to make too confusing or unclear to be understandable) an argument and misdirect us from its faults, even when there is no equivocation per se. The same could be said of vagueness. We'd do well to discuss them both a bit more here.

First, it will be useful to distinguish between ambiguity and vagueness. You often hear these words used interchangeably, to indicate a general lack of clarity. Strictly speaking, however, a word or phrase is **ambiguous** when it has more than one meaning and the context in which it is used does not adequately indicate which of those multiple meanings is intended.

Whole statements can be ambiguous in any number of different ways, but we can distinguish two main types. **Semantic ambiguity** arises from a particular word or phrase that has multiple meanings (again without sufficient context to determine which is intended). **Syntactic ambiguity** arises from ambiguity in the structure of the sentence itself.

The following exchange from Donald Trump's meeting with the *Washington Post*'s editorial board in March 2016 centers on a question of semantic ambiguity, especially over the word "incorrect," which can mean either inaccurate or morally problematic. Trump had called for the "loosening" of libel laws in America, and the *Washington Post* asked him to clarify:

> [Frederick] RYAN [*Washington Post* Publisher]: But there's standards like malice is required. Would you weaken that? Would you require less than malice for news organizations?
>
> Donald TRUMP: I would make it so that when someone writes incorrectly, yeah, I think I would get a little bit away from malice without having to get too totally away. Look, I think many of the stories about me are written badly. I don't know if it's malice because the people don't know me.
>
> Stephen STROMBERG, EDITORIAL WRITER: How are you defining "incorrect?" It seems like you're defining it as fairness or your view of fairness rather than accuracy.
>
> TRUMP: Fairness, fairness is, you know, part of the word. But you know, I've had stories that are written that are absolutely incorrect.[4]

An example of syntactic ambiguity also comes to us from the campaign trail in March 2016, specifically this tweet from Bernie Sanders: "I don't believe we should be punishing millions of people with outrageous levels of student debt. That shortsighted path must end." Now, is Sanders saying that we should punish people *who have* outrageous levels of student debt, or is he saying that we should not use outrageous levels of student debt as a punishment (perhaps for poor financial decisions during college)? I don't imagine Sanders endorses either of these things, but it is not entirely clear here which he intended to address. Notice, though, that the ambiguity in the tweet does not result from the ambiguity of any particular word or phrase, but rather from the structure of the sentence that Sanders used.

A word or phrase is **vague** when there is an unsettled range of application for it. Genuine vagueness does not arise when people disagree about the proper application of a word or phrase so much as when a reasonable person will have to admit to some "gray area" in its application. So, for example, this is Indianapolis Colts owner Jim Irsay (quoted in *USA Today* in 2016) on the health risks of playing professional football: "I believe this: that the game has always been a risk, you know, and the way certain people are. Look at it. You take an aspirin, I take an aspirin, it might give you extreme side effects of illness and your body . . . may reject it, where I would be fine. So there is so much we don't know." You'll likely recognize in this statement a fallacy we discussed

<hr>

[4]"A Transcript of Donald Trump's Meeting with the *Washington Post* Editorial Board." Washingtonpost.com, 21 March 2016.

earlier, namely, questionable analogy. The risks of playing football are just not like the risks of taking aspirin. But the argument may have enjoyed some initial plausibility because of the vagueness of "risk." Usually we don't apply this word to something just because it has the remotest chance of causing harm. There is almost nothing on Earth that doesn't. Rather, a risk is something that carries a certain level of possible harm. But where is the threshold for that level? Is going for a walk on a busy street taking a risk? Probably not. Is wingsuiting? Yes. (Look up this craziness if you need to.) How about taking an aspirin? Playing professional football?

Vagueness appears in a couple of different forms. We can have vague predicates such as "is tall." It seems pretty clear that an adult male in 2017 is tall when he's 6'5". It is also clear that he's not tall at 5'4". But what about 6'? Or if you think that is still tall, what about 5'10"? If that is clearly not tall, what about 5'11"? 5'10.5"? As you can see, for each of us there will be some range of heights where it just won't be clear to us if the predicate applies or not.

We also use words that refer vaguely such as "novella," "city," or "glance." There just can't be (at least given the way we commonly use these terms) a clear line of demarcation between a short story and a novella, or a novella and a novel; between a large town and a small city, or between a mere glance and full look.

So when is ambiguity and vagueness problematic? The answer (not trying to be funny here) is, unfortunately, somewhat vague. Ambiguity and vagueness are problematic when they are used intentionally to make a questionable claim seem better than it really is or when they prevent us from being able to tell what is really being claimed at all.

By way of preview, recognizing this problematic sort of ambiguity or vagueness will be especially important later in the text when we consider arguments and rhetoric in advertising and news media in greater detail (Chapters 10 and 11). Ambiguities are especially common in news headlines, mostly because they are (of necessity) short and thus able to provide less context. For instance:

- From hngn.com in 2016: "Heart Attacks Are Affecting Younger and Fatter Americans." (Is the average American who suffers a heart attack younger and fatter than he or she used to be, or are more Americans, who happen to be younger and fatter, having more heart attacks than others?)
- From the *New York Daily News* in 2010: "S.C. Dems Split over Surprise Senate Nominee Alvin Greene, Accused of Flashing Porn at Co-ed." (Did Alvin Greene flash porn, or was this poor woman flashed by the entire South Carolina Democratic Party?)
- From the *Toledo Blade* in 2016: "Volunteers Look to Serve Others at Easter Dinner." (Are volunteers serving dinner to other people, or are they serving a horrifying dinner made of other volunteers?)

Interestingly, terms that can be used either relatively or absolutely, like "Rich" and "Poor", sometimes cause trouble. Poverty, for instance, is exceedingly unpleasant anywhere, at any time. But the poor in the United States today are richer in absolute terms with respect to material wealth than the vast majority of people who lived in days of old or who live today in the so-called Third World countries in Africa, Central and South America, and Asia. This important truth is masked by the fact that the term *poor,* in its relative sense, does apply to those Americans who are poor compared to other Americans, though they may be rich compared to most people who lived in the past or who live in Third World countries today.

Finally, vagueness can be especially problematic in advertising, especially as it can lead consumers to think a claim for a given product is stronger than it really is. Sometime in the late 1990s or early 2000s, every other deli in New York City became a "gourmet" deli. A little later they were all "organic" as well. But how much organic produce does a store need to offer in order for it to be an organic market? What does a store need to sell in order to be gourmet? After a while, these terms were used by so many stores (and so many that had no reasonable claim to either title) that they lost all meaning and effectiveness.

BUT AMBIGUITY OFTEN SERVES USEFUL PURPOSES

Students sometimes get the idea that ambiguity, and certainly equivocation, are always bad. But they aren't. Ambiguous uses of language, especially metaphorical ones, can be employed for all kinds of good purposes. The well-known psychologist Carl Rogers, for example, used ambiguity effectively in the following passage to emphasize a point:

> As a boy I was rather sickly, and my parents have told me that it was predicted I would die young. This prediction has been proven completely wrong in one sense, but has come profoundly true in another sense. I think it is correct that I will never live to be old. So I now agree with the prediction that I will die young.[5]

Ambiguous uses of language also serve to grease the wheels of social intercourse. Benjamin Disraeli, the nineteenth-century British prime minister, often used ambiguity to soften his replies to letters, while still coming close to being truthful, as in his reply to an unsolicited amateur manuscript: "Many thanks; I shall lose no time in reading it." (In most other contexts, of course, equivocation of this kind is rightly considered to be rather sneaky.)

Ambiguity also serves very useful purposes in literature, particularly in metaphoric passages. It enables writers to introduce multiple meanings quickly into a text in a way that adds significance to what is being said by drawing attention to often rather subtle connections without hitting us over the head with them. For example, the title of William Faulkner's *Light in August* may plausibly refer to the quality of sunlight in late-summer Mississippi (where the novel is set), to a house fire that occurs in the novel, or to the "light" of revelation of one sort or another, a constant theme of the novel. The title "works" in a sense because it captures all three of these at once.

Again, the difference between these acceptable, even laudable uses of ambiguity and the problematic kind is that in none of these acceptable cases is an argument or claim made to seem better than it really is. Rather, the ambiguity is used to better display the richness of the argument or claim in question.

---

[5]Rogers, Carl. *The Carl Rogers Reader*. New York: Houghton Mifflin, 1989. Reprint of article in *Journal of Humanistic Psychology* (Fall 1980).

4. Other Common Rhetorical Devices

Let's now look at a few of the many other rhetorical devices that are frequently used to manipulate the unwary or less knowledgeable. (This does not mean that these devices cannot be used in the service of truth and justice!)

TONE

Good writers or speakers try to choose the **tone** best suited to their audience, as students are taught to do in writing classes. Tone expresses attitudes or feelings—of compassion, anger, levity, humility, congeniality, and so on—and can be quite powerful when employed properly in argumentative passages. Using the proper tone, even though doing so clearly plays to emotions, isn't like arguing fallaciously or from premises known to be false, but rather is just a matter of common sense; arguments aren't won by unnecessarily ruffling the other guy's feathers.

But tone can be employed for nefarious purposes, not just virtuous ones. Lawyers addressing juries are masters of the art, as are politicians addressing constituents. Success in politics requires knowing how to use the tone of "Mom and apple pie" rhetoric when addressing, say, families of soldiers returning from overseas duty, and humor when dealing with matters of a lighter nature. Here, for instance, is an excerpt from the veto by Adlai Stevenson, then governor of Illinois, of a bill to protect birds by restraining the roaming of cats:

> It is in the nature of cats to do a certain amount of unescorted roaming. . . . That cats destroy some birds, I well know, but I believe this legislation would further but little the worthy cause to which its proponents give such unselfish effort. The problem of the cat versus the bird is as old as time. If we attempt to resolve it by legislation, who knows but what we may be called upon to take sides as well in the age-old problem of dog versus cat, bird versus bird, or even bird versus worm. In my opinion, the state of Illinois . . . already has enough to do without trying to control feline delinquency.

Just the right touch to put the quash on a bill that members of the legislature cared little about anyway. By using elevated language to explain his decision on a rather minor matter, and by carrying the consequences of the vetoed bill's logic to ridiculous lengths, Stevenson managed to undermine the opposition with gentle humor and without offending anyone. (Stevenson, by the way, was rightly famous for his ironic humor; witness his remark when accused of being an "egghead": "Eggheads of the world unite; all we have to lose are our yolks.")

Contrast the tone of the Stevenson veto with the following excerpt from the best-known speech by Winston Churchill, a master at the trade. It is taken from the end of an address to the British Parliament in the summer of 1940, during the darkest days of World War II, when the British expected to be invaded by German armies flush with recent and spectacular victories in France—a time when most observers believed Britain was about to be crushed by German military power:

> We shall not flag nor fail. We shall go on to the end. We shall fight . . . on the seas and oceans; we shall fight with growing confidence and growing strength in the air. We shall defend our island whatever the cost may be; we shall fight

on beaches, landing grounds, in fields, in streets and on the hills. We shall never surrender and even if, which I do not for the moment believe, this island or a large part of it were subjugated and starving, then our empire beyond the seas, armed and guarded by the British fleet, will carry on the struggle until in God's good time the New World, with all its power and might, sets forth to the liberation and rescue of the Old.

The point of Churchill's rhetoric was to buck up the courage of the British people—to stiffen their resolve to fight in the face of terrible odds—and the tone of his speech, not to mention its content, accomplished exactly that. (Incidentally, Churchill's address was not recorded; the recording frequently heard of this momentous speech is by someone else, later.)

SLANTING

Slanting is a form of misrepresentation. In one version, a true statement is made so as to imply or suggest something else (usually either false or not known to be true). For example, a defense lawyer may try to blunt damaging testimony by stating, "All this proves is that . . ." or "Since we willingly admit that . . . ," implying that the testimony is of little importance when in fact it is quite damaging. Or an advertisement may say, "Try our best-quality knife, *only* $9.95," implying that the price is very low when in fact it may be just the ordinary price.

Slanting creeps into objective news reports, as in this example from a *Wall Street Journal* article (1 February 2012) explaining super PAC donations to candidates. "In Iowa and Florida, the pro-Romney PAC unleashed a torrent of negative ads that helped dent Mr. Gingrich's poll numbers." The phrase "unleashed a torrent" suggests a virulent attack on an opponent, but the explanation of Gingrich's expenditures that followed is benign. "Mr. Gingrich's super PAC has spent a total of $4.4 million on ads, while his campaign has spent $2.7 million on ads." No mention here of *his* campaign's "torrent" of attack ads on Romney in Florida. A subtle slant, but one that creates a bias.

Slanting also can be accomplished by a careful selection of facts. (So slanting often involves the fallacy of suppressed evidence, discussed in Chapter 3.) For example, the authors of most U.S. history texts used in public schools select facts so as to sanitize American history as much as they can (given the general stricture against wandering too far from the straight and narrow). The point of public school history texts, after all, is not to produce disaffected citizens. Slanting, also, subtly promotes textbook biases. Now that multiculturalism has nudged out Eurocentrism, history books tend to romanticize Native Americans, for instance, and criticize the actions of white settlers. The word *massacre* is invariably used to describe whites attacking Native Americans, but not when the situation is reversed and settlers are the victims of atrocities committed by Native Americans.

It's no secret that political parties slant information to favor their agendas. Under the second President Bush, for example, health information on government websites was subtly changed to reflect the administration's ideology. On the National Cancer Institute website, the statement that there was "no association between abortion and breast cancer" was changed to "the evidence is inconclusive." And the website for the Centers for Disease Control and Prevention used to explain that condoms could protect people effectively from HIV infection, but the revision claimed that "more research is needed."

Slanting sometimes goes under the name *suggestion* or, in some cases, the more pejorative name *innuendo.* The latter term might well be applied to Jeffrey R. Tucker, who wrote the following about Trump for *Newsweek* in 2015: "Because Trump is the only one who speaks this way, he can count on support from the darkest elements of American life. He doesn't need to actually advocate racial homogeneity, call for whites-only signs to be hung at immigration control or push for expulsion or extermination of undesirables. Because such views are verboten, he has the field alone, and he can count on the support of those who think that way by making the right noises." Tucker here stops short of saying that Trump does (or would, for votes) endorse segregation or "extermination," and if pressed, he could deny that he was making any such claim. The nice thing about slanting, so far as practitioners of the art are concerned, is that you can always deny that you implied or suggested what you in fact have implied or suggested.

Suggestion Can Be Dangerous

Monroe C. Beardsley was one of the first to write a textbook dealing strictly with critical reasoning (as opposed to formal logic). In this excerpt from his book Thinking Straight, *he explains an example of* suggestion:

On November 30, 1968, the *New York Times* reported on the construction site for a new jetport in the Everglades, 40 miles from Miami:

> *Populated now by deer, alligators, wild turkeys, and a tribe of Indians who annually perform a rite known as the Green Corn Dance, the tract could someday accommodate a super jetport twice the size of Kennedy International in New York and still have a one-mile buffer on every side to minimize intrusion in the lives of any eventual residents.*

A more horrible example of suggestion could hardly be found. First, note that by putting the Indians in a list with deer, alligators, and wild turkeys, the writer suggests that they belong in the same category as these subhuman species. This impression is reinforced by the allusion to the "Green Corn Dance," which (since it is irrelevant to the rest of the story) can only suggest that this kind of silly superstitious activity sums up their lives. And the impression is driven home sharply at the end when we get to the need to "minimize intrusions on the lives of any eventual residents"—the Indians, of course, can hardly be counted as real residents.

—*Thinking Straight. 4th ed. Englewood Cliffs, N.J.: Prentice Hall, 1975.*

WEASEL WORDS

Weasel words (or phrases) are locutions that appear to make little or no change in the content of a statement while in fact sucking out all or most of its content. (Weasels often suck out the content of eggs without breaking their shells.) Typical is the use of the terms *may* or *may be,* as in this example from a student paper: "Economic success *may be* the explanation of male dominance over females" (italics added). Using the expression *may be* instead of the straightforward verb *is* protected the student from error by reducing the content of her statement close to zero. What she said is consistent with the economic success of males *not* being the reason for male dominance. By the way, note the assumption that males do dominate females in the last analysis, a contention some males (and females!) would deny. The term *arguably* is another weasel word frequently employed to spruce up weak arguments. The student quoted here might just as well have protected herself by stating that "Economic success *arguably* is the explanation for male dominance over females."

Weasel words are the stock and trade of most politicians when discussing controversial issues—and they can be subtle. For example, when President Obama went to Ohio in 2011 to spread the good news about the improved economy of the automobile industry, he had this to say on his weekly radio address: "Chrysler has repaid every dime and more of what it owes American taxpayers for their support during my presidency."[6] Literally this was true. Chrysler *did* repay the $8.5 billion that the Obama administration lent the corporation—but not the $4 billion loan from the Bush administration. Obama weaseled out of that one.

FINE-PRINT DISCLAIMERS

Another common trick is to take back unobtrusively in the (usually) unread fine print what is claimed in the most easily read part of a document. Schlock insurance policies are notorious for their use of this device. They tout wonderful coverage in large type while taking it away in the fine print. When private property is damaged by earthquakes, tornadoes, or hurricanes, for instance, people usually think they are sufficiently insured against damage from natural disasters, but they often discover to their chagrin that upfront promises of replacement cash are severely limited in the fine print of their insurance policies.

Advertisers regularly use very small asterisks to direct readers to the bottom of ads, where they find out, say, that to get the "low-low" airline fare, tickets must be purchased 21 days in advance and cover a stay over at least one Saturday, and also learn that "other restrictions may apply" (note the weasel word *may*, hiding the fact that they do).

Fine-print disclaimers have become so odious that advertisers have begun to play on the fact with a bit of humor, announcing (as some Lexus auto commercials did) that their lawyers have gone into paroxysms of joy while writing the fine print that is then scrolled across the TV screen (very quickly, so it can't be read—but that's part of the humor).

A variation of the fine-print disclaimer is the sneaky stipulation buried in contracts. A blatant example of this fine-print finagling occurred in the case of a fellow named Jim Turner, who rented a car in Connecticut, but discovered when he returned it to the car rental company that he had been charged $450 because of a stipulation in the contract that "fined" the driver $150 every time the speed exceeded 79 miles per hour. His car had been tracked by satellite over seven states! Alas, poor Mr. Turner didn't read the fine print in the contract when the agent asked him to sign his initials by the X.

Another variation on the fine-print disclaimer gambit is the *reinterpretation ploy*. Having said what turns out to be unpopular, or perhaps offensive, the best strategy for a politician often is just to reinterpret the ill-advised remark. On one of the tapes released by Gennifer Flowers, Bill Clinton is heard making a remark that clearly implies he thought Mario Cuomo (then governor of New York) acted like a mafioso. When the

---

[6]Cited in: Kessler, Glenn. "President Obama's Phony Accounting on the Auto Industry." *Washington Post,* 6 June 2011.

tapes became public, an embarrassed Clinton apologized, which is the right thing to do when caught with . . . uh . . . one's pants down, but also stated that "I meant simply to imply that Governor Cuomo is a tough, worthy competitor," which was a clever, but somewhat shady, reinterpretation of his remarks.

EVASION (AGAIN)

Recall our conversation of evasion in Chapter 3. There we focused on the practice as part of a fallacious argumentative strategy. Its prevalence, however, means that we should consider it again here as an unfortunate rhetorical device. It is sometimes shocking how often people get away with evasion in public life. An issue or question can be *evaded* by *wandering from the point* or by snowing one's audience with an immense amount of detail in the hope that they either won't notice or at least won't press the point.

Whenever politicians debate one another, evasion is on full display. We could use any major debate over the last decade, but this is a particularly good example: In the first Republican debate of the 2016 primary season, moderator and Fox News anchor Chris Wallace had this exchange with Ohio governor and presidential candidate John Kasich:

> WALLACE: Governor Kasich, I know you don't like to talk about Donald Trump. But I do want to ask you about the merit of what he just said. When you say that the American government is stupid, that the Mexican government is sending criminals, that we're being bamboozled, is that an adequate response to the question of illegal immigration?
>
> KASICH: Chris, first of all, I was just saying to Chris Christie, they say we're outspoken, we need to take lessons from Donald Trump if we're really going to learn it. Here is the thing about Donald Trump. Donald Trump is hitting a nerve in this country. He is. He's hitting a nerve. People are frustrated. They're fed up. They don't think the government is working for them. And for people who want to just tune him out, they're making a mistake.
>
> Now, he's got his solutions. Some of us have other solutions. You know, look, I balanced the federal budget as one of the chief architects when I was in Washington. Hasn't been done since. I was a military reformer. I took the state of Ohio from an $8 billion hole and a 350,000 job loss to a $2 billion surplus and a gain of 350,000 jobs.
>
> WALLACE: Respectfully, can we talk about illegal immigration?
>
> KASICH: But the point is that we all have solutions. Mr. Trump is touching a nerve because people want the wall to be built. They want to see an end to illegal immigration. They want to see it, and we all do. But we all have different ways of getting there. And you're going to hear from all of us tonight about what our ideas are.
>
> WALLACE: All right, well, Senator Rubio, let me see if I can do better with you . . .

By the way, it needs to be said that not all wandering from the point is evasive. We have to say this here because the many asides in this textbook (like the one you're reading right now) definitely are not intended as obfuscations, but merely as remarks about related or secondary matters that, it is hoped, the reader will find either interesting or informative.

*"Let me answer your question about farm subsidies
by saying a few words about Benghazi."*

David Sipress The New Yorker Collection/The Cartoon Bank

*After an attack on the U.S. embassy in Benghazi, Libya, the Obama admin-
istration and especially then-Secretary of State Hillary Clinton came under
constant fire from political opponents for their handling of security in Libya,
the attack itself, and its aftermath.*

5. Language Manipulators

People manipulate language for all sorts of reasons: to flatter, to impress, to persuade, to obfuscate, and to distort the truth—to name a few. Sometimes language manipulation is benign, but when it is done to benefit those in power, it can undermine the rights of others. Often the point of redefining language is to circumvent legal stipulations or to justify inequities—as noted below.

When the torture scandal at Abu Ghraib hit the news, officials in the Bush adminis-tration claimed it was the work of a few bad apples, but skeptics dug deeper and came up with the Justice Department's interpretation of existing laws banning torture abroad (posted on the *Washington Post* website, June 14, 2004). In Section 2340 of the U.S. Criminal Code, torture is defined as any act "specifically intended to inflict severe phys-ical or mental pain or suffering . . . upon another person within his custody or physical control." The Justice Department's legalistic explanation (written in June 2002) was that "mere" pain wasn't enough. "Physical pain amounting to torture must be equivalent in intensity to the pain accompanying serious physical injury, such as organ failure, impairment of bodily function, or even death."[7] This interpretation seems to make torture legal, unless it is extreme.

As for the fate of interrogators "who might arguably cross the line drawn in Section 2340" and be charged with torture—not to worry: They could claim they acted out of "necessity" or "self-defense," pleas that "would potentially alleviate criminal liability." In other words, they could get off the hook.

THOSE WHO CONTROL THE DEFINITIONS . . .

Calling something by just the right name is crucial when you want to bend the law in your favor, influence public opinion, or justify funny business of one kind or another. For example, employers who want to pay employees less than the legal minimum wage or escape contractual obligations to provide health and other benefits to employees need only categorize them as *subcontractors* and arrange paperwork accordingly. Minimum wage laws in the United States apply to employees but not to subcontractors; union-brokered agreements concerning employee health insurance don't cover subcontractors.[8] Attempts at this kind of chicanery via definition occasionally have been overturned by the courts, but often they are successful.

The food industry is plagued with misleading labels initiated by special interest groups who change the meaning of words used to describe food. For example, in 2003, the House and Senate passed a huge federal spending bill with the last-minute provision that meat, poultry, and dairy products could be labeled "organic" even if the animals were fed partly or entirely nonorganic feed. This rider was added to the bill on behalf of Fieldale Farms, which complained about the supply of organic feed (though organic farmers say that what is really at issue is the price, not the supply—which is sufficient). So when does organic mean organic?

Closer to home, college administrators manage to cope with shrinking budgets by hiring lots of cheap labor, often referred to as *adjunct faculty* to distinguish them from "tenure-track" professors. Teachers hired as adjunct faculty earn a good deal less per course than do their tenured colleagues; receive many fewer, if any, fringe benefits; and don't enjoy similar job security. This division of labor can be thought of as an academic analogue to the "downsizing" that goes on in the business world.

On a worldwide level, rich nations manage to undercut the labor force of poor ones by manipulating the language of international agreements to their advantage. Farm subsidies unfairly undercut the agricultural industry of developing countries, particularly in Africa, where most farmers are desperately poor, partly because they cannot compete with the subsidized products from the United States and European Union (EU). A world trade agreement was drawn up to prevent this situation from occurring, but the United States and the EU managed to slide out of it by simply using different language for export subsidies. For instance, instead of violating the agreement with "trade-distorting"

---

[7]Taken from: "Small Comfort." *Washington Post,* 15 June 2004.

[8]While billionaire Bill Gates was becoming the richest person in the world, his Microsoft Corporation was using the subcontractor ploy to stiff over a thousand of his employees out of several perks other employees were entitled to. At one time or another, Microsoft has been embroiled in court battles over employee classification since 1990.

subsidies by paying farmers according to the amount they produce, the EU gives them direct grants that have almost the same effect on the price of these crops as before but are now called "non-distorting" because grants are determined by the amount of land a farmer owns and how much the land produced in the past.[9] Thus the EU is able to under-cut the labor force of developing countries without breaking the trade agreement.

Although the U.S. Constitution grants Congress the sole right to declare war, this has rarely deterred American presidents from waging war without obtaining any such decla-ration. As we noted earlier in the chapter, they have simply renamed their escapades or declared them not to be wars. The American wars in Korea and Vietnam were described (at least in their early stages) as "police actions" since no "war" had been declared. Assuming the December 1990 congressional measure allowing President Bush (the elder) to carry out United Nations (UN) resolutions did indeed constitute a declaration of war, even though it didn't actually say we were declaring war, then that Gulf conflict is very likely the only legal war out of at least five fought by the United States since World War II.

In 2002, Congress gave President Bush (the younger) authorization to use the armed forces as he considered necessary to defend our country's national security against the threat of Iraq and to enforce the UN Security Council resolutions with regard to Iraq. Thus Congress gave Bush the authority to wage war on Iraq but managed to avoid a

---

Just "Folks"

How much can you squeeze out of a single word, like folks, for example? A lot, according to Susan Anthony. In a trenchant analysis of the dumbing down of America, she explains how the ubiquitous use of folks is symptomatic of the erosion of cultural standards in this country.

The word is everywhere, a plague spread by the President of the United States, tele-vision anchors, radio talk show hosts, preachers in megachurches, self-help gurus, and anyone else attempting to demonstrate his or her identification with ordinary, presumably wholesome American values. Only a few decades ago, Americans were addressed as people or, in the more distant past, ladies and gentlemen. Now we are all folks. . . . [as in "our prayers go out to those folks" or "I've been in contact with our homeland security folks."]

The specific political use of folks . . . designed to make the speaker sound like one of the boys or girls, is symptomatic of a debasement in public speech inseparable from a more general erosion of American cultural standards. . . . Look up any impor-tant presidential speech in the history of the United States before 1980 and you will not find one patronizing appeal to folks. Imagine: "We here highly resolve that these folks shall not have died in vain . . . and that government of the folks, by the folks, for the folks, shall not perish from the earth."

—*The Age of American Unreason.* New York: Pantheon, 2008. 3–4.

---

[9]For more on this, see the (London) *Guardian,* 3 June 2003.

congressional declaration of war. This equivocation enabled Congress to pass the buck and avoid criticism if the war went badly.[10]

In the war in Afghanistan, the Bush administration classified as "enemy combatants" hundreds of suspected al Qaeda and Taliban fighters detained by the United States at Guantanamo Bay Naval Base. Had they been called "prisoners of war," they would have been entitled to release when the war was over, but as "enemy combatants," not only could they be detained indefinitely for questioning without charge, they couldn't challenge their imprisonment in court, nor were they entitled to any other constitutional rights. The case to reverse this decision was appealed for years until it finally worked its way up to the Supreme Court in 2008. In *Boumediene v. Bush,* the Court ruled that aliens detained as enemy combatants in Guantanamo have a constitutional right to challenge their detention in American courts. Will this ruling stand, or will the term *enemy combatants* morph into another category that manages to slide past the law?

When President Obama took office, his administration immediately began rebranding military activities without necessarily changing the policies.[11] Cut from the vocabulary were favorites of the Bush administration like "surge," "enemy combatants," and "war on terror." As Senate majority leader Harry Reid said when Obama increased troop levels in Afghanistan, "Whatever you do, don't call it a surge." So tens of thousands of troops were sent to Afghanistan, but it wasn't a "surge." Captives were still held at Guantanamo Bay, but they weren't "enemy combatants." The War on Terror morphed into "overseas contingency operations." And the controversial U.S. Patriot Act (a euphemism if there ever was one) that allowed eavesdropping without warrant was renamed the Terrorist Surveillance Program. One of the first items on a new president's agenda is to revise the lexicon to make it seem as though it reflects a change in policy.

Sometimes common sense prevails, and redefinition backfires. In 2015, presidential candidate Ben Carson had the following exchange with *Meet the Press'* Chuck Todd (NBC, September 20, 2015):

> CHUCK TODD: Should a President's faith matter? Should your faith matter to voters?
>
> DR. BEN CARSON: Well, I guess it depends on what that faith is. If it's inconsistent with the values and principles of America, then of course it should matter. But if it fits within the realm of America and consistent with the Constitution, no problem.
>
> CHUCK TODD: So do you believe that Islam is consistent with the constitution?
>
> DR. BEN CARSON: No, I don't, I do not.
>
> CHUCK TODD: So you—
>
> DR. BEN CARSON: I would not advocate that we put a Muslim in charge of this nation. I absolutely would not agree with that.

This last comment understandably caused a bit of controversy for Carson, so much in fact that he felt the need to clear up just how he was using the word "Muslim." For that

---

[10]See: Dorf, Michael C. "Is the War on Iraq Lawful?" Web. 19 March 2003. http://writ.news.find-law.com/dorf/20030319.html.

[11]See: Baker, Peter. "The Words Change, if Not the Policies." *New York Times,* 3 April 2009.

he chose the much more sympathetic environs of the conservative-leaning *Sean Hannity Show*. From that conversation the very next day (Fox News, September 21, 2015):

> HANNITY: OK. But, well, then so basically the controversy is over in that sense. You're saying, did you mean to say "radical Islamist" or one that supports a form of government as is practiced in Muslim countries, is that more what you meant to say?
>
> CARSON: Well, you know, that was implied in the comment, because I prefaced that by saying I don't care what religion or faith someone belongs to if they're willing to subjugate that to the American way and to our Constitution, then I have no problem with it. That's what I said before that.

That's not exactly what he said, but okay. Hannity declared the controversy over, so nothing to see here, right? Carson just meant "radical Islamist" by "Muslim." The meaning that he just made up was implied, somehow. We can definitely agree that it would be bad to have a radical Islamist in the White House. But let's go back to the original conversation on *Meet the Press,* right from where we left off:

> CHUCK TODD: And would you ever consider voting for a Muslim for Congress?
>
> DR. BEN CARSON: Congress is a different story, but it depends on who that Muslim is and what their policies are, just as it depends on what anybody else says, you know.

So putting all this together, we have to conclude that Ben Carson might well vote for a radical Islamist (or, as he likes to say, "Muslim") for Congress. But that's surely not what he'd like us to conclude. As much as this is a lesson in the perils of backtracking through redefinition, it is also yet another lesson that politicians will often say just about whatever they think they can get away with at the moment they're saying it.

When lesser-known people manipulate language to their own ends, though, it often slips under the radar. Take, for instance, a German teenager, Helene Hegemann, who infused her best-selling novel about clubbing and drugging in Berlin with passages lifted from other writers' works. When her plagiarism was discovered, her response was to turn it on its head. "There's no such thing as originality anyway, just authenticity." (Whatever that means.) No apology given, despite the uproar it caused, and no consequences, either. In fact, the book was nominated for a $20,000 fiction prize at the Leipzig Book Fair. By claiming that she didn't feel she was stealing "because she put all the material into a completely different and unique context," she managed to doublespeak her way out of blame. How many students could get away with that one?

When language is manipulated, it isn't always easy to determine whether there is some sort of sleight of hand going on. For years, the psychologist Thomas Szasz campaigned against the use of the expression *mental illness,* on grounds that there is no such thing as *mental* illness. Declaring John Hinckley "not guilty by reason of insanity" after his attempt to assassinate President Reagan was for Szasz just an extreme example of what happens when we take the analogy between physical illness and alleged mental illness seriously. (He did believe, however, that sometimes what is thought of as mental illness really is physical dysfunction.)

But Szasz is in the minority on this point, with the result, he claimed, that various kinds of serious abuses of civil rights occur. One is that close relatives of the "mentally ill" often are able to have them "hospitalized for treatment" against their will. Forcing people into institutions in this way is a practice some see as not unlike the one that used to be common in the Soviet Union of confining political opponents in "mental institutions." In a similar vein, Szasz argued, "we call self-starvation either *anorexia nervosa,* a *hunger strike,* a *suicide attempt,* or some other name, depending on how we want to respond."

Well, then, is Szasz right about this? A number of psychologists find his position modestly persuasive, while the majority do not. The reason for this split of opinion is that good arguments can be made on both sides of the issue, making it difficult to choose one over the other. Which choice we should make may well depend, as Szasz noted, on how we wish to deal with whatever circumstances our decisions affect. (Philosophy students might note the connection of this sort of case to the age-old conundrum about whether, when every part of an old ship has been replaced over the years by a new part, it is still the same ship; the answer, at least a third of this writing team believes, is that it depends on who we wish to say "built" a ship repaired in this way, not on any truth written in the sky.)

THOSE WHO FRAME PUBLIC POLICY

Redefining words is one way to influence public opinion; another is to use loaded language to evoke a worldview that persuades people to adopt policies—even if these policies go against their own interests. Over the past decade, George Lakoff, a professor of linguistics at the University of California, Berkeley, has become well known (and controversial) for developing a theory about the science and art of framing the debate that has attracted attention across the political spectrum.

> *Conservative, n.* A statesman who is enamored of existing evils, as distinguished from the Liberal, who wishes to replace them with others.
>
> —AMBROSE BIERCE *(THE DEVIL'S DICTIONARY)*

Lakoff defines frames as "mental structures that shape the way we see the world. As a result, they shape the goals we seek, the plans we make, the way we act, what counts as a good or bad outcome of our actions. In politics our frames shape our social policies and the institutions we form to carry out policies."[12]

We recognize frames through language, and since people usually make decisions about politics based on their values, the language creates the frame that evokes those

---

[12]Lakoff, George. *Don't Think of an Elephant.* White River Junction, VA: Chelsea Green Publishing, 2004. xv.

values. Lakoff uses as an example the loaded phrase "tax relief," conjured up by Republicans to hype their campaign for tax cuts (a neutral, but accurate term). The notion of relief suggests that there is an affliction that must be removed. Those who remove the affliction are the good guys; those who oppose it, the bad guys. The "frame" taps into the voters' value systems, and they, in turn, buy into the idea. Meanwhile the media repeats the phrase over and over until it enters the political lexicon.

In recent budget battles, the term "tax relief" has continued to evolve in ever more creative ways. When Democrats proposed closing special interest loopholes in the tax code to regain billions of dollars lost to offshore tax havens, house Republicans labeled it a "tax hike," vowing that such tax increases cannot pass in the House. Buried by this doublespeak is the fact that companies use these gimmicks to avoid paying taxes already levied on them—in no sense are they tax hikes. But the frame hoodwinks people into believing that they are. Other examples include the ominous-sounding "death tax" and the emotionally charged "partial birth abortion," loaded phrases that nudge voters into supporting tax cuts and banning third-term abortions.

Democrats invented their own political frames. When Republicans threatened to eliminate the filibuster procedure that Democrats were using to prevent a quick confirmation of Bush-appointed judges, the Democrats framed their attack as an "abuse of power." Day after day they hammered away at the message that they were fighting for democracy against a Republican abuse of power that was not what our founders intended. This frame evoked the worldview that we value democracy and want to preserve it. Republicans were attempting to undermine democracy by eliminating the filibuster, an American birthright that is central to our republic. In fact, the filibuster is a parliamentary procedure (not a birthright) that is typically used to prevent the Senate majority from ending a debate. The Democrats were actually breaking tradition in using it to block the confirmation of an entire slate of judges. Nonetheless the public was persuaded, and Republicans backed down under pressure.[13] It's not surprising, though, that Republicans had no qualms about using this trick repeatedly to block the Democratic agenda once Barack Obama became president.

Whether or not we agree with Lakoff's theory, there is enough truth in it to make us wary of the way politicians use language to manipulate us to side with them on critical issues.

Psychologists use the term *framing effects* to describe similar phenomena that influence our decisions. For instance, weight-conscious people are more likely to eat hamburgers described as 90 percent lean rather than 10 percent fat, even though the amount of fat is the same in either case. Charities rake in more money when they urge donors to give pennies a day rather than dollars per year. People are more likely to spend money described as a bonus (because it is extra income and thus dispensable) and more likely to save money described as a rebate (because it implies a return on money spent within their income that should not be squandered). And, of course, advertisers regularly rely on framing effects to manipulate consumers into buying their products.

---

[13]For more on this see: Bai, Matt. "The Framing Wars." *New York Times Magazine,* 17 July 2005—an in-depth discussion of Lakoff's theory.

6. Some Subtle Issues

Sometimes our use of language can manipulate, evade, or bend claims in more subtle ways. Like the rhetorical devices we discussed just now, these are not necessarily always bad things, but they're certainly things about which we need to be aware as we approach rhetorical and argumentative texts and speech.

USE AND MENTION

We do lots of different things with words. We state claims, issue commands, ask questions, make declarations, perform ceremonies, express attitudes, and unleash exclamations. We use individual words to refer to people, objects, actions, properties, ideas, forces, feelings and (almost) all other sorts of things. One thing that we can refer to with a particular word is the word itself.

Philosophers and linguists offer us a useful distinction between *using* a word to refer to something and *mentioning* the word—roughly speaking, referring to the word itself. In written language, we have certain conventions to distinguish use and mention, most notably quotation marks or italics. We'll just use quotation marks here. So we clearly use the word "chair" in the sentence "Please have a seat in this chair." And we mention the word "chair" in the sentence " 'Chair' has five letters." We are highly unlikely to make a mistake in a case like this. We can't sit on words; and chairs can have seats, legs, armrests, backs, etc., but not letters. You may be surprised, though, how much confusion and trouble we can get up to when we don't sufficiently appreciate this distinction.

One example comes to us from Fox News (June 22, 2015, via a transcript on Foxnews.com):

> I'm David Webb, in for Sean [Hannity] tonight. Thank you for joining us.
>
> Over the weekend, during a podcast with a comedian, Marc Maron, President Obama sparked controversy during a discussion about race when he used the n-word to convey his point. Listen to this.
>
> (BEGIN AUDIO CLIP)
>
> PRESIDENT BARACK OBAMA: Racism, we are not cured of it, clearly. And it's not just a matter of it not being polite to say (DELETED) in public. That's not the measure of whether racism still exists or not. It's not just a matter of overt discrimination. We have to—societies don't overnight completely erase everything that happened 200 to 300 years prior.
>
> (END AUDIO CLIP)
>
> WEBB: So is the dialogue you just heard advancing Americans' discussion about race? Joining me to respond, criminal defense attorney Eric Guster, executive director of TheTeaParty.net, my good friend, Niger Innis, and Fox News contributor Deneen Borelli. Ladies first. Deneen, President Obama's comments and the dignity of the office.
>
> DENEEN BORELLI, FOX NEWS CONTRIBUTOR: It's outrageous, David. I think he has absolutely lowered the standard in terms of being president of the United States. He made no mention of racism in America when he ran for president not once but twice. And I have dubbed him today rapper-in-chief for using such language.

Had President Obama *used* such language, this may have been a real controversy and something deserving of leading a national news segment. But of course, he did no such thing.

QUOTATIONS

We just discussed one application of quotation marks. A far more common use, of course, is marking off when we are referring to someone else's words rather than using our own. But quotations have their own pitfalls and opportunities for chicanery.

One common deceptive use of quotations involves distancing ourselves from claims we would like to make ourselves but know it's inopportune to do so. This sort of rhetorical move is especially common in politics, and facilitated by Twitter's "retweeting" function. This, for instance, was sent from Donald Trump's account in 2015 (and then was subsequently deleted): " '@mplefty67: If Hillary Clinton can't satisfy her husband what makes her think she can satisfy America?' " This is clearly not an appropriate joke for a presidential candidate to make. But is it any different because he's just quoting @mplefty67?

We should be particularly suspicious when someone doesn't attribute the quote to a particular person, but instead appeals to what "they" say. Trump got a question on *Meet the Press* similar to the one that tripped up Ben Carson, about whether he'd be comfortable with a Muslim president. His reply: "I mean, some people have said it already happened, frankly. But of course you wouldn't agree with that." Trump can claim, then, that *he* isn't intimating that President Obama is secretly Muslim, he's just helpfully reporting on what "some people" have said.

Of course, quoting without attribution is no worse than misquoting someone—whether we're making an opponent's claims worse than they are (leading to the "straw man" fallacy discussed in Chapter 3) or making some authority seem more amenable to our position than they actually are. During the 2016 campaign, Ted Cruz's spokesman Rick Tyler shared a video of Cruz's opponent Marco Rubio saying something not quite intelligible to a Cruz staffer who was reading a Bible. The subtitles on the video had him

JOEDATOR

"You have the right to remain silent. Anything you say can be taken out of context and put on Twitter and then it'll be a whole thing."

saying the Bible has "not many answers." Apparently, Rubio actually said the Bible has "all the answers." To Cruz's credit, Tyler lost his position over the incident.

Perhaps not as egregious as the manufactured quote, quoting out of context can be just as deceptive a practice. In 2016, the *Los Angeles Times* printed a headline that was sure to grab the attention of fans of the television show *The Office:* "Jenna Fischer was 'genuinely in love' with 'Office' costar John Krasinski." Fischer and Krasinski played characters whose romantic relationship was a major part of the show's plot. Here, though, is Fischer's complete quote: "John and I have real chemistry. There's a real part of me that is Pam and a real part of him that's Jim. And those parts of us were genuinely in love with one another." That quote, which sounds much more like a claim about a good *acting* relationship, is a far cry from what the headline (or, indeed, the body of the story) suggests.

One more note on quotations. People often use common expressions, or "sayings," and think they're quoting something like common sense. Indeed, a recognized expression too often counts for more than an actual argument. This is one of our odder habits. A claim is not more likely to be true because it is often repeated. Sometimes the results of this are illogical, and sometimes they're ridiculous. Take, for instance, the way people commonly refer to "the exception that proves the rule," as when they want to dismiss an exception to a favored principle. "Well, that's the exception that proves the rule." But exceptions refute the generality of rules, not prove them. The expression's original (and reasonable) usage does not mean that an exception to a rule proves it to be true. Rather, the expression meant that indicating an exception suggests that there is a (non-universal) rule in the first place—not that the rule holds universally. So, for instance, when a teacher says "a student who does not turn in a draft cannot turn in a final paper," there is an implication that students (at least those who do turn in a draft) can turn in a final paper.

THE PASSIVE VOICE

At some point, probably, a composition teacher has told you that you should write in an active rather than passive voice. So you should write "I want to do well" rather than "doing well is wanted by me," and even "the butler murdered the lord of the house" rather than "the lord of the house was murdered by the butler." As stylistic advice, this is probably a bit fussy. But this is not only a stylistic issue.

Because it makes the subject of a sentence the person or thing being acted upon rather than the one doing the acting, the passive voice allows speakers a grammatical trick for distancing them from unpleasant admissions. The public non-apology apology has become something of a cliché: "mistakes were made" rather than "I made mistakes." The offender, but not the offense, disappears from the sentence.

As one of a plethora of available examples, consider this from a statement from Congressman Randy Weber apologizing for a tweet that compared President Obama to Hitler (remember the guilt by association fallacy):

> I need to first apologize to all those offended by my tweet. It was not my
> intention to trivialize the Holocaust nor to compare the President to Adolf Hitler.
> The mention of Hitler was meant to represent the face of evil that still exists in
> the world today.

Notice how different the whole thing would have sounded in a consistently active voice:

> I need to first apologize to all those my tweet offended. I did not intend to
> trivialize the Holocaust nor to compare the President to Adolf Hitler. I meant
> the mention of Hitler to represent the face of evil that still exists in the world
> today.

This is not to say that we should reject as duplicitous every use of the passive voice. But when the context clearly calls for an active voice—say, in a public apology—we should be suspicious when someone drops out of a sentence entirely when they should be the subject of it.

If you disagree with this section, just remember that it was written with the best intentions.

7. Language Revision

Languages aren't artificial products constructed by "linguistic experts" in some laboratory or think tank. They are living, changing products of human intelligence designed to perform various functions, including not just communicating ideas from one person to another, but also issuing commands, asking questions, and certifying relationships (as in wedding ceremonies). This being the case, languages tend to mirror the foibles, aspirations, loyalties, and (alas!) prejudices of those who speak them. English is no exception. Like all languages, English undergoes revision on a regular basis.

THE REFORM OF SEXIST LANGUAGE

In the past 20 or 30 years, a minor revolution has taken place in the United States, as well as many other countries, in the attitudes of most people toward members of minority groups and women. Inevitably, this revolution has been mirrored in the linguistic practices of those caught up in it.

But the most extensive linguistic changes of this kind have been those reflecting the changing attitudes of most people concerning relationships between men and women and the roles played by women in society. A large majority of previously common sexist locutions have disappeared from everyday speech. This linguistic change has occurred very quickly, as these things go, no doubt in part because of the persistent demands of women's rights advocates. But it also has happened quickly because of the swiftness with which attitudes toward women and their roles in society have changed, and because of the speed with which women have entered fields previously reserved primarily for men.

Not so long ago, when the overwhelming majority of those in high office were men, it may have made some sense to refer to these people as business*men* and congress*men.* But in this day and age, with increasing numbers of women taking on these roles, it makes much less sense. In addition, there is a general realization that these sexist terms imply not just that those holding these offices always are male, but also, and wrongly, that only males are supposed to, or are competent to, fill them. The old sexist language implies in subtle but persuasive ways that positions of power should be *manned,* not *personed* or *womaned,* and this in turn implies that only men are capable of holding these important positions. Thus, substituting nonsexist words for the old sexist terms puts women on an equal linguistic footing with men that not only reflects their growing equality but also helps make it possible. Our thoughts about the world—how it works and how it should work—always are framed in language; sexist locutions tend to introduce sexist thoughts into our minds.

So today, people who head committees or departments are generally called *chairs,* not *chairmen* ("I would like to address the chair about . . ." or "The chair has ruled that . . ."). Similarly, people who deliver the mail tend to get called *letter carriers,* not *mailmen.* We say *firefighter* instead of *fireman* and *police officer* rather than *policeman.* The term *man* and its many derivatives now often are replaced by *people, person,* and the like. Publishers don't cotton to manuscripts that contain locutions like "Of course, a *man* might be described as taking a . . ." when it would be more accurate to say "*Someone* might be described as taking a . . ." or to phrases like "even if *he* is willing to allow . . ." when what is meant is *he or she.*[14]

One of the more interesting language changes accompanying the feminist revolution has been the widespread use of the term *Ms.,* intended to serve when the marriage status of a woman is not considered relevant. The point of this change was to foster equal treatment of the sexes. Men, whether married or single, have always been referred to by the same term, *Mr.,* whereas women have had to be called either *Miss* or *Mrs.,* depending on their marital status. In magazine and newspaper articles, the trend is to drop the title entirely and simply refer to women by their last names—the way men always have been. A similar, and perhaps much more significant change, is the fact that women nowadays don't always take on the last name of their mate, although, interestingly, they still usually do (while men rarely do). But even when women do adopt their husband's last name, they often also hang onto their own, so that, for example, we refer to Hillary *Rodham* Clinton, not just Hillary Clinton.[15]

But an even more important language change may be the elimination of locutions like this one, once typical of the language encountered in all sorts of places, including public school history textbooks: "Pioneers moved west, taking their wives and children with them." That made all of the pioneers into men, while women and children were just accessories. A text written today would get it right and say something like "Pioneer families moved west."

On the other hand, things can get carried too far. It would be unnecessary, wouldn't it, for Germans to stop referring to their homeland as the *Fatherland,* or Englishmen—that is, citizens of England—to their *mother tongue?* What purpose would be served by replacing *Uncle Sam* with *Aunt Sarah?* And why worry about using the term *manhole* when talking about those round excisions in streets and avenues, as did the Public Works Departments of several American cities? (Would it be wrong to change biblical references to God from the *He* employed in the original versions to some more neutral

---

[14]Both of these examples are taken, alas, from a journal article coauthored back in the bad old days by a male coauthor of this text.

[15]However, the increasingly common practice of adding a name by hyphenation (and passing both on to children) is not sustainable. What happens if everyone does it? Well, then in the next generation, two people with hyphenated last names will have kids, and those kids will have four names. Their kids will have eight and in just eight generations we'll all have 256 last names. Filling out forms is onerous enough as it is. One suspects that another convention must be around the corner.

term?) The term *humankind* seems an apt substitute for *mankind*, but somehow the "era of ordinary people" doesn't have the same ring as the "century of the common man."

In any case, the changes in linguistic style brought on by the feminist revolution have also raised questions of aesthetic taste—of what sounds right or wrong rolling off the tongue or when reading a book. The expression *her or his,* to take one example, rings false, perhaps because it calls attention to the avoidance of *his* (used to mean *his* or *her*) or of *his or her,* and thus detracts from what is being said. Good taste sometimes dictates other sorts of moves, for instance, employing plural rather than singular pronouns, thus saying things like, "when students read their textbooks . . ." rather than "when a student reads his textbook . . ." (That's one reason for the plethora of plural expressions that occur in this textbook. Note, by the way, that the term *congressperson* nowhere appears on these pages, although *member of Congress* is used quite often.)

Interestingly, no one seems overwrought by the fact that Liberty always is portrayed as a woman. (Think, for instance, of the Statue of Liberty in New York Harbor.) Note also that, although there are lots of complaints about sexist terms like *waitress* and *actress,* no one seems bothered by the equally sexist term *widower.* Women still receive an award each year for best *actress.* And freshmen still are called *freshmen.* Ah, well.

PC (POLITICALLY CORRECT) TERMINOLOGY

The revolution concerning gender rhetoric is part of a larger movement that also has dramatically changed the ways in which we speak of minorities. As attitudes have changed, language, inevitably, has followed suit.

The result is that certain locutions have become "in," while others are "out." Some are politically correct (PC), some politically incorrect. Careers have been wrecked by publicly using expressions like "fat Jap" and "Nigra." It would be political suicide today to say publicly, as someone did in the 1970s, when then Governor Tribbitt (Delaware) hired a woman as his press secretary at $20,000 a year, "If he wants to pay $10,000 a mammary, that's his business." We aren't supposed to use phrases like *admitted homosexual* (because it implies that being a homosexual is bad) or *tidal wave of immigrants* (because of its negative implication concerning immigrants).

On the whole, of course, changes of this nature are all to the good and are applauded by just about everybody. But problems do arise, and it is quite possible that an excess of zeal causes some of them. At Stanford University, students can be punished for violating speech codes designed to suppress racist, sexist, and homophobic speech that carries no legal penalty in the "real" world. An administrator at the University of California, Santa Cruz, was even wary of phrases like a "nip in the air" and "a chink in one's armor" because certain of these words could be construed as racial slurs in other contexts.

Sometimes the attempt to be PC defies all logic. The reading passages of the New York State Regents English exam were edited to delete anything that might make "any student feel ill at ease when taking the test." For example, all references to Judaism were cut from an excerpt from a work by Isaac Bashevis Singer about Jewish life in Europe! In one revision, for instance, "most Jewish women" was changed to "most women." For this PC passage, the New York State Regents were given the NCTE Doublespeak award for 2002.

And sometimes these kinds of sweeping changes can produce truly bizarre results. In one infamous episode, the American Family Association decided to set up a program that would automatically change the word "gay" to the word "homosexual" in wire

GREGORY

"We're trying to come up with a less offensive term for 'political correctness.'"

Alex Gregory The New Yorker Collection/The Cartoon Bank

service stories before publication on its news website OneNewsNow. That seemed to work out for them and their audience until American sprinter Tyson Gay started to make headlines prior to the 2008 Olympics. At that point—well, you can guess what happened: "Tyson Homosexual was a blur in blue, sprinting 100 meters faster than anyone ever has . . . Homosexual qualified for his first Summer Games team and served notice he's certainly someone to watch in Beijing . . . 'It means a lot to me,' the 25-year-old Homosexual said. 'I'm glad my body could do it, because now I know I have it in me.' "

Are we getting a bit overzealous in our, shall we say, *linguistic cleansing?* It no doubt is a good idea, now that the children of unwed parents are not looked down upon, to stop referring to them as *bastards,* thus getting rid of the unfair opprobrium of that nasty term. And why not change the name of the Italian Welfare Agency to the *Italian-American Community Service Agency*?

But is there anything wrong with calling "mixed-breed" dogs *mongrels,* "visually impaired" people *blind,* or the "psychologically impacted" *insane*? Don't those who call the *Sports Illustrated* swimsuit issue *pornographic* rob that word of its legitimate meaning? (Is there a risk here that the door will be opened to wrongheaded legislation?) Was Newt Gingrich just being polite when he said President Bill Clinton was "factually challenged" instead of calling him a liar? (Was he just trying to be cute, snide, or clever?)

Although quibbling about the trivial use of PC language continues, the more serious issue of political correctness toward certain minority groups may be eroding. Now that immigration has once again heated up in the wake of the Great Recession, and multiculturalism has come under attack with the rise in Islamophobia after 9/11, PC has been winding down. In the debate over whether to change the Constitution to deny citizenship to children born in this country of immigrant parents, terms like *anchor babies* are now widely used as slurs—this one implying that illegal immigrants have babies here to improve the parents' chance of getting citizenship. No PC is evident there. The same

---

What Is in a Name?

Sometimes it takes a bit of consideration to determine how to distinguish the genuinely offensive from the object of PC overreaction. Current controversies over Native American sports team names provide particularly interesting cases.

It seems like overkill to object to a team name like the Atlanta *Braves* (though the Braves' icons, mascots, and chants may be another story). If the Braves have an inappropriate name and the Golden State *Warriors* do not, and if the Kansas City *Chiefs'* name is problematic but not that of the Sacramento *Kings*, then it can only be because any such reference to Native American culture is offensive, and that is at least not obvious.

A slightly harder case may be the Cleveland *Indians*. At least one author of this text finds it a little uncomfortable to name a team after an entire people. Coupled with the problematic nature of "Indian" as a name for that people, and the fact that we're referring to a current culture, there seems to be a relevant difference between the Cleveland *Indians* and, say, the Minnesota *Vikings* or the USC *Trojans*.

One name that seems obviously offensive is the Washington *Redskins*. Indeed, a growing number of sportswriters and commentators have begun to refuse to use the name, instead referring to the team just by their city.

What do you think? Where should an appropriate line be drawn? What exactly is the difference between "Redskins" and "Indians" or between "Indians" and "Braves"? Is there a relevant difference?

---

goes for widespread attacks on Muslims, who are increasingly targeted by well-funded anti-Islamic groups peddling hate and fear on websites and blogs. When slurs and hate speech filter into the national dialogue, PC collapses into prejudice and scapegoating—exactly what it was created to prevent.

Summary of Chapter 7

1. Most words have emotive meanings (in addition to cognitive meanings). Words like *oppression, kike,* and *bitch* have more or less negative emotive overtones; words like *spring, free,* and *satisfaction* have positive emotive overtones; and words like *socialism, marijuana,* and *God* have mixed overtones.

2. Con artists use the emotive side of language (1) to mask cognitive meaning by whipping up emotions so that reason is overlooked and (2) to dull the force of language so as to make acceptable what otherwise might not be. The latter purpose often is accomplished by means of *euphemisms* (less offensive or duller expressions used in place of more offensive or emotively charged locutions).

3. Claims and arguments are often made unnecessarily unclear, and sometimes made to seem more plausible or cogent than they really are by virtue of ambiguity or vagueness within them. Ambiguities in statements may be semantic or syntactic. Ambiguity and vagueness are often unavoidable and sometimes even desired, but they should not be used to hide conceptual or logical faults.

4. Common rhetorical devices often are used in a slippery manner. ***Examples:*** *Slanting* words and expressions ("All this proves is that . . ."); *weasel words* that suck out all or part of the meaning of a sentence ("Economic success may be . . ."); *fine-print disclaimers* that take back part of what was originally asserted ("Tickets must be purchased 30 days in advance, subject to availability . . ."); *evasion* that, for example, may mask failure to respond to questions (Sarah Palin wandering from the point of the question about whether she had the national security credentials to serve as vice president). Note that employing the right tone can be used to mask lack of cogent reasoning or content or to sway audiences via emotional appeals.

5. People often use a number of subtleties of language to help them manipulate claims and arguments. Confusing use and mention, chicanery with quotations, and relying on the passive voice are three common problems.

6. The meanings of words and expressions sometimes are changed so as either to get around or to take advantage of laws, rules, or customs. ***Example:*** Calling an employee a *subcontractor* to avoid paying a minimum wage or Social Security taxes. But it isn't always easy to determine whether terms have been used rightly or wrongly. ***Example:*** Psychologists disagree about whether it makes good sense to use the expression *mental illness,* because they disagree about whether the implied analogy to physical illness is useful or accurate. Loaded language can "frame" issues and thus influence the way we think about public policy. ***Example:*** Calling tax cuts "tax relief" or estate tax "death tax."

7. The social revolution that changed the roles played by women in society, as well as the attitudes of most Americans concerning male-female relationships, has resulted in matching linguistic changes. ***Examples:*** Replacing expressions in which the term *man* is used to refer to people in general by more neutral words such as *person;* using *Ms.* in some cases instead of *Miss* or *Mrs.;* not repeatedly using *his* to mean *his* or *her;* or switching to the plural form to avoid this use of *his.* (Note that when use of dechauvinized language may ring a bit false—*her* or *his* can sound somewhat forced—there always are aesthetically acceptable ways to avoid sexist locutions.) But do we go a bit too far when we start talking, say, about *personhole* covers?

8. The linguistic revolution that has replaced sexist language with locutions that are more congenial with today's attitudes and beliefs also has changed many of the ways in which we refer to members of minorities and other groups, as well as to activities in several important areas of life. Using current lingo, we can say that some ways of speaking are *politically correct* (PC), others not. ***Examples:*** The terms *Native American, physically challenged,* and *Latino* are "in"; *Indian, crippled* (or *handicapped*), and *Hispanic* (used to refer, say, to Mexican Americans) are "out." In some cases, the PC revolution may have gone a bit too far. But some PC language is eroding for the wrong reasons now that immigrants are coming under attack and Islamophobia is on the rise.

MindTap®   **Visit MindTap for more readings and resources.**

EXERCISE SET 7-1

In the run-up to the 2008 presidential election, Barack Obama gave a speech, "A More Perfect Union," hailed by many people as one of the most important speeches on race and the American experience since those given by Martin Luther King. Evaluate this excerpt and explain why it might be effective, persuasive rhetoric. Consider the language (positive and negative), tone, examples, repetitions of words and phrases, choice of pronouns, and anything else you can think of. Conclude with a discussion of the world-view it reflects.

[W]e have a choice in this country. We can accept a politics that breeds division, and conflict, and cynicism. We can tackle race only as spectacle—as we did in the O.J. trial—or in the wake of tragedy, as we did in the aftermath of Katrina—or as fodder for the nightly news. . . . We can pounce on some gaffe by Hillary Clinton as evidence that she's playing the race card, or we can speculate on whether white men will all flock to John McCain in the general election regardless of his policies.

We can do that.

But if we do, I can tell you that in the next election, we'll be talking about some other distraction. And then another one. . . . And nothing will change.

That is one option. Or, at this moment in the election, we can come together and say, "Not this time." This time we want to talk about the crumbling schools that are stealing the future of black children and white children and Asian children and Hispanic children and Native American children. This time we want to reject the cynicism that tells us that these kids can't learn; that these kids who don't look like us are somebody else's problem. The children of America are not those kids, they are our kids, and we will not let them fall behind in a 21st century economy. Not this time.

This time we want to talk about how the lines in the emergency room are filled with whites and blacks and Hispanics who do not have health care, who don't have the power on their own to overcome the special interests in Washington, but who can take them on if we do it together.

This time we want to talk about the shuttered mills that once provided a decent life for men and women of every race. . . . This time we want to talk about the fact that the real problem is not that someone who doesn't look like you might take your job; it's that the corporation you work for will ship it overseas for nothing more than a profit. . . .

I would not be running for president if I didn't believe with all my heart that this is what the vast majority of Americans want for the country. This union may never be perfect, but generation after generation has shown that it can always be perfected. And today, whenever I find myself feeling doubtful or cynical about this possibility, what gives me the most hope is the next generation—the young people whose attitudes and beliefs and openness to change have already made history in this election.

1. Louisiana license plates feature the motto "Sportsman's Paradise." Is this sexist? Defend your answer.

2. Over the past decade, the term *illegal alien* has been euphemized as "undocumented worker" or even "guest without status." What is the point of these euphemisms, and who would be most likely to use them?

*3. Translate the following statement, found on the back of a Hallmark greeting card, into everyday lingo:[16]

   Printed on recycled paper. Contains a minimum of 10% post-consumer and 40% pre-consumer material.

   Aside from the euphemistic use of language in this statement, is there something a bit sneaky going on here?

4. Here is a passage from a thankfully out-of-print edition of the U.S. history textbook *America: Its People and Values:*

   A friendly Indian named Squanto helped the colonists. He showed them how to plant corn and how to live in the wilderness. A soldier, Captain Miles Standish, taught the Pilgrims how to defend themselves against unfriendly Indians.

   How is language used to slant this account? In what other ways is it slanted? Rewrite the passage from the point of view of the "unfriendly Indians" (that is, Native Americans) in question.

5. Explain in plain English Annette Koloday's "reconceptualization" of the term *family* in this quote from her book *Failing the Future: A Dean Looks at Higher Education in the Twenty-First Century* (this passage was nominated for the Doublespeak Award, *Quarterly Review of Doublespeak,* January 2002):

   To conceptualize what I am calling the "family-friendly campus" means reconceptualizing what we include in the term family. The family in the twenty-first century will no longer be identified by blood ties, by legalized affiliations, by cohabitation, or by heterosexual arrangements.

   How, then, would you define family?

*6. Translate into plain English the following remark by Admiral Isaac C. Kidd when he was chief of navy matériel:

   We have gone with teams of competent contract people from Washington to outlying field activities to look over their books with them . . . to see in what areas there is susceptibility to improved capability to commit funds.

7. An animal rights organization wants to replace the term *pet owner* in San Francisco laws with the expression *pet guardian,* because the term *owner* implies that animals are property. Defend or challenge their view on this.

---

[16]Starred (*) items are answered in a section at the back of the book.

8. Several groups opposed to legal abortions, as well as a few state legislatures in recently enacted laws, refer to a fetus as an *intact child*, a *partially born infant*, or an *unborn child* (see, for example, the March–April 2000 edition of *Extra!*).

   a. What is the point of their use of these locutions instead of the medical term *fetus*?

   b. To which sections or topics of this chapter is this example relevant?

EXERCISE SET 7-3

For each of the following statements, say whether it contains semantic ambiguity, syntactic ambiguity, or vagueness. Is this ambiguity or vagueness detrimental to understanding and/or evaluating the claim? Briefly explain your answer.

1. From HillaryClinton.com: "Hillary Clinton will be a small business president."

2. Headline from MLB.com: "Bryant sustains mild ankle sprain on bases."

3. From KansasCity.com: "Prince's genius was underrated, yet he still stood out among giants."

*4. Overheard on subway: "I wish I could be a professional basketball player, just like my boyfriend."

5. Headline from the *New York Daily News*: "NCAA Bans Trojans from Bowls."

EXERCISE SET 7-4

1. Find at least one good example of an inappropriate name (for example, *subcontractor*) that is applied so that the law, a custom, or whatever deals with them differently, and explain the chicanery. (No, you aren't supposed to "find" the example in this textbook.)

2. Check your local newspaper, magazines, television programs, the Internet, or some such; find at least two examples of doublespeak or jargon, and translate them back into plain English.

3. Do the same with a particularly obtuse use (as opposed to a "mention") of academese from one of your textbooks (*definitely* not from this one!).

4. Do the same with respect to sexist locutions, but this time translate into PC language.

EXERCISE SET 7-5

*1. Each chapter in this text starts out with a few (hopefully) apt quotes. But doesn't one of the quotes that starts this language chapter use one of the devices railed against in this chapter? Which one might this be? If it doesn't, why doesn't it?

If it does, wasn't it a mistake to use this quotation? Explain. (By the way, does a different one of these quotes commit the fallacy slippery slope?)

2. Previous editions of this text have been criticized by some for implying that in some cases the recent linguistic revolution has gone a bit overboard. This edition contains the question "Why worry about using the term *manhole* when talking about those round excisions in streets and avenues, as did the Public Works Departments of several American cities?" Should we worry? Why, or why not?

3. Do you think universities should develop speech codes designed to suppress racist, sexist, and homophobic speech on campus? Write an argument for or against this policy.

Evaluating Extended Arguments

8

> *The prejudice against careful analytic procedure is part of the human impatience with technique which arises from the fact that men are interested in results and would like to attain them without the painful toil which is the essence of our moral finitude.*
>
> —Morris R. Cohen
>
> *There is no expedient to which a man will not resort to avoid the real labor of thinking.* —Sir Joshua Reynolds

MindTap® Visit MindTap for more readings and resources.

Our principal topic in this chapter is the evaluation of extended passages, or **essays**, that argue to a conclusion. Up to this point, we've considered mainly short arguments, and these primarily to illustrate fallacious reasoning or manipulative uses of language. But in daily life, we frequently encounter longer passages, generally containing several related arguments, offered in support of a thesis—the overall conclusion of the passage.

We should recall, however, that there are other kinds of persuasive essays in addition to the argumentative variety. Even simple description or narration often is used for this purpose. For example, in his essay "A Hanging," George Orwell argues with some force against capital punishment simply by graphically describing a hanging and one person's gut-wrenching response to it. (The ongoing abortion debate is studded with detailed descriptions of aborted fetuses.) And just explaining something may effectively persuade others to our point of view. An article on chlorofluorocarbons, for instance, may simply describe how these chemicals deplete the ozone layer, thus increasing our chances of getting skin cancer, and yet convince readers of the implied conclusion that the use of Freon in refrigerators and other modern equipment should be stopped. In Chapter 13, we will consider fiction as an alternative source of arguments.

But our main concern in this chapter will be rhetoric in which there is an explicit and clear attempt to present reasons for conclusions. We need to remember, however, that a conclusion can be argued for in various ways. We may, for example, weigh the merits and demerits of a possible course of action, instead of just presenting favorable reasons. A **pro and con argument** of this kind can be very effective because it tends to answer questions or objections the reader or listener may have about the thesis being argued for. This also is why essays often provide a **refutation to counterarguments**, as in the case of politicians who, after arguing for their position, may then go on to say, "Now my opponent will no doubt respond _____; but I say _____," and then attempt to refute their opponent's objections. An essay may also argue for a course of action by showing that likely alternatives are less desirable, which means arguing by a **comparison of alternatives**.

Note, by the way, that a legitimate appeal to experts in a field may count as a reason for accepting their conclusions, even in the absence of an account of their reasoning processes. During World War II, for example, President Roosevelt accepted the conclusion of physicists Leo Szilard and Albert Einstein (conveyed to the president in a famous letter) that it was possible to build an atomic bomb, even though Roosevelt, like every other layperson, would have been unable to comprehend the reasoning behind their conclusion (which, no doubt, is why the two scientists didn't bother to provide it).

Finally, note that essay writers frequently employ more than one of the methods just mentioned. They first may argue, for instance, by a general comparison of alternatives and then, finding the alternative that seems to be the most attractive, zero in on it for a more careful analysis. Or they may provide reasons that support the essay's thesis and are in turn supported by expert opinion.

1. The Basic Tasks of Essay Evaluation

There are almost as many ways to evaluate extended passages as there are evaluators. What works best for one person may not work so well for others. And time and interest always need to be taken into account. Even so, there are guidelines that most people find of value, in particular, those who initially have a bit of trouble handling lengthy or complicated passages. (Most of the discussion that follows will deal with written passages, but applies also to those that are verbal.)

The next few sections of this chapter describe a method for evaluating essays when the topic being dealt with is of great importance and we have the time necessary to do a thorough job. In daily life, of course, these two conditions are not often met. But getting good at a method like the one described here is a good way to become adept at the quicker kinds of evaluations that we do frequently have to make in everyday life.

FIND THE THESIS AND KEEP IT IN MIND

The most important thing is to *locate the thesis*—the main conclusion of the argument. The thesis isn't always obvious because the passage may be poorly written, or because the thesis may be implied but not explicitly stated, or simply because the author may build up to it and reveal it only near the end of the work. The thesis is the point of an essay, so you have to keep it in mind to determine whether sufficient *reasons* are provided for accepting it. In many sports, the trick is to keep your eye on the ball; in evaluating extended passages, the trick is to keep your mind's eye on the thesis, so that you can better judge whether the reasons do, or don't, adequately support it.

FIND THE REASONS THAT SUPPORT THE THESIS

Obviously, then, the next task after locating the thesis is to *find the reasons*—the *premises*—that are provided in support of the thesis. Again, this will be hard or easy depending on the author's style and competence. But it may also be hard because the reasons themselves are supported by reasons, so that the sheer complexity of an extended passage makes analysis difficult.

Typically, however, it isn't all that hard to see what the thesis of an essay is and to discover the principal reasons offered in its support. For example, a newspaper columnist arguing for the thesis that cigarettes should be made illegal supported his conclusion by pointing out that cigarette smoking kills millions of people; then supported that claim by presenting statistics concerning smoking and heart disease, cancer, and emphysema; and then claimed that anything so bad for us should be illegal. The logical structure of his essay thus was something like this:

> *Thesis:* Cigarettes should be made illegal.
> *Reasons:* 1. Cigarette smoking is deadly.
> 　　　　　 2. Anything so deadly should be illegal.
> *Support for 1:* Statistical proof linking smoking cigarettes with heart disease, cancer, and emphysema.

The columnist assumed (wrongly) that most people would accept his second reason without further justification.

IDENTIFY THE EVIDENCE

Effective extended arguments usually provide evidence, or support, for the reasons they present. That is, they provide reasons for believing their reasons. In the cigarette example, statistical evidence was cited in support of the claim that cigarette smoking is deadly. But many other sorts of evidence may be appealed to, including authoritative pronouncements, examples, personal experiences, generally accepted facts or common knowledge, and so on. In the Szilard/Einstein letter mentioned before, the evidence for the conclusion that an atomic bomb could be built was just the authority of the letter's authors. Someone might defend the claim that cigarette smoking is deadly simply by appealing to what by now is common knowledge—that it causes lung cancer, heart disease, and so on. A powerful argument against war might well contain specific examples of wars—for example, World War I—that produced incredible misery with little else to show for them.

In a sense, of course, all reasons or premises offered in support of a thesis constitute evidence in its favor. The important point here is that reasons themselves often need, and receive, supporting evidence. Indeed, good essay writers always support reasons in this way except when confident that readers will accept them without further argument.

Sometimes, especially with particularly intricate or complicated arguments and those with multiple sub-arguments, it may be useful to provide a diagram to visualize the argument's logical structure—i.e., what supports what. In most cases, a very simple diagramming scheme will do. For instance, you may separate individual claims and represent the support relationship between them with arrows. So we might diagram the argument about cigarette smoking (not itself a very complicated one or one that we would *need* to diagram, but a handy example) this way:

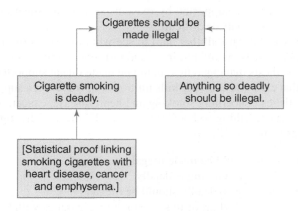

IDENTIFY RESPONSES TO LIKELY OBJECTIONS OR COUNTERARGUMENTS

The sample essay concerning cigarette smoking did not discuss likely objections or counterarguments, but essays often do. The cigarette essay, for instance, might have raised and argued against the objection that we have a right to risk shortening our lives by smoking, or taking other sorts of risks, if we want to. If this objection had been included in the essay, then it would have been important to note and take account of it.

Notice that the objection in question is not so much an objection to the main conclusion, but to the second premise. But if we have no reason to accept the second premise, then the support that the first premise provides is severely diminished, if it doesn't disappear entirely.

In our visualization scheme, we may want to account for objections with another sort of symbol. Use whatever works best for you, but one simple way would be to put a line through the arrow between an objection and the claim to which it is objecting. The overall amended argument might be visualized this way:

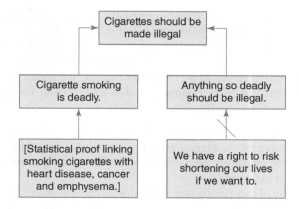

SKIP WHATEVER DOESN'T ARGUE FOR (OR AGAINST) THE THESIS

People write essays to persuade other people. So they sometimes include irrelevant material if they think it will help them to persuade others. This kind of "flavoring" material makes reading more fun, but it shouldn't influence the assessment of an argument.

ADD RELEVANT INFORMATION OR REASONS

Everything needed to prove a thesis is *never* included in an essay, no matter how long it may be. There is no point in trying to prove things that are obvious or generally accepted. Good writers try to provide just the information their audiences will need in order to see the merit of the writer's point of view. For instance, someone writing about education for an audience of teachers doesn't need to prove that plenty of students graduate from high school today without having developed sufficient ability in reading, writing, and basic arithmetic. Every teacher knows that.

Of course, writers, being human, often fail to do the best job of supporting their theses. They often overlook important evidence, or they reason incorrectly to a conclusion that can be supported by better logic. Good critical thinkers try to evaluate the best version of an argument, adding material that its author may have neglected. By the same token, of course, good reasoners also bring to bear whatever negative evidence or reasons they may know about.

CONSIDER TONE AND EMOTIVE LANGUAGE

Although tone and emotive language are not part of the formal elements of argument, they are subtle manipulators that deserve attention, particularly when considering a strongly emotive topic or one that uses irony or humor to persuade. When Adlai Stevenson argued against a state senate bill to restrain cats (quoted in Chapter 7), his droll exaggeration of the consequences was part of the persuasive power. The idea that the state senate might be "called upon to take sides in the age-old problem of dog versus cat, cat versus bird, or even bird versus worm" made the bill seem just plain silly and thus not worth passing.

One way to identify these hidden persuaders is to underline or circle the emotive words or humorous phrases and then see how they nudge the reader into agreeing with the writer's thesis. Becoming aware of these expressions helps us guard against their undue influence.

Now, just because a claim is stated in particularly emotive language does not necessarily mean that it is without argumentative value, so we should not reject such claims
outright any more than we should allow ourselves to be persuaded simply by their rhetorical draw. Rather, we should try to translate highly emotive language into something
a little more neutral-sounding so we can better evaluate the actual claims in question.

Consider this excerpt from a Hillary Clinton speech from June 2015 in which she
contrasts herself with current Republican candidates:[1]

> These Republicans trip over themselves promising lower taxes for the wealthy
> and fewer rules for the biggest corporations without regard for how that will
> make income inequality even worse. We've heard this tune before. And we
> know how it turns out.
>
> Ask many of these candidates about climate change, one of the defining threats
> of our time (cheers, applause), and they'll say: "I'm not a scientist." (Laughter.)
> Well, then, why don't they start listening to those who are? (Cheers, applause.)
>
> They pledge to wipe out tough rules on Wall Street, rather than rein in the
> banks that are still too risky, courting future failures. In a case that can only be
> considered mass amnesia. They want to take away health insurance from more
> than 16 million Americans without offering any credible alternative. (Booing.)
> They shame and blame women, rather than respect our right to make our
> own reproductive health decisions. (Cheers, applause.) They want to put im-
> migrants, who work hard and pay taxes, at risk of deportation. (Booing.) And
> they turn their backs on gay people who love each other. (Cheers, applause.)
>
> Fundamentally, they reject what it takes to build an inclusive economy. It
> takes an inclusive society. (Cheers, applause.) What I once called "a village"
> (cheers) that has a place for everyone.
>
> Now, my values and a lifetime of experiences have given me a different vision
> for America. I believe that success isn't measured by how much the wealthiest
> Americans have, but by how many children climb out of poverty . . . (cheers, ap-
> plause) How many start-ups and small businesses open and thrive . . . How many
> young people go to college without drowning in debt . . . (cheers, applause) How
> many people find a good job . . . How many families get ahead and stay ahead.

We can restate these claims this way:

"The Republicans promise lowering taxes, and lowering taxes increases income
inequality. They do not adequately consider scientists' views on climate change. They are
in favor of deregulation of Wall Street banks, which is risky. They are against publicly
funded health care. They are against legalized abortion. They are in favor of deporting
undocumented immigrants. They are against gay marriage.

My policies consider more people. I favor economic policies that focus on bringing
income for families with children above the poverty line, encouraging small business
development, making college more affordable, and decreasing unemployment."

No one would win an election with speeches as dry and dispassionate as this, but
if we want to consider Clinton's argument for her election rather than the persuasive
flourish of her presentation of that argument, it's just these claims (and the support they
provide) that we should evaluate.

---

[1]From a CNN.com transcript, 13 June 2015.

COME TO AN EVALUATION

While evaluation is logically the last thing we need to do when dealing with an argumentative passage, good critical thinkers start evaluating from the word go. They keep in mind questions such as, Do I already accept this thesis? Does it fit well with what I already know and believe? If not, in what way is the argument fallacious, and why? What sort of reasons or evidence might change my mind? And they continue to evaluate as they go along, bearing in mind questions such as: Is this reason acceptable without further justification? Does that reason really defend the thesis at hand? Do the facts alleged seem plausible, given my background beliefs? Has the writer forgotten a serious counterargument or omitted important counterevidence? Is the use of tone and emotive language unduly persuasive? It's true that a completely confident judgment about a work can't be reached until an essay has been thoroughly examined, but it still is useful to make provisional evaluations right from the start. This enables a reader to engage actively rather than passively with the essay and its arguments. It is always best to imagine ourselves as in a kind of dialogue with a writer, mutually engaged in the activity of testing beliefs and arguments in order to determine what is true and what isn't.

Successfully bringing relevant background information to bear is clearly key to good evaluations, but other relevant thoughts often play an important role. We often simply don't know enough to come to a confident evaluation but still may be able to speculate intelligently by thinking about the right questions that need to be raised either for or against a particular thesis. For example, one of the important reasons often given in favor of laws requiring capital punishment for heinous crimes is that these laws will act as a deterrent—criminals may think more carefully before committing murder if they know conviction means death. This sounds like a very plausible reason given the strength of the urge most of us have to stay alive. But does it in fact work this way? Not knowing the answer may be a good reason for withholding judgment, or for seeking further information, or for at least only *provisionally* assuming that the threat of death deters criminals more than do lesser penalties. The point here is that coming to a justified evaluation requires us to think of what it would be useful to know that we don't as yet know—it requires us to raise the right sorts of questions. (Raising questions of this kind, of course, also serves as a guide to research that might have to be undertaken.)

When the entire structure of an extended argument has been figured out, its relevant passages will divide into those that are argued for within the essay and those that are not. The latter are the writer's basic *assumptions*—starting points—assumed without being justified. When evaluating an extended passage, you need to ask and answer three vital questions, corresponding to the three basic requirements of cogent reasoning (discussed in Chapter 1):

1. Are the writer's assumptions and stated reasons justified by what you already believe?
2. Do you know other relevant reasons or arguments? (If so, then you need to add them before coming to a final conclusion as to the essay's cogency.)
3. Do the reasons (plus any relevant material you may have added) justify acceptance of the thesis—that is, is the reasoning valid?

If an assumption or reason is not supported by your background beliefs, if you know of relevant information that refutes or casts doubt on the thesis, or if the reasoning is not completely valid (taking into account material you may have added), then clearly you should not be convinced by that particular extended argument. It may be, of course, that your background beliefs neither support nor conflict with an argument's assumptions or reasons, in which case you can neither accept nor reject the argument's thesis; you need to withhold judgment or delve further into the matter.

A note of caution: It is common for some of the subsidiary arguments in a long essay to be cogent, while others are fallacious. When this is the case, reason dictates accepting only the untainted portions of the overall argument. But it would be wrong to automatically toss out the whole extended argument—wrong to reject the thesis of the essay—if that thesis can stand on the basis of the legitimate portions of the essay (along with relevant material you may have added from your background beliefs). This point often is characterized as one of *charity*—of being fair to the other side on an issue—but it also is an important requirement of good critical reasoning.

2. The Margin Note and Summary Method

The **margin note and summary method** is a good method to use when an evaluation has to be right. The idea behind this method is that a summary can be more easily worked with than the longer work from which it is drawn, provided the summary is *accurate*. (Making a summary helps us to remember things better and thus is a good study technique—one, in fact, that instructors often use when preparing class material.)

The margin note and summary method has four basic steps:

1. Read the material to be summarized.
2. Read it through again, this time marking the important passages with an indication of their content written in the margin. (The point of the first reading is to enable you to spot the important passages more accurately when you read through the material a second time. First readings often don't catch the drift.) Margin notes need not be full sentences or grammatically correct. They may contain abbreviations or whatever shorthand notes you care to employ.
3. Use the margin notes to construct a summary of the passage, indicating which statements are premises (reasons) and which conclusions, so that the structure of the passage's argument is laid bare.
4. Evaluate the essay by evaluating your summary, checking back and forth to be sure there are no significant differences between the essay and your summary.

Two things need to be remembered about the margin note and summary method. First, when we skip portions of a passage, we make a judgment that the passed-over material is relatively unimportant. It takes practice and skill to know what to include and what to omit, and even those with a good deal of experience may differ on such matters. (This does not mean, however, that anything goes!) Second, margin notes and summaries are shorthand devices; they should be briefer than the passages they summarize—if possible, a good deal briefer. The risk in this process, obviously, is falsification. We don't want to commit the straw man fallacy by making judgments about the shortened version that would not be valid for the original.

3. Extended Evaluation of an Argument

An extended evaluation examines an argument in some detail, using the critical thinking tools covered throughout this text. The first step is to summarize the article using the margin note method explained in the previous section. Then identify the thesis, the reasons and the main points of the argument. Provide a diagram if necessary.

The next task is to determine whether the argument should be convincing. Do the reasons really defend the thesis, or are they fallacious? Is the evidence plausible? Has the writer included important counterarguments? Is the use of emotive language persuasive or manipulative? Is the worldview convincing? These sorts of questions should be asked about each smaller argument as well as about the argument as a whole.

It is important to keep in mind that there is no such thing as a perfectly reasoned, totally convincing argument (though there are plenty of really bad ones out there). Even brilliant thinkers slip up once in a while or get carried away with their own rhetoric. A good analysis determines what is convincing and what is not, then comes to an overall evaluation of the argument.

Here is a condensed version of an argument on capital punishment by probably the most famous trial lawyer of the twentieth century, Clarence Darrow, followed by an evaluation. One of Darrow's most celebrated cases was his defense of Richard Loeb and Nathan Leopold, two teenagers who pled guilty to kidnapping and murdering a 14-year-old boy. The prosecution was determined to hang the killers, but Darrow's brilliant 12-hour summation, an eloquent attack on the death penalty, was so effective that the presiding judge wept at its conclusion and gave Leopold and Loeb a life sentence instead of the death penalty. (An interesting footnote on Darrow is that no client of his was ever executed.) The following essay was published a few years after the trial. Although written in the first half of the twentieth century, the arguments Darrow made are still used by death-penalty abolitionists today. Given his legendary prowess in a court of law, one might think his arguments were airtight, but even the great Darrow lapsed into fallacious reasoning and used purely rhetorical tricks to persuade.

The Futility of the Death Penalty[2]

. . . It is my purpose in this article to prove, first, that capital punishment is no deterrent to crime; and second, that the state continues to kill its victims, not so much to defend society against them—for it could do that equally well by imprisonment—but to appease the mob's emotions of hatred and revenge. . . .

Behind the idea of capital punishment lie false training and crude views of human conduct. People do evil things, say the judges, lawyers, and preachers, because of depraved hearts. . . .

If crime were really the result of willful depravity, we should be ready to concede that capital punishment may serve as a deterrent to the criminally

---

[2]Darrow, Clarence. "The Futility of the Death Penalty." *Verdicts Out of Control.* Eds. Arthur and Lila Weinberg. Chicago: Quadrangle Books, 1963. 225–234. This essay first appeared in *The Forum,* September 1928. By permission of the Estate of Clarence Darrow, all rights reserved.

inclined. But it is hardly probable that the great majority of people refrain from killing their neighbors because they are afraid; they refrain because they never had the inclination. Human beings are creatures of habit; and, as a rule, they are not in the habit of killing. The circumstances that lead to killings are manifold, but in a particular individual the inducing cause is not easily found. In one case, homicide may have been induced by indigestion in the killer; in another, it may be traceable to some weakness inherited from a remote ancestor; but that it results from *something* tangible and understandable, if all the facts were known, must be plain to everyone who believes in cause and effect.

Of course, no one will be converted to this point of view by statistics of crime. In the first place, it is impossible to obtain reliable ones, and in the second place, the conditions to which they apply are never the same. But if one cares to analyze the figures, such as we have, it is easy to trace the more frequent causes of homicide. The greatest number of killings occur during attempted burglaries and robberies. The robber knows that penalties for burglary do not average more than five years in prison. He also knows that the penalty for murder is death or imprisonment. Faced with this alternative, what does the burglar do when he is detected and threatened with arrest? He shoots to kill. He deliberately takes the chance of death to save himself from a 5-year term in prison. It is therefore as obvious as anything can be that fear of death has no effect in diminishing homicides of this kind, which are more numerous than any other type.

The next largest number of homicides may be classed as "sex murders." Quarrels between husbands and wives, disappointed love, or love too much requited cause many killings. They are the result of primal emotions so deep that the fear of death has not the slightest effect in preventing them. Spontaneous feelings overflow in criminal acts, and consequences do not count.

Then there are cases of sudden anger, uncontrollable rage. The fear of death never enters into such cases; if the anger is strong enough, consequences are not considered until too late. The old-fashioned stories of men deliberately plotting and committing murder in cold blood have little foundation in real life. Such killings are so rare that they need not concern us here. The point to be emphasized is that practically all homicides are manifestations of well-recognized human emotions, and it is perfectly plain that the fear of excessive punishment does not enter into them.

In addition to these personal forces which overwhelm weak men and lead them to commit murder, there are also many social and economic forces which must be listed among the causes of homicides, and human beings have even less control over these than over their own emotions. . . . the United States has gathered together people of every color from every nation in the world. Racial differences intensify social, religious, and industrial problems, and the confusion which attends this indiscriminate mixing of races and nationalities is one of the most fertile sources or crime.

Will capital punishment remedy these conditions? Of course it won't; but its advocates argue that the fear of this extreme penalty will hold the victims of adverse conditions in check. To this piece of sophistry, the continuance and increase of crime in our large cities is a sufficient answer. No, the plea that capital punishment acts as a deterrent to crime will not stand. The real reason why this barbarous practice persists in a so-called civilized world is that people still hold the primitive belief that the taking of one human life can be atoned for by taking another. It is the age-old obsession with punishment that keeps the official headsman busy plying his trade.

And it is precisely upon this point that I would build my case against capital punishment. Even if one grants that the idea of punishment is sound, crime calls for something more—for careful study, for an understanding of causes, for proper remedies. To attempt to abolish crime by killing the criminal is the easy and foolish way out of a serious situation. Unless a remedy deals with the conditions which foster crime, criminals will breed faster than the hangman can spring his trap. Capital punishment ignores the causes of crime and, like the methods of the witch doctor, it is not only ineffective as a remedy, but is positively vicious in at least two ways. In the first place, the spectacle of state executions feeds the basest passions of the mob. And in the second place, so long as the state rests content to deal with crime in this barbaric and futile manner, society will be lulled by a false sense of security, and effective methods of dealing with crime will be discouraged. . . .

[W]hile capital punishment panders to the passions of the mob, no one takes the pains to understand the meaning of crime. People speak of crime or criminals as if the world were divided into the good and the bad. This is not true. . . .

Human conduct is by no means so simple as our moralists have led us to believe. There is no sharp line separating good actions from bad. The greed for money, the display of wealth, the despair of those who witness the display, the poverty, oppression, and hopelessness of the unfortunate—all these are factors which enter into human conduct and of which the world takes no account. Many people have learned no other profession but robbery and burglary. The processions moving steadily through our prisons to the gallows are in the main made up of these unfortunates. And how do we dare to consider ourselves civilized creatures when, ignoring the causes of crime, we rest content to mete out harsh punishments to the victims of conditions over which they have no control? . . .

Even now, are not all imaginative and humane people shocked at the spectacle of a killing by the state? . . . How can the state censure the cruelty of the man who—moved by strong passions, or acting to save his freedom, or influenced by weakness or fear—takes human life, when everyone knows that the state itself, after long premeditation and settled hatred, not only kills, but first tortures and bedevils its victims for weeks with the impending doom?

For the last hundred years the world has shown a gradual tendency to mitigate punishment. We are slowly learning that this way of controlling human beings is both cruel and ineffective. . . . There is no doubt whatever that the world is growing more humane and more sensitive and more understanding. The time will come when all people will view with horror the light way in which society and its courts of law now take human life; and when that time comes, the way will be clear to devise some better method of dealing with poverty and ignorance and their frequent byproducts, which we call crime.

ANALYSIS[3]

In "The Futility of the Death Penalty," Clarence Darrow argues against capital punishment because it is "no deterrent to crime" and it is the state's attempt "to appease the mob's emotions of hatred and revenge." His overall argument is valid and often persuasive, but he sometimes reasons fallaciously, and though he uses language effectively, he also uses it cleverly, to manipulate the reader. He is at his best, however, when he urges us to consider the humane worldview at the heart of his argument.

Darrow's first premise, that capital punishment is no deterrent to crime, is hypothetical, based on common sense and his own background experience as a defense lawyer. Darrow himself concedes that "no one will be converted to this point of view by statistics of crime" partly because "it is impossible to obtain reliable ones." Although recent studies seem to provide some statistical corroboration that the death penalty is a deterrent, Darrow's reservations about crime statistics are just as relevant today as they were then. According to the Death Penalty Information Center, the homicide rate in states without the death penalty has been consistently lower than in states with the death penalty over a 20-year period from 1990 to 2009. However, these findings suggest the fallacy of questionable cause, since the states cited may have had a higher rate of murder to start with and may have instituted the death penalty to reduce the number of homicides.

Instead of using questionable statistics to make his point, Darrow reasons that most killers are not deterred by the death penalty when they kill in the heat of the moment—during attempted burglaries, in sex-related quarrels, or in cases of uncontrollable rage. Our own background beliefs would probably confirm his assumption that people aren't likely to think of the consequences under these circumstances. But he is guilty of suppressing evidence when he dismisses the idea of premeditation in his claim that "men deliberately plotting and committing murder in cold blood have little foundation in real life." Countless examples of premeditated murder could be used to refute this claim, but the most obvious in Darrow's case is the gruesome crime committed by his own clients, Leopold and Loeb, who systematically planned to commit the perfect crime to kidnap and murder their 14-year-old victim.

---

[3]We are skipping here some of the intermediate steps like making margin notes, providing a summary or making a diagram. We do so only to focus attention on the result. As an exercise, you may want to take up these other steps to re-create how we came to these results.

His argument that a "great majority of people refrain from killing their neighbors . . . because they never had the inclination" probably applies to most people but doesn't take into account those who *do* have the inclination to kill and who *are* deterred by the fear of punishment.

There is some truth to his second premise that the state continues to kill its victims to appease the mob's emotions of hatred and revenge. Politicians do, indeed, pay attention to the attitudes their constituents have about capital punishment. In Texas, for instance, candidates who take a stand against the death penalty would have a hard time getting elected. But Darrow relies more on provocative rhetoric than reasoning to make his point. He argues that those who favor the death penalty are a "mob," incited by "hatred and revenge," and the state is a murderer in the questionable premise that "the state itself, after long premeditation and settled hatred, not only kills but first tortures and bedevils its victims for weeks with the impending doom." By presenting the criminal as the "victim," he transforms the entire legal process—from the interrogation, to the trial, sentencing, and appeals—into torturous treatment of the murderer, all of which evade the issue that a real victim is dead at the hands of a killer.

Darrow's argument is driven by highly emotive, often persuasive language, used to engage the reader in his crusade. His tone is characterized by compassion for the hapless killer and moral outrage at the harsh retribution exacted by the state. Capital punishment is condemned as a "barbarous practice," the "easy and foolish way out of a serious situation." Those who favor it are "moralists" with "crude" notions of human conduct, people with the "primitive belief" that executing the killer will atone for the murder. To counter these uncivilized tendencies in human nature, Darrow describes right-thinking people as "imaginative and humane," "shocked at the spectacle of killing by the state." This is an effective ploy to jar the reader into seeing the state in a different light—as a killer not far removed from the murderer it condemns. Less persuasive is the linguistic sleight of hand he reserves for the criminals, whom he repeatedly refers to as "victims"—of social forces, emotional drives, or biological quirks—implying that they commit crime through no fault of their own because of the questionable premise that their behavior is the result of "conditions over which they have no control."

Perhaps more than anything else, Darrow's argument stands or falls on his worldview, which encompasses his attitude toward the criminal class and the responsibility of society in dealing with it. Darrow's philosophy of determinism is evident throughout when he claims that homicides may be "traceable to some weakness inherited from a remote ancestor" or "the result of primal emotions" or "uncontrollable rage," or that criminals are "victims of conditions over which they have no control." Although it is true that we have no control over the environment we are born into or the genes we inherit, most of us believe that we not only can but should control our actions, despite the problems inherent in our background. A more compelling reason for abolishing capital punishment is rooted in his humane worldview that a civilized society should not sink to the level of the criminal, that it should resist the primitive urge to exact retribution, and that it should deal with criminals in a humane manner, by mitigating punishment and trying to remedy the conditions that foster crime. In this way, he appeals to our better natures and presents his most convincing argument.

4. Dealing with Value Claims

By now, it should have become clear how often the reasons presented in favor of a thesis are at least in part about values, not facts. It is a *fact,* for example, that sugar sweetens coffee; it is a *value judgment* that sweetened coffee tastes better than unsweetened. It is a fact that the Earth goes around the sun once every 365 days or so; it is a value judgment that, other things being equal, those who give to the poor are better people than the Scrooges who don't. (Note the slanting word used in the previous sentence.)

When someone argues, say, that vacations are better taken in the spring, because spring is the best time of the year, that person uses a value judgment as a reason (premise) supporting the conclusion that vacations are best taken in the spring. (Note, by the way, that this conclusion is itself in part a value judgment, as are all conclusions that depend on at least one reason that is a value judgment.)

Value judgments typically are justified, or defended, in ways that are different from judgments about facts. Someone who claims, for example, that gold does not rust can support that claim by citing the fact that nothing made of gold has ever been observed to rust and that all attempts to rust gold have failed. But the person who says that gold makes beautiful jewelry has to cite a different sort of evidence—for example, that people generally like the look of gold jewelry. That is why many philosophers say that value judgments concern matters that are *subjective,* while judgments about alleged facts deal with matters that are *objective.*

The idea that values are subjective is captured nicely by the saying that beauty is in the eye of the beholder, and by the old precept that there is no disputing about taste. According to these maxims, the fact that some people like string beans, or Bach fugues, while others don't, doesn't make those who do or those who don't wrong. By way of contrast, those who make a nonvalue, factual claim—for instance, that the Earth is flat (so-called "flat earthers")—are wrong; the rest of us who believe that it is spherical (well, extremely close to being spherical) are right. (Yes, there are people who still, in this day and age, believe that the Earth is flat. Recall the discussion of self-deception in Chapter 6.) Merely believing that something is a fact doesn't make it a fact; nor is such a belief justified in the absence of evidence (experience about something relevant) to support that belief.

It's true, of course, that lots of philosophers would argue against the idea that value judgments are by their nature subjective. Some would say, for example, that beauty is in the object, not just in the eye of the beholder, so that the person who doesn't see the beauty in beautiful objects is like someone who is color blind.[4] (One of the points of a philosophy course in which value judgments are discussed is precisely to deal with controversies of this kind.)

---

[4]Such philosophers may appeal to the evidence of our own disagreements over such matters. Take a food you find particularly delicious and another that you find repugnant. Now you meet someone who holds the opposite judgments. It is likely that you will simply say that this person has different tastes, not that those tastes are somehow wrong. But what about the person who says that the latest issue of *Captain America* is more beautiful than the ceiling of the Sistine Chapel? Or that the novel *Twilight* is more beautiful than Shakespeare's *Twelfth Night*? It seems to many of us that something has gone wrong in these latter judgments. If so, then judgments of beauty in art or otherwise are not quite as subjective as judgments of taste in food.

Fortunately, when the value judgments relevant to an argument are about beauty, or taste, or other aesthetic matters, we generally can come to an evaluation without having to deal with underlying philosophical issues like the one about objectivity versus subjectivity. Suppose, for example, that some people in a community want to make uncovered auto junkyards illegal, on the grounds that they constitute an "eyesore." Voters don't need to decide whether being an eyesore is an objective or a subjective property to figure out how to vote. They can just find out whether most people find them to be ugly, or at least whether they themselves see junkyards as a good deal less than attractive. (There may, of course, be good reasons against banning open auto graveyards, but that is another matter.) The point is that, in these cases, we can appeal to something subjective—namely, whether we see junkyards as ugly or not—without answering the underlying questions about whether the ugliness of something is in the thing itself or merely in the eyes of the beholder.

But other sorts of questions about values often have more pressing practical consequences, the prime case being those involving *moral values*. If it is true that moral values are subjective, then policy and personal conduct decisions that involve them can be justified simply by appealing to evidence that most people hold these values. Enslaving people and working them to death then become morally wrong just because virtually everyone finds this sort of behavior wrong or unfair. But if moral values are objective, judgments about them cannot be defended in this way. Subjective feelings become irrelevant if moral principles are objective—if there is something outside us, be it biblical commandments, natural rights, the greatest good for the greatest number, or whatever, that determines which actions are right and which are wrong.[5] Thus, those who hold that moral standards are objective need to think carefully as to what sorts of justifications—appeal to cultural norms, natural rights, religious principles, or something else—they believe should count in assessing moral claims and whether these allegedly objective standards in turn can be justified without appeal to subjective values or standards.

The point here, however, is that when someone makes a moral value claim in an argument, it may be crucially important to find out what makes that person hold the value in question. Those who argue against legal abortions, for example, often present as their principal reason the claim that taking a human life is morally wrong; but if their justification is the biblical commandment "Thou shalt not kill," then those who do not accept the Bible as the ultimate authority on moral matters have not been given a persuasive reason for accepting this claim about the immorality of taking a human life.[6] Similarly, those who argue in favor of legalizing prostitution often claim that a woman has a right to use her body in any way that she sees fit; but if their justification is a

---

[5]All of these, and many other allegedly objective factors, have been argued for, and against, by philosophers and theologians.

[6]Note that appeals to authorities such as the Bible can be tricky. With respect to the abortion case, for instance, it has been argued that the original Hebrew has been mistranslated and that what the commandment says is better translated as "Thou shalt not *murder*," so that the question remains as to whether abortion is murder—immoral killing. There also is the problem that most who deny the legitimacy of abortion believe certain kinds of killing are justified—for instance, in wartime or in self-defense; those who believe this would have to show why killing fetuses is not also sometimes justified.

theory of objective natural rights, then those who reject the idea of objective rights have not been given a satisfactory reason for being in favor of legal prostitution.

In any case, good critical reasoners accept premises that contain moral value judgments only if those judgments conform to their own moral standards. This does not mean, of course, that moral standards and values are exempt from challenge. Those who believe, say, that it always is morally wrong to violate legally enacted legislation may see the matter differently if laws are enacted forbidding the practice of their own religion, or forcing acceptance of another faith.

It also needs to be noted that there often are no simple principles—say, those like the Ten Commandments—to apply in determining moral right and wrong. It seems morally right to many people that income should be proportionate to what one produces, a standard encapsulated in the idea that one should reap what one sows. According to this *principle of just desserts,* the fruits of a cooperative effort ought to be distributed according to the relative contributions of the various parties, whether in labor, capital, or whatever. But even supposing this idea is accepted, how are just desserts to be determined in actual cases? How do we compare, for instance, the efforts of a corporate chief executive officer who oversees the successful introduction of a new product with the engineers who designed and perfected that product, or with workers on the line who actually produce the goods? How do we compare the contributions of those who put up the money (stockholders) with those of company executives or production line employees?[7]

That said, even if we can't (or at least don't and probably won't) agree on fundamental principles, there are a few rules of moral reasoning that we all seem to endorse—at least those of us who engage in moral argument in the first place. First, we agree that acting morally is acting on some kind of generalizable rule. Whatever the wrongness of an action consists in, it applies to other similar actions in similar circumstances. Second, we agree that we have a duty to apply those rules consistently. There are surely exceptions to just about any rule, but we do not allow *arbitrary* exceptions to moral rules. If it is wrong for one person to lie in order to get out of some mild embarrassment, then it is wrong for anyone to lie in order to get out of some mild embarrassment. When it comes to morality, no one has special privileges.

Finally, it is important to remember that those who go through life without carefully examining and questioning their moral principles run the same risk of mistake as do those who fail to acquire accurate factual beliefs about how things work in this complicated world of ours. This is true even if the subjectivist view of moral right and wrong is correct, for it still could well be that a person's unexamined feelings about this or that moral issue will fail to agree with how that individual might see the matter after giving it careful thought or after bringing to bear relevant background information. The first thought that virtually all of us have about infanticide, to take an interesting case, is that it always and everywhere is the worst sort of murder; but thinking carefully about the hard choices life presents to some parents has changed the minds of more than a few thinking and even compassionate individuals.[8]

---

[7]For more on this topic, see: Kahane, Howard. *Contract Ethics: Evolutionary Biology and the Moral Sentiments.* Lanham, MD: Rowman & Littlefield, 1995.

[8]It sometimes happens that the only alternatives open to parents in poor societies, or societies in the throes of famine, are to do away with a newborn child so as to be able to keep their other children alive or else to see all of their offspring slowly starve to death.

5. Evaluating Ironic Works

Jonathan Swift, author of *Gulliver's Travels,* wrote a famous satire called "A Modest Proposal," in which he suggested that the Irish should raise babies to be eaten in order to solve the myriad problems confronting that famine-stricken land back in the eighteenth century.

But the point of his essay, of course, was completely other than that people should literally carry out the plan he proposed. He was, to be plain, using **irony**—that is, saying one thing, but meaning something entirely different. So when evaluating ironic works, it is a mistake to take them literally; you need to evaluate them in terms of their underlying message. Swift's point was to force his British audience to face the mass starvation and misery in Ireland that British policies had produced; his ironic suggestions were intended to shock his audience into a recognition of what they were doing in Ireland.

Irony often is combined with humor or exaggeration to form a potent weapon in the hands of a master at the trade. Telling us what is true in a funny or exaggerated way makes it harder to deny than if it is put to us in a straightforward, serious manner. Ironic writing is particularly effective in penetrating the kinds of self-serving psychological defenses—denial, rationalization, and so on—that were discussed in Chapter 6.

Summary of Chapter 8

Chapter 8 concerns the evaluation of extended arguments—essays.

1. Most types of essays are straightforwardly argumentative, but some—for instance, descriptive or explanatory essays, sometimes even fictions—may mask their theses in one way or another. ***Example:*** Orwell's essay, "A Hanging."

2. Essays may argue by considering reasons *pro and con* a thesis, by providing a *refutation to counterarguments,* or by making a *comparison of alternatives,* as well as simply by presenting *reasons (premises)* in support of a *thesis.*

3. There are several guidelines to use in evaluating argumentative passages: (1) Find the thesis and keep it in mind as you read; (2) find the reasons (premises) that support the thesis, and (when there are any) the reasons for the reasons, and so on, taking into account the evidence presented; (3) identify responses to likely objections or counterarguments; (4) skip whatever doesn't support (or argue against) the thesis; (5) add relevant information, pro or con, that you may know of; (6) consider the tone and emotive language; and (7) come to an evaluation.

4. Coming to an evaluation consists primarily in asking and answering three questions, corresponding to the three basic requirements of cogent reasoning introduced in Chapter 1: (1) Are the writer's (or speaker's) assumptions and

stated reasons justified by what you already believe? (2) Do you know other relevant reasons or arguments? (If so, they need to be added to the mix.) (3) Do the reasons (plus any added material) justify acceptance of the thesis—that is, is the argument then valid?

5. The *margin note and summary method* is a useful way to clarify the main ideas of an essay before analyzing it. This method has four steps: (1) Read the material carefully; (2) read it again and add margin notes at the relevant spots in the essay; (3) construct a summary (and diagram if needed) from the margin notes; and (4) evaluate the summary, making sure to bring relevant information to bear.

6. Reasons offered in support of a thesis may be about *facts* or about *values*. Claims about values typically are justified differently than those about facts. It often is said that facts are *objective,* values *subjective.* On this view, the shape of a gold ring, for example, is an objective fact about the ring itself; the beauty of the ring is "in the eye of the beholder." A contrary view is that values inhere in the valuable objects themselves, so that they too are objective. Among value claims, those about *moral* matters tend to be both controversial and important. If moral values are subjective, then moral claims can be justified by evidence that the writer or speaker, or most or even all people hold that value. But if moral right and wrong are objective facts, then how people feel about them is irrelevant, and something outside our feelings—for example, biblical commandments— need to be appealed to in order to justify a particular moral claim. So when one is evaluating arguments containing moral claims, it often is important to try to find out what makes the writer or speaker make such a claim and to then assess the claims in view of one's own moral standards, however one has arrived at them. Of course, one's own moral standards should not be exempt from challenge and improvement. Those who accept, say, the Ten Commandments need to see that they do not automatically answer all questions—they don't answer all economic ones, for example—and thus are in need at the very least of interpretation and perhaps also augmentation. Careful consideration of a standard may lead to a change of mind, say, about abortion or infanticide, in view of the dire situations some people find themselves in.

7. Ironic essays argue for a point indirectly and thus are not to be taken literally. (For example, Swift did not espouse the eating of Irish babies.) The point in irony is not to present reasons for a conclusion so much as to get readers to see something clearly that they may have overlooked, or not paid sufficient attention to, or defended against by some sort of self-serving self-deception. An honest evaluation of ironic writing requires us to determine whether, as implicitly claimed, we have overlooked or denied something important.

EXERCISE SET 8-1

Here are several short passages (taken from longer works). Reveal the structure of each passage, including reasons that support the thesis, reasons for the reasons, counterarguments, extraneous material, and so on, as in this simple example. (Remember, sometimes a reason or thesis may be implied.) If you find it helpful, make a diagram to display the structure of the argument.

Example

Original passage (from an essay by Baruch Brody on the abortion issue):

There is a continuity of development from the moment of conception on. There are constant changes in the foetal condition; the foetus is constantly acquiring new structure and characteristics, but there is no one state which is radically different from any other. Since this is so, there is no one stage in the process of foetal development after the moment of conception which could plausibly be picked out as the moment at which the foetus becomes a living human being. The moment of conception is, however, different in this respect. It marks the beginning of this continuous process of development and introduces something new which is radically discontinuous with what has come before it. Therefore, the moment of conception, and only it, is a plausible candidate for being that moment at which the foetus becomes a living human being.

Rewritten Passage

Reason (premise): After the moment of conception, there is a continuous development of the human fetus, with no one state being much different from the next.

Conclusion: No moment after conception can be selected as the moment the fetus becomes a human being. (This conclusion then becomes a reason [premise] in the larger argument.)

Reason (premise): The moment of conception introduces something radically different from what came before.

Conclusion (thesis): The moment of conception is the only plausible moment when the fetus becomes a human being.

Diagram

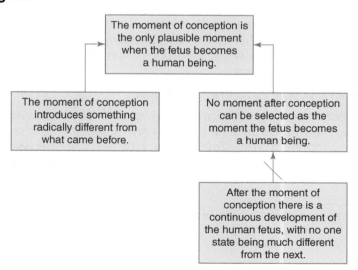

1. Payday loan stores prey on low-income people and drive them into debt. There are now so many of them that they outnumber most fast-food franchises. Companies with names like EZ Money and Check Into Cash give two-week loans with no credit checks, but they charge huge fees. It's not uncommon for a company to charge a fee of $22 per two weeks for every $100 borrowed; at this rate a $500 loan would rack up an annual interest rate of 572 percent. Loan companies like this take advantage of poor people who are desperate to make ends meet from one paycheck to the next. Borrowers begin by taking out one loan to tide them over, and then another if they still run short, and then another. For example, one woman had to take out loans from four different companies and wound up paying $600 in finance fees alone for a debt of $1,300. Borrowers like this, who live on the margin as is, are driven deeper and deeper into debt by the loan shark practices of payday stores. This is little better than thievery and should be stopped. State governments should prohibit payday lending. It's bad enough that these borrowers are living on the edge. Loan companies that take advantage of them are unconscionable. (Data taken from: Leland, John. "Payday Loans, Nonprofit Style, Emerge to Mixed Response." *New York Times,* 28 August 2007.)

2. Excerpt from "The Case for Censorship," by Roger Kimball. *Wall Street Journal,* 8 October 2000:

   ... What's wrong with a little censorship? Until quite recently all sorts of things were censored in American society. There were very strict rules about what you could show on television and in movies, what you could describe in books and what you could reproduce in magazines. Were we worse off then?

   ... There are plenty of reasons to support government censorship when it comes to depictions of sex and violence. For one thing, it would encourage the entertainment industry to turn out material that is richer erotically.... Another reason ... is that it would help temper the extraordinary brutality of popular culture.

   ... [Society] has an interest in protecting the moral sensibility of its citizens, especially the young. Freedom without morality degenerates into the servitude of libertinage. Which is why judicious government censorship is not the enemy of freedom but its guarantor.

*3. Thomas Paine, in his classic *The Age of Reason:*[9]

   Revelation is a communication of something which the person to whom that thing is revealed did not know before. For if I have done a thing, or seen it done, it needs no revelation to tell me I have done it or seen it, nor to enable me to tell it or to write it. Revelation, therefore, cannot be applied to anything done upon

---

[9]Starred (*) items are answered in a section at the back of the book.

earth, of which man himself is the actor or the witness; and consequently, all the historical and anecdotal parts of the Bible, which is almost the whole of it, is not within the meaning and compass of the word "revelation," and therefore, is not the word of God.

4. **From Sandra A. Arnold's "Why Slaves' Graves Matter,"** *New York Times,* **2016:**

   Our country should explore ways to preserve the public memory of enslaved Americans. Their overlooked lives are an inextricable part of the historical nar-rative of our country—and not simply because they were the "beneficiaries" of the 13th Amendment. We should remember enslaved Americans for the same reason we remember anyone; because they were fathers, mothers, siblings and grandparents who made great contributions to our nation. Regardless of our country's history or our ambivalence about the memory of slavery, we can choose to remember the enslaved—the forgotten. They offer our contem-porary society examples of resilience and humanity. Preserving their memory contributes to our own humanity.

5. **From a 2013 opinion piece at the** *Huffington Post* **by Dr. Helene Pavlov, on a proposed ban on large sugary drinks in New York City:**

   The reaction to the mayor of New York's recent proposal to limit large-sized sugary drinks is one of those "seems like common sense" examples. Decreas-ing sugar and salt in our diet seems like common sense; however, the "man on the street" interviews indicate that people think otherwise. People believe that, "The government should not be telling us what to do!" Really? I appreci-ate and agree that government should not be dictating what we eat or how we conduct our lives. However, government assumes some responsibility for informing us about what we can do to keep ourselves and the rest of society safe and secure. The law tells us we cannot commit homicide, we cannot drive at unsafe speeds, we cannot drink or text while driving, we must wear seat belts and buckle up our kids, etc. The government is responsible for making us aware of environment dangers and informing as to how to stay safe and healthy.

6. **Philosopher John Locke, in his classic** *The Second Treatise on Government:*

   Though the earth and all inferior creatures be common to all men, yet every man has a property in his own person; this nobody has any right to but himself. The labor of his body and the work of his hands, we may say, are properly his. Whatsoever then he removes out of the state that nature has provided and left it in, he has mixed his labor with, and joined to it something that is his own, and thereby makes it his property. It being by him removed from the common state nature has placed it in, it has by this labor something annexed to it that excluded the common right of other men. For this labor being the unquestionable property of the laborer, no man but he can have a right to what that is once joined to, at least where there is enough and as good left in common for others.

7. From an article on genetically engineered foods, by John B. Fagan:[10]

Giant transnational companies are carrying out a dangerous global experiment by attempting to introduce large numbers of genetically engineered foods widely into our food supply. Because genetic manipulations can generate unanticipated harmful side-effects, and because genetically engineered foods are not tested sufficiently to eliminate those that are dangerous, this experiment not only jeopardizes the health of individuals, but could also lead to national health threats. . . . Tampering with the genetic code of food is reckless and poses a serious threat to life. It could easily upset the delicate balance between our physiology and the foods that we eat. There is already ample scientific justification for an immediate ban on genetically modified foods in order to safeguard our health.

8. Philosopher Sidney Hook, on recovering from a near-fatal stroke triggered by an angiogram used to diagnose heart disease:

A few years ago, I lay at the point of death [following the stroke]. . . . At one point my heart stopped beating; just as I lost consciousness, it was thumped back into action again. In one of my lucid intervals during those days of agony, I asked my physician to discontinue all life-supporting services or show me how to do it. He refused. . . .

A month later I was discharged from the hospital. In six months I regained the use of my limbs [and voice]. . . . My experience . . . has been cited as an argument against honoring requests of stricken patients to be gently eased out of their pain and life. I cannot agree. . . . As an octogenarian, there is a reasonable likelihood that I may suffer another "cardiovascular accident" or worse. . . . It seems to me that I have already paid my dues to death—indeed . . . I suffered enough to warrant dying several times over. Why run the risk of more?

Secondly, I dread imposing on my family and friends another grim round of misery similar to the one my first attack occasioned. My wife and children endured enough for one lifetime. . . .

EXERCISE SET 8-2

In general, we do not read poetry with the intent of constructing a summary and then evaluating for cogency. We read out of love for effective poetic expression. Nevertheless, it is a fact that poems often argue for a conclusion. Andrew Marvell's wonderful (one might say "Marvell-ous") poem "To His Coy Mistress" is a case in point. Clearly, there would be no point in constructing a detailed summary of this, or perhaps any, poem, citing every bit of support given for the reasons provided for its thesis. So in

[10]Fagan, John B. "Genetically Engineered Food: A Serious Health Risk." Physicians and Scientists for Responsible Application of Science and Technology (PSRAST). Web. http://www.psrast.org/jfhealth.htm.

this case, after first reading the poem for the enjoyment of the experience, simply state in a general way and in your own words the poem's thesis; the reason, or reasons, provided in its support; and a rough idea of the support provided for the reason or reasons.

To His Coy Mistress

Had we but world enough, and time,
This coyness, Lady, were no crime.
We would sit down and think which way
To walk and pass our long love's day.
Thou by the Indian Ganges' side
Shouldst rubies find: I by the tide
Of Humber would complain. I would
Love you ten years before the Flood,
And you should, if you please, refuse
Till the conversion of the Jews.
My vegetable love would grow
Vaster than empires and more slow;
An hundred years would go to praise
Thine eyes and on thy forehead gaze;
Two hundred to adore each breast,
But thirty thousand to the rest;
An age at least to every part,
And the last age should show your heart.
For, Lady, you deserve this state,
Nor would I love at lower rate.
But at my back I always hear
Time's winged chariot hurrying near;
And yonder all before us lie

Deserts of vast eternity,
Thy beauty shall no more be found,
Nor, in thy marble vault, shall sound
My echoing song; then worms shall try
That long preserved virginity,
And your quaint honor turn to dust,
And into ashes all my lust;
The grave's a fine and private place,
But none, I think, do there embrace.
Now therefore, while the youthful hue
Sits on thy skin like morning dew,
And while thy willing soul transpires
At every pore with instant fires,
Now let us sport us while we may,
And now, like amorous birds of prey,
Rather at once our time devour
Than languish in his slow-chapped power.
Let us roll all our strength and all
Our sweetness up into one ball,
And tear our pleasures with rough strife
Through the iron gate of life,
Thus, though we cannot make our sun
Stand still, yet we will make him run.

EXERCISE SET 8-3

The Declaration of Independence contains a thesis and reasons supporting that thesis. Get a copy of that important document, and (1) determine what its thesis is and (2) list the reasons provided in defense of that thesis. Is the argument inductive or deductive? What is the worldview?

EXERCISE SET 8-4

1. The analysis of Darrow's argument in Section 3 is one person's evaluation and may not agree with your own. In what ways would you agree or disagree with it? Analyze the premises, reasoning, language, and worldview of Darrow's argument and come up with your own evaluation.

2.   Provide a similar analysis and detailed evaluation of Martin Luther King, Jr.'s "Letter from a Birmingham Jail," which is available at many places online. Pay special attention to the following features of this argument:

(a) King's criteria for distinguishing between just and unjust laws

(b) King's argument that we have a duty to disobey unjust laws

(c) King's claim that we have a duty to disobey these laws "openly, lovingly, and with a willingness to accept the penalty."

3.   Find a two- to three-page argument in a magazine or online and evaluate it, using the critical thinking tools covered in the text.

EXERCISE SET 8-5

In a *New York Times* op-ed piece (16 April 2008), James Alan Fox argues that colleges and universities are creating an "unwarranted and unhealthy level of fear" by beefing up campus security with measures that might well be ineffective. Fox, a professor of criminal justice and law at Northeastern University, believes that colleges are overreacting to shootings at Virginia Tech and other institutions by developing security measures like lockdowns and mass notification "that not long ago would have been considered unnecessary, if not absurd." Lockdowns, or plans to seal off buildings to prevent a gunman from moving from one place to another, "may do little to prevent casualties . . . [since] almost all college shootings have taken place in one location." They have the added disadvantage of preventing a potential victim from fleeing the building that has been sealed off. Mass notification may be equally ineffective. Emergency sirens could be set off by other causes other than gunfire, and text message alerts on cell phones wouldn't reach a lecture hall full of students required to turn off cell phones. Professor Fox argues that security measures like these raise the level of student fear without providing reliable protection. He does believe in taking sensible precautions, like having an adequate security force and well-trained staff members, but he thinks colleges have overreacted to violence on campus, creating fear and apprehension that undermine the "carefree atmosphere of campus life." Would you agree or disagree? Has Professor Fox's arguments changed your views at all? Do some research on security measures at your campus and evaluate them for effectiveness.

EXERCISE SET 8-6

In Exercise Set 8-1, number 6, you were asked to summarize excerpts from the writings of philosopher John Locke.

1.   Indicate which of his assertions, if any, in his essay concern values, moral or nonmoral.

2.   Use the summary of the article that you constructed before, along with your beliefs about any value statements the essay in question may contain, to come to an evaluation of Locke's view on the matter, indicating where you think his argument is weak, where strong, and what your overall evaluation is, making sure, of course, to explain why you think so.

EXERCISE SET 8-7

In the fall of 2003, Californians were asked to vote on Proposition 54, a measure that prohibits state and local governments from classifying any person by race, ethnicity, color, or national origin. Your task is to evaluate the argument for Proposition 54 and decide whether you would vote for or against it.

Argument in Favor of Proposition 54[11]

"What is your race?"

African-American? Mexican-American? Asian-American? White? Native American? Or, the mysterious "other?"

If you're like most Californians, you're getting tired of that question.

Californians are the most racially and ethnically diverse people in the world— and we are proud of it. We are also among the most independent; and we resent being classified, categorized, divided and subdivided based on our skin color and the origin of our ancestors.

When you're asked to check a government form with row after row of these rigid and silly little "race" boxes, have you ever just wanted to say, "None of your business; now leave me alone?" Proposition 54 seeks to eliminate racial categorization, by the government, in all areas except medicine, health care and law enforcement.

The advocates of racial categorization maintain that you have no right to privacy concerning your ancestry and racial background. They see no problem if your employer or school officials label you AGAINST YOUR WILL often without telling you—or charge you with "racial fraud" if their "racial" definitions are different from yours.

Dare we forget the lessons of history?

Classification systems were invented to keep certain groups "in their place" and to deny them full rights. These schemes were not invented by the Civil Rights movement! They were anathema to it. In fact, former Supreme Court Justice Thurgood Marshall once said, "Distinctions by race are so evil, so arbitrary and invidious that a state bound to defend the equal protection of the laws must not involve them in any public sphere."

Throughout history, government-imposed racial classifications have been used to divide people. They have been used to set people against each other. The slave owners and segregationists of the American past knew it when they labeled European Jews a separate and inferior "race"; American judges knew it when they had to determine if Asians or part-Asians were white or non-white for the purposes of naturalization. Now, the advocates of racial categorization tell us that government-imposed racial categories will somehow yield the very opposite of what they were originally intended to do! They insult our intelligence!

The unrelenting daily racial categorization of people by the government is one of the most divisive forces in American society. It is constantly emphasizing our

[11]*California Statewide Special Election.* California Secretary of State Official Voter Information Guide. Web. http://voterguide.sos.ca.gov/past/2003/special/propositions/2-3-2-arguments.html.

minor differences, in opposition to our better instincts that tell us to seek our common interests and common values.

It's time for a change!

The government should stop categorizing its citizens by color and ancestry, and create a society in which our children and grandchildren can just think of themselves as Americans and individuals.

The colorblind ideal—judging others by the content of their character rather than the color of their skin—is more than a dream in California; it is central to the definition of who we are as a people, because, in California, we don't just dream; we do what others dream of doing.

Vote "YES" on Proposition 54 (www.racialprivacy.org)!
Ward Connerly, University of California Regent
Martha Montelongo Myers, Columnist
Joe Hicks, Human Relations Consultant

1. Using the margin note and summary method, or whatever method works best for you, construct a summary of the excerpt, and then identify the thesis and the main premises.

2. Critically evaluate the article, using your summary as your guide, making sure that your evaluation accurately reflects the excerpt itself, as well as your summary.

3. Drawing on your background knowledge and beliefs, decide how you would vote on this issue and defend your decision.

EXERCISE SET 8-8

Today, political columnists such as Gail Collins and Maureen Dowd use a combination of irony and humor to make points about the current social/political scene. Here is an example, written in 1999 by the late and sadly missed Arthur (Art) Hoppe.

Our Deserving Rich

Let us pray that not a hand is laid on the $792 billion tax cut passed by the House when the Senate takes it up today. Never has a piece of legislation been so pure in its concept, so efficient in its means, so right on the mark.

As you may have read, the Republican measure passed by the House proposes giving 79 percent of the income-tax reductions to the richest one-fifth of our citizens and .03 percent to the poorest. The richest's take would average $4,592, while the poorest would haul in $15.

It is high time we recognized the tremendous contributions the rich have made to this great land of ours. Hitherto, we have punished them for their well-earned money. The harder they labor and the more they make, the more we penalize them financially. What sort of a message does this send to every little tad in the land?

At the same time, we have rewarded the poor for their inability to find well-paying jobs. The less money they make, the more we subsidize them with our taxpayer dollars. There can be no doubt that they take far more from us than they give.

Let's ask ourselves: What has poverty ever done for America? The answer is absolutely nothing. Do the poor endow the symphonies and operas that flood our souls with musical grandeur? Of course not. Do they build the museums that increase our knowledge of the world or the galleries where hang the masterpieces of human creativity? Do they donate vast acreages of untouched land as a heritage for generations yet unborn? Don't be silly.

How many poor people have adopted a highway or saved a baby harp seal? Their commitment to the environment is infinitesimal at best. Indeed, rather than devoting themselves to improving our surroundings, they go out of their way to make our cities and towns far less inviting.

Their ghetto tenements, their sleazy housing projects and their skid row hotels are a blight on the landscape. Generally speaking, their wardrobes are tasteless, if not downright appalling. And those who live in the country have a penchant for littering their yards with unsightly collectibles such as broken-down washing machines and rusted-out cars.

Contrast this utter disregard for our sensibilities with the care the rich lavish on their surroundings. How pleasant it is to stroll through a wealthy neighborhood, graced with high flower-bedecked walls, verdant hedges and stately cast-iron fences.

How pleasing to the eye is the sight of an immaculately tuxedoed man and his bejeweled wife in her haute couture gown stepping from a limousine to attend a culture-improving function. Never could a poor person hope to equal their gratifying splendor.

Yes, as we would say in the rosy Ronald Reagan days, "It's morning in Palm Beach."

So hail the Republicans! Let us take comfort in the adage that the rich will always be with us—at least as long as the Republicans are in power. As for the Democrats, they would foolishly squander our hard-won budget surplus on Social Security, Medicare and other give-aways to the less successful members of our society.

Let's admit that the Democrats were not totally defeated. In what was obviously a last minute compromise, the Republicans agreed to give the poor families that $15. I can't for the life of me think why. It will only encourage them.[12]

1. What is Hoppe's point—his unstated thesis?

2. Why does Hoppe bash the poor and praise the rich? What is the point of such questions as "What has poverty ever done for America?" or "Do the poor endow symphonies and operas that flood our souls with musical grandeur?"

3. In your opinion, is he on target or not? Explain.

4. Does he make you take account of something that you already knew or that you hadn't paid sufficient attention to or appreciated the significance of? If so, explain. If not, why not?

---

[12]From Art Hoppe, "Our Deserving Rich," *San Francisco Chronicle*, 28 July 1999. © *San Francisco Chronicle*. Reprinted by permission.

MindTap®   **Visit MindTap for more readings and resources.**

Writing Cogent (and Persuasive) Essays

9

> *There are no dull subjects. There are only dull writers.* —H. L. MENCKEN
>
> *He can compress the most words into the smallest idea of any man I ever met.* —ABRAHAM LINCOLN
>
> *Learn as much by writing as by reading.* —LORD ACTON
>
> *A deluge of words and a drop of sense.* —JOHN RAY

MindTap® **Visit MindTap for more readings and resources.**

The discussion in Chapter 8 should make clear the essential contents of an argumentative essay: a thesis (grand conclusion) and reasons (premises) supporting the thesis. It also should be clear that in most cases the reasons themselves need to be supported by evidence or secondary reasons and that it often is useful to consider and refute likely objections.

But it should quickly become evident that writing a cogent and effective essay is much more difficult than summarizing and evaluating someone else's effort. Writing is character forming; it does indeed make evident the truth that writing is nature's way of letting us know how sloppy our initial thoughts on a topic often are. There are three reasons for writing essays, and one is without doubt that it is the very best way to sharpen sloppy thoughts into ideas that are clear, sensible, and well supported by good reasons and evidence. (The other two are to convince others and—obviously—to satisfy course or other requirements.)

1. The Writing Process

Experienced writers tend to keep their basic goals firmly in mind as they write and, indeed, as they prepare to write. They usually develop a plan of attack designed to meet their goals, but they don't generally move relentlessly from one idea to the next. Rather, they frequently revise their original plans in the light of new evidence or ideas or in the face of unexpected difficulties. One task often interrupts another. (Interestingly, editing seems to have a higher priority with most experienced writers than any other writing task and tends to interrupt others at any time. Having used an inaccurate word, for example, writers tend to put aside whatever they are doing and search for one that is more precise.) The point is that for most people, essay writing is a convoluted process, not a straightforward, linear one.[1] Skilled writers constantly rework their ideas as they plan and then write. The process itself leads to discovery, including, alas, the discovery of the inadequacy of our previous thoughts.

2. Preparing to Write

Students generally are asked to write short argumentative essays on specific topics—for instance, literacy in the United States, or legalizing marijuana. Suppose your assignment is to write an essay on the topic of regulating the possession of firearms.

The first task is to determine what the precise thesis of your essay will be. Gun regulation might involve restricting the carrying of handguns to specific places or perhaps only to specified individuals. Your thesis might be for, or against, the legal possession of automatic, quick-firing weapons, or it might focus just on handguns such as pistols.

Once you have provisionally decided on a thesis, your research and greater thought on the matter may well urge a change of mind, perhaps even a switch from pro to con, or vice versa. Unless a precise thesis is forced on you, say, by your instructor, the very process of thinking about the topic and investigating the evidence and the reasonings of others is likely to motivate you to revise your thesis in one way or another. Poor thinkers often decide on a thesis and hang on to it no matter what the evidence seems to indicate, as though changing one's mind indicates failure. Good thinkers realize that changing one's mind *for good reason* is the hallmark of intelligent thought. In the case of laws concerning firearms, for instance, evidence about the incredible destructive firepower of handheld automatic weapons such as Uzis might convince you to argue for the banning of these weapons.

After you have provisionally selected a thesis and have developed reasons and evidence in its favor, it often is useful to construct an outline of the essay that is to be the finished product. It's true, of course, that we all are different. Some people do better just starting out writing, doing research, and even altering their thesis as they go along rather than following the order suggested here. (Recall the earlier remark about writing being a convoluted process.) But most writers, in particular those with little experience, find it useful to do a good deal of preparation, including the construction of an outline,

---

[1]There have been a very few exceptions to this rule, the philosopher Bertrand Russell, interestingly, being a case in point. His handwritten first drafts, with extremely few changes here and there, often were used by publishers to set final type. We ordinary writers can only examine these drafts with a sense of awe, not with the intent to acquire the knack ourselves.

before starting to write the essay itself. (That is an important reason why essays written the night before they're due seldom get good grades—the fact that they are "off the top of the head" is obvious to instructors.) At the very least, an outline should include a provisional thesis and the principal reasons and supporting evidence expected to be presented in its favor. Outlines need not be written in grammatically correct or even whole sentences. Phrases and key words often are sufficient. But it is a good idea for inexperienced writers to state the thesis and principal reasons in complete sentences.

Calvin (of the Calvin and Hobbes duo) found it overly tedious having both to write an essay about bats and to do research on the topic, but research—diligent research—usually is essential. When doing research, take notes (including citations!) of pertinent evidence—statistics, examples, the opinions of experts, and so on. Regularly review what you have discovered in the light of your thoughts on the topic to see how the evidence supports, or undermines, your thesis or important reasons. If research undermines your thesis, it obviously needs revision (making the thesis narrower, perhaps) or a significant change in the reasons you intend to offer in its support. *Never simply ignore counterarguments or reasons!*

Some reasons involve legal matters that require us to review the law and interpretations of it. For instance, many arguments address issues that involve constitutional law (such as abortion, gun control, pornography, and so on). Because the Constitution often is used to support either side of an argument, it needs careful interpretation to be persuasive. For this reason, it's a good idea to research judicial opinion (the majority and dissenting opinions of high-court judges) in court cases addressing the issue you are writing about. Consulting expert opinion will help you understand the kind of careful deliberation needed in arguing complex legal matters.

Of course, you don't want to snow readers with a mountain of reasons or evidence. Plan to stick to your best reasons—those that reflect your most convincing evidence. Remember, though, that not all reasons are based on factual research or evidence. When relevant, moral convictions and standards, or beliefs about aesthetic or other values, constitute very good reasons indeed. For instance, the belief that taking the life of animals solely for our own purposes—for food or for furs—is morally wrong certainly is relevant to issues concerning the treatment of animals.

Finally, before starting to write an essay, make sure that its thesis follows logically from the reasons (premises) you intend to offer in its support. After all, validity—deductive or inductive—is an absolutely necessary condition of cogent argument. And reasons that do not genuinely support a thesis are useless.

3. Writing the Essay

Argumentative essays can be structured in several ways. One way is to present the opposition's argument in some detail, then refute it point by point, emphasizing your position as you go along. Another is to present reasons for and against a proposition, but wait until the end of the essay to draw conclusions that persuasively argue your position. Organizing arguments in these ways, however, can be tricky for students learning the craft. Too often the tendency is to drift off message or to present the opposition's argument so persuasively that it seems more convincing than your own. The best way for most students to structure an argument is to state the thesis in the introduction, present the reasons point by point in the body—taking care to refute the opposition when appropriate—and drive home the thesis at the end in an emphatic conclusion.

THE INTRODUCTION

A good introduction engages the reader's attention and lays the groundwork for the essay's thesis, which usually is stated toward the end of the introduction but may be placed at the beginning. The point of the introduction is to start persuading readers to accept your thesis, perhaps before it is even stated. (Remember, you have two goals in mind. One is to write an essay that is cogent. The other is to persuade readers to accept your thesis. A perfectly cogent essay that is not well written may very well not convince many readers.[2]) An essay can be introduced in all sorts of ways—with a quotation from an authoritative source, for instance, or a personal example that supports your position on the issue.

Once you capture the reader's attention, state the thesis and two or three major reasons in its support. Starting the essay in this way prepares the audience to read the body of the essay intelligently. Although it isn't necessary to include the main reasons after the thesis, doing so helps to keep both the writer and the reader on track.

Many writers find it particularly difficult to start essays. They often place *such* importance on the first few sentences that they end up with overlong introductions in overwrought language. We have two pieces of advice on this: First, avoid platitudes and grandiosity. One of the authors of this text implores his students each semester not to begin essays with "So-and-so was one of the greatest philosophers in history." But each semester, a couple of students just can't help themselves. Second, if you're having trouble starting an essay, don't stare at a blank screen waiting for inspiration. Start in the middle and work your way back. Often, the right introduction isn't any clearer than the right conclusion until the rest of the essay has been worked out, written, reworked, and rewritten to its final form.

THE BODY OF AN ESSAY

The body of an essay develops the reasons and evidence offered in support of the essay's thesis. How much support is needed depends on how resistant the intended audience is likely to be (or how much space is available to make your case). You don't want to hit people over the head with what they already believe or know. Support for each reason can take many forms (to be discussed in detail later in the chapter), but in brief, the reasons need to be persuasive, the evidence convincing, and the arguments logical.

If the opposition has a reason you think important enough to address, then bring it up by all means and either refute it or concede that it may be right—but not right enough to sink your argument.

THE CONCLUSION

The conclusion of an argumentative essay usually restates the thesis. If the essay is rather long or complicated, the main points may need to be summarized. But avoid the temptation to introduce new ideas. The conclusion is the place to draw your argument to a close with an emphatic statement of your position on the issue.

---

[2]Recall our discussion about "winning" arguments in Chapter 1.

Here, now, is what an entire essay might look like. It is rather short as essays go, intended primarily to serve as an example, but it nevertheless does a satisfactory job of clearly presenting and defending a thesis. The topic was purposely chosen to provoke some controversy and invites an essay in rebuttal.

Why Bother with College?

Introduction, ending with thesis and reasons.

Is college worth it? Not according to 57 percent of Americans, who claim that our system of higher education fails to give students "good value for the money they and their families spend."[3] Times are tough and life is short, so why waste it on college when all you get for your money is a load of debt? A friend of mine graduated from state university last year, and he still cannot get the kind of job his anthropology major prepared him for. Instead, he works at McDonald's for $7.60 an hour and lives at home with his parents, buried under a $30,000 debt. That is not going to happen to me. I am halfway through my freshman year and plan to drop out. Going to college makes no sense economically and does little to prepare most students for the job market: It is too expensive, the job-related courses I should take don't interest me, and besides, practical experience in the business world is worth more than an academic education.

Reason #1, followed by supporting evidence: high cost of a college education and extensive student debt.

Most Americans agree that a college education costs too much. According to a Pew Research Center survey, 75 percent say college is too expensive for most people in this country, and the cost keeps going up.[4] Each year the College Board releases figures on the average cost of a higher education. In 2011–12, for example, in-state students in public colleges paid $17,131 for tuition, room, and board per year—and that reflects an 8.3 percent increase in tuition plus a 6 percent increase in room and board over the previous year.[5] That would be about $68,500 total if the cost stayed the same, but, of course, it won't. It has been spiraling up for years. The increase in tuition alone is 5.1 percent beyond inflation over the previous five years. As far as private colleges go, the $38,500 price tag per year is so far beyond my wallet that it doesn't compute.

Increasing costs for most students means deepening debt. According to Consumer Reports the average debt per student in 2011 was $22,900, up 47 percent from the previous decade, taking inflation into account.[6] That is a lot of money. Many college grads have trouble getting jobs to begin with or wind up working for

---

[3]"Is College Worth It?" *The Pew Research Center.* 15 May 2011. 4 April 2012.
[4]Id.
[5]"New College Board Trends Reports Price of College Continues to Rise Nationally." *College Board.* 25 October 2011. Web. http://press.collegeboard.org/releases/2011.
[6]"2011 College Grads Have Highest Average Debt to Date." *Consumer Reports.Org.* 16 May 2011. Web. http://news.consumerreports.org/money/2011/05/2011-college-grads-have-highest-average-debt-to-date.html.

minimum wage in jobs they are vastly overqualified for—like my friend, for example, whose salary before taxes is $15,200. With that paltry paycheck he can't afford
to pay down his debt. And since he will probably have to retrain for work in another
field, he will run up an even bigger debt. College was a waste of time for him.

Reason #2, followed by a list of hot careers that don't interest the writer.

Another major drawback is that the courses designed to prepare students for success
in the job market don't interest me. According to a College Board report, the hottest
careers from 2008 to 2018 for graduates with bachelor's degrees are in education,
accounting, and computers.[7] Elementary, middle, and high school teachers are right
up there along with accountants, auditors, and computer analysts. None of these fields
interests me. What I really want is a liberal arts major, but that won't prepare me for the
job market. In fact, only 56 percent of all graduates in the class of 2010 got any jobs at all,
and those who did earned a median starting salary of $27,000, down 10 percent from
graduates in 2006–7.[8] These depressing statistics don't motivate me to stay in school.

Concession to the opposite side, which the writer then refutes.

I admit that there are a few advantages to getting a college education. It would
expand my knowledge, develop my communication skills, and probably make me
into a well-rounded person. If I took more English classes, I would write better, and
a philosophy course would help me reason more clearly. A few classes in history
wouldn't hurt, either, to give me a better perspective on current affairs. But these are
all things I can learn on my own without the exorbitant cost of college—knowledge
is free at the local library, after all. Another advantage widely touted for getting a
degree is that college grads earn more money than high school grads. However, an
economist for the Brookings Institution once argued that the numbers are skewed
because smarter kids are more likely to go to college to begin with. It stands to reason that if these smart, ambitious kids decided to go into business rather than college, they would have a good chance of succeeding on the job as well.

*Reason #3, with an explanation of practical experience gained on the job, and examples
of college dropouts who succeeded brilliantly in business.*

A college education may provide academic grounding, but it doesn't give the practical experience that the business world does. It doesn't teach you the skills you
need in the job market—like how to sell a product or how to develop a business
network. You learn skills like this by going to work. Maybe you fail some of the time,

---

[7]"Hottest Careers for College Graduates." *College Board.* 29 March 2012. http://www
.collegeboard.com/student/csearch/majors_careers/236.html.
[8]Rampell, Catherine. "Many with New College Degree Find the Job Market Humbling." *New
York Times,* 18 May 2011. Web. http://www.nytimes.com/2011/05/19/business/economy
/19grads.html.

but that is another practical lesson to be learned—how to turn business failures into success stories. Failure in college is a stain on your transcript, but not in business. Besides, a bachelor's degree really isn't necessary to succeed in business. Two titans of our times, Steve Jobs and Bill Gates, were college dropouts. So was Mark Zuckerberg, the Facebook CEO. In fact, 15 percent of the Forbes 400 richest people in the country are either college dropouts or high school graduates.[9] Only 5.3 percent have PhDs. Of course, I'm no Steve Jobs, but I could learn to be a pretty good entrepreneur with a small business of my own. President Obama was right when he told Congress, "Everyone here knows that small businesses are where most new jobs begin." The sooner I get there, the better.

Conclusion that emphatically restates the thesis.

Going to college is fine for students who have the money and the time. I have neither. The price tag is too high and the payoff too paltry. Given my financial situation, it makes more sense to gain practical experience in the workplace where I am earning money, not giving it away to an academic institution. Since far more professions require on-the-job training than classroom learning, it stands to reason that someone with ambition and brains can succeed.

---

[9]"Billionaire University: Education of the Forbes 400." *Forbes.com*. 16 January 2012. Web. http://www.forbes.com/forbes/2012/0116/leaderboard-education-billionaires-forbes-400-university.html.

4. Supporting Reasons Effectively

Perhaps the most difficult part of writing an argument is to provide convincing evidence. It's not enough to have sensible reasons to begin with. You need to convince the reader that those reasons are worth believing. Here are a few guidelines.

PROVIDE CONCRETE EVIDENCE

When possible, provide evidence that is specific. Use examples, cite statistics, compare or contrast relevant material, and draw on factual information. Reasons are more likely to be convincing when they can be verified by specific information than when they are explained in terms of generalities.

Specific information of this kind is usually drawn from these three sources:

1. *Personal experiences:* Suppose your thesis is that the food served at school should be improved. In this instance, you, yourself, have had personal experiences that can be used to support your position. Every time you have eaten lunch in the cafeteria, the food has been terrible: The bread is hard as a rock, and the spaghetti tastes like rubber. Citing these personal experiences provides good support for your reasons, though usually other kinds of evidence are needed as well.

2. *The experiences of others:* When using this type of evidence, you need to make sure that their information is accurate. You know what your own experiences are, but judgment is required in evaluating what others claim has happened to them. (Sad, but true.)

3. *Authoritative sources:* These include such sources as reference books, journals, and people who have extensive knowledge about a subject—experts. But here, too, judgment must be used. Reputable encyclopedias, dictionaries, and handbooks on specific subjects can usually be relied on with respect to bare facts or matters that are not politically controversial. You have to be more careful with magazines, newspapers, television programs, and particularly the Internet because people can put anything online they want to and claim to be authorities when they aren't.

Note this important point: *Authoritative sources must always be credited,* either in a footnote or in the text itself. And direct quotations must always be indicated by the use of quotation marks. Using someone else's material without acknowledging the source constitutes **plagiarism**, an extremely serious offense.

PROVIDE TRANSITIONS

A good essay obviously has to have a logical structure, but you also want to write so that one thought flows into another—so that the logical structure of your essays is easy to follow. Transition terms and expressions highlight the flow of an essay, helping readers to know what to expect next—to know which expressions serve as reasons and which as conclusions and, in general, how things hang together. Note the use in the sample essay of the words *but, however, instead, besides,* and *of course,* and the expressions *for example, another advantage is,* and *it stands to reason that.*

THINK YOUR POSITION THROUGH CAREFULLY

Having to write so as to convince others—much more than speaking extemporaneously— is an excellent way to get clear in your own mind as to where the truth lies. Writing a good argumentative essay requires mental discipline—the ability to see through the natural tendency to hang on to opinions once formed, even in the light of their inadequacy—to root out inconsistencies and fuzzy beliefs, and to arrange thoughts into a coherent whole.

CONSIDER YOUR AUDIENCE

Writers who seriously intend to influence others have to keep their audience firmly in mind. It's all too easy to forget the audience as we sit alone at a desk scribbling away (well, these days, also tapping away). But experienced writers learn that they must always write with the intended readers in mind. Past failures—having had manuscripts rejected, severely criticized, or simply passed over by others—motivate them to figure out who they are writing for and how best to engage the interest of that particular audience.

> The plural of anecdote is not evidence.
>
> —BILL LOCKYER, ATTORNEY GENERAL OF CALIFORNIA

Block Those Metaphors!

Metaphor is a time-honored linguistic device. In the hands of careful writers, it often can express ideas swiftly and more effectively than more literal language. The trouble is that writers often go overboard in their enthusiasm for this linguistic tool. Here is an example from the writings of Guy Gugliotta in the Washington Post *(carried as one of the* New Yorker's *occasional metaphoric overkill items):*

> *There was no time, Acting Chairman Matthew F. McHugh (D-N.Y.) said last week, and the committee was tired of stoking public outrage with fortnightly gobbets of scandal. It decided to publish everything it had left, warts and all.*
>
> *Now everyone is tarred with the same ugly brush, and the myth that forever simmers in the public consciousness—that the House shelters 435 parasitic, fat-cat deadbeats—has received another shot of adrenalin.*

This little snippet also illustrates another writing no-no: the use of obscure words few readers can be expected to understand. Or did you know what gobbet means without having to look it up?

One way to develop a sense of audience is to have one immediately at hand. Much has been written about the importance of writing with an audience in mind, but this advice needs to be augmented by actually having others respond to your work. In college, papers are usually directed to an audience of one—the teacher who evaluates your work and provides valuable advice intended to improve your writing ability.

However, what do you do in the hazy prewriting stage when you have the glimmer of an idea but aren't sure whether it will work, or when you have thought of a thesis and reasons but don't know whether they are convincing? In this stage of the writing process, it is helpful to try your ideas out on other people. Their feedback will give you a sense of audience response. Some teachers divide their classes into response groups so that students can discuss their ideas and read drafts aloud to each other. Some schools have tutors who can act as an audience. The point is to use whatever resources happen to be available so as to become accustomed to addressing a real audience.

Here are some questions to ask about the audience:

1. What is your intended audience?
2. What are their worldviews and background beliefs?
3. What tone is appropriate?

Think of how different your approach would be if you were arguing for gun control either to a group of mothers or to a local gun owners' organization. Most likely their worldviews and background beliefs would differ considerably, and undoubtedly the gun owners would be harder to convince than the mothers. Once you have the audience firmly in mind, you can begin to see what reasoning and evidence would be most likely to persuade and what tone would be appropriate.

Reprinted by permission of Paul Miller

STRENGTH OF CLAIMS: THREADING THE NEEDLE

When we talk about the "strength" of a claim, we may be referring to the overall value of a claim. In this sense, strong claims make for a strong (i.e., a cogent and persuasive) argument, and it makes no sense to wonder if a claim is *too* strong. But there's another sense of "strength" for which we do have to worry about our claims being too strong.

In this second sense, the "strength" of a claim means something like its boldness. Take the claim "Steph Curry is the best point guard in the NBA." This claim is stronger than "Steph Curry is possibly (or maybe, or probably, or likely) the best point guard in the NBA," and weaker than "Steph Curry is necessarily (or definitely, or without doubt) the best point guard in the NBA."

Also, a claim involving a group can be weaker or stronger depending on how many members of the group the claim is about. The universal claims "All politicians are liars" and "No politicians are liars" are stronger than the particular claims "Some politicians are liars" and "some politicians are not liars."[10]

Writers often make the mistake of using claims that are either too weak or too strong. A claim that is too weak provides insufficient evidence for the conclusion to which it is a premise. A claim that is too strong is too difficult to defend with further premises. Choosing claims that are adequately supportive of their conclusions but that are also defensible can be a tricky business.

Say for instance that you want to argue that Denzel Washington deserves a lifetime achievement award at the Oscars. Well, the claim that Washington is the greatest actor of his generation would be terrific evidence for this conclusion. But this would be awfully difficult to demonstrate, and not just because such matters are somewhat subjective. You could instead claim that he is a very good actor. I can't imagine anyone would disagree with this much weaker claim, but it does not do much to support the conclusion. There are lots of very good actors and actresses who don't quite deserve lifetime achievement awards. What about the claim that Washington is *one of* the greatest actors of his generation? This claim, while not quite as compelling as evidence, is more defensible than the

---

[10]Recall our discussion of claims like these in the section on syllogisms in Chapter 2.

strongest claim. And while it is not quite as easy to demonstrate as is the weakest claim, it provides better support for the conclusion.

Unfortunately, choosing the right premise is not always as easy as just identifying a claim intermediate between the weakest and strongest options. Say you wanted to argue that some politician is a liar but had no evidence that he or she told any specific lies. Of course the claim that some politicians are liars is easy to defend, but it doesn't provide much help. Neither, though, does the claim that most or even nearly all politicians are liars. This one may well be in the minority. To make this particular argument, nothing else will do but "all politicians are liars." But this claim is much too strong to be defensible (unless all that is meant is that all people are essentially liars—but then the conclusion is awfully trivial). This particular argument, then, probably needs to be abandoned.

By and large, the best strategy is to look for the weakest claim that provides adequate support for your conclusion rather than the strongest claim you think you can defend. In nearly all cases, though, paying attention to the strength of your claims will help you craft better arguments. (Notice the relative weakness of both of the claims in this paragraph.)

REWRITE! REWRITE! REWRITE!

The difficulty of arranging thoughts coherently is an important reason why rewriting almost always is necessary. One author of this text, in fact, often tells his students that "good writing is good editing." When writing a critical essay, we often realize that our thoughts aren't as focused or penetrating as we supposed. The writing process itself constitutes an important part of the reasoning process.

That's why most writers, definitely including the authors of this text, construct the first draft of an essay as a learning, or thinking, device. They do the best job they can on the first draft and then critically evaluate it as they would an opponent's essay. The next draft then can take account of what has been learned, perhaps by introducing new reasons and arguments that aren't open to the criticisms made of the first draft.

But one thing is clear. Only a few of the very best writers can construct a really good critical essay in one draft. Writers like philosopher Bertrand Russell (recall that his manuscripts often showed only a word or two changed here and there to mark the transition from first to final draft) are extremely rare in this world. The rest of us have to write at least two drafts, usually more, to get our thoughts into good order and to express them so they can be easily understood by others. And you shouldn't be surprised to find out that learning to do this well takes . . . practice, practice, practice.

Perhaps the chief difficulty of rewriting—for everyone, but especially for less experienced writers—is just in properly reading and evaluating your own work. The trick (and it's not an easy one) is to read what you've written as though it were someone else's. After all, *you* know what you meant to say, but that doesn't mean your audience will. Putting yourself in the place of your audience as best you can goes a long way toward making your writing clearer and more understandable.

When you go back to your writing, always ask yourself if you've stated everything as clearly as you can. To really appreciate the importance of this, try to find something you wrote a few years ago. Is everything there as clear to you now as you thought it was then? One thing that helps in this task is to give yourself some time and (psychological) distance between drafts of a paper. Looking again with "fresh eyes" can often be quite illuminating. (This is another reason to avoid procrastination!)

Good Writers Respect Their Audience

F. L. Lucas, once fellow and lecturer at King's College, Cambridge University, stressed the writer's obligation to readers in his essay "What Is Style?" from which this excerpt is drawn:[11]

The writer should respect his readers; therefore [he should behave with] courtesy.... From this follow several other basic principles of style. Clarity is one. For it is boorish to make your reader rack his brains to understand. One should aim at being impossible to misunderstand—though men's capacity for misunderstanding approaches infinity. Hence Molière and Po Chui tried their work on their cooks; and Swift on his men-servants—"which, if they did not comprehend, he would alter and amend, until they understood it perfectly." Our bureaucrats and pundits, unfortunately, are less considerate.

Brevity is another basic principle. For it is boorish, also, to waste your reader's time. People who would not dream of stealing a penny of one's money turn not a hair at stealing hours of one's life. But that does not make them less exasperating. Therefore, there is no excuse for the sort of writer who takes as long as a marching army corps to pass a certain point. Besides, brevity is often more effective; ... And because one is particularly apt to waste words on preambles before coming to the substance, there was sense in the Scots professor who always asked his pupils—"Did ye remember to tear up that fir-r-st page?"

---

[11]*Holiday* magazine, March 1960.

Student Essay Bon Mots

Here are a few extreme examples from student essays to serve as a reminder that good writing requires care and—yes—extensive revision. (Our thanks to English students at Knowname College.)

The elementary school I first attended was racial towards minorities.
(Poorly expressed thought.)

Women have sat on the back burner long enough.
(Unfortunate figure of speech.)

She was a rabid typist.
(Malapropism.)

Secondly, the American school system is more loose, thus encouraging students to be creative rather than Japanese.
(Faulty comparison.)

Every day at 4:00 thousands of people evacuate on their jobs.
(Poor choice of words and construction.)

The octopus of communism spread its testacles over the continent.
(Really!)

Do punctual errors count?
(Yes, they do.)

He resorts to name calling and puts himself on a peddle stool.
(What a motor-mouth.)

A broader view also prevents the student from charging blindly into a brick wall of unconceptuality.
(Block that metaphor!)

I have a fool-time job.
(Freudian slip?)

The vowels we made at the alter.
(Double display of ignorance.)

I am in favor of capital punishment particularly in cases of murder and rape and aggravated napping, child or otherwise.
(Unintended humor.)

> And here are a few gems culled from Jaime O'Neill's article "The Goal Is Garbage In, Writers Out" (*San Francisco Chronicle*, September 4, 2005):

"I believe in my second amendment that is the right to bare arms."
"I have this udder glow of happiness."
"I placed a reef on my grandmothers' grave."
"My ex-best friend is so stuck on herself. She's like a pre-Madonna."
"I was in the mist of studying when my cell phone rang."

Ah, well, everyone can't go to the head of the class in this doggy dog world. But at least we all can have self-of-steam.

Summary of Chapter 9

The essential contents of an argumentative essay are a *thesis* and *reasons (premises)* supporting the thesis. Usually, reasons need to be supported in turn by evidence or secondary reasons.

1. Experienced writers tend to keep their basic goals in mind as they prepare to write, developing a plan of attack to meet those goals, revising their original plans in the light of new evidence or unexpected difficulties. But they don't generally write in a linear fashion; writing tends to be a convoluted process.

2.   The first task when preparing to write is to determine precisely what your thesis will be. Later, of course, you may change your mind, perhaps by narrowing the topic or zeroing in on it more carefully. While preparing to write and during the writing process itself, changing one's mind for good reasons is the hallmark of intelligent thought.

   After selecting a thesis and developing your principal reasons in its support, you may find it useful to construct an outline of the proposed finished product. When doing the generally inevitable research, be sure to take notes, including reference citations. If research undermines your thesis or reasons, you must revise. Never simply ignore counterarguments or reasons. Before starting to write, make sure your thesis follows logically from the reasons you intend to offer in its support.

3.   Argumentative essays typically divide into three parts. The *introduction* generally states and lays the groundwork for the thesis, either before or after stating it explicitly. The *body* of the essay should contain the reasons and evidence, perhaps also reasons in support of the reasons. It is likely to be more convincing if it contains examples. If counterarguments are to be discussed, the right time to do so is in the body of an essay; and similarly for comparing or contrasting with other ideas. The *conclusion* of your essay may restate the thesis or perhaps provide a short summary of the essay's most important points.

4.   The point of writing an argumentative essay is to persuade readers to accept your thesis. To do so, effective writers provide convincing reasons and supporting evidence. They also keep the reader firmly in mind by considering the background beliefs of their audience and the appropriate tone to take given that audience.

5.   Good writers also try to achieve a natural flow by providing readers with transition words and expressions such as *but, although, for instance,* and *nevertheless.*

   But (note the transition word), however well planned an essay may be, rewriting almost certainly will be necessary. A first draft may thus serve as a learning device, so that later drafts can take account of what has been learned.

6.   When writing an argumentative essay, choose claims that are neither too strong (and therefore cannot be adequately defended) nor too weak (and therefore cannot provide adequate support for their conclusions).

7.   Think your position through carefully and revise the essay as you reexamine your ideas. (You may find that your ideas change in the writing process itself.) Write and rewrite until your essay says just what you want it to say.

EXERCISE SET 9-1

One good way to get practice in writing well is to critique poor writing. Here is a tiny (142 words) tongue-in-cheek essay from the delightful book *Ordinary Money* by Louis B. Jones (New York: Viking, 1990). For many years, Jones was a reader for freshmen English and other college writing courses. As a warm-up exercise, explain the various writing bloopers, of the kind that might move your instructor to make negative margin comments—blunders that Jones constructed into his little "student-written" essay (described by one of the book's characters as "complete bull___, but Ohrbach [the instructor] never notices"):

> The comparison/contrast of the Greeks and Romans is a very important comparison/contrast. Since the beginning of time, people have pondered this question. In the hustle-bustle world of today, the comparison/contrast of the Greeks and Romans is very important and relevant. For example, the Romans were after the Greeks and therefore they had a more technology-oriented advancement. For example, they had plumbing and flush toilets and they had lead in the pipes which made everybody gradually insane. For example, Caligula, which caused the Decline and Fall of the Roman Empire. Another comparison/contrast of the Greeks and Romans is, the Greeks were very sane. For example, Plato and other world-famous philosophers pondered the greatest question of all time. Plato believed that everything was ideal. This is still true today. . . .

EXERCISE SET 9-2

Here are many issues that should be of some interest to college students. Select one and, bearing in mind the writing suggestions just discussed, write an essay (about 1,000 to 1,500 words), taking one side or the other of the issue. Then write a critical analysis in reply to your own essay (as though you were a competent—and fair!—opponent attacking your position). And then rewrite your original essay to try to take account of your own criticisms. Think of your fellow students, not your instructor, as your audience. Pick a topic that will let you show how well you can reason about a complicated issue. Do not pick an issue that you think has an obviously right solution to it. For example, do not select number 10 if all you are going to say is that of course we should not offer abstinence-only sex education, because we all have the right to learn about contraception. Every issue is more complicated than that, and there always are serious pros and cons to consider. This is a difficult and very important assignment; it absolutely cannot be done satisfactorily the night before it is due—if for no other reason than that a certain amount of research very likely is in order. (Your instructor definitely and without doubt will quickly tell when reading your essay if it's a last-minute concoction.)

1. Should speech codes be instituted in colleges and universities to fight racism on campus?

2. Should undocumented workers be allowed to get driver's licenses?

3. Should affirmative action with respect to the education or employment of women and minorities be the law of the land? (If you write on this topic, you

must carefully explain what you mean by "affirmative action," and you should restrict your topic either to education or to employment.)

4. Should colleges and universities support big-time football and basketball teams?

5. Should colleges and universities permit teachers and students to carry guns on campus?

6. Are the salaries paid to movie stars and sports stars too high? If so, what should be done about this? If not, what exactly justifies the amount of money paid to them?

7. Should stem cells from embryos be used in medical research?

8. Should the Supreme Court have ruled that all or part of the Affordable Health Care Act is constitutional?

9. Should alleged terrorists be read their Miranda rights to remain silent and to have an attorney present during questioning—before they are interrogated?

10. Should high school courses in human sexuality offer abstinence-only sex education and eliminate discussion of contraception?

11. Should women be required to register with the Selective Service System along with men?

12. Should voters be required to show government-issued photo IDs in order to vote at the polls?

13. Florida now has a Stand Your Ground law that lets a person use deadly force if he or she believes it is necessary to prevent death or great bodily harm to himself or herself or someone else. Under these circumstances, the person using force cannot be prosecuted. Once you have researched the law and understand the particulars, write an argument for or against it.

14. Increasingly colleges and universities are encouraging students to take unpaid internships for academic credit at for-profit companies, even when the companies use the students to replace regular employees rather than give them on-the-job experience that internships are meant to provide. Argue for or against this practice.

15. Current law penalizes people who distribute to minors "harmful matter," like pornography, alcohol, and cigarettes, but it doesn't restrict the sale of graphically violent and first-person shooter video games (where the player advances the game by killing). Should legislation be enacted to prohibit the sale of these games to minors?

16. In recent years, some pharmacists have refused to fill prescriptions for birth control pills or devices, arguing that their religious or moral beliefs prevented them from doing so. Should pharmacists have the legal right to refuse this service?

17. As of spring 2001, discoverers of human genes are allowed to patent their discoveries, so that, for instance, certain tests for a propensity to breast cancer

cannot be conducted on your genes without paying a royalty to the patent holder. The principal argument in favor of gene patenting is that allowing it dramatically increases the incentive to discover such genes. Should we allow human genes to be patented?

18. Most scientists believe that increased use of fossil fuels (coal, oil, and so on) is leading to increases in global warming that will have adverse effects such as raised sea levels and the inundation of low-lying coastal areas. But some scientists deny this is true, and a very few argue that the good effects of global warming will outweigh the bad ones. Take sides in this debate.

EXERCISE SET 9-3

1. In recent years, many European and Middle Eastern governments have debated whether to forbid people from wearing certain types of Islamic dress like the niqab, a face veil with slits for the eyes, and the burqa, a garment that covers the entire body from head to toe. The French parliament has overwhelmingly approved banning the niqab and the burqa, the Dutch have enacted a burqa ban, and the Turks have banned Muslim head scarfs at university. Those in favor of the ban argue that wearing Islamic garb is degrading to women and presents a security risk because it masks a person's identity. Those opposed maintain that it is a violation of religious freedom and stigmatizes Islamic people.

    Much has been written about this issue in recent years that can easily be researched in periodicals and on the Internet. Examine the reasons given on both sides and write an argument for or against a full or partial ban of Islamic dress. Include persuasive evidence to support your reasons.

2. Online courses have become so popular that nearly 25 percent of all college students took such courses in 2012. These courses work well for students who live far from a campus or have jobs and cannot attend regularly scheduled classes. They offer everything a conventional classroom provides except live participation. But some educators worry that the virtual classroom is no substitute for the real thing. They argue that electronic conversations can't match classroom discussions where students are stimulated by the spontaneous exchange of ideas and by professors who are better able to clarify and channel discussions in person than online.

    Interview students who have studied online and professors who have taught these courses. Use the evidence you gather, along with current research on the subject, to support an argument for or against taking courses online.

3. According to the *Los Angeles Times* in 2015, upwards of 20 million Americans download music illegally through peer-to-peer sites. And a 2013 study by the "brand protection" firm NetNames found that in just one month, 432 million people (or at least unique users) searched for copyright-infringing material. Critics of this practice liken music "piracy" to theft, cite (potentially) billions of dollars in lost revenue, and claim that music piracy inhibits creative output by taking a means of income away from would-be musicians. Defenders argue

that unlicensed downloading allows many more people access to music they wouldn't otherwise be able to afford, and that far from being a limiter of creativity, this practice encourages creativity by spreading musical inspiration further and exposing more people to different kinds of music.

Write an essay arguing for or against greater regulation of and penalties for peer-to-peer sharing of copyrighted music.

4. In the ongoing debate about the rights of alleged terrorists imprisoned in U.S. territory, the main issue is whether those prisoners, classified as enemy combatants, should be detained indefinitely without a writ of habeas corpus. This constitutional right allows prisoners to ask the court to determine whether they are being lawfully imprisoned. When the Supreme Court ruled in 2008 (*Boumediene v. Bush*) that enemy combatants held in U.S. territory are entitled to this right, it ruled against the Bush administration policy that disallowed it. However, there continues to be much controversy over the issue.

    Examine the literature on this subject, particularly rulings and dissents of the Supreme Court and lower courts. Then write an argument defending the position you find most convincing.

5. A Florida technology company has developed a computer ID chip that could be implanted inside the body. The implant, about the size of a grain of rice, can be encoded with a wide range of information—everything from secret codes to sensitive medical data. Such a device would be invaluable to the medical community for giving emergency workers access to an unconscious patient's medical history, but it raises questions about privacy rights. Lee Tren, a senior attorney for a privacy advocacy group, cautioned that "you always have to think about what the device will be used for tomorrow. . . . At first a device is used for applications we all agree are good, but then it slowly is used for more than it was intended."

    Write an argument either defending or rejecting the use of embedded ID chips.

6. Here are brief arguments for and against public colleges and universities soliciting private funding from corporations and wealthy benefactors. Take a stand on this issue and write an argument defending your position. Good sources of information might be professors, department chairs, and deans in your own school.

    An argument for soliciting private dollars is that state and federal budget cuts have been so severe in the past decade that public schools have had to look to the private sector for funding in order to ensure a high-quality education, to do cutting-edge research, to replace outdated equipment, and to upgrade deteriorating buildings.

    The opposition argues that private funding transforms public schools into appendages of private industry, preoccupies the faculty with fund-raising instead of teaching, pits one department against another, and undermines the curriculum through corporate influence.

7. DDT, once used to control malaria-bearing mosquitoes, has been banned for decades because of its harmful effect on animals and humans. Fish-eating birds, in particular, were threatened with extinction from eating fish that had concentrated DDT in their tissues. But humans eating contaminated fish were afflicted

as well, accumulating DDT in their systems and passing it onto their babies through breast milk. Since the chemical has been banned, however, malaria rates in developing countries have soared, and a movement is underway to start spraying houses in these countries to protect people from mosquitoes carrying the disease.

Do some research on this subject and write an argument for or against using DDT in developing countries to prevent the spread of malaria.

8. In recent years, WikiLeaks has released confidential State Department material on an unprecedented scale to selected media sources like the *New York Times* and the *Guardian*. WikiLeaks justifies these disclosures on the grounds that they hold the government more accountable and thus improve our foreign policy. But those who disagree argue that secrecy is essential to foreign relations and that leaks in confidential information will damage our diplomatic relations and thus our foreign policy will suffer.

Argue for or against the WikiLeaks practice of disclosing confidential State Department material.

9. As part of a movement toward "effective altruism," some people have recently argued that those who would dedicate their lives to doing good should work to secure the most lucrative employment they can and then donate as much of their income as they can to the charities that produce the most good. As most such charities need money more than they do volunteers, this strategy would produce the most good. Critics claim that this strategy is dangerous, as it would expose the would-be do-gooder to the temptation of spending the money he or she earns. Another argument from critics is that the strategy relies too heavily on assumptions about others' proper use of donated funds.

Argue for or against this strategy for people who genuinely want to dedicate their lives to helping others.

EXERCISE SET 9-4

The tragic shootings at Virginia Tech in 2007 by a psychotic student raised questions about the way colleges and universities deal with mentally ill students. Warning signs of Cho Seung Hui's troubled mental state surfaced well over a year before the killings. Mental health officials knew of his suicidal tendencies, two women students complained to the police about annoying contacts initiated by Cho, and several English teachers informed university officials about his deeply disturbing writing, full of violent images, persecution, and anger. Yet the university was limited in taking action by federal privacy and antidiscrimination laws. Colleges and universities are restricted by the disabilities act from screening prospective students for mental health problems. They cannot put a student on involuntary medical leave on the grounds of mental illness, nor can they notify parents of their child's mental condition or release medical records without the student's consent. Although these laws are designed to curtail discrimination and the invasion of privacy, they make it harder to detect seriously disturbed students like Cho and to take the steps necessary to prevent violent behavior. While not all of the incidents can be attributed to previously detectable mental illness, there have been dozens of similar shootings at American colleges and universities since this one at Virginia Tech.

Consider the complex issues involved and write an argument for or against amending laws that restrict colleges and universities from dealing with students who have serious mental illness.

EXERCISE SET 9-5

We live at a time when surveillance technology is so advanced that we can easily be spotted in public places by video cameras, or tracked by GPS devices, or identified by software with face recognition. In fact, the former head of public policy at Google, Andrew McLauglin, said at a Stanford conference in 2007 that he expected public and private agencies to request Google to post live, online surveillance fields worldwide within a decade. Alarmed at the increasing scope of public surveillance, privacy rights advocates argue that this invasion of our privacy violates the Fourth Amendment, which prohibits unreasonable search and seizure. But their opponents claim that we have no reason to expect privacy when we are in public places; rather we should welcome surveillance technologies, because they prevent and discourage crime as well as provide evidence for criminal investigations.

Examine these and other reasons as well as the evidence on either side of the issue. Then write an argument on the position you find most convincing.

EXERCISE SET 9-6

In a bitterly contested case, *Citizens United v. Federal Election Commission*, the Supreme Court made a landmark ruling that the government may not prohibit political spending by corporations or unions in elections. Although banned from giving money directly to candidates, they are not restricted from making unlimited contributions to independent political committees (later dubbed super PACs). The case was decided on First Amendment grounds, with the majority arguing that political expenditures are a form of speech, and since corporations are made up of individuals, they are entitled to the same free speech protection as individual citizens. In defense of the ruling, Justice Anthony Kennedy wrote, "If the First Amendment has any force, it prohibits Congress from fining or jailing citizens, or associations of citizens, for simply engaging in political speech." The dissenting opinion argued that the Court's ruling threatened to corrupt democracy by allowing corporate money to flood the political system. As Justice John Paul Stevens wrote, "A democracy cannot function effectively when its constituent members believe laws are being bought and sold."

Review the First Amendment. Then look up the majority opinion written by Justice Kennedy and the dissent by Justice Stevens. Examine their arguments carefully and decide which ones are the most convincing. Write an argument for or against the Court's ruling using your own reasons and evidence as well as those of the justices. And remember to cite sources.

EXERCISE SET 9-7

In a very well-known, often-reprinted lecture, "The Idea of a University," Cardinal John Henry Newman (1801–1890) argued that the principal work of the university is to provide a liberal education, not merely, or even primarily, professional training. He said that a liberal education:

> gives a man a clear conscious view of his own opinions and judgments, a truth in developing them, an eloquence in expressing them, and a force in urging them. . . . it prepares him to fill any post with credit and to master any subject with civility.

Do you agree with Cardinal Newman's assessment of a liberal education and agree that the primary job of a university (or college) is to provide such an education? Write an essay defending your opinion.

EXERCISE SET 9-8

High-tech cheating has increased dramatically now that almost all students have access to the Internet. Some examples: About 70 students from an Introduction to Congress course at Harvard (some irony here, we suppose) were forced to leave school for a year after a highly publicized cheating scandal in 2012. And in 2015, a professor at Stanford brought cheating allegations against some 20 percent of a large introductory course. These were just some of the incidents that happened to make the news, probably because of the combination of a surprising number of students involved and the prestige of the schools. The problem, though, is widespread. One recent study suggested that some 68 percent of undergraduates admit to having cheated. Plagiarizing from online sources is a common offense, and the prevalence of smartphones, tablets, watches, etc., make policing cheating in the classroom all the more difficult.

It has been suggested that this new wave of cheating is due in part to there being a relatively low risk of detection and even more to the lenient nature of punishments when caught. In view of this and the fact that cheaters do harm to those who do not cheat, would you approve expulsion from college for first-time proven cheaters? Or flunking the course? Or suspension for one semester? Defend your answer.[12]

In the mid-90s, a number of schools and districts accepted televisions and VCRs (a bygone precursor to the DVD) from Channel One in exchange for showing Channel One educational programming—including commercials—in the classroom.

---

[12]See the article by Ted Wallach, *San Francisco Chronicle*, 14 August 2000.

MindTap®   **Visit MindTap for more readings and resources.**

"In the marketplace of ideas, we may not have the best ideas, but we have the best marketing."

Advertising: Selling the Product

10

MindTap® Visit MindTap for more readings and resources.

A dvertising is so obviously useful that it's surprising it has such a bad name. Ads tell us what is new and what is available, where, when, and for how much. They tell us about a product's (alleged) quality and specifications. All for free, except for the effort of reading or paying attention.

Yet there are legitimate gripes about advertising. Ads don't tell us about product defects. They often mislead, either via exaggeration or, occasionally, downright lies. And because some products are advertised more heavily or more effectively than others, ads tend to skew our choices in unreasonable ways.

It also has been argued that advertising increases the costs of goods to consumers. It isn't uncommon for a quarter, or even a third, of the price of an item to be due to advertising costs, and critics have argued that this constitutes a tremendous waste.

But this charge is misleading. Advertising does cost a great deal of money, and this expense has to be factored into the costs of finished goods. Nevertheless, advertising greatly reduces the prices of those goods in the marketplace compared to what they would cost were advertising abolished or greatly

restricted. It does so because it lowers production costs by making mass production profitable, thus enabling producers to obtain a mass market. In short,
advertisers advertise because it reduces the costs of *selling goods.* It is not an
accident that virtually all businesses advertise; they do so because they don't
know of a better or cheaper way to sell their products. Those who argue otherwise generally forget that if a company doesn't advertise, it will have to increase
other selling costs, especially sales commissions. (Advertising also has been
objected to on the grounds that it gives an unfair advantage to large organizations when they compete against smaller ones, but objections of this kind raise
issues best left unexplored here—for example, about the desirability of large
versus small businesses.)

It is worth noting, though, that advertising techniques and markets have
changed dramatically over the past forty years. In 1965, companies poured
most of their advertising dollars into the three major TV networks: ABC, NBC,
and CBS, the market that reached 80 percent of the prime target audience—the
18- to 49-year-olds. Today, most Americans have more than a hundred channels
to choose from and the high-tech tools to mute or bypass ads altogether. Since
fewer people read newspapers and magazines (once major marketing outlets)
and more turn to the Internet for information and entertainment, the advertising industry has had to reach far broader and much more complex markets than
ever before. But advertisers are nothing if not inventive. So over the years, ad
agencies have metamorphosed into marketing companies that hawk their products through public relations promotions, in-store displays, and direct mail gimmicks. They use product placement, show ads in movie theaters, and inundate
the Internet with pop-up ads and TV commercials that stream on (and on and
on) to websites like YouTube and Facebook, giving them an eternal shelf life.
And the lines between marketing, advertising, and public relations are further
blurred as companies scramble to take advantage of the massive echo of social
media and the ever-elusive viral video. But no matter how glitzy or numerous
the innovations are, the bottom line is that they still manipulate consumer
attitudes about beauty, status, relationships, and sex, using age-old gimmicks to
sell us the goods.

1. Are Advertisements Arguments?
Examples of Rhetoric?

We do not generally think of advertisements, be they on TV, in website banner ads, in
newspapers, or in subway cars, as being *arguments.* In fact, it may not be clear that
advertisements are really meant to be persuasive in the sense that, say an opinion piece in
a newspaper is. Why, then, give them a whole chapter in a book about logic and rhetoric?

The answer is a little complicated, and has more to do with how we treat advertising than with its purpose.

There are at least two senses of "persuade." In one sense, we persuade someone when we cause a certain *action*, as when we say things like "I was persuaded to eat by the dinner he put in front of me." Persuasion to action does not require rationality or reasons. We even talk about "persuading" animals to do certain things. In the other sense, we persuade when we change someone's *beliefs,* as in "I persuaded the class that the test was unfairly constructed." This is the sense of persuasion with which we're concerned in a study of public rhetoric. We employ arguments to persuade people of certain conclusions on the basis of premises.

So in which sense are advertisements meant to persuade us? Are they meant to get us to do certain things or to believe certain things? Fundamentally, we have to say that advertisements are meant to have us do certain things, usually to spend money on particular products or services. If an advertisement causes us to buy a particular product, does the advertiser really care *how* that happened? Does it *really* matter to them if we come to believe in the value of what they're offering? Or is the important thing just that we buy it?

This does not mean that we (the consumers) should treat advertisements as agents of persuasion only in the first sense. We have an interest in being persuaded to the kinds of actions advertisers want to us to take only on the basis of beliefs. In fact, we have an interest in being persuaded to this sort of action only on the basis of *rational* beliefs. We therefore have an interest in *treating* advertising as though it were attempting to persuade us to belief on the basis of argument. When we do so, we become better consumers.

But if advertisements are arguments (or if we are to treat them that way), then what kind of arguments are they? They certainly do not have clearly laid-out premises and conclusions. But many arguments, as we've discussed, have unstated conclusions. Advertisements are plausibly arguments that almost always have the unstated conclusion: "You should buy this product or service." When we think of advertisements this way, many of them start to look ridiculous. Paraphrasing Gillette: "You should buy our brand of shaving razor because . . . jet fighters and explosions!" Paraphrasing Axe Body Spray: "You should buy our product because women, who have all of the sophistication and discernment of wild deer, will become uncontrollably attracted to you if you do." Paraphrasing innumerable ads for clothes, airlines, yogurt, apartment buildings, phones, you name it: "You should buy our product because you'll have something in common with a person who represents to you what you would like to be."

Now to be fair, a lot of advertising is not really meant to convince you to buy a product or service so much as it is to make sure you *remember* the product or service. But then, of course, we should ask ourselves: should we spend our money on something just because we happen to remember its name?

2. Promise and Identification Advertisements

Virtually all ads are one or another (or both) of two basic kinds. **Promise advertisements** promise to satisfy desires or allay fears. All you have to do is buy the product advertised (remove bad body odor by using Old Spice deodorant; enjoy life more by driving a Ford

Explorer). Most promise ads provide "reasons why" the product will do the job or do it better than competitors (Kleenex tissues are softer; a bowl of Total cereal has more vitamins and minerals). Then there are ads that promise to satisfy our bodily needs, like the taglines for Snickers candy bars, "When You're Hungry, Reach for a Snickers" or "Hungry, Why Wait?" The implication is that Snickers is a food that will satisfy hunger when, in fact, the only food value is in a few peanuts—the rest is sugar, chocolate, nougat, and caramel, none of which will ward off hunger for long. But this immensely successful campaign boosted sales 3½ percent, no small amount for the best-selling candy bar in the world. This campaign was so successful, in fact, that Snickers has built most of its subsequent marketing around the idea that Snickers is a great cure for hunger. A later campaign revolved around the tagline "You're Not You When You're Hungry." These sometimes-clever ads basically suggested that hunger causes undesirable personality changes and that Snickers can help solve that. Of course, putting 27 grams of sugar (about nine sugar packets) into an empty stomach may not have the advertised effect of getting us on a more even keel.

> Promise, large promise, is the soul of advertising.
> —SAMUEL JOHNSON

Identification advertisements sell the product by getting us to identify with the product. They are a kind of promise ad, since they promise that somehow or other you will be better off using the product. But the promise is made indirectly through identification with respected institutions or individuals (or occasionally simply by fostering identification with the product directly). We all tend to identify with our own group and with those whom we respect—people who are famous, rich, accomplished, unusually brave, or powerful. Identification ads take advantage of this very human trait. Recall our discussion of celebrity endorsement ads back in Chapter 3. As irrational as it may be to take Taylor Swift or Beyoncé to be soft-drink authorities, these ads do work on us. And this is precisely because we identify with the famous people they feature and thus with the products they tout; we become like them in some small way by using the same products they do.

Identification ads—indeed, all ads—work for another interesting reason. When people shop, say, in a supermarket, they tend to purchase products whose brand names are familiar to them. Few of us, for example, will buy a brand of toothpaste we have never heard of or never seen advertised; we buy a brand we recognize even though we know no other "reason why" we should buy that brand and not a competing one. (When was the last time you chose a brand with which you were not familiar through advertisements over one you knew well?)

3. Things to Watch Out for in Advertisements

The good news about advertising, you will recall, is that it often provides true and useful information about products and entertains us with humor, storytelling, or just nice scenes or sentiments. Time enjoyably spent is time not completely wasted. *Recent*

Examples: Android's adorable "Peaceful Co-existence" TV spots that feature (at least apparent) friendships between unlikely pairs of animals; Geico's "Unskippable Family" ad that plays with our newfound ability to skip ads; and (a slightly older ad, but a personal favorite that you should definitely look up) Ikea's "Lamp" ad from 2002.

The bad news about advertising stems from the increasing ability of advertising geniuses—and some of them, alas, *are* geniuses—to manipulate audiences via sophisticated psychological ploys. Everyone realizes how others are conned by advertising, but most of us think that we somehow are exceptions. Young people, including college students, often deny that they are influenced by advertising. They typically say that they don't wear designer jeans or Adidas shoes because of advertising, but rather that they just "like" these products, self-deceptively ignoring the effect of advertising on their preferences. In fact, *no one* is immune to the influence of advertisements. (A Madison Avenue bigwig owned up to this when he said, "Even I fall for the stuff.") So we all are faced with the problem of how best to use advertising without being used. One way is to become familiar with the advertising devices and gimmicks used to appeal to our weaknesses, prejudices, and emotions unguided by intelligence. No doubt we'll still get taken now and then, but perhaps less often and with less seriously harmful consequences.

ADS INVITE US TO REASON FALLACIOUSLY

We've already noted that ads often feature celebrity endorsements to manipulate us into buying the product. They thus invite us to commit the fallacy appeal to authority. We don't stop to think whether Taylor Swift really does prefer Coca-Cola to Pepsi, or whether she just gets paid to say she does. Anyway, what difference would it make to you if she didn't drink soft drinks at all? (*Consumer Reports* taste tests, by the way, show that hardly anyone can distinguish between Pepsi and Coke. Can Taylor Swift? Can you? *Hint:* In several actual classroom tests conducted by one of the authors of this text over a period of years, students consistently failed to distinguish their favorite brands of beer from competing brands.)

In the case of Taylor Swift advertising Coke, it seems obvious that she is no authority on the taste of soft drinks, which, anyway, certainly are a matter of individual preference. But some celebrity ads are different, sports equipment endorsements being a case in point. Before the sex scandal shattered the image of Tiger Woods, he dominated the golf scene and was thought to be one of the greatest golfers of all time. So his endorsement of Nike's Tour Accuracy golf balls carried great weight with golf duffers intent on improving their scores. But in fact, Woods doesn't use these ordinary golf balls in tournaments. Instead, he hits custom-made balls not available to the general public (as do, by the way, some other pro golfers who endorse other brands).

After the scandal erupted, Woods's advertising appeal evaporated, confirming multiple studies showing that most successful celebrity endorsements depend on a tight fit between the celebrity and the product. In Woods's case, the fit was intensified. Not only was he an iconic golfer, he was the embodiment of ideal virtues. A genius at the game, he appeared to be hard working, dedicated, disciplined, and tough-minded—an ethical, reliable man. In other words, his virtues as well as his prowess persuaded consumers to buy the sports products he endorsed. And that, of course, is the best sell of all. Consumers are inclined to trust a virtuous celebrity—even though he isn't virtuous and doesn't use the product he is hawking. So for a while no one has used the slogan "Go on. Be a Tiger."

It should be clear by now that ads generally are designed to invite us to overlook their *suppression of evidence.* They tell us the good features of products but always hide their product's warts. (Why should they do otherwise?) Cigarette ads contain probably the most obvious examples of this fallacy, given what we know about the lethal effects of smoking. When R. J. Reynolds Tobacco launched a feminine version of Camels called Camel No. 9, you can be sure the ads made no mention of the fact that far more women die of lung cancer today than breast cancer. Instead, they played up the feminine appeal of the cigarette, giving it a name that evokes images of perfumes like Chanel No. 19 and packaging it in pink and green floral boxes labeled "light and luscious." Getting women to identify with a brand that has long played to male smokers has put Camels in competition with its biggest competitor for the female market, Virginia Slims, whose classic slogan, "You've Come a Long Way, Baby," ironically reflected the fact that women, indeed, have come a long way—in catching up with male mortality rates for lung cancer.

> *There is an art to making whole lies out of half truths.*
>
> —CHRISTY MATHEWSON (BASEBALL HALL OF FAME PITCHER
> WHO WAS PAID TO ENDORSE TUXEDO PIPE TOBACCO)

Advertisements are also common homes for fallacious appeals to popularity and tradition—and sometimes both, as when Ford on their website touts the value of their F-Series truck by claiming that it has been the best-selling truck in America for 35 years. But these are just some of the fallacies that are especially common in advertising. You can find just about any of the fallacies we discussed earlier in one ad or another.

Some ads, though, use fallacious reasoning humorously and aren't meant to be taken seriously. A good example is this BMW ad: "Doctors say increased activity slows the aging process. Coincidentally, BMW drivers are ten years younger than other luxury car drivers." This humorous use of cause and effect was not an example of *questionable cause* because it was not intended to be taken literally. Nor was this clever blurb for American Coach Lines, "If men were meant to fly, God would have lowered the fares." Nonetheless, both ads are intended to manipulate prospective customers into buying the products.

ADVERTISEMENTS POUND HOME SLOGANS AND MEANINGLESS JARGON

How, though, should we categorize the fallacious reasoning that leads people to be swayed by endlessly repeated, mostly empty slogans? *Classic Examples:* "Because You're Worth It" (L'Oréal); "Think Different" (Apple—with the "ly" dropped at Steve Jobs's insistence); "The Ultimate Driving Machine" (BMW); "I'm Lovin' It" (McDonald's).

Slogans run the range from the modestly informative ("Miller Light: Great Taste, Less Filling") to the somewhat suggestive ("Chevrolet. Like a Rock") to the completely irrelevant ("Nike: Just Do It"). In general, they work because they are repeated endlessly, so that they become ingrained in our minds. In the days before television, which is primarily a visual medium, singing commercials did the job on radio. There can be very few people over 70, for example, who could not at the drop of a hat sing the Rinso soap flakes jingle they heard belted out on radio countless times lo these many years ago: "Rinso white, Rinso bright; happy little washday song!"

> The most brilliant propaganda must confine itself to a few points and repeat them over and over.
>
> —ADOLF HITLER

Slogans that tout products as "the official" something or other are an interesting special case. The NFL, for example, has an official soft drink, beer, insurance carrier, wireless carrier, hotel, credit card, shipping service, and pizza. What exactly does all of this mean? In fact, becoming "official" merely means paying for the privilege of being identified with another brand. All of these companies paid through the nose to be the official whatever of the NFL. In 2015 alone, the NFL and its teams brought in $1.2 billion in sponsorship revenue. Another wrinkle in the "official" gambit is the naming of sports arenas and stadiums after companies that buy this privilege (Coors, Citibank, AT&T, etc.)

ADS PLAY ON WEAKNESSES AND FEARS

Many ads depend on the consumers' weaknesses or fears for their effectiveness. *Examples:* Ads for deodorants, mouthwashes, hair restorers, hair colorers, and so on. Some of these ads do have the virtue of being informative (Just for Men does darken gray hair), but in many cases the product doesn't do the job advertised (Aquafresh does very little, if anything, for bad breath, since most bad breath originates elsewhere; it does, though, kill some mouth bacteria). In many other cases, the advertised product doesn't do the job any better than competing products (Mylanta isn't any better at counteracting stomach acidity than Maalox, Gelusil, or several other brands; Energizer and Duracell batteries are equally good).

There is nothing wrong with having a product that solves a problem or allays a fear and letting people know about it. But many advertisements create, exaggerate, or exacerbate fears in order to sell just the right thing to save us from the problem we didn't know we had. Consider an ad for the "Guardzilla" (yes, really), a wide-angle in-home video recording system with night vision and motion detection that triggers a siren, alerting you remotely to movement. The ad begins with ominous music and a shadowy figure breaking into a home. "How do you know," the voice-over says, "if your home is secure? How do you know that your family is safe? How do you really know what is going on at your house when you're away?" Scary. So scary and dire is the situation, in fact, that your suburban two-bedroom house needs a security system suitable to Fort Knox.

The beauty-product industry has always been a leader in creating problems to solve for their customers. Who knew before seeing an ad for an eyelash curler that their eyelashes were too straight? Who knew their hands looked too old before seeing antiaging hand cream? Who told us we needed more hair here, less there, none over there, lighter hair, darker hair, thicker hair, thinner hair, or someone else's hair if not the companies that profit from compounding our anxieties about appearance?

Calvin & Hobbes Watterson./Universal Press Syndicate.

ADS EMPLOY SNEAKY RHETORIC, PHOTOS AND LAYOUTS

In particular, *weasel words* are quite common in advertising. When an ad says the product *"fights* bad breath," it's wise to assume it doesn't *cure* bad breath, because if it did, the ad would make this stronger, less weaseling claim. Similar remarks apply to claims such as *"helps* control dandruff with regular use," "gets dishes *virtually* spotless," and so on.

We also need to watch out for sneaky uses of *comparative* and *evaluative* terms, like *good, better,* and (best of all) *best.* The term *best* at best translates into "tied for first with all other leading brands." The "lowest fare to Europe" may turn out to be the standard fare every airline charges. And when an ad says, "No one sells ___ for less," you can be pretty sure others sell for the same price. And then there is that wonderful term *free,* itself perfectly unsneaky, but so often used to lure the gullible (all of us in weak moments) into thinking they're getting something for nothing.

But these kinds of ads aren't as sneaky as fine print disclaimers that let the manufacturer off the hook. The dietary supplement industry, for example, makes a huge profit hyping health products in ads that don't exactly say they treat a condition but make claims that lead people to believe they do. Fine print disclaimers do little to dissuade consumers—instead, they provide regulatory loopholes for the manufacturer. For instance, an ad claiming a product is an "amazing new joint health supplement" that is "clinically shown to quickly improve mobility and joint comfort" doesn't really say it treats arthritis but suggests it does.[1] Then the fine print disclaimer lets the manufacturer off easy when it says in tiny print, "This statement has not been evaluated by the Food and Drug Administration. This product is not intended to diagnose, treat, cure or prevent any disease." A wary consumer would be wise to check out those "clinical trials," by the way, to see if they have been published in legitimate scientific journals or are just the marketing ploys of health care hucksters.

---

[1]From an informative article about diet supplements: "The Bad News About Products, Too Good to Be True." *Tufts University Health and Nutrition Letter.* September 2009.

Misleading language is just one of the sneak factors in ads. Photos are even more deceptive. Take, for instance, ads for diet pills endorsed by celebrities air-brushed to a size 2, or cruise ads with Photoshopped landscapes. Then there are the food ads that "enhance" products to look believably scrumptious, but are in fact really inedible.[2] In mouthwatering photos of luscious meals, for example, the spaghetti is actually glued to the fork to keep it in place, the ice cubes in frosty drinks are acrylic imitations, and the ice cream smothered in syrup is a slab of lard doused with Karo syrup. More subtle deceptions are the visual cues that tweak our brains into Pavlovian responses when we watch chocolate syrup streaming over caramel candy with the sexy voice-over "Chocolate." It is safe to say that nothing ever tastes as good as it looks in the ad.

Deliberate Deception

A Charles Schwab commercial shows a satisfied couple talking about their successful investments with the brokerage firm. Then a three-second statement appears on the screen with about ten lines of print, starting with the information that the people telling their story were real customers of Schwab. But only a speed reader could get to the end fast enough to read the sentence revealing that the customers were paid for their testimonials.

Finally, there is the layout. When does an ad not look like an ad? When it's laid out like a news article—as it was, for instance, when the *Los Angeles Times* ran a front-page ad for an NBC drama, *Southland*, that was framed as a news report.[3] The only sign of its real intent was an NBC logo with the label "advertisement" in small print. Another issue ran a four-page ad for the movie *The Soloist* laid out in the form of a news article in the entertainment section. A case could be made that the struggling *Times* was desperate for money, given the recent massive cuts to its newsroom, and maybe an occasional lapse is forgivable in marketing something as trivial as entertainment. (Still, 100 reporters signed a letter of protest.) Marketing entertainment as news may not be a serious deception, but framing a sales pitch that way for fraudulent herbal remedies, say, most certainly would be.

It is often even more difficult to distinguish advertising from original content on popular websites. The *New York Times* features ads that look like *Times* content on its site, though at least it segregates them in a "From Our Advertisers" section. The *Huffington Post,* on the other hand, has advertising right alongside content, distinguishable only via a small "Presented by . . ." note. The line between content and advertisement is even less clear at Buzzfeed, where "Promoted" pieces appear in just the same format as the site's

---

[2]Taken from an interesting article on the tricks of the trade in food ads: Segal, David. "Grilled Chicken, That Temperamental Star." *New York Times,* 9 October 2011.

[3]See: "In Advertisers We Trust." *Extra!* May 2010.

All of us come from someplace else.

Just once, you should walk down the same street your great-grandfather walked.

Picture this if you will.

A man who's spent all his life in the United States gets on a plane, crosses a great ocean, lands.

He walks the same streets his family walked centuries ago.

He sees his name, which is rare in America, filling three pages in a phone book.

He speaks haltingly the language he wishes he had learned better as a child.

As America's airline to the world, Pan Am does a lot of things.

We help business travelers make meetings on the other side of the world. Our planes take goods to and from six continents. We take vacationers just about anywhere they want to go.

But nothing we do seems to have as much meaning as when we help somebody discover the second heritage that every American has.

⊚PAN AM.
America's airline to the world.

See your travel agent.

Source: Pan American World Airways

Advertising tends to concentrate on marginal needs, desires, and fears at the expense of many more important ones. Indeed, a frequently heard charge against advertising is that it increases the already strong tendency of people in industrial countries to become preoccupied with buying and consuming goods. (Note the humorous bumper sticker WHEN THE GOING GETS TOUGH, THE TOUGH GO SHOPPING.) *Occasionally, however, an ad comes along that reminds us of what (for most of us) are much more important values, even though we tend to forget them in the hustle and bustle of everyday life. This Pan Am ad is one of those rare ads that tend to push us in the right direction. Yes! If we can afford it (and more of us could if we spent less on lesser needs), just once, we should walk down the same street our great-grandfather walked. (Pan Am went belly up in the early 1990s, but for other reasons.)*

own material. The situation is worse still at sites where the same people who create the original content also write the ads. When even the voice of an author doesn't change between a news item and an ad, there is a significant opportunity for deception.

ADS DRAW ON TRENDY ISSUES IN THE NEWS

Issues that grip the country are fertile ground for advertisers, who use them to play on our fears and desires. For instance, America's waking up to its own obesity epidemic and the resulting trend of health-conscious eating has created some very strange claims among food companies and chain restaurants. McDonald's, for instance, touts the health benefits of its salads in one ad and then mocks salads in another to advertise its Big Mac.

Sometimes advertisers' fear-mongering around current issues can be absurdly over the top. Take the print ad for the "Patriot Power Generator 1500" (yes, really). It begins with a large banner that reads "Former CIA Official Warns: ISIS Terrorists Could Cripple America's Electric Grid! How will you keep your family safe when the power goes out? And it <u>Will</u> go out."

Advertisers also pounce on changing social norms, but rarely have the courage to drive such changes. A number of brands got some free press by being among the first to feature gay and lesbian couples in roles usually reserved for straight couples. But except in rare instances and in very specific markets, this didn't happen until social attitudes toward gay rights had already radically changed.

ADS WHITEWASH CORPORATE IMAGERY

Whenever an ad sells a company's image instead of a product, you have to wonder what is going on. With the popularity of environmental issues on the rise, corporations that have a major impact on the environment have sponsored an increasing number of "green" ads. DuPont's classic "seal-slapping" ad captures the flavor of these eco-friendly spots. This one features a scenic shoreline with dolphins diving, penguins waddling, sea lions clapping (you get the idea)—all to the melodic strains of Beethoven's "Ode to Joy." Just visible on the horizon is an oil tanker. The voice-over tells us, "recently DuPont announced that its energy unit would pioneer the use of new double-hulled tankers in order to safeguard the environment." Not long after the ad appeared—with its happy sea creatures cavorting in an eco-friendly environment—the EPA issued a report that DuPont was far and away the largest emitter of toxic waste.

Sometimes advertising is *just* about corporate image rather than incitement to buy anything. Do you ever wonder why a company like Archer Daniels Midland (ADM) spends money on national advertising? ADM, primarily an agricultural processing company, sells very few products directly to consumers—and those products are generally not mentioned at all in their ads. So why advertise? Well, one reason is that they can—ADM's annual revenues are often in excess of $80 billion. The other reason is that ADM is seemingly always in one PR crisis or another, be it scandals involving price fixing, antitrust violations, or a whole slew of environmental problems. Some of this may be inevitable given ADM's size and reach, but that is just the image they want to escape. Their advertisements portray them as a caring partner to small farmers, a real backbone of rural America and champion of its values. In one recent campaign, ADM named itself "the biggest little company out there." As a mainstay of the Fortune 500 (usually in the top 30–40) list of America's largest companies, it's probably safe to just call them a big company.

ADS USE AND PROMOTE STEREOTYPES

There's a kind of mystery surrounding the way toys are advertised to children. Some toys are marketed only to boys and some only to girls. Why in the world would an advertiser want to ignore half of its potential buying (or at least, demanding) population? If you were a maker of toy trucks, wouldn't you want to sell those trucks to as many parents as you could, those buying for girls as well as for boys? If you made dollhouses, wouldn't you want the money of boys' parents just as much as the money of girls' parents?

The answer is that advertisers know there is more money to be made trading on the stereotypical expectations of parents and children. But of course, the advertisements themselves do as much as anything else to encourage and perpetuate those stereotypes. And this is not a good thing. Judith Elaine Blakemore, a professor of psychology and expert in the development of gender roles, speaking about her research to the National Association for the Education of Young Children, said: "We found that girls' toys were associated with physical attractiveness, nurturing, and domestic skill, whereas boys' toys were rated as violent, competitive, exciting, and somewhat dangerous. The toys rated as most likely to be educational and to develop children's physical, cognitive, artistic, and other skills were typically categorized as neutral or moderately masculine. We concluded that strongly gender-typed toys appear to be less supportive of optimal development than neutral or moderately gender-typed toys." and that "[i]f you want to develop children's physical, cognitive, academic, musical, and artistic skills, toys that are not strongly gender-typed are more likely to do this."[4] Parents have to go out of their way to insist on this, though, as most marketing to children is still very gendered.

We find similar patterns in advertising to adults. How often do you see household cleaning products advertised using male actors? How often are women behind the wheel in pickup truck advertisements? Racially targeted advertising may be less common today than it used to be. But it is still illuminating to have a look at different ads for the same product in various markets where advertisers expect different demographics.

UBIQUITOUS ADS AND SENSORY OVERLOAD

Marketers are nothing if not resourceful. What with conventional reading material and TV watching on the wane, they can no longer count on reaching consumers through established media like magazines, newspapers, and TV. Instead they are taking a

---

[4]Blakemore, Judith Elaine. "What the Research Says: Gender-Typed Toys." Web. http://www .naeyc.org.

scattershot approach, plastering ads all over the place.[5] Microsoft advertised on tray tables on board US Airways planes; Geico on subway turnstiles; Continental Airlines on Chinese food cartons and pizza boxes; Perry Ellis on shirt boxes and hanging bags at dry cleaners. And how about this for a mini-marketing gem: CBS was stamping the names of CBS television shows on supermarket eggs. Then there are the video screens that have appeared in taxicabs and elevators, ostensibly to provide news but heavily larded with ads. Ads are even projected on the sides of buildings, and old-fashioned billboards are being converted into digital screens that change messages throughout the day.

Even ostensibly "commercial free" media often isn't. Popular movies and Internet-only programs have the same for-a-price product placements that we've come to expect on network television. Netflix's *The Ranch,* for instance, quickly starts to feel like a Budweiser ad with a laugh track. And recent James Bond movies often seem like action-packed catalogs for all sorts of products.

Given the intense marketing barrage with which we live, we cannot possibly process all of the ads to which we're exposed on a daily basis. Most of them pass us by without grabbing our attention, at least consciously. Advertisers, then, have to go further and further to inundate the street, the Internet, and the airwaves with their images and slogans in the hopes of capturing our collective attention, or at least saturating our subconscious with their messages.

PUFFERY IS LEGAL, BUT NOT DECEPTIVE ADVERTISING

Finally, it's worth noting that what is called "puffery"—generalized, vague, or exaggerated claims, particularly when asserted humorously—is legal. *Example:* The claim by BMW to be "The Ultimate Driving Machine." (Litigation does very occasionally arise concerning borderline cases.) However, ads can overstep legal boundaries and make fraudulent claims. The cigarette industry, in particular, has come under fire for deceptive advertising. For example, in spring 2003, Philip Morris was found guilty of consumer fraud in its ads for "light" cigarettes. Judge Nicholas Byron ruled that the company intentionally misled the public into thinking that Marlboro Lights and Cambridge Lights were "less harmful or safer than their regular counterparts" and ordered the company to pay $10.8 billion to the plaintiffs. This is one of several lawsuits brought against cigarette companies in recent years.

It may be, though, that current restrictions on deceptive advertising and marketing are less than sufficient. In 2014, the Supreme Court allowed a suit brought by Pom Wonderful (a seller of pomegranate juice) against Coca-Cola for false advertising to move forward. It seems Minute Maid (owned by Coke) sold a brand labeled "Pomegranate Blueberry" that prominently featured pomegranates and blueberries in the label artwork. The problem was that the juice consisted of only 0.3 percent pomegranate juice and 0.2 percent blueberry juice; 99.4 percent of the juice came from much less expensive apples and grapes. However, in 2016, a jury found in favor of Coke—probably because

---

[5]Examples taken from: "Anywhere the Eye Can See, It's Now Likely to See an Ad." *New York Times,* 15 January 2007.

Coke was technically in compliance with FDA labeling requirements. Perhaps it is time to revisit those requirements?

ADVERTISING TO CHILDREN

Targeting children has become a tricky business for advertisers. Consumer advocates have become more vocal about the evils of marketing to kids, and regulators have pressured various industries to soft-pedal their ads.[6] Given the rise in childhood obesity, food marketers, in particular, have come under fire, with the result that some companies, like Coca-Cola and Hershey, have actually agreed not to advertise to children. But advertisers are nothing if not creative, and though they proceed with caution, they have developed strategies to bypass regulations with ads that don't look like ads at all. Instead, they are framed as games or contests or events that "engage with" kids rather than sell directly to them. So you have magazines like *Sports Illustrated Kids* inventing such programs as "Sports Dad of the Year," sponsored by Wendy's, or design-your-own games for Goldfish, the Pepperidge Farm cracker. This subtle sell may seem innocuous, but not to those opposed to commercials for kids, who worry that children are brainwashed into identifying with the brand. Of course publishers in favor of ads for kids (for obvious reasons) dismiss these concerns with the argument that children have to get used to the commercial world they live in—and the earlier, the better. Really? Tell that to a mother in the supermarket who is battling her kid for the box of Cocoa Puffs he just yanked off the shelf.

4. The Upside of Ads

Although most ads hawk consumer goods, a few actually attempt to educate us or warn us against harmful activities. Partnership for a Drug-Free America has aired a series of ads aimed at combating drug use in this country. The ads, targeting young people as well as parents, focus on the harmful effects of drugs ranging from Ecstasy to marijuana to alcohol. For example, one set of TV spots focuses on embarrassing or disturbing moments that teen drug users experience as a result of their habit. One ad shows a girl trying to conceal a drug-induced nosebleed that starts suddenly in class. Another features a boy inadvertently dropping a drug packet on the counter of a fast-food restaurant. A more shocking series of ads appeals to the vanity of teens by running photographs of young adults who are long-term users in fashionable but grotesque poses that highlight the disfiguring effects of methamphetamines. For instance, under the caption "Body by Crystal Meth," a young man stands, hand on hips, revealing a skeletal body ravaged by drugs. Ads aimed at parents urge them to monitor their kids' activities and social life. They feature parents asking questions like "Where are you going after school?" or "What are your plans after soccer?" Companion ads show older, grateful teens who realize in hindsight that all those irritating questions their parents asked managed to deter

---

[6]Clifford, Stephanie. "A Fine Line When Ads and Children Mix." *New York Times,* 15 February 2010.

them from using drugs. Clearly the message is that parents should be involved in their kids' lives by asking questions and by knowing what they do, whom they hang out with, and where they go. We can only hope that all the advertising devices and gimmicks used so effectively to market goods and services will be just as successful at discouraging drug use among teens.

Public service announcements crafted like ads are another strategy used to publicize wrongdoings and bring about change. As part of an effort to ferret out insider trading on Wall Street, the FBI ran a one-minute video featuring Michael Douglas, well known for playing the criminal financier Gordon Gekko—whose mantra was "greed is good"—in the film *Wall Street*. In the video, Douglas drives home the message that insider trading is illegal. "The movie was fiction, but the problem is real," he says. By using a megawatt celebrity like Douglas, the FBI hoped to bring the crime to the attention of the public and encourage whistle-blowers to report illegal activity in the financial world.

All that Glitters . . .

Luxury used to be for the happy few, but now it is hawked to the mass of consumers. Even ordinary products are hyped with inflated language to give them luxury status. James B. Twitchell comments on this trend in "Luxe Populi," San Francisco Chronicle, May 20, 2007.

> *. . . [T]he consumers of the new luxury have a sense of entitlement that transcends social class, a conviction that the finest things are their birthright. Never mind that they may have been born into a family whose ancestral estate is a tract house in the suburbs, near the mall, not paid for, and whose family crest was downloaded from the Internet. Ditto the signet ring design. Language reflects this hijacking. Words such as gourmet, premium, boutique, chic, accessory and classic have loosened from their elite moorings and now describe such top-of-category items as popcorn, hamburgers, discount brokers, shampoo, scarves, ice cream and trailer parks.*

---

5. Targeted Advertising and Big Data

Not long ago, which ads you saw depended entirely on where you were or what media you sought out. You saw the same ads as anyone else who went to those places or engaged with that media. Today, a great number of the ads you see are targeted much more specifically to you—or, to be more exact, to the marketing profiles established by your past behavior.

You may look at the same website at the same time as someone sitting next to you and see entirely different banner ads. If you're curious (and don't mind giving a marketing firm some identifying information), there are sites where you can view your own marketing profile. Data collected about you comes from your credit card spending, search engine and website history, and social media posts, as well as your financial history. It may include your race, gender, where you live, what you typically purchase, your interests, income, debt, and much more. This data is collected, organized, and packaged by large firms and sold to potential advertisers.

As targeted advertising improves and the "big data" industry grows and matures, there are some advantages to the consumer. As long as we're being bombarded with ads, they might as well be ads that speak to our wants and needs. And many social media platforms are free to consumers because their owners make money from the data collected from them. But the collection and distribution of personal data also raises (for many of us) uncomfortable privacy concerns. We will return to this issue in Chapter 12.

The Shopping Mall as Marketing Tool

Theatricality, illusion, pretense, manipulation, and artifice are the essence of the mall setting. The shopper must buy . . . Every possible design tool is aimed at behavioral control, to make the shopper visit more often, stay longer, and buy more. Pathways are contrived to require her to walk past the maximum number of shopping outlets en route to the planned destination, tempting her to suspend judgment and yield to impulse. Attention-getting banners, vivid signs, dramatic lighting, seductive color schemes, lush plantings, upbeat music, and soothing sounds provide intense sensations, alternately stimulating and relaxing the visitor until she is freed from normal restraints and caught up in the mood of buying.

—Rifkind, Carole. "America's Fantasy Urbanism:
The Waxing of the Mall and the Waning of Civility."
*Dumbing Down: Essays on the Strip Mining of
American Culture*. Eds. Katharine Washburn and
John F. Thornton. New York: W. W. Norton & Co., 1997. 261.

---

6. Political Advertising

By now, just about everybody knows that political candidates and issues are marketed in pretty much the same way as breakfast foods and laundry detergents. This means that appeals to reason are scarce, while emotional appeals are rampant.

In the very old days, only candidates for local office could reach more than a tiny fraction of their prospective constituents—via "whistle stop" campaigns in which they made speeches before small audiences and "pressed the flesh." Billboards, lawn signs, newspaper ads, posters, patriotic bunting, and that sort of thing were extremely important parts of any successful campaign.

But the average voter never heard the actual voices of candidates running for high office or, except for some presidential candidates, ever saw their pictures or photographs. Political parties and platforms thus loomed much larger than they do today. Charisma didn't travel very widely.

Things began to change early in the twentieth century with the introduction of electronic devices and other means of mass communication devices, starting with methods for printing pictures in newspapers and continuing with the widespread ownership of radios. Franklin Roosevelt was the first president to fully understand and gain significant political advantage from the miracle of radio; his "fireside chats" were an immensely successful public relations instrument, and his voice was instantly recognized by virtually everyone in America in those days.

But the changes in political rhetoric and tactics that came after World War II dwarfed those that preceded it. A large increase in the number of primary elections reduced the power of political parties and party "bosses," and, much more important, television brought candidates and their pitches into living rooms across the nation. Political campaigns were changed forever (as was pretty much everything else—but remember the saying that "The more things change, the more they remain the same"). Within a few years, image makers, which means advertising experts, reigned supreme.

The first presidential candidate to make full and effective use of the new medium was Dwight D. Eisenhower. His successful 1952 campaign against Adlai Stevenson featured short television commercials like the following example, part of a series of TV spots in which General Eisenhower read from letters sent in by "citizens" asking questions that Eisenhower then "answered":

> *Citizen:* Mr. Eisenhower, what about the high cost of living?
> *General Eisenhower:* My wife, Mamie, worries about the same thing. I tell her it's our job to change that on November 14.[7]

No need for Eisenhower to tell viewers *how* he planned to change it.

Of course, Eisenhower conveyed an almost perfect image—war hero and father figure—and most people therefore strongly identified with him. War heroes, father figures, and candidates with charisma, like John Kennedy, are very hard to beat. When Kennedy ran for office, his father, whose connections in Hollywood dated back to the 1920s, hired professionals experienced in using effective film production techniques to hype the candidate as a symbolic role model—a strong, courageous hero—and to capitalize on his undoubted glamorous appeal. Nowadays, candidates who project a less appealing image can, and frequently do, overcome their handicaps by hiring image makers to attractively tailor their campaigns *and their personalities.*

Image makers have honed their craft over the years. They have learned, for example, that negative ads attacking one's opponent can be dynamite. Mudslinging isn't new, of

---

[7]Ogilvy, David. *Confessions of an Advertising Man.* New York: Atheneum, 1963. Ogilvy quotes Eisenhower as moaning between takes, "To think that an old soldier should come to this." Note that the device used is a promise to satisfy a strong desire (for lower prices) without providing a single reason for believing that the promise would be kept.

"Sally, Jim — you'll handle daily speech writing.
Vince, as usual, will be in charge of attack ads."

Chris Wildt/Cartoon Stock

course. John Adams was labeled a closet monarchist, Thomas Jefferson was derided because he didn't enlist in 1775 (!), and Abe Lincoln was dubbed "Honest Abe." And in one of the most vicious presidential campaigns in history, John Quincy Adams was accused of pimping for the czar of Russia. But that was nothing compared to the mud slung at his opponent, Andrew Jackson, who was called a murderer, a drunk, a biga-mist, and—get this—a cannibal. The charge? He massacred a village of peaceful Native Americans, had a dozen bodies dressed to barbecue, and ate them for breakfast the next morning! So when we lament the onslaught of negative ads, let us not forget that our political history is steeped in mudslinging. The difference is that television and the Internet have brought it to a far wider audience, and thus made it more effective. One of the first TV spots to use this technique to full effect—the 1964 "Daisy/Girl/Peace" spot—also is probably the most famous of all political TV commercials. It ran just once as a paid advertisement, but received so much comment that it was broadcast several times as a news item. (It was once believed that this commercial was never run again because of a public outcry against it, but in fact the original plan was to run it just once and then to garner free repeat TV coverage, which is exactly what happened.)

The Attack Ad Industry

Negative campaigning has been honed to a fine art. Just about every political campaign involves people who are opposition researchers, a polite term for political hitmen (or women). Here is a description of the process by one such fellow who finally became so demoralized by the whole business that he dropped out and wrote a book about it:

Step I: The political hitmen dig up the dirt.
Step II: The dirt is then given to the pollsters, who through sophisticated polling can determine which pieces of dirt are the most damaging in the minds of the voters.
Step III: The pollsters give their results to the media advertising folks, who put the most damaging two or three negative issues into the TV, radio, and direct-mail pieces that do their best to rip their political opponent into shreds.

—Marks, Steven. *Confessions of a Political Hitman.*
Naperville, IL: Sourcebooks, Inc., 2007.

That final step only hints at the warped genius of ad writers who transform pages of research into 30- or 60-second spots that crucify the opposition in sound bites the public can easily grasp and often believe.

> *Orthodontics and the hair dryer have become vital to the achievement of political power.*
>
> —LEN DEIGHTON

The spot starts by showing a very young girl picking petals from a daisy while counting, "1, 2, 3, 4, 5, 7, 6, 6, 8, 9, 9," at which point there is the voice-over of a man counting, "10, 9, 8, 7, 6, 5, 4, 3, 2, 1, 0," followed by the blast of an atomic bomb on the screen and the voice of President Lyndon Johnson saying, "These are the stakes—to make a world in which all God's children can live—or to go into the dark. We must either love each other or we must die." Then another voice-over: "Vote President Johnson on November 3rd. The stakes are too high for you to stay home."

The point of this commercial was to picture Johnson's opponent, Republican Senator Barry Goldwater, as an extreme hawk all too willing to push the button, while Johnson is portrayed as a responsible "peace" candidate. Is it an accident that this best known of all political spots also is one of the most vicious, inaccurate, and unfair? Fortunately, it sank into the quagmire of history, where it belonged.

For the next few decades, Congress enacted various campaign-finance reforms to regulate campaign spending and limit the influence of wealthy people or interest groups on elections. Electioneers struggled to bend reform laws—not too hard to do, since money, like water, finds ways to trickle in. As restrictions eased through various court cases, political action committees (PACs) thrived by bundling contributions (to comply with legal restrictions on donations). The law required that they be independent of candidates' official campaigns, but in fact, they functioned as arms of campaigns, with money and clout to influence elections.

PACs are in the business of running primarily negative ads. One, with the innocuous title of National Security PAC, came up with a lulu during the 1988 presidential campaign between George H. W. Bush and Michael Dukakis. Probably the second-most notorious ad in modern history (after the Daisy ad), the Willie Horton ad featured a mug shot of Horton, an African American convicted murderer who escaped from a Massachusetts prison while out on a weekend furlough pass. He later raped a white woman and stabbed her fiancé. The ad played on voter anxieties about race and crime and was widely criticized for its racist content, but it helped demolish Michael Dukakis, who supported the furlough act when he was governor of Massachusetts.

In retrospect, however, those were the good old days, when negative ads were used but didn't dominate campaigns. In 2010, though, the Supreme Court lifted restrictions even more drastically in *Citizens United v. Federal Election Commission,* when it ruled that corporations, unions, and individuals could contribute to super PACs without limit as long as they didn't fund candidates directly. Then, as night follows day, unprecedented sums of money poured into political campaigns and negative ads went viral.

Negative attack ads funded by large third-party sources are becoming more commonplace in political arenas where we just didn't see them 10 or 15 years ago. According to an article in the *New York Times,* in 2014, Justice Robin Hudson of the North Carolina Supreme Court faced an opposition to her reelection with over $1 million in funds. A good deal of that money was spent on negative ads during the primary, including one that claimed she was "not tough on child molesters" and that she "sided with the predator" (charges she called "outrageous"). A group called "Justice For All NC," not her opponents in the race, funded those ads. For whatever it's worth, $1 million later, Hudson was reelected after all.

Obvious political smears are the tip of the iceberg, though, in undermining political opponents. Less obvious techniques involve the visuals and the pacing. For example, an editor can make a candidate look less attractive by cropping the photo and going tighter on the face or by draining the color to black and white and reducing the action to slow motion. Editors have enormous power. They can—and do—manipulate every element of an ad in ways so subtle that most viewers have no idea that they, themselves, are being manipulated.

> *You can fool some of the people all of the time, and those are the ones you need to concentrate on.*
>
> —GEORGE W. BUSH, QUOTING ROBERT STRAUSS (IN A SPOOF) AT THE 2001 GRIDIRON DINNER

> *Most people are eternally taken in by the myth and rhetoric of democracy. . . . What we have now is an increasingly uneducated public—especially in what used to be called civics—dealing with evermore complex issues with which they are unequipped to knowledgeably deal. . . . We have a population ripe for manipulation by powerful public relation firms and political consultants who are expert in sound bites and seductive imagery.*
>
> *—BRECHIN, GRAY. IMPERIAL SAN FRANCISCO: URBAN POWER, EARTHLY RUIN. BERKELEY: UNIVERSITY OF CALIFORNIA PRESS, 1999.*

Although voters have complained repeatedly about negative ads, the media continue to run them—because they work. Ideally, people would study the candidates' records and vote rationally on the basis of their credentials; instead, too many people sit mesmerized in front of their television sets or computers, passively absorbing the sound bites they get from infotainment and its ubiquitous commercials—including negative political ads. It's no wonder campaigns resort to using these ads. They actually grab the viewers' attention in ways that information about the candidates' records or positions almost never does. So when we complain about the onslaught of negative ads, let's remember that political campaigns would never waste money on them if there weren't a receptive audience ready to absorb their messages.

As must be evident by now, political campaigns are indistinguishable from advertising campaigns. In fact, one of the most successful factors in selling a product, brand recognition, is just as effective in marketing a candidate; but in politics the brand name is often a recognizable family name of a politician whose father, uncle, or husband has served in public office. Most recently there was George Bush the father, then Bill Clinton, then George Bush the son, then Hillary Clinton, who lost the race for the White House but did receive the Democratic nomination in 2016. Voters recognize the family name and feel comfortable with it much as they do with brands like Ivory soap or Campbell's soup. This tendency to favor candidates with dynastic names has deep roots in American politics. Before the Bushes and the Clintons, the Kennedys dominated the dynastic field, with John, the president, then Bobby and Teddy, the senators, and a raft of their offspring in Congress and state governments. Before them was Teddy Roosevelt and his distant cousin Franklin Delano Roosevelt, and so on, all the way back to John Adams, the second president, and his son John Quincy Adams, the fourth president. It seems that voters often put more stock in the family names of prominent politicians than they do in the candidate's qualifications, a fact not lost on political advertisers.

I'm not an old hand at politics. But I am now seasoned enough to have learned that the hardest thing about any political campaign is how to win without proving that you are unworthy of winning.

—ADLAI STEVENSON (1956)

What one candidate learned from two (failed) runs at the presidency.

Of course, most candidates don't bear the name of a famous forebear and have to market other attributes. One of the most important ploys in marketing candidates is image making, and one of the most effective formats for candidates to sharpen their image is presidential debates. The presidential debates provide candidates with the largest audiences they will be able to advertise to during a whole election campaign. (Nowadays, of course, a tradition has been established so that candidates pretty much are forced to debate or lose face.) Political debates are hardly a new idea—think of the famous debates between Abraham Lincoln and Stephen Douglas. But the first presidential debates, between Richard Nixon and John Kennedy, did not take place until 1960. Kennedy is generally seen as the winner because he exhibited "vigor" and youth and exuded great charisma, whereas Nixon appeared to be overcautious and a bit sneaky. (Nixon later complained that his makeup was incorrectly applied—a very important point.) The debates generally are credited with being the crucial factor in Kennedy's extremely narrow victory (we pass over the controversy concerning alleged chicanery in counting votes in Texas and Illinois), but not because his proposals and comments were any better than those of Nixon. It has often been claimed, in fact, that people listening to the debates on the radio tended to credit Nixon with the win, while those who watched on television overwhelmingly gave the win to Kennedy.[8]

In all of the presidential debates so far, just as in the Nixon-Kennedy debates, it has been *image,* not reasoning or displays of intelligence or character, that has determined the winners. The 1988 debates between the first George Bush and Michael Dukakis illustrate this nicely. When Dukakis failed to respond with instant outrage to CNN commentator Bernard Shaw's famous question about what Dukakis would do if his wife were raped, his chances of winning the election pretty much flew out the window.

In 2016, the Presidential debates seemed to have little effect on the eventual outcome of the race. Polling showed that Clinton "won" each of the three debates. Trump appeared unprepared in the first debate. The second was dominated by the recent revelation of an audio recording in which Trump bragged about sexually assaulting women. He had a better time of it in the third debate before creating negative headlines by refusing to agree to accept the results of the election should he lose. The debates themselves, however, were mostly long on insults and vitriol, short on substance and meaningful content. They likely had a net effect of further turning off an already frustrated electorate. In the end, of course, Clinton's victories in the debates were either exaggerated or they were insufficient to carry her to victory in the general election.

---

[8]An interesting article in *Slate* (Greenberg, David. "Rewinding the Kennedy-Nixon Debates." *Slate,* 24 September 2010) attempts to dispel this claim as a popular myth.

ELECTION POLLS—A SPECIAL CASE

Finally, no account of campaign rhetoric could be complete without mention of the role of polls in elections. No serious candidates for high office these days would open their mouths without having first tested the wind via polls. Whatever may be the case after they have won, when running for election, smart candidates make their pitches conform to what the polls indicate about voter sentiments and prejudices. During campaigns, at any rate, successful politicians generally are followers, not leaders. They waffle because they have to in order to get elected. It's always better to tell voters what they want to hear, not what the candidate genuinely intends to do if elected.

Polls tell candidates how to advertise; their media experts build campaigns in terms of what they learn from polls; blind advertising bit the dust a long time ago. In the 2012 campaign, for example, the polls gave advertisers information they needed to market their candidates to the undecided voters who were considered so important in the campaign. To reach these voters, advertisers focused their efforts on ten or so swing states that could decide the election. As the campaigns heated up, some voters in these states got more than a dozen robocalls a day that pounded away at poll-driven issues like the ailing economy, the failing housing market, and the health care law. But those who lived in the big states (like California, Texas, and New York), where the vote was predictable, saw much less advertising for the candidates.

When Is a Poll Not a Poll? When It's an Ad

When we think of politicians polling the electorate, we think of a campaign trying to gauge public opinion on some matter in order to craft its message (or, what's worse, in order to determine what positions the candidate should claim to have). But not all polls are really meant to do this.

"Push polls" are a much-too-common tactic in today's political landscape. In a push poll (which isn't really a poll at all), people are made to think that they are providing information about their views when in fact someone is trying to change their views via the questions that are being asked. These questions are often about a given candidate's opponent, as in "would you vote for so-and-so if you learned that he or she . . ."

In one particularly repugnant example of this, some Republican primary voters in the 2000 presidential election received phone calls asking if they would vote for John McCain if they "knew he had fathered an illegitimate black child." Karl Rove, then an operative for the Bush campaign, was responsible for this strategy.

Of course not every push poll preys on the very worst racist tendencies of voters, but they all appear to be something they are not. And they provide a good opportunity for a campaign to engage in this sort of dirty tactic without putting their name to it—unless the subject is savvy enough to ask. Sometimes, though, they call the wrong person. In 2014, former Labor Secretary Robert Reich happened to be on a caller's list:

I was phoned the other night in the middle of dinner by an earnest young man named Spencer, who said he was doing a survey.

> *Rather than hang up, I agreed to answer his questions. He asked me if I knew a soda tax would be on the ballot in Berkeley in November. When I said yes, he then asked whether I trusted the Berkeley city government to spend the revenues wisely.*
>
> *At that moment I recognized a classic "push poll," which is part of a paid political campaign.*
>
> *So I asked Spencer a couple of questions of my own. Who was financing his survey? "Americans for Food and Beverage Choice," he answered. Who was financing this group? "The American Beverage Association," he said.*
>
> *Spencer was so eager to get off the phone, I didn't get to ask him my third question: Who's financing the American Beverage Association? It didn't matter. I knew the answer: PepsiCo and Coca-Cola.*[9]

Push polls are likely here to stay as they are both effective and much cheaper than actual polls. Why are they cheaper? Because no one is collecting data on responses.

---

[9]Reich, Robert. "Berkeley Speaks Out Again, This Time in the Soda Wars." *San Francisco Chronicle*, 21 September 2014.

Well, then, if virtually all political rhetoric is guided by expediency, why pay attention to it? If we can expect candidates to waffle, even to lie, why hear them out? The answer is that even waffling and lies can tell those of us who read between the lines a great deal about how candidates may perform if elected to office: Which sorts of lies they tell and what kinds of campaign promises they make tell us something about which groups and positions a candidate is likely to favor if elected. The promises made by Barack Obama and his advocates during the 2012 presidential campaign were different from those made by Mitt Romney and his advocates, because different constituencies were being appealed to.

Nevertheless, it is true in the political arena at least as much as anywhere else that actions speak louder than words. It has to be true that a candidate's past performance is almost always a better guide to future performance than is his or her political rhetoric. Smart viewers of the political scene always evaluate current political advertising in the light of past performance. So a sensible evaluation of political rhetoric requires us to bring to bear good background information (nothing new here). (The other key ingredient, aside from background information is, of course, the desire and attempt to be intellectually honest—to set aside prejudices of all kinds and come to fair, cogent evaluations.)

IMAGE BUILDING AS CAMPAIGN RHETORIC

Politicians don't just campaign via paid advertisements or after they have thrown their hats into the ring. Image building is a day-in, day-out task—indeed, in terms of time spent, perhaps a successful politician's principal task. Of course, for those holding high office, particularly for the leader of a nation, image building often coincides with ceremonial duties. For instance, when George W. Bush referred to the War on Terrorism as a crusade at one point, he was photographed with all manner of religious figures from fundamentalist Christian delegates at the Southern Baptist Convention to the pope in the Vatican. Candidates challenging incumbents don't have the opportunity to improve their images via ceremonial activities, one reason incumbents are hard to unseat.

Incumbents also have an advantage when it comes to garnering media coverage via press conferences. President Roosevelt was perhaps the first American president to exploit this kind of image-building opportunity, but the technique was perfected by President Kennedy, who, unlike Roosevelt, had television at his beck and call. Since Kennedy's time, presidential news conferences have generally been scheduled so as to gain the president free exposure on evening TV news programs. Because presidents are coached beforehand, they have ready-made "answers" to all likely questions, and they rarely are forced into on-the-spot improvisations.

FURTHER DEVELOPMENTS

Many years ago, virtually all political advertising was for candidates running for office. But with the advent of ballot initiatives and referendums—propositions put before voters for their direct decision—*issue advertising* entered the scene, and over the last decade it has become an extremely important kind of political advertising, because voters in many states and localities now are regularly asked to decide all kinds of controversial issues. Interested parties now spend millions advertising their views on these measures. The U.S. Chamber of Commerce, for example, ran an anti-Obamacare ad in Missouri, claiming the health care act will kill jobs. "Call Claire McCaskill [Missouri senator]," the voiceover intones, "and tell her Missouri doesn't need government-run health care." Ads like this generate floods of letters and calls to elected representatives.

Even wars are marketed to the public. The first Gulf War, generally thought to be the first war tailored for the mass media, was "branded" "Operation Desert Shield" much the way brand names are given to toothpaste or cereal. The second war, "Operation Iraqi Freedom," was promoted by state-of-the-art marketing techniques that launched the "conflict" (not the war) with "shock and awe" (instead of bombing), wrapped it in patriotism and morality (stressing good versus evil), and downplayed the ugly realities with euphemisms like "decapitation strategy" (for kill Saddam Hussein). War propaganda has a long history, of course, but current marketing savvy has raised it to new heights (or sunk it to new depths, depending on your point of view). We can only roll our eyes at the Alice-in-Wonderland approach to marketing wars displayed by Andrew Card (the second Bush's chief of staff) when he told the *New York Times* that the administration had waited until after Labor Day (2002) to make its case for military action in Iraq because "from a marketing point of view you don't introduce new products in August."

TELEPHONE AND INTERNET ADVERTISING

The great increase in negative telephone advertising that has occurred in the past few years is one of the more unfortunate recent developments in political advertising. The device itself is old, perhaps first being used on a large scale in 1946, when Richard Nixon first ran for Congress. A typical call in that telephone campaign went like this: "This is a friend of yours, but I can't tell you who I am. Did you know that Jerry Voorhis [Nixon's incumbent opponent] is a communist?" (Click.) Nothing much changes. Nowadays robocalls are standard procedures in political campaigns, and bugged voters regularly in 2016.

But some things *are* changing. A study conducted by the research firm Borrell Associates estimated that, given trends over the last few cycles, Internet advertising spending in the 2020 campaign will reach $3.3 billion. That will still be short of what is spent on television ads these days, but as a percentage of campaign spending, online advertising is clearly going up relative to television.[10] By analyzing data on the browsing habits of millions of computer users, campaign strategists identify voters most likely to side with their candidate. By 2016, internet communication was drastically changing both campaign tactics and campaign economics. Donald Trump relied heavily on Twitter and other free sources of mass communication, so much so that he was able to spend considerably less money than predecessors on television spots and other costly forms of advertising. Trump dominated numerous news cycles by tweeting what many saw as outrageous statements. However, the facts that this strategy was ultimately successful and cost effective make it likely that it will be replicated in future elections.

The upshot of all these various ways to advertise is that the 30-second TV spots that played the major role in elections to high office during the previous 45 years or so have now become just one of several important devices used to influence the electorate (although still the most important). By the 2012 election, tens of millions of Americans were tuning in to at least one presidential debate, and at least that many hear candidates give their spiels on TV talk shows. What this digital age has in store for us next is an interesting and exceedingly important question, to which politicians and their media masters would very much like to know the answer. (So should we, so as to better defend ourselves against deceptive or emotively driven advertising.)

Summary of Chapter 10

1. Most ads can be divided into either of two groups. *Promise ads* promise to satisfy desires or allay fears. **Example:** Use Old Spice deodorant and get rid of body odor. *Identification ads* sell the product by getting us to identify with the product. **Example:** The Virginia Slims cigarette ads, "You've Come a Long Way, Baby," tailored to specific audiences.

---

[10]Lapowsky, Issie. "Political Ad Spending Online Is About to Explode" Wired.com, 18 August 2015.

2. Ads are plausibly—and more importantly, *usefully*—thought of as arguments whose conclusions are that we should buy the product or service in question.

3. Although ads provide us with useful information about products, often in an entertaining way, they also are designed to manipulate us via sophisticated ploys.

    a. They invite us to reason fallaciously. ***Example:*** Appeals to the authority of famous figures such as Beyoncé and Taylor Swift on soft drinks.

    b. They employ repetitive slogans and meaningless jargon. ***Example:*** "Nike: Just Do It."

    c. They play on our weaknesses, prejudices, and fears. ***Example:*** The "Guardzilla" TV commercial and many (most?) beauty product ads.

    d. They use sneaky rhetoric, including fine print disclaimers and weasel words. ***Examples:*** Using the word *free* when the product isn't free; weaselly expressions like "fights bad breath."

    e. Ads draw on trendy issues. ***Example:*** The low-fat, low-sugar, low-salt, low-carb ads aimed at overweight Americans.

    f. They whitewash corporate imagery. ***Example:*** ADM's "biggest little company out there" campaign.

4. Although most ads hawk consumer goods, a few actually attempt to educate us and warn us against harmful activities. ***Example:*** The ads aimed at combating drug use in this country.

5. Targeted advertising strategies and the "big data" industry have changed the way we experience advertising, but also raise serious concerns about privacy.

6. Political candidates and issues are sold in pretty much the same way as any other products.

    a. In the age of television, elections are won or lost via exposure on the tube, whether in debates, paid 30-second TV spots, press conferences, or whatever. And it is *image,* not rationality, that often wins in this arena. Increasingly, image makers have focused on negative advertising. Although mudslinging has long been a part of our political history, attack ads are far more extensive and effective than ever before. ***Examples:*** The Daisy/Girl /Peace TV spot that portrayed Barry Goldwater as too trigger-happy to be trusted with the nuclear bomb button; the Willie Horton ads that helped sink Michael Dukakis.

    b. It also should be noted that the campaign rhetoric of candidates running for high office generally is guided by the results of polls. It's always safer to tell voters what they want to hear, not what candidates intend to do if elected. That is why we can expect candidates to lie, exaggerate, or otherwise distort when necessary to curry the favor of voters. (But savvy voters still can learn from political rhetoric by reading between the lines and paying attention to past performance, so as to figure out what candidates are likely to do if elected.)

MindTap® **Visit MindTap for more readings and resources.**

c. Politicians in a democracy "campaign" virtually all of the time, not just when actually running for office. They always have to be intent on projecting the right *image* to the voters, and once in office, they have several standard ways of doing this. One is by performing the ceremonial duties of their office well; another is by holding press conferences.

d. Views on issues now are advertised just like candidates. The point is to influence voter preferences and thus legislation that is before Congress or state or local legislatures. ***Examples:*** the anti-Obamacare ad sponsored by the Chamber of Commerce.

e. The Internet has become increasingly important in marketing politicians. Not only do campaign strategists advertise their candidates online, but by analyzing the browsing habits of millions of users, they are able to target people open to political persuasion.

EXERCISE SET 10-1

Here are several advertising snippets (usually including the main ploy). Evaluate each of them for honesty, cogency, and the like, and point out uses of the various kinds of gimmicks and devices (humor, jargon, etc.) discussed in the text. Identify any fallacies.

1. Woman in a cigarette ad: "Until I find a real man, I'll settle for a real smoke."

*2. Burger King sign: "10 FREE French Fry Certificates for only $1.00."[11]

3. Calvert Gin ad: "Dry, Drier, Driest, Crisp."

4. Ad for a car: "You can love it without getting your heart broken."

5. Apple ad: "Think different."

*6. Part of a Nike commercial: "You don't win silver; you lose gold."

7. From a 2014 ad for Jolly Time Pop Corn: "Jolly Time Pop Corn has been endorsed by celebrities since the early 1950's by Bob Hope, Ozzie and Harriet, Alan Ladd & Family, and Danny Kaye. Famous radio and television personality, Arthur Godfrey, declared it 'the world's best popcorn.'"

8. Ad for presidential coins: "Every reader of this newspaper who beats the order deadline will still get one of the last never-circulated Golden Presidential Dollar Coins free with each sealed vault tube at just twenty-eight dollars plus shipping."

9. Proactiv commercial: "Got acne? Just ask your boyfriend what to do. Oh, that's right, you don't have a boyfriend."

---

[11]Starred (*) items are answered in a section at the back of the book.

*10. The principal part of a newspaper ad sponsored by the U.S. Council for Coconut Research/Information featuring a photo of Martin Agronsky: "The truth told by a famous U.S. television personality: Whoever says coconut oil's 'poisoning' America isn't supported by facts. . . . In fact, an on-going medical study in a Boston hospital has turned out some strong evidence that the 'fatty acids' of coconut oil could be beneficial to human health. America's intake of coconut oil fats is a lot less than what you think. The FDA [Food and Drug Administration] commissioner testified recently before the U.S. Congress that less than 1.5% of U.S. total fat intake is made up of coconut oil. . . ."

11. Newspaper ad for the Massachusetts State Lottery: "There's a good chance you could win the Numbers Game today. Just ask the 12,000 people who won yesterday. . . . The only thing that's hard to do is lose. When this many people win, how can you lose?"

12. Notice on the package of Elizabeth Arden Ceramide Time Complex Capsules: "Take your skin back in time to the future of a younger tomorrow."

EXERCISE SET 10-2

1. Apple ads have been among the most successful in the history of advertising. Examine a wide range of these ads on the Internet, starting with the text-heavy spots in the 1970s, followed by the strong, visual ads in later years that have almost no text at all. How does the evolution of these ads reflect new generations of consumers? Explain the appeal of an early ad and a later one. In what ways are they promise and/or identification ads? What ploys do they use to sell Apple products? Are there any fallacies involved? An entire generation of consumers seems to have loved these ads. Why?

2. How about the following excerpts (paraphrased) from a *Wall Street Journal* commercial:

Twenty-five years ago, two very similar young men graduated from the same college and started work at the same company. Returning to college for their 25th reunion, they still were much alike—happily married, three children, and so on—but one was manager of a small department in the company, the other was the company's president.

The difference that made the difference was in what each of these two men knew and how they made use of that knowledge: one read the Wall Street Journal; *the other did not.*

*3. Here is a United Airlines TV commercial (used by permission of Leo Burnett Co.):

Ben (the boss, addressing his sales force): I got a phone call this morning from one of our oldest customers. He fired us. After 20 years. He fired us. He said he didn't know us anymore. I think I know why. We used to do business with a handshake—face to face. Now it's a phone call and a fax—get back to you later. With another fax probably. Well folks, something's gotta change. That's why we're gonna get out with a little face-to-face chat with every customer we have.

> *Salesman:* But Ben, that's gotta be over 200 cities.
>
> *Ben:* I don't care. Edward, Ryan, Nicholas . . .
>
> *Voice-over:* If you're the kind of business that still believes personal service deserves a lot more than lip service, . . . welcome to United. That's the way we've been doing business for over 60 years.
>
> *Salesman:* Ben, where're you going?
>
> *Ben:* To visit that old friend who fired us this morning.
>
> *Voice-over:* United. Come fly the friendly skies.

Do you think this was a successful commercial? Why, or why not? Is this primarily a promise or an identification ad?

4. A letter from a travel company included this note on the envelope: "Lowest Fare Advertised on Holland America Guaranteed." Assume, as is likely, that this ad for Holland America (a large cruise ship company) is true. Is there something about this blurb that should make you suspect that the rates quoted are not the lowest you can get? Explain.

5. One of the classic ads in the Pepsi-Coke advertising competition is set some time in the distant future and shows a teacher taking his students to an archeological site containing artifacts from the late twentieth century. He explains the various objects while his students drink cans of Pepsi. One of them holds up a bedraggled Coke bottle and asks the teacher what it is, to which the teacher responds, after much puzzled thought, "I've no idea." A great commercial (why? what is its pulling power?), it brings to mind the way in which ordinary items from a time and place can reveal a great deal to discerning investigators (doing the archeological equivalent of reading between the lines).

6. Advertisements, if you can believe Marshall McLuhan, contain a treasure trove of clues about our times. If you were an investigator who came across records containing most of today's advertisements a thousand years hence, what might you learn from them about life in the early twenty-first century? Explain.

EXERCISE SET 10-3

1. Create a magazine ad for a product: (1) Decide which product it will be, (2) decide on an intended audience for your ad, and (3) design the picture and the copy. Use the ad to make a sales pitch to the class. Then ask students why they would or wouldn't buy the product, based on your ad, and analyze the ad's appeal, or lack of same. (Doing this will make you better appreciate the creative ability of professionals in the advertising business.)

2.   Compare two ads for the same or similar products in magazines with very different audiences (for instance, *Vogue* and *Time* magazine or *Sports Illustrated*). Explain how the intended audience influenced the ad design and sales pitch.

3.   For each the following fallacies, find at least one ad that is an instance of it: Appeal to Authority, False Dilemma, Questionable Premise, Tokenism, Irrelevant Reason, Equivocation, Appeal to Popularity, Appeal to Tradition, Hasty Conclusion, Questionable Cause, and Questionable Analogy.

4.   Find ads that reinforce and/or play upon stereotypes. Are these ads problematic for this reason?

EXERCISE SET 10-4

1.   Find an ad that has strong emotional appeal for you and try to figure out why you find it so engaging. Once you have done so, decide whether you would purchase the product, and explain your decision. (Be honest. Think carefully about it. No off-the-top-of-the-head goody-goody.)

2.   Go through a bunch of ads on some kind of product that interests you—cars, cosmetics, sports gear, whatever—and choose the one you would like to buy based on what you are told in these ads. Then do some research in *Consumer Reports, Consumers Digest,* or any one of several publications that specialize in product comparisons. On the basis of your research, decide whether you would still purchase the item you selected. Explain your decision.

3.   Visit a shopping mall or department store and examine the ploys used to seduce people into buying products. Consider subtle as well as obvious marketing devices and explain why you might be tempted to buy them.

4.   Here is part of a comment made by John Kasson: "Advertising . . . has become . . . a way of telling us not just what we should buy but how we should live, how we should associate the advertised objects with ourselves."

   Is Kasson right? Or do ads primarily appeal to already-existing desires and lifestyles? It is obvious, for example, that we cannot have a desire to play computer games like Nintendo before they exist, but do most ads touting products merely tell us about new ways to satisfy old desires, or do they create new ones, or perhaps just strengthen existing desires so that we spend more on them than we should? Do ads, say, for designer jeans and other fashion clothes just reinforce existing preferences? (Defend your answer.)

5.   In his book, *Business Civilization in Decline,* Robert Heilbroner claims that advertising is "the single most value-destroying activity of a business civilization." Would you agree or disagree with this statement? Write an argument defending your position.

6.   Imagine that you live in another country (or on another planet, for that matter) and know nothing about the United States except what you see in ads. What values and attitudes do you think Americans might have? Support your response by using ads as evidence.

7.   (This one will take some time.) Create a new email address, web presence, and online persona (with activity). How is this "person" advertised to? How is it the same and how is it different from the ads you currently see?

EXERCISE SET 10-5

Write two letters to one of your senators or representatives in Washington, D.C., in one taking a short, strong stand on an issue of importance to you, in the other taking an equally strong but different stand (completely opposite, if possible) on the same issue. Compare the two replies that you get. (Remember that you can't expect instantaneous replies.) Send each letter from a different address and use different names (because some members of Congress keep track on computers).

EXERCISE SET 10-6

Examine a political commercial for the visual effects, the pacing, and other nonverbal elements, and analyze how they either enhance a candidate's image or undermine it (in a negative ad).

EXERCISE SET 10-7

These days, the mass media (in particular, newspapers and magazines) spend a modest amount of time and effort covering and evaluating the political advertisements, especially TV spots, of candidates for high office. Look into some of this reporting; then (1) present and explain the content of at least two such analyses of advertisements for candidates in your state or locality and (2) evaluate their accuracy and cogency.

EXERCISE SET 10-8

In an article with the provocative title "Nuke 'Em" (*New York* magazine, June 25, 2012), Frank Rich argues that negative advertising is an essential part of political campaigns. Although he concedes that it is universally deplored, he defends it as powerful marketing that must be used in campaigns. "The president, any president," he writes, "should go negative early, often, and without apology if the goal is victory." Except for a few notorious examples, he claims attack ads are soon forgotten. What matters is not the mudslinging, but the victory—winning the presidency. In other words, the end justifies the means.

Do some research on the way negative advertising influences presidential campaigns. Then write an argument for or against using it.

"You know, it's O.K. to skip a news cycle."

Managing the News

11

MindTap® Visit MindTap for more readings and resources.

The news media have been going through a huge transformation comparable to what it went through with the advent of television. For the past several years, Project for Excellence in Journalism[1] has been tracking and analyzing significant trends and changes in the industry. Technological

---

[1]For a detailed analysis of emerging trends. see "The State of the News Media 2015," provided by the *Project for Excellence in Journalism.* Web. http://www.journalism.org/.

advances have created new ways for people to access the news, and as a result, traditional news outlets have been shrinking. In 2006, 55,000 people worked in American newsrooms. By 2013, that number was down to 36,700. Worse still, it seems another metropolitan daily or two go out of business every year, and scores more have had to reduce their print schedule. One notable victim was the New Orleans newspaper the *Times-Picayune*, which carried on heroically during Hurricane Katrina. Dozens of staff members rode out the storm in the newspaper's offices, filing stories until they were forced to evacuate to another site, where they continued posting updates on conditions in the city. This is the kind of stuff that wins Pulitzers (which, in fact, it did), but alas, the once-mighty paper has had to reduce its print version to three days a week.

There is a glimmer of hope in all this gloom, though. More news outlets have moved successfully to digital subscriptions, rather than simply giving the news away online, and network and cable news audiences have grown somewhat in 2011 after a decade of decline. One online news source that has done exceptionally well in recent years is *Bloomberg News*, a publication geared mainly to financial markets, but loaded with national and international news. While most media outlets are downsizing, *Bloomberg* is snapping up some of the best journalists in the business from top-rated newspapers across the country.

For much of the news industry, though, economics is still a major problem. For the past century, advertising has been the main source of revenue, but with the growth of advertising on the Internet and the shift of classified ads to free sites like Craigslist, income from these sources is drying up—the newspaper industry has lost more than half its ad revenue since 2006, despite gains in such revenue on digital products. As a consequence, major investors are reluctant to finance newsrooms adequately, and large cuts in staff are inevitable. Now that most people are getting the news online, particularly on mobile devices (according to a 2015 Pew Research study, smartphones are now in the pockets of 64 percent of American adults), advertisers are following the audience. This change in news venues is a mixed blessing. The good news is that more people than ever have access to the news. The bad news is that a handful of technology giants are consolidating their power to control as much of the digital world as they can by devising the operating systems, browsers, email services, and so on—all of which provide detailed personal information about Internet users (more about this later). Then there is the worrisome possibility that these Internet giants will acquire major news companies and be in a position to control the content. It is one thing for Jeff Bezos, the CEO of Amazon, to purchase the *Washington Post,* or for Facebook or Apple to partner with various newspapers in content-distribution deals. It would be quite another for a single company to manage content, distribution, and access all at once. Just imagine, for instance, how much control of information a company like Google would have if it were able to direct all of its search engine traffic to its own news sources.

New trends in journalism require us to be even more vigilant in thinking critically about the way the news is managed and presented to the public. Although there is more and better news out there than ever before in history, not all of the more is better. The trick is to know how to separate the wheat from the chaff and, thinking of the remark above by Adlai Stevenson, concentrating on the wheat. (Another bit of bad news is that masses of people pay more attention to news schlock than to news pearls.)

1. The Media and the Power of Money

In France, the expression is *cherchez la femme* ("look for the woman"). In America, at any rate, and perhaps in France and just about everywhere, a more apt expression would be "follow the money."

THE POWER OF THE PEOPLE

The one overriding fact about almost all news sources is that they are businesses. They exist to make money. They sell a product and we buy it. Or we don't, in which case they go out of business. This means that we, the viewers of television programs, users of websites, listeners to the radio, and readers of newspapers and magazines, have the most important say as to what sorts of news stories are reported in the mass media and how they are presented. That is why, for instance, the mass media so often play up relatively unimportant events while slighting more important ones—most people tend to be more interested in certain kinds of relatively trivial goings-on than in extremely important events. A case in point is the low priority often given to foreign news (unless, of course, the United States is involved, as in the Afghanistan War, or a major upheaval occurs, like the Arab Spring). Since the news is now driven by ratings and foreign news ranks low in public interest, overseas coverage has been in decline. The number of foreign correspondents employed by news organizations has dropped precipitously since 2003, with nearly all newspapers closing some of their foreign bureaus and some doing away with them entirely. Notably, McClatchy, owner of over 30 major newspapers across the country, announced in 2015 that they would be closing all of their foreign bureaus. One result of this trend is that foreign news is coming from fewer and fewer sources, which means less coverage of world events overall, not to mention fewer unique (and informed) perspectives on those events. What we get instead are more sensational new stories, reality shows, celebrity gossip, and a host of other trivial news that audiences seem to thrive on.

Since large audiences also tend to be quite provincial, the mass media concentrate on national affairs and home-grown celebrities, slighting news events from other countries. Similarly, because they are more interested in lighthearted material, human-interest stories, and fantasy than in hardheaded reality, human interest also tends to crowd out more important matters. For instance, in late August 2013, the world was just becoming aware of the extent of a horrific chemical attack in Ghouta during the then-escalating Syrian civil war. Stories were also still being filed about the Egyptian military's violent crackdown on demonstrators earlier in the month. But much more American coverage, commentary, and outrage was spent on a particularly salacious performance by Miley Cyrus at the MTV Video Music Awards.

As mentioned in Chapter 6, large numbers of people are superstitious or believe in pseudosciences of one kind or another, and we all are wishful thinkers to some degree. That is why many TV programs feature so many more pseudoscience programs than they do those concerning genuine science. It is particularly troubling when popular TV personalities feature dubious medical advice and pseudoscientific claims. Perhaps most notably, Dr. Mehmet Oz, famous for his appearances on *The Oprah Winfrey Show* and later his own *Dr. Oz* program, has made a career out of peddling dangerously pseudoscientific medical advice. Millions of people receive this advice dispensed from his television and radio shows. Many fewer are familiar with the rebukes he received from the U.S. Senate for his irresponsible endorsement of potentially unsafe weight-loss products. And fewer still are aware of the 2014 *British Medical Journal* article that found (from a random sampling) that less than half of his medical advice was supported by evidence and only about a third was established by evidence the researchers considered even somewhat believable. We might wonder why his massive audience remains unaware of his poor reputation in the medical community. The more disturbing question, though, is this: if his audience were aware of his reputation, would they care? That is to say, does someone like this get to be on TV because they are considered an appropriate authority, or do they become considered an appropriate authority because they're on TV?

Calvin and Hobbes © Watterson. Reprinted with permission of Universal Press Syndicate.

Reporting or Taking Dictation?

Stephen Colbert skewered the media in this satiric send-up at the annual White House Correspondents dinner (quoted in Extra! Update, *June 2006).*

Here's how it works: The president makes decisions. He's the decider. The press secretary announces those decisions, and you people of the press type those decisions down. Make, announce, type. Just put 'em through a spell check and go home. Get to know your family again. Make love to your wife. Write that novel you got kicking around in your head. You know, the one about the intrepid Washington reporter with the courage to stand up to the administration. You know—fiction!

Needless to say, the press was not amused.

THE POWER OF ADVERTISERS

The media are beholden not just to the people, but also to advertisers. Advertising revenue is the most important source of income for virtually all newspapers and magazines, and also the principal source for television stations and networks. Since money translates into power, the media must cater to the interests of advertisers as well as to those of the general public. Commenting on this fact years ago, H. G. Wells, in his classic *Outline of History,* remarked:

> [T]hose fathers of America thought also that they had but to leave the Press free, and everyone would live in the light. They did not realize that a free press could develop a sort of constitutional venality due to its relations with advertisers, and that large newspaper proprietors could become buccaneers of opinion and insensate wreckers of good beginnings.

Wells would not be a bit surprised at the way things have been going on the tube. For several years, the main problem with advertising was that it was drying up. Recently, however, the news media other than print journalism have made some financial gains since the steep losses of 2008–2009. Ad revenues increased for many (but not all) cable, network and local TV providers, but the biggest increase by far was in online advertising, which shot up 18 percent in 2014 compared to 2013.[2]

Online advertising has become more complicated for the news industry now that digital news relies on technology companies like Google or Facebook or YouTube to attract their audiences. These new players not only get a cut of the revenue, they usually control the most important information—data about the audience, which means that they can target advertising to suit individual users. Because these companies have the technology to recognize the tastes and preferences of users, advertisers have more power than ever before in persuading people to buy their products. It also means that the news industry has less control of its future now that it increasingly relies on technology companies who understand the audience best and can deliver the news consumers want as well as attract advertising revenues.

In order to increase advertising revenue and to maintain their autonomy, news organizations will have to make more effective use of digital advertising to survive. To do this, they may well resort to the lucrative business of gathering consumer data, just as the technology companies are doing. This raises the question of whether they will violate the trust of their audience. Because advertisers have always been important to the media, the issue now isn't just that advertisers may have undue influence, but that they are fed data on consumers that may seriously undermine their privacy.

Online advertising is just one of many ways advertisers make their power felt. Now that the 30-second commercial doesn't have the appeal it used to, they are using subtle ploys, like product placement and "news releases." One company, Citizens Bank, persuaded the venerable *Philadelphia Inquirer* to let it sponsor (that is, pay for) a column emblazoned with their green Citizens Bank banner. Although the *Inquirer*'s editor had qualms about renting out editorial space to an advertiser, he promised that the newspaper staff would have "complete independent control" of the column. Well, maybe.

---

[2]This section includes more information from the 2015 report by the Project for Excellence in Journalism.

Other ways the media cater to advertisers is by suppressing news that reflects badly on them or their products, and by touting advertisers' products free as "news" items. When an editor for the *Pioneer Press* (publisher of many papers in suburban Chicago) ran a review critical of a restaurant that advertised in the *Press,* she was told by higher-ups that the paper was "not in the business of bashing business." A while later, a favorable review of the same restaurant was written by someone in the marketing division—not a journalist (*Extra!* May–June 2004).

THE POWER OF GOVERNMENT

Government has the right and often the power to regulate business activity. It thus can harass a news agency by being strict about the rules it sets up (it usually isn't) and the licenses it requires. The mere threat of government action has a "chilling" effect on the media. It is true, of course, that the U.S. Constitution guarantees freedom of the press as one of several freedoms necessary to make a representative government function. And various Supreme Court decisions provide added protection for the press. For instance, our laws protect journalists against libel suits, particularly by government workers, and against government censoring in advance anything the media want to report, except certain kinds of classified information. But more important, the media are free to advocate controversial, even dangerous ideas—a freedom allowed in few other countries. Despite these legal protections, the government has ways of restricting the freedom of the press, and has done so with increasing regularity since September 11, 2001.

Just about every administration tries to muzzle the media in one way or another, and the Obama administration is no exception. For instance, in 2009, Congress proposed a national shield law that allowed reporters to protect confidential sources that provided information vital to important news stories. Before subpoenaing a journalist to reveal these sources, prosecutors would be required under the bill to use every other method possible to find the source of the information. So many journalists had been subpoenaed after 2001 (and four were jailed for refusing to reveal sources) that advocates for reporters lobbied Congress to pass this national shield law. But the Obama administration responded with major revisions that watered down the bill. One such provision was that journalists would not be allowed to protect sources of news items that might cause "significant" harm to national security. However, the judges who determined whether indeed the information was harmful would be "instructed to be deferential to the administrative opinion." Thus the bill would offer little protection and eventually was scrapped.

But government censorship doesn't end with classified information. Administrations can, and often do, suppress information that doesn't conform to their political agenda. For example, when Dr. Richard Carmona, the former surgeon general in the Bush administration, testified before a congressional oversight committee in 2007, he made the startling revelation that political appointees censored his speeches and prevented him from expressing his views on comprehensive sex education, emergency contraception, and the science on stem cell research, among other things. Two other former surgeons general testified as well about the political interference of presidents they served under, but nothing approached the constraints placed on Dr. Carmona, who not only had to manipulate scientific information to suit the political landscape, but was ordered to mention President Bush's name three times on every page of his reports!

Governments have other ways of managing the news. One way is to censor material alleged to be obscene, which is not covered by the First Amendment. The problem comes in trying to determine legally what is obscene. The Federal Communications Commission (FCC) sidesteps this issue by levying fines and revoking licenses, not by censoring material. In recent years, the FCC has raised its fines considerably for obscenity and indecency. CBS was fined $550,000 after Janet Jackson's breast was famously bared during her halftime Super Bowl performance in 2004 with Justin Timberlake (who euphemistically called it a "wardrobe malfunction"). Although this incident did not literally involve "speech," the public outrage it sparked, along with other similar incidents, spurred the FCC to set a stricter standard for determining indecent behavior and obscene language. This issue has been in and out of the courts since Jackson's bared-nipple debacle. Public outcry grew louder when celebrities let fly coarse comments, as Nicole Ritchie did at an awards ceremony aired by Fox, and when a seven-second bare buttocks scene aired on ABC's *NYPD Blue*. Complaints over these "fleeting expletives" (FCC talk for spur-of-the-moment obscenities) convinced the FCC to ramp up its fines to $325,000 an episode. The case bounced back and forth in the courts until the Supreme Court finally ruled in 2012 against the FCC on the grounds that the incidents occurred before the FCC put its new policy in place, and thus Fox and ABC weren't given fair notice. But this narrow ruling didn't address the First Amendment issue of regulating indecency in the media, and the issue will probably surface again.

Government officials also can, and do, manipulate the news by playing favorites among reporters, leaking only to those newspeople who play ball in return. Since leaks are such a large source of media information (see the discussion of news-gathering practices a few pages forward), reporters have to think twice before crossing their government informants. Similarly, reporters have to be careful in press conferences not to ask embarrassing questions or follow-up questions; those who are too brash or persistent don't get called on in future. Hillary Clinton's State Department administration was especially adept at manipulating coverage by controlling access and information. Advance copies of speeches and access to the Clinton family were traded for favorable stories, often with language suggested directly by Clinton's office. Reporters at institutions as respectable as the *Atlantic* and *Politico* seem to have gone along all too willingly. For what it's worth, it took *Gawker*'s probing, seven years, and multiple Freedom of Information Act requests for this journalistic malfeasance to come to light.

Although many items leaked to the media are on target, the fact that their sources can be concealed gives government officials a good deal of power. They can rig stories to serve their own interest without being accountable. But if sensitive material is leaked that the government does not want released, it can, and often does, threaten reporters with criminal prosecution unless they reveal their sources. If reporters comply, however, they lose their credibility and their sources dry up, so they almost always refuse to cooperate. But failure to do so may result in their being subpoenaed to reveal their sources. If they refuse, they may be convicted. With a jail threat hanging over their heads, reporters may be deterred from using controversial, confidential sources.

Another way the government manages the news is by issuing prepackaged reports that can be slipped into 90-second slots in the local news. Presidents Bush and Obama both used this ploy to get their messages out or to put a positive spin on the news, packaging it as though it came from traditional reporting. The Bush administration hyped all kinds of policies from regime change in Iraq to Medicare reform, often featuring government officials with scripted answers to scripted questions without any critical overview or comments. This covert propaganda, broadcast around the country without citing government as its source, is on the rise now that the news media are on the skids, and news staffs are shrinking.

Of course, no U.S. government agencies have censoring powers that are anywhere near those regularly exercised in quite a few foreign countries. In China, Myanmar (Burma), Liberia, and many other countries, news media rarely are allowed to criticize governmental policies or actions. Middle East governments were especially repressive during the Arab Spring revolts. At the start of the uprising in Egypt, TV viewers around the world saw thousands of protestors pouring into Tahrir Square in Cairo and thousands more fleeing the country.[3] But state-controlled TV showed life proceeding as usual, with pictures of the steady traffic flow over a Cairo bridge and empty streets below office buildings. When the uprising intensified, state TV linked the protests to lawlessness, reporting that thousands of criminals were released from jails and neighborhoods were overrun by looters. Regular newscasts assured viewers that the government was in charge, quelling the insurgents and restoring order. Predictably, the government attempted to muzzle other media sources by cutting off Internet service and shutting down Al Jazeera.

Worse still, reporters in dangerous countries are often threatened, even murdered, in the line of duty. According to the Committee to Protect Journalists (CPJ), 1,173 journalists were killed between 1992 and 2015. The CPJ website (cpj.org) chronicles abductions and murders, citing in grisly detail the signs of torture (like body bruises and broken fingers), gunshot wounds, and beheadings. A quick look at this website is enough to deter any aspiring journalist from working as a foreign correspondent in hostile territory.

THE POWER OF THE MEDIA

The media are not simply beholden to the three powerful groups just discussed. They themselves are a genuinely separate power faction. This is particularly true of the mass media: television, radio, major newspapers and magazines, and so forth. Investigative reporters can, and sometimes do, unearth governmental chicanery as well as stories not in the best interests of advertisers, although we have gone to some pains to show why they often hesitate.

This doesn't mean that the media constitute a monolithic, organized group, but rather that individual mass media organizations have a certain amount of power and that, taken as a whole, the mass media have great power and frequently common interests. Cases such as the *Washington Post* Watergate exposés, which set in motion events that drove Richard Nixon from office, are well known. Going back even further to the Vietnam War, the press turned the tide of public opinion when journalists began reporting that the chaos and destruction they witnessed on the battlefield was nothing like the official upbeat version. This may seem like ancient history, but it set an important precedent that

---

[3]Fahim, Kareem. "State TV Offers Murky Window into Power Shift, with Few Protesters in Sight." *New York Times,* 1 February 2011.

continues to this day (with notable exceptions, like the media's failure to question the Bush administration's rationale for the Iraq War).[4]

During and after World War II, the press rarely questioned the judgment or truthfulness of our military leaders, but as the Vietnam War churned on, journalists became disillusioned with the war and its leaders when they saw what was really happening on the ground. They wrote about it forcefully and photographed it graphically. These reports were so upsetting that President Kennedy tried to persuade certain major newspapers to pull outspoken reporters out of Saigon. (Presidents Johnson and Nixon used similar tactics.) Future administrations learned from this experience that if they let journalists roam the battlefields unescorted, the news coverage might be very bad indeed, so they herded reporters into supervised "pools" during the Gulf War and embedded them in military units during the Iraq War.

But controlling access to the action in Iraq and imposing other official restraints didn't succeed in muzzling the media once they got over their initial patriotic fervor. Just as they had in Vietnam, reporters started filing gritty dispatches about car bombings, assassinations, rampant militias, and failed politics. And just as previous administrations had tried to control the press in Vietnam, the Bush administration fought back, excluding some reporters from official briefings, refusing others the chance to embed, classifying a mountain of material as top secret, and serving up its own optimistic version of the war. The media didn't cave in, however, and became probably the single most influential force in turning Americans against the war. For better or for worse, the media wields immense power in swaying public opinion.

A recent example of the power that media can exert is the 2010 publication of the whistle-blowing WikiLeaks material by the *New York Times*. The difference between this publication and previous ones is the sheer scale of information released—a whopping 250,000 confidential government documents that ranged from secret military reports to impolitic comments by U.S. diplomats in foreign countries. Although WikiLeaks had been publishing leaks for several years, it only gradually made its way into mainstream media. But it hit the big time in 2010 when the *Times, Der Spiegel* in Germany, and the *Guardian* in England simultaneously published reports of secret military operations in Afghanistan after hundreds of hours spent analyzing and confirming the documents.[5] When the WikiLeaks material hit the newsstands, it stunned the country and gave Americans who were already weary of the war more reason to call for an end to it.

Often, though, the news media tend to report the same stories while ignoring others that may never come to light unless some publication chips away at them for years before they catch fire (as happened when the *Washington Post* exposed the Watergate scandal). A recent example is the way the *Guardian* has investigated Rupert Murdoch's

---

[4]For more on this see Filkins, Dexter. "A Skeptical Vietnam Voice Still Echoes in the Fog of Iraq." *New York Times,* 25 April 2007.

[5]Before releasing the material, the *Times* showed it to the State Department to identify any confidential sources that might compromise national security, and then edited out the information, a procedure commonly followed by responsible news organizations when dealing with major leaks. But that doesn't mean the government managed to censor the publication. The editorial staff decided what material it would publish. As might be expected, the Obama administration opposed it and tried to undercut the leak about military operations in Afghanistan, but to little avail.

British tabloid, the *News of the World*, for illegal phone hacking to get sensational stories. For decades, Murdoch, arguably the most powerful media mogul in history, has wielded immense power over British politicians by using his tabloids as a bully pulpit to punish or reward them. In recent years, he has expanded his empire to the United States, where News Corporation, his U.S. company, took control of the *Wall Street Journal* and Fox News, outlets that have given him more power to influence American politics than any other single person in the media.

Like the biblical David pelting stones at Goliath, the *Guardian* doggedly followed leads for years on phone-hacking reporters who tapped into conversations of celebrities and the royal family. The public found this salacious gossip amusing but inconsequential until the *Guardian* broke the news that hackers had tapped the cell phones of a murdered 13-year-old and the families of soldiers who died in Iraq and Afghanistan. Soon after, the *New York Times* and *Vanity Fair* jumped on the story, and suddenly it had legs. The usual denials and cover-ups surfaced, like News Corp. laying the blame on a "few rotten apples" and the editor of the *News of the World* claiming she knew absolutely nothing about the phone hacking that had been going on under her nose for years. When Murdoch was questioned by members of Parliament, he said was shocked—yes, shocked!—at the illegal activity endemic in his organization.

The press kept digging and gradually revealed that the scope of the phone tapping was far greater than anyone imagined—thousands of phones were hacked. Prominent politicians were hand-in-glove with Murdoch, and some senior officers in Scotland Yard had a cozy relationship with editors of the *News of the World*. As one revelation led to another, Murdoch decided to shut down the tabloid, not so much to eliminate a rogue newspaper as to buy time to repair the damage.

Of course, one media giant's power has to compete with that of the others. CBS's power to determine what will be shown on its network programs is held in check by the identical power wielded by NBC, ABC, Fox, CNN, and the rest of its competitors, not to mention competitors in the print media, just as the power of one politician may be reduced by the power of others and by the power of the media. Vive le competition!

Every country has its own influential media, of course. A good case in point, given our current involvement in the Mideast, is the increasing importance of the media in the Arab world. Probably the most influential network in that area is Al Jazeera, established in 1996 by the British-educated, progressive emir of Qatar. The network reaches over 35 million people and is reputed to have as much power as the *New York Times*. With its nonstop coverage of the protests that swept through the Arab world, it has been a major influence in galvanizing popular rage against Middle East dictators. Because it has trumpeted the common struggle against oppression of people throughout the region, it has become a lightning rod for political factions in the Middle East. When it covered the uprisings in Tunisia, Lebanon, and Egypt, reporters were either harassed or driven out of the country, but through local contacts, Al Jazeera managed to broadcast grainy cell phone pictures of police violence. Middle East factions weren't the only ones that wanted Al Jazeera muzzled; Western governments have been deeply suspicious of the motives behind its sympathetic coverage of Hezbollah and Hamas and of its tendency to broadcast Arab anger at Israel. Since all this ferment makes for riveting television, Al Jazeera's continuous coverage of Arab protests, often shared with other media outlets, has had a profound influence as the "Arab Spring" unfolded before our eyes.

In 2013, Al Jazeera launched Al Jazeera America, a cable news channel in the United States. The channel promised less shouting, more investigative news, longer and more in-depth pieces, and more diverse and nuanced perspectives than its competitors CNN, Fox News, and MSNBC. Al Jazeera America failed to attract audiences and ended its broadcast in 2016, a reminder that big news is big business, and the bottom line almost always determines who survives. Which brings us to . . .

THE POWER OF BIG BUSINESS

The days are long gone when most business in countries like the United States was conducted by individuals or small organizations. "Ma and pa" stores have given way to Walmarts and Safeways. Individual doctors hanging out their shingles have been replaced by group practices and HMOs. Most family farms have been replaced by huge agribusinesses. These days, virtually all industries are dominated by large corporations—especially by huge multinational conglomerates. Large corporations, individually and collectively, thus have great power, which they exercise almost exclusively in the interests of maximizing their own profits.

Corporate power affects the dissemination of news in two ways: first, by getting the viewpoints of big business reported favorably in the mass media; second, by preventing conflicting viewpoints from being reported or stressed. This censoring power of large corporations stems in part from their power as advertisers (a point already discussed). Large corporations, after all, are by far the largest advertisers in the mass media. But it also stems from the power money has in the political arena (a point to be discussed later). When the mass media cooperate with political power, they thus indirectly also cooperate with large corporate interests. Furthermore, the mass media themselves have become controlled in large part by very large media conglomerates, which often are parts of even larger corporate structures (a point also to be discussed shortly). In general, the interests of media conglomerates coincide with those of other large businesses—for example, in favoring lower wages for low-level employees—so that the mass media tend to have a built-in bias in favor of big business. (Interestingly, many conservative commentators regularly accuse the media of having a left-wing bias.)

The result is that news and opinion in the mass media tend to be skewed strongly to the interests of the rich rather than the poor or middle class. Ordinary people, of course, also have great power in determining how the mass media portray the world—they can switch channels or otherwise tune out. They also can go to non-mass media news and opinion sources (yes, these will be discussed shortly), but most people do not do so, one reason being that the average person does not understand how the news is slanted in the interests of those with great political power.[6] (Another reason is that large numbers

---

[6]The idea is widespread in America that there are no social classes in the land of the free and the home of the brave. The truth in this idea is that in every generation, some individuals move from lower into higher economic classes, even occasionally into the highest. The falsehood in this idea is that most of those born into rich families remain rich, and most of those born into average- or lower-income households never become rich. Class membership in large industrial democracies is not carved in stone in the way it was in the monarchies of old, but this surely does not mean that there are any truly classless societies on this planet, other than in tiny hunting-and-gathering groups.

of people—in particular, those in the lower half of the economic pecking order—tend to concentrate on their own personal lives and problems and to be inattentive when it comes to the important economic and political issues of the wider community, even though a good deal of what happens in their lives is seriously influenced by what happens in the broader social arena.)

Most big city dailies have "business" sections that report the goings-on of large corporations and of the various financial markets—almost exclusively from the point of view of investors and other large money interests. But no daily newspapers have labor sections or report on business from the point of view of individual workers or, except on occasion, organized labor. Similarly, several business news programs are aired on TV during the day (when MSNBC is devoted almost exclusively to stock market goings-on), but no labor programs or programs regularly reporting from the point of view of ordinary workers. (But consider the fact that a majority of daytime TV audiences prefer to watch the soaps, sports news, and sitcom reruns. How, then, could a labor channel be a paying proposition?)

However, when the economy slides into a recession and people lose their jobs, foreclosures multiply, and retirement funds dwindle, the media pay attention. Until 2011, labor union stories had been underreported for decades—a reflection of the decline in power of organized labor since its heyday from 1955 to 1967. But as the Great Recession lingered on and state budgets dwindled, unions suddenly leapt into the news when the governor of Wisconsin decided to cut bargaining rights and benefits to public workers to close gaps in the state budget—a measure later supported by the state Supreme Court. No one expected this isolated incident to spark the kind of national attention it got. But times were tough and workers throughout the country were threatened with reduced benefits or job loss, so the massive response to this action forced the media to address union issues at length.

The result was a public debate on the plight of organized labor. Pro-union advocates argued that the slow slide of workers out of the middle class was partly the result of dwindling union membership in the private sector. (According to the Bureau of Labor Statistics, union membership was down to 11.1 percent of wage and salary workers in 2015 from 20.1 percent in 1983. Only 6.7 percent of private sector workers belonged to a union in 2015). Although organized labor is stronger in the public sector, the argument

Keep Digging

David Halberstam (one of the most respected journalists in recent years) on the importance of investigative reporting:

You have to keep digging, keep asking questions, because otherwise you'll be seduced or brainwashed into the idea that it's somehow a great privilege, an honor, to report the lies they've [those in power] been feeding you.

—Quoted in: Herbert, Bob. "Working the Truth Beat." *New York Times*, 30 April 2007.

was that all unions were threatened nationwide now that a dangerous precedent had been set when they were stripped of bargaining rights in Wisconsin. Antiunion forces were quick to point out union abuses like blatant increases in overtime pay, unreasonable job protection, and crippling retirement benefits that threaten to undermine corporate budgets. Articles on both sides appeared, not only in editorial and business sections, but on the front page as well—unprecedented coverage of union issues.

Another segment of society usually given short shrift in the media is the plight of poor people in our country. According to the U.S. Census Bureau, in 2010, 46.2 million Americans lived below the federal poverty line, defined as $22,314 for a family of four—the highest number of poverty stricken people in 52 years. Until recently, however, coverage of poverty was a blip on the radar except during holidays and times of disaster (like Hurricane Katrina). But as the recession deepened and millions of people slid into poverty, the media addressed the issue. Stories about housing foreclosures, job losses, food banks, and homeless people cropped up on a regular basis. The poor population, once centered in urban areas, spread to the suburbs—long considered the bastion of the prosperous middle class—straining the resources of local government to provide social welfare. When poverty becomes that widespread, the media pay attention, particularly in an election year.

Media biases regarding historically marginalized groups came under scrutiny in two different ways in 2014 and 2015 as the Black Lives Matter movement caught on in cities across the country. First, many activists pointed to long-term underreporting on violence against African Americans in the United States as a contributing factor to the perpetuation of such violence. Second, protests held (at least in part) under the "Black Lives Matter" banner—especially those in Ferguson and Baltimore—were allegedly misreported as being more riotous and violent than they were.[7]

This brings us to one of the news media's deepest biases—a bias in favor of the sensational. When news agencies have to compete for audiences in order to survive, there is a natural incentive to tell the story that attracts the most attention rather than the one that is most accurate or honest. That doesn't mean that every newspaper eventually becomes the *National Enquirer* and every news site becomes *TMZ*. But if there are two ways of telling a story, one that focuses on the substantive and one that focuses on the sensational, it's the rare news provider that consistently chooses the former.

POWER TENDS TO COOPERATE WITH POWER

Although the interests of big business and government often coincide with those of the media, sometimes they do not. Scandals may sell newspapers and increase TV news audiences, but they also tend to sink political careers. What is bad for Microsoft may be good for CNN.

In a majority of cases, however, it's better for the various power factions to cooperate rather than to fight. That is why, for instance, reporters covering the White House

---

[7]For examples of such criticism, see: Taibi, Catherine. "What's Not Working in Media's Coverage of Baltimore." *Huffington Post,* 28 April 2015. See also: Hannah-Jones, Nikole. "How the Media Missed the Mark in Coverage of Michael Brown's Killing." *Essence,* 12 August 2014.

quickly learn which sorts of questions can be asked at presidential press conferences, how far follow-up queries can go, what sorts of editorial comments they can make in news reports, and the like. Journalists who don't play the game, who persist in challenging the standard self-serving replies to their questions, don't get called upon in the future. Columnists who tear into an administration in Washington with a great deal of gusto are less likely to receive leaks or other tidbits.

Sometimes an organization's coverage of the news is compromised by its own business partnerships with the subjects of that coverage. A striking example of this came in 2013 when ESPN bowed out of a joint project with PBS covering concussions in football and the NFL's response to them. ESPN initially claimed that the decision had nothing to do with their partnerships with the NFL—including incredibly lucrative televising rights. But the *New York Times* later reported (to absolutely no one's surprise) that the NFL had directly pressured ESPN to not participate in the story.

NEWS AS ENTERTAINMENT

For all the reasons discussed so far, the news has increasingly become a source of entertainment more than an information source. Because money is the bottom line, because vested interests like big business and government shape the news to their advantage, and because the public wants entertainment more than information, news items tend to morph into Hollywood action, disaster, or horror stories. And often, important stories go underreported until they are sensationalized.

A good example is U.S. news coverage of the Ebola outbreak in West Africa in 2014 and 2015. The severity and human cost of the epidemic—which was the largest of its kind in the disease's history—were woefully underreported until America saw its first cases. Then you would have thought we were all doomed. Hours upon hours of coverage flooded cable news channels and news websites, very little of which did much to educate the public about Ebola, its risks, or the genuine health crisis in West Africa. Much more time was spent tracing the movements of a doctor who contracted the disease helping patients in Guinea and then returned to New York, along with wild speculations about the risks to those who may have been in contact with him. These stories were often produced with the techniques and conventions of a blockbuster disaster movie. As Deane Marchbein of Doctors Without Borders said to healthjournalism.org, "a reckoning is due. Instead of focusing on the medical literature and the facts related to Ebola, many of your colleagues fanned the hysteria and the frenzy and the fear. An opportunity to educate, inform and reassure was, to a great degree, missed." In the end, two people actually contracted Ebola in the United States, and both recovered.

At least the Ebola coverage was tied to a genuine health issue of public concern, albeit with excessive hype, but much of the news nowadays has drifted downward to infotainment.[8]

Tabloid television has been on the rise ever since 24-hour news channels emerged in the 1980s. To maximize profit, cable producers made use of increasingly sophisticated methods of tracking viewer preferences in content and time slots. The result is a mishmash of hardcore news and tabloid fodder. Over the years, sensational coverage of cases

---

[8]See "The News Merchant," *Atlantic,* September 2010, for an excellent article on agents who broker tabloid news.

like the murder trials of O. J. Simpson or Amanda Knox have skyrocketed cable ratings and boosted profits. Nowadays the demand for salacious stories is so great the networks vie for a first crack at them. This competition has spawned a tier of middlemen— network bookers, who chase after stories about strangled coeds, kidnapped children, serial murderers, and a whole range of bloody, tragic cases. They then broker deals between the networks and the newsworthy people. This, by the way, enables networks to claim that they don't pay sources directly for news, a practice long considered corrupting because it undermines the credibility of the source. Instead they pay the agent, a sleight of hand that barely masks the negotiation. If this descent into tabloid journalism is unsettling, though, we have to remember that the networks are responding to the will of the people. They give viewers what they want.

An important lesson to be learned from what has been said so far in this chapter is that the news, as presented to us by the mass media, tends to misdirect our attention away from important, underlying, day-to-day occurrences and trends in favor of "breaking news" (assassination of a foreign leader, Super Bowl coverage); "human interest" stories, particularly celebrity coverage; and what the powerful want to tell us.

It hasn't always been this way. In the years before media mergers and increasing demands that news divisions show a profit, the coverage of celebrities was a small part of mainstream news. *Extra!* (October 1997) reported that Elvis Presley's death in 1977 was covered in 29 minutes over the following five weekdays. When John Lennon was killed in 1980, his murder received 50 minutes over the same period of time. But coverage of Princess Diana's death in 1997 totaled 197 minutes on nightly newscasts over a five-weekday period—almost two-thirds of all nightly news coverage in the first week of September 1997. Fast forward to 2009, when Michael Jackson died—60 percent of the news coverage was devoted to his life story and death compared to 10 percent coverage of the bloody protests in Iran over disputed elections (according to an analysis by Project for Excellence in Journalism). Of course, the public's fascination with human-interest stories doesn't always result in celebrity news drowning out other more important items, but, in fact, it often works that way.

2. News-Gathering Methods Are Designed to Save Money

The all-important fact about the mass media, as we have been at pains to point out, is that they are in business to make money, not lose it. When they regularly spend more money gathering the news than they take in, they go out of business. One result is that true investigative reporting tends to get slighted, because it is so very expensive in time, effort, and thus money. More "efficient" news-gathering techniques are used whenever possible, even though spending greater amounts of money might produce more accurate accounts, not to mention dredge up dirt the powerful are trying to hide. Media people generally do try to be careful in what they report so as not to leave themselves open to libel charges, and (in most cases) because of a desire to adhere to professional ethics. But they rarely get to dig below the surface.

The principal way in which news is gathered is through established "beats." The major wire services, television networks, and a few top newspapers and magazines routinely assign reporters to cover the major news-developing institutions—the White House, Congress, and so on. At the local level, they cover city hall, the police, and the like. Roving reporters are assigned to cover breaking stories in business, medicine, and so on, by interviewing interested parties—representatives of large corporations giving press conferences, "experts" in relevant fields, union leaders.[9] In effect, then, *most news is given to reporters by government officials or by others who have or represent power or wealth.* Further, as a condition of interviewing officials, reporters often have to show them drafts of the articles for quote approvals, which gives the interviewed officials veto power over what statements can be included. The news thus is bound to reflect established interests much more than those of the general public, given that it is the rich and powerful who have the means to call press conferences, provide video footage, or issue fancy press releases or control the quotable material.[10]

Tabloid "Journalism"

Pete Hamil, on the trend of journalists to degenerate into gossip hounds:

[Reporters in the 1950s] were conscious of their limitations; they knew that they never once had turned out an absolutely perfect newspaper, because the newspaper was put out by human beings. But in their separate ways, they tried very hard never to write anything that would bring the newspaper shame. They would be appalled at the slovenly way the word "tabloid" is now used. [Tabloid describes the shape of the page, not the content.] They didn't pay whores for stories. They didn't sniff around the private lives of politicians like agents from the vice squad. Even in large groups, on major stories, the photographers didn't behave like a writhing, snarling, mindless centipede, all legs and Leicas, falling upon some poor witness like an instrument of punishment. Somehow, they found ways to get the story without behaving like thugs or louts.

—Hamil, Pete. *News Is a Verb.*
New York: Random House, 1998.

That is an important reason why *very few important news stories in the mass media result from true investigative reporting!* It's much easier, quicker, and cheaper to interview heads of government agencies or representatives of big business than it is to find

---

[9]Experts can be found on every side of virtually all issues. Which experts are consulted depends on the way in which a story is to be slanted, and that, of course, usually is determined by the various factors we have been considering in this chapter.

[10]An important exception to this rule is that ordinary people often are interviewed to impart "human interest" to stories that otherwise reflect the opinions and viewpoints of power or money. Another exception is the coverage of local news events such as fires—reporters actually go to the scene and interview those affected by the event.

out what actually is going on by tedious digging. (It's also safer; recall the discussion a while back about the power of government and why power tends to cooperate with power.)

In another alarming trend, many newspapers, networks, and stations are ending local beats. We discussed earlier the damage closing foreign bureaus does to coverage of world events. The situation is perhaps even more critical at the local level. For instance, when there is no one on a dedicated City Hall beat, there is no one well positioned to uncover malfeasance and impropriety in local government. This is not just because no one is looking. In many cases, it takes the expertise of the beat reporter to know *where* to look and what to look *for*.

There is a bit of good news on the topic of true investigative reporting. In recent years, newspapers, and occasionally TV and radio programs, have been recycling items from non-mass media magazines and from the major newspapers (which have set up syndicates for this purpose to compete with feature syndicates). Reprinting someone else's investigative efforts is a good deal cheaper than digging on one's own. So items from the *Washington Monthly*, the *Atlantic*, the *New Republic*, the *National Review*, and other non-mass media publications, as well as from the *New York Times*, the *Washington Post*, and the *Los Angeles Times*, appear now and then in local rags and on network news programs.

3. News Reporting: Theory and Practice

People don't often stand back and look carefully at what they're doing from a wider perspective; they don't often theorize about their activities. On the whole, media workers do so more than most, but their theories frequently are self-serving.

NEWS REPORTING IS SUPPOSED TO BE OBJECTIVE, NOT SUBJECTIVE

Until well into the twentieth century, American journalists covered the news from politically biased points of view, following the eighteenth- and nineteenth-century models that date back to the American Revolution. Alexander Hamilton took full advantage of the freedom of the press set forth in the Bill of Rights to expound his Federalist philosophy and attack his opponents in the Republican Party (not to be confused with the current political party). He, in turn, was vilified in opposition newspapers by such stalwarts as John Adams and James Madison. But in the early part of the twentieth century, journalism evolved into a more politically independent profession and attempted to report unbiased news, relegating opinion-based articles to the editorial pages. (Many European countries, though, still use the partisan model. In England, for example, the *Guardian* tends to champion liberal causes; the *Times*, conservative ones.)

However, both conservatives and liberals claim that the other side dominates the news. In the 1970s, to offset what conservatives believed was a liberal bias in the press, they launched magazines like the *National Review* and *Commentary* to get their message out and to begin to influence news coverage. Later, conservative think tanks and television networks emerged, along with talk shows hosted by right wingers like Rush Limbaugh and Laura Ingraham. Liberals were slower to respond, maybe because the media did seem more liberal until the late 1970s. But gradually liberal think tanks sprang up, as did news programs and political comedy shows like *The Daily Show* and *The Colbert Report* that skewered the opposition on both sides and began to influence a more youthful audience than the more traditional programs did.

But even news coverage that strives to be unbiased cannot be completely objective. Reports of facts generally depend on somebody's judgment that they are facts. A reporter must reason to the facts, or at least report someone else's reasoning to the facts, just as one reasons to anything else. Facts are not like fruit on trees, to be plucked at one's leisure.

The idea that media hands should not make value judgments is foolish. They *must* make value judgments, if only about which items are important enough to be featured, which should be mentioned only briefly, and which should be tossed into the round file (where most items that go over Associated Press wires end up). The point is that *editing,* one of the chief tasks performed by media workers, requires value judgments about the relative importance of events.

In any case, theory is one thing; practice, another. Practice is driven primarily by the various forces we have been at pains to describe and only to a small extent by abstract theory. The theory of objectivity serves as a convenient cover under which this can be done. Its cash value is that reporters are motivated to stay within the narrow, middle-of-the-road social consensus when they make judgments or draw conclusions. So one effect of the theory of objectivity is to discourage the reporting of nonestablishment or nonconsensus points of view, satisfying instead the desires of media audiences, advertisers, and others who have great power. Objectivity turns into not rocking the boat.

It's also true, and worth noting, that journalists often confuse objectivity with its close relative—being evenhanded. Thus journalists and news agencies fall into the problem that critics call "false balance." It has become common practice, for example, for the major networks to present rebuttal from the "other side" when they carry major presidential addresses, so that both major parties get their say. Comments about the truth of whatever is at issue tend to get lost. And objectivity is not valuable if it is at the expense of truth. Do we want our news media to report on what is happening in the world, or only on what two opposing sides say is happening? *Another example*: In the name of "balance" and "objectivity," news media have for a long time given too great a voice to climate change deniers, despite overwhelming scientific consensus to the contrary. In 2014, an independent audit by the BBC Trust found that the BBC was guilty of exactly this. If a news organization as respectable as the BBC can fall into this "false balance" trap, few are immune.

Note, by the way, how the expression "other side" masks the fact that there are *many* sides to most issues and that the viewpoints championed by the two major political parties often run the range only from A to B. During the 2016 presidential campaign, for example, the mass media breathlessly covered the Democratic and Republican candidates, but did very little reporting on candidates of the Green, Libertarian, and other "minor" parties. Even attempts at evenhandedness regarding just the two major parties are giving way to one-sided coverage on some TV news programs. Now that the public's interest in the news media is on the wane, cable TV

Figuring Out the Story

Robert Caro, journalist and biographer, told this anecdote about the advice an editor gave him when he was assigned his first story on the paper. Caro was just a copy boy then, but because all the other reporters were busy, the editor asked him to cover a controversial development at City Hall. This brief piece of advice embodies the basic principles of good journalism.

"OK, here's what you do," the editor said, "You go down to City Hall and listen for a while until you think you know what's going on. After the meeting, talk to whoever is opposing this plan to find out why. Then you go to the developer to get his side of the story. If you're confused, go back to the opponents and ask more questions. Keep going back and forth until you've figured out the story. Got it?"

—Quoted in "Read All About It—But Where Exactly?" *San Francisco Chronicle*, 17 June 2007; a perceptive evaluation of the current state of journalism.

outlets are experimenting with ways to build audience appeal by replacing conventional newscasts with opinion-based coverage. Fox News has done this for years, of course, but now MSNBC has a string of liberal news programs like *All In with Chris Hayes* and *The Rachel Maddow Show*.

NEWS IS SUPPOSED TO BE SEPARATED FROM ANALYSIS AND IN-DEPTH REPORTING

The theory of objectivity requires that facts be reported separately from conclusions or evaluations (which are thought of as "subjective"). But this separation of news from analysis further aggravates a defect already in evidence in most media reporting: *the failure to tie what happens to any explanation as to why it happened and why it is important.*

For instance, in 1998, when Hurricane Mitch wreaked havoc in Honduras, Guatemala, and Nicaragua, the mass media reported horrendous destruction and a large number of deaths. But they failed to explain *why* the destruction was so great. To do that, they needed to explain how the Central American policies of the United Fruit Company and of the United States in the 1950s and 1960s led to intense deforestation that undermined the landscape. They failed to stress the important point that this deforestation, undertaken to replace local farmers with large-scale agriculture, was a major part of the cause of the massive flooding and landslides that resulted when Hurricane Mitch hit. See, for example, *Counterpunch,* November 1–15, 1998—a left-wing, non-mass media publication—or many good histories of Central America. Moral: To know what is really going on, you can't rely on the mass media.

Typically, when covering a story, a reporter consults those directly involved or affected by it. Writing, say, about civil service employee salaries, a reporter would very likely interview civil servants who, naturally, will say that their salaries are lower than for comparable jobs in industry; and critics who, having raised the issue, can be expected to say that the salaries in question are higher than in the nongovernment business world. In fact, this routine has been gone through several times in recent years. Most reporters, of course, have no idea which side is right—they don't know enough about the topic to make an intelligent judgment. They don't know, for example, whether civil service job specifications truly describe what happens on the job day to day. How could they, given that the topic they investigated the week before might have been water pollution in Pennsylvania, while next week's topic will be job flight to Mexico?

Although the theory of objective news reporting often tends to deter journalists from saying what they believe or even know to be true, as just described, it doesn't absolutely forbid the mixing of news with evaluation or analysis. In fact, reporters have a modest amount of freedom to spout off, at least when no toes of the powerful are being stepped on. Nevertheless, the impossibility of being experts on every topic they must investigate, coupled with the need to seem authoritative, whether they know what they are talking about or not, often produces rather mixed results. For example, the journalists embedded with the troops during the Iraq and Afghanistan wars reported a piece of the action as they experienced it, but they had no concept of the big picture. And since much reporting was instantaneous, aired on television or radio as it was happening, they had no time to sort through the information and give it context. As a result, the audience got a slice of the battle but little evaluation or analysis that would come from mature deliberation over time.

> Thoughtfully written analysis is out, "live pops" are in. . . . Hire lookers, not writers. Do powder-puff, not probing, interviews. Stay away from controversial subjects. Kiss a___, move with the mass, and for heaven and the ratings' sake don't make anybody mad. . . . Make nice, not news.
>
> —DAN RATHER (OF CBS'S *EVENING NEWS*)

THE OPINIONS OF THE "RIGHT" AUTHORITIES TAKE PRECEDENCE

Since the reporters who gather the news are not usually experts in the fields they have to cover, they must, and do, seek out expert opinion. The trouble is that experts can be found on all sides of virtually every issue that is even mildly controversial. Which experts they consult thus becomes crucially important, and that is usually determined by just a very few factors.

Perhaps the most important consideration is whether an expert's opinions might be unpopular either with the intended audience or with advertisers or other power groups. Experts with views that might raise too many hackles tend to be overlooked (or, sometimes, used as foils). Mainstream experts dominate the field. These days, for example, positions on race, gender differences, pollution problems, and so on, generally have to stay within bounds set by the concern to be "politically correct" (PC).

Not all experts are trustworthy, however. When personal interest conflicts with public duty, ethical attitudes can disintegrate. This is exactly what happened when a group of high-ranking military officers were recruited by the Pentagon to sell the Iraq War to the American public. The *New York Times* ran a devastating, well-researched exposé of how these retired military experts became purveyors of Pentagon propaganda.[11] The article charted their activities in detail from the run-up to the war through the 2008 surge. Dubbed "key influentials" by the Pentagon, these military analysts were well-decorated, authoritative commentators who framed the way the audience should interpret the war. They didn't simply give objective descriptions of warfare in the battle zones or explain the capabilities of military hardware; they passed on the administration's ideology and helped establish its priorities. True, many of them believed that the war was justified and, since they had devoted their lives to the military, were understandably reluctant to criticize it. Nonetheless, there were powerful incentives for them to play along. Some were defense lobbyists, others were involved with helping companies win military contracts, and still others were board members of military contractors. What their willing participation gave them was access to power and influence and the opportunity for lucrative business deals. Eventually the Pentagon recruited over 75 retired officers, although some became disenchanted over time, and others were only briefly involved. Most of them appeared on Fox News and to a lesser extent on NBC, CNN, and other stations.

Thus, viewers who thought they were getting an objective analysis of the war were really getting a sell job. When journalists in Iraq began filing reports about the rise of insurgencies, the shortage of armor, the corruption of Iraqi security forces, and so on, the counterforce was the military analysts, briefed with Pentagon talking points, who assured the public that all was well. And the Pentagon monitored their media appearances, taking them to task if they criticized the war effort even mildly.

Meanwhile, the networks not only remained in the dark about the extensive interaction between the Pentagon and the military analysts, but they didn't seem to know that some analysts had business relationships with the Pentagon that could create conflicts of interest. And so the public was hoodwinked.

For two years the *New York Times* battled with the Defense Department, finally suing it successfully to gain access to 8,000 pages of documents describing the interaction between the Pentagon and the military analysts. So the news finally came out that these so-called experts were little more than shills for the Pentagon. This story, by the way, is journalism at its best—a trenchant analysis of government corruption, well substantiated by evidence.

---

[11]See: Barstow, David. "Message Machine: Behind TV Analysts, Pentagon's Hidden Hand." *New York Times,* 20 April 2008.

SELF-CENSORSHIP

The theory that news reporting should be objective does not require that all of the news, even all of the very important news, be reported. During wartime, for example, national security takes precedence. When U.S. troops were poised to invade Afghanistan in 2001, the media knew a full day in advance the exact time that the strikes would begin, but virtually no major media organization reported this information in the news. Even in peacetime, the media sometimes voluntarily suppress news out of a sense of duty. Perhaps the most famous instance of this kind occurred during John Kennedy's time as president, when the *New York Times* decided not to print reliable information about the impending attack on Cuba by U.S.-trained forces intent on overthrowing Fidel Castro.[12]

Sometimes, though, self-censorship happens for the worst of reasons. Charles and David Koch are billionaire brothers and longtime funders of conservative politicians and causes. If America has kingmakers, these are they. David Koch is also a board member and significant contributor to WNET, the New York City public television station. After a public television–funded film called *Park Avenue: Money, Power and the American Dream* ruffled Koch's feathers, another documentary that had been promised similar funding, this one about the influence of large donors on American Elections titled *Citizen Koch,* suddenly had its funding and distribution deal cut off. The good news is that the filmmakers were able to instead fund the film through a Kickstarter campaign. But it is troubling that even decisions about *public* television documentaries are determined by the influence of the rich and powerful few.

Also in 2013, Bloomberg News created some controversy when editors killed a story (and later suspended its writer) that was critical of China for fears that it would damage the news agency's relationship with the Chinese government.

But those who see self-censorship as automatically evil might consider the right of individuals to privacy in their nonpublic life. At what point does one draw the line? A person in the public eye is still, after all, entitled to a private life. Anyway, things are not as bad here as in, say, England, where the press hounded Princess Diana up to her death and continues to cover every move of her sons Prince William and Prince Harry.

In days long gone, the media felt more constrained in its reporting of the private lives of important public figures. It was well known to some in the press, for example, that both before and after his marriage—as a congressman, senator, and president—John Kennedy was quite a ladies' man. But the media, on the whole, chose not to divulge this feature of his private life. In those days, matters of this kind were usually passed over, even though they would have found an eager audience. With the advent of the Internet, though, the media no longer have the power to suppress details about the private lives of politicians and celebrities. Gossipy blogs and provocative photos crop up on Facebook, YouTube, and other social networks, eroding the line between public and private lives. As intimate details about public figures flood the Internet, the public no longer seems to take notice of information that once was off limits—a radical shift in attitude. (We'll discuss these issues in greater detail in the next chapter.)

---

[12]The invasion turned into a fiasco that was terribly embarrassing to the Kennedy administration. Kennedy himself is alleged later to have had the chutzpah to take the *Times* to task for this self-censorship on grounds that publication of the story by the *Times* might have resulted in the aborting of that ill-fated venture!

Last year, 300,000 Americans were arrested for smoking an herb that Queen Victoria used regularly for menstrual cramps.

It's a fact.

The herb, of course, is *cannabis sativa*. Otherwise known as marijuana, pot, grass, hemp, boo, mary-jane, ganja—the nicknames are legion.

So are the people who smoke it.

By all reckoning, it's fast becoming the new national pastime. Twenty-six million smokers, by some accounts—lots more by others. Whatever the estimate, a staggeringly high percentage of the population become potential criminals simply by being in possession of it. And the numbers are increasing.

For years, we've been told that marijuana leads to madness, sex-crimes, hard-drug usage and even occasional warts.

Pure Victorian poppycock.

In 1894, The Indian Hemp Commission reported marijuana to be relatively harmless. A fact that has been substantiated time and again in study after study.

Including, most recently, by the President's own Commission. This report stands as an indictment of the pot laws themselves.

And that's why more and more legislators are turning on to the fact that the present marijuana laws are as archaic as dear old Victoria's code of morality. And that they must be changed. Recently, the state of Oregon did, in fact, de-criminalize marijuana. Successfully.

Other states are beginning to move in that direction. They must be encouraged.

NORML has been and is educating the legislators, working in the courts and with the lawmakers to change the laws. We're doing our best but still, we need help. Yours.

Used with permission of NORML.

Ad censorship. NORML marijuana ad rejected by Time *and* Newsweek, *accepted by* Playboy.

4. Devices Used to Slant the News

So far, we have been considering why the media slant the news and how that affects story selection. Now let's take a brief look at a few of the many devices used to accomplish this task. (The examples are taken primarily from newspapers and magazines, but television, radio, and news websites have their analogues.)

STORIES CAN BE PLAYED UP OR DOWN

Breaking news of immense interest, like the killing of Osama bin Laden, for instance, is always played up in the news. Reports of the risky mission carried out in the dead of night by the elite Navy Seals riveted the entire nation. Gory photos of mangled bodies in blood-soaked rooms flickered across TV screens as commentators described the stealthy assault on the bin Laden compound. This is the stuff that newsrooms love. And the secrecy of the mission, hidden even from the Pakistani government, made it all the more tantalizing. But not all news is that compelling. Often stories are played up because of audience interest or media bias. If the interest isn't there, the story may be buried by placing it on page 59 or by packing the undesirable material toward the end of an otherwise acceptable story.

Calvin & Hobbes © Watterson. Reprinted with permission of Universal Press Syndicate. All rights reserved.

Of course, the most obvious way to bury the news is simply to ignore it. Bad news becomes no news when the media doesn't cover it. Project Censored, a media watchdog, noted in their 2012 report that one of the least-reported stories in 2011 was that the U.S. military had developed software to create fake online personas that behave like real people on social media, in order to spread American propaganda in the Middle East. These fake people, who have convincing histories and backgrounds of their own, are apparently weapons of psychological warfare used to encounter the online presence of al Qaeda and other extremists resisting American presence in the Middle East. We are assured that it would be unlawful to unleash these fake people in U.S. social media, so it's not going to happen here—we hope.

Other, less dramatic omissions occur as well. For instance, newspapers often inform readers about which movies are drawing the largest audiences, which records are selling best, and so on. But the *New York Times,* for obscure reasons of its own, routinely excludes religious books (Bibles and so forth) and "romance" (Harlequin) paperbacks from its lists of best-selling books, even though together these two kinds of publications account for a very large slice of the book market.

MISLEADING, SENSATIONAL, OR OPINIONATED HEADLINES CAN BE USED

Many more people read the headlines on stories than read the accounts that follow. So even if an account itself is accurate, a misleading or sensational headline (generally not written by whoever wrote the news report itself) distorts the news for many readers. For example, a *Los Angeles Times* headline (June 16, 2010)—

"Debate Grows Over Afghanistan Drawdown Plan"

—implied that opposing points of view would be given on whether the United States should pull out of Afghanistan.[13] But the article's sources were U.S. military officials and John McCain—all of whom had serious reservations about a withdrawal timeline. No mention was made of the opposing position held by 53 percent of the American public at the time, who thought the war wasn't worth fighting. So the "debate" in the headline was no debate, but the opinion of promilitary sources on one side of the issue.

Often, slanting through headlines is more subtle. For instance, in 2016, Facebook faced some national scrutiny following accusations that the company suppressed conservative-friendly news in its "Trending Topics." In the same 24 hours (May 9–10) and operating with essentially the same information, various news media provided different headlines for the story:

- "Conservatives Accuse Facebook of Political Bias" (*New York Times*)
- "Facebook Rebuts Criticisms about a Bias against Conservatives" (*Wall Street Journal*)
- "Former Facebook Staffers Say Conservative News Is Deliberately Suppressed" (FoxNews.com)
- "Report Claiming Bias in Facebook 'Trending' Topics Sparks Social Media Outcry" (*Reuters*)
- "You Won't Read This on Facebook: Site Censors the News" (*New York Post*)
- "Senate Republicans Rush to Investigate Allegations of Facebook News Bias— Still Refuse to Hold Hearings for SCOTUS Nominee" (Salon.com)
- "Did Facebook Bury Conservative News? Ex-Staffers Say Yes" (*Washington Post*)
- "Report: Facebook Suppresses Conservative Outlets, Amplifies 'Black Lives Matter'" (Breitbart.com)

Notice that all of these headlines could be accurate, but their various uses of language paint different pictures. What exactly is the story about which the public needs to know? Is it about bias at Facebook, accusations of bias at Facebook, or certain responses to accusations of bias at Facebook? If you knew nothing about these sources, what would you guess about their own political leanings from the headlines above?

---

[13]Cited in *Extra!* August 2010.

IMAGES CAN SLANT THE NEWS

Image has been important in American politics since before George Washington refused a crown and declined a third term as president because he didn't want to create the wrong image. Abraham Lincoln played up his image as a rail-splitting back woodsman reared in a log cabin in the Illinois wilderness. But in those days, news traveled slowly and photography was either nonexistent (in Washington's time) or in its infant stages (in Lincoln's). With the advent of television, visual images began to dominate the scene. Starting with John F. Kennedy and his photogenic family, the emphasis on visual imagery began to increase. Today image triumphs over content for most people.[14]

Now that photos can be transmitted instantaneously around the world, the power of imagery has enormous impact internationally as well as nationally. Knowing full well the effect of disturbing pictures on the public, the second Bush administration refused to allow coverage of the flag-draped coffins that were returned from Iraq to Dover Air Force Base, Delaware. But provocative photos tend to slip through the cracks no matter how carefully they are guarded. (The coffin footage eventually surfaced.) The most notorious example of the Iraq war was the graphic photos of U.S. soldiers abusing and humiliating Iraqi prisoners at Abu Ghraib. The *60 Minutes II* airing of this footage sent shock waves around the world. Americans were horrified, Iraqis were alienated, and the popularity of the Bush administration plummeted in the polls. The Arab media were quick to respond. Although some of the coverage was evenhanded, media outlets opposed to U.S. intervention used the photos to inflame anti-American feelings. In the case of Abu Ghraib, the image was the story.

On April 25, 2015, the leftist news website CommonDreams.org ran a story about the aforementioned protests in Baltimore following the death of Freddie Gray in police custody earlier that month. Under the headline "Baltimore Rally Aims to Ensure Latest Death of Black Man at Hands of Police Won't 'Be in Vain,'" Common Dreams ran a picture of a multiracial crowd of peaceful protesters holding signs. The same day, the right-leaning Breitbart.com displayed a picture of two men, one white, one black, engaged in a fistfight in front of a Baltimore bar. Breitbart's headline read: "War Zone: Baltimore Erupts into Violence, Chaos as #BlackLivesMatter Riots Rage." Both of these photos were taken from reputable sources (the *Baltimore Sun* and Associated Press, respectively) and both show events that actually happened in Baltimore around the same time. But they were chosen to tell the story that each site wanted to tell. They were both presented as though they were indicative of the mood and tenor of protests in Baltimore at the time. In an age when people rely more and more on visual imagery for the news, it is no exaggeration to say that photos have far greater impact than the written word. They just can't be relied upon to tell a more objective or accurate story.

FOLLOW-UP STORIES CAN BE OMITTED OR PLAYED DOWN

There are a number of reasons why follow-up stories rarely make headlines. The first is that they are more difficult to obtain than breaking news stories. It takes much less time and effort to record the fact that a bank has failed than to follow up details of an ensuing court

---

[14]For more on this, see: Wahl, Richard C. "The Triumph of the Image." *Columbia Review of Journalism,* November–December 2003.

case against its directors. The second is that the public (and media) conception of "news" is what is new, and follow-up stories seem like just more of the same, or just plain humdrum.

Breaking news is often sensationalized, but follow-up stories usually aren't sexy enough to grab the audience's interest, so the media ignore them. For example, from August to October 2010, the media ran a story that electrified the public about 33 Chilean miners trapped in a coal mine in San Jose, Chile. Their drama unfolded in painstaking detail, covering their special diets and exercise routine, the rescue efforts of engineers and drill operators, and the families and friends camped out above ground anxiously waiting for their return. When a half-mile shaft was finally constructed through solid rock and the rescue was imminent, the entire world cheered as they struggled to the surface. They had endured underground longer than survivors of any other mine accident, and they were rewarded with acclaim and showered with gifts—like motor bikes from Kawasaki, and $15,000 each from a Chilean businessman. But that was the end of the story. Everyone assumed that they lived happily ever after, and no follow-up stories appeared to contradict this perception. A year later, though, on the anniversary of the rescue, a few scattered articles in papers such as the *New York Times* and the *Guardian* mention that most of the miners had returned to poverty, and some were worse off, suffering from psychological and physical trauma after the ordeal. Little was made of their tragedy, and most people thought they continued to thrive. Then in 2015, the *Guardian* reported that nine of the miners had filed suit against their attorneys for poorly advising them and theft of profits from *The 33,* a film based on their ordeal starring Antonio Banderas, as well as other productions and publications inspired by their story. Stories, like the lives they cover, usually keep going after substantial press interest in them has faded. We will have to wait (and hope) for subsequent follow-ups.

One reason for the paucity of follow-up stories is that most of us have short attention spans. Except for "ongoing" stories—wars providing the best examples—people tend to tire of any topic quickly. When bored, it's all too easy to flip the switch to another channel or to put down the newspaper and instead watch some tawdry reality show.

Well, no one can be in favor of boredom. The problem is that in the vast majority of cases, the time-consuming details make all the difference. Ten-second news sound bites aren't all that different from "Chevrolet—the Heartbeat of America" or "Magnavox—Smart, Very Smart." Short and easily remembered usually drives out long and complicated. That may well be the chief reason relevant background information and follow-up tend to be in short supply.

Occasionally, though, the media makes a concerted effort to follow through on old stories. One example is the *Lincoln Journal Star* in Nebraska, whose editor, Peter Salter, decided to fill in the Monday edition (traditionally thin on news) with follow-ups on old stories in their files.[15] Reporters took turns writing about any item of interest in the paper's archives and came up with a wide range of topics. The column, called "Epilogue," covered such items as a woman who had half her brain removed surgically ten years earlier (she lost the use of the right side of her body but learned to walk and talk again), and a man jailed five years previously for impregnating and marrying a 13-year-old (they were still married and had three children). The stories were so popular

---

[15]Fenwick, Alexandra. "Darts and Laurels." *Columbia Journalism Review,* September–October 2010.

that they consistently made the front page, and they were so unusual that the *Columbia Journalism Review* awarded the paper a "laurel" for doing systematic follow-up on stories, a rare practice in journalism.

POINTS OF VIEW CAN BE CONVEYED VIA CARTOONS AND COMIC STRIPS

According to the old saying, a picture is worth a thousand words, which may account for the ability of cartoons and comic strips to effectively—graphically—make a point. In any case, it most certainly accounts for the large number of these pertinent cartoons that have been reprinted in this particular textbook. A clever practitioner of the cartoonist's art can puncture prejudices and force us to open our eyes to unpleasant truths in a way that few others can match.

The *Doonesbury* strip, crafted by Garry Trudeau, deserves special mention here because it has been in the forefront of a minor trend on newspaper comic pages to feature strips that at least occasionally touch on social or political issues rather than just tickling the funny bone. A classic cartoon and a particular favorite of the authors of this text (one of whom is a UCLA alum) is the 1994 *Doonesbury* series that poked fun at the hiring of junk bond ex-con Michael Milken to teach a business course at UCLA. In one panel, Milken is pictured saying, "Who is Professor Milken, the genius who created a new world of financial instruments? Well, I'm many things, of course. But most of all, I'm a survivor. After a 98-count indictment and a 6-count plea bargain, I'm still here— and with $1 billion to show for it!" after which students repeat his code: "Greed works! Crime pays! Everybody does it!" In another strip, Milken states what must certainly be his actual opinion on the matter: that government attempts at regulation are a joke and government employees no match for "a true visionary and his defense team." Students are shown booing the student who has the temerity to ask a pertinent question: "As the key player of the greatest criminal conspiracy in the history of finance, do you think justice was served by your brief stay in a country club prison?" Interesting, isn't it, that this cartoon is just as relevant today as it was when it first appeared.

Unfortunately, this ability of comic strips to graphically make a point sometimes results in their being censored. *Doonesbury,* of course, bites the dust now and then. But even normally nonpolitical strips occasionally get the axe. For example, when a young boy in the *For Better or for Worse* comic strip summoned the courage to tell his parents that he was gay, the resulting furor came as a shock to the strip's creator, Lynn Johnston. The series of strips on this theme ran for just 10 days but was censored during that time in 40 papers, with 20 more canceling the strip outright. In Memphis, Tennessee, to cite just one city, about 2,000 readers canceled their subscriptions to the *Commercial Appeal* because that paper ran the strips they objected to. Johnston was flooded with mail, both pro and con, and stung by the anger and hate some letters exhibited. She wrote the series, she said, because several friends had died from AIDS, and one of her closest gay friends recently had been robbed and killed. "He was nothing more than a wonderful person and a good friend to me," she said. "My intent was to show that Lawrence [the gay boy in the strip] was different but that he's still the kid next door, still a member of the community, someone who should be judged on his moral character, not his genetic code."[16]

---

[16]See, for instance, the *San Francisco Examiner,* 25 April 1993.

Aaron McGruder's Boondocks *sometimes gets in trouble for its political satire.* Extra! *(December 2001) noted that this strip along with several others were pulled from some newspapers after September 11 because it was critical of U.S. foreign policy.*

In the United States, controversial cartoons may be censored or criticized, but they don't galvanize people into committing violent protests as they sometimes do in other countries. Cartoons featuring the Prophet Muhammad have incited violent protests from Islamists for almost a decade. When a Danish newspaper printed cartoons caricaturing Muhammad a few years ago, a group of fundamentalist Muslim clerics urged Middle Eastern embassies to demand a meeting with the Danish prime minister. He refused, and the protests escalated into violence. Hundreds of Iraqis demanded an apology from the European Union, Palestinians stormed through European buildings in Gaza and burned German and Danish flags, and thousands of Syrians torched the Danish and Norwegian embassies in Damascus. More recently, *Charlie Hebdo*, a French satirical weekly newspaper, released a cartoon cover on the Internet of an upcoming issue that featured Muhammad in a turban saying "100 lashes if you don't die laughing!" Hours before the issue was published, an arson fire swept through the Paris office of the newspaper, gutting the interior. After publishing more cartoon depictions of Muhammad (and featuring a novel many claim is Islamophobic) the *Charlie Hebdo* offices were attacked by gunmen in 2015. Twelve people were killed. It may be in poor taste to print these sorts of depictions given how many people are so deeply offended by them. But of course, even the deepest and most personal offense is never justification for murder.

5. Television and the Internet

For the last half of the twentieth century, television was by far the most important mass medium. More households own television sets than bathtubs and showers. (Interesting facts: The average number of TVs per household is 2.5, and 31 percent of Americans own four or more TVs.) It would be hard to overestimate the effects of television on everyday life. (One thinks, for a parallel, of the ways in which the automobile has transformed the world.)

Consider, for instance, the ways in which news reporting has helped break down prejudices. It was a very important event indeed the first time a woman, Barbara Walters, read the evening news to us on national TV, and an equally important event the first time an African American, Max Robinson, did so. In recent years, the number of TV commentators with diverse backgrounds has grown. When Barack Obama and Hillary Clinton vied for the Democratic presidential nomination, race and gender issues dominated campaign coverage as never before. To address these issues, cable news stations brought in seasoned minority analysts who hadn't had much exposure in the mainstream media. TV exposure also influenced the public's attitude about homosexuality. Although gay newscasters had long kept their sexual orientation under wraps, all that changed when news anchors such as Anderson Cooper publicly acknowledged being gay.

But perhaps the most graphic illustration of television's power to change the world is in its effect on the nature of war and associated diplomacy. It is a commonplace today that television shortened American involvement in the war in Vietnam through its living-room coverage, but insufficient notice has yet been taken of the way in which TV influenced the conduct of the Gulf War, the Iraq War, and the war in Afghanistan. The American government and its coalition allies were exceedingly careful to reduce the number of casualties, not just of their own forces but also of enemy civilians, in a way that (in the long history of warfare) has rarely, if ever before, been true. Compare that, for instance, with the American and British record of mass bombings of civilians in World War II, when television was not peeking over every general's shoulder.

Even sitcoms and the other prime-time entertainment programs sometimes have positive effects—in addition to providing entertainment—a case in point being their role in reducing ethnic and gender prejudice, one of the great improvements that has taken place in the United States (and most other democratic nations) since World War II. African Americans are portrayed as middle-class workers, not just as janitors or (the very expression is odious) cotton pickers, and women as business executives, not just housewives.

> Television is the first truly democratic culture—the first culture available to everybody and entirely governed by what people want. The most terrifying thing is what people do want.
>
> —CLIVE BARKER

Calvin & Hobbes © Watterson. Reprinted with permission of Universal Press Syndicate. All rights reserved.

When we think of the mass media, it's important to remember that at least one-third of American adults are or come close to being functionally illiterate. For them, and for many others, a picture is worth more than a thousand words. So for the mass of people, by default, television is the best news source. (Note, by the way, that it's much easier to become a couch potato and endlessly watch the tube than it is, say, to search the Internet for interesting material.)

But capturing and informing this kind of mass audience requires extremely tight editing (matched in print only by advertisements). The average attention span is short, and comprehension limited. TV does a better job than the other media in editing the news so that it can be understood, somewhat, by most Americans. However, a recent trend in cluttering the screen with multiple images tends to undermine otherwise concise editing. Even the most focused viewer gets distracted by split-screen pictures with headlines underneath and crawling commentary at the bottom.

THE INTERNET

For the past several years, the audience growth in Internet news has outpaced growth in any other news source—not surprising, now that nearly three-quarters of U.S. adults own laptops or desktop computers and 64 percent own smartphones. The advantages of using the Internet are obvious. It can be, and often is, more up to date than the best reference books; it allows people everywhere to read some of the best newspapers and magazines in the land; and it often is more readily available than books or other print media. The world of online journalism continues to expand. All of the major media outlets have Internet presences, including broadcast networks, cable networks, newspapers, and news magazines. In addition, Google News provides access to English-language news sites around the world. An outgrowth of the Google search engine, Google News draws on stories from 4,000 news sites, updating items on a second-by-second basis.

For an in-depth look at the news, websites have the capability of offering extensive links to background sources like archived material and related stories, interviews, or photographs. In this way, websites can provide much more information than a newspaper or magazine article. For instance, when the *New York Times* ran an article revealing that President Obama personally oversaw drone attacks on top terrorists, the online version was studded with links to related sources.[17] With a flick of the finger, readers could access Obama's counterterrorism record, the legal case for killing America citizens who are al Qaeda operatives, Obama's speech defending his policies, and editorials questioning the power of presidents to make such attacks. This deep background fleshed out the report on a very controversial subject in ways that a newspaper or magazine article could never do, giving the *Times'* users a chance to examine related sources and judge for themselves the morality and legality at issue.

Although the Internet is a wonderful source of information, the downside is that it spawns so much more schlock than even the TV networks do. It takes a rather sophisticated user to separate the wheat from the chaff. Of course, this is always a problem; the point is that it becomes more urgent to be able to do this well online. (Instructors

---

[17]Becker, Jo and Shank, Scott. "Secret 'Kill List' Proves a Test of Obama's Principles and Will." *New York Times,* 29 May 2012.

regularly tear their hair out when students turn in papers based on second-rate Internet sources.) The Internet is now inundated with bloggers and citizen reporters, and though they sometimes have more expertise in a particular field than career journalists, they often express strong biases that professionals try to avoid in straight news reporting.

6. The Non-Mass Media to the Rescue

The mass media are a reasonably good source of information about breaking stories—speeches made by important officials, fluctuations in the Dow, bills passed by Congress (but not about a bill's value, or who benefits and who is harmed!), and so on. Television does these stories rather well, at least when it can get good visuals. But for detailed, sophisticated, in-depth accounts, and for analysis that doesn't just parrot what powerful people are saying, the non-mass media are indispensable.

Strengths and Weaknesses

Todd Oppenheimer, a seasoned journalist, on the limitations of "citizen journalists" who report news on the Internet:

. . . [I]t's one thing (a good idea) to use citizen journalists for material from the field, such as on-the-scene accounts from a Hurricane Katrina, or soldier diaries from the trenches of Iraq. It's quite another (a bad idea) to expect amateurs to figure out who is telling the truth about Iraq, or which priests have committed pedophilia. Stories in this later category obviously require skill in a host of exacting tasks, such as interviewing evasive sources, understanding how and where bureaucracies hide evidence and writing a narrative that is compelling yet properly sourced. . . .

In every field, standards are devised and continually refined by the profession's senior members. These masters earn their wisdom through years of challenging, often painful experiences. Their duty is to pass on their lessons to up-and-comers, who should serve some demanding period of apprenticeship. This is how every profession achieves its high ideals. In the media's case, those standards involve strong writing, fairness and independence, thoroughness and accuracy, ethics and astute judgment.

—From "Read All About It—But Where Exactly?" *San Francisco Chronicle*, 17 October 2007; an insightful article about the current state of journalism

The commercial networks do feature several rather good investigative, in-depth programs—namely *60 Minutes, Nightline,* and *20/20.* But the Public Broadcasting Service (PBS) provides the best television news—best without doubt, for in-depth reporting and analysis on programs like *The News Hour, Charlie Rose* (for penetrating interviews on a wide range of topics) and *Washington Week* (for news analysis). Indeed, in most ways, PBS is perhaps the brightest spot on the television spectrum. But those viewers who are on cable, which means most people, can also click on the Discovery Channel, the National Geographic Channel, Arts and Entertainment, C-Span, and, of course, CNN, which still gives its viewers a reasonably well-balanced account of the news. Then there are the two NBC news channels, the Fox News Channel, and for science, *Nova* (PBS), an excellent, high-level program that examines cutting-edge issues in science.

Nevertheless, TV still easily is eclipsed by the few good daily newspapers and especially by small-circulation magazines and journals. The mass media, even the big-city newspapers, generally focus on what is current, in the air, neglecting the underlying forces that ultimately determine what will be big news at a later date.

In addition, they often cover important stories that slide under the radar. For example, *Extra!* a media watchdog that evaluates news coverage, reported on the mass media's failure to cover adequately the startling testimony on wiretapping by Former Deputy General James Comey in May 2007.[18] The story is not only gripping but reveals a disturbing behind-the-scenes attempt to ambush the Justice Department. When U.S. Attorney General John Ashcroft was hospitalized for gall bladder surgery in 2004, Comey, as acting attorney general, refused to sign an extension of the controversial wiretapping program partly because it was considered illegal by the Justice Department's legal counsel. In a scene right out of a film noir, the White House chief of staff at the time, Andrew Card, and counsel Alberto Gonzales hurried to Ashcroft's bedside to persuade the very sick man to overturn Comey's ruling. Meanwhile, Comey and FBI director Robert Mueller got wind of the ambush and rushed to the hospital to intervene. But Ashcroft rallied his strength, rose to the occasion, and dramatically quashed the attempt. The media could have had a field day with this sensational, important story, but they didn't. Although the *New York Times* and *Newsweek* mentioned it in 2006, Comey's testimony before the Senate Judiciary Committee a year later got little notice except from a *Washington Post* editorial critical of the president for proceeding with a program that the Justice Department itself considered illegal. As *Extra!* points out, this significant scandal never even appeared in most of the mass media. This is the type of revelation that the non-mass media bring to our attention. (See an annotated list of publications at the end of the book for examples, and for some thoughts by the authors of this text concerning some of these important information sources.)

Finding out what is really going on, however, isn't so much a matter of mass versus non-mass media as it is of learning how to be selective—learning how to separate pearls from schlock. Those interested in science, for example, would do well to avoid newsstand magazines that pander to the appetite so many people have for stories about ESP and other matters on the edge of legitimate science and that try to sensationalize science to increase sales. (Will stories about "close encounters of the third kind" ever go away?)

The point is that the non-mass media contain lots more pearls per square inch and are, on the whole, a good deal more sophisticated in their discussions of what is going on in the world than are newspapers, TV, and even mass-sales books. Best-selling books—for instance, those concerning politics, economics, and the like—often are shallow or sensationalist.

---

[18]Hart, Peter. "Illegal Yes—But Not Newsworthy." *Extra! Update,* June 2007.

Of particular note are the self-serving memoirs of "distinguished statesmen," such as Dick Cheney, that are often little more than bald-faced attempts to rewrite history in their favor. Presidential memoirs, supposedly written by former presidents, are perhaps the most self-serving of these tomes. *Example:* Ronald Reagan's *An American Life* (Simon & Schuster, 1990), apparently written by Robert Lindsey (whom Reagan credits by saying "Robert Lindsey, a talented writer, was with me every step of the way"). Also, Bill Clinton's *My Life* (Knopf, 2004), written in longhand by Clinton himself, he claimed, played up his triumphs and played down his failures (as do most presidential memoirs), George W. Bush's *Decision Points* cherry-picked his successes and skipped passed his failures (though he did admit that he has a "sickening feeling" over the failure to find weapons of mass destruction in Iraq).

We should note, by the way, that National Public Radio (NPR) does a better job of presenting the news and analysis than does any television channel or most other radio outlets. Some examples of their regular programs are *All Things Considered, Talk of the Nation, BBC World News, Fresh Air, Science Friday,* and *As It Happens,* an excellent Canadian news program broadcast widely in the United States. For news media coverage *of* the news media, including a number of the issues we discuss in this chapter, NPR's *On the Media* is a terrific source.

One particularly encouraging development over the last few years has been the emergence and increased prominence of so-called "nonprofit newsrooms." In the absence of a clear and effective business model for providing quality news, it may be that the proper model is not treating news-gathering as a *business* at all. One interesting example is *ProPublica,* an organization that focuses on investigative journalism and is funded by contributions rather than advertising or subscriptions.

Another bright spot is the emergence of largely online "hyperlocal" newsrooms. Funded either by advertising or contributions, these sites sometimes have full staffs, filling in some of the gaps left by discontinued local beats.

6. News Media Concentration

During the past 30 years or so, dramatic changes have been taking place in the news business. Perhaps the most important of these is the ever-increasing concentration of media ownership, and thus power, in fewer and fewer hands.

The first and much smaller concentration of media power occurred way back in the late nineteenth century with the development of newspaper chains—the most important, perhaps, being the one put together by William Randolph Hearst and fictionalized in the movie classic *Citizen Kane.* The power of these early media magnates is illustrated in that film by a scene in which a journalist sent to Cuba in 1898 reports back that there is no sign of war in Cuba, only to be told that Kane (Hearst) would supply the war. (The scene is a takeoff on what is held by some to be true: that U.S. involvement in the Spanish-American War was in large part due to the Hearst publications' sensationalistic journalism. More likely, though, it was just one of many factors leading to that one-sided, unprovoked, war.)

The power of the Hearst media empire was illustrated again in 1941 when Hearst forced RKO, the producer of *Citizen Kane,* not to show that film in its theaters nationwide. The threat was to refuse ads listing any RKO theater offerings in Hearst's many newspapers around the country, which would have caused RKO a tremendous financial loss.

This blacklisting of *Citizen Kane* nicely illustrates the great censorship potential of concentrated media power. But back in those days, all big cities had more than one newspaper so that no small group or individuals could effectively control the newspaper business. (It was not until the 1950s that television usurped the role of newspapers as the principal news source for a growing majority of people in the United States and Canada.)

> The founders of this country believed a free and rambunctious press was essential to the protection of our freedoms. They couldn't envision the rise of giant megamedia conglomerates whose interests converge with state power to produce a conspiracy against the people. I think they would be aghast at how this union of media and government has produced the very kind of imperial power against which they rebelled.
>
> —MOYERS, BILL. "ON MEDIA AND DEMOCRACY."
> *NATION*, 15 DECEMBER 2003

Today's media conglomerates are a good deal more worrisome than were the newspaper chains of old, because they concentrate power into an extremely few hands in all of the major news media—television, radio, mass-circulation magazines and newspapers, and the Internet. Independent newspapers still exist in some cities and towns, but their number shrinks every year, and most big cities now are down to just one daily paper, usually owned by a large and powerful chain. So today, a single individual may control quite a few TV outlets as well as newspapers and magazines.

Equally troubling is the fact that the giant media empires have multiple business interests outside the news media world that provide enormous opportunity for product sales and promotion. The ruling principle of these megacorporations is the bottom line, not the best possible dissemination of news. Here is a list of some of the holdings of the top three of these huge media giants:

- **Comcast** has majority ownership of NBCUniversal, Telemundo, CNBC, Universal Pictures, online platforms like Daily Candy and Fandango, XFINITY TV and Internet, TiVO, VeriSign and Comcast Interactive Media.
- **Walt Disney** owns ABC (*ABC Network News*, *Prime Time Live*), 80 percent of ESPN, dozens of radio stations, Walt Disney Pictures (including Pixar animation), Hyperion Books, Disney Publishing Worldwide, Disney Interactive Media Group, and Disney Music Group.
- **News Corporation and 21st Century Fox** constitute Rupert Murdoch's international conglomerate, and include Fox Networks, STAR India, Twentieth Century Fox Film, the international Shine Group, over two dozen U.S. television stations, Direct Broadcast Satellite Television which includes the international Sky TV channels, as well as numerous print holdings.

Then there are gigantic newspaper corporations like Gannett, Tribune, and the New York Times; book publishers like Bertlesmann, Pearson, and Hachette, and Internet giants like Google and Yahoo. And let's not forget Time Warner, which has a hand in just about facet of media.[19]

Well, then, why should the rest of us care about this concentration of media power into fewer and fewer hands? Doesn't size, after all, yield efficiency? Aren't large news companies better able to afford large staffs of reporters gathering news items around the world? The answer to both of these questions may well be yes. But three other nagging questions immediately arise. Will being *able to afford* larger staffs automatically translate in practice into larger staffs? Will greater efficiency generally translate into better news reporting or simply into greater profits? Will media moguls resist the temptation to further their own interests, including the interests of their own nonnews subsidiaries, at the expense of news quality and fair evaluation? The answer to all of these questions, unfortunately, seems to be *no*.

Item: When cartoonist Dan Wasserman made edgy fun of the Boston Museum of Fine Arts (MFA) and Bank of America (a massive corporate contributor), the *Boston Globe* literally stopped the presses to pull the editorial cartoon scheduled to run on the

THE FINAL MERGER

Mick Stevens The New Yorker Collection/The Cartoon Bank

[19]Much of the information in this section comes from the *Columbia Journalism Review*'s excellent resource at http://www.cjr.org/resources. Check back there for updates on this list, as media companies have a habit of changing hands, breaking up and merging with some regularity.

day that the opening of the MFA's new wing was to be celebrated.[20] In the run-up to the opening, the *Globe* had covered the MFA expansion at length and in depth—including a 56-page magazine commemorating the event with a full-page ad from Bank of America. Why was the cartoon pulled? Because it showed an MFA exhibition of all the houses Bank of America foreclosed on!

Since megacorporations are profit driven and risk averse, one consequence of their dominating the industry is that the quality of programming has gone down in recent years, so instead of getting high-caliber, innovative sitcoms like the Mary Tyler Moore productions in the 1970s, for example, we get reality TV—cheap thrills that cost a fraction of a good sitcom to produce. Even more important, though, is that big media have the ability to limit the free exchange of ideas and thus undermine democracy. Because they are able to control the news, they can (and do) limit the range of information and debate from diverse sources, slant the news to their advantage, and kill stories that threaten their own interests.[21]

Item: When *Frontline* showed the documentary "Hand of God," their PBS affiliate in Brownsville, Texas, KMBH, claimed it didn't get the video feed in time to air the program in January 2007. But critics, knowing the station was owned by the Roman Catholic diocese of Brownsville, suspected the real reason was that the documentary dealt with child molestations by Catholic priests.

Another disturbing issue closely connected to the concentration of media power in a few companies is the cozy relationship between media giants and corporate America. Project Censored did a study of media interlocks with big corporations and found that all 118 board members of the ten largest media companies sat on boards of 288 national and international corporations.[22] Not only that, but eight out of 10 of these media companies had board memberships in common with each other. The *Washington Post* and NBC, for instance, both had board members with seats on J. P. Morgan and Coca-Cola. The *New York Times* and Gannett had members with seats on Pepsi.

These interlocking connections raise obvious conflicts of interest. How likely is a network or newspaper to play down or ignore news stories harmful to companies with close ties? Very likely. And how tempting would it be to play up the products and images of these companies? Tempting, indeed. Take, for example, an NBC *Today* show (April 30, 2007) that featured Matt Lauer making glowing comments about Boeing aircraft in a segment shot at their Everett, Washington, factory. His "full disclosure" that Boeing is owned by NBC's parent company, General Electric, was a blip on the screen compared to the footage given to the favorable coverage of Boeing's 777s. Viewers were assured that the planes would make flying more comfortable, safer, and cost effective and would

---

[20]Kennedy, Dan. "What Was Missing from Today's *Boston Globe*." *Media Nation,* 14 November 2010.

[21]For more on this, see: Turner, Ted. "My Beef with Big Media." *Washington Monthly,* July–August 2004. Turner focuses in particular on the way big media increasingly shut out independent entrepreneurs with diverse points of view but not enough cash or clout to compete with the big guys.

[22]For a full discussion and list of overlaps between media giants and corporations, see: Phillips, Peter. "Big Media Interlocks with Corporate America." *Project Censored,* 2 May 2010. Web. http://www.projectcensored.org/.

boost the U.S. economy. Not only that, employees loved making this "great product." The sign-off, "If it ain't Boeing, we ain't going," added the final touch. With news stories like this, "why bother with commercials?"[23]

AN AFTERWORD

All is not lost, though. While it is true that media giants can have a corrupting influence and the public's demand for sensationalism can fuel the gutter press, it is also true that good journalism still exists and continues to have a significant effect on our collective understanding and attitudes. As Ben Bradlee, legendary editor of the *Washington Post* wrote, "There is much to criticize about the press, but not before recognizing a ringing truth: the best of the American press is an extraordinary daily example of industry, honesty, conscience, and courage, driven by a desire to inform and interest readers."[24]

Over the past 50 years, the media have exposed significant wrongdoings, sometimes at considerable risk. Think back to two blockbusters—the Pentagon Papers and the Watergate scandal. When the *New York Times* published excerpts of the Pentagon Papers revealing that the Johnson and Kennedy administrations had systematically lied to the public and Congress about starting and expanding the war in Southeast Asia, it blew the lid off the Vietnam War. Then along came the Watergate scandal, painstakingly unearthed over two years by the *Washington Post,* which culminated in the resignation of President Nixon under threat of impeachment. Explosive stories like these require the kind of courage and sense of mission to expose deception in government that represents the best in journalism.

While these iconic stories have gained lasting fame, thousands of others have appeared in the national and local media, revealing not only corruption and deception in government and business (such as the seemingly ceaseless reporting on the 2,522-and-counting public corruption convictions in New York State since 1970), but stories about the heroism of everyday citizens (like *Pittsburgh Magazine*'s 2011 feature on Dr. Jim Withers, who has provided "house call" medical services to Pittsburgh's homeless for decades) or news about the plight of regions where disaster strikes (like the *Times-Picayune*'s valiant reports of conditions in New Orleans as Hurricane Katrina battered the city and flooded the newspaper offices). At their best, the news media are an invaluable source of information and analysis. While there is much to criticize, there is also much to praise.

Summary of Chapter 11

1.   The news media have been going through a huge transformation. Technological advances like the Internet have created new ways for people to access the news, and as a result, traditional news outlets have been shrinking. These new trends in journalism require us to be even more vigilant in thinking critically about the ways the news is managed and presented to the public. The one overriding fact

---

[23]Example from "Fear & Favor 2007." *Extra!* March–April 2008.

[24]From *A Good Life*, Ben Bradlee's autobiography, an absorbing insider account of journalism in the last half of the twentieth century.

about all news sources is that they are businesses intent on making money. So they have to satisfy their audiences, advertisers, and governments.

They cater to their audiences by simplifying the news to make it more easily understood—by breaking news items into small sound bites that stay within the average attention span in length and by arranging coverage of news so as to conform to audience interests and prejudices.

The media cater to advertisers by suppressing news that reflects badly on them or their products and by touting advertisers' products free as "news" items. **Example:** the *Pioneer Press* quashing a review critical of a restaurant that advertised in the paper.

The media also has to take account of the power of government to harass them by rescinding licenses, restricting access to government records, censoring information that doesn't conform to their political agenda, playing favorites in the dissemination of news, and fining networks for broadcasting indecent material. **Example:** the half-million-dollar fine slapped on CBS for airing Janet Jackson's indecent exposure during her halftime Super Bowl performance. The media often give in to this power of government by treading more carefully in criticizing government actions. **Example:** reporters at press conferences who are careful not to ask overly pointed follow-up questions. Another way the government manages the news is by inserting into newscasts prepackaged reports that get their message out or put a positive spin on the news. (Note that the power of government to censor is much greater in many other countries than in the United States and in some other industrial democracies.)

But the mass media have a good deal of power of their own, stemming from their ability to expose and publicize whatever they care to. **Famous example:** the *Washington Post*'s dogged exposé of the Watergate scandal that forced President Nixon to resign in disgrace.

The business world—in particular, very large corporations—have a large say in the dissemination of news. They often use this power, first, to suppress stories unfavorable to their own narrow interests and, second, to get favorable stories included in media presentations. This power of big business stems from its power as advertisers (to withdraw advertising), from its ability to influence politicians and governments (principally through "campaign contributions") and from its ownership of a good deal of the mass media.

Of course, in practice the media tend to try to satisfy all of the various power factions and not to needlessly throw their weight around. It almost always is more profitable to cooperate with power than to fight it. **Example:** politicians and the media cooperating to produce sound bites: The pols get exposure, and the media get cheap footage to show on the evening news. Unfortunately, the news has increasingly become a source of excitement and entertainment more than useful and important information, as evidenced in the media's coverage of the recent Ebola outbreak.

Since the bottom line is, as they say, the bottom line, news-gathering methods tend to be designed to save money, which means that regular beats are set up to gather the news from those able to regularly supply it (the rich and powerful and the government). True investigative reporting is very costly and thus relatively less common than a mere gathering of the news from other sources. ***Example:*** the regular attendance at presidential press conferences as compared to the amount of journalistic digging below the surface.

2.   For reasons already mentioned, the media tend to misdirect audience attention away from important, underlying issues and events to human interest stories. In doing this, they tend to take advantage of the average person's lack of a good sense of proportion. ***Example:*** playing up celebrity scandals and playing down or ignoring serious issues.

3.   The media's theory of objectivity, to which lip service is widely paid, requires that news stories be separated from speculations, judgments, evaluations, and the like, which are considered to be subjective. But this theory is off the mark. Facts don't just lie around waiting to be picked up; reporters must reason to the facts. Similarly, decisions as to what will be covered and what will not depend in part on value judgments, so that news and evaluations cannot be completely separated.

In practice, however, the theory of objectivity simply keeps the media from straying too far in their judgments and evaluations from the mainstream social consensus. ***Example:*** their attempts to be objective by being "evenhanded" merely result in our hearing what the Democrats have to say as compared to the Republicans.

Because the theory of objectivity says that news reporting must be separated from judgments, speculation, and background information, the mass media tend to be short on explanations as to why things happen as they do. Of course, reporters cannot be expected to be experts on every topic they cover. But they still want to appear to be authoritative—to appear to know what they are talking about whether they do or don't.

The media generally want to play it safe when featuring expert opinion. They want to satisfy all relevant power factions, if possible. So they tend to consult establishment figures, including media bigwigs, and not to annoy their audiences. The result often is silly pontificating. ***Example:*** the political correctness of almost all political discussion on TV.

Note that the media sometimes act as self-censors, either out of patriotic intent (as in wartime), or in order to placate their audiences or advertisers, or to avoid the possibility of libel. ***Example:*** *Bloomberg News* killing a story critical of China out of fears of damage to its relationship with the nation.

4.   The media need to slant the news can be accomplished in quite a few different ways: playing a story up or down, using a misleading or sensational headline, omitting or playing down follow-up stories, using (or not using) emotive language, using suggestive photos and other imagery, and using cartoons to convey a point of view. ***Example:*** the wide range of headlines used to describe allegations of political bias at Facebook.

5.   Television is the town crier, certifier, and grapevine. It is the chief medium on which political contests are fought and news about major events such as wars is disseminated.

The result is that the television industry has greater power than the other media and indeed can and does influence the course of events in the world on which it reports. ***Example:*** the way in which TV coverage of the Iraq War influenced the public to support it early on and turn against it as coverage became negative.

Even prime-time television entertainment sometimes has positive features. ***Example:*** It has helped to break down prejudices against ethnic and religious groups and women—portraying African Americans and women in important jobs in the business community. Note also the positive effects of employing African Americans and women on TV news programs. (TV also is superior in explaining the news to ordinary people on the street.)

6.   For the past several years, the audience growth in Internet news has outpaced growth in any other news source. It offers an unparalleled opportunity to access the news, obtain useful information, and participate in public discourse. But because of all the schlock on the Web, we have to be vigilant in thinking critically about the way the news is reported or managed. ***Example:*** "citizen reporters" or bloggers expressing strong bias or misrepresenting the news.

7.   Although the mass media are a modestly good source of breaking news, smaller-scale outlets are much better at analysis, at supplying background information, and at investigative reporting.

PBS is a relatively good source of news, generally better than most mass media outlets, particularly in providing background information and analysis. But lots of small-circulation magazines are significantly better than PBS and CNN, being crafted so as to appeal to more sophisticated audiences. ***Example:*** the *Washington Monthly* coverage of politics.

But the point is selectivity, not mass versus non-mass media. This is true not only with respect to television, newspapers, radio, and magazines, but also to books. Popular books tend to be of lighter weight than some that are less popular, because mass audiences tend to be rather unsophisticated. ***Example:*** *Discover* magazine, which hokes up science in the attempt to make it interesting to a mass audience. Note that presidential memoirs and those of other high government officials tend to be particularly shoddy products. ***Example:*** President Bush cherry-picking his successes in *Decision Points*.

8.   The intense concentration of media power in the hands of giant conglomerates is one of the more ominous recent developments in the media business. ***Example:*** Walt Disney owning ABC, dozens of radio stations, hundreds of Disney stores, and so forth. Although size theoretically can yield efficiency and better news coverage, in general it hasn't worked that way so far.

EXERCISE SET 11-1

1.   In April 2007, two days after a psychotic student, Cho Seung Hui, went on a tragic rampage killing 33 people at Virginia Tech, NBC received a package in the mail from the killer that included an 1,800-word diatribe, along with photos and

videos of himself making threats and waving guns and other weapons. NBC aired portions of the material on the *Nightly News* that were quickly picked up by other networks, newspapers, and the Internet. The ethical issues raised by releasing this footage were widely debated. Although NBC took care to edit out disturbing content, it was criticized in some quarters for its insensitive handling of the material and for doing precisely what the psychotic killer intended—getting his deranged message out to the public. But others argued for full disclosure and criticized the network's editing.

2. Write an essay or debate the question whether NBC should have suppressed the material altogether or released all the footage uncensored. Or should it have done exactly what it did—aired an edited version?

EXERCISE SET 11-2

When Barack Obama was campaigning for the Democratic presidential nomination, CBS News.com received so many ugly remarks about the senator that the network decided to block all comments on its stories about him out of concern for the latent racism and the safety of the candidate. (Obama had been assigned Secret Service protection the previous week.) But CBS allowed comments on stories about all the other candidates. The network was criticized for denying him the publicity and for suppressing useful discussion about the candidate. Do you think CBS made the right decision?

EXERCISE SET 11-3

1. Evaluate the coverage in your local newspaper of a particular event or issue of national importance, with respect to (1) objectivity, (2) original versus secondhand reporting, (3) use of headlines, (4) establishment or mainstream point of view compared to minority opinions, and (5) any other matters discussed in this chapter.

2. Do the same for a recent issue of *Time, Newsweek, U.S. News & World Report,* or one of the online magazines such as *Salon.*

3. Do the same for an ABC, NBC, or CBS national evening news program.

4. Get a recent copy of the *Economist,* a British news magazine that widely circulates in the United States and Canada. Select a story in it about a particular event, and compare how it is handled with the way it is dealt with in one of the major American news magazines.

5. Compare news reporting on the BBC world news program carried on NPR with news reporting on any network TV or radio station. Which is better, and why?

MindTap®   **Visit MindTap for more readings and resources.**

6. Watch several episodes of any popular hospital TV drama (there are always a few) and explain how doctors and the medical industry are portrayed. Be sure to explain how their portrayal is similar to and different (if it is) from the real medical world. Do you think these programs influence how viewers tend to see doctors and medical care?

7. How are the elderly and teenagers portrayed on network TV programs, both in news stories and, especially, in popular entertainment programs? Back up your conclusions with details. How about women as compared to men?

8. Check the front page of a single issue of your local newspaper and determine as best you can the sources of their stories. (In the case of wire stories—Associated Press, Reuters, and the like—try to determine their sources.) How many of these stories are based primarily on a single handout or speech, how many were compiled from several such sources, and how many from reporters going out and finding for themselves what is going on?

9. Read through a single issue of three non-mass media magazines, one liberal (for instance, the *Nation*), one conservative (say, the *National Review*), and one libertarian (for example, *Reason*). Are their points of view evident? How do you think they compare to mass media magazines such as *Time* or *Newsweek* or to network national TV news programs?

10. How do you think the news would be presented to us if the federal government controlled and managed the mass media? Be specific and defend your answer with some thoughtful analysis.

11. Suppose that you owned a local television station or newspaper, or a whole television network. Would you report the news any differently from the way that the outlets in your area do now? If so, how, and why? If not, why not? (Assume that, although you may be rich, you can't withstand losses forever. And be realistic, not goody-goody.)

12. Many more women are working in the mass media today than in the old days, but fewer women than men rise to the top. Do you think the fact that men hold so many of the top positions in the mass media and thus make most of the important policy decisions seriously influences work conditions and news content in ways that would be different if women were equally represented in news media high management? If so, how? If not, why not?

13. For the energetic: Go to the library or the Internet and dig through back issues of some mass media publication and evaluate its coverage over time of some important, underlying, or long-term national issue or problem (for example, under- and unemployment, crime, pollution). Defend your evaluation.

14. Also for the energetic: Write your own news story about a personal event that truthfully makes you look bad. Write it as though it were to appear in your local or school newspaper, including headlines and the rest. Now rewrite the story to show your part in it in the best light possible without actually lying. Compare the two. Was this little exercise educational? (Answer: Definitely, if you did it well.)

15. Examine the photographs accompanying a news story and explain how they slant the news.

16. The thrust of the discussion about the recent intense concentration of media power into fewer and fewer hands was that on the whole this is bad for the effective dissemination of the news. We noted, for example, that the chief concern of these large corporations is the bottom line, not the best presentation of the news. But isn't it possible, perhaps even likely, that these megacorporations will find that the highest profits are obtained by best satisfying their audiences, thus putting all of us (collectively) into the driver's seat—being given the sort of news coverage we most prefer? And if so, isn't that all to the good? So why worry about the concentration of media power that has been taking place lately?

"We need to rethink our strategy of hoping the Internet will just go away."

Tom Toro The New Yorker Collection/The Cartoon Bank

New Media, Cyberculture, and Public Discourse

12

> [T]he explosion of information has changed everyone's life, nowhere more than on the Internet. Now, think about the Internet, how rapidly it's become part of our lives. In 1969 the government invested in a small computer network that eventually became the Internet. When I took office, only high energy physicists had ever heard of what is called the Worldwide Web . . . Now even my cat has its own Web page. —PRESIDENT BILL CLINTON, 1996

> [W]e're seeing the spread of broadband throughout the country. Access has gone from 7 million subscriber lines in 2000, to 28 million last year. That's rapid growth. Yet, on a per capita basis, America ranks 10th amongst the industrialized world . . . The goal is to be ranked 1st when it comes to per capita use of broadband technology. It's in our nation's interest. It's good for our economy. The spread of broadband will not only help industry, it'll help the quality of life of our citizens. —PRESIDENT GEORGE W. BUSH, 2004

> We cannot solve the problems in government and we cannot solve the problems that we face collectively as a society unless we, the people, are paying attention. And in an age in which people are getting information through digital platforms, through the Internet, where people's attention spans have shrunk, it is critical that all of you who are shaping this environment are spending time thinking about how are we getting people—how are we getting citizens engaged, and you, yourselves have to be engaged and spend some time thinking about it. —PRESIDENT BARACK OBAMA, 2016

MindTap® Visit MindTap for more readings and resources.

Let's say you have a strong opinion on some matter of immediate social importance, one that you want to share with as many people as you can. If you found yourself in a Greek city in, say, the fifth century BC, and assuming you're a free male above the age of 18, you could voice your opinion in the Assembly and be heard by as many as were in attendance. You would likely plan your speech, refine, and practice it so you could be ready when the herald asked if anyone wished to speak. If your speech were particularly memorable, perhaps its key points would be repeated. Perhaps you'd be asked to perform it again in a less formal setting. Someone may even write some of it down. But almost certainly your speech and the arguments and claims you make in it would be forgotten—and so lost to posterity—as quickly as they were said.

After the movable-type printing press was introduced (during the fifteenth century in the West, but hundreds of years earlier in the East), you could express such a view in a pamphlet, assuming that you were among an elite minority with access to education and therefore were literate, and further that you had access to a press and the funds to buy paper and ink. Your view would reach more people—perhaps into the hundreds, thousands if you were lucky—and be preserved as long as you could keep the pamphlets in circulation. By the eighteenth century, you could reach even more people so long as you owned or wrote for a newspaper. In order to justify the cost and/or keep your job, you would have to carefully plan, write, and rewrite everything you said.

Fifty years ago, you could reach even more people (and much faster) over the radio or on television, but you needed to be among the very select few with access to the reins of these media. And everything you said—and now the way you said it—had to be carefully planned and orchestrated (and of course you'd have to be careful not to offend your advertisers or the FCC!).

Today, you need only a finger, a phone, and maybe 30 seconds of reflection to reach (potentially) hundreds of millions of people. And all of those millions of people can reach back to you, too.

If you were to go back and look at previous editions of this book, you'd find that the Internet has taken on greater and greater significance in these pages, especially in the two preceding chapters on advertising and the news. Check back in with us for the 26th edition, and you'll likely find no reference whatsoever to any hardcopy publishing (except maybe as part of a history lesson!). But changes to news reporting and advertising are just a couple of facets of a seismic shift in public discourse brought on by advances in communication technology. In this chapter, we'll look at some of the other significant ways in which "new media," "cyberculture," and our "digital age" are changing—for better and for worse—the ways in which we communicate, debate, argue, discuss and think about our public lives.

> In short, the tools of rhetoric provide procedures for moving back and forth between the worlds of database and narrative.
>
> —JAMES A. BROWN, JR., IN *ETHICAL PROGRAMS: HOSPITALITY AND THE RHETORICS OF SOFTWARE*

All too often, discussions about modern public discourse—and especially as it is shaped by new technology—present pictures that are either too rosy or too bleak. The Internet itself is either a great democratizing force that uplifts every voice and is ushering in a new era of reason, or it is a magnet for our basest instincts, the dimming of rhetoric to our least common denominator, and a megaphone for the worst among us. Both of these positions are a little extreme, but they also both have some truth in them. At any rate, we won't try to settle these issues here. Love it or hate it, barring some great calamity, digital mass communication is here to stay, even as it constantly changes. Our present task will be to track some of those changes and to consider some ways of responding to them.

Sound Familiar?

It seems probable that the first books printed with movable metal type came from Holland in the second quarter of the fourteenth century. But the man who perfected the technique, if he did not invent it, was the printer of Mainz, [Johannes] Gutenberg . . . Its use spread quickly to other German towns, and traveling German printers introduced it into Italy, Spain and France. William Caxton, the first printer of English books, learned his art in Cologne and Bruges. . . .

By the end of the fifteenth century the works of humanists, religious radicals, and classical authors could thus be printed and quickly disseminated throughout Europe. But printing was from the first not a philanthropy for the benefit of learning or revolution; it was a business . . .

By the beginning of the sixteenth century, however, the new as well as the old learning was being printed in abundance . . . The works of the religious reformers came to be in some instances best sellers. Erasmus's Praise of Folly was such a success, and together with Luther's Ninety-Five Theses revealed the power of the new invention in spreading new ideas as well as preserving old ones. The press did away with the progressive corruption of texts at the hands of a succession of copyists. It made, of course, for a wider and quicker dissemination of every kind of information. It changed the methods of instruction in the schools by minimizing the emphasis upon oral instruction. But as long as the vast majority of people did not know how to read its influences were severely limited. And since it cast a magic spell upon the printed page leading to the popular belief that what it printed must be true, its effects, when people read at all, were not necessarily beneficial. But there are very few who would wish to do without the printing press, despite all the difficulties that its gradual improvement has introduced.

—JAMES THOMPSON AND EDGAR JOHNSON
FROM *AN INTRODUCTION TO MEDIEVAL
EUROPE 300–1500*, 1034–5

In what ways does the impact of the movable type printing press mirror the impact of the internet? In what ways are they different?

1. Discourse in a Digital Age

Whenever a new form of communication technology is introduced, there is an exciting but somewhat awkward period when norms, expectations, and standard practices are less established than the adoption of the technology. We are living in such an era now, with the difference that our communication technologies are *constantly* changing, so that the norms of public discourse are constantly playing catch-up. Still, we can identify some trends and patterns.

SPEED, BREVITY, AND CONSTANT CHANGE

In 1968, William F. Buckley and Gore Vidal, intellectual icons of the political right and left, respectively, had a heated series of televised debates during the Republican and Democratic National conventions. These now-infamous debates each lasted about 15 minutes, and the participants (the term "combatants" may be better) were able to spend a good amount of time preparing what they would say and how they might respond. Each claim and counterclaim was months in the making, and many resonated for months after the fact.

In 2015, Hillary Clinton and Jeb Bush, both presidential candidates at the time, had another combative public political disagreement. This one, though, consisted of dueling Photoshop alterations to Twitter posts and campaign logos, as shown in these screenshots. This battle played out over eight hours and—almost certainly— did not involve the candidates themselves so much as staff members in charge of social media.

Hillary Clinton ✔
@HillaryClinton

⚙   👤+ Follow

Cost won't be a barrier to an education. Debt won't hold you back. Read Hillary's plan: hrc.io/college

$1.2 trillion

The amount 40 million Americans owe in student debt.

New College Compact

Source: Twitter, Inc.

Jeb Bush ✔
@JebBush
⚙ 👤 Follow

@HillaryClinton

100%

The increase in student debt under this Democratic White House.

Hillary Clinton: mortgaging the future of college grads for 4 more years.

Source:Twitter, Inc.

Hillary Clinton ✔
@HillaryClinton
⚙ 👤 Follow

.@JebBush Fixed it for you.

F

The GRADE GIVEN TO FLORIDA FOR COLLEGE AFFORDABILITY under JEB BUSH'S LEADERSHIP.

SOURCE: CENTER FOR PUBLIC POLICY AND HIGHER EDUCATION 2006

Source:Twitter, Inc.

Jeb Bush ✔
@JebBush
⚙ 👤 Follow

.@HillaryClinton fixed your logo for you.

Source:Twitter, Inc.

When Cleveland Browns running back Jim Brown retired from football in 1966, he did so with a two-page private letter to the owner of the Browns followed by a press conference, which was then followed by an extended meeting with a reporter from *Sports Illustrated*. Seattle Seahawks running back Marshawn Lynch announced his retirement in 2016 by tweeting (wordlessly) a picture of cleats hanging from a telephone line (i.e., he had "hung them up," as the saying goes).

These cases exemplify two of the most significant changes in contemporary public discourse: speed and brevity. Communication that required a good deal of planning and multiple channels of delivery can be achieved today with a few keystrokes. What once required half an hour or many pages now is communicated within 140 characters or a single photo.

Changing norms are producing changing appetites, expectations, and behaviors. A 2015 study (funded by Microsoft; take that for whatever it's worth) found that average attention spans have dropped precipitously since just 2000. We've gone from 12 seconds to eight seconds. *Eight* As most media pointed out when reporting on this study, a goldfish's attention span clocks in at around nine seconds. *Seven* The shortened attention span both results from and demands shorter bursts of information and argument. *Six* This is not necessarily a bad thing, as we are able to take in more content and from more sources in a shorter amount of time. *Five* But we should at the same time worry that we're collectively losing some important nuance and details about what we receive. *Four* At the very least, we must rely more heavily on authorities and trust our information sources to a greater degree. *Three* Especially when we spend less time considering what they're claiming, this puts us at greater risk of being taken in by bad claims and arguments. *Two . . . One . . . what were we talking about?*

We shouldn't be too quick, though, to pronounce the longevity of trends, especially in an atmosphere of constant change. In fact, there is an identifiable push against the fast and the short. Longform journalism and extended multipart documentaries are currently enjoying something of a renaissance. "Binge-watching" is a form of entertainment consumption that has only come into existence as web-based content providers, such as Netflix and Amazon Prime, began to offer whole series runs at once. Similarly, websites like Longreads.com aggregate long-form content from around the web for an audience eager for more substantial articles (though with some ironic results, they maintain a Twitter presence as well).

Still, we should ask what it means for public rhetoric that it is—in the main—coming faster and in shorter bursts. One thing it means is that we are able to consume more information and hear from more people than ever before. We'll call that the good news. The bad news is that we've created a breeding ground for certain kinds of fallacies and irrational behavior. Perhaps you've noticed that none of the examples of fallacies in the previous chapters come directly from websites' comments sections or Internet discussion forums. This is not because fallacies are difficult to find there—far, *far* from it. Instead, the discourse common to Internet comments is so vitriolic, irresponsible, and absurd that its irrationality has become something of a cliché and therefore too easily dismissed. But, just for fun (a depressing, hope-killing, soul-draining kind of fun), try to identify the fallacies and/or psychological impediments to cogent reasoning involved in each of the following comments, all from one 24-hour period (April 19–20, 2016). Granted, some comments you see on sites like these are from trolls desperately seeking outraged responses. And it's possible we've missed some sarcasm in one or two cases. Otherwise, this is part of what we collectively had to say online that day:

- *At FoxNews.com:* "What determines a person's wealth most often has to do with their IQ. Smart people tend to make smart choices in life and low IQ people tend to make poor choices, thus influencing their financial outcome. Of course there are exceptions but in general this is true. If you were to give 1000 people who make over 100K a year an IQ test and also give 1000 people who make less than 50K a year and IQ test, the results would show the higher earners were more intelligent humans on average."

- *At Politico.com, on (we think) Ted Cruz:* "Just send the Tea Nazi back to Texas . . . where nutty fruit cakes are always in style."
- *At WashingtonTimes.com, on a story about students at Harvard Law School who claimed that tuition at the school is racially biased:* "Blacks need to pay for whites' tuition as a matter of racial justice. After all, whites didn't invent slavery—but whites did END slavery. Blacks owe us."
- *At MSNBC.com on a story about the move to replace Andrew Jackson with Harriet Tubman on the $20 bill:* "Replacing the founders of this great country is nonsense! Without them we wouldn't even be having this conversation!"
- *At HuffingtonPost.com on a story about a statewide anti-LGBT law in North Carolina:* "If you want to cure the hate problem in the legislature stop voting for republicans. Republicans have never ever done anything for the middle class, ever. There are only two kinds of people that vote republican, millionaires who live off the dividends of their investments, and dupes!"

We could go on, of course, but you get the idea.

THE OLD MEDIA TRANSFORM

The kinds of changes we just described provide an opportunity for new media players to enter what was once a very closed market, and require long-standing media producers to transform themselves. There are three main ways that we can notice such changes: (1) content shifts from one format to another, (2) the roles of primary and secondary media production change hands, and (3) practices established in newer forms of media change expectations for older forms.

Perhaps the most glaring change in public discourse over the last 20 years has been the shift in content to new forms and formats. We have already discussed the decline of newspapers and print magazines in the digital age. A few major magazines, the sort that were once mainstays of newsstands across the country, have abandoned print entirely for a second life online. This may be the beginning of what is now an inevitable process. Scot Finnie, *Computerworld* editor-in-chief, had this to say about taking his magazine all-digital in 2014: "It's sad to lose anything that has endured so long. But we are merely taking part in the natural evolution of the media industry, like so many great publications before us. Trains, after all, were once powered by coal and steam; *Computerworld* is moving from paper to electrons." Other sources have only ever been online but perform many of the functions once reserved for ink-and-paper publications. When you're deciding what movie to see, is your first stop the review section of your local paper, or Rotten Tomatoes? When you decide which movie to see, do you look at the listings in the paper. or Fandango? Then if the unrealistically opulent lifestyles of the characters in the movie were to rouse your envy, would you look for a new apartment in the paper's classifieds or on Craigslist? At the same time, no major newspaper or magazine could exist today without a strong online presence. According to the *New York Times*'s own numbers, their weekly average digital circulation in 2013–2014 was almost twice that of print. Their online readership continues to increase as their print readership continues to decrease. It seems "the gray lady" (a longtime nickname for the *Times*) is not so gray anymore.

It is no wonder, of course, that the news business is moving online. Who today waits until the next morning for their breaking news? Who pays for a classified ad and then waits patiently for it to appear? Who writes a letter to the editor in the hopes that it is one of the few chosen for publication in the coming days? And who would rather read a movie review without a clip to go along with it? But there has also been a major change in the roles played by various media players. Not long ago, online-only entities would most likely aggregate, distribute, or comment upon content that was gathered or produced for newspapers, magazines, television networks, or movie studios. But now it is not uncommon for the evening news to lead with stories first broken by Gawker, Deadspin, or even TMZ. And newspapers now review shows produced for Netflix and Amazon alongside reviews for shows on HBO and NBC.

There also continue to be changes in the kinds of content the old media provides, often in response to audiences' new expectations. You can see this in the changing style of campaign flyers, which with each cycle look more like candidates' websites; in the tendency of news reports in papers and on television to end in invitations to explore the issue more on the provider's website; and in the pleas of advertisers to have audiences "like" or "follow" their products on social media.

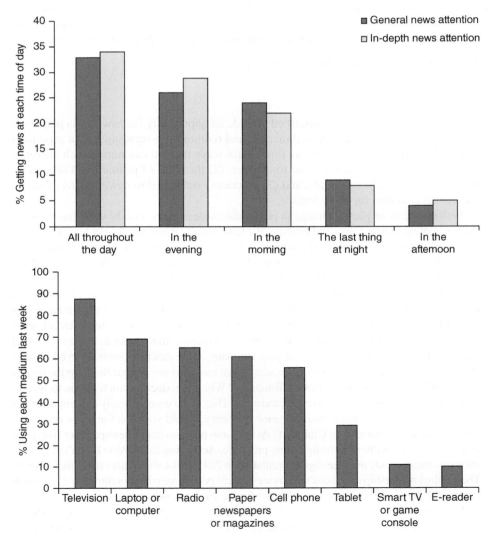

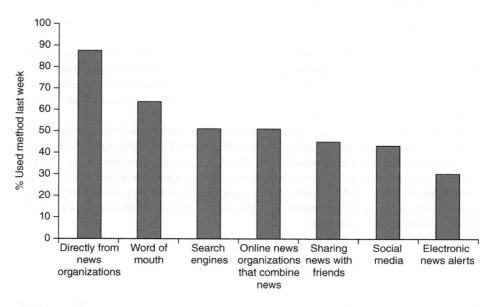

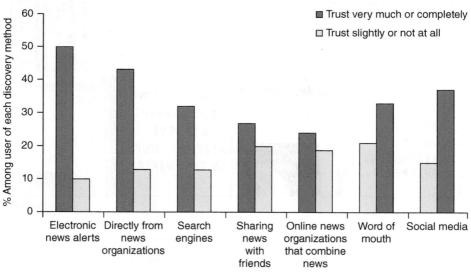

News Reception Behavior, via the American Press Institute

THE NEW MEDIA EMERGE (AND EMERGE, AND EMERGE . . .)

WARNING: By the time you read this section, it will be hopelessly out of date.

You may have to ask your parents about Compuserve and America Online and an older sibling about MySpace and Napster. You'll have to tell your kids about Facebook,

Twitter, Snapchat, Vine, Instagram, etc., and they'll explain the value of some other newer, better form of social media.

One thing all these have in common is that they lack direct correlates in the world of old media. If Facebook has an analog analogue, it's some combination of personal ad, diary and self-portrait. For Twitter, it's a bullhorn so low on batteries that it only lasts for a minute or so. But these analogies are poor, and do no justice to the great reach we have in these social media platforms.

Perhaps the most striking change between the "old" and "new" media is the blurring of the line between producers and consumers of content. Public discourse today is more of a dialogue than it has been since before the advent of mass communication. Our present condition is much more like a meeting in a village square than the largely one-way communication provided by books, radios, newspapers, and televisions. Only now, the potential reach of our views, beliefs, and arguments is not the furthest person in earshot, but the person half a world away.

© Yumi Sakugawa

Jason Gainous and Kevin M. Wagner note in their 2014 book *Tweeting to Power: The Social Media Revolution in American Politics:* "Newspapers and television networks choose what to cover, what questions to ask, even what not to convey to the public, presumably using journalistic ethics . . . Social media has no obvious gatekeeper. While this is a limitation of sorts, it is a very low threshold established by the virtually uncountable number of posts on social media like Twitter and Facebook every day . . . Social media is an incredible aggregator of sortable information that is virtually free for millions of people. Each individual in a social network chooses whether to read, redistribute or even add to each stream of information that comes to them" (*Tweeting to Power,* 11).

THE MORE THINGS CHANGE . . .

Let's go back to those televised debates between Buckley and Vidal in 1968. In the most infamous exchange of those debates, Vidal called Buckley a "crypto-nazi," at which Buckley lost his temper entirely and called Vidal a "queer" while threatening to assault him. This was hardly high-minded political dialogue, and certainly shocked ABC's network audience. But it was great for ratings, something ABC desperately needed at the time. Ratings meant advertisers, advertisers meant money, and ABC was lagging behind its competitors at the time.

As we've been discussing, a lot has changed about public discourse since 1968, but two features of that moment should look awfully familiar to us. First, we should recognize the ease with which these two people (who allegedly should have known better) slipped into ad hominem name calling and ad baculum threats. Second, we should also be familiar with the fact that their debate occurred in the context of a perpetual contest for eyes and ears, and the information and arguments were provided as much in service to a corporate as to a public interest.

Today there are two places where people tend to become their worst selves: the Internet, and their cars. It seems that whenever some of us are faced with a situation that is social and yet involves some distance away from face-to-face contact, they forget all civility, sympathy, and generosity. Buckley and Vidal at least were facing each other directly. How many people who would never in a million years willingly enter into a heated confrontation with a stranger on the street have no compunction about abusively attacking someone on Reddit or YouTube? The answer is "a whole lot," judging by the comments on such sites and the relative paucity of public shouting matches.

The question of corporate control of digital information and speech is a little trickier. In the last section we compared the atmosphere of public discourse online to a village square. And it is certainly more like that than the condition not long ago when mass communication was reserved for the very few that were granted access to the means. But the village square analogy only goes so far. Unlike in the village square (or at least our idealized version of it), speech online is—for most of us—facilitated by platforms delivered by corporations with the aim of generating money. This is not problematic per se. Nothing about the profit motive demands anything like untoward censorship. In fact, that sort of thing would probably be very bad for business. Still, we should be cognizant that in the background of this marketplace of ideas is an economic marketplace. And we should recognize that the Googles, Twitters, and Facebooks of the world are not providing their platforms (only) for the betterment of humanity.

> There was a first "Oh, no!" moment. That was the first time I saw spam pop up. It could have been as early as '79. A digital-equipment corporation sent a note around announcing a job opening, and we all blew up, saying, This is not for advertising! This is for serious work!
>
> —"FATHER OF THE INTERNET" VINT CERF IN *ESQUIRE*, 2008

THOSE LEFT BEHIND

As of 2016, over 88 percent of Americans have home Internet access, but worldwide, it's less than 50 percent. Without consistent, reliable access to the Internet, whole populations of peoples can be left behind, both culturally and economically.

NET NEUTRALITY

For much of the Internet's history, content providers, end users, and the service providers (ISPs) have operated under an assumption that all traffic should be treated equally in terms of speed and access. This is the principle of "net neutrality." Recent revelations of ISPs slowing or speeding uploads and/or downloads to and from certain sites and services (depending on partnerships or other economic relationships, of course) has understandably caused a good amount of public concern.

Citing the value of net neutrality, the FCC has sought to fine ISPs for these practices, and President Obama called for broadband services to be regulated in much the same way that we regulate utilities like gas and electricity companies. Opponents argue that this sort of regulation would set a dangerous precedent of government oversight of the Internet and its content.

A plethora of organizations have popped up to support one or the other side of this issue, usually funded by the corporations that stand to benefit from their position being advanced.

As we've seen, at its worst cyberculture is degrading, mean-spirited, and an incubator for irrationality. But at its best, it can in fact be our first real shot at the democratization of public discourse. But that laudatory goal can't be meaningfully achieved unless many more people have sufficient access.

2. Privacy, Celebrity, and Anonymity

Changes to the nature of rhetoric in the digital age have occurred along with changes to the ways we think about ourselves as members of a digital public. Some of the significant trends of the last 20 years may seem somewhat contradictory at first glance. At the very least, it is difficult to fit them into a simple narrative. This is certainly the case when we consider the shifting balance between our private and public lives. On the one hand, so much of what once was the purview of only close friends and family—vacation pictures, personal stories, where we are and what we're doing at almost any given time—is now available to strangers everywhere. And on the other hand, many things that we once did openly—discuss current events, shop, enjoy entertainment—are now often done under the cover of anonymity.

There may be another kind of tension between our tendency to allow corporations to access (and sell!) all kinds of information about us while fiercely guarding our Internet privacy from the government. Of course, it makes a great deal of difference whether disclosures of and access to personal communications and data are voluntarily given or not. But one can't help but wonder if some of our concern over privacy in one context ought to carry over to the other.

These apparent conflicts in our thinking about our public lives may reflect a deeper uncertainty. Namely, we're just not sure how to think about the Internet and our role in it.

For instance, let's take just that part of the Internet we call "the Web."[1] Is it more like a book that we read privately, or like a street we walk down in public? We do read websites (at least sometimes) in our own homes with the door closed, and so maybe we should have an expectation of privacy when we do so. But we also do our shopping and communicate with any and all strangers who may care to pay attention. My right to privacy does not extend to not being observed walking into a store or watched while I speak on a street corner. So for the purpose of understanding our public lives and right to privacy therein, should we think of the Web (and maybe the Internet as a whole) as a book or a street?

> *Being always-on is not just about consumption and production of content but also about creating an ecosystem in which people can stay peripherally connected to one another through a variety of microdata.*
>
> —DANAH BOYD IN "PARTICIPATING IN THE ALWAYS-ON LIFESTYLE"

Another oddity of our public lives now follows the changing nature of celebrity. Where once the only path to fame was through specific channels and offices, it seems as though just about anyone can become famous these days. Famous actors and actresses were (in a sense, anyway) chosen by studio heads and casting directors. Famous writers went through publishers, editors and agents. Famous musicians had to be "discovered" by A&R reps and approved by record labels and radio stations. To be sure, these channels are still in place, but you can also become famous by posting just the right video of yourself on YouTube or writing just the right blog post, and thus bypass all of these steps. It seems like the paths to celebrity would therefore be easier and more open. And yet that all-important virality is awfully hard to come by. Despite lots of claims from consultants and marketing "experts," the ingredients for Internet sensation remain mysterious, and there appears to be something almost random about contemporary celebrity.

> *In the future, everyone will be world-famous for 15 minutes.*
>
> —ATTRIBUTED TO ANDY WARHOL
>
> *Many people have noted just how prophetic this famous quote now seems.*

The authors of this text may be admitting to being out of touch here, but like many people who grew up in a world without social media, we cannot for the life of us figure out why so many people want to watch other people play video games, or how it is that America's appetite for cat videos and crudely Photoshopped images of celebrities seems endless and boundless. But perhaps that is just the lesson to be learned here. If one, two

---

[1]The terms "Internet" and "World Wide Web" are often used interchangeably, but there is a useful and significant distinction. The Web is just that part of the larger Internet that utilizes HTTP language and is accessed through browser applications. The Internet is the massive network through which we communicate in a variety of different ways.

WE LIVE IN PUBLIC (FILM), DIRECTOR ONDI TIMONER, 2009

In documentary filmmaker Ondi Timoner's 2009 film *We Live in Public,* the life and work of early Internet pioneer Josh Harris is used as a meditation on our increasingly connected and un-private lives, both online and off. The film follows the early days of the Internet in which Harris created "Pseudo.com," the first entirely online programming network and a precursor to YouTube. Ahead of his time, the dial-up connections in use in the early 1990s weren't efficient enough to carry the broadcasts and most of the country was still off-line, leading to the nascent network's demise. Undaunted, Harris created a work of performance art entitled "Quiet," in which participants were chosen to live in an underground environment in New York City and provided food and entertainment in exchange for their every move being videotaped, 24 hours a day. The initial good humor in the environment soon sours as the constant exposure—participants were able to watch each other as well as be watched—starts to wear on the psyches of those involved. The resulting documentary, fashioned from over 5,000 hours of footage, much of it culled from the "Quiet" material, serves as a cautionary tale of where the combination of Internet and surveillance culture would end up in our own society and holds a dark mirror up to our present, overexposed moment.

or twenty Internet sensations pass us by, there will be that one that catches and holds our attention. And if you can grab the attention of one out of twenty people online, you're a star.

3. Speaking Directly to the Public

However one becomes a public figure, certain features of the relationship between these people and their publics has changed as well. At one time public figures had reasonable expectations of distance and privacy. Their private lives could be kept separate from whatever work made them well known, and the public expected to have access to the latter and not the former. And their communications with the masses were filtered through a process that often involved some combination of journalists, editors, speechwriters, managers, public relations teams, or others.

Some of the erosion of privacy came well before the Internet age, with tabloid "journalists" stalking celebrities, and political reporting over the years looking more and more like gossip pages. But the Internet has accelerated both of these trends. More importantly, though, it has allowed public figures to speak directly to the public, for better or for worse.

BYPASSING TRADITIONAL GATEKEEPERS

Through their websites and Facebook pages, politicians, celebrities, and corporations are able to speak directly to their audience without having their words edited or commented on by journalists or other intermediate parties. However, nothing has moved this trend along more than Twitter. When Madonna at the height of her stardom in the 1980s and 1990s had something to say to her fans, she likely contacted her agent, who got together with some PR people; they all chose a magazine and a journalist; there was an interview, some editing, and maybe some negotiating; and eventually the message was out on newsstands. Today, Rihanna picks up her phone. Seconds later, her 59.5 million followers (as of this writing) can read what she has to say.

The advantages to bypassing the traditional gatekeepers can be enormous. Reporters edit comments and choose quotes. They ask potentially embarrassing follow-up questions and can press when an answer is incomplete. It is no wonder, then, that the *Players' Tribune*, a website established by Derek Jeter around the time of his retirement, has no lack of contributions. The *Players' Tribune* publishes written pieces and posts videos directly from athletes. The site looks like any number of sports news sites. But sports fans reading it (and other sites like it) should be a little extra dubious about what they read. Without journalists, questions, follow-ups, or fact-checking, athletes at the *Players' Tribune*, like everyone on Twitter, are free to be as self-serving as they like.

THE RISKS OF DIRECT COMMUNICATION

There are, of course, risks to direct communication. In 2008 and 2009, a group of Los Angeles teenagers (later dubbed the "Bling Ring") broke into the mansions of area celebrities ultimately making off with millions of dollars' worth of property. They knew when to strike largely by following their victims on Twitter, Facebook, and the like. With constant updates about where they were and what they were doing, the thieves knew exactly when their houses would be empty.

In 2003, Barbra Streisand sued a website that posted a picture (among thousands of others) of her beachfront home in a piece about coastal erosion. Her claim was that the picture invaded her privacy and she wanted it taken down. At the time, fewer than ten people had viewed the picture. Because of the suit and the publicity surrounding it, hundreds of thousands of people flocked to the site to view the offending picture. This backfiring strategy of attempting to suppress some information online and therefore calling attention to it was dubbed (by Mike Masnick at Techdirt.com) the "Streisand Effect."

Perhaps most people have learned lessons from these incidents in the years since. But in the absence of public relations gatekeepers and with immediate access to mass communication—day or night, sober or not—embarrassing tweets and posts are a constant. Sometimes the response is a quick and thorough apology along with a frantic attempt to delete and bury the problematic missive. When Prince died suddenly in 2016, Cheerios tweeted out an image that said "rest in peace" against a purple background with the "i" dotted with a Cheerio. General Mills, the maker of Cheerios, quickly apologized and deleted the tweet because it was afraid it was being "misinterpreted." Genuine corporate grief or not, the complaint is that they were using the musician's death to associate themselves with him and ultimately sell some cereal. That seems like a pretty good interpretation.

Another approach is to dig in and double down on the original mistake. In 2010, former governor Sarah Palin urged "peaceful muslims" to "refudiate" something or other (it isn't quite clear). What is clear, though, is that "refudiate" isn't a word. She deleted the post, then came back to point out that languages evolve and Shakespeare coined new words as well. Of course, Shakespeare didn't do so in error and then try to delete the evidence of having done so. Also, Palin comparing her use of language to

Shakespeare's may be a *bit* of a questionable analogy. And yes, languages do evolve, sometimes because of errors (Merriam-Webster recently added a previously incorrect use of "literally" to its possible definitions of "literally," which is literally troubling). But that doesn't justify every misuse and mistake. That's because languages evolve over time and through widespread changes in use, not whenever Sarah Palin uses the wrong word.

And then there is the oft-used "my twitter/website/facebook page etc. was hacked" claim, though this has been so *over*used that no one really believes it anymore (if they ever did). This was attempted for a short time by Anthony Weiner (remember him from Chapter 6 and his "Carlos Danger" fame).

Sometimes social media mistakes are just baffling. Just before July 4, 2014, American Apparel posted this to their Tumblr account:

americanapparel ⇄ plzstic ▸   Source: truangles

#Smoke #Clouds

11,004 notes

Source:Tumblr

But that's not a fireworks display. That's a picture of the 1986 explosion of the space shuttle *Challenger*. The image was quickly removed after an immediate public outcry. One hopes, of course, that this was an honest—if egregious—mistake, and not a case of a company reasoning that all publicity is good publicity.

Another kind of mistake organizations make involves overestimating the maturity or decency of its online public. When Britain's Natural Environment Research Council needed to name a massive new research ship in 2016, it solicited the Internet's help. Public suggestions and a subsequent online poll produced a clear winner: "Boaty McBoatface." At the time of this writing, the government was threatening to overrule the vote and use a more "suitable" name. Here's hoping democracy prevails this one time. But sometimes such results are not so funny. Also in 2016, Microsoft launched "Tay," an "artificial intelligence" program that would interact with people on social media and mimic their conversational habits. Of course, within 24 hours, Tay was tweeting out the very worst sort of racist, misogynistic, anti-Semitic garbage the Internet has to offer. Now, to be fair, Microsoft and "Tay" were victims of widespread trolling more than widespread hate speech—though the fact that *that* was the modus operandi is troubling in itself.

4. Using and Misusing Mass Communication

So how are we to develop a consistent approach to a rhetorical environment distinguished by constant change and seeming contradictions? First and foremost, a new rhetorical environment does not require a new set of logical standards. An argument invalid in the Agora of ancient Greece is invalid printed on a pamphlet, spoken over the radio, recited on television, or posted on Facebook. And a fallacy committed at a dinner party is the same when tweeted and retweeted to millions.

Where we may need a different kind of strategy is in evaluating individual claims. Our recommendations are caution, verification, and selectivity. First, we should be *cautious*. That something looks official does not mean that it's correct. That a source has been correct in the past does not make it reliable. Second, no matter what the source, we should always endeavor to *verify* what is said. That is, everything should be held with something less than absolute conviction until we have a number of independent sources for it. Finally, we should be highly selective about the sources that we accept.

> *The problem with internet quotes is that they are often inauthentic.*
>
> —ABRAHAM LINCOLN (VIA A POPULAR MEME)

When you want information on some topic that you know nothing or relatively little about, what is your first source? We can't say for sure, of course, but judging from its average of some 18 billion visits per month, it's probably Wikipedia. And Wikipedia gives us a good opportunity to apply our strategy. First, we should approach what we read on Wikipedia with caution, but not necessarily skepticism. A highly publicized (and sometimes contested) 2005 study in the journal *Nature* found that Wikipedia was about as reliable in its science entries as the *Encyclopedia Britannica*. But of course, unlike the *Encyclopedia Britannica,* Wikipedia can be edited by the public. Errors are corrected at a surprisingly brisk rate, and clearly many people take their role as Wikipedia editors seriously. But the possibility of error and even malfeasance remains. One thing that Wikipedia has going for it is its insistence on citations and policy of not allowing original research. So if you think you've found an answer to your question in Wikipedia, have a look at the citation and follow the link. That is, verify the claim in question. But how do we know we can trust the Wikipedia editor's source? That is where selectivity comes in. How respected is the source in the field in question? Are there any obvious conflicts of interest? Are there further links and citations for the claim you're trying to track down? This process may seem daunting, but, to appropriate an old phrase, eternal vigilance is the price of Internet freedom.

"I just feel fortunate to live in a world with so much disinformation at my fingertips."

Peter C. Vey The New Yorker Collection/The Cartoon Bank

In general, anonymity, bias, and implausibility are all red flags that we should never ignore. And while the approaches that we suggest will not save us from being taken in by bad information or bad actors, they may give reason a fighting chance.

Summary of Chapter 12

1.   As with other advancements in communication technology, those of our "digital age" have brought about massive changes in public discourse. Three of the most significant such changes consistently involve who is able to speak to the public, how many people can be reached, and how quickly communications can be made.

2.   The norms and modes of public discourse today are marked by three key features: speed, brevity, and constant change. The effects of these features (including some push back against them) are widespread—for better and for worse.

3.   Old media sources—newspapers, television programs, magazines, etc.—are integrating their traditional modes of communication with new ones. Digital distribution of news, for instance, is becoming more and more something done online.

MindTap®   **Visit MindTap for more readings and resources.**

4.   Meanwhile, new media sources appear (seemingly) every day, many of which deliver not just new platforms for public discourse, but entirely new ways of communicating with the public.

5.   Despite all of these constant changes, certain issues and concerns about public discourse linger. Chief among them are the tone of discourse (especially our propensity for ad hominem attack) and the corporate control of the means of public communication.

6.   Public life today is full of seeming contradictions, most notably in our attitudes toward privacy, celebrity, and anonymity.

7.   Another key change in discourse today is that public figures can bypass traditional gatekeepers like reporters and public relations "experts" to speak directly to the public. This can be advantageous for them and for us, though it does have its pitfalls.

8.   We do not need a new strategy for evaluating arguments in the new communications environment. Invalidity is still invalidity. But evaluating individual claims may require some extra effort, especially some extra caution, verification, and selectivity.

9.   We should not exaggerate the cultural, economic, or social benefits of the digital age until it reaches more people around the world.

EXERCISE SET 12-1

1.   Earlier in the chapter, we quoted a number of Internet comments without providing the name (or screenname) of the commenters. This was not an easy decision. On the one hand, it does not seem appropriate to call out someone who is not a public figure in a text like this. But on the other hand, these people did make their declarations public and open to comment from anyone. What do you think? Would it have been more appropriate to include the names? Defend your answer in a short essay. And if you feel strongly about the issue, send us your response.

2.   Recall our conversations about vitriolic rhetoric and anonymity online. Imagine that instead of being able to create anonymous accounts on social media and other platforms, everyone was assigned an Internet handle like a Social Security number, and those handles were publicly attached to you. You could not post or act anonymously at all. How might discourse online change? Would these changes be for the better? And if so, would they be worth giving up the ability to act anonymously? Defend your answers in a short essay. Then write another short essay taking up the (or an) other side.

3.   Do as thorough a job as you can of investigating yourself online. Who *are* you online? What impression do you give? What would a prospective employer (or date, maybe) think of you just from what they could find? If someone might get

the wrong impression about you, how can you fix that? If someone cannot get any impression of you at all, is that a problem?

4. If possible, go back to some arguments you made online—preferably things that are still available for some public (or semipublic) audience to see. Evaluate that argument for validity. Do you commit any fallacies?

5. Let's combine the last three exercises: Imagine that everything you've ever written, argued, posted, or said online came attached to your actual name and face? What might prospective employers think of you then? Is your answer to #3 significantly different from your answer to this question? If so, is that (morally or otherwise) problematic?

6. Find some dispute online between two people, both of whom are committing fallacies, using overly emotive language, and/or reducing themselves to vicious personal attacks. (Unfortunately, this shouldn't be hard.) Now, to the best of your ability, write out arguments for *both* positions that are valid and contain reasonably well-founded premises. What would public discourse be like if we all were able to do this?

"By God, for a minute there it suddenly all made sense!"

Argument and Rhetoric in Fiction

> *Literature is the safe and traditional vehicle through which we learn about the world and pass on values from one generation to the next. Books save lives.* —LAURIE ANDERSON
>
> *In documentaries there's a truth that unfolds unnaturally, and you get to chronicle it. In narratives, you have to create the situations so that the truth will come out.* —AVA DUVERNAY
>
> *If people are rotting and starving in all directions, and nobody else has the heart or brains to make a disturbance about it, the great writers must.* —GEORGE BERNARD SHAW
>
> *Then shall we carelessly allow the children to hear any old stories, told by just anyone, and to take beliefs into their souls that are for the most part opposite to the ones we think they should hold when they are grown up?* —PLATO
>
> *[L]iterary art has in common with all other texts the fact that it speaks to us in terms of the significance of its contents. Our understanding is not specifically concerned with its formal achievement as a work of art but with what it says to us.* —HANS-GEORG GADAMER
>
> *We live in a box of space and time. Movies are windows in its walls.* —ROGER EBERT

MindTap® Visit MindTap for more readings and resources.

A number of times in this book, we have used fictions as examples, sometimes as presenting arguments, sometimes as presenting a certain worldview. We have taken it for granted that fictions *can* do these things, and left open the question of *how* they do them. We will try to fill in these gaps here.

There are many different and varied sources of argument and rhetoric, but narrative art forms like films and novels happen to have immense cultural importance for us. The stories we tell communicate values and norms between people, between groups of people, and between generations. And those who tell them well have an extraordinary ability to affect public attitudes and opinions. This is the *rhetorical function of fiction* and is where we begin our discussion.

1. Fictions as Arguments

Many philosophers, critics, and others deny that fictions can be arguments. To be clear, no one denies that fictions can *contain* arguments. An argument can be spoken in a bit of dialogue between two characters or described elsewhere in the narration. The issue at hand is whether or not the fiction itself can (in some sense or other) *be* an argument. And if this is to be of interest to us, the argument must be about the actual world in which we live rather than (only) the fictional world of characters and their actions.

It is easy to see, then, why many people have doubts about this idea. After all, fictions are made up. How could something contrived from imagination speak to issues in the real world? More importantly, we engage in argument (ideally) to come to some new knowledge about the world. So how does describing some *other* world move us any closer to knowledge about our own? Perhaps in its simplest form the worry is this: fictions are false (at least in the sense that they do not accurately describe the world), so how can fictions lead us to something true on the basis of something false?

At the same time, we seem to assume that fictions can do just this. We often speak about "the point" of movies, or say that a novel "argues that . . .," or that a play "makes the claim that . . ." Don't we *want* to be able to say that *Uncle Tom's Cabin* makes (and perhaps *is*) an argument against actual slavery? Or that *Frankenstein* makes an argument against actual scientific advancement unchecked by morality? Or that the *Hunger Games* books and movies make a case against actual state oppression and a voyeuristic attraction to violence?

There are lots of ways of reconciling this apparent tension, many of which are quite amenable to the view that fictions don't in fact make (or present) arguments at all. However, there are at least three ways that fictions can and do make arguments that are relevant to us and our lives.

> Art is a lie that makes us realize truth, at least the truth that is given us to understand.
>
> —PABLO PICASSO

FICTIONS AS ALLEGORIES

The first and perhaps most familiar way that fictions can speak to real-world issues is by being analogues or allegories for them. Here, the audience is supposed to first recognize some similarity between the fictional world and their own. Then, on the basis of the recognized similarity, the audience should conclude that the real world shares some further feature of the fictional. Fictions, then, can act as a vehicle for the "argument by analogy" that we discussed in Chapter 5. In these cases, the characters and/or events of the fiction stand in for actual people and/or events.

Some examples will help make this clearer. One famous such allegorical work is Jonathan Swift's *Gulliver's Travels,* particularly the first section, "A Voyage to Lilliput." It's here that Gulliver is shipwrecked, taken in by the tiny Lilliputians, and embroiled in their court politics and international quarrels. As narrator, Gulliver describes the Lilliputians' practice of deciding important offices by acrobatic feats, their civil strife over the height of shoe heels, and their prolonged quasi-religious war with neighboring Blefuscu over the sanctity of competing methods of breaking eggs. Critics have long disagreed about whether or not (or to what extent) Swift meant for certain characters in his tale to represent specific people. What is clear is that Swift is satirizing eighteenth-century British partisan politics and international conflicts, lampooning their absurdities and magnifying their ills. "A Voyage to Lilliput" is, among other things, like a political cartoon in prose.

Much the same sort of thing could be said about George Orwell's *Animal Farm,* though its themes and treatments are a few shades darker. *Animal Farm* tells the story of a revolt among animals on a farm and the descent of their revolution into the same conditions against which they were rebelling. With *Animal Farm,* Orwell makes a point about power, corruption, and popular revolutions in general. But he has in mind the 1917 Soviet revolution in particular. The novella is an argument against the Stalinist corruption of socialist ideals, and a powerful one at that.

> What I have most wanted to do throughout the past ten years is to make political writing into an art. My starting point is always a feeling of partisanship, a sense of injustice. When I sit down to write a book, I do not say to myself, "I am going to produce a work of art." I write it because there is some lie that I want to expose, some fact to which I want to draw attention, and my initial concern is to get a hearing. But I could not do the work of writing a book, or even a long magazine article, if it were not also an aesthetic experience.
>
> —GEORGE ORWELL, "WHY I WRITE" (1946)

We find similar sorts of arguments in movies as well. Take the 1997 movie *Starship Troopers.* It was advertised at the time as a campy science fiction action movie. It is that, but it is also an allegorical criticism of martial patriotism and the seductive simplicity of fascism.

The examples above are all pretty fantastic (as opposed to realistic) stories. But we can find allegorical arguments even in works based on true stories. In these cases, one set of actual events "stands in" for another. A classic example of this is Arthur Miller's play *The Crucible.* Miller's play is based on records of the events surrounding the infamous seventeenth-century Salem witch trials. But even if these are the events it depicts, the play is *about* the "Red Scare" of the late 1940s and early 1950s. The central claim of the play—which would have been obvious to its original 1953 audience—is that the fears of communist infiltration that Senator Joseph McCarthy and others used to ruin lives (through blacklisting and publicly humiliating hearings) were at the time as ill-founded and destructive as the residents of Salem's fear of witches and the trials that followed. This was a timely and powerful argument, and one that ultimately won out. Notice that today calling some proceeding a "witch trial" and describing it as "McCarthyist" mean roughly the same thing.

FICTIONS AS MODELS

We often praise fictions for being "true to life" and their characters for being "realistic." We also praise fictions for having plots that evolve out of the nature of the characters. Combining these qualities of (at least good) fictions provides another, slightly different way in which fictions can be arguments.

Let's begin with a recognizable example: Shakespeare's *Macbeth*. Even if you haven't read or seen a production of *Macbeth*, you are likely familiar enough with the main thrusts of the story: Macbeth's ambition is spurred by three witches' prophecy that he will be king of Scotland, so he and Lady Macbeth conspire to kill the king. Preserving the throne and thwarting another of the witches' prophecies requires more killing. Madness ensues, and the Macbeths end up defeated and dead. Of course, this absurdly short synopsis does no justice to the value of the play itself, in large part because no synopsis can capture just how recognizable Macbeth's newfound but overwhelming ambition is to us. It is an extreme version of something we can see in ourselves. Now, ambition is normally thought of as a good thing, and yet the series of tragedies in the play result directly from the Macbeths being overcome by that recognizable ambition. In this case, then, we can learn that ambition is—or at least can be—the enemy of the good.

In general, another way a fiction can provide an argument about the real world is when these two things are present:

1. Characters in the fiction are like us in some relevant way.
2. Certain events in the story result directly from these traits of the characters.

When we have these two things, we can learn something about ourselves from the stories. And because in the fictional world events can result directly from the traits of certain characters instead of the randomness of chance or the necessity of natural laws, we sometimes think of fictions as being even better teachers than the real world. We don't mean to suggest that fictions like *Macbeth* should be read only as arguments. But it is both plausible and valuable to think of them *in part* as being such arguments.

> Nothing can please many, and please long, but just representations of general natures . . . the pleasures of sudden wonder are soon exhausted, and the mind can only repose in the stability of truth.
>
> —SAMUEL JOHNSON

Another example: one author of this text learned in this way from a number of William Faulkner's novels and short stories. Faulkner's characters are like us in their varieties of brilliance, fragility, and dangerousness. Many of the events of his stories spring directly from these seeds, especially from the way people with these shared traits engage with one another. This almost always happens under the shadow of past social traumas, most notably slavery and the Civil War. The results are usually disastrous.

The argument that emerges here is that because we are collectively so much like Faulkner's characters in certain ways, and because the stories unfold as a result of those shared traits, our real world is like his fictional world in this important respect: past social traumas can be as psychologically damaging to a community as individual traumas are to a given person.

The Clint Eastwood movie *Unforgiven* does something similar. Many of the central characters in *Unforgiven* are actively, sometimes desperately trying to change who they've been by changing their reputation—for instance, fashioning themselves as coldhearted gunslingers when they are not, or as pig farmers when they're really coldhearted gunslingers. In just about every case, these characters assume that changing what others think they are will then change what they actually are, and will somehow turn them into who they think they should be. Again, the results are disastrous, as one by one, everyone returns to their own nature and almost everyone ends up dead. Because the tragic story results from this identification of reputation with individual character, and because we often make such an assumption ourselves, *Unforgiven* is able to make an argument against making this identification in the actual world.

There is a clear similarity between these cases and those described in the last section. But these are not exactly allegories. The characters in these stories model certain features of us all rather than represent or stand in for certain people.

Vigilante: *You're full of hatred.*

Officer: *Sorry to disappoint you. Hatred wasn't part of my education. I was taught liberty, equality, fraternity.*

V: *Water, gas, electricity.*

O: *You don't [care] about rules, do you . . . ?*

V: *Sure I do, but I want them to be the same for everyone.*

O: *They are, and I'm here to make sure that they're followed.*

V: *You're a dog who bites for his master.*

O: *Just when rules aren't followed*

. . .

O: *Is burning people's cars gonna change anything?*

V: *You know any other way for us to get heard?*

O: *Not right now, no.*

—DIALOGUE FROM THE MOVIE *DISTRICT B13*,
TRANSLATED AND SLIGHTLY SANITIZED

There are arguments being made here in this bit of dialogue, but there is a sense in which the entire movie (in addition to being a fun and somewhat silly action flick) is part of another conversation on these same topics. That is to say, there is on the one hand the points being made by these characters within the story, and on the other the point being made by the filmmakers in having their characters say what they say and do what they do.

FICTIONS AS THOUGHT EXPERIMENTS

If you've taken an introduction to philosophy course, you're likely familiar with arguments via thought experiment. The philosopher John Locke, for instance, argues against identifying ourselves with our bodies using what is now a famous thought experiment. He asks us to imagine a prince and a cobbler switching memories, psychological characteristics, dispositions, inclinations, etc. So one night the prince goes to sleep in his castle, and the cobbler goes to sleep in his house. Someone wakes up in the castle with the prince's old body and the cobbler's memories and someone wakes in the house with the cobbler's body and memories of having been the prince. So how should we describe this situation? Who woke up in the castle? Did the cobbler wake up in the prince's body, or did the prince wake up with the cobbler's memories? Locke thinks the former is correct and that just about everyone would agree. And if so, we have an argument for one particular answer to the age-old question of personal identity. If the prince wakes up in the cobbler's body, then what matters for personal identity is psychological rather than physical continuity. Crucially, the conclusion reaches beyond this particular imagined case. The conclusion is not just that this prince's and this cobbler's identities are essentially tied to the continuity of certain psychological states rather than their bodies. The conclusion is that this is true for us as well.

This conclusion is still, alas, quite uncertain and debatable. Thankfully, we don't have to settle the issue here. All we need to recognize is that Locke does indeed make a genuine argument about the real world with a fictional (in fact, a quite fantastical) example. Sometimes popular fictions do much the same sort of thing.

Let's return to Shakespeare for our first example. One way of reading *Hamlet* is as an extended argument whose conclusion is that inaction is the enemy of justice. (Again, it would be awfully unfortunate if this is the *only* thing we got out of reading the play!) It may be clearer that there is such an argument than exactly how such an argument works. We submit that it works something like Locke's thought experiment. Shakespeare presents this scenario in which the king of Denmark is murdered by his brother Claudius, who then takes the queen for a wife and the crown for himself. Prince Hamlet then, charged with securing justice and revenge, waits, stammers, questions, doubts, and goes through (what are, on sober reflection) the oddest contrivances to "catch the conscience of the king." Much has been made over the years of Hamlet's procrastination, with serious disagreement over its causes and meaning. But the frustration we feel with Hamlet is just about universal. Our frustration is not only the fear that Hamlet's inaction will allow Claudius to escape justice, but that justice is somehow underserved just by the delay itself. "Justice delayed is justice denied" as the saying (which postdates Shakespeare) goes. We come to be convinced of this via our experience of *Hamlet*. And if we think this is true of the fictionalized Denmark that Shakespeare creates, we must also think it is true in the actual world—just as we must think it true in general that we are not essentially our bodies if we think that one particular prince can wake up in a particular cobbler's body.

Sometimes a "thought experiment" like this can occur in something less than an entire work of fiction, say in a particular scene or plotline. Take Mark Twain's *The Adventures of Huckleberry Finn*. There's a moment in that novel after Huck has helped Jim escape slavery that Huck has a kind of crisis of conscience in which he wonders if he's done the wrong thing by "stealing" Jim. Everyone, after all, would say that what he's done is wrong. But he decides that he must do it regardless of the consequences to his conscience or even his soul. We admire Huck for this, and may realize in the process that personal conscience is more important than public morality.

THE FORM OF ARGUMENTS IN FICTION

One more worry about fictions as arguments may be that fictions can't present arguments because they do not have the right form. Arguments contain premises in support of conclusions, but fictions are the telling of stories. Can something present an argument when it looks so much like mere exposition?

To start to answer this question, let's first remember a discussion we had way back in Chapter 1. Some arguments are presented without their conclusions. Advertising, we said later, is best thought of as arguments with unstated conclusions. This does not mean that these arguments don't have conclusions, only that their conclusions are not stated outright. The conclusion is rather something the arguer expects the audience to draw on their own.

Other arguments have unstated premises. You've probably heard a teacher say something like, "You should take some time to study for the exam, because if you want to do well on this exam, you'll need to study." There is an unstated premise here that you do, in fact, want to do well on the exam. We have to *interpret* what is spoken aloud to make explicit what was intended but not said outright.

Now, can we have an argument without stated premises *or* conclusion? These cases often call for more involved acts of interpretation, but there are such arguments. Many cartoons are arguments of just this sort. Consider the interpretive work that must go into understanding the following:

© Mike Lynch

If this cartoon presents an argument, then it does so with unstated premises and conclusions. The best interpretations of it uncovers those unstated claims. One way to understand the argumentative content of this cartoon may be:

1. People who are bullied at home often deal with that by being bullies at work.
2. People who are bullied at work often deal with that by being bullies at home.
So, 3. There are some terrible ironies about the perpetuation of bullying.

There is no reason in principle why the same sort of interpretations could not be appropriate for some fictions as well.

EVALUATING ARGUMENTS IN FICTION

Recognizing when a work of fiction is presenting an argument requires—as we just suggested—some interpretation. When the correct interpretation of a fiction includes recognizing an argument it makes, we can evaluate that argument using the same criteria we would for arguments that are stated outright.

A slightly trickier question arises, though, when we wonder how to view the fictional work as a whole once we've ascertained the cogency of the argument it presents. Here there is a stark difference between the work of fiction and the persuasive essay. An essay that makes nothing but fallacious arguments is a bad essay no matter how well it is written or presented. But a good movie or novel may make a bad argument. In evaluating a work of fiction, we are typically concerned with far more than its rhetorical or logical value. Indeed, we often (and justly) criticize works of fiction for being overly didactic, for emphasizing some lesson at the expense of qualities of form or style.

That said, a bad argument may make a work of fiction a little worse just as a good argument may make it a little better. But this will be one factor among many that count toward a work's overall value, and we should not expect a general rule for weighting it against others. Fortunately, this is a problem for critics and not one we have to settle today.

2. The Persuasive Power of Fiction

Even if fictions are sometimes the conduits for arguments as we described above, this is not the only way that they affect public opinion and attitudes. The persuasive power of fiction is in fact *much* broader than just their argumentative function. Here we'll consider a number of other means of public persuasion available to fictions and their makers.

WORLDVIEWS IN FICTIONS

Perhaps the most obvious way that fictions persuade is by presenting us with a particular worldview (recall our conversation of worldviews in Chapter 1). Identifying a fiction's worldview is often easier than identifying the features that communicate it. But when we immerse ourselves in the world of a fiction, we immerse ourselves in the worldview assumed by and presented in it.

Sometimes we create fictions in order to present a particular worldview. Other times, worldviews are implicit in fictions just by virtue of the fact that fictions are made by people whose particular perspectives are (perhaps necessarily) informed by the worldviews they happen to have.

> If the writer exists for any social good, his role is that of preserving in art those human values which can endure by confronting change.
>
> —RALPH ELLISON

Consider, for instance, John Steinbeck's *The Grapes of Wrath* and Ayn Rand's *The Fountainhead*. Published less than five years apart, the worldviews presented by these novels could not be more different (nor could the novels' respective quality, but that's another matter entirely). Rand's story about firebrand architect Howard Roark is a testament to the individuality and personal achievement of a "great man" in the face of the stifling obstacles society puts in his way. Sure, Roark is a rapist and he blows up a public housing complex, but he does these things *his* way. The enemies of individuality and success in *The Fountainhead* are followers, sycophants, and socialists, the last coming in for special disfavor. No wonder the book has become must-read material for libertarians.

The Grapes of Wrath seems to come to us from the very other end of the political spectrum. The Joad family travels from Oklahoma to California after the "Dust Bowl" farm they've worked is foreclosed on by the bank. The hard road to California ends in despair, desperation, and exploitation at the hands of farm owners and the authorities with whom they collude. Sure, two of the Joads are (or end up being) killers, but their killings are simply the results of a system built to oppress the masses and stifle their

Pictorial Press Ltd / Alamy Stock Photo

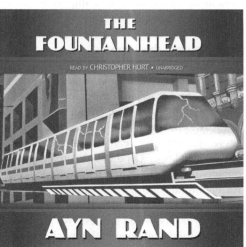

© Blackstone Audio

collective will so that a few may prosper. No wonder the book was criticized for being socialist propaganda.[1]

No one is saying that reading *The Fountainhead* will make you a libertarian or that reading *The Grapes of Wrath* will make you a socialist (though surely both of these things have happened before). Rather, we have here two novels that have been at least somewhat persuasive of the worldviews they present.

Not all worldviews presented in fictions will be as stark as these. Contrast, for instance, the conceptions of power and human nature evident in the television series *House of Cards* and *The West Wing*. Both programs are about fictional American presidencies. On *The West Wing*, though, the powerful are largely good and capable, and even their "enemies" are mostly well-meaning people who happen to have a different political agenda. On *House of Cards*, the powerful are by and large monstrously ambitious (consider sometime the similarities between *House of Cards* and *Macbeth*) and their enemies—especially anyone who might be confused for a "good guy"—mostly end up dead or imprisoned. Comparing *The West Wing* and *House of Cards*, one immediately notices how much the former is concerned with specific policies and their moral implications, while both policy and morality seem to be mostly incidental in the latter. What, then, do these two shows *say* about us and our leaders?

SYMPATHY, EMPATHY, AND IDENTIFICATION

Fictions sometime seem to be better at persuading us to a particular worldview than even the best straightforward arguments (i.e., arguments without unstated premises or conclusions) for them. One important reason for this involves our emotional reactions to fictional characters. Our feelings regarding characters are often very similar to (if not precisely the same as) our feelings for or about actual people. We'll focus here on three common ways this happens.

The first is sympathy. We sympathize with someone when we feel *for* them. We recognize their pains, discomforts, or losses, and this makes us feel something toward or about them. So, as we sometimes say, our "heart goes out" to people. There seems to be something missing from our appreciation of *The Grapes of Wrath* if we feel nothing for the Joads and something wrong with the way we view *Les Miserables* if we fail to feel some sympathy for Jean Valjean. As Pixar has demonstrated again and again, our sympathies need not extend only to creatures like us in situations in which we could imagine ourselves. Watch the first half hour or so of *Wall-E* and see if you don't feel something for the titular robot.

Empathy is somewhat different. When we empathize, we feel along with someone. Empathy is a two-step process. We put ourselves in the place of a character and then feel what we think someone in that position would feel. So when we read *To Kill a Mockingbird* (a story largely *about* empathy) we feel Scout's fear, curiosity, and outrage because we imagine ourselves in her condition. We feel the effects of the injustice done to Tom Robinson because we imagine ourselves in his. And we feel Boo Radley's isolation and loneliness because we imagine what it would be like to be in his place.

---

[1]Lest there be any confusion, we're *not* suggesting that libertarians are generally sympathetic with rapists and bombers, or that socialists generally sympathetic with killers.

In addition to feeling for and feeling with characters, we also identify with them. That is to say, we see ourselves *in* them in some regard. Particular fictional characters share certain characteristics with us (or at least with the way we like to think of ourselves). Noticing that draws us into the life of that character as depicted in the fiction. We tend to view the events of the story from the perspective of that character. The authors of fictions will often craft their stories in ways that invite identification with one particular character or another. In literature, probably the surest route to an audience's identification with a particular character is to write the story first-personally from that character's perspective.

Sympathy, empathy, and identification often go hand in hand, and one can lead to another. In fact, sometimes it is difficult to know exactly how we feel about/toward/with a particular character or what the source of that feeling is. The present point, however, is that all of these things tend to make us more susceptible to adopting the worldview presented by fictions. This is not always a bad or unreasonable thing to do. Were it not for everyone's ability to empathize and identify with Eliza, Tom, and other characters in *Uncle Tom's Cabin,* the book could never have had the social impact that it did.

Other fictional objects of identification and empathy are somewhat more curious. We empathize with Walter White more than we would a meth dealer we read about in the paper. And we identify with Michael Corleone and Tony Soprano far more than we could Lucky Luciano or John Gotti. Some people even report feeling for Hannibal Lecter, when no such feeling would exist for actual psychotic serial killers. Now, some of this can be chalked up to the fact that in fictions we often come to know more about the characters than we ever do about real people in similar circumstances. But it is also just in the nature of our responses to fictions that we are more likely to have feelings like these.

DESENSITIZATION AND NORMALIZATION

Another way that fictions can have a profound effect on our attitudes and beliefs comes more from the central role they collectively play in our cultural lives than from anything specific to individual fictions. What we see, read, or hear depicted in fictions often becomes incrementally more acceptable to us. This does not even need to result from our personally engaging with a fiction. Popular fictions move the needle on important social issues in ways that are hard to measure but can nonetheless be profound.

To be sure, the content of popular fictions largely depends on what is socially acceptable, but it can also help determine what is socially acceptable. In 1970, there had been no long-standing depictions of single working women on television. It simply wasn't done. *The Mary Tyler Moore Show* changed that, and in the process helped incrementally change social expectations of and attitudes toward women. Another first came a few years later when *The Jeffersons* introduced an interracial couple. And in the 1990s, the creators of *Ellen* and *Will and Grace* pushed other boundaries by centering shows around gay characters.

Today it seems crazy to think that a show about a single working woman might have caused a stir. That a television couple is interracial is hardly a fact worth commenting on, and we can (or maybe we're close to being able to) have lead characters who happen to be gay without it being all that significant that they are *gay* characters.

Again, we shouldn't overestimate the power of the sitcom here. The struggle for social equality is much more difficult and complicated than that. But by the same token, we should not underestimate the power of fictions to move these things along. The ubiquity of single working women, interracial couples, and gay characters in fiction today is not just a reflection of changing times. These shows helped push such changes in the first place.

The principal way this happens is through a process of desensitization and normalization. Just like people who are allergic to bees can be desensitized to the effects of venom by injecting small doses of venom over a period of time, a society can be desensitized to things it finds shocking or startling by being exposed to it over time. Opposition to professional women, interracial marriage, and gay rights would probably have deflated much faster if every workplace had at least one lesbian openly in an interracial relationship. But in the absence of that, the fictions with which we live—especially those in the public eye week in and week out—provided a nice alternative.

Over time, desensitization gives way to normalization. So these pioneering sitcoms helped us get over the shock of progress, and then these sorts of characters became commonplace. And what was once incredible becomes normal.

3. The Downsides to Fiction's Power to Persuade

Alas, not all is rosy and light when it comes to the rhetorical function of fiction. Deep concerns about fiction, and especially about its power to persuade are at least as old as Plato's *Republic* (fourth century BC) and as current as any other socially significant issue.

Plato's concern in the *Republic* is twofold. First, he was very worried about the negative effects that engaging with fictions can have on our character, especially for writers and actors, but also for audiences as well. Those effects may be especially pernicious because of the very subtle—and therefore often unnoticed—way that they come about. The claim here is not that we're going to watch *Game of Thrones* and then go out and become murderers, torturers, and rapists. It is rather that performing the roles probably made the *Game of Thrones* actors a little bit worse, and it makes us a little bit worse to immerse ourselves in the story and identify with its unsavory characters. This moral-psychological thesis is interesting, to be sure, but it is not something we need to settle here.

The second concern is a little more pressing for us. It is that fictions are *more* persuasive than rational argument. Even if fictions implicate arguments in one or more of the ways described above, we tend to be persuaded by fictions more than we would the cut-and-dried presentation of the same arguments. One reason for this, as we've already discussed, is the powerful psychological effects of sympathy, empathy, and identification. But just as importantly, our guards are down when we engage in fiction. When we watch a political debate, we are primed to evaluate the validity of the arguments that the candidates make and question their premises. We also may wonder about the worldviews in the background of the policies the candidates advocate. But we don't tend to do any of these things when we read a novel, and they're even more rare when we watch movies. And so if we are persuaded with our guards down, we are more likely to be persuaded when we shouldn't. We are then, perhaps, more likely to be taken into believing something false, because what we're seeing or reading is not purporting to be true in the first place.

Plato's prime example was Homer, the author of the *Iliad* and the *Odyssey*. Plato accused Homer of providing false impressions of gods and men, and of telling stories that made audiences more cowardly, less pious, and generally less virtuous. Just as importantly, he argued that his contemporaries made a grave error in being persuaded by Homer's great poetic talent to think of him as an expert in the subjects about which he wrote.

Homer was an awfully bold target at which to aim. At the time of Plato's writing, Homer was the "teacher of the Greeks." Homer had a kind of cultural significance that nothing today could match—imagine for starters a kind of combination of the Bible, Shakespeare, and *Saturday Night Live*. And while we may not have any current work of fiction that is quite so influential, we still should wonder about the relationship between fictions and social attitudes. Especially: to what extent do fictions get to be popular because they express attitudes and exhibit worldviews that are already popularly held, and to what extent are popularly held attitudes and worldviews shaped by popular fictions?

If we take seriously the possibility that fictions shape worldviews, we have to take Plato's concerns seriously. And we are left, then, with two choices. First, we could seriously diminish the role that fictions have in public life and replace them with rigorous arguments and philosophical inquiry. This was Plato's preferred solution, but it likely strikes us as both drastic and implausible. More importantly, we'd lose all that we do and should value about (at least our best) fiction. The second choice is to make the subtle persuasive effects of fiction a little clearer, to engage with fictions with our guards a little more up, primed to question their persuasive effects even as we enjoy the stories and their telling. This chapter, then, is a small step toward that goal.

4. Rhetoric in Various Forms of Storytelling

Having discussed some of the ways in which fictions work as rhetoric generally, we'll now consider some of the ways that particular forms of storytelling affect and persuade us.

LITERATURE

It is no accident that most of the examples we've used in this chapter come from literature. For one thing, certain novels, plays, and poems are the narrative artworks with which we're most likely to all be familiar. Almost everyone had to read at least one of *Moby Dick, To Kill a Mockingbird, Hamlet, The Great Gatsby,* or *The Grapes of Wrath* in high school. More importantly, though, there are two features of our engagement with literature that make its rhetorical effects especially strong.

The two features we have in mind are *sustained involvement* and *close attention*. First, it simply takes longer to read a novel than to watch a movie. Unless we are extremely familiar with it already, it also takes longer to read a play than to see the same play in a theater. It almost always takes much more time to read a novel than an essay or opinion piece that might make the same point. As a result, we spend more time engaged

"His volumes speak silences."

Bruce Eric Kaplan The New Yorker Collection/The Cartoon Bank

A pun on the expression "his silence speaks volumes." Notice that an assumption behind this joke is that it is a defect of a novel that it doesn't have something to say.

in the world of the fiction and the worldview presented in and by the narrative. We cannot help but be influenced more by those things with which we spend more time.

But it is not only the time spent engaged with literature that matters to its rhetorical effects. It is also the nature of that engagement. While we can have a movie on in the background while we clean the apartment or let our mind wander to an important upcoming meeting while playing a video game, reading a poem or novel requires our total attention. That is to say, it makes sense to say that we watched a movie while cleaning or that we were thinking of other things while playing the game. But when we catch ourselves daydreaming in the middle of a novel, we have to go back to where we were when the daydream started. This is because our eyes may have been scanning over words, but we can't be said to have been "reading" at all. The work of literature thus demands our undivided attention, and as such has a unique ability to capitalize on that attention in the form of influence.

Consider the scene at the end of Camus's *The Stranger* (a book we've mentioned before) when Meursault finally explodes in anger at the priest who has come to save his soul before execution. There the protagonist delivers a kind of disjointed existentialist soliloquy, which on its own would sound like the ravings of a madman. And perhaps it is that. But having been through Meursault's story to that point, having our attention fixed on his (seemingly) detached amoralism for so long (though it's a short novel), we instead see something revelatory in this moment, and something philosophically significant in what we might otherwise have dismissed.

Or, if you've read *Anna Karenina,* you may remember the farmer Levin and his two brothers, one a writer and intellectual with whom Levin tries to keep up in conversation concerning contemporary metaphysics, and the other (at least at one point) a committed communist with whom Levin has uncomfortable political confrontations. These conversations between Levin and his brothers involve conflicts between morality and class interests and between rational deliberation and faith. On their own, the discussions are not all that productive or illuminating, and they serve more to establish Levin's character than anything else. But in the context of the novel as a whole, which we're able to grasp only through very long and close attention, we see that these conversations mirror themes that are important throughout, and involve questions that are better treated implicitly *by* the fiction than explicitly *in* it.

If *The Stranger* and *Anna Karenina* are only in your future, perhaps *Harry Potter* is in your past. Despite its fantastical storylines, the novels do suggest worldviews that are relevant to us muggles. The worldview presented by *Harry Potter* is one that values loyalty, free thinking, skepticism, a healthy distrust of authority, and an unwillingness to judge others too quickly. These things are clear to us when we watch the movies for a couple of hours at a time, but they are much more present to us when we read the novels. Having our full attention on that world for 4,224 pages, we become as immersed in a worldview as we are in the story that presents it.

MOVIES

While movies may not demand our attention or put us in contact with a given worldview for quite as long, their audiovisual nature may be said to put us in more direct contact with the fictional worlds being depicted—and therefore with the worldviews that underwrite them. Specifically, depictions of characters and events in a novel are—we might say—mediated by the interpretation of symbols (i.e., printed words) and the imagination of readers. In a movie, what is depicted is somewhat more directly *shown* to an audience.

There is thus something qualitatively different about seeing and hearing a movie, and that experience is uniquely immersive. Think about the experience of going to a movie. There are announcements, advertisements, and maybe previews beforehand, but once the main feature is about to start, the lights go down in the theater, maybe the curtain widens, people (ideally) turn off their phones and cease conversation. We recognize that movie time is separate from normal time through these signals, not unlike religious services that begin and end with ceremonies to mark the change back and forth between secular and sacred time.

And while we don't want to take the analogy too far, movies have come to hold a place in our cultural lives that was once interwoven with religion. In ancient Greece, for instance, plays were held at religious festivals attended by all who could. They would be discussed over dinner parties and on the street for weeks and months to come. So they had their religious function, and they also served to unite and communicate to Greek culture.

For much of the twentieth and early twenty-first centuries, the movie has played two of those three important roles. Going to the theater is not a religious event, but our movies provide both a shared cultural experience and a means of communicating our culture—especially its prominent worldviews—to one another, and across generations.

If you have the means and want to make a claim that will reach as many people and as persuasively as possible, you'd do well to produce a movie rather than make a speech or write an editorial. Consider this: how often do you make a point by referencing a line from an essay, an editorial, or even a play or novel? If you did, is it likely that your friends would pick up on and understand the significance of the reference? Now, how often do you use references to movies? How often do you do so reflexively, without necessarily even being aware that you're doing it? For better or for worse, the views expressed in and by movies take on an air of plausibility by virtue of their familiarity and cultural resonance.

This is why people from every side of the political spectrum are especially concerned about the political content of fictional movies. This usually manifests in accusations of "bias." So Christopher Nolan's *Batman* trilogy is criticized for being an apologetic for a conservative agenda, and James Cameron's *Avatar* is called liberal propaganda. The popularity of these movies and the comparatively subtle nature of the political messages they contain mean that opponents of those messages may have good reason to be concerned about them.

Perhaps in part because of their visceral nature and natural fit in the medium, horror movies are often particularly well suited to fulfilling a rhetorical function. This is

Moviestore collection Ltd / Alamy Stock Photo

especially clear when we consider movies in these genres as allegories for prominent social fears. At one time, addiction, mental illness, and domestic violence were "private matters" in America. Increased awareness of these things and their devastating effects created (with good reason) a newfound concern about them. It was in this environment that Stanley Kubrick's *The Shining* was such a critical and public success. Fears of uncontrollable and unpredictable terrorism in 2008 surely had something to do with the success of *Cloverfield*. And in too many examples to count, cultural clashes within American society get played out in movies where innocent urbanites are terrorized by backwoods psychopaths or naive small-town folk are caught in the horrors of the big city. Our claim is that movies like these do more than just reflect cultural conditions; they go as far as anything else in helping create and shape these conditions in the first place.

Moviestore collection Ltd / Alamy Stock Photo

TELEVISION

Some of the rhetorical value of movies comes from the expectation that movies are more likely than other moving-image media to be artistically and culturally significant, and that the others are more likely to be mere entertainment. But if this expectation was ever warranted, it is less and less so every year as scripted television continues to improve and mature. And as the quality of television increases, so too does its capacity for rhetorical and argumentative value.

This is not to say that television has not had such value in the past (think of *M*A*S*H* or *All in the Family*, for instance) or that all television is getting better (networks are still churning out stupid sitcoms and pointless dramas). But recently, popular shows like *The Riches, The Wire,* and *Breaking Bad* have done artful jobs of presenting (often conflicting) worldviews. And it is no surprise that television fictions have taken as much political heat as movies—*24* and *Downton Abbey,* for instance, have been attacked from the left, while *Girls* and *Transparent* are attacked from the right.

Until recently, it has been the norm that story arcs on television shows last one or two episodes. Many shows today will cover a single story in a whole season, or even throughout the lifetime of the program. Especially as the storytelling on television becomes more long form and its quality (again, on the whole) improves, the rhetorical value of television interestingly emerges from two qualities we've already ascribed to literature and movies. Like literature, we are exposed to a fictional world and its world-view for a longer time on television. Especially as television content is increasingly made available (or originating) online, the "binging" experience may be as sustained as the experience of reading a novel. And of course, like movies, the experience is both visually and aurally immersive.

One advantage television has over movies and novels is the capacity for currency. Novels usually take years to write, edit, and distribute. Movies sometimes take even longer to write, produce, shoot, edit, etc. But many television shows go through these kinds of processes every year. This gives them a greater ability to respond to and comment on current events. In a kind of extreme case, episodes of the animated show *South Park* are often produced start to finish in as little as a week or less. This gives the creators of *South Park* the ability to weigh in (and weigh in they do) on *very* current topics.

The combination of all these things may well make television (including shorter-form online shows) a preferred medium of fictional argument and rhetoric over the coming decades. None of the above should suggest, however, that television has only recently acquired its rhetorical function. Looking back on the history of television, there is nothing that better illustrates the importance of attending to this function than children's television. Whole generations of kids learned important and valuable life lessons from *Sesame Street* and *Mister Rogers.* They learned about how to (and why we should) be kind, generous, forgiving, brave, honest, and understanding of people unlike ourselves. But there is no less learning going on for kids who only watch violent cartoons. *What* they learn is just more concerning.

VIDEO GAMES

The last medium for fiction that we'll consider here is the video game. The features of video games that make them especially adept at exposing us to particular worldviews and attitudes are the facts that we are often—if in a limited way—participants in creating the stories that unfold, and that we actually control some of the actions of a character or characters, and therefore can come to identify with them more strongly. Notice, for instance, that people will often refer to the characters they control in the first person.

These features, along with the tendency of popular video games to be particularly violent, have led to much consternation about their increased significance in popular culture. We can just imagine the horror Plato would feel regarding the massively popular *Grand Theft Auto*. And *Grand Theft Auto*, with its cartoonish and pseudo-comical depictions of violence and crime, is hardly the most concerning. In a 2015 game called *Hatred,* you play as a deranged mass murderer and progress through the game by killing innocent bystanders, often in brutal ways. No one is claiming that *Hatred* will turn its players into actual mass murderers, but players should ask themselves what the point of *Hatred* is and what worldview they are immersing themselves in.

But the medium itself is value-neutral, and some video games use just these features to increase our sensitivity to and feeling for others rather than make naked appeals to our baser instincts. An online game called *Coming Out Simulator* makes a particularly powerful case for sensitivity to the difficulty gay and lesbian teenagers face in coming out to homophobic parents. It seems unlikely that experiencing the depiction of such an event in a novel, movie or television show would have quite the same emotional impact as playing as the character as he tries to navigate this emotional minefield.

> *Gamers want to know: Where, in the real world, is that gamer sense of being fully alive, focused, and engaged in every moment? Where is the gamer feeling of power, heroic purpose, and community? Where are the bursts of exhilarating and creative game accomplishment? Where is the heart-expanding thrill of success and team victory? While gamers may experience these pleasures occasionally in their real lives, they experience them constantly when they're playing their favorite games.*
>
> *The real world just doesn't offer up as easily the carefully designed pleasures, the thrilling challenges, and the powerful social bonding afforded by virtual environments. Reality doesn't motivate us as effectively. Reality isn't engineered to maximize our potential. Reality wasn't designed from the bottom up to make us happy.*
>
> *And so, there is a growing perception in the gaming community:*
> *Reality, compared to games, is broken.*
>
> —JANE MCGONIGAL FROM *REALITY IS BROKEN:*
> *WHY GAMES MAKE US BETTER AND*
> *HOW THEY CAN CHANGE THE WORLD*

Summary of Chapter 13

1. Fictions can make arguments by being allegories, models, or thought experiments that speak to real-world situations and problems. These arguments are often implicit, as neither their premises nor their conclusions are stated outright. As such, identifying, analyzing, and evaluating these arguments requires quite a bit of interpretation.

2. Fictions also persuade through the presentation of particular worldviews. They are able to do this in part through our sympathy, empathy, and identification with fictional characters, and also through the desensitization and normalization that can go on through exposure to fictions.

3. Fictions can sometimes be even more persuasive than explicit argument, and therefore we run the risk of allowing the subtle effects of engagement with fiction to replace rational deliberation.

4. Different forms of storytelling have different rhetorical advantages. For instance, literature requires our sustained involvement and close attention; movies are visually and aurally immersive and have a great deal of cultural significance; television has some of the advantages of both literature and movies, and it benefits from a capacity for currency; and video games are uniquely participatory and therefore they're especially immersive and conducive to identification with fictional characters.

EXERCISE SET 13-1

1. Take a work of fiction with which you are very familiar and identify an argument made by (i.e., through) the work. Is this argument made by virtue of the work being an allegory, a model or a thought experiment? Should we find this argument persuasive? Why or why not?

2. Do the same thing with one or more of the following novels: *Slaughterhouse-Five* (Kurt Vonnegut), *Sula* (Toni Morrison), *The Brief and Wondrous Life of Oscar Wao* (Junot Diaz) or Movies: *Taxi Driver* (Martin Scorsese), *Do the Right Thing* (Spike Lee), *Two and Two* (Babak Anvari).

3. Earlier in the chapter we compared the worldviews presented by *The West Wing* and *House of Cards*. Watch a couple of episodes of each show. How do they match up with your own views of politics and human nature? Is *The West Wing* too naive? Or is *House of Cards* too cynical? Defend your answer with examples from the shows and from real life.

4. Is it true that fictions can be more persuasive than rational deliberation? If so, does this give us reason to be concerned about the fictions to which people are exposed? And if *that* is true, does that give a society the right (or even the responsibility) to determine which fictions its members are exposed to? Does

your view of such censorship change if just applied to fictions available to children? Defend your answers to these questions in a complete essay.

5.   Compare the rhetorical advantages and disadvantages of two or more forms of fiction. Which do you think has the greater ability to persuade? Does this ability come from the form's capacity to present implicit arguments or display particular worldviews?

Appendix: More on Cogent Reasoning

1. More on Cause and Effect

In Chapter 1, we said a few words about how inductive reasoning is used to discover causal relationships—to discover how one thing causes another. But just as in the case of most interesting concepts, that of causation is really a cluster of related concepts, mostly with blurred edges. Recall our previous conversation about necessary and sufficient conditions as they relate to conditional claims (in Chapter 2). When we call one thing the cause of another, we can mean simply the *sufficient condition* for bringing it about. In this sense, the cause of Marie Antoinette's death was being guillotined—having one's head cut off certainly suffices to bring about death.

On the other hand, we often mean by the cause of a thing or event whatever is a *necessary condition* for bringing it about. Striking a match on a rough surface (thus heating it) can be thought of, for example, as a necessary condition of the lighting of a match, even though it is only part of what must be true for the effect—the lighting of the match—to occur. It is a necessary condition, but not a sufficient condition: Matches also need to be dry and struck in the presence of oxygen if they are to light. Being in the presence of oxygen and being dry and being heated together constitute both the necessary and the sufficient conditions for a match to light.

The point here is that, even though striking a match (heating it) cannot alone cause a match to light, we still in everyday life talk as though striking a match is what makes it light. It usually makes perfectly good sense to say, for instance, that the match lit because it was struck on a rough surface (which heats the match to the required temperature), even though a match struck on a rough surface in a vacuum will not light (because of a lack of oxygen). But we would not say, for example, that it lit because it was in the presence of oxygen. The difference, roughly speaking, is *human agency*—in everyday life, it's easy to make a match light by striking it (heating it), but we can't usually make it light by providing oxygen. (For one thing, the oxygen already is there; for another, the match still won't light because ordinary air temperatures are too low.)

Also of interest is the fact that we sometimes need to distinguish between *proximate causes* and those that are more *remote*. Suppose that a truck jackknifes on an icy highway, blocking three of four lanes, and that an auto, call it auto *A*, has to swerve into the unblocked lane and that another auto, *B*, then crashes into auto *A*. The ice on the road would be said to be the proximate cause of the truck's jackknifing but a much more remote cause of the accident between autos *A* and *B*.

The difference between proximate and remote causes can be important in everyday life, in particular in legal cases. Clearly, auto *A*'s swerving into the last unblocked lane is a proximate cause of the crash between *A* and *B*, yet the driver of *A* may well not be held responsible, since his need to go into that lane was caused by more remote events. The guilty party more likely will be held to be the driver of the truck for driving without sufficient care on an icy highway.

This example brings to mind the fact that, in everyday life, a given effect can be explained in terms of more than one cause. Which one we select usually depends on our particular interest in that effect. In assessing blame, say, in the case of a knife murder, we don't care about the neural and muscular causes of the murderer's arm movement, but we do care very much about his having consciously willed to do the act. A biologist, on the other hand, might be very interested indeed in neural firings in the guilty party's body, and in a court of law might well testify to neural and muscular causes of the knife blow. So it makes sense to say either that the willing caused the event or that the neural firings and muscle contractions did so.[1]

2. Scientific Method

Scientific method is just common sense writ large, sharpened, fine-tuned, and applied (in the best cases) with creative persistence and patience. There is nothing mysterious or impenetrable about how scientists go about justifying their hypotheses.

Common sense requires that beliefs about the nature of the world be justified, more or less, by cogent arguments, as discussed in earlier chapters. Scientists have no other way, no magic formulas or wands, for coming to justified beliefs about the nature of the world. Science's "secret" lies in the persistent accumulation of knowledge by thousands (now literally millions) of practitioners who have required of each other the elimination so far as is possible of the shoddy, wishful thinking that peppers everyday reasoning. The rules of the scientific game force scientists to reject unjustified theories[2] and to give

---

[1]For more on causation and related matters, see Hausman, Alan, Kahane, Howard, and Tidman, Paul. *Logic and Philosophy*. 12th ed. Boston: Wadsworth, Cengage Learning, 2013.

[2]Scientists use the terms *theory* and *hypothesis* in at least two ways. In one sense, both of these terms refer to untested speculations or to insufficiently confirmed patterns. In another, they refer to well-established, well-confirmed, and accepted patterns. The second sense is synonymous with the expressions "scientific law" and "law of nature."

up their most cherished ideas when experience shows that they are false (or unsupported by good evidence).

Typical scientific theories result from a complicated mixture of deductive and inductive arguments, but the key arguments are inductive. Good scientists try to find *patterns* in what they have observed so far, in particular in their scientific experiments,[3] and project these patterns via inductive reasoning to larger slices of reality. In everyday life, common sense reasons by inductions from past experiences that sugar sweetens, vinegar sours, bread nourishes, and drought kills crops. Scientists, using the same commonsense methods, but much more persistently and stringently, conclude that copper conducts electricity, cigarette smoking causes cancer, Earth's path around the sun is an ellipse, and radioactive substances have half-lives. (They also, of course, use viewing instruments they have learned to construct by means of inductive reasoning—telescopes, microscopes, X-ray machines, and so on—that we ordinarily don't have at our disposal in daily life.)

So science is just the accumulated knowledge gained by huge numbers of individuals observing nature, proposing theories (patterns) that explain what has been observed, and testing by additional observations to confirm their theories (hypotheses). When scientists claim to have discovered a new pattern, others will try to duplicate their findings; when they succeed, a theory tends to be accepted into the scientific canon; when they cannot successfully duplicate the findings, a theory will be discarded, or at least modified so as to take account of what has been learned by the failure to confirm. It is this that distinguishes science from pseudoscience: A scientific theory predicts what will be experienced under certain conditions; if it is not experienced, the theory must be rejected or revised to conform to what has been discovered. Those who believe in pseudosciences—for example, extrasensory perception—cling to theories that are disconfirmed by experience and that do not make successful predictions about what will be experienced in the future.

Speaking of pseudoscience brings to mind the fact that a truly scientific theory must conform not just to evidence directly supporting it, but also indirectly to all scientific theories whatsoever. Pseudosciences, on the other hand, never conform to the whole body of scientific knowledge or even, sometimes, to ordinary everyday thoughts. Creation science, for example, asserts that all human beings except for Noah and his family perished about 5,000 or so years ago in the biblical flood. This means that all of the human genetic variety we see today—all racial differences—must have evolved in just a few thousand years from the common Noah family stock, and this contradicts everything we know about how human beings, or any mammals, evolve and propagate. So anyone who accepts creation science on this point must reject virtually everything known about genetics, along with a great deal of the rest of modern biology.

Note, by the way, that failure to confirm a proposed scientific theory does not mean that the attempt to do so was of no value. On the contrary, failure can be very revealing; indeed, it often is more enlightening than success. For example, the failure of experiments conducted in the 1880s to prove the existence of an "ether," believed in those days by scientists to be

---

[3]A scientific experiment is just a kind of deliberately arranged experience. Instead of waiting for an event to happen, scientists arrange for it to happen, perhaps in their laboratories. For instance, they may mix two chemicals in the laboratory that rarely, if ever, are found mixed in nature, to see the result. But whether an event is "found" in the laboratory or found in "nature" is irrelevant to scientific procedure.

the medium through which light (and other electromagnetic waves) traveled through space, led to a crisis in Newtonian physics that was finally resolved by Einstein's special theory of relativity. So, in a sense, one of the most important scientific advances of the twentieth century grew out of the failure to confirm a previously widely accepted scientific theory.

Students often misunderstand this aspect of scientific investigation. They often object, for example, to biological research done on animals because what works with respect to other animals frequently does not do so in the case of human beings; students often see this as proof that animals were made to suffer with no offsetting increase in knowledge about how human diseases can be conquered. They don't understand that failures of this kind may lead investigators away from a wrong path and on to a right one. (They also often overlook the many cases in which, say, drugs that work well on close mammalian relatives also do so when tried on human beings.) This is not to say that these benefits necessarily outweigh animals' suffering. That is a difficult moral question that we are not addressing just now. Note, by the way, that those who champion pseudosciences generally do not learn from failures to confirm their theories; they tend simply to sweep this sort of counterevidence under the nearest metaphorical rug.

Pseudoscientists also tend to ignore ways in which their theories run counter to simple facts and ideas about how things work that we all hold in everyday life. Creation science, for example, fails to take account of what we all know about the abundance of species in today's world. There are thousands of mammal species, thousands of bird species, thousands of amphibian and reptilian species, and millions of insect species, all of which could not have fit into one ark that even today's technology might with great effort construct. So even forgetting that lions can't be expected to lie down with lambs; forgetting that the ark would have had to be stocked with an incredible amount and variety of food and water so animals would not starve or dehydrate; forgetting that literally millions of plant species would have had to be collected; forgetting the physical impossibility of Noah and his family going around the world to collect all of these animals and plants and food; forgetting about bacteria and viruses; and forgetting fussy details about getting rid of huge amounts of fecal material, it should be clear that the creation science story violates not just dozens of extremely well-confirmed, high-powered scientific theories, but also all kinds of everyday ideas about how the world works, *while predicting nothing about what sorts of (earthly!) experiences the future may hold for us!* The scientific theory of evolution, on the other hand, is consistent with every other well-confirmed scientific theory and has predicted all sorts of things that have been and continue to be discovered to be true, including how and where fossils might be found, and so on.

Finally, let's take a look at a rather simple and truly scientific theory—the "sea-of-air" hypothesis—and at how scientists test and confirm their hypotheses. The theory was proposed by the seventeenth-century mathematician and physicist Evangelista Torricelli, a disciple of Galileo. It was well known then that water can be pumped from a well only from a maximum of about a depth of 34 feet (without the aid of auxiliary power); Torricelli proposed to explain this and other facts by his theory that a sea of air surrounds the surface of Earth and presses down on it because of the force of gravity, just as water presses down on something at the bottom of the ocean. Pumps thus can raise water from a well (at most) to a height of about 34 feet, Torricelli theorized, because of this *air pressure.*

Torricelli's theory can be, and was, confirmed by performing several different sorts of experiments. For instance, if the limit that water can be pumped from a well is about

34 feet, and if mercury is about 14 times heavier than water (it is), then if the sea-of-air theory is correct, it follows that air pressure will hold up a column of mercury only $^1/_{14}$ as high as a column of water. So we can confirm the sea-of-air hypothesis by constructing a mercury device (we call these things *barometers*) and finding that this is the case. Torricelli's followers also confirmed his theory by testing at higher-than-sea-level elevations where, according to the sea-of-air theory, a column of mercury should be held up a lesser amount than at sea level, because there is less air pressing down on the mercury. (We now use this fact in other ways—for instance, in measuring fluctuations in air pressure at a given elevation, part of the knowledge needed to predict changes in the weather.) Notice, by the way, that had the results of experiments not conformed to Torricelli's theory, his hypothesis would not have been accepted by the scientific community.

The point of all this is twofold. First, scientific method is not some mysterious entity; and second, although in practice it leads to extremely complicated experiments and arguments, the basic underlying patterns of scientific inquiry are rather simple. We also should mention that the incredibly diverse evidence that supports scientific theories is the reason why they are so reliable and why we should not reject what science has to say on any subject without having *extremely good reasons* for doing so.

3. Criteria for Theory Selection

In the preceding section we stressed that the scientific method provides a reliable means of coming to true hypotheses (or theories). But often even the best available methods of data collection and testing do not yield one clear and definitive answer. So how exactly do we choose one theory over competitors? Crucially for our purposes, lessons learned from scientific contexts can provide valuable insights into the logic of everyday explanatory judgments.

Debate over the proper criteria for theory selection and especially the proper weighting (or prioritizing) of them is long-standing and ongoing. We offer here a few of the more likely candidates for any good list:

1. *Explanatory Power:* Almost certainly the first criterion for a thesis is that it explains more of the data in question than competing theories. Why do we formulate theories in the first place if not to explain certain relevant data? In almost all cases, we should choose the theory that explains more of the data.
2. *Plausibility:* If two theories are equally good at explaining the data, we ought to choose the one that is more plausible prior to considering that data. Sometimes, of course, we have to accept the seemingly implausible when there is no more plausible theory that explains the data as well. But all things being equal, we should reject the theory that forces us to amend more—or more fundamental—beliefs.
3. *Consistency:* Some things we cannot accept no matter how well they seem to explain what we observe. These things rise above the merely implausible and into the absurd. For many of us, the best example of an unacceptable absurdity is an inconsistency: the truth of two or more claims that cannot be true at the same time. If that's right, then consistency is a requirement of any acceptable theory.
4. *Simplicity:* All things being equal, we should prefer the simpler theory over the more complex. In practical terms, this means we should reject the theory

that forces us to take on more new beliefs that are not required to explain the data.

5. *Utility:* Two theories may come out relatively equal on all the criteria so far and differ only in what we can *do* with them. We should then choose the theory that leads to more practical benefits, like opening up new lines of research, suggesting new policies, or otherwise guiding our actions.

To see how these criteria can work outside of a scientific context, let's look at a fictional but indicative argument. This is an inductive argument of a kind we call an "argument to the best explanation":

> Tommy Malone, the most prominent bookmaker in town, was found shot in his car last week. Mayor Smith owed Malone a lot of money after the Super Bowl and Smith alone knew where Malone would be the night of his death, because the two were planning to meet then. Also, no gun was recovered at the scene, but a gun whose barrel matches the caliber of the murder weapon was found in the Mayor's office. We can reasonably conclude that Mayor Smith murdered Malone.

Now let's imagine that we are considering this theory that Smith murdered Malone against some competitors, namely:

> #1 Malone committed suicide.
>
> #2 Madame Mysterio, the local psychic, murdered Malone (knowing by virtue of her psychic powers where he would be and that suspicion would fall on Mayor Smith).
>
> #3 Mayor Smith unjustifiably killed, but did not murder Malone.
>
> #4 Someone else with a motive broke into Mayor Smith's office in City Hall, stole his gun and saw on his calendar when and where he was to meet Malone. This person then killed Malone before the mayor showed up, then broke back into City Hall, replaced the gun and successfully covered up both break-ins and the murder.
>
> #5 Mayor Smith killed but did not murder Malone. "Murder" implies guilt, and guilt implies free will. But we have no free will.

All of these other theories can be rejected pretty quickly in favor of our preferred hypothesis. But why exactly? The answer is that each one runs afoul of one of our criteria for theory selection:

Theory #1 does not explain as much of the data. If Malone killed himself, where is the gun?

Theory #2 is less plausible. We would have to first believe in psychic powers like those described in order to accept this theory.

Theory #3 is inconsistent. What does "murder" mean if not *unjustified killing*?

Theory #4 is less simple. We must take on a much greater number of new beliefs in order to choose this theory over the one in question.

Theory #5 is less useful. The possibility and/or actuality of free will is a deeply problematic issue in philosophy. And it may well be that if we do not have free will, none of us are genuinely culpable for what we do. But recognizing this does nothing to help us determine what to do with Mayor Smith if he killed Malone to avoid a debt. It can't be that we must settle the larger philosophical problem every time we're faced with a question of individual guilt.

4. Calculating Probabilities and Fair Odds

Billions of dollars are legally wagered on games of chance each year in the United States, and billions more are wagered illegally. The popularity of Atlantic City, Reno, and Las Vegas testifies to the fact that many millions of people in America gamble every year. Yet most who gamble have no idea how to calculate fair odds, one reason almost all gamblers lose in the long run. (Another reason, of course, is that the odds on all legal gambling games, including in particular slot machines and state lotteries, are rigged against the player—the odds *always* favor the house.)

Legitimate, fair odds depend on the *likelihood* (*probability* or *chances*) that a given outcome will occur. For example, when you flip a symmetrical coin, the chances are *one out of two*, or ½, that the coin will land heads up because there are two possibilities, and both are equally likely. *Fair odds* on heads thus should be even money—one to one—and someone who bets a dollar and wins should win a dollar. (Note, though, that very few coins are absolutely symmetrical. They tend to be very slightly heavier on one side or the other. Also notice that the dice at places like Las Vegas are specially made to be as close to symmetrical as possible. Just any old pair of dice will not do, because of possible numbers "bias" favoring some numbers over others.)

Most games of chance are designed to present players with a specific number of equally likely alternatives, or combinations of alternatives, on which they must wager. To find the *probability* of combinations of outcomes, simply divide the number of favorable outcomes by the total number of possible outcomes, favorable or unfavorable. (Remember, though, that this works only in cases in which all individual outcomes are equally likely and outcomes are *independent* of each other—a matter to be discussed soon.)

Suppose we want to calculate the chances of getting a 7 on the next toss of an honest (symmetrical) pair of dice. There are exactly 36 possible outcomes on each toss, of which exactly 6 add up to 7 (namely, the combinations 1 and 6, 2 and 5, 3 and 4, 4 and 3, 5 and 2, and 6 and 1). So the probability of getting a 7 on a given toss equals $6/_{36}$, or $1/_6$. Out of six tosses, the average wagerer will win once and lose five times. That is why fair odds on 7 in a dice game are 5 to 1, and why someone who wins a dollar bet should win $5.

At a casino, someone who bets a dollar is required to place it on the table, so that, if winners were paid fair odds, they would get back $6—their own dollar plus $5 in winnings. But no casino in history has ever paid fair odds. Gambling establishments are in business to make money, not to run fair games of chance!

At Las Vegas and other places where gambling is legal, perhaps the best odds for average players are at the dice tables. Slot machines provide the worst odds (except for wagers on sporting events or horse races). Yet the slots are without doubt the most popular way to lose money at every legal gambling casino. But state lotteries very likely offer players (one is tempted to say "suckers"!) the worst odds of any legal popular games of chance, since they pay back in winnings only from one-half to at best two-thirds of what they take in.[4]

Anyway, probabilities being what they are, when the odds are less than fair, virtually everyone who gambles must lose in the long run. But people being as so many of us are, all sorts of foolish theories have gained wide currency among those who like to gamble. The most foolish theory, of course, is that there is something called luck, and that in certain situations, luck is on our side.

But there are also two other, more sophisticated theories that should be mentioned. One is the belief that doubling a bet after a losing play, say, at the dice table, assures victory in the long run even when the odds are stacked against you. After all, you must win sooner or later, thereby recouping all losses plus a nice profit.

Alas, there is no gambling Santa Claus. First, the odds are against you on every play; doubling the bet cannot change that fact. Second, unless you are a Bill Gates or a Warren Buffett, the house always has a very much larger pile of reserve cash than you do and therefore can withstand a greater run of losses. In the battle between house and gambler, the gambler thus almost always gets wiped out first by a streak of bad luck.

---

[4]That is why playing a state lottery amounts to paying a voluntary state tax. Thomas Jefferson, among other illustrious figures, favored lotteries for that very reason. Ordinary taxes are compulsory; lottery "taxes" are completely voluntary. Good point. Of course, human nature being what it is, plenty of people who regularly toss money away on state lotteries complain bitterly about having to pay state sales and income taxes.

(There are old stories and even a song about "the man who broke the bank at Monte Carlo," but if it ever happens, it is a rarity.)

According to a variation of the double-the-bet gambit, a bet made after previous losses should cover just what has been lost so far plus just a small amount extra—say, the amount of the first bet—so that if you bet $2 on the first play and lose, the second play is for $4, the third for $8, and so on until you win, at which point you start over with a $2 bet. This method certainly increases the average number of plays until a gambler will get wiped out, but it still can't change the inevitable failure lurking in the distance. This method also has the disadvantage that, even if you beat the odds and end up a winner, you've just won the tiny amount of your initial wager. (A friend of the authors of this text tried this system at Las Vegas several years ago—at $10 a pop—and actually lasted over two hours before losing her bankroll.)

The other cute fallacy that gamblers fall for is to believe that the less often, say, a 7 has shown up lately at the dice table, the more likely it is that it will show up on the next toss of the dice. The odds, gamblers are fond of saying, have to "even out." Wait until 7 has not shown up for a specified number of tosses—say, ten in a row—and then bet heavily on 7.

The trouble with this system is that each toss of the dice is *independent* of every other toss, which means that what happens on one toss is independent of what happens on any other. The point is that the dice don't know (or care!) what has shown up on previous tosses. The conditions that determine the odds on any given toss determine them to be the same for all tosses, no matter how previous tosses turned out. The dice, after all, are still the same symmetrical devices obeying the same laws of physics on every toss.

True critical reasoners, of course, don't need to know anything about correct odds to be sure that systems like this don't work. The house is in business to win; if they let you play, you can bet your system is no good.[5]

Although the theory about how to calculate fair odds in general is quite complicated, there are a few simple rules that cover most common cases. Using the lowercase letter *a* to stand for a first event or outcome, *b* for a second, and *P* as shorthand for probability, here are four such rules:

Restricted conjunction rule:

If two events are *independent* of each other (the occurrence of one has no effect on the occurrence of the other), then the probability of both occurring is equal to the probability of the first times the probability of the second. In symbols, this reads:

$P(a \ \& \ b) = P(a) \times P(b).$

---

[5]There have been very few exceptions to this rule. One occurred many years ago when card-counting systems were devised for blackjack that changed the odds so that they were in favor of adept card counters. At first, casinos refused to let card counters play—they actually kept lists— but then they simply increased the size of blackjack decks or used mechanical devices spewing out an endless series of cards, thereby ruining the card-counting game. (The card counters proved to be not much of a problem, because extremely few players were sufficiently adept at keeping track of cards played, and anyway, the idea that there is a way to beat the odds is good for business.) Another exception also occurred many years ago when college students discovered the tiny bias of a particular Las Vegas casino roulette wheel by patient observation over several days. They were allowed to win several thousand dollars, because of the great publicity, before the house ruined the game simply by changing the wheel.

For example, the probability of getting two 7s in a row with a fair pair of dice is equal to the probability of first getting a 7 ($1/6$) times the probability of 7 on the second toss ($1/6$), and thus is $1/6 \times 1/6 = 1/36$.

General conjunction rule:

$P(a \ \& \ b) = P(a) \times P(b$, given that a occurs$)$.

For instance, the probability of drawing two spades in a row out of an at-first-complete deck of cards is equal to the probability of drawing the first spade ($13/52$, because 13 of the 52 cards in a deck are spades) times the probability of drawing a second one, given that the first spade is not replaced in the deck ($12/51$), and thus is $13/52 \times 12/51 = 1/17$.

Restricted disjunction rule:

If a and b are mutually exclusive events (an outcome cannot be both a and b), then:

$P(a \ \text{or} \ b) = P(a) + P(b)$.

For example, the probability of drawing a spade or a heart on a given draw is equal to the probability of drawing a spade (¼) plus the probability of drawing a heart (¼), and thus is ¼ + ¼ = ½. (Drawing a spade and drawing a heart are mutually exclusive because no card can be both a spade and a heart.)

General disjunction rule:

$P(a \ \text{or} \ b) = P(a) + P(b) - P(a \ \& \ b)$.

For instance, the probability of getting at least one head in two tosses equals the probability of getting a head on the first toss (½) plus the probability of doing so on the second toss (½) minus the probability of getting heads on both tosses (¼), and thus is ½ + ½ − ¼ = ¾. (Note that we can't just say it is equal to ½ + ½.)

It should be obvious, by the way, that the probability of a contradiction equals zero, and of a tautology (logical truth), one.

EXERCISE A-1

*1. What is the probability of getting either 2 or 12 on a given toss of an honest pair of dice?[6]

2. How about one or the other in two tosses?

3. What is the probability of getting a red jack, queen, or king with an ordinary deck of cards on one random draw?

*4. If a state lottery paid fair odds, how much should a $2 wager pay a winner who picked the correct five-digit number?

5. Can we use the general disjunction rule in cases in which the events are mutually exclusive, as in the spade/heart example just mentioned? Explain your answer, and give an example.

---

[6]Starred (*) items are answered in a section at the back of the book.

EXERCISE A-2

Here is a "system" promoted in a book on gambling.[7] (A tiny part of the system has been omitted here.) Explain why it doesn't work (hard question, but well worth figuring out).

There is only one way to show a profit. Bet light on your losses and heavy on your wins.

Bet minimums when you're losing.

You recoup losses by betting house money against the house, not your own. When you win with a minimum bet, let the winnings ride and manage to come up with a few more wins. . . .

Bet heavy when you're winning.

Following a win with your minimum bet, bet the original minimum plus the amount you won. On a third win, drag [keep] the minimum and bet the rest. You now have a one-minimum-bet profit on the round, regardless of what happens. . . . As soon as you lose, go back to the minimum bet. . . .

Always make your heavy bets with the other fellow's money, not your own.

The worst thing you can do betting house money against the house on a bet is break even on that particular wager. Actually, you've lost money on the round—but it was money that you got from the other fellow, not part of your original venture money. . . .

Don't limit your winnings.

Always ride out a winning streak, pushing your skill to the hilt. . . .

Quit on a losing streak, not a winning streak.

While the law of mathematical probability averages out, it doesn't operate in a set pattern. Wins and losses go in streaks more often than they alternate. If you've had a good winning streak and a loss follows it, bet minimums long enough to see whether or not another winning streak is coming up. If it isn't, quit while you're still ahead.

---

[7]*Gambler's Digest: The World's Greatest Gambling Book.* 2nd ed. Ed. Clement McQuaid. Iola, WI: DBI Books, 1981.

Answers to Starred Exercise Items

These answers certainly are not presented as revealed truth. They represent the authors' thoughts on the matter, which it is hoped will prove useful to the reader.

4. *Premise:* We are sinners all.
   Implied premise: All sinners should forbear to judge (others).
   Conclusion: We all should forbear to judge (others).

5. *Premise:* We would get rid of crime syndicates.
   Premise: The government would rake in billions in taxes.
   Conclusion: Drugs should be legalized.

8. *Premise:* Michael Vick has paid the penalty for his criminal behavior and has made amends by volunteering with the Humane Society.
   Premise: He is a great quarterback.
   Conclusion: His criminal record shouldn't prevent him from getting into the Hall of Fame.

1. *Premise:* If we keep burning so much coal and oil, the greenhouse effect will continue to get worse.
   Premise: But it will be a disaster if it happens.
   Conclusion: So we've got to reduce our dependency on those fossil fuels.

4. No argument. This is a narrative of summer activities plus an *explanation* of why the author will be seeking work outside a casino.

10. *Premise:* We all think ourselves so abundantly provided with good sense that we don't desire any more.
    Implied premise: If everyone is satisfied with the amount of good sense he or she has, then good sense must be equally distributed.
    Conclusion: Good sense is equally distributed.

    (The bit about it being the most equally distributed item is, we can assume, a rhetorical flourish. By the way, do you suppose Descartes was being a bit ironic?)

EXERCISE SET 2-4

4. Disjunctive syllogisms have the form

   A or *B*

   Not *A*

   B

   If we replace the *A*s by the *sentence* "Snow is white" and the *B*s by the *sentence* "Snow is pink," we get the following argument:

   Snow is white or snow is pink.

   Snow isn't white. (Not snow is white.)

   Snow is pink.

   The term *or* in this disjunctive syllogism serves as a *sentence connective* (grammarians would say it serves as a coordinating conjunction); it connects whole sentences. In this case, it connects the sentences "Snow is white" and "Snow is pink." "Snow is white or snow is pink" is said to be a *compound sentence* composed of the two *atomic sentences* "Snow is white" and "Snow is pink," joined together by the sentence connective *or*.

   Contrast this with the following syllogistic form and argument:

   All *S* are *M*. All sinners are betrayers.

   All *M* are *P*. All betrayers are untrustworthy.

   All *S* are *P*. All sinners are untrustworthy.

   In this case, we replace the *S*s, *M*s, and *P*s not by the whole sentences but by parts of sentences—namely, sentence *subjects* or sentence *predicates*. The term *are* serves not as a sentence connective but rather as a *verb* (the verb *to be*); it connects the subject of a sentence with its predicate. In the case, say, of the atomic sentence "All sinners are betrayers," the verb *are* connects the subject *sinners* with the predicate *betrayer* to form the atomic sentence "All sinners are betrayers." (The term *all* serves as a *quantifier*, indicating how many sinners, but that is another story, discussed in formal logic texts.)

EXERCISE SET 2-5

3. Contingent. It certainly is not a contradiction, and it also is not a tautology because there is no law of logic that forbids one from running for both president and vice president in the same election. (Is there a legal law of the land?)

EXERCISE SET 3-1

1. Appeal to authority. Doctors are specialists in medicine. They don't necessarily know anything more about moral issues than anyone else. Anyway, don't we all need to make up our own minds about moral matters?

2. Straw man. This was a cheap shot that misrepresented Obama's position by distorting a minor segment of his stimulus plan.

8. Questionable premise: Trump here is suggesting that the United States should not take in refugees from Syria because doing so will be the destruction of civilization as we know it. Coming just after terrorist attacks in Brussels, the clear implication is that attacks like these

will be the destruction of civilization. Let's start with the fact that terrorist attacks in the West, as awful as they are, have not yet meant the destruction of civilization or anything remotely close to it. And given the very long history of such atrocities, it is at least a bit alarmist to think they will now. Also, there is no reason to think that closing our borders to refugees will make us significantly safer from such terrorist attacks. Trump could not possibly have known this at the time, but none of the Brussels attackers were Syrian refugees. The question is, though, why did he race to make such a sweeping generalization?

14. Appeal to authority, questionable premise, suppressed evidence. A doctor who is setting guidelines shouldn't be profiting from a company who stands to benefit from those guidelines. Under those circumstances, his authority may be suspect. And it is questionable that banning conflicts of interest would limit the number of doctors available for work. After all, 44 percent of the medical evaluators were conflict free. Finally, the fact that some well-regarded doctors conducted company-sponsored research doesn't mean that they remained untainted or that they were essential for setting the guidelines.

17. Suppressed evidence. Most of us are in our own home a lot more than we are in these other places. The rape rate per unit of time is much greater in the other places mentioned by Dr. Brothers than in one's own home.

20. No fallacy if this was a humorous jab at the practice of collecting and reporting on endorsements. But the story was treated with apparent seriousness. It may (MAY!) be news that someone appearing in a Cruz ad is voting for another candidate. But usually we are interested in *endorsements* as potential guides to how we should vote. The endorsement itself is a kind of appeal to authority. And being a former adult film actress who later appeared in a commercial does not quite qualify someone as an authority in governance or politics. This is not to say that this particular woman is necessarily not qualified to give a meaningful endorsement, only that CNN did nothing whatsoever to establish that she is.

24. Inconsistency. Doesn't the phrase "heritable disposition" mean a disposition caused by a genetic inheritance?

32. Questionable premise and possibly either/or. It is certainly questionable to refer to WikiLeaks as a "high-tech terrorist," whether you are for or against its unauthorized publication of classified information. An either/or fallacy is conceivable if the argument is couched in terms of two possible alternatives, one good, the other bad.

EXERCISE SET 4-1

4. Irrelevant reasons.

6. Slippery slope.

10. This is one of those juicy quotes that is loaded with fallacies. For starters, there are the ad hominems—calling the student a slut and prostitute. Then there is the straw man in Limbaugh's claim that she is asking Congress to pay her for having sex, a gross distortion of her argument that the schools should provide coverage for contraception. On top of that is the irrelevant reason that because she is asking for coverage, she must be a prostitute. Throw in a couple of questionable premises, and you've got a veritable minefield of fallacies.

14. Equivocation. You don't have to make the past or future present in thought. What you make present, the "it," is thoughts about the past or present. The term *it* is used equivocally, the first use denoting the past or present and the second the thought of the past or present.

24. Equivocation. To imagine our own death is to visualize what it would be like to experience it. In this sense, we can and do imagine our own death. Freud changes the meaning of *imagine* so that to imagine it, we would have to not visualize it, which, of course, is impossible.

33. Irrelevant reason, ad hominem, questionable premise. Even if all our poor people were fat, which they aren't, it doesn't logically follow that food stamps should be cut. This is just a cheap shot at welfare recipients.

EXERCISE SET 5-1

6. Students taught this way could be, and very likely are, different from "average" students in having more concerned parents (than average), more affluent parents, homes in which books and the like form a larger part of life, and so on. We already have good reason to believe that "booked" households produce children who generally score higher than average. The point is bringing background beliefs to bear. You may have specific, relevant background beliefs, as above, or just general ones that should lead you to have some doubts about the implication of the stat—that home teaching is better than public schools.

EXERCISE SET 5-2

1. Questionable analogy. First of all, Governor Perry is comparing a genetic *disposition* (to alcoholism) to a genetically *determined* sexual preference. More importantly, though, he is comparing alcoholism, which we can all agree is a bad thing, to homosexuality, which (at the very least) we do not all agree is bad. You might also reasonably say that this is a small sample or anecdotal reasoning. He's making very broad statements about genetic dispositions to alcoholism and alcoholic behavior based solely on his own case.

12. Misuse of statistics and hasty conclusion. This poll was taken shortly after highly covered terrorist attacks in Paris and San Bernardino, California. From Gallup's own analysis: "The terrorist attacks in San Bernardino and Paris have altered how Americans view the problems facing the U.S. . . . Whether terrorism remains atop the list of Americans' concerns or recedes in the coming months likely will depend on the government's response to the terror threat as well as the occurrence, or the lack, of major attacks in the U.S. or elsewhere." We can't draw general conclusions about the present state of American politics from a poll taken at such a time. Furthermore, the poll (as O'Reilly himself suggests) was asking participants about their views of what America's most important problems are. It did not determine the extent to which concerns over those problems are "driving American politics."

20. Questionable premise and hasty conclusion. The first part of the premise, that same-sex marriage is contrary to divine law, may not seem fallacious to someone with a conservative, religious worldview, but the second half, that it is contrary to natural law, certainly is questionable and leads to the hasty conclusion that same-sex marriage should be illegal. Furthermore, even if something is (or we happen to think something is) "contrary to divine and natural law," this does not mean that it should be forbidden by our laws as well. For instance, many people think that dishonoring one's parents, not observing holy days, and idolatry are contrary to divine command, but very few think we should create civil laws against these practices. At the very least, this is not an inconsistent set of beliefs.

EXERCISE SET 5-3

1. Questionable analogy. Here's an example for which some background information is essential. (Precise figures aren't necessary.) On a trip to Saturn, the *Titan 4, Cassini,* carried 72.3 pounds of plutonium—the most carcinogenic substance known to man—with far greater radioactivity than was in the Chernobyl reactor at the time of its meltdown. The failure rate of *Titan 4* is 1 in 12.5. If *Cassini* disintegrated at its closest point (500 miles) in encircling the Earth, scientists estimate that millions of people would die—vastly more than the fatalities in a car crash. It's also worth noting that the chances of having an accident when driving a car are very much less than 1 in 12.5.

7. Questionable statistics. Having extolled scientists for their generally correct handling of statistics, here is a case where they goofed. The problem isn't that a rough statistic did not follow from their evidence, but rather that precise ones such as 968.1 billion tons of carbon stored 18,000 years ago did not. Note, for instance, that they estimated how much carbon dioxide was locked within plants, and so on.

10. Suppressed evidence. (1) Superstition is more accurately defined, in part, as belief without good evidence, or in the face of contrary evidence. (So the article changed the meaning of the term *superstition,* and some readers may have been guilty of falling for the fallacy equivocation.) (2) Some of the greatest scientists may have been superstitious, Isaac Newton being perhaps the best candidate. But the parts of their beliefs that became incorporated in science were not superstitions, Newton again furnishing perhaps the best example. (3) In addition, a great deal of what scientists once accepted, *on good evidence,* they now reject, or have modified or sharpened, because of better evidence (for example, the rejected ether theory). Rejecting or modifying well-supported theories because of better evidence in favor of more accurate theories is the heart of science and is definitely not superstition.

14. No fallacy. His analogies are apt.

20. Hasty conclusion. The evidence cited certainly is relevant to the question and favorable to Pierce's claim that the ads caused a rise in teen smoking, but it is not conclusive. Many other factors were at work (was there a similar increase in the use of other harmful drugs such as alcohol or marijuana?) and need to be evaluated along with the ads. In the absence of further evidence that the ads cause teenage smoking, this appears to be an instance of post hoc ergo propter hoc. Also questionable statement: Why isn't banning cigarette ads a First Amendment issue? It's true that we don't think a ban on ads for illegal substances would violate the First Amendment prohibition on censorship of speech, but, on the other hand, we wouldn't be inclined to agree that nothing can be advertised that causes serious illnesses (for instance, high-fat foods).

21. Hasty conclusion. There certainly are plenty of good background reasons for concluding that raising the speed limit will increase traffic fatalities. But we can't automatically credit the 55-mph speed limit with reducing fatalities. (For one thing, that limit was generally flouted anyway; for another, cars have been made safer, and perhaps drivers on average are more sober.) Still, it would have been a good guess, based on background beliefs, that increases in speed would result in increases in fatalities. (Experience so far is mixed as to whether in fact the new higher maximum speed limits have resulted in increased highway deaths.)

23. Questionable analogy. The issue is not the similar sizes of California and Iraq, but the populations. There are 35 million Californians but only 140,000 U.S. soldiers in Iraq. California homicides would amount to 125,000 if people in that state were actually killed at the same rate as our soldiers were dying in Iraq.

EXERCISE SET 5-4

Questionable cause/hasty conclusion. To begin with, if we subtract the U.S. figures, the stats look much different (suggesting the criminal population in the United States is high for other reasons). Also, Ireland, with 88 percent church attendance, has a lower jail rate than four of the six low-church nations and lower than the average. This raises all kinds of questions. Are the Irish secret sinners? Are their police incompetent? How many criminals are behind bars in the United States because they committed victimless crimes (such as smoking dope) or because of race prejudice?

In any case, the statistics cited completely fail to support the implication that churchgoing leads to criminal behavior, nor do any other statistics known to the authors of this text.

EXERCISE SET 7-2

3. Translation: Printed on paper that is at least 10 percent recycled, with a minimum of 40 percent new material.

   Is there something sneaky about this? Yes, indeed. Starting out with the statement "Printed on recycled paper" leads one to suspect that the item is printed on 100 percent recycled paper, thus playing to those who like to use recycled materials. The bit about post- and preconsumer materials is bound to be confusing to most of these people, who will then rely on the (misleading) first statement—the one they can understand. At the same time, the manufacturer is protected from fraud by the statements about pre- and postconsumer materials.

6. What the good admiral said in militaryese was that navy teams had gone around the country trying to find ways to get naval installations to spend more money. (It was close to the end of the fiscal year, and the navy had not used up its appropriation for that year. Yes, bureaucracies, with very few exceptions, do work this way.)

EXERCISE SET 7-3

4. This is an instance of syntactic ambiguity. It is not semantic ambiguity because the intended meaning of each of the words is clear enough, but there are at least three possible meanings given the sentence's structure: (1) the speaker wants to be a professional basketball player and the boyfriend is a professional basketball player, (2) the speaker wants to be a professional basketball player and the boyfriend also wants to be a professional basketball player, or (3) the speaker wants to be a professional basketball player and the boyfriend also wants the speaker to be a professional basketball player. The context is so limited here (just something overheard on the subway) that the ambiguity really is detrimental to understanding what is meant.

EXERCISE SET 7-5

1. Actually, two of the sayings might be challenged. Charles Beardsley's quote may be thought to be doublespeak, and the Chinese proverb clearly does use the pronoun *he* when people in general are meant. But Beardsley deliberately employed "pompous prolixity" in order to rail against that very kind of language. And it makes not a great deal of sense to change ancient sayings (or should we commit to flames the King James version of the

Bible with its sexist sayings, such as "He that is without sin among you, let him first cast a stone at her"?).

Confucius's precept does exaggerate the slipperiness of the slope he describes. But it is slippery!

EXERCISE SET 8-1

3. *Thesis:* None of the historical or anecdotal parts of the Bible are the word of God.

Reason (premise): What I've seen (or know?) needs no revelation.
Conclusion: Revelation is that which reveals what we don't know (haven't seen) before.
Reason: Revelation is that which reveals what we don't know (haven't seen) before.
Conclusion: Revelation can't tell us about earthly things men could witness.
Reason: Revelation can't tell us about earthly things men could witness.
Conclusion (thesis): None of the historical or anecdotal parts of the Bible count as revelation. (Paine assumed an equation between revelation and the word of God.)

EXERCISE SET 10-1

2. Clearly there's a contradiction here. Certificates that cost $1 aren't free.

6. This Nike commercial wins the *Logic and Contemporary Rhetoric* "Most Absurd Commercial of the Decade" Award for telling those who have just proved to be the second best at an activity (perhaps by the tiniest margin) among the several billion people on the planet that they are losers, instead of crediting them with their great accomplishment. (The underlying offensive message is captured by Vince Lombardi's famous remark, "Winning isn't everything; it's the only thing." Compare that to "It isn't whether you win or lose but how you play the game.")

10. Appeal to authority. Agronsky is no authority on the subject. Straw man. No one claims coconut oils are "poisoning" America. Suppressed evidence. (1) Although some fats are healthier than others, coconut oil is low on the healthy list. (2) It is total amount of fat intake that is most important. (3) No single fat source supplies more than a small portion of total intake of fat, so that "only" 1.5 percent coming from coconut oil proves nothing. The point is that it's prudent to reduce one's total amount of fat intake well below the national average and to reduce intake of some kinds of fat—coconut oil being a prime example—more than others. (4) If true that the fatty acids in coconut oil are beneficial, that would be a good reason to prefer this oil to others—say, when cooking. But this claim is generally not accepted by the medical profession. On the contrary, fats such as olive oil seem to be the most beneficial.

EXERCISE SET 10-2

3. This commercial points to a profitable use of air travel—to foster face-to-face business relationships. That is why this has been an extremely successful ad—it reminds business executives of the value of catering to customers in person. But the commercial gives no reason to fly United instead of other airlines. (The implied reason that United flies to more than 200 locations is not a good reason for choosing United. For one thing, some other airlines fly to that many cities; and for another, what difference does it make if you intend, say, to fly to Chicago, whether the airline you choose also flies to 199 other cities

or just to half that many?) Jargon-type slogan. "United. Come fly the friendly skies." Identification. Casting the right actors for TV commercials is crucial, and this ad does it beautifully. Ben is someone most people in business will identify with.

EXERCISE FOR THE ENTIRE TEXT

You didn't really expect an answer to this one, did you? (If you did, go back to page 1 of Chapter 1 and start reading—carefully this time.)

EXERCISE SET A-1

1. Since it isn't possible to get both 2 and 12 on a given toss, we can use the restricted disjunction rule. And given that the probability of getting a $2 = \frac{1}{36}$ and of a $12 = \frac{1}{36}$, the probability of getting 2 or $12 = \frac{1}{36} + \frac{1}{36} = \frac{2}{36} = \frac{1}{18}$.

4. There are 100,000 five-digit numbers, each one equally likely to be picked. Thus, the odds on any given number are 100,000 to 1. So a winning $2 bet should pay $200,000 plus the $2 wagered. (None do. But note that in lottery cases of this kind, how much is paid to winners usually depends on how many people pick the correct number and whether there was a winner of previous plays. When there is no winner for several plays and the pot becomes very large, the number of people who play increases dramatically [people are not always rational!], so that, even though the amount of prize money increases, the probability that there will be several winners increases, thus dividing each winner's share. Of course, when the odds against winning anything are 100,000 to 1, the chances of winning are so miniscule that it is a waste of time to play. It almost never makes sense to wager at such poor odds, even if they are statistically in your favor; doing so loses you the opportunity to profit in some more likely ways. Human irrationality makes most of us see things differently, but that's just one of the tendencies that a good rational thinker fights against.)

Bibliography

Asterisks indicate works mentioned in the text.

Cogent Reasoning

Carroll, Lewis. *Symbolic Logic and the Game of Logic*. New York: Dover, 1958.

Dewey, John. *How We Think*. Lexington, MA: Heath, 1910.

Govier, Trudy. *A Practical Study of Argument*. 7th ed. Boston: Wadsworth, Cengage Learning, 2010.

*Hausman, Alan, Kahane, Howard, and Tidman, Paul. *Logic and Philosophy*. 12th ed. Boston: Wadsworth, Cengage Learning, 2013.

Kahane, Howard. "The Proper Subject Matter for Critical Thinking Courses." *Argumentation* 3 (1989).

Lemmon, E. J. *Beginning Logic*. Rev'd. G. N. D. Barry. Indianapolis, IN: Hackett, 1978. (A strictly formal logic text.)

Toulmin, Stephen E. *The Uses of Argument*. Updated ed. Cambridge: Cambridge University Press, 2003.

*Plato. "Apology" in *Complete Works*. Ed. John M. Cooper. Indianapolis, IN: Hackett, 1997.

Fallacious Reasoning

*Bentham, Jeremy. *The Handbook of Political Fallacies*. New York: Harper Torchbooks, 1962. (A reprint of a classic nineteenth-century tract.)

Broad, C. D. "Some Fallacies in Political Thinking." *Philosophy* 29 (April 1950). (Interesting article by an important twentieth-century philosopher.)

*Cerf, Christopher, and Navasky, Victor. *The Experts Speak: The Definitive Compendium of Authoritative Misinformation*. New York: Pantheon, 1984.

*Dixon, Paul. *The Official Rules*. New York: Delacorte, 1978.

Ekman, Paul. *Telling Lies: Clues to Deceit in the Marketplace, Politics, and Marriage*. New York: Norton, 1992. (Fascinating book that will help readers to perceive when they are being lied to.)

*Fireside, Daniel, Miller, John, and Snyder, Bryan. *Real World Macro: A Macroeconomics Reader from Dollars and Sense*. 25th ed. Boston: Dollars and Sense, 2008. (How statistics can be manipulated, in particular by the federal government.)

Hamblin, C. L. *Fallacies*. Newport News, VA: Vale, 1986. (A reprint with new preface of the definitive history of fallacy theory.)

Huff, Darrell. *How to Lie with Statistics*. New York: Norton, 1954.

*Jackson, Brooks, and Jamieson, Kathleen Hall. *UnSpun: Finding Facts in a World of Disinformation*. New York: Random House, 2007.

*Kahane, Howard. "The Nature and Classification of Fallacies." In *Informal Logic: The First International Symposium.* Eds. J. Anthony Blair and Ralph H. Johnson. Inverness, CA: Edgepress, 1980.

Miller, James Nathan. "Ronald Reagan and the Techniques of Deception." *Atlantic Monthly* February 1984. (Nice illustration of how statistics can be misused for political advantage.)

Morgan, Chris, and Langford, David. *Facts and Fallacies: A Book of Definitive Mistakes and Misguided Predictions.* Exeter, England: Webb & Bower, 1981. (One of several excellent books illustrating expert feet of clay.)

Morgenstern, Oscar. "Qui Numerare Incipit Errare Incipit." *Fortune* October 1963. (Still one of the best explanations of how government statistics on business and such can be and are manipulated for political purposes.)

Smith, H. B. *How the Mind Falls into Error.* New York: Darby, 1980. (Reprint of the 1923 edition.)

Thouless, Robert H. *Straight and Crooked Thinking.* New York: Simon & Schuster, 1932.

Wheeler, Michael. *Lies, Damn Lies, and Statistics: The Manipulation of Public Opinion in America.* New York: Dell Laurel, 1977.

Impediments to Cogent Reasoning

Batholomew, Robert E., and Goode, Erich. "Mass Delusions and Hysterias: Highlights from the Past Millennium." *Skeptical Inquirer* May–June 2000. (Fascinating article on human irrationality during the just-completed thousand years. Great companion to the Charles MacKay book listed later.)

*Bentham, Jeremy. *The Handbook of Political Fallacies.* New York: Harper Torchbooks, 1962. (A reprint of a classic nineteenth-century tract.)

*French, Christopher C., Fowler, Mandy, McCarthy, Katy, and Peers, Debbie. "Belief in Astrology: A Test of the Barnum Effect." *Skeptical Inquirer* Winter 1991.

Gardner, Martin. *Fads and Fallacies in the Name of Science.* New York: Dover, 1957. (The classic debunking of pseudoscience.)

———. *Science: Good, Bad, and Bogus.* Buffalo, NY: Prometheus, 1981. (Debunking of pseudoscience.)

*Gilovich, Thomas. *How We Know What Isn't So.* New York: Free Press, 1991.

*Goffman, Erving. *The Presentation of Self in Everyday Life.* New York: Anchor, 1959. (A classic.)

*Goleman, Daniel. *Vital Lies, Simple Truths.* New York: Simon & Schuster, 1985. (The best understandable explanation of recent scientific ideas about self-deception, its biological functions, and the unconscious.)

MacKay, Charles. *Memoirs of Extraordinary Popular Delusions and the Madness of Crowds.* New York: Harmony, 1980. (Reprint of 1841 edition, with foreword by Andrew Tobias. An excellent account of several disasters—the Crusades, the seventeenth-century Dutch tulip madness, the South Sea Bubble—driven by mass hysteria.)

Nickell, Joe. *Inquest on the Shroud of Turin.* Buffalo, NY: Prometheus, 1982. (An example of sanity on a foolishness-provoking topic.)

Nisbet, Robert. *Prejudices.* Cambridge, MA: Harvard University Press, 1986.

Peirce, Charles Sanders. "The Fixation of Belief." *Popular Science Monthly* (1877). (A classic article by America's premier philosopher.)

Sagan, Carl. *The Demon-Haunted World.* New York: Random House, 1996. (A protest by an eminent astronomer against superstition and the uncritical acceptance of pseudoscientific claims.)

Shermer, Michael. *Why People Believe Weird Things: Pseudoscience, Superstition, and Other Confusions of Our Time*. New York: Freeman, 1997.

Twain, Mark. *Mark Twain on the Damned Human Race*. Ed. Janet Smith. New York: Hill & Wang, 1962. (The great American humorist on all sorts of human foibles. If you think of Sam Clemens as just a writer of stories, you should read this book. For one thing, it will make evident to you how ridiculous it is to censor *Huckleberry Finn* on grounds of racism.)

Vyse, Stuart A. *Believing in Magic: The Psychology of Superstition*. New York: Oxford University Press, 1997.

Language

*American Philosophical Association (APA). *Guidelines for Non-Sexist Use of Language*. (Publication of the APA, available from their national office in Washington, D.C.)

*Carroll, Lewis. *Alice's Adventures in Wonderland*. New York: New American Library, 1960. (Reprint. The Reverend Dodgson, by the way, was a first-rate logician.)

"Guidelines for Equal Treatment of the Sexes in McGraw-Hill Book Company Publications." (Eleven-page, in-house statement of policy that has been generally adopted in the publishing business.)

Hall, Edward T. *The Silent Language*. New York: Doubleday, 1973.

*Jacoby, Susan. *The Age of American Unreason*. New York: Pantheon Press, 2008.

*Lakoff, George. *Don't Think of an Elephant*. White River Junction, VT: Chelsea Green Publishing Co., 2004.

*———. *Moral Politics: How Liberals and Conservatives Think*. Chicago: University of Chicago Press, 2002.

*Lutz, William. *Doublespeak Defined*. New York: HarperCollins Publishers, Inc., 1999.

———. "Notes toward a Description of Doublespeak." *Quarterly Review of Doublespeak* January 1987.

*Orwell, George. *Nineteen Eighty-Four*. New York: New American Library, 1949. (Shows how language control helps control thoughts and thus behavior.)

*———. "Politics and the English Language." In *A Collection of Works by George Orwell*. New York: Harcourt Brace, 1946.

Postman, Neil. *Amusing Ourselves to Death: Public Discourse in the Age of Show Business*. New York: Penguin, 1986.

Solomon, Norman. *The Power of Babble: The Politician's Dictionary of Buzzwords and Double-Talk for Every Occasion*. New York: Bantam Doubleday Dell, 1992.

Evaluating and Constructing Extended Arguments

Cavender, Nancy, and Weiss, Len. *Thinking/Writing*. Belmont, CA: Wadsworth, 1987.

Flew, Antony. *Thinking Straight*. Buffalo, NY: Prometheus, 1977.

Lanham, Richard. *Revising Prose*. New York: Scribner's, 1979. (A good guide to clear writing.)

St. Aubyn, Giles. *The Art of Argument*. Buchanan, NY: Emerson, 1962. (A beautifully written little book on argument.)

Writing Cogent (and Persuasive) Essays

*Hayes, John R., and Flower, Linda S. "Writing as Problem Solving." *Visible Language* 14: 396–398.

*Kahane, Howard. *Contract Ethics: Evolutionary Biology and the Moral Sentiments*. Lanham, MD: Rowman & Littlefield, 1995. (Helpful in bringing value judgments to bear when evaluating arguments.)

Advertising

Baker, Samm Sinclair. *The Permissible Lie*. Cleveland, OH: World, 1968.

*Beiler, David. *The Classics of Political Television Advertising: A Viewer's Guide*. Washington, DC: Campaigns and Elections, 1986. (Companion guide to a 60-minute videocassette containing some of the great TV campaign spots. Great fun and educational, too.)

Benn, Alec. *The 27 Most Common Mistakes in Advertising*. New York: AMACOM, 1978.

*Clark, Eric. *The Want Makers*. New York: Viking, 1988.

*Collins, Thomas L. *Beyond Maximarketing*. New York: McGraw-Hill, 1994.

Faucheux, Ron. "How to Win in '94." *Campaigns and Elections* September 1993. (Interesting to compare with how campaigns were run in 1994.)

*Feldstein, Mark. "Mail Fraud on Capitol Hill." *Washington Monthly* October 1979.

Glatzer, Robert. *The New Advertising: The Great Campaigns from Avis to Volkswagen*. New York: Citadel, 1970.

Hopkins, Claude. *Scientific Advertising*. New York: Crown, 1966. (Reprint of one of the classics on advertising.)

Iyengar, Shanto, and Ansolabehere, Stephen. *Going Negative: How Political Advertisements Shrink and Polarize the Electorate*. New York: Free Press, 1996.

Jamieson, Kathleen Hall. *Dirty Politics: Deception, Distraction, and Democracy*. New York: Oxford University Press, 1992. (How campaigns dominated by 30- and 10-second TV spots fail to provide voters with adequate information.)

———. *Packaging the Presidency: A History and Criticism of Presidential Campaign Advertising*. 2nd ed. New York: Oxford University Press, 1992.

*Kilbourne, Jean. *Deadly Persuasion: Why Women and Girls Must Fight the Addictive Power of Advertising*. New York: Simon & Schuster, 1999.

*Lemann, Nicholas. "Barney Frank's Mother and 500 Postmen." *Harper's* April 1983.

*Marks, Steven. *Confessions of a Political Hitman*. Naperville, IL: Sourcebooks Inc., 2007.

McGinnis, Joe. *The Selling of the President 1968*. New York: Trident, 1969. (Still the best inside account of a presidential campaign—Nixon's successful run for the presidency.)

*Ogilvy, David. *Confessions of an Advertising Man*. New York: Atheneum, 1963.

Preston, Ivan. *The Great American Blowup: Puffery in Advertising and Selling*. Madison: University of Wisconsin Press, 1975. (Interesting account of what legally qualifies as mere puffery rather than false advertising.)

Rowsome, Frank, Jr. *They Laughed When I Sat Down*. New York: Bonanza, 1959. (Perhaps still the most interesting book on the history of advertising.)

*Sabatim, Karry J., and Simpson, Glenn R. "When Push Comes to Poll." *Washington Monthly* June 1996.

Savan, Leslie. *The Sponsored Life: Ads, TV and American Culture*. Philadelphia: Temple University Press, 1995.

Stauber, John, and Rampton, Sheldon. *Toxic Sludge Is Good for You: Lies, Damn Lies, and the Public Relations Industry*. Monroe, ME: Common Courage Press, 1995.

*Washburn, Katharine, and Thornton, John, eds. *Dumbing Down: The Strip-Mining of American Culture*. New York: Norton, 1996.

In addition to the books already listed, several excellent videocassettes are available from Campaigns and Elections, Washington, D.C., including the June 1986 *The Classics of Political Advertising* (with an accompanying booklet by David Beiler); *Prime Time Politics*, a 1989 cassette primarily concerned with the 1988 elections; and *The 25 Funniest Political TV Commercials* (actually, not all that funny, but instructive). There also are several other modestly interesting videocassettes available, including *30-Second Seduction*, a 1985 cassette by Consumer Reports.

Managing the News

Bagdikian, Ben. *The Media Monopoly,* 4th ed. Boston: Beacon, 1992.

Bennett, James. "The Flack Pack: How Press Conferences Turn Serious Journalists into Shills." *Washington Monthly* (November 1991).

*Bradlee, Ben. *A Good Life*. New York: Simon & Schuster, 1995.

Cohen, Jeff, and Solomon, Norman. *Adventures in Medialand: Behind the News, Beyond the Pundits*. Monroe, ME: Common Courage Press, 1993.

Cohen, Richard. "Making Trends Meet." *Washington Post Magazine* 28 (September 1986). (How *Time* and *Newsweek* exaggerate and invent trends and fashions.)

Crossen, Cynthia. *Tainted Truth: The Manipulation of Fact in America*. New York: Simon & Schuster, 1994.

Croteau, David, and Hoynes, William. *By Invitation Only: How the Media Limits Political Debate*. Monroe, ME: Common Courage Press, 1997.

Day, James. *The Vanishing Vision: The Inside Story of Public Television*. Berkeley: University of California Press, 1995. (A good account of how and why public television [PBS] succeeds in some ways and comes short in others.)

*El-Nawawy, Mohammed, and Iskandar Faraq, Adel. *Al-Jazeera: How the Arab Network Scooped the World*. Boulder, CO: Westview Press, 2002.

Fallows, James. *Breaking the News: How the Media Undermine American Democracy*. New York: Pantheon, 1996. (Important book by an editor of *U.S. News & World Report*.)

Faludi, Susan. *Backlash: The Undeclared War against American Women*. New York: Bantam, 1991.

Fineman, Howard. "The Power of Talk." *Newsweek* 8 (February 1993). (How "call-in democracy"—TV and radio talk shows—is influencing elections and the legislative process.)

Hansell, Saul, and Harmon, Amy. "Caveat Emptor on the Web." *New York Times* 26 February 1999.

Hausman, Carl. *Lies We Live By: Defeating Double-Talk and Deception in Advertising, Politics and the Media*. New York: Routledge, 2000. (One of the best books on these related topics.)

Hess, Stephen. "Television's Self-Fulfilling News." *Washington Post* National Weekly Edition 30 October–5 November 1989. (How TV shops around for expert opinion that conforms to the view they want to air.)

Hitt, Jack. "Warning: CIA Censors at Work." *Columbia Journalism Review* July–August 1984.

*Jensen, Carl, and Project Censored. *Censored: The News That Didn't Make the News—and Why*. New York: Seven Stories Press, 1996. (A [hopefully] yearly publication about censored news stories.)

*Knightly, Phillip. *The First Casualty*. New York: Harcourt Brace Jovanovich, 1975. (The first casualty in war is, of course, truth.)

Levine, Richard M. "Polish Government versus the Workers: Why TV Is the Prized Weapon." *TV Guide* 7 November 1981. (An illustration of how important TV has become for politics everywhere.)

Lieberman, David. "Fake News." *TV Guide* 2 (February 1992). (How video press releases, created by public relations firms, are surreptitiously slipped into TV news programs.)

McChesney, Robert. *Corporate Media and the Threat to Democracy*. New York: Seven Stories Press, 1997. (Interesting critique of corporate media power, plus some suggestions for improving the fairness and accuracy of the mass media.)

Miller, John J. "MLK, Inc." (How the Martin Luther King family is making big bucks by charging high permission fees to reprint from King's "I Have a Dream" speech and other writings, thereby inadvertently acting as censors.)

Perkins, Ray, Jr. *Logic and Mr. Limbaugh*. Chicago: Open Court, 1995. (A nifty account of how Rush Limbaugh mangles truth and logic.)

*Perry, David L. "No Way to Celebrate." *Columbia Journalism Review* July–August 1990. (On how increasingly large jury awards in libel cases are putting a chill on investigative reporting.)

Smiley, Xan. "Misunderstanding Africa." *Atlantic Monthly* (September 1982). (How government intimidation and interference mangles news from Africa. An old article, but not that much has changed.)

Waters, Frank. *The Earp Brothers of Tombstone*. Lincoln: University of Nebraska Press, 1976. (The most accurate account of the exploits of the famous "Wild West" Earp brothers, Wyatt and Virgil, including a reasonably accurate account of the so-called "gunfight" at the O.K. Corral. A good antidote to the baloney the media dish out on this and other aspects of western U.S. history.)

*Zepezauer, Mark, and Naiman, Arthur. *Take the Rich Off Welfare*. Tucson, AZ: Odonian, 1996.

In addition to the books just listed, there are several excellent videocassettes on managing the news, perhaps the most revealing being *Fear and Favor in the Newsroom,* distributed by California Newsreels, dramatically illustrating how corporate power influences news coverage.

New Media, Cyberculture, and Public Discourse

There are many good resources for and discussions on this topic, and new ones are coming out every month. The following list should be read as something of a sampling, or starting point.

Abramovitz, Melissa. *How Are Digital Devices Impacting Society?* San Diego, CA: ReferencePoint Press, 2015.

Beasley, Berrin, and Haney, Mitchell. *Social Media and the Value of Truth*. Lanham, MD: Lexington Books, 2013.

Brown, James. *Ethical Programs: Hospitality and the Rhetorics of Software*. Ann Arbor: University of Michigan Press, 2015.

Franklin, Seb. *Control: Digitality as Cultural Logic*. Cambridge, MA: MIT Press, 2015.

Gainous, Jason, and Wagner, Kevin. *Tweeting to Power: The Social Media Revolution in American Politics*. Oxford and New York: Oxford University Press, 2014.

Rowell, Rebecca. *Social Media: Like It or Leave It*. North Mankato, MN: Compass Point Books, 2015.

Argument and Rhetoric in Fiction

Aristotle. *Poetics*. Trans. Joe Sachs. Newburyport, MA: Focus Publishing, 2006.

Carroll, Noel. "Art and the Moral Realm." In *Art in Three Dimensions*. Oxford: Oxford University Press, 2010.

Gaut, Berys. "Art and Knowledge." In *The Oxford Handbook of Aesthetics*. Ed. Jerrold Levinson. Oxford: Oxford University Press, 2003.

Lamarque, Peter, and Olsen, Stein Haugom. *Truth, Fiction and Literature: A Philosophical Perspective*. Oxford: Clarendon Press, 1994.

*McGonigal, Jane. *Reality Is Broken: Why Games Make Us Better and How They Can Change The World*. New York: Penguin, 2011.

Mikkonen, Jukka. "On Studying the Cognitive Value of Literature." *The Journal of Aesthetics and Art Criticism* 73.3 (2015): 273–282.

*Plato. *Republic*. Trans. G. M. A. Grube and C. D. C. Reeve. In *Complete Works*. Ed. John M. Cooper. Indianapolis, IN: Hackett. 1997.

Selected List of Periodicals

One of the themes of this text is that good reasoning requires reasonably accurate background beliefs, and one of the best ways to acquire a good stock of general information and theory is by reading some of the literally thousands of periodicals—magazines and journals— that are readily available these days. Here is a selected list of (primarily) non-mass media periodicals, the majority concerned mostly with social-political issues, the media, or science, which the authors of this text happen to dip into at least now and then. (The comments represent our opinions and are not to be taken as some sort of revealed truth.) Most of these publications have websites. For a complete list of magazine reviews, see *Magazines for Libraries,* ed. Cheryl LaGuardia, available in the reference section of most college libraries.

American Spectator: A wild-swinging, right-wing publication that has as its mission "to provide its unique view of American conservative politics, with a keen sense of irreverence." The writing is often humorous, particularly in regular columns like "Current Wisdom," "Political Hay," and "High Spirits."

Atlantic Monthly: One of the best general magazines, with some excellent articles and fiction. It always covers foreign affairs and the Washington scene, plus a wide variety of articles on everything from the London Olympics to the continuing saga of JFK's mistresses. *Examples*: "Why Women Still Can't Have It All" and "The Last Days of Foie Gras," in the July–August 2012 issue.

Black Enterprise: A business magazine oriented toward African Americans in the business world whose mission has always been centered on "closing the black wealth gap and financially empowering African-Americans." It regularly covers such topics as family finances, money management, business opportunities, and home ownership.

Bloomberg BusinessWeek: A good business magazine, written for those in business on a level that the general reader can appreciate and understand. In addition to a wide range of business articles, it covers social issues and lifestyles. Editorials are generally moderate in their position.

Columbia Journalism Review: One of the best journalism publications, full of interesting, newsworthy articles as well as articles on the field of journalism and a particularly good book review section. *Example:* The cover story of the July–August 2012 issue: "Women, 40 Years Later." Other articles include "Piecemeal Existence" on the tough job market for young writers, and "Cell Coverage" on the jailhouse reporting of a convicted murderer.

Congressional Digest: A monthly publication providing impartial coverage of the pros and cons on controversial issues before Congress, as well as legislative and judicial background information. *Example:* The June 2012 issue that summarizes and debates the federal response to violence against women.

Consumer Reports: Publication of Consumers Union, an unbiased, nonprofit organization, and a very good source of information about consumer products. All products it tests are purchased, no free samples are accepted, and no revenue comes from outside advertising—all of which make for objective, dependable reviews.

Discover: Perhaps the best of a bad lot of mass media popular science magazines. Articles cover research from all science disciplines, profiles well-known scientists, reviews books, and reports on other science related issues. *Examples:* Articles on the environment ("Great Floods" and "Conspiracy of Winds") and biology ("Microbes You Can't Clean Away") in the July 2012 issue.

The Economist: A very informative British newsweekly, well-respected internationally for articles on business and economics, world politics, science, technology, and the arts. *Examples:* Articles in the July 14, 2012, issue on election laws ("Voting Right, Voting Wrong"), prostitution in France ("On the Game"), and cholera in Cuba ("Under Observation").

Editor and Publisher: Important trade magazine and a good source of information about how those in the business see things. Its newsy articles are aimed at industry leaders.

Environmental Nutrition: A very good, concise newsletter on diet, nutrition, and health that covers a wide range of topics, including food safety, nutrition comparison charts, herbal remedies, and best buys in brand-name foods. It is edited by a team of doctors, nurses, academics, and other health professionals.

Extra! The best magazine on the media, the main publication of FAIR (Fairness and Accuracy in Reporting). *Examples:* A special section on Iran and war in the June 2012 issue, including "U.S. Media Duck Legality of Attacking Iran" and "Lost in Translation."

Free Inquiry: Secular humanist publication that defends the importance of free inquiry in all areas of human endeavor. *Examples:* Articles on controversial topics like the use of religious-based charities in the secular sphere, and homosexuality and atheism in the U.S. armed forces.

Harper's: Very good general monthly, with some of the best writing on politics and culture in the country. The Harper's Index is famous for its illuminating statistics and facts about a wide variety of subjects. *Examples:* July 2012 articles "Breeds of America," on current attitudes about race, and "Nature's Perfect Package," on euphemistic food labels.

Harvard Health Letter: An eight-page newsletter containing reasonably reliable medical information. The editorial board is staffed with doctors in different specialties, but the writing is geared to the general public.

Index on Censorship: A chronicle of censorship around the world that acts as a political forum with an international outlook. *Example:* Recent articles addressing suppression of freedom of expression in the United Kingdom and Internet privacy issues.

In These Times: Left-wing, socialist publication. Analyzes social, environmental, and economic justice in popular movements and discusses politics that shape our lives, but the magazine is critical of the left when writers think it is warranted.

Mother Jones: Successor to *Ramparts,* radical left viewpoint, with occasionally very good exposés. Investigates politicians, corporations, and governments, sometimes irreverently, and champions environmentalism. *Examples:* July–August 2012 articles "Undoing Citizens United" and "Follow the Dark Money."

The Nation: Long-established left-wing magazine, very much improved under the current editor and now very good indeed. It covers politics extensively, as well as economics and the arts, and has a searchable index of items in every issue from 1865 to the present. *Examples:* July 16/23, 2012, articles "Mitt Romney and the Gilded Age," "The *Washington Post*'s Problem," and "Is There Freedom after Torture?"

National Geographic: The long-established special-topic magazine. While tending to make the world look somewhat better than it is, it nevertheless has interesting articles, with very good, sometimes stunning, visuals about interesting places around the world. *Examples:* August 2012 articles "Life After Wounded Knee" and "Tibet's Golden Worm."

National Review: Perhaps the most interesting conservative magazine. It covers mainly current political issues, with a long cover story for each issue as well as columns, book reviews, and political cartoons. *Examples:* Articles in the July 9, 2012, issue, "The Immigration Population," "The Bush-Obama Years," and "Sex and the Social Scientist."

Natural History: A publication of the American Museum of Natural History. An attractive magazine with good nature photography, featuring articles written by scientists or naturalists for a general audience.

Nature Conservancy: Magazine sent to contributors to the Nature Conservancy, a nonprofit organization that purchases land in the attempt to preserve natural habitats. *Examples:* July 2012 e-newsletter articles "Artists Find Inspiration in Nature" and "Honoring the Military Who Honor Nature."

New Internationalist: Excellent, very left-wing publication intent on reporting issues of world poverty and inequality and the unjust relationship between the powerful and the powerless. *Examples:* The July 2012 issue articles, "Can Co-operatives Crowd Out Capitalism?" and "What Would Che Say about Co-ops?"

New Republic: Long-established liberal (sort of) political magazine, but recently more middle-of-the-road. *Examples:* July 12, 2012, articles, "Why I Wish Obama Would Stop Inviting Me to Dinner" and "Mormons on the Potomac."

Newsweek: Mass media, general news weekly recently made over with updated graphics and more celebrity profiles. Trendy, good for summarizing a week's happenings, but generally fails to scratch the surface. *Examples*: the July 16, 2012, issue includes "Champagne Flows While Syria Burns," "Hey, Buddy, Can You Spare $20 Million?" and a profile of the late Nora Ephron.

New Yorker: A very good general magazine, with funny cartoons (several reprinted in this text-book), great photos, plus information on goings-on in New York City. *Examples:* Articles in the June 25, 2012, issue include, "Unpopular Mandate: Why Do Politicians Reverse Their Positions?" "Adversity Basketball," and a review of the book *Barack Obama: The Story*.

New York Review of Books: Very good left-wing publication with excellent, indeed sometimes superb, lengthy reviews and articles. *Examples:* July 12, 2012, articles, "American Male Nov-elists: The New Deal," "Burmese Days," a review of books by Burmese authors, and "In Mitt Romney's Schoolroom," and a review of Diane Ravitch's book *A Chance for Every Child*.

Nutrition Action Healthletter: Publication of the Center for Science in the Public Interest. An excellent source of information about food and health. Each issue tends to focus on topics in the news.

Politico.com: Online magazine covering national political news (about Congress, elections, lob-bying, etc.) Started by two former *Washington Post* staffers, it has brought some big-name journalists on board. *Examples*: On July 19, 2012, "Rupert Murdoch Warms on Romney" and "YouTube Restores Romney's Ad."

Reason: Perhaps the most interesting of the libertarian (pro-free-enterprise, con-big-government) publications. *Examples:* Recent articles cover topics like the fiscal soundness of the Affordable Care Act and perspectives on medical marijuana in Los Angeles.

Salon.com: Online magazine with a liberal slant that focuses on U.S. politics but covers a range of issues from technological advances to book, music, and film reviews. *Examples:* July 20, 2012, articles "The Tiny GOP Zone of Decency," "America's Grand Tax Lie," and "Journalism v. Propaganda."

Science News: Very good weekly, packed with information about what is new in science. *Examples:* Articles in the July 14, 2012, issue, "Alzheimer's May Be Prion Disease," "Volcanoes Belch Up Ozone—Depleting Bromine," and "Mosquitoes Remade."

Scientific American: Excellent science monthly, often difficult going for lay readers, but worth the effort. *Examples:* the July 2012 issue includes "Secrets of the HIV Controllers," "Witness to an Antarctic Meltdown," and "Machines That Think for Themselves."

Skeptical Inquirer: Publication of the Committee for the Scientific Investigation of Claims of the Paranormal—the best periodical on pseudoscience. *Examples:* Articles in the July–August 2012 issue, "The Social and Symbolic Power of AIDS Denialism," "Political Myths That Influ-ence Voters," and "Why the GOP Distrusts Science."

Slate.com: A liberal online magazine of news, culture, and politics—plus *Doonesbury* cartoons. *Examples:* July 20, 2012, articles "How Obama Defies Gravity" and "Nice Assassination" on the killing of high-level Syrian officials.

Time: Mass media general news weekly. Trendy, but often doesn't scratch the surface. *Examples*: Articles in the July 23, 2012, issue, "The Insidious Enemy" on military suicides, "The Syrian Arms Race," and "Definite Particle" on the Higgs boson particle.

Utne Reader: Reprints "the best of the alterative press" and is perhaps itself the best of the maga-zines that reprint material from other magazines. *Examples:* Articles in the July–August 2012 issue, "The PhD Now Comes with Food Stamps," "The Other Arctic," and "Life in the Bike Lane."

Vanity Fair: A style magazine filled with lush celebrity photos and reams of ads that also features some serious, in-depth articles on a wide range of topics from business and politics to litera-ture and film. *Examples*: Articles in the June 2012 issue, "Murdoch's Civil War," "Unearthing Obama," and "A Splash of Marilyn."

Washington Monthly: One of our favorite magazines on how our political system works. It offers a balanced approach to a wide-range of issues. Examples: Articles in the July–August 2012 issue, "How to Save Our Kids from Poverty in Old Age" and "The Slow-Motion Collapse of American Entrepreneurship."

Wire: Magazine publication of Amnesty International, reporting on government torture around the world. (Reading this publication makes one appreciate living in a democratic society.)

Wired: Online magazine on computing, the Internet, and other areas of science and technology. *Examples:* July 2012 articles "How I Accidentally Kickstarted the Domestic Drone Boom" and "New Videogame Lets Amateur Researchers Mess with RNA."

Women's Health Watch: A very good Harvard University health letter for women. *Examples:* July 2012 articles "8 Secrets to a Good Night's Sleep," "What Clinical Studies Can Do for You," and "I Can't Eat That!"

World: A weekly newsmagazine reporting from a right-wing Christian perspective. *Examples:* July 28, 2012, articles, "Ice Age-4: Continental Drift," "Hope in the Heartland," and "Democracy and Dualism" on the Muslim Brotherhood victory in Egypt.

Glossary

ad hominem   An attack on one's opponent rather than one's opponent's **argument**. (An *ad hominem* argument, literally, is an argument "to the person.")

affirming the consequent   Arguing in a way that has the following invalid form (also called *asserting the consequent*):
1. If *A* then *B*.
2. *B*.
3. *A*.

ambiguity   The condition of a word, phrase, or statement when it (a) has more than one possible meaning and (b) the context of its use does not adequately indicate which of those meanings is intended.

analogical reasoning   Reasoning from the similarity of two things in several relevant respects to their similarity in another.

appeal to authority   Using the word of an authority, alleged or genuine, when we should not.

appeal to force   attempting to convince someone of the truth of a claim by way of threatening or showing bad consequences of not believing (or not appearing to believe) it.

appeal to ignorance   Claiming that something is true because there is no good evidence that it is false. (Traditionally known as *argumentum ad ignorantiam.*)

appeal to popularity   Arguing that something is good or true on evidence that it is popular or widely believed.

appeal to tradition   Claiming that some practice is good or at least acceptable because it has been done for some time.

argument   One or more statements (premises) offered in support of another statement (a conclusion).

argumentative essay   A passage (usually consisting of at least several paragraphs) that argues for a **conclusion**.

background belief   A belief that is brought to bear in evaluating an **argument's** cogency.

begging the question   Assuming as a premise some form of the very point that is at issue—the conclusion we intend to prove.

biased statistics   Fallaciously **reasoning** from a sample that is insufficiently representative of the population from which it is drawn.

categorical proposition   A proposition (statement) that asserts or denies a relationship between a **subject class** and a **predicate class**.

cause (of an event)   Something necessary to bring about a particular result, or part of what is sufficient to bring it about.

cogent reasoning   **Valid reasoning** from justified premises (**warranted premises**) that include all likely relevant information.

cognitive meaning   The part of the meaning of a word or expression that refers to things, events, or properties of one kind or another.

comparison of alternatives   Arguing for a course of action by showing that likely alternatives are less desirable.

composition   The fallacy in which it is argued that a particular item must have a certain property because all or most of its parts have it.

concatenated reasoning   Reasoning that employs several inductions and deductions, concluding to a pattern that fits what has been observed so far.

conclusion   What the **premises** of an **argument** are claimed to prove.

contingent statement   A statement that is neither necessarily true (a **tautology**, **logical truth**) nor necessarily false (**inconsistent**, a **contradiction**).

contradiction   A statement that is necessarily false (**inconsistent**, a contradiction), or a group of statements that taken together are inconsistent.

correct   A criterion of **cogent reasoning** requiring that the premises of an **argument** genuinely support its conclusion, either deductively or inductively. (See also **valid**.)

culture lag   The tendency of practices and beliefs to persist long after whatever conditions made them useful or sensible have disappeared.

deductively valid   An **argument** that guarantees that if all its premises are true, then its conclusion also must be true, because the claim asserted by its conclusion already has been stated in its premises, although usually only implicitly.

deductively invalid   Any **argument** that does not have a **deductively valid** form.

delusion   A strong belief held despite strong evidence invalidating it.

denial   Denying the existence of painful situations, thoughts, or feelings or reinterpreting them to make them seem less threatening.

denying the antecedent   Arguing in a way that has the following invalid form:
1. If *A* then *B*.
2. Not *A*.
3. Not *B*.

dilemma   An **argument** that presents two alternatives, both claimed to be bad.

disjunctive syllogism   A **deductively valid argument** having the following form:
1. *A* or *B*.
2. Not *A*.
3. *B*.

division   The fallacy in which it is assumed that all (or some) of the parts of an item have a particular property because the item as a whole has that property.

either–or fallacy   Mistakenly **reasoning** from two alternatives, one claimed to be bad (to be avoided), so that we ought to choose the other alternative in particular when there is at least another viable alternative.

emotive meaning   The positive or negative overtones of a word or expression.

equivocation   Use of a term in a passage to mean one thing in one place and something else in another.

evading the issue   A fallacy in which a question at issue is avoided (usually) while appearing not to.

exposition   An explanation of an issue, idea, or other specific subject.

fallacious reasoning   Reasoning that is not **cogent**, because it suppresses relevant evidence, contains a **questionable premise**, or is invalid.

false charge of fallacy   Wrongly accusing others of a fallacy.

false dilemma   A dilemma that can be shown to be false because either one of its **premises** is false or there is a third alternative.

faulty comparison   A questionable analogy.

form (of an argument)   Its logical or grammatical structure.

guilt by association   Judging someone guilty solely on the basis of the company that person keeps.

hasty conclusion   The fallacious drawing of a **conclusion** from relevant but insufficient evidence.

herd instinct   The tendency to keep our beliefs, and thus our actions, within the bounds of what society as a whole will accept.

higher-level inductions   Very general inductions that can be used to evaluate those that are less general.

hypothetical syllogism   A deductively valid **argument** having the following form:
1. If A then B.
2. If B then C.
3. If A then C.

identification advertisement   An ad aimed to motivate its intended audience to identify either with a particular product or with the product's manufacturer or distributor.

inconsistent   Contradictory.

indirect proof   An **argument** in which the opposite of a desired conclusion is assumed as a **premise**, leading to a **conclusion** that is false, contradictory, or patently absurd, justifying acceptance of the desired conclusion.

induction   **Reasoning** that a pattern of some sort experienced so far will continue into the future.

induction by enumeration   An **inductively valid argument** moving from a premise stating that all so far examined As are Bs to the conclusion that all As whatsoever are Bs.

inductively valid   Correctly **reasoning** that a pattern experienced so far will continue into the future.

irony   Locutions that literally say one thing although their intended meaning is something else, usually opposite to its literal meaning.

irrelevant reason   A broad fallacy category containing several narrower fallacies in which a **premise** of an **argument** is irrelevant to its **conclusion**.

logical indicator   A word or phrase used to indicate the logical function of a particular statement, especially to distinguish premises and conclusions.

logical truth   A statement that is necessarily (logically) true; a statement that can be proved to be true by logic alone.

loyalty   Unwavering allegiance to one's group.

major term   The predicate of the **conclusion** of a **syllogism**.

margin note and summary method   A method for evaluating an extended passage by constructing a summary of that passage and evaluating the summary.

middle term   The term that occurs once in each **premise** of a **syllogism** but not in its **conclusion**.

minor term   The subject of the **conclusion** of a **syllogism**.

modus ponens   A deductively valid **argument** having the following form:
1. If *A* then *B*.
2. *A*.
3. *B*.

modus tollens   A deductively valid **argument** having the following form:
1. If *A* then *B*.
2. Not *B*.
3. Not *A*.

mood (of a syllogism)   The classification of a **syllogism** depending on the kinds of propositions (A, E, I, or O) it contains.

obfuscate   To be so confused or opaque as to be difficult to understand.

particular affirmative proposition   A proposition having the form "Some *A*s are *B*s"; an I proposition.

particular negative proposition   A proposition having the form "Some *A*s are not *B*s"; an O proposition.

partisan mind-set   An attitude of strong, often biased, allegiance to a faction, cause, or person that results in viewing everything in terms of "us" versus "them."

plagiarism   Verbatim, or close to it, use of someone else's writings without acknowledging the source, making it appear to be one's own material.

population   In inductions by enumeration, statistical inductions and some other forms of inductive reasoning, the instances about which we draw a conclusion based on observation of samples from them.

predicate class   The items referred to by the predicate of a **categorical proposition**.

prejudice   Thinking ill of others without sufficient warrant, particularly members of a specific group, race, or religion.

premise   A **reason** offered in support of an **argument's conclusion**.

pro and con argument   An **argument** that considers **reasons** in favor of and against a thesis or conclusion.

procrastination   Putting off for tomorrow what common sense tells us needs to be done today.

promise advertisement   An ad that promises to satisfy desires or allay fears.

provincialism   A limited perspective shaped by the ideas, interests, and kinds of behavior favored by the groups with which we identify.

pseudoscientific theories   Theories that are without scientific foundation.

questionable analogy   **Reasoning** by an analogy that is not apt, not justified.

questionable cause   Labeling *A* as the cause of *B* on evidence that is insufficient, negative, or unrepresentative, or is in serious conflict with well-established high-level theories.

questionable premise   Accepting a less than believable **premise** or other statement.

quibble   To attempt to take advantage of the failure of one's opponent to cross every *t* and dot every *i*, to spell out what should be taken for granted.

rationalization   A psychological ploy we use to justify our actions or beliefs, however wrong, by coming up with self-satisfying but incorrect **reasons** to explain them.

reasoning   Inferring from what we already know or believe to something else; the conclusion reached by reasoning.

reasons   Statements (**premises**) offered in support or acceptance of another statement (**conclusion**).

reductio ad absurdum proof   An **argument** in which the opposite of an untenable **conclusion** is assumed in order to show that the conclusion is false, contradictory, or patently absurd.

refutation to counterargument   An attempt to refute one's opponent's **argument**s against one's own position.

sample   In inductions by enumeration, statistical inductions and some other forms of inductive reasoning, the observed instances on which we base a conclusion about a larger population.

scapegoat   One who is blamed for the ills of the world.

self-deception   Consciously believing at a deeper level what we know to be dubious.

semantic ambiguity   Ambiguity in a statement that arises from the ambiguous meaning of a word or phrase in that statement.

slanting   A form of misrepresentation in which a true statement is made to suggest something else (usually either known to be false or not known to be true). Also, the careful selection of facts so as to imply something else (usually something false).

slippery slope argument   Objecting to a course of action on the grounds that once it is taken, another action, and then perhaps still others, are bound to be taken; or arguing that whatever would justify taking the first step would justify the others, where, given that the last step is not justified, then neither is the first.

slippery slope fallacy   Arguing that a slope is slippery without providing good **reasons** for thinking that it is. (Also see **slippery slope argument**.)

small sample   Drawing **conclusions** about a population on the basis of a sample that is too small to be a reliable measure of that population.

statistical induction   An induction that moves from the **premise** that a certain percentage of a sample has a particular property to the **conclusion** that the whole population from which it is drawn has the same percentage of that property.

stereotype   A conventional oversimplification, often negative, of characteristics that describe a specific group of people.

straw man   A fallacious form of **reasoning** in which an opponent's position, or a competitor's product, is misrepresented or a weaker opponent is attacked rather than stronger ones.

subject class   The items referred to by the subject of a **categorical proposition**.

superstition   An irrational belief, based on biased evidence or on small or unrepresentative samples, that ignores logical evidence to the contrary.

suppressed evidence   The fallacy in which evidence contrary to one's position is neglected, overlooked, or slighted.

suppression   Avoiding thoughts that are stressful by either not thinking about them or by thinking nonstressful thoughts.

syllogism   An **argument** containing exactly three **categorical propositions**, two of them **premises**, one a **conclusion**.

syntactic ambiguity   Ambiguity in a statement that arises from the statement's structure.

tautology   A statement that is logically, or necessarily, true or so devoid of content as to be practically empty.

thesis   The conclusion of an extended argumentative passage; its **conclusion**.

tokenism   Mistaking a token gesture for the real thing, or accepting a token gesture in lieu of something more substantive.

tone   The attitudes or feelings expressed by a passage.

traditional wisdom   Accepting an unsuitable practice because doing so follows a traditional or accepted way of doing things.

two wrongs make a right   Justifying a wrong by pointing to a similar wrong done by others, usually by one's accuser.

universal affirmative proposition   A proposition having the form "All *S* are *P*"; an A proposition.

universal negative proposition   A proposition having the form "No *S* are *P*"; an E proposition.

unrepresentative sample   Fallaciously **reasoning** from a sample that is insufficiently representative of the population from which it is drawn.

vagueness   The condition of a word, phrase or statement that has an unsettled range of meaning or application

valid   A criterion of cogent **reasoning** requiring that the **premises** of an **argument** genuinely support its **conclusion**, either deductively or inductively.

warranted premise   A **premise** that is believable given one's background beliefs and other evidence.

weasel word   A word that appears to make little or no change in a passage, while in fact sucking out most of its content by being so **equivocal** or qualifying that it negates the substance of what is being said.

wishful thinking   Believing what we would like to be true, no matter what the evidence.

worldview   The most important of one's background beliefs (including those about morality, God, the "meaning of life," etc.), usually but not always very general; one's philosophy.

Index